CHICAGO STUDIES IN THE HISTORY OF AMERICAN RELIGION

Editors

JERALD C. BRAUER

AND MARTIN E. MARTY

A CARLSON PUBLISHING SERIES

For a complete listing of the titles in this series,
please see the back of this book.

Toward a Tradition of Feminist Theology

THE RELIGIOUS SOCIAL THOUGHT OF ELIZABETH CADY STANTON, SUSAN B. ANTHONY, AND ANNA HOWARD SHAW

Mary D. Pellauer

PREFACE BY MARTIN E. MARTY

CARLSON
Publishing Inc

BROOKLYN, NEW YORK, 1991

Please see the end of this volume for a listing of all the titles in the Carlson Publishing Series *Chicago Studies in the History of American Religion*, edited by Jerald C. Brauer and Martin E. Marty, of which this is Volume 15.

Library of Congress Cataloging-in-Publication Data

Pellauer, Mary D.
    Toward a tradition of feminist theology : the religious social
thought of Elizabeth Cady Stanton, Susan B. Anthony, and Anna Howard
Shaw / Mary D. Pellauer.
        p.   cm. — (Chicago studies in the history of American
religion ; 15)
    Thesis (Ph. D.)—University of Chicago, 1980.
    Includes bibliographical references and index.
    ISBN 0-926019-51-1 (alk. paper)
    1. Feminist theology—History of doctrines—19th century.
2. Sociology, Christian—United States—History—19th century.
3. Feminism—Religious aspects—Christianity. 4. Stanton, Elizabeth
Cady, 1815-1902. 5. Anthony, Susan B. (Susan Brownell), 1820-1906.
6. Shaw, Anna Howard, 1847-1919. 7. Suffragettes—United States-
-Biography. I. Title.   II. Series.
BT83.55.P45   1991
230'.082—dc20   91-28029

Typographic design: Julian Waters

Typeface: Bitstream ITC Galliard

Case design: Alison Lew

Index prepared by Scholars Editorial Service, Inc., Madison, Wisconsin, using NL Cindex, a scholarly indexing program from the Newberry Library.

Printed on acid-free, 250-year-life paper.

Manufactured in the United States of America.

Contents

An Introduction to the Series ix
Preface *by Martin E. Marty* xiii
1991 Preface xv
Acknowledgments xix

I.   Introduction 1
II. Elizabeth Cady Stanton:
     Toward a Theology for a Feminist Civil Religion 15
III. Elizabeth Cady Stanton, Continued:
     More Rational Religion 105
IV. Susan Brownell Anthony:
     Toward a Theology for a Feminist Praxis 153
V.   Anna Howard Shaw:
     Toward a Theology for a Feminist Christianity 219
VI. Conclusion 285

Epilogue: On Having a Tradition 305
Notes 317
Bibliography 379
Index 413

An Introduction
to the Series

The *Chicago Studies in the History of American Religion* is a series of books that deal with topics ranging from the time of Jonathan Edwards to the 1970s. Three or four deal with colonial topics and three or four treat the very recent past. About half of them focus on the decades just before and after 1900. One deals with blacks; two concentrate on women. Revivalists, fundamentalists, theologians, life in the suburbs and life in heaven and hell, the Beecher family of old and a monk of new times, Catholics adapting to America and Protestants fighting one another—all these subjects assure that the series has scope. People of every kind of taste and curiosity about American religion will find some books to suit them. Does anything serve to characterize the series as a whole? What does the stamp of "Chicago studies" mean?

Yale historian Sydney Ahlstrom in *A Religious History of the American People*, as influential as any twentieth-century work in its field, pays respect to the "Chicago School" of American religious historians. William Warren Sweet, the pioneer in such studies (beginning in 1927) at Chicago and, in many ways, in America at large represented the culmination of "the Protestant synthesis" in this field. Ahlstrom went on to name two later generations of Chicagoans, including the seminal Sidney E. Mead and major figures like Robert T. Handy and Winthrop Hudson and ending with the two editors of this series. He saw them as often "openly rebellious" in respect to Sweet and his synthesis.

If, as Ahlstrom says, "a disproportionate number" of historians have some connection with the Chicago School, it must be said that the new generation represented in these twenty-one books carries on both the lineage of Sweet and something of the "openly rebellious" character that scholars at Chicago are encouraged to pursue. This means, for one thing, that the "Protestant synthesis" does not characterize their work. These historians question the canon of historical writing produced in the Protestant era even as many of them continue to pursue themes shaped in a Protestant culture. Few of them concentrate on the old "frontier thesis" that marked the early years of the school. The shift for most has been toward the urban and pluralist scene. They call into question, not in devastating rage but in steady patterns of inquiry, the received wisdom about who matters, and why, in American religion.

So it is that this series of books focuses on blacks, women, dispensationalists, suburbanites, members of "marginal" denominations, "ethnics" and immigrants as readily as it does on white men of progressive urban bent in mainstream denominations and of long standing in America. The authors relish religious diversity and enjoy discovering the power of people once considered weak, the centrality to the American plot of those once regarded as peripheral, and the potency of losers who were once disdained by winners. Thus this series enhances an understanding of an America overlooked by the people of Sweet's era two-thirds of a century ago when it all, or most of it, began.

Rebellion for its own sake would not long hold interest; it might tell more about the psychology of rebels and revisers than about their subject matter. Revision, better than rebellion, characterizes the scholars. Re+vision: that's it. There was an original vision that characterized the Chicago School. This was the contention that in secular America and its universities religion mattered, as a theme in the national past and as a presence in the present. Second, it argued that the study of religious history belonged not only in the seminaries and archives of denominations, but also in the rough-and-tumble of the secular university, where no religious meanings were privileged and where each historian had to make a case for the value of his or her story.

Other assumptions from the earliest days pervade the books in this series. They are uncommonly alert to the environment in which expressions of faith occur. That is, they do not take for granted that religion comes protected in self-evidently important and hermetically sealed packages. Churches and denominations are porous, even when they would be sealed off; they cannot be understood apart from the ways the social environs effect them, but their power to effect change in the environment demands equal and truly unapologetic treatment. These writers do not shuffle and mumble and make excuses for their existence or for the choice of apparently arcane subject matter. They try to present their narrative in such ways that they compel attention.

A fourth characteristic that colors these works is a refusal in most cases to be typed in a fashionable slot labeled, variously, "intellectual" or "institutional" history, "cultural" or "social" history, or whatever. While those which concentrate on magisterial thinkers such as Jonathan Edwards are necessarily busy with and devoted to his intellectual achievement, most of the books deal with figures who cannot be understood only as exemplars in a sequence of studies of "the life of the mind." Instead, their biographies and circumstances come very much into play. On the other hand, none of these writers is a reductionist who sees religion as "nothing but" this or that—"nothing but" the working out of believers' Oedipal urges or expressing the economic and class interests of the subjects. Social history becomes in its way intellectual history, even if the intellects are focused on something other than the theologians in the traditions might like to see.

Some years ago *Look* magazine interviewed leaders in various denominations. One was asked if his fellow believers considered that theirs was the only true faith. Yes, he said, but they did not believe that they were the only ones who held it. The editors of this series of studies and the contributors to it do not believe that the "Chicago School," whenever and whatever it was, is the only true approach to American religious history. And, if they did, they would not hold that Chicagoans alone held it. To do so would imply a strange solipsistic or narcissistic impulse that would be the death of collegiality in the historical field. They have welcomed the chance to be in a climate where their inquiries are given such encouragement, where they find a company of fellow scholars in the Divinity School, the History Department, and the Committee on the History of Culture, whence these studies first emerged, and elsewhere in a university that provides a congenial home for massed and massive concentration of a special sort on American religious history.

While the undersigned have been consistently involved, most often together, in all twenty-one books, we want to single out a third person mentioned in so many acknowledgment sections, historian Arthur Mann. He has been a partner in two or three dozen religious history dissertation projects through the years and has been an influential and decisive contributor to the results. We stand in his debt.

Jerald C. Brauer
Martin E. Marty

Editor's Preface

Connecting women and religion, in an era of feminist scholarship, often gets reduced to two or three themes. Such historians measure religious barriers and achievements by accounting for the ordination of women to clerical status, or the absence of such ordination. Others write histories of patriarchy and the suppression of women on religious terms; they lack evidence for such suppression only if they can overlook mountains of documents. In both cases, the majority of such studies equate religion with a church, synagogue, or some other institution. On such terms, this book would be beside the point.

Mary Pellauer deals with three pioneering feminists known best for their participation in the struggle for woman suffrage in the United States. Elizabeth Cady Stanton, Susan Brownell Anthony, and Anna Howard Shaw have to be central to any canon, portrayed in any gallery, of creative and accomplished feminists in America. They had little to do, most of the time, with "organized religion," except to see it as representing a power bloc that stood in their way or on which they could selectively draw for talent and articulation. Yet Pellauer sees them as religious thinkers.

To do this, of course, she needs more expansive definitions of religion than those that tend to equate religion with specific institutions, as often has been the case in both folk wisdom and unimaginative sociology of religion. To her credit, let it be said that she does not define religion so broadly that it becomes meaningless; if everything is religious, one might say, nothing is religious. She does the defining with such clarity and consistency that I would not wish to corrupt her approach, and I commend the early pages of this book to the reader for that effort. Her definition is compelling and anyone who accepts even a major portion of it will see how inventive and persistent were these three leaders in their religious expression.

This book is the only one in this series that did not take rise in the context of historical studies alone. James M. Gustafson, a theorist of religious ethics without peer, coadvised it and helped the author bring to high visibility the ethical issues involved in Stanton's, Anthony's, and Shaw's feminist, political, and religious expressions. So she is not content with accounting for their contributions to the suffrage battles, the way we historians might be tempted to be. Instead, she moves on to heavily weighted themes like "justice" and "freedom," and treats them with a sophistication that should please social and intellectual historians alike.

Today theologians and philosophers of religion do not characteristically turn to these women when they write histories of religious thought in America. Their near contemporaries—William James, Josiah Royce, the early John Dewey, Walter Rauschenbusch—receive first notice. Only as the definition of religion expands are scholars seeing that social thinkers like George Herbert Mead and Jane Addams need religious attention. It is hard to picture that, after Pellauer has made her mark, they can overlook these impassioned and often-changing women. To use terms fashionable since their time, they were paradigm-breakers and -makers, and what they came up with can be realized decades later though it was long obscured by their more formal contributions to the politics of suffrage.

Speaking of fashion, it has been customary in scholarly circles to keep the word "I" out of formal works. In the present circumstances "I" am happy to note that Pellauer allows herself an appearance in the final pages. This book represents a moment of development in the feminist movement and in the life of the author, developments that have corollaries in the lives of readers, be they men or women, who also make a transit through these times of change. What I find especially appealing is the way she turns to the concept of "tradition" for expounding. Using her three subjects as mentors and her own encounters as exemplary or representative, she throws light on issues that Stanton, Anthony, and Shaw opened but that remain urgent.

Martin E. Marty

1991 Preface

I finished writing this work eleven years ago. In the intervening time, both feminist theology and women's history have flourished. I cannot hope to provide a guide to that literature mushrooming and blossoming throughout the academic garden. I have added some new footnotes to works that substantially enrich our understanding of these figures or these issues.

Readers may wish to know that my interpretation may be controversial. Where I have claimed these suffragists as part of a tradition of feminist theology, two recent scholars have claimed that Stanton and Anthony are secular. Ellen Carol DuBois, *Elizabeth Cady Stanton, Susan B. Anthony: Correspondence, Writings, Speeches* (Ithaca: Cornell University Press, 1981) made this claim for Stanton, Kathleen Barry for Anthony (*Susan B. Anthony: A Biography*, New York: New York University Press, 1988). The footnotes point to these disagreements. But aside from these specifics, there is a larger issue to notice.

Both authors appear to understand religion in narrow ways—as other-worldly, for instance, or as evangelical rather than liberal. These misunderstandings arise, I believe, from a combination of these scholars' own presuppositions about the present women's movement and the lack of conceptual frameworks adequate for women's religiousness. Feminist theologians are especially familiar with the latter problem. Since I struggle with this issue at length in the introduction, I will add only two points here.

If we do not have adequate terms for understanding women's religiousness, then it follows that we do not have adequate terms for understanding women's secularity either. At the very least, when women withdraw from Christianity, we must not leap to the conclusion that they have become a-religious or secular. More narrowly, when women are not affiliated with a particular form of Christianity, we must not conclude that they are irreligious. Or, when women are critical of the patriarchy in Christianity, we must not conclude that they have become either nonchristian or secular.

These concerns are extremely serious for nineteenth-century women. True Womanhood, for our Victorian forebears, was defined by its piety as well as by its purity, domesticity, and submissiveness. Piety by its nature was uncritical. When we identify religiously critical women as secular, in effect we nod our heads in thoughtless agreement with this Victorian stereotype. As Anthony wrote in one of her diaries, she was called "infidel" merely for having a different faith. It is a faith that takes a careful and creative eye to see. If one is mesmerized by evangelicalism, by supernaturalism, or merely by conventional notions of religion, especially for women, we will never see it. This is extremely serious. It is not that being secular or irreligious is a bad thing, though perhaps it is not to be so taken for granted as twentieth-century people think.

These misjudgments verge on historylessness about women and religion. Historylessness in this area removes issues about women's religious faith or perceptions from the realm of choices, or it narrows the choices rather than expanding our view of the options and nuances. I find this troubling both for women—since we are struggling today to widen rather than restrict our possibilities—and for religion, which aims to enrich, complete, or supplement human existence rather than to flatten it out. If we cannot see the creative alternatives to patriarchal religion that were woven, quilted, or cobbled together by these feminist foremothers, then perhaps we cannot see our own either.

One achievement of this study is that it provides us with a clear and nuanced view of the religious and ethical differences between these three suffragists. This leads me to think that its method might indeed be a tool worth using. Three figures is a good number. One alone would not show anything about differences. With more than three, I probably could not have gotten a "thick description" of the figures involved. These differences among our foremothers please and delight me as surely as those I find in today's movement. (More, they invite me to seek out nuances among women today to emphasize and celebrate.) I hope that readers too will be cheered and enlivened by the specific contrasts between these women.

These three suffragists are not the only figures in a tradition of feminist theology, of course. Maybe they are not even the most important. It may be that the most important figures in this tradition will be Asian, African American, Hispanic, or Native American women, rather than white, middle-class women. A recent womanist theologian, retrieving the theologies of Sojourner Truth and Jarena Lee, points out that in Black women's experiences of the triple oppression of race, sex, and class, "the particular connects up with the universal" in a way that can be whole without being abstract. (See Jacquelyn Grant, *White Women's Christ and Black Women's Jesus: Feminist Christology and Womanist Response*, Atlanta: Scholars Press, 1989.)

We will not have a clear sense of the proportions of this tradition until we get more of it dug out, dusted off, pieced together again, and shared. Recent work in the psychology of memory tells us that remembering is creative, an act of imagination. Surely that's also true in history.

Mary D. Pellauer
March, 1991

Acknowledgments

Many people have offered me human resources on which to draw in the course of this lengthy work, both in emotional support and intellectual stimulation. It is difficult for me to disentangle the relative importance of emotional and intellectual streams that made it possible to do this work, and I am pleased with that entwinement.

Alan B. Anderson's intellectual nudging at me during the early years of my graduate study slipped me into new territories of the mind that I have only too slowly explored. Without his teaching and advisement at the Divinity School of the University of Chicago, this project would never have been. Simultaneously, the creation of the Ecumenical Women's Centers of Chicago, with its focus on ministry by women to women and its early feminist theology study group, was a source of comfort, challenge, and creativity, as women from the seminaries, the churches, and the city began to affirm the religious dimensions of the women's movement in the early 1970s; Rev. Florris Mikkelsen, Rev. Becca Kutz, Rev. Julie Less (then Wagstaff), Rev. Robin Mattison, Ann Rathbun, and Lois Gehr Livezey all deserve recognition for the strength of those early years. Lois and I taught together at several seminaries in the Chicago area in those early days, and her unflagging human support together with her process theology perspective have enabled me to see theological issues in new ways.

James Gustafson and Martin Marty coadvised this thesis, and a more felicitous pair of colleagues could not be imagined for this ethics project in a historical context. Their patience with the various drafts of this study and their cooperation, as ethicist and historian, in working through the material of ethics in a historical context, have drawn this book through its darker days.

Several feminist colleagues in religion have read drafts of this material. The comments of Beverly Wildung Harrison of Union Theological Seminary have been immensely constructive in disentangling the places where intellectual and editorial confusions intersected. Barbara Andolsen, an ethicist working with the same primary materials in the woman suffrage movement, is one of the few colleagues whose acquaintance with and interest in this field paralleled my own. The Rev. Carol Adams of Dunkirk, New York, caught several errors as well as serious intellectual issues in her nets as she read. The Union Theological Seminary students who were so kind or so misguided as to join my course in the history of feminist religious thought helped me to see points of interest within this body of work that I had not previously noted: my gratitude to Rev. Joyce Soltzfus, Rev. Karen Ziegler, Julie Aegerter, Rev. Ginny Bergfalk, Tom Kiesel. The Rev. Fay Ellison added pastoral contributions to my flagging spirits.

To Mary Daly I owe a debt of another sort. Her daring and creativity are unmatched among our contemporaries in feminist theology. However much I finally part company with her, I do not count agreement in content high among the reasons for respect. Daly's thoughts lured many women beyond acquiescence in patriarchal religion, beyond the passive consumption of religious theories produced elsewhere. In many ways this work is the merest footnote to her achievements. Even a footnote, however, may eventually lead elsewhere.

The librarians at the Schlesinger Library and the Library of Congress were helpful in the ways that truly good librarians are. In addition, the staff at the Library of Congress introduced me to members of the Anthony family whose interest in this project redoubled my efforts. The conversation and comments of Dr. Susan B. Anthony and Charlotte Anthony Szabo about this material, especially with regard to Chapter Four, encouraged and stimulated my work.

Finally, there is David W. Pellauer, whose name I have chosen over my father's name. The irony of scholarly acknowledgments to spouses has frequently been noted by feminists. In many feminist circles to speak of a male contribution to one's personal or professional growth is considered a sign of unhealthy dependency on the oppressor. But it is only fair of me to record my debt to David. He believed in me and my work even when I did not; he did the laundry and the child care almost uncomplainingly and yet did not become my "wife"; his honest struggles with equality and love have helped me to see myself in a new light. Thus he has taken his place among the many sisters who have participated in the transformation of my life. There are few men of whom I can say such a thing.

Toward a Tradition of Feminist Theology

If it is true that all thought begins with remembrance, it is also true that no remembrance remains secure until it is condensed and distilled into a framework of conceptual notions within which it can further exercise itself. Experience and even the stories which grow out of what men [*sic*] do and endure, of happenings and events, sink back into the futility inherent in the living word and the living deed unless they are talked about over and over again. What saves the affairs of mortal men [*sic*] from their inherent futility is nothing but this incessant talk about them, which in its turn remains futile unless certain concepts, certain guideposts for future remembrance, and even for sheer reference, arise out of it.

Hannah Arendt, *On Revolution*

Introduction

This book explores the religious social thought of three leaders in the woman suffrage movement in the United States of America—Elizabeth Cady Stanton, Susan Brownell Anthony, and Anna Howard Shaw. These three figures are well known as suffragists; their impact on the organized drive for women's rights, and particularly the vote, has been central to understanding and describing that movement. In this work I investigate a side of these women that has been far less adequately scrutinized—the ethical and theological dimensions of their thought and work. Indeed, it is my contention that without a grasp of the religious aspects of the work of these women, it may be seriously questioned whether they have been adequately understood at all.

In light of the mass of previous scholarship about the woman suffrage movement, this is a serious and fundamental contention. To clarify and specify this assertion are the objectives of the twofold hypothesis that has guided this study: (1) there is an internal and reciprocal relationship between each figure's social analysis and her religious perspective; (2) this relationship between social and religious thought is most clearly illuminated by a focus on justice in each woman's view, as the pivot point, so to speak, between the social and religious dimensions. To elucidate this twofold hypothesis in turn requires the formulation of certain theoretical guideposts by which to delineate the meaning of the terms "social," "religious," and "justice." To provide guidelines for the use of these terms forms the major burden of this introductory chapter.

It is no exaggeration to claim that these women are part of a hitherto unrecognized tradition of feminist theology. Each of them found aspects of the situation of women, and women's struggle for equality, crucially relevant to structured reflection on religious realities. They were by no means of one mind as to the terms and categories most appropriate to this task—no more than are, let us say, Mary Daly, Rosemary Radford Ruether, or Sheila Collins among feminist theologians of the 1970s. Yet there is enough resemblance to the work of Daly, Ruether, and Collins that we may see real continuities across the intervening decades. There is, in fact, an extraordinary amount of material in the work of each one of these women that is useful to the contemporary feminist interested in religion—not to mention the historical theologian who may have been under the impression that there were little data in theology originating from women in the nineteenth century.

These comparisons with feminist theology, that enterprise of the 1970s, are more than superficial. Mary Daly has claimed that the women's movement itself is an ontological revolution, a religious reality in its own right. It is more than a little startling to the women of the last decade, like myself, a bit shaken and intrigued by the novelty of Daly's claim, to find that *each* of the women featured in this study had similar ideas a century earlier—in three different sets of terms, none of them resembling Daly's use of Tillich or Roman Catholic theology. Furthermore, these three case studies are the merest beginnings to what I now judge to be an unrecognized tradition of theological reflection by women prior to the 1970s. It is not unusual for scholars in the area of religion to claim in conversation that the material simply is "not there" prior to this women's movement. The research for this study and my other teaching in religious history has convinced me of the contrary: the problem is not that there is too little, but rather too much, material.[1]

It may be that one reason this religious tradition of suffragist argument has gone unnoticed stems from the fact that, in Hannah Arendt's phrase from the epigraph, the conceptual "guideposts for future remembrance" were not present before the rise of feminist theology. Those conceptual guideposts were not established during the movement. Major male theologians did not give the movement substantial attention. No feminist of the last century wrote a systematic theology in multiple volumes. Formal theological training for women opened up only under the impact of the suffrage movement itself and its contiguous social influence. The very terms on which the figures in this study viewed religion may have contributed to reading such religious themes out of the historical record. As I show below in some detail, the social emphasis implicit in these positions did not lend itself to viewing the construction of explicit theological schemes as an urgent task. If hastening the advent of the Kingdom of God on earth by social and moral reform was the business of religion—to choose a well-known example from the nineteenth century's panoply of rhetorics—we might well conclude that the more religious one was on such a view, the less likely one was to be found writing a theology about it.

2

These brief remarks are frankly speculative. Whatever the reasons for the lack of attention to such religious positions—and sexism itself in the religious communities and scholars of religion is by no means a minor contributing factor—we have today compelling reasons for remembering these religious perspectives, methods of inquiry available to bring them to light, and intellectual tools by which to assess them. What are the questions and challenges inherent in the investigation of the religious social thought of three leaders of the North American woman suffrage movement?

Thesis and Method of This Inquiry

This study proceeds by way of the in-depth treatment of the thought of each of the three individuals featured in it—Stanton, Anthony, Shaw. In each case that follows, an internal analysis of the writings of each figure is the primary task—the careful, close internal reading dear to scholarship. Attention to what Kenneth Burke might call the "grammar"[2] of each woman's thought has been less practiced than some other modes of analysis; it is itself a useful and illuminating aspect of this thesis. A recognizable intellectual style emerges from the work of each of these three suffragist leaders.

This in-depth treatment does not require an intellectual leap of faith that each figure is utterly consistent and systematic. Even incoherence and changes of opinion over the course of a career can be instructive. But I do claim that there is a "quasi-systematic"[3] nature to the intellectual achievements of these figures that warrants this approach—as I think the ensuing chapters demonstrate. Whether this internal coherence is in the eye of the beholder or really there cannot be fruitfully debated outside the specific attention to the thought of each particular figure. It is less internal inconsistency that is the stumbling block to this approach than the "occasional" nature of Anthony's thought. And even in her case—perhaps especially in her case—the approach taken here more than pays off.

The perspective by which I have elucidated these three figures is not developmental or chronological, however, except where the development of positions through time and events was crucial to the logic of arguments and to the coherence and persuasiveness of such perspectives. Stanton's position on the churches, for example, shifted considerably across the span of her career, with discernible consequences for her systematic thought. Anthony's aphorisms and insights were more thoroughly determined by the time and nature of the occasion on which she spoke; yet she too can be profitably understood in more systematic terms if we see that the occasional nature of her theory was in line with the more practical, political, understandings of herself and her struggle. Shaw frequently spoke of the lessons learned by reformers in the course of reforming activity; but it is difficult to see that the basic building blocks of her position ever really changed in the course of her career. The focus in this work on the internal logic of the religious social thought of these three women can, I believe, encompass these shifts and developments through time without excessive distortion.

This study has proceeded under the aegis of a department of ethics and society. This is perhaps a contingent disciplinary lodgement in the arbitrary world of academic compartments; it might well have taken place in a department of American church history or intellectual history. Nonetheless, from my perspective the social-ethical home of this work is more than coincidental. Religious social thought is peculiarly the preoccupation of social ethics in a divinity school. Either term in that nebulous phrase, and the relations between them, may well bear focused scrutiny in its own right. Hence the first half of the hypothesis of this work: there is an internal and reciprocal relationship between social analysis and religious perspective in each woman's thought. It is the second half of that hypothesis, however, that marks this work as particularly appropriate to a field of social ethics: the relationship between social analysis and religious perspective is most clearly illuminated by a focus on justice. My objectives as a scholar in this area extend far beyond the exposition of the internal logic of these three suffragists to a concern for the substance of justice on issues pertaining to sexism and other social questions. My aims, like those of these suffragists themselves, are more normative and interpretive than simply descriptive.

These normative and interpretive concerns do not exempt this work from the ordinary guidelines of the working historian even in the fields of religion. To lay before the reader the religious social thought of these three women, to do justice to each woman's own perspective, to bring to light relevant comparisons, to indicate the sorts of evidence available for my exposition, to make critical assessments—these aims of this study fall within the usual canons of the writing of history.

Nonetheless, it is particularly as an exercise in social ethics that this book is able to delineate the relationships in the work of these women between views of the social order and of religion, and their emergence as one whole focused on justice. This is not to say that individual historians or theologians are less

4

passionately concerned with justice than is the social ethicist; personal commitments are not what is at stake in such a point. It is rather the stance of this field as a discipline of practical inquiry that disposes the social ethicist to attend to dimensions of both social analysis and religion in their interrelation to justice. While this work is clearly a contribution to the history of feminist theology, it is no less a contribution to the field of social ethics.

Even coherent exposition requires a framework within which to proceed. The purely miscellaneous recounting of opinions does not advance one's understanding. The cataloging of suffragist opinions on this or that topic was indulged enough in the nineteenth century—and it contributed, I believe, to the oblivion into which these works fell. Anyone who has read Ida Husted Harper's three-volume biography of Anthony will be aware, I think, of the truth expressed in the citation from Hannah Arendt. An unstructured recitation is extraordinarily unmemorable, even though its incidents may thrill a later reader. The remainder of this introductory chapter focuses firmly on the conceptual "guideposts" Arendt speaks of as necessary even to the act of remembrance. If this is a study in religious social thought, what do we understand by "religious" and "social" in this subject matter? And how are we to be guided in combining them with each other?

Social Analysis: Defining a Social Issue

It is striking that the social thought of the suffragists under scrutiny did not investigate the American social order with questions of a broad, general nature in mind. They did not, for example, begin by queries about self and society, or about the nature of social institutions. They did have positions on some of these points, but they were developed not for their own sakes, but in the course of arguing other matters. They concerned themselves intensely with certain aspects of the social order and with a social movement designed to transform these specific points. Their social thought, in other words, was largely focused upon a particular social issue.

Feminists call this social issue by various names—sexism, male chauvinism, patriarchy, sometimes misogyny. Of these terms, only the latter pair was available in the nineteenth century, and they were not often used by Stanton, Anthony, and Shaw. As we shall see in the central chapters of this work, these suffragists were not unmindful of the quandaries of how to delineate, with insight and economy of expression, the complex of points with which they

5

struggled. Stanton, for example, spoke of "every invidious distinction of sex," and later in her life, of the "bias of sex." Anthony, from her abolitionist background, occasionally used phrases like "sex-slavery." Shaw spoke of the discrepancy between the republic's ideals and its practice; she knew and used "feminism." Whatever they called it, however, the social thought of these women was articulated and shaped, centered, on a particular social issue.

Social issues are notorious for the controversy and contention attendant upon them. We recognize this obvious point when we speak, for example, of the point "at issue" between persons in conflict.[4] For purposes of this book I assert here that there is a "focal region"[5] to such controversies—the matrix of interconnected points for which and about which the woman suffrage movement struggled. I call this focal region of social contention the "definition of the issue"—that is, the social issue.[6] I address and analyze the various definitions of the issue put forward by three major proponents of suffrage.

The focal region of these suffragists' social analysis was not limited to the suffrage pure and simple. The vote was only one, though a pre-eminent one, to be sure, of the goals sought by the advocates of women's rights. The Seneca Falls "Declaration of Sentiments" numbered eighteen grievances before the public. At least one of its authors, Elizabeth Cady Stanton, claimed that its aim was to cover the entire expanse of relevant human experience. Suffrage theorists argued for a variety of programs that provided the context for the meaning, the ethical status and importance, of any particular goal such as the vote.

According to these same suffragists, injustice and justice were the ethical stakes of the movement. Yet despite the importance of these ethical terms, one may search long and hard for precise definitions of them, or for systematic statements of the meaning of justice. Each of these women concentrated her efforts on the injustice before her.[7] To thematize and scrutinize such terms we need a somewhat indirect, oblique, mode of approach to the use of justice.

For the purposes of this inquiry I propose that the relations between injustice and justice within the social analysis of any one of these women may be profitably viewed as a "question-and-answer" structure. The question-and-answer structure of theological argument is familiar from Paul Tillich's method of correlation.[8] The issue may be seen to be analogous to the theological "question": What is the problem? Or, in this context, What is the injustice? The "answer" corresponds to the proposals advanced for its resolution. In the case of social movements such as the suffrage cause, the proposal for justice is the "answer" to the problem of injustice.

Within this inquiry, this structure of correlation is not the correlation between human questions and the answers of the Christian message. Both question and answer appear within the thought of each suffragist. But the notion of question and answer, mutually interdependent in structure and content, is especially helpful here. The answer, the form and content of justice, did not always receive the same detailed attention as did the question or the injustice. It can, however, be inferred from their work and writings, *if* we see that there is a "fit" between notions of injustice and notions of justice just as the answer "fits" the question. Thus in this work I may be able to cast some light on specific proposals for justice, by backing into them, as it were.

Tillich's question-and-answer structure also draws our attention to the variety of possible interrelated questions and answers of theological disagreement. If the theological question is formulated as death, a theological structure is erected locating this problem in a matrix and determining its answer (eternal life). This is a very different theological structure from one in which the question is articulated as guilt or meaninglessness. One theological tradition or church may of course contain several varying theological questions and answers.

Similarly, in contention about the social order, there may emerge differing notions of the questions, the injustice, within one social movement. The kinds of activities and particular structures of the social order named as the problem, the question, may vary considerably from activist to activist; and the shape of justice proposed will vary accordingly.

This is precisely the case with the three leaders studied here. Stanton described a fourfold bondage whose central meaning was the denial of women's individuality. Anthony's analysis highlighted three areas of concern in the American society, whose organizing center was not individuality but powerlessness. Shaw saw the issue in yet another way, as a case of the inconsistency between ideals and practice. Therefore the presumptive unity of these suffragists disappears—though not entirely, as we shall see—into a conflict of interpretations. These differing modes of defining the issue had important political, ethical, and religious consequences for the movement. To focus on these differing kinds of social thought is one of the gains achieved by the method of scrutiny I employ.

Religion and Theology

Many suffragist controversies concerning religion focused on the biblical and particularly the Pauline injunctions to women. These "traditional" discussions never disappeared altogether as years passed. But another strand of argument, much more difficult to understand, also appeared most dramatically as the century wore on. The Rev. Anna Garlin Spencer, for example, declared that the new philanthropic professions, such as social work and social science, were "as sacred as ministry was of old."[9] She also spoke of the "humanizing of religion" as a result of a "more womanly influence."[10] Mary Craigie, chair of the National American Woman Suffrage Association's Committee on Church Work, established in 1903, thought that social and moral reform advancing the Kingdom of God on earth "constituted" the work of the churches.[11] Her pamphlet *Christian Citizenship* called this shift to "twentieth-century religion" a transition comparable to the industrial revolution in economics.[12] The Rev. Ida C. Hultin asked rhetorically, "What is education for, what is religion for, but as a means to the development of humanity?"[13] Or as the laywoman Harriet Taylor Upton put it, "If it is not religion to promote a cause that will make men better and women wiser, then what is it?"[14] Finally, Ednah Cheney's address to the Symposium on Religion of the 1888 International Council of Women asserted that the entire week's work regarding the political, social, and legal disabilities of women had been religious; she was not accustomed to cordoning religion off into churches and special days.[15]

Such examples could be multiplied. If we confine ourselves to the figures under investigation in this work, the same dynamics may be seen. Anthony rose to agree with Cheney, citing the release of the oppressed as a divine activity. Stanton referred to the ballot box as a "holy of holies" and saw chaos everywhere that human beings did not walk in line with the true cosmic laws regarding the sexes. The Rev. Anna Howard Shaw believed democracy was an emanation from the Infinite, and criticized Christianity for not recognizing that "life itself is a religion."

These notions raise fundamental problems for the historian's understanding of the religious discussions of the woman suffragists. They suggest that the cogency and appropriateness of accepted distinctions will not be adequate to my material. If some proponents of suffrage believed that such activities as social work, voting, snapping chains of bondage, "life itself" were religious in nature, then we have a radical question of the scholarly framework within which to locate, articulate, understand, and perhaps explain religion in this social movement. Conventional notions alone, such as references to God-language, the Bible, clergy, or churches, will not suffice, though they must also be included.

There are other intellectual constraints on my proposed notions of religion. It is implicit in these examples that the heuristic devices regarding religion in this study must also illumine the focus on action and social change.[16] What is needed, in other words, is a "generic" concept of religion that can do three things at once: include the "secular" motifs mentioned above; allow for the unfolding of several differing religious views; and direct our attention to social and political dimensions of life.

I propose, therefore, that wherever and whenever in these three women's thought, considerations of the "really real," the "way things really are," are brought to bear, that we are entering the realm of religion.[17] When we discover intertransposable "models of" and "models for" reality such that ethos (the dimension of action) and worldview (the image of the cosmos) are linked together to form an "unbreakable inner connection," we are entering the realm of religion. The "reality" to which one refers is an intensified, magnified, purified reality—just as it is when one doubles the phrase, "the really real."

This unbreakable inner connection, however, should not be understood a priori as a simple, reductionist, or deductive connection.[18] There is room for creativity within religion in such a view. As Stanton argued, if woman's emancipation could not occur within the former religious perspective, then it too must change—die or disappear, if need be. I therefore speak of religious symbols as "redescribing"[19] the "really real." "Redescription," on this view, directs attention to the transformative dimension of this creative religion in this social movement.

If intensification of the real through redescription is what religion amounts to in this study, what then might we say regarding theology? It is crucial to note that several figures were extremely critical of theology per se. Stanton, for example, distinguished between not only true and false religion, but between religion and theology. Religion was healthy and natural, but theology she identified with gloomy speculation regarding an afterlife; as such it contributed to the perversion of religiousness in women. Anthony too rejected creeds and dogmas, though in different ways from her old friend. To put it bluntly, the Victorian era did not allow theology to women; but equally these feminists saw theology as part of the problem.[20]

Of the women who are the central figures in this study, only Anna Howard Shaw had formal theological training. Stanton and Anthony never set foot in a theological school. I look to them here not as exponents of fully articulated and well-rounded theological systems, as we look to figures such as Barth or Tillich.[21] My use of the term "theology" here is rather intended to highlight precisely the *structured character* of such religious thoughts, feelings, and statements made by these suffragists—the internal relationships between ideas, their coherence, the particular building blocks each employed, and the alternative consequences of such building blocks when related in differing ways to different notions. This implicit structure deserves the name of "theology."

That such positions were not always self-consciously articulated in their internal structure created problems for the woman suffrage movement. Stanton, the most "philosophical" of these figures, attained a degree of clarity and coherence to which many of us could aspire; Anthony, the "occasional" theorist, less so—but her hints and pointers are more creatively suggestive than much of Stanton.

Each woman understood herself to be "liberal" in religion. They were not specific or definite about what the designation meant. More than any particular positive program, it indicated a demurral from orthodoxy. Each in her own way, however, affirmed broadly God's unity and benevolence, in opposition to stern divine judgment upon creatures steeped in original sin, and in opposition to the uniquely mediating role of Jesus. As one might expect from such a notion of God, they all affirmed human nature and human efforts. They all refused to accept religious authorities external to the self—though they were not of one mind as to whether the self's rational, active, or emotive capacities were the source of its religious discernment. Traditional discontinuities between revealed and natural religion, or between nature and supernature, were no longer sharply held. All of them believed that some version of reform activity was indistinguishable from the highest and best revelation of a divinity. The self-consciousness, sophistication, consistency, and passion with which they held such notions varied widely. The relationships they postulated between such views and the churches' versions of religion were also diverse. Women who agreed on a very abstract set of principles like these might differ as to whether they constituted the "true" meaning of Christianity or were in contradiction to Christianity.

Yet these women were liberals with a difference; they were feminist liberals. The topics they explored in a religious fashion were unusual—woman's right to think (Stanton), sisterhood (Anthony), or the spirituality of those involved in the women's movement (Shaw).[22] Further, we can see ways in which liberalism itself was problematic to such figures. Stanton's confused attempts to establish grounds on which to descry in the same event general progress that was at the same time a regress for women is a notable case in point. To choose another example from Stanton's rich corpus, when she identified the doctrine of sin as a masculine product, she implied that self-respecting women *had to be* liberals in religion.[23]

To focus on the relationships between the social analysis and the religious perspective brings to light a point intrinsically interesting and even crucial for feminist theology: It was these women's perception of sexism in the social order, and their efforts to combat it publicly, which pushed them into theological creativity. They were not always equipped to refine their insights into systems, or to follow them to their final implications. But it is my wager that they were right on target at precisely this point—for sexism was, and is, a central theological and ethical problem. Each of these women glimpsed this fact and spoke of it in her own vocabulary.

Within this framework the distinction between religion and the social analysis is *not* that the first prescribes and the second describes, as though it were a distinction between value and fact. This is emphatically not the case. The definition of the issue describes; the religious symbols redescribe. The notion of the issue prescribes operational standards for action; the religious symbol, to employ an inelegant neologism, "represcribes." Fact and value appear in *both* terms of this inquiry, in both religion and the definition of the issue. But they are, as it were, reordered or even "re-presented," when considerations of the really real are brought to bear.

Justice

Neither the social analysis nor the religion in each figure's work can be reduced to the other, nor exhausted in the explication of the other dimension. There is always more social analysis that can be derived from the religious view, and more to the religious view than can be poured into the particular social analysis. Yet, when these two areas are brought into conjunction with each other, they mutually illumine and provide insight into the other dimension—without for that matter being exhausted.

Hence, this project's focus is on *justice*, the area of the intersection of social analysis and religious view. To see justice in the light of the full social analysis and full religious view results in a richer appreciation of the content of that concept in each woman's thought. The use of the question-and-answer

11

structure on the side of the social analysis alerts us to the multiplicity of ethical positions regarding justice among these three figures. Stanton's natural law position firmly attached justice to a fundamental cosmological view. Anthony's ethics of conscience resulted in a position we may call *Fiat Justitia Pereat Mundus*. Shaw gave pride of place to aspiration and responsibility in her ethical reasoning.

Each one of these women embedded justice within a larger frame of reference. They explored the relationships between justice and deity, cosmos, or the Christian tradition. They thus found grounds for the reality and urgency of justice within a religious frame of reference. They established the warrants for the truths of their suffrage arguments, and found sources of human transformation toward justice, in some religious and theological aspects of their positions.

These theological frameworks were articulated not primarily for their own sakes but for the purposes of explicating and securing justice. The theological points were not cut loose from their moorings in the ethical and social perspectives. Both the religious perspectives and the social analyses in this work had one goal—to point American society toward justice. Hence, the perspective regarding justice is a particularly apt locus in each woman's framework of thought to view the intersection between social thought and religious thought.

The reflections and public work of these three figures are instructive and intriguing for contemporary ethics. None of these women was a moral philosopher, but each had a distinctive style of ethical reasoning. Each found it important to characterize questions of injustice with assertions of empirical reference to the society in which she lived; and yet each found reason also to "refer" to cosmological, biblical, or spiritual themes by which to illuminate her ethical and social perceptions and action. In this interplay among social description, ethical awareness, and theological reflection, an ethicist like myself finds an expanded view of moral perspectives and finds reasons to ponder whether we have construed the discipline of ethics in ways that are too constricting. In addition, one advantage of this work is to note ethics as practiced by people who were not "professionally" concerned with that discipline. The moral reasoning and moral activity of ordinary people might well find a greater foothold within our arena of attention.

Each chapter is structured in the same fashion. Because of the nature and scope of Stanton's work, I have for convenience divided the consideration of her position into two chapters, but the fundamental structure is identical to those which follow. After some preliminary remarks comes a brief biographical sketch of each figure to set the context for the exposition. These biographical summaries also contain notes regarding sources and source problems for this figure's work. The social analysis, or definition of the issue, is then described in some detail. Following this social analysis I pause to inquire regarding the relations of the question-and-answer structure of injustice and justice. In each case this analysis pushes onward to the religious or theological position taken by each woman. Hence I proceed to a reconstruction of that figure's religious view, once again in some detail. Finally, this exposition is followed by critical remarks.

As the chapter titles indicate, these three women possessed rather different theological views. I have called Stanton a "theologian for a feminist civil religion," Anthony a "theologian for a feminist praxis," and Shaw a "theologian for a feminist Christianity." Relevant comparisons are made in the course of each of the central expository chapters.

The conclusion inquires as to the distinctions and similarities among these figures along the schema employed in my analysis—the definition of the issue, the religious view, the view of justice in each one. Its focus is less on further comparisons and contrasts among these three figures than on the most salient problems and questions that surface from this material for future feminist reflections with regard to social analysis, views of justice, and theological reflection: the relationship between women's experience and science, between action and justice, and between theology and the women's movement. Finally, I could not leave this work without appending an epilogue concerning the overall shape and importance of this material. The work of these three women is an invitation to further theological reflection, to outlining the importance of women's history to the future of constructive feminist ethics and feminist theology.

TWO

Elizabeth Cady Stanton: Toward a Theology for a Feminist Civil Religion

Enlightenment is man's release from his self-incurred tutelage. Tutelage is man's inability to make use of his understanding without direction from another. Self-incurred is this tutelage when its cause lies not in lack of reason but in lack of resolution and courage to use it without direction from another. *Sapere Aude!* "Have the courage to use your own reason!"—that is the motto of enlightenment. . . . . That the step to competence is held to be very dangerous by the far greater portion of mankind (*and by the entire fair sex*)—quite apart from its being arduous—is seen to by those guardians who have so kindly assumed superintendence over them.

Immanuel Kant, "What is Enlightenment?"

So long as women are not represented in the government they are in a condition of tutelage, perpetual minority, slavery.

Elizabeth Cady Stanton, *History of Woman Suffrage*

In terms of contributions to feminist theory, Elizabeth Stanton is the most important of the figures considered in this study. She has been called the "chief intellectual architect of American feminism"[1] and the "boldest thinker and most outstanding leader of the first generation of feminists."[2] More than any other theorist of the movement, it was she who set the terms on which the feminists of the nineteenth century made their case to the American public. She wrote so much,[3] on so many differing aspects of the suffrage struggle, with such insight, that it was hard even for her detractors to escape her influence. In addition, she wrote so well that her political prose commands respect regardless of what one finally thinks of her views. To deal adequately

15

with Stanton's thought would require a full-length treatment in itself. Failing that, I will treat her more fully than the figures who follow.

The chief injustice faced by the suffrage movement according to Stanton was the denial of the individuality of women's persons. A system of caste and class based on sex legislated for all women regardless of their individual merits or activities. She aimed her struggle against "every invidious distinction of sex"—and "invidious" invariably meant those distinctions which hampered the individual woman in the development of her capacities. For Stanton individuality was a metaphysical first principle as much as a political principle, and it was meant to undercut all discussions of women from the point of view of the "incidental relations of life" (such as wifehood and motherhood). Stanton also integrated into her system the masculine/feminine "elements" of civilization (or of the universe). They were, however, always strictly subordinated to the sheer solitariness of individuals and hence to individual rights.

Such brief and bald statements must immediately be qualified, for Stanton's analysis of women's situation aimed to be both detailed and comprehensive. She sought to delineate "the nice shades and degrees of woman's wrongs, and the central point of her weakness and degradation,"[4] in a way that covered "the whole range of human experience."[5] To achieve this comprehensive goal, she articulated a "fourfold bondage"—in family, politics, civil society, and religion. To Stanton the "central point" of women's situation was that this fourfold bondage presented systemic obstacles to the development of women as individuals.

Stanton's religious evolution was nearly as complex as the social analysis she did so well. She began her feminist career at Seneca Falls, announcing her allegiance to Christianity and her belief that the Bible, the greatest of all books, was ever on the side of freedom. The following years of her suffrage activities led her to assert that the church was a "police institution" that had done more to degrade woman than all other adverse influences combined. Nor were the other world religions able to point to a better record.

Critical analysis of Stanton's religion requires a distinction between an "early" and a "late" Stanton. One major theme was her changing assessment of the Christian churches. Alienation from received Christianity, however important it was, did not exhaust the transition. The controversies surrounding the Fourteenth and Fifteenth Amendments to the Constitution, the well-known "Negro's Hour" debates, led her to contest the ethical and religious value of self-sacrificing love in order to concentrate on women's self-assertion. Fundamental to this change was her growing sense of the devastation of women's physical bodies, particularly the notion that maternity was a "curse" attributable to the fall of Eve in the Garden of Eden.

The case for individual rights, however, remained constant in Stanton's thought. Indeed, her arguments were so classic as to warrant calling her an "Enlightenment feminist."[6] Many of her speeches opened with the arraignment of the tyrant, Custom, before the "bar of Common Sense." She was tireless in pointing out that great nature's laws were transgressed by the social order's strictures on women. "*Sapere Aude*" was translated into women's idiom as Stanton was converted to a more rational religion, one that insisted on her right to think. She appealed to each woman's right to think as her own authority, to cosmic laws that were natural and immutable, to the status of woman as "imaginary Robinson Crusoe," and a watchmaker God. In the context of the late nineteenth century, this religion of the Founding Fathers and their European counterparts was radically out of step with mainstream American religion—especially as Stanton became ever more anticlerical. It was perhaps inevitable that she embraced the Free Religious Association.

Like many of the Founding Fathers, Stanton identified democratic politics and religion so closely that we must see her as an exponent of a "civil religion." As one of her exceptionally clear articles put it, "the American idea of individual rights [is] more sacred than any civil or ecclesiastical organizations."[7] Fundamentally, equality, symbolized by the right to vote, was a religious idea, a divine idea. As in many of Stanton's antiecclesiastical statements, there was a sense in which equality was also a Christian idea, for it was "uttered on Calvary" as well as "framed into statutes by the Fathers of '76." As religion and politics came together for Stanton in the upward progress of civilization toward the divine ideal, she was clear that human beings could be "as gods." It was unthinkable that true religion, as opposed to the false faiths promulgated by Christian doctrine, would oppose any moral advance or truths. Politics was a high art, "the most exalted of all sciences." Religion was, as she misquoted Matthew Arnold, "science tinged with emotion."

Stanton's career and thought were full and complex enough in their development over time to require a brief overview as a guide to the analysis that follows. "Toward Free Religion" offers a sketch of her biography and theoretical evolution through the decades. The remainder of this chapter is devoted to Stanton's view of the social issue, the fourfold bondage in family, state, church, society. Because Stanton's religious metamorphosis is fundamentally related to her social view, I begin with her critique of the religions of man. "The Perversion of the Religious Element in Women" depicts in detail the movement of Stanton's theoretical and practical critiques of the churches. "The Man Marriage and Nothing More" investigates her view of injustice to women in family and marriage. "The Tyrant Custom" presents her perspective on women's situation in "civil society," that is, in education, dress, character, work. "The Degradation of Disfranchisement" is Stanton's case for the vote as the chief arena of her political strand of bondage, in some ways the culmination of all her arguments. In each section I pay special attention to ways these "strands" of bondage were interwoven.

This social analysis aimed at portraying adequately the injustice that the suffrage movement fought. Hence I conclude this chapter by inquiring as to the shape and nature of the justice that "fits" this ethical question as a theological "answer" fits its theological "question." "Injustice and Justice" summarizes and analyzes the view of justice buried in Stanton's social analysis. This consideration then opens out into her constructive religious perspective. The next chapter analyzes Stanton's theology in greater detail.

Toward Free Religion

Elizabeth Cady (1815-1902) was born into the family of a stern upstate New York judge. The family was Scotch Presbyterian, a branch of Christianity she remembered as gloomy, dogmatic, and formal. Educated at Troy Female Seminary, one of the earliest serious courses of study for girls, she had an early formative brush with the second Great Awakening. Charles Grandison Finney himself presided over the revivals in the school, located in the "burned-over district" of New York.

> Owing to my gloomy Calvinistic training in the old Scotch Presbyterian Church, and my vivid imagination, I was one of the first victims. . . . Fear of the judgment seized my soul. Visions of the lost haunted my dreams. Mental anguish prostrated my health. Dethronement of my reason was apprehended by friends.[8]

Despite this soul-searching, Stanton was *not* one of the great evangelist's success stories.[9] Her efforts to "repent and believe" only made her ever more unhappy. The Cady family, alarmed at her state of mind, presented her with a change of scene (a trip to Niagara) and some theoretical demystification of

18

the revival process. The conversation and reading centered on phrenology and "many other liberal works."[10] Her brother-in-law explained in a scientific manner to the young victim

> the nature of the delusion we had all experienced, the physical conditions, the mental processes, the church machinery by which such excitements are worked up, and the impositions to which credulous minds are necessarily subjected . . . he helped us to understand these workings of the human mind and reconciled us to the more rational condition in which we now found ourselves.[11]

The home of Gerrit Smith, prominent abolitionist, was Stanton's entrée into both the abolitionist struggle and her marriage. There Stanton encountered abolitionists in contention with the received tradition of Christianity— Garrison, Phillips, May, Greene, Foster, Abby Kelley, the Motts, John Browne, black people on the Underground Railway, and her future husband. Henry Stanton, a member of Finney's Loyal Band of abolitionist theological students, took his new wife to the World Anti-Slavery Convention in 1840 in England. There Stanton witnessed one of the early public debates on women's equality. Despite the strong support of several American male colleagues, the women delegates were relegated to observing the convention's work from behind a balcony screen. Lucretia Mott and Elizabeth Stanton made their first acquaintance here, one that Stanton later remembered as initiating her into her "right to think"—the same right exercised by Luther, Calvin, and John Knox.

Henry Stanton practiced law in Boston between 1843 and 1847. In that center of reform and religious ferment, his wife's continuing intellectual quest found substance adequate to her talent. She attended conversations on the model established by Margaret Fuller (though Fuller herself had left Boston) with Elizabeth Peabody, Alcott, Zane, Wright, Johnson. She appreciated so much Theodore Parker's lectures on religion[12] that she heard them a second time; she regularly attended his church. The Stanton family was close to Whittier, and moved in circles containing William Henry Channing, Emerson, Lowell, Hawthorne, Dana, Brownson.[13]

In 1848, in upstate New York once again, Stanton and Mott renewed their acquaintance. The result was the Seneca Falls Convention on the rights of women, whose Declaration of Sentiments became the broadside statement of the organized women's rights movement. Stanton shocked that assembly with a resolution demanding women's enfranchisement—the only resolution that was not voted unanimously. Her earliest recorded speech declared her a

Christian. She believed that the greatest of all books was ever on the side of freedom, and she embarked on the exegesis of St. Paul to prove her point—the first of a series of biblical interpretations she used to make her case. In 1851 Stanton met the young Quaker schoolteacher Susan B. Anthony; their friendship became the collaboration of a lifetime's suffrage agitation.

The years before the Civil War found Stanton at home with her growing family (seven children) and a spouse who himself was deeply involved in reform. Even these years she turned to good account for the cause: "It is not in vain that in myself I have experienced all the wearisome cares to which woman in her best estate is subject."[14] She spent three years working for a women's temperance organization; broadening the platform to include women's rights, divorce, and the church met with such opposition that she left that arena for women's rights alone. In this period, she spoke of "two types of Christianity"—the practical (reforming) type, and the devotional (conservative) type—and left little doubt that she was of the former sort. The radical themes of her social analysis included divorce and marriage laws and women's rights to their earnings and to the custody of their children.

To meet the challenge of the Civil War the suffragist movement transmuted itself into the League of Loyal Women, petitioning Congress for immediate abolition of slavery. The supporters of women's rights waited upon the peace, believing that their efforts for the nation would win them the vote. The Kansas campaigns of 1867 were among the last occasions of suffragist unity. Supporters of antislavery and women's rights had come together for two brief years in the American Equal Rights Association. The Fourteenth Amendment, introducing the word "male" into the U.S. Constitution for the first time, simultaneously introduced discord into the AERA. The debates over "the Negro's Hour" produced several fateful results.

First, Stanton and Anthony formed the National Woman Suffrage Association (NWSA). They opposed the passage of any federal amendment that would so drastically exclude women, while the American Woman Suffrage Association (AWSA), led by women such as Julia Ward Howe and Lucy Stone, wanted to consolidate the gains of the antislavery struggle, believing that women would eventually have their "hour" as well. The split between these two groups persisted until 1890, when they merged into the National American Woman Suffrage Association (NAWSA).

Second, from this time onward, Stanton vacillated between universal suffrage and other partial suffrage proposals that might be made to enfranchise some women. To Stanton's perspective, educated women were being passed over for "Sambo," as she called black men. She painted dreary pictures of the further degradation that women were to experience with this change.

Third, the attack by Wendell Phillips on the Stanton-Anthony wing of the movement pushed Stanton away from certain traditional Christian vocabularies. He accused the opponents of the Fourteenth and Fifteenth Amendments of "selfishness"; almost immediately, Stanton stopped using the language of self-sacrifice for women in favor of the language of self-assertion, a difference that was to become marked between the feminists of the AWSA and the NWSA.

Fourth, *The Revolution*, owned by Anthony but edited by Stanton with Parker Pillsbury, melded fiery abolitionist attacks on the church with fiery feminist attacks on the church. Pillsbury covered, for example, the Free Religious Conventions; the journal published selections and reviews from such men as Comte and Lecky. Further, several ordained clergy and religious journals took up their cudgels against the magazine.[15]

During the 1870s Stanton was a regular on the Lyceum Bureau circuits. Already in her sixties during the nation's centennial, she, along with Anthony and a younger protégée, interspersed their lectures and NWSA conventions with work on *The History of Woman Suffrage*. That project soon outgrew its initial modest projection as one volume, and lasted through the 1880s.

Though her earliest brushes with creative movements in American religion were with Finney's evangelicalism and Boston transcendentalism, by this period Stanton was a full-fledged free thinker. She gave lectures to the Free Religious Association and quoted approvingly from that association's journal, *The Index*. Beginning in 1878 she sponsored resolutions in suffrage conventions "to rouse women to a realization of their degraded position in the Church."[16] A typical question of her articles and speeches was "What has Christianity done for Women?" The answer was, less than nothing. Indeed, she saw the church as a "police institution"[17] and called for a new religion. Among her friends were such outspoken infidels as Robert G. Ingersoll, Moncure Conway, and the English atheist and secularist Charles Bradlaugh. Her later years took her frequently to Europe, where her son Theodore and her daughter Harriet (the only two children to follow in their mother's footsteps) resided. Many of her religious materials from her later life were published by the Open Court Press, the Chicago freethinker's publishing arm. She increasingly left aside discussions of emotion for reason, and spoke of science and scientific laws in relation to religion. The notion, attributed to the Bible, that maternity was a curse was among the most strenuous reasons that she embarked on the project of *The*

21

Woman's Bible, reading the higher criticism, and gathering a committee of women to comment on the text.

Already advanced in years when the suffrage rupture was healed with the merger of the two organizations, Stanton became the first president of the NAWSA. This was largely Anthony's doing, who always sought to point away from herself and toward her esteemed friend. It was also a largely honorary position.[18] After her departure from the chair in 1892, she continued sending letters and writing articles. The publication of Volume 1 of *The Woman's Bible* provoked a storm of controversy in the NAWSA in 1896, resulting in a vote that amounted to censure. But by 1902, at her death at age eighty-seven, she was promptly hailed from near and far as the "eldest statesman" of the cause that once had brought her so much opprobrium.

Stanton had spent the last fifty years of her long life concentrating on the cause of woman suffrage. Her active involvement with conventions and organizations waxed and waned in various periods of her life; her religious evolution led her outside the bounds of traditional Christianity.[19]

Women's Individuality Denied in a Fourfold Bondage

It is frequently said that a major failing of the woman suffrage movement was its single-minded concentration on the vote. This was hardly true of Elizabeth Cady Stanton, herself one of the most ardent advocates of women's right to vote. In her last years, Stanton argued to Anthony that

> our association cannot be too broad. Suffrage involves every basic principle of republican government, all our social, civil, religious, educational, and political rights. It is therefore germane to our platform to discuss every invidious distinction of sex in the college, home, trades, and professions, in literature, sacred and profane, in the canon as well as the civil law.[20]

This was no last-minute piece of wisdom from an old woman reconsidering errors she had earlier committed. For, she continued, "at the inauguration of our movement we numbered in our Declaration of Sentiments eighteen grievances covering the whole range of human experience."[21] All her life efforts were devoted to such a broad attack. To seek equality everywhere, to include every woman,[22] to discuss every invidious distinction of sex, on the basis of every basic principle of government and human rights—these formulations indicate the sweep of her "suffragist" aims.

To translate this comprehensive aim into a political program, Stanton analyzed women's situation into four major categories—family, society, politics, and religion. This multidimensional analysis represented a complex vision of the American social order. Each division of the American order could be analyzed on its own terms; each could be demonstrated to be interwoven in the other three. As she put it,

> Here, then, is a fourfold bondage, so many cords tightly twisted together, strong for one purpose. To attempt to undo one is to loosen all. . . . To my mind, if we had at first bravely untwisted all the strands of this fourfold cord which bound us, and demanded equality in the whole round of the circle, while perhaps we should have had a harder battle to fight, it would have been more effective and far shorter.[23]

Hence, "all reforms are interdependent . . . whatever is done to establish one principle on a solid basis, strengthens all."[24] As each strand perpetuated the others in this holistic analysis, "to undo one is to loosen all."

Stanton thought that "in all the struggles of the human race there has never been one more complicated than the present demand for equality for woman."[25] One reason for this complexity was that this was the only reform in which "no appeal to the self-interest of the dominant powers can be made."[26] These complications were also apparent in Stanton's struggle for terms by which to characterize the issue. At times she spoke of the "invidious distinction of sex."[27] At others she referred to the "bias of sex."[28] On these occasions she was also likely to speak of women as a class or caste. She also used the "antagonism of sex"[29] to describe hatred and contempt for women. Antagonism of sex was "subtle and contradictory in its influence" because "the more intimate the personal interests, the more bitter the antagonism,"[30] as one saw in the family and the church.

These complications also arose within her view of the issue, for at different times in her life Stanton seemed to believe that one of these four was more basic than the others. In the 1850s, for example, she wrote that the marriage relationship was "the starting point."[31] Even so, the other three realms were intertwined within her argument regarding marriage and family: "Our present lives, our religious teaching, our social customs on the whole question of marriage and divorce are most degrading to woman."[32] When she argued the primacy of the ballot, likewise, she continued the use of the fourfold typology.

After the vote was won, she asserted, "the rest they will surrender at discretion. Then comes equality in Church and State, in the family circle and in all social customs."[33] Later in her life she cited religious emancipation as the "first great step in the elevation of woman."

The four cords were twisted together "strong for one purpose," to deny the individual rights of women. As we shall see, each strand of bondage was brought back to the natural capacities of the solitary individual woman. These individual faculties were denied, dwarfed, stunted, distorted, and undeveloped by the "spirit of caste and class," the aristocracy of sex, the white male interpretation of the Bible, the conventions of custom. All group-based behavioral distinctions, "the invidious distinctions of sex," denied to individual women the merits of their personal achievements or the chances of their personal development.

In each section that follows, I shall summarize the salient points in Stanton's analysis of each strand of the "fourfold bondage," paying particular attention to the sorts of arguments used, and to the interrelated character of these dimensions in her work.

A. The Perversion of the Religious Element in Woman

Stanton's first suffrage speech at Seneca Falls in 1848 proclaimed her Christian beliefs and her assurance that the greatest of all books was ever on the side of freedom. In contrast, her later life's message was that "Bible and Church degrade woman" and that there was no hope for their transformation. She dated her own change from the convention of 1878, when she and her allies presented resolutions designed to rouse women to an indignation at the churches equal to that which they felt in other areas of life.[34] These changes were dramatic and substantive ones. We need, however, to scrutinize the terms of such shifts, for in certain respects the anti-Christian character of her later statements obscures the continuity of themes and assertions throughout Stanton's long career.

Hence this section is directed toward exploring the perversion of the religious element in woman, the critical social analysis of the functioning of one strand of the fourfold bondage.[35] Some emphases in Stanton's understanding of the abuse of women's faith came visibly to the fore as she grew more impatient with Christianity. But the language of the distortion of women's religious nature was constant throughout decades. Comments in *The*

Even in Christian countries woman's position was "infinitely inferior" to that of man. Stanton set herself to dispute the intellectual, moral, and physical superiority of man to woman. "Man's intellectual superiority cannot be a question until woman has had a fair trial"[42]—that is, after a century of her participation in colleges and professions.

> When woman, instead of being taxed to endow colleges where she is forbidden to enter—instead of forming sewing societies to educate "poor, but pious," young men [—]shall first educate herself, when she shall be just to herself before she is generous to others; improving the talents God has given her, and leaving her neighbor to do the same for himself, we shall not then hear so much about this boasted superiority.[43]

In fact, sewing societies for the theological education of young men were "one of the greatest humbugs of the day."[44] He, the "great, strong, lazy man," was supported by downtrodden woman, "poor, friendless, robbed of all her rights, oppressed on all sides," who "must go ignorant herself."

> There is something painfully affecting in the self-sacrifice and generosity of women, who can neither read nor write their own language with correctness, going about begging money for the education of men.[45]

Men—"bless their innocence"—represented themselves as rational and women as emotional. Stanton reinterpreted the fall of Adam to dispute such claims. Eve was told by Satan that "the sphere of her reason should be enlarged," while Adam merely ate the apple because "his love for Eve prevailed. . . . Which, I ask you, was the creature of the affections?"[46] This might well stand as the first of Stanton's efforts to cope with the biblical heritage of comments and laws with regard to women. Later her speech undertook to wrestle directly with the Bible on questions of marriage. "Must we not obey our husbands? Does not the Bible so command us?" Not so, said Stanton, "you have not rightly read your Bible."[47] The creation story said "their name" was Adam; both "first parents" had equal dominion over the earth. It was St. Paul who had to be met head on. His remarks on women's obedience were the stumbling block, but one past which Stanton nimbly found her way.

> It needs but little consideration to see how limited this command of St. Paul must be, even if you give it all the weight which is usually claimed. "Wives, obey your husbands in the Lord." Now as the command is given to me, I am of course to be the judge of what is "in the Lord," and this opens a wide field of

> escape from any troublesome commands. There can be no subordination where the one to whom a command is given is allowed to sit in judgment on the character of the command.[48]

Since an entire lecture would be required to deal with the Bible arguments, it was "enough to say that that best of Books is ever on the side of freedom, and we shrink not from pleading our case on its principles of universal justice and love."[49] From the vantage point of Stanton's later strictures on the Bible, which could not be made "in plain English" to exalt womanhood, this statement is astonishing. Similarly, she claimed, in answer to a point regarding whether women would go to war, "I believe in Christ. I believe that command 'resist not evil,' to be divine."[50]

It is not surprising, then, that this essay spoke of the suffering and self-sacrifice of women in terms that made women morally better than men, for woman was "early schooled in self-denial and suffering." Ministers, lawyers, physicians, politicians were everywhere seen in "some sad, soul-sickening deed." Hence man was inferior to woman "in every moral quality, not by nature, but made so by a false education." The duty of the day was to raise men to women's moral level. "It is as much his duty to be kind, self-denying and full of good works, as it is hers. . . . I would not have woman less pure, but I would have man more so."[51]

Nonetheless, there were some moral and religious changes that needed to be made, even in woman herself.

> Let woman live as she should. Let her feel her accountability to her Maker. Let her know that her spirit is fitted for as high a sphere as man's, and that her soul requires food as pure and exalted as his. Let her live *first* for God, and she will not make imperfect man an object of reverence and awe. Teach her her responsibility as a being of conscience and reason, that all earthly support is weak and unstable, that her only safe dependence is the arm of omnipotence, and that true happiness springs from duty accomplished. Thus will she learn the lesson of individual responsibility for time and eternity.[52]

This lesson, it seemed, was the lesson that heroic Joan of Arc had learned, to whom Stanton turned for her concluding reflections.

> Her success was philosophical, in accordance with the laws of the mind. She had a full faith in herself and inspired all those who saw her with the same. Let us cultivate like faith, like enthusiasm, and we, too, shall impress all who see and hear us with the same confidence we ourselves feel in our final success. There

seems now to be a kind of moral stagnation in our midst. . . . Verily, the world waits the coming of some new element, some purifying power, some spirit of mercy and love.[53]

This new element was womanhood. "As in woman all have fallen, so in her elevation shall the race be recreated."[54] Just as Joan of Arc had her voices, so voices came to woman "daily from the haunts of poverty, sorrow, degradation and despair." Women were called to work with all the downtrodden because they had some special skills. "There are deep and tender chords of sympathy and love in the hearts of the down-fallen and oppressed that woman can touch more skillfully than man."[55] These concluding remarks were designed to muster religious motives to do good works in general. "The same religious enthusiasm that nerved Joan of Arc to her work nerves us to ours."[56]

As president of the New York State Woman's Temperance Convention in 1852, Stanton was more explicit about her call to women to withdraw their support from churches:

And lastly, inasmuch as charity begins at home, let us withdraw our mite from all associations for sending the Gospel to the heathen across the ocean, for the education of young men for the ministry, for the building up of a theological aristocracy and gorgeous temples to the unknown God, and devote ourselves to the poor and suffering about us. Let us feed and clothe the hungry and naked, gather children into schools, and provide reading-rooms and decent homes for young men and women thrown alone upon the world. Good schools and homes where the young could ever be surrounded by an atmosphere of purity and virtue, would do more to prevent immorality and crime in our cities than all the churches in the land could ever possibly do toward the regeneration of the multitude sunk in poverty, ignorance, and vice.[57]

Later that year she honed her charges against the representatives of Christianity. Writing once more on the subject of education, her proposals modulated into criticism of the Christian churches. The separation of the sexes in all departments of life was part of the reason men did not see that women were moved by the same needs and thoughts. The "unoccupied women of fashion," left alone in the evenings while their menfolk went to political rallies or taverns, could not even turn to their religion for comfort, for "their theology is too gloomy and shadowy to afford them much pleasure in contemplation; their religion is a thing of form and not of life, so it brings them no joy or satisfaction."[58]

Education societies for the clergy came in for their share of rough language. They were especially absurd, since "among the clergy we find our most violent enemies—those most opposed to any change in woman's position." She included the whole Benevolent Empire, which was filled with men "living like so many leeches, on the religious element in our nature." "Priestcraft," as present in Protestantism as in Catholicism, abused women's religious faith by manipulating women's emotions, as we have seen. She conjured her countrywomen to withdraw the widow's mite from the support of such societies, but now for their *own* benefit, their own cause.

> Instead of any further efforts in behalf of a pin-cushion ministry, I conjure my countrywomen to devote themselves from this hour to the education, elevation, and enfranchisement of their own sex. If the same amount of devotion and self-sacrifice could be given in this direction now poured out on the churches, another generation would give us a nobler type of womanhood than any yet molded by any Bishop, Priest, or Pope.[59]

Her conclusion resembled that of many latter-day feminist theologians who rely on sociological understandings of the relationship of religion to other institutions: religion reinforced woman's bondage, completing and intensifying her degradation, rather than *causing* it, as she later claimed.

> Woman in her present ignorance is made to rest in the most distorted views of God and the Bible and the laws of her being; and like the poor slave, "Uncle Tom," her religion, instead of making her noble and free, and impelling her to flee from all gross surroundings, by the false lessons of her spiritual teachers, by the wrong application of the great principles of right and justice, has made her bondage but more certain and lasting, her degradation more helpless and complete.[60]

While Stanton's language was not as radical as it was to become later, it was nevertheless too radical for her contemporaries. The following year, in the Woman's State Temperance Organization, Stanton was forced to defend herself for attacking the church. Her response is worth citing at some length because this phase of Stanton's religious thought is little known and because this statement marks a crucial stage in the development of her thought. Two types of Christianity appear, each relatively complete in itself.

> But why attack the Church? We do not attack the Church; we defend ourselves merely against its attacks. It is true that the Church and reformers have always

been in an antagonistic position from the time of Luther down to our own day, and will continue to be until the devotional and practical types of Christianity shall be united in one harmonious whole. . . . I find no special fault to find with that part of humanity that gathers into our churches; to me, human nature seems to manifest itself in very much the same way in the Church and out of it. Go through any community you please—into the nursery, kitchen, the parlor, the places of merchandise, the market-place, and exchange, and who can tell the church member from the outsider? I see no reason why we should expect more of them than other men. Why, say you, they lay claim to greater holiness; to more rigid creeds; to a belief in a sterner God; to a closer observance of forms. The Bible with them, is the rule of life, the foundation of faith, and why should we not look to them for patterns of purity, goodness and truth above all other men? I deny the assumption. Reformers on all sides claim for themselves a higher position than the Church. Our God is a God of justice, mercy, and truth. Their God sanctions violence, oppression, and wine-bibbing, and winks at gross moral delinquencies. Our Bible commands us to love our enemies; to resist not evil; to break every yoke and let the oppressed go free; and makes a noble life of more importance than a stern faith. Their Bible permits war, slavery, capital punishment, and makes salvation depend on faith and ordinances. In their creed it is a sin to dance, to pick up sticks on the Sabbath day, to go to the theater, or large parties during Lent, to read a notice of any reform meeting from the altar, or permit a woman to speak in the church. In our creed it is a sin to hold a slave; to hang a man on the gallows; to make war on defenseless nations, or to sell rum to a weak brother, and rob the widow and the orphan of a protector and a home. . . .

We must not expect the Church to leap en masse to a higher position. She sends forth her missionaries of truth one by one. All of our reforms have started there. The advocates and opposers of the reforms of our day, have grown up side by side, partaking of the same ordinances and officiating at the same altars; but one, by applying more fully his Christian principles to life, and pursuing an admitted truth to its legitimate results, has unwittingly found himself in antagonism with his brother.

Belief is not voluntary, and change is the natural result of growth and development.[61]

Thus in 1853 Stanton's posture was already defensive, but she still found grounds for common cause with the Christian churches. The churches had provided the matrix, the original principles of reformers. The practical type of Christianity merely applied its Christian principles to life "more fully" than the devotional type. There was not a disagreement in substance between them. Stanton's patience with the ecclesiastical institutions here was in stark contrast to her later position. The notion that the practical reformers were developed in the churches was not a call for the churches as such to change. Reformers grew "one by one," in unwitting antagonism to the devotional Christian next to them in the pew. She finally relieved the churches of responsibility for their position by her comment that "belief is not voluntary." She hoped that these two types would be "united in one harmonious whole."

Nevertheless, one can see in this statement hints of Stanton's later rupture with the churches. Each type of Christianity was relatively complete—two types, two Gods, two Bibles, two creeds, one of them higher than the other. It is a temptation of hindsight to say that it was only a matter of time before she ceased to say that these were two branches of Christianity and began to say that they were two types of religion, one true and one false. In fact, for all Stanton's anticlerisy, late or early, she always wavered precisely on grounds similar to these in 1853. In her freethought stage she continued to maintain that the great principle(s) of Christianity and of feminist reform were the same, though what they consisted in was not always spelled out. (Freedom of individual judgment and equality in creation were frequent items of their similarity.) That a noble life was of more importance than a stern faith, that ethical axiom of the liberal Protestantism of the age, was a notion she later developed at some length.

Stanton wavered between self-assertion and selflessness in this earliest period. In the chair of the temperance organization, she urged that sincere women workers "shall ever lose sight of self; each soul will, in a measure, forget its own individual interests in proclaiming great principles of justice and right."[62] As late as 1869 she claimed that women's self-sacrifice and self-denial were Christ-like. Most marriages reversed the injunctions of St. Paul regarding families.

> Take the multitudes of drunkards, licentious men and criminals, married to sober, virtuous and refined women, and consider in what single point of view their relation to their wives can correspond to that of Christ and the church. The self-sacrificing mother in such households, who, by constant toil, feeds and clothes her children, and brings them up in habits of industry, who, in rain and sleet and snow, follows her wretched husband to his haunts of vice, at the midnight hour, and, with a divine love and patience, guides his unsteady feet to their far off home, surely, she is the Christ that smooths the rough road and illumines life's dark journeys all through.[63]

This likening woman to Christ on the basis of her self-sacrificing love utterly contradicted Stanton's earlier comments. As early as 1856 she had articulated a general rejection of self-sacrifice for women and placed that rejection in the context of a religious critique.

> For what man can honestly deny that he has not a secret feeling that where his pleasure and woman's seems to conflict, the woman must be sacrificed; and what is worse, woman herself has come to think so too. She believes that all she tastes of joy in life is from the generosity and benevolence of man; and the bitter cup of sorrow, which she too often drinks to the very dregs, is of the good providence of God, sent by a kind hand for her improvement and development. This sentiment pervades the laws, customs, and religions of all countries, both Christian and heathen.[64]

Sometimes she claimed that the woman who said she had all the rights she wanted was not only ignorant but selfish. At other times she claimed that a woman needed to learn to be just to herself *before* she could be generous to others.[65]

Stanton's early firm belief that the Bible was ever on the side of freedom and justice ran into opposition. In 1854, writing to the women of New York, she sounded notes that indicated women's religious convictions were impeding their participation in the suffrage struggle. "Let no religious scruples hold you back," she urged. The short piece attacked briefly on a variety of fronts. The conflict of interpretations was central in Stanton's mind. "The writings of St. Paul, like our State Constitutions, are susceptible of various interpretations." Certain of those interpretations were "man's interpretations," not woman's. On the one hand, she urged women to ignore Paul altogether, because to "any thinking mind, there is no difficulty in explaining those passages of the Apostle as applicable to the times in which they were written, as having no reference whatever to the Women of the nineteenth century."[66] If not biblical literalism, then what? Stanton replaced the law written in the text with the law written by God on the inner soul. Indignation against injustice moved one past human codes and creeds into personal accountability directly to God.

> But when the human soul is roused with holy indignation against injustice and oppression, it stops not to translate human parchments, but follows out the law of the inner being, written by the finger of God in the first hour of its creation.[67]

Woman "falsified herself and blasphemed her God" when she refused to demand equal rights.

Clearly more had to be done directly with the "white male interpretation" of the Bible. Over the next decade Stanton devoted considerable effort to establishing that the Bible supported women's freedom on a variety of fronts. She gave specific lectures on biblical topics.[68] The early volumes of *The Revolution* are especially rich with Stanton's religious thought. She wrote a series on the women of the Bible, which pointed out how "strong-minded" they were.[69] The female figures in the Bible made it all the more remarkable that "so many persons still insist that both the letter and the spirit of the Book are opposed to the political, religious, and social equality of woman."[70] I have already noted above Stanton's treatment of St. Paul. Let us glance at her transitional interpretation of the creation stories. Stanton was well aware that there were two separate creation stories.[71] Genesis 1:27-28 was her single most frequently cited biblical text; like many feminists after her, she took her fundamental bearings from the simultaneous creation of the sexes. In the early pages of *The Revolution* Stanton edged closer to a scientific approach to these questions.

> There is a great deal of fine-spun theorizing about the creation of man and woman, but there is no reason in the light of science, for not supposing that the male and female of the human family were a simultaneous creation, as in the case of all the lower animals.[72]

The Eden story was "of course allegorical." It had nonetheless to be treated, since the opposition relied on it so heavily. "All admit that before the fall our first parents were equal." Stanton's critique of the interpretation of the aftermath of the fall was an ethical one. The opponents' view had to be that there was "some somerset of the moral laws of the universe" in order to conclude that "woman fell the farthest, became an inferior being, and has been in subjection ever since to man, and must be to the end." This Stanton characterized as "twaddle," and if such arrant nonsense needed an answer, it was a Christian answer:

> The old dispensation has passed away. No condition of things, laws, or customs recorded in that ancient system previous to the advent of the Messiah, have any authority today; they are all superseded in the Christian civilization.

That meant appealing to the "general spirit of Christianity," rather than to proof-texts in isolation or to the obsolete "customs of the Oriental nations."

A year later Stanton went farther. A letter from "Peter and Paul" expressed religious objections to suffrage based on the fall story. "Peter and Paul" had evidently met Stanton in a convention, and were taken with her, for their letter was good-natured, even affectionate, as well as patronizing: "Now, you know how in the beginning, woman voted on the apple question." In answer, she refused to attribute the sin and evil of the world to Eve's action, claiming instead that it was beneficial. The influence of Positivism is apparent in her response. She viewed Eve's action as the beginning, the sine qua non of science, which would not have been possible in the innocence of Eden.

> I disagree with Peter and Paul as to the effect on civilization of the action of woman at that ancient polling booth, the apple tree, where our first parents and his Satanic Majesty held council together. That act was the unlocking to the human family of all the realms of knowledge and thought; but for that, Moses and Aaron, Samson and Solomon, Columbus, Newton, Fulton and Cyrus Field, would have been to this hour listlessly sunning themselves on the grassy slopes of Paradise, ignorant of the laws of their being and everything beyond their own horizon. Yes, when Eve took her destiny in her own hand and set minds spinning down through all the spheres of time, she declared humanity omnipotent, and today thinking people are wrapt in wonder and admiration at the inventions and discoveries of science, the grandeur of man's conceptions and the magnitude of his works.[73]

Stanton had been reading Comte, and it is to her shift in religious views I now turn.

2. From The Revolution to The Woman's Bible

The editorial policies of *The Revolution* were not always clear or apparent to a later reader. Parker Pillsbury and Elizabeth Stanton wrote most of its material, it seems, though additional authors were drawn into its pages later. It reprinted news related to women from other periodicals, frequently in order to point to a lesson in the presuppositions of an author or in the mechanisms of the social order that were out of line with the "theory." It also reprinted material its editors found of particular interest to the cause.

Two sections of Comte's positive philosophy that pertained to the "feminine influence of positivism" were translated for its pages. In Comte's "scientific" view, man represented force and reason; woman, affect and love. Love was the only truly moral power. From this rational scientific perspective the sexes were ever complementary to each other. (She represented the social, he the selfish virtues on one reading.) That "in every respect it is as simple companion of man that positivism honors woman, irrespective of maternal functions" must have been welcome words to Stanton, who had ever argued that maternity was the less universal fact. Similarly, the view of upward progress in the theory, which saw human existence as "devoted to universal perfectionment, and elevates to the highest rank moral perfectionment," must have been congenial to her.[74] Most crucial to the development of Stanton's later religious thought was Comte's rendition of the sexes' complementarity as fundamental to attaining the acme of progress: "The natural differences of the sexes, happily completed by their social diversities, renders each one of them indispensable to the moral perfectionment of the other."[75]

Stanton's comments regarding Comte's work have a specific stamp to them. The elements of masculine and feminine and the great laws of the cosmos were the two aspects of his thought she integrated with her own. A scant six months after these Comte selections appeared in *The Revolution*'s pages, Stanton admitted to having changed her position altogether. Suddenly she "saw that stronger arguments could be drawn from a difference in sex, in mind as well as in body."[76] From this time forward she asserted that there was "sex in soul" as well as in body, an idea she found in various scientific authorities ("as Swedenborg, and Comte, and Holcombe . . . all admit").[77] It followed from "sex in soul" that men could not represent women anywhere in the social order, for they could not partake of the specific qualities of women's thought.

> Man is but half a complete being, with but half an idea on every subject, and yet he has undertaken to govern the world according to his fragmentary ideas, never dreaming that woman's thought, everywhere, was necessary to his success. Need anyone wonder at the disorganization of the state, the church, and the home under a dynasty so incomplete and one-sided?[78]

Interestingly, woman's thought here was identified with that of the *mother*, as it seemed regularly to be from this point on. "Our false customs and philosophies, our unjust laws, gloomy theologies, and social abominations call loudly for the revivifying influence of the mother, and in every department of science and life."[79]

The natural laws that Comte had established were the other real attraction of his system, a motif readily assimilable to Stanton's republican natural law stance. Here Stanton's language assumed a form that persisted throughout her career.

The beauty of Comte's system to us is that it is based on immutable laws, governing not only the solar system, the vegetable, mineral, and animal world, but the human family, all moving in beautiful harmony together, while the seeming friction and discord of our daily life are but our blundering efforts to bring ourselves into line with these laws.[80]

Comte's was a scientific case that demonstrated what Stanton had long claimed, that moral laws and material laws were not distinct from each other, nor were the former any less fixed and sure than the latter. (Her early temperance speeches had used a "medical metaphor": the wise doctor of the social realm would point to the true causes of what others merely attacked as symptoms.) Stanton's scientific rationalism extended itself more deeply into her ethical and religious arguments for the suffrage.

There were, however, other building blocks that were to fall into place in these short years before 1870. An editorial in a Catholic magazine set Stanton to clarify her thoughts regarding religion and politics. Its author claimed that suffrage was not a natural right; that the family was deteriorating in American life; that the remedy for many social wrongs was to be found in the Catholic stress on authority. This piece incensed Stanton, who found it un-American. Unlike her successor, Shaw, when the ballot box, "the symbol of that great idea of equality," was attacked, Stanton sprang to its defense.

There was a complexity about her case that is crucial for understanding her "more rational religion." She did not use the language of "essential" and "positive" religion, but clearly something like that distinction underlay the ways she identified and distinguished that which was truly sacred from the conventionally religious (and conventionally political) life of the day. Religion and government were distinct from each other, yet the idea of equality was the locus of their identity at their highest moments. "The American idea" was that individual rights were "more sacred than any civil or ecclesiastical organizations." (The Catholic idea of authority was inimical to this American idea; if it "finds lodgment in the minds of this people, we ring the death-knell of American liberties.") Inasmuch as they were separate from each other, there were distinct criteria of judgment to be brought to bear on both religion and government.

A religion is pure only as it dignifies man, lifts him above fear and superstition, and leaves him free to think.

A government is just only when the whole people share equally in its protection and advantages.[81]

Individual rights and equality were more basic than either of these merely temporal and mortal phenomena. Nonetheless these fundamental, more sacred ideas found specific expression in both churches and government.

> Its outgrowth in the church, is discussion, dissension, and division into endless sects and creeds and canons, all good, it shows life and thought there. Its outgrowth in the state is a determination on the part of the whole people to have a voice in national questions involving the interests of all alike.[82]

The right to vote provided a bulwark of natural self-sovereignty. Its purpose was "to throw round one's self new outposts of individual sacredness."

This great idea of equality and individual rights was also identified with the Christian tradition and the Revolution in their highest and best manifestations. Its "divine power" even drew the human race and deity closer together.

> The ballot-box is the symbol of that great idea of equality, uttered on Calvary, echoed by the exiles of liberty through ages, and framed into statutes by the Fathers of '76. Its divine power is fast clearing away the rubbish of caste and class between man and man, between the creature and the Creator.[83]

The Catholic author deprecated action in this world to improve the human spiritual lot; Stanton became more explicit about her this-worldly hopes of paradise implied by the notion of drawing nearer to the creator.

> We are taught to pray, "Thy will be done on earth as it is in heaven." If the thing cannot be done, why waste breath asking for it? I believe, by a knowledge of God's laws, of political, moral, and social science, we can make a paradise for the race in this world. Progress is the law of life, things are greatly improved since the days of Noah, and to what point of elevation a few centuries more will lift the race there is no telling. . . . We do not yet fully appreciate the power of the ballot nor all that we can accomplish by a wise use of it.[84]

Finally, Stanton identified the case dearest to her own heart with this civil religion, with the Reformation and the Revolution, in one fell swoop:

> This great idea of equality, now making such radical changes in the state and the church, will in its progress, revolutionize our homes also. The present rebellion of women and children against injustice and oppression is just as philosophical as that of Luther against the church, and the American colonies against Great Britain.[85]

That the human race were to be as gods once they had begun the upward climb through the ballot box (and education) is something I return to more fully below. To Stanton the ballot box was a holy of holies; voting was a religious duty to be exercised religiously in more than a debased sense of that word. Anything that kept women from this sacred dimension of life, sometimes the "most exalted" of all, was clearly a perversion of the religious element of her nature. The suffrage cause was religious *not* because of St. Paul's injunctions or any biblical text, but intrinsically so, on its own grounds. That Christianity was itself to be measured against this standard—and not the other way around—was here presented clearly for the first time in Stanton's career.

One other incident from the epoch of *The Revolution* was necessary to complete the transition. The controversies over the "Negro's Hour" and the publication of Mill's *The Subjection of Women*, pushed Stanton beyond the language of self-sacrifice as a virtue for women. Wendell Phillips, one of the men Stanton most admired, charged that the women's rights movement, unlike anti-slavery, was a selfish movement. Stanton denied the moral difference between the two movements.[86] A scant two months later, she clarified her thinking regarding selfishness in an essay contrasting self-sacrifice and self-assertion. Delicacy, fainting, and hysteria had gone out of fashion; now "Woman's Pet Virtue" was self-sacrifice. This notion of woman's moral character had been so thoroughly internalized (as we would say today) that it was no wonder that more women did not join the struggle.

> This has been theoretically presented to woman so long by crafty, selfish teachings as the acme of her virtues, and so patiently practiced, that all women have fallen into a kind of inane apathy over their slavish condition; and a religious cant, in its acceptance, as divinely ordained, that it is the most hopeless and humiliating feature of their present degradation.[87]

This mistaken notion of the "acme of her virtues" was directly responsible for the worst conditions that prevailed among women, the cause of

> this annual holocaust of womanhood, from weakness, weariness and vice; from overwork, unhappy marriages, excessive maternity, prostitution, and from a humiliating dependence on man for her daily bread. The mass of women sacrifice themselves to their clothes, houses, children, fashion, custom, and their fathers, brothers, or husbands at home.[88]

Rather than "ministering to the animal wants of those around them," Stanton called women to realize that "a woman's first duty is to herself; to develop all the powers and capacities of her own soul and body, to secure health, happiness, and freedom." This assertion went hand in hand with Stanton's familiar claim that "womanhood is more than wifehood or motherhood, because it is a more universal fact." Self-development was always to be discussed in terms of individuality rather than the "incidental relations" of social role.

This series of claims regarding woman's moral duty to herself was directly tied to the indictment of false religion.

> The religious faith of woman has been so perverted and played upon, that she really has come to think that the chains that hold the mother of the race slaves to their own sons, were forged by the hand of the living God.[89]

Stanton had not yet slipped outside the tradition altogether. She pointed to the active virtues and moral heroism of Christ in contrast to his suffering:

> In conversation with a highly educated woman, not long since, we chanced to speak of the provoking patience with which women endured wrongs they could easily escape, if they only had a little more will-power. "Ah," said she, "that is the Christ in them!"
> We felt then, and still feel that she was wrong in her conception of the character of Jesus, ever brave and heroic, entrenching himself on high moral principle, denouncing to the death, the vices and crimes, the opinions and customs of his day and generation. What in his humanity he could not escape, he bore with a patient grandeur that commands our love and admiration, but where resistance was possible he verified his words, that he came not to bring peace on earth, but a sword.[90]

Any language praising or encouraging the self-sacrifice or self-denial of women was henceforth banished from Stanton's feminist theory and feminist theology. This theological and ethical stance, which virtually became the credo of NWSA stalwarts, was one of the reasons for its rift with the Boston AWSA feminists, to whom the language of service to others remained fundamental.[91]

Unprinted speeches of the late 1860s and early 1870s are good indicators of another transition in Stanton's thought. The perversion of the religious element in women went farther than the indictment of priestcraft or concern for woman's self-assertion. Gloomy theology and otherworldliness were particularly emphasized as Stanton called for something like a social gospel. I have noted that "the practical type" of Christianity was devoted to generalized reform: slavery, capital punishment, war, temperance, and women's rights appeared among the list of good causes in the noble life. From *The Revolution* onward, she added prisons and asylums, the cause of the poor, and political economy. To change these conditions in this world was more important than speculations about the hereafter. Surveying the situation of the poor, she found the first step toward the transformation of their condition to be "cultivating the religious conscience of the people" as to the sinfulness of "these broad inequalities among mankind" and as to practical work.

> Let the missionary spirit of the Christian world begin with the heathen of their own country towns, neighborhood, with the high duties of this life which they know and understand, instead of that which is to come of which they know nothing. Let them give more thought to their outward conditions, their bodies, instead of cultivating such undue anxiety about their souls. Let them understand that the facts and duties of this life are of primal importance to all speculations about the hereafter.[92]

This was, notice, a call for the reform of Christianity. The poor should no longer be taught by the churches "lessons of satisfaction and patience with the humiliating conditions in which they find themselves there" in favor of a good life in heaven. "They should be roused . . . to secure their rightful share of the good things on this green earth." There was an explicitly Christian theological argument constructed to secure this program.

> Let the all pervading love of charity of the command, "Love thy neighbor as thyself" be the text for all the sermons until the practical duties involved in that universal sentiment be thoroughly understood and enforced. When justice takes the place of charity, no alms-giving will be needed. The essential element of the mission of Jesus was equality. That was the theme of all his discourses, the essential oneness of humanity the cornerstone of the Christian religion. Yet how little its apostles dwell on this central truth. Faith in abstractions counts for more than morality in all life's relations.[93]

During the 1870s she explored the relationship of the churches to "The True Republic." Otherworldliness and obedience to authority belonged to "the feudal past when humanity was cheap," and not to the American republic. "The errors of the church have consisted all along in substituting the customs of ignorance for the wisdom of nature in worshipping the invisible, forgetting the visible, in dignifying symbols and degrading man." Happily, in the new age "science is fast changing our theology and metaphysics." If the church was to keep up with the times, "forms, dogma, and abstractions" must be replaced by "moral science." Unfortunately the church of Stanton's age was not up to this measure.

> We find the whole world stirred up today with the discussion as to whether the Pope is infallible when any man or woman with two grains of common sense knows he is not. . . . It is of very little importance whether the Pope is infallible, the conception of the Virgin Mary immaculate, whether children should be sprinkled when babies or dipped when twenty-one, whether the devil has a personality or hell a locality.[94]

All these dogmas "drop of their own weight as the mind perceives truth and its relations to the universe." But Stanton's critique went far beyond the irrelevance of these doctrinal matters. Since Christians at the North and the South alike found theological rationales for their positions on slavery, "Our late civil war resulted in no small measure from the vacillating position of the church." Hence, she held "every minister of the gospel" responsible for the carnage and cruelty of that war as surely as every politician.

She called the churches "to give some thought to these practical everyday questions and show us what science and religion united . . . can do" on such issues as the subjection of woman, labor and capital, prohibition, war, finance, free trade, land monopoly, jails, prisons, capital punishment, and criminal legislation. The relations of capital and labor called forth some of her most passionate language. Since the world was "always ready to quote Bible in favor of oppression," she proposed to quote the Bible against oppression. She then built a case for changing the economy based on the prohibitions against usury. To be deeply involved in all these questions was "notably the office of the Christian teacher and philosopher." She concluded by recommending that the money spent on building magnificent churches should be put into making lighter the burdens of the poor. "To give the congregations in our churches all over the land some suggestions on their moral duties on these questions would do more to Christianize this nation than all the nice disquisitions or abstractions that occupy so much thought and time in our pulpits today."[95]

In the 1880s and 1890s the themes of Stanton's transition came together in a series of sharp attacks on religious ideas and institutions. Science, free thought, self-development, natural law in this world combined into a denunciation of Christianity—and all the other religions of the world, for that matter. Whatever form of religion did not teach the equality of the sexes was a false faith to be roundly condemned, deserted, opposed. She stopped calling for the reform and redirection of the churches in the light of their own teachings and proclaimed that the teachings themselves were irredeemable. Resolutions to that effect were proposed in the NWSA in 1885:

> *Whereas*, The dogmas incorporated in the religious creeds derived from Judaism, teaching that woman was an afterthought in creation, her sex a misfortune, marriage a condition of subordination, and maternity a curse, are contrary to the law of God as revealed in nature and the precepts of Christ; and,
> *Whereas*, These dogmas are an insidious poison, sapping the vitality of our civilization, blighting woman and palsying humanity; therefore,
> *Resolved*, That we call upon the Christian ministry, as leaders of thought, to teach and enforce the fundamental idea of creation that man was made in the image of God, male and female, and given equal dominion over the earth, but none over each other. And further we invite their cooperation in securing the recognition of the cardinal point of our creed, that in true religion there is neither male nor female, neither bond nor free, but all are one.[96]

In defense of these resolutions (eventually tabled after a long and heated discussion), Stanton made two separate and differently argued appeals. The first claimed that there was a "natural equilibrium" of the sexes distorted by the current state of affairs, and particularly in the history of Christianity. In effect, it was an argument for the "integration" of the sexes in all human activities; "segregation" in Christianity was its fatal flaw.

> Those people who declaim on the inequalities of sex, the disabilities and limitations of one as against the other, show themselves as ignorant of the first principles of life as would that philosopher who should undertake to show the comparative power of the positive as against the negative electricity, of the centrifugal as against the centripetal force, the attraction of the north as against the south end of the magnet. These great natural forces must be perfectly balanced or the whole material world would relapse into chaos. Just so the masculine and feminine elements in humanity must be exactly balanced to redeem the moral and social world from the chaos which surrounds it. One might as well talk of separate spheres for the two ends of the magnet as for man and woman; they may have separate duties in the same sphere, but their true place is together everywhere. Having different duties in the same sphere, neither can succeed without the presence and influence of the other. To restore the equilibrium of sex is the first step in social, religious, and political progress. It is by the constant repression of the best elements in humanity, by our false customs, creeds, and codes, that we have thus far retarded civilization. . . .

If one-half the effort had been expended to exalt the feminine element that has been made to degrade it, we should have reached the natural equilibrium long ago. Either sex, in isolation, is robbed of one-half its power for the accomplishment of any given work. This was the most fatal dogma of the Christian religion—that in proportion as men withdrew from all companionship with women, they could get nearer to God, grow more like the Divine Ideal.[97]

These strictures on Christianity were matched in the second phase of the argument by Stanton's points against other world religions, which were not better off in this regard. (Her autobiography claims that she refused the attribution of such dogmas to Judaism alone, but lost to other members of the convention.[98]) Undoubtedly she had in mind arguments made by the rival suffrage organization, the AWSA, that of all the world's religions, Christianity had done far more to advance woman's cause than the others, mere relics of barbarism. This Stanton refused strongly: world religions were equal in their degradation of womankind. Religion itself as a human force had a particular role to play in enforcing and reinforcing the situation of women:

You may go over the world and you will find that every form of religion which has breathed upon this earth has degraded woman. There is not one which has not made her subject to man. . . . What power is it that makes the Hindoo woman burn herself on the pyre of her husband? Her religion. What holds the Turkish woman in the harem? Her religion. By what power do the Mormons perpetuate their system of polygamy? By their religion. Man, of himself, could not do this; but when he declares, "Thus saith the Lord," of course he can do it. So long as ministers stand up and tell us that as Christ is the head of the church, so is man the head of the woman, how are we to break the chains which have held woman down through the ages? You Christian woman can be held in such bondage. Observe to-day the work women are doing for the churches. *The church rests on the shoulders of women.* Have we ever yet heard a man preach a sermon from Genesis 1: 27-28, which declares the full equalities of the feminine and masculine element in the Godhead? They invariably shy at that first chapter. They always get up in their pulpits and read the second chapter.

Now I ask you if our religion teaches the dignity of woman? It teaches us that abominable idea of the sixth century—Augustine's idea—that motherhood is a curse; that woman is the author of sin, and is most corrupt. Can we ever cultivate any proper sense of self-respect as long as women take such sentiments from the mouths of the priesthood?[99]

Stanton not only denied that the church had contributed even "one impulse of freedom,"[100] she charged that the church had been in all ages, "a powerful police institution," to rob the poor, to suppress free thought, to make martyrs of noble men and women[.] When has it ever risked its own safety to fight the battles of the people against the oppressions of the State? When, by wise counsels as a united body, has it ever averted the settlement of one vexed question by war?[101]

When the "indignant masses" wake up to the truth of the situation, "They will repudiate the Church and the creeds that have so long held them in bondage." What was true for the poor and laboring people was true for women. "How little strong men dream of all they suffer in a sincere belief of the gloomy doctrines of our Christian theology!" The fear of hell and an angry God were singled out by Stanton in conjunction with the story of the fall. That women believed that because of them "all this misery entered the world, and hence the pangs of maternity were to be their punishment" was cruel and absurd.

Among the reading Stanton did in these later decades were works by Comte, Spencer, Matthew Arnold, and the historian Lecky. She was confirmed in her growing emphasis on rationalism,[102] which led her to join forces with the Free Religious Association. It also brought forcefully to Stanton's attention the witchcraft persecutions of the late Middle Ages. Her pamphlets of this period vent her rage at the dramatic suffering of women throughout history in ways that *The Woman's Bible*, for all its scornful and strong language, never did. "Women endured such persecutions and tortures that the most stolid historians are said to have wept in recording them; and no one can read them today but with a bleeding heart."[103] These painful scenes of history were directly connected to Christian teachings regarding sin.

> Out of the doctrine of original sin grew the crimes and miseries of asceticism, celibacy, and witchcraft, woman becoming the helpless victim of all the delusions generated in the brain of man.[104]

It was because of original sin that there was "nothing so cheap as womanhood in the commerce of the world."[105] The analogies of slavery were left behind as Stanton discovered metaphors directly pertinent to women's experience. Suttee was the most prominent of these:

> What is true in this case [suttee] is true of women of all ages. They have been trained by their religion to sacrifice themselves, body and soul, for the men of their families and to build up the churches. We do not burn the bodies of the women of today; but we humiliate them in a thousand ways, and chiefly by our theologies. So long as the pulpits teach woman's inferiority and subjection, she

can never command that honor and respect of the ignorant classes needed for her safety and protection. There is nothing more pathetic in all history than the hopeless resignation of woman to the outrages she has been taught to believe are ordained of God.[106]

Orthodox religion drove women to despair and death, to asylums with religious melancholia. "Men can never understand the fear of everlasting punishment that fills the soul of women and children."[107] Nor can they understand the scars left by the notion that maternity was a curse: hence, the Bible project. "The Church has done more to degrade woman than all other adverse influences put together. And it has done this by playing on the religious emotions (the strongest feelings of her nature) to her own complete subjugation."[108]

The Woman's Bible project was the culmination of Stanton's critique of the Judaeo-Christian heritage. In concert with a group of women, she undertook to write commentaries on those sections of Scripture which particularly bore on woman's status. The project was several years in the making, partly due to the reluctance of others to join; partly from Stanton's advanced age; partly, it seems, because she took time to read some of the higher criticism in preparation for it. She understood this work as continuous with the higher criticism. "As the 'higher criticisms,' written by learned scholars and scientists, are not familiar to women, our comments in plain English may rid them of some of their superstitions."[109]

That the project was an occasion for Stanton to demystify what she saw as crude speculation no doubt accounted for a part (but only a part) of the vehemence of the clerical response. Her first principle, by this time clear in her own mind, was that "every form of religion which has breathed upon this earth has degraded women."[110] Since it was to the Bible that the clerical opponents of woman's emancipation repaired for their case, that text was an appropriate object of feminist scrutiny. While from a systematic point of view, the realm of religion was merely one strand in the cord of fourfold bondage, it was more than simply an equal perpetrator with the other areas of life. "The religious superstitions of women perpetuate their bondage more than all other adverse influences."[111]

All the material in the Old and New Testaments that argued, rationalized, degraded women, or otherwise perpetuated oppression, Stanton declared to be simply the work of all too fallible man—read, "male." She relentlessly mocked such notions as superstitious, outmoded, barbaric relics of human savagery.

She found much that in her opinion was too degraded to be circulated at all; the censoring hand was particularly offended by the story of Sodom and Gomorrah, as unworthy of a place in *The Woman's Bible*. "Indeed the Pentateuch is a long painful record, of war, corruption, rapine, and lust."[112] If one considered the Bible "as a mere history of an ignorant, undeveloped people" there would not be such a problem, but when divine authorship, inspiration, moral lessons were allegedly to be found in it, "we must judge of its merits by the moral standards of· today."[113] This Stanton proceeded relentlessly to do.

Here, as elsewhere, Stanton did accord the truth of the first account of creation that declared the simultaneous creation of both sexes in the image of God. The second account was a "mere allegory, symbolizing some mysterious conception of a highly imaginative editor."[114] Sarah possessed no heroic virtues worthy of our attention; neither she nor her husband bothered to speak the truth when they could lie. Rebekah suffered from "the extreme of individual selfishness"; Rachel's capacity for theft and deception, the perfidy and dishonor of Potiphar's wife, the "perpetual tutelage"[115] of women under the Jewish law—all came under Stanton's ire. Her strongest statements of the corruption of the Old Testament were reserved for those passages in which Israel was enjoined to destroy all men, women, and children in its possession of Canaan or its conflicts with other nations.

> The utter contempt for all the decencies of life and all the natural personal rights of women should destroy in the minds of women at least, all authority to superhuman origin and stamp the Pentateuch as emanating from the most obscene minds of a barbarous age.[116]

The New Testament evidently did not engage Stanton's imagination or anger so fully. The commentaries were in many cases simply paraphrases of the text at hand, unlike the excurses occasioned by the Pentateuch. Interestingly, the story of Mary and Martha was omitted; and Galatians 3:28 did not appear under Stanton's commenting hand. For moral reasons, Stanton disclaimed the divinity of Jesus on the grounds that this would disqualify him as "a worthy example for imitation."

> By showing us the possibility of human nature he is a constant inspiration, our hope and salvation; for the path, however rough, in which one man has walked, others may follow. As a God with infinite power he could have been no example

to us; but with human limitations we may emulate his virtues and walk in his footsteps.[117]

The parables that teach self-development instead of sacrifice, like the parable of the talents, were lauded. Phoebe's status was pointedly remarked. Especially prominent in Stanton's mind were the Pauline injunctions to women to be subordinate to their husbands or to keep silence in the churches.

She summed up the case very simply. The Bible taught woman's degradation. No refuge was to be found in "false translations, interpretations, and symbolic meaning." No amount of learned reading, no higher criticism, no devious arguments or references to the original languages could redeem it. "Whatever the Bible may be made to do in Hebrew or Greek, in plain English it does not exalt and dignify woman."[118]

The most fundamental reason for this was central to the Christian tradition: it was the fall and hence the need for a savior. The many notions of sin and the corresponding salvation from sin were the pivots of her case.

> The real difficulty in woman's case is that the whole foundation of the Christian religion rests on her temptation and man's fall, hence the necessity of a Redeemer and a plan of salvation. As the chief cause of this dire calamity, woman's degradation and subordination were made a necessity.[119]

"Thus," as she concluded, "the bottom falls out of the whole Christian theology."[120] The case did not, however, end there.

> If, however, we accept the Darwinian theory, that the race has been a gradual growth from the lower to a higher form of life, and that the story of the fall is a myth, we can exonerate the snake, emancipate the woman, and reconstruct a more rational religion for the nineteenth century, and thus escape all the perplexities of the Jewish mythology as of no more importance than those of the Greek, Persian, and Egyptian.[121]

This points to the outlines of Stanton's positive alternative case, "a more rational religion," to which I turn in the following chapter.

The Woman's Bible brought Stanton little thanks from pious Victorians, and little more from her suffragist allies.[122] The NAWSA convention of 1896 voted 53-41, over Anthony's protests, the following resolution of repudiation of her project:

> *Resolved,* That this Association is non-sectarian, being composed of persons of all shades of religious opinion, and that it has no official connection with the so-called "Woman's Bible," or any theological publication.[123]

Such opposition by her colleagues (including Shaw) did not deter Stanton from continuing to call for suffragist action in the religious sphere.

Again in 1901, her letter to the convention urged action, both practical and theological, in the churches. She sharpened her case against those suffragists who claimed such agitation would antagonize clergy, who were moving in increasing numbers to support the suffragists. "It matters little that here and there some clergyman advocates our cause on our platform, so long as no religious organization has yet recognized our demand as a principle of justice."[124] She recommended that women all over the country form committees to visit clergy to press women's claims on them. Such groups should clearly include a theological revision among their aims; it would not be sufficient "if they gave their adhesion to the demand for political equality, so long as by scriptural teachings they perpetuate our racial and religious subordination."[125] Stanton sought a full theological transformation as well as an organizational change. The lessons of the degradation and subordination of women were to be "relegated to the ancient mythologies"[126] and another theology take its place.

From Seneca Falls to *The Woman's Bible* was a long journey indeed. The perversion of the religious element in woman was comprehensively surveyed. The thoroughness of her aims pushed Stanton to the consideration of non-Western religions as well as to the fundamental assumptions of orthodox theology. These were no easy, flip assertions made by someone with no stake in the Christian tradition. She described her own experience, looked deeply at the lives of women around her, studied, analyzed, reflected about the causes of the subjection of women. Finally the practice of the churches counted as much as their theory, and the theory was clearly wanting. "If the Bible teaches the equality of Woman, why does the Church refuse to ordain women to preach the gospel, to fill the offices of deacons and elders, and to administer the Sacraments, or to admit them as delegates to the Synods, General Assemblies, and Conferences of the different denominations?"[127] Good questions indeed. But she did more than to ask good questions. She went on to create her own theological statement to prove that the inequality of women bore only "the impress of fallible man" and not that of Deity.[128]

B. The Man Marriage and Nothing More

Stanton's autobiography records that it was not the example of the Grimké sisters among antislavery advocates, or exclusion of women at the World Anti-Slavery Convention, or any other external event, which pushed her into organizing and acting on her convictions about the status of women. Rather, it was domesticity in Seneca Falls. Setting up house, dealing with servants, exposure to wife-beating among her neighbors all combined with Stanton's earlier learnings to produce a women's rights convention.

> I now fully understood the practical difficulties most women had to contend with in the isolated household, and the impossibility of woman's best development if in contact, the chief part of her life, with servants and children. Fourier's phalansterie community life and co-operative households had a new significance for me. Emerson says, "A healthy discontent is the first step to progress." The general discontent I felt with woman's portion as wife, mother, housekeeper, physician, and spiritual guide, the chaotic conditions into which everything fell without her constant supervision, and the wearied, anxious look of the majority of women impressed me with a strong feeling that some active measures should be taken to remedy the wrongs of society in general, and of women in particular. My experience at the World's Anti-slavery Convention, all I had read of the legal status of women, and the oppression I saw everywhere, together swept across my soul, intensified now by many personal experiences. It seemed as if all the elements had conspired to impel me to some onward step. I could not see what to do or where to begin—my only thought was a public meeting for protest and discussion.[129]

The Seneca Falls Declaration of Sentiments contained several demands concerning marriage and family—especially the status of *femme coverte*, married women's property rights, custody of children, and the laws of divorce. Stanton's particular vision of these questions drove her to single out divorce as especially urgent. Along the way she developed a complex and in some respects surprisingly contemporary view of the issues involved—including wife-beating, sexuality, women's loss of name in marriage, hints at shared housework, and some little-known arguments for free love. An early letter to Anthony states that "this whole question of woman's rights turns on the pivot of the marriage relation."[130] Even more emphatically, "the right idea of marriage is at the foundation of all reforms."[131]

Stanton made early forays into the question of divorce in her temperance movement days. "Justice and mercy demand a legal separation from drunkards

. . . a unity of soul alone constitutes and sanctifies true marriage." Any legal or conventional coercion of two immortal souls, aside from their love, was "false to God and humanity."[132] At the woman's rights convention of 1854, she honed and systematized her appeal. Her address to the lawmakers of New York, demanding a revision of the state constitution, began with echoes of Tom Paine: "The tyrant, Custom, has been summoned before the bar of Common-Sense." The rhetoric of the Founding Fathers was to be applied where they had never applied it: to the family.[133]

The order that Stanton proposed for considering such topics was important. The only adequate procedure was to begin with "woman as woman" before proceeding to "woman as wife," "woman as widow," and "woman as mother."[134] The first of these was the straightforward argument for the ballot and jury duty, but each of the other sections was designed also to present an additional case for the vote.

Regarding "woman as wife," Stanton began on a characteristic note. "Your laws regarding marriage . . . are in open violation of our enlightened ideas of justice and of the holiest feelings of our nature."[135] If marriage was a "Divine Relation," then human legislators should not, could not, meddle with it, "for the prerogative belongs to God alone, who makes men and women, and the laws of attraction, by which they are united." If, on the other hand, marriage was a civil contract, then it was to be ruled in the same reasonable light as other contracts. The remainder of the section pointed out the absurdity of a civil contract that brought "instant civil death to one of the parties."[136] The laws relating to marriage made woman, the same woman who was "blessed and honored" by the rhetoric of the day, into an "ignoble, servile, cringing slave," whose wages, bodily safety, peace of mind, and self-determination were sacrificed in law to her husband, no matter if he were a "confirmed drunkard, a villain, or a vagrant."[137] Should she inherit property, under progressive New York State legislation, she had no ability to protect it; like the widow, the woman inheriting property was taxed without her consent and participation. Hence, these arguments drove to the point of the ballot for the woman considered in her roles as wife and widow.

Lastly, the "woman as mother" argument similarly castigated the laws of the day. "Nature has clearly made the mother the guardian of the child; but man in his inordinate love of power, does continually set nature and nature's laws at open defiance."[138] Fathers not only assumed custody of the children, but had the right to apprentice or beat them at will. A woman could protect her child "neither at home nor abroad," where the liquor traffic and other abominations flourished. Woman's influence and moral power could be effective only when it could "speak through the ballot-box."[139]

The closing arguments were directed toward the age-old question, "What do you women want?" They are noteworthy here for Stanton's case that the "radical difference in sex" presupposed by the era was the major stumbling block to men's understanding the logic and justice of women's rights arguments.

It is impossible to make the Southern planter believe that his slave feels and reasons just as he does—that injustice and subjection are as galling to him—that the degradation of living by the will of another, the mere dependent on his caprice, at the mercy of his passions, is as keenly felt by him as his master. If you can force on his unwilling vision a vivid picture of the negro's wrongs, and for a moment touch his soul, his logic brings him instant consolation. He says, the slave does not feel this as I would. Here, gentlemen, is our difficulty: When we plead our cause before the law-makers and savants of the republic, they can not take in the idea that men and women are alike. . . .

If you, too, are thus deluded, what avails it that we show by your statute books that your laws are unjust—that woman is the victim of avarice and power? What avails it that we point out the wrongs of woman in social life, the victim of passion and lust? You scorn the thought that she has any natural love of freedom burning in her breast, any clear perception of justice urging her on to demand her rights.[140]

She assured the lawmakers that "burning indignation" filled woman's soul in reading law books; women were humiliated that lawyers learned in school "these ideas of one-sided justice." Women felt the same love of freedom and had the same "clear perception of justice," as the above quotation indicated, as any man. Hence,

Christ's golden rule is better than all the special legislation that the ingenuity of man can devise: "Do unto others as you would have others do unto you." This, men and brethren, is all we ask at your hands. We ask no better laws than those you have made for yourselves. We need no other protection than that which your present laws secure to you.

In conclusion, then, let us say, on behalf of the women of this State, we ask for all that you have asked for yourselves in the progress of your development, since the Mayflower cast anchor beside Plymouth Rock; and simply on the ground that the rights of every human being are the same and identical.[141]

On other occasions, however—and most noticeably in private correspondence—Stanton could severely qualify the notion that the sexes feel and think alike on such topics. A letter to her sympathetic cousin, Gerrit Smith, claims that he had "spoken well for a man whose convictions on this subject are the result of reason and observation." But this was not enough.

> [T]hey alone whose souls are fired through personal experience and suffering can set forth the height and depth, the source and center of the degradation of women; they alone can feel a steadfast faith in their own native energy and power to accomplish a final triumph over all adverse surroundings, a speedy and complete success.[142]

She invited him to perform a "thought-experiment." "You claim to believe that in every sense, thought, and feeling, men and woman are the same." Well, then, "suppose yourself a woman." Suppose yourself educated and interested in the great political questions of the day; you are condemned to silence. You read "from the Bible down to Mother Goose's Melodies" sentiments that degraded you. "Every passion of the human soul, which in manhood becomes so grand and glorious in its results, is fatal to womankind."[143] Suppose you were the wife of a confirmed drunkard—indeed, suppose something virtually unspeakable about this relationship. Stanton hinted at the hidden history of women's sexuality in marriage:

> I might take you through many, many phases of woman's life, into those sacred relations of which we speak not in our conventions, where woman feels her deepest wrongs, where in blank despair she drags out days, and weeks, and months, and years of silent agony.[144]

Indeed, in the face of "the sacred right of a woman to her own person, to all her God-given powers of body and soul," all other rights, such as the right to vote, to hold property, to speak in public, "sink into utter insignificance." She skirted as well the notion of contraception: "Did he [man] ever take in the idea that to the mother of the race, and to her alone, belonged the right to say when a new being should be brought into the world?"[145] The notion that "maternity was the one and sole object of a woman's existence" made a variety of reforms impossible. "Here, in my opinion, is the starting-point; here is the battleground where our independence must be fought and won."[146] Women may have seemed to be content with life as it was given in the period. But "we suffer in our own persons, on the gallows, and in prison walls."[147] In the face of this direct experience of life's emergencies and pains, chivalry was the merest cant.

Stanton edged into shared housework as well:

> Divines may preach thanksgiving sermons on the poetry of the arm-chair and the cradle; but when they lay down their newspapers, or leave their beds on a cold night to attend to the wants of either, I shall begin to look for the golden age of chivalry once more.[148]

As for the alleged dependence of women on men, it was a mockery. Prefiguring what was to become the statement of "Solitude of Self," Stanton wrote of the women who depended "on their own hands" and their mother love to get through life:

> It is into hands like these—to these who have calmly met the great emergencies of life—who, without the inspiration of glory, or fame, or applause, through long years and faithfully and bravely performed their work, self-sustained and cheered, that we commit our cause. We need not wait for one more generation to pass away, to find a race of women worthy to assert the humanity of women, and that is all we claim to do.[149]

This strong sense that women "suffer in our own persons," especially regarding questions of family and marriage, but certainly in all the great emergencies of life, later was articulated as the means of women's access to justice, the place in this work where Stanton's religious views and her social analysis intersect. It functioned as a principle of verification of Stanton's later speech on divorce as well. In the face of the opposition to her position from many erstwhile allies, she comforted herself that "the sad women who struggled up to press my hand and who were speechless with emotion, know better than our noble Phillips or politic editors who has struck for them the blow in the right place."[150]

Stanton laid further building blocks into her case regarding the degradation of women in marriage before her full-blown arguments for divorce were crafted into place. Analogies from slavery were never far from her pen on the subject of women's situation in marriage.

> Marriage, as we now have it, is opposed to all God's laws. It is by no means an equal partnership. The silent partner loses everything. . . . She is nameless, for a woman has no name! She is Mrs. John or James, Peter or Paul, just as she changes masters; like the Southern slave, she takes the name of her owner.[151]

Others might consider this strong language for such a seemingly trivial point. Yet the loss of a woman's name in marriage functioned as "the symbol of the most cursed monopoly on this footstool; a monopoly by man of all the rights, the life, the liberty, and happiness of half of the human family—all womankind."[152]

The positive side of this case rested on the notions of God's laws in creation. These laws implied equality, the utter individuality of each woman, and her consequent right to self-development rather than self-sacrifice.

> Marriage is a divine institution, intended by God for the greater freedom and happiness of both parties—whatever therefore conflicts with woman's happiness is not legitimate to that relation. Woman has yet to learn that she has a right to be happy in and of herself; that she has a right to the free use, improvement and development of all her faculties, for her own benefit and pleasure. The woman is greater than the wife or the mother; and in consenting to take upon herself these relations, she should never sacrifice one iota of her individuality to any senseless conventionalism, or false codes of feminine delicacy and refinement.[153]

The longer Stanton dwelt on the subject of marriage, the more vehement her rhetoric became. "So long as our present false marriage relation continues, which in most cases is nothing more nor less than legalized prostitution, women can have no self-respect, and of course man will have none for her; for the world estimates us according to the value we put upon ourselves."[154] This comment, however, came from a private communication to Anthony, and it was in those letters that most of her radical thinking regarding sexuality was to be found—particularly in the decades after the Civil War, when the charges of free love drove most suffragist critiques of marriage underground.

It was finally in 1860, at the last woman's rights convention before the war, that Stanton presented ten resolutions to establish firmly woman's rights to divorce. It was not only a "right, but a duty" to abolish any relationship that did not "produce or promote human happiness." "Mental or moral or spiritual imbecility" were, like physical impotence, sufficient ground for divorce. An unfortunate marriage was a calamity, but "not ever, perhaps never, a crime." Human errors in the selection of business partners, teachers, ministers, lawmakers were no different from those of selection of marital partners. The children born "in these unhappy and unhallowed connections" proceeded "from beneath" rather than from above. Growing up in an "atmosphere where love is not the law, but where discord and bitterness abound" distorted their moral natures. Thus the human race was bound into a "weakness and depravity that must be a sure precursor of its ruin, as a just penalty of long-violated law."[155]

The argument for these resolutions painted a picture of American marriages that was a far cry from the roseate glow that surrounded the word "home" in mid-century society. Her religious position departed significantly from the Puritan and Calvinist heritages in its repudiation of human "degradation and total depravity." This meant that "man" was "above" all governments and institutions, whether churches or politics, and "above" all positive laws. The implications of this humanist notion were formulated in a fashion consonant with her philosophical leanings: "In the settlement, then, of any question, we must simply consider the highest good of the individual."[156]

Marriage laws were to be seen in the light of the cases of family "violence, debauchery and excess," the cold hearthstones "where the fires of love have all gone out." The woman in such relationships was frequently "unconscious of the true dignity of her nature, of her high and holy destiny." In such "legalized marriages of force and endurance," her children "see the only being on earth they love, dragged around the room by the hair of her head, kicked and pounded, and left half dead and bleeding on the floor."[157] Equally relevant to her case, however, were the social phenomena that were to become an obsession of later eugenicists—"asylums for the blind, the deaf and dumb, the idiot, the imbecile, the deformed, the insane . . . the bylanes and dens of this vast metropolis," presumably the results of these marriages "from beneath" rather than from above.

The moral of such tales was to point out "how fearful a thing it is to violate the immutable laws of the beneficent Ruler of the Universe."[158] This human wretchedness was in heartrending contrast to "God's arrangements," which were "perfect, harmonious, and complete," stamped with "immutability, perfection, and beauty." In the true marriage, love was the "vital essence" and "the talisman of human weal and woe."[159] "Thus far we have had the man marriage and nothing more"; we Americans have never tried marriage as "a contract made by equal parties to live an equal life, with equal restraints and privileges on either side"[160] in which the "gauge of womanhood" came from the "solemn convictions of our own souls, in the higher development of the race."[161]

Stanton did not, however, stop with divorce. She went, as it were, "all the way." A little-known, privately delivered speech of 1869 argued that free love was "logically" related to woman suffrage. It is interesting not only because of Stanton's boldness in broaching that Victorian unspeakable, but also for the ethical premises on which the case was built and for its religion. This was the period of *The Revolution* and Stanton's changing ideas of religion. She closed the speech with a call for a "new Catholic Church," a rather surprising conclusion.

That such a change in her reasoning was entwined with the divorce speeches was made clear from its opening words. "I have said in the preceding lecture [on divorce] that what I advocated and claimed would not destroy but would simply improve and perfect marriage."[162] That, it appears, was wrong. Marriage "as a compulsory bond enforced by the law and rendered perpetual by that means" would be disturbed indeed. Woman suffrage advocates should "be at once therefore and emphatically warned that they mean logically if not consciously . . . social equality, and next freedom, in a word, Free Love, and if they wish to get out of the boat they should for safety get out now."[163]

The appeal to free love was a conscious appeal to the principle of freedom. Stanton reflected on her observations of married couples in the women's rights movement. Even those marriages, consciously based on equality of the sexes, were disastrous. She questioned the sufficiency of a principle of equality. Equals could, it seemed, oppress each other equally.

> I know parties, man and wife, who have labored hard and honestly for almost a lifetime and together on behalf of what has been known as women's rights . . . and thoroughly believing in the equality of the sexes, neither of whom dared say their souls were their own, making each other mutually and equitably the most abject slaves, simply because each had claimed and established the right of ownership over the other and because each had in ignorant good faith conceded the right; had in a word abdicated their own individual sovereignty, sinking it in the vortex of marriage. . . . They live the lives, these married couples generally, of mutual spies and tyrants over each other, and it is the most subtle form of slavery ever instituted, because it is seemingly so fair, buried as it is in mutual agreement and not incompatible with the full concession of the equality of the parties to this mutual treaty of self stultification.[164]

Not merely equality and social recognition were necessary, "though both these must be had." The only remedy for such a state of affairs was "freedom from all unnecessary entanglements and concessions, freedom from binding obligations involving improbabilities, freedom to repair mistakes: to express the manifoldness of our own natures; and to progress or to advance to higher planes of development."[165] Even fidelity in monogamy was "just as much free love as the most unlimited variety or promiscuity." Freedom could abide no obstacles such as arguments regarding its bad uses, which were merely "the unavoidable friction of the machinery, the bad investment which goes to profit and loss in the business of progress."

There was a progression of principles within the woman suffrage struggle: first equality, then freedom. Freedom was not enough, either; it needed wisdom, "the whole science of the subject," which included its right use, presumably from within rather than by external regulation. Further, it needed virtue, the love of each other's well-being and of the good and the true. And, she concluded,

> one other want, a new religion—a religion that shall be to all these blooms of human nature what the string which binds the stems of the flowers is to the bouquet. The day was when religion was allied with all that was most progressive in human affairs. Today it has somehow got on the wrong side and has been retarding and obstructive.
>
> The last want then is a new catholicity which shall not merely tolerate but which shall advocate and enforce by its influence all that reform shall aspire after and all that science shall discover and define—in a word, the new Catholic Church, in this radical and progressive signification of the term.[166]

This was an underground argument, and it remained underground—particularly as Victoria Woodhull embroiled the woman suffrage movement of the 1870s in the Beecher-Tilton case and its attendant cries of "free love." Though she publicly opposed the calumniation of the Irish leader Charles Parnell for his relationship with a married woman, and always argued that "social" relationships had to be regulated by women alone, since they bore the children, it seems true that such radical arguments were driven out of the center of the suffrage struggle. Stanton was not above profiting from this conservative turn. "The free love scare has made suffrage respectable."[167]

Though free love was a purely private notion, Stanton did not cease to call for other revisions of the family. To secure a true republic required that the home life of the nation's citizens be consonant with its democratic polity.

> How can we hope to ground republican citizens in the broad principles of justice and equality if we teach the doctrine in the family that there must be one divinely ordained head, "who can do no wrong," to rule and reign absolutely, no matter how disastrous the dynasty may be. This idea was in harmony with that of the Church and State in the feudal regime, but it is all out of joint with a republican form of government and the Protestant religion that recognizes the right of individual judgment in all things temporal and spiritual.[168]

What did that republican form of government in the family entail? The first group of conclusions had to do with the "woman as wife." It meant "the wife's personal freedom, private judgment, pecuniary independence, and equal partnership." The wife's lack of personal freedom was "the last and most subtle type of slavery to be banished from the earth, the last link in the hoary chain of oppression that has so long crippled the human race."

The status of women as wives and mothers had far-reaching implications for the republic also because of the example and influence on the children. "As the mother's moral stature decides that of her sons, if statesmen are to have clear ideas of justice, they must not be cradled in oppression."[169] She saw the rebelliousness of the young as proof that self-government was grounded in nature. "Childhood is one long struggle against arbitrary power, one continued protest in favor of self-government."[170] The conclusion of such arguments was clear. In a republic, the family also must be an "experiment in self-government" where each member

> must be trained in the a b c of individual rights. Each must learn the exact limits of his own rights and the boundary line beyond which he cannot go without infringing on those of another. This will necessarily involve most patient educational work and prolonged discussion, immense self-control, and constant yielding one to another, the will in all cases being subordinate to a sense of justice and equality. This lesson well learned in childhood and in youth is the best possible preparation for good citizens for the State.[171]

Provoked by proposals to render the divorce laws of the states homogeneous, Stanton returned to this question in the 1890s. She feared that such practices would eviscerate the more liberal codes and hence be detrimental to women. "The States that have more liberal divorce laws are for women today what Canada was for the fugitive in the old days of slavery."[172] As in her earlier years, she argued that in some cases divorce was not merely a right but a duty. "Divorce is not the foe of marriage. . . . One might as well speak of medicine as the foe of health."[173] In keeping with the condemnation of the churches in this period of her life, she was adamant in wishing to keep the public out of the clutches of the "icy fingers of the Canon law."[174] She had few positive words for the ecclesiastical positions on divorce. "The less latitude the Church has in our temporal affairs, the better."[175] The marriage contract was reinterpreted. The pronouncement, "What God hath joined together, let no man put asunder," did not actually join the couple, since only "real attraction or a religious sense of loyalty to one another" could do that.

Those harmonious marriages "where the parties are really companions for each other" did not need the law to hold them together. Other marriages, based on money, position, "mere sensual gratification," were already based on defiance of the natural law; so to legislate for these cases made no sense either. "The time has come when the logic of facts is more conclusive than the deductions of theology."[176] In other words, little had changed in the fundamental premises of her perspective. Woman's enfranchisement was "the primal step in deciding the basis of family life."[177] It was "folly to talk of the sacredness of marriage and maternity" until women were more than inferiors and subjects. The central claim was that "the true standpoint from which to view this question is individual sovereignty, individual happiness."[178]

"The Man Marriage" was, in Stanton's view, disastrous for women, for the offspring, and for the prospects of the republic itself. She spelled out this view with the nuances and subtleties she sought in perspectives on woman suffrage. While her focus was frequently divorce, she explored sexuality, property laws, the dramatic emergencies of human life, the feelings of the sexes, the changes in women's names, housework, the training of children, all in the context of the familial strand in the cable of the fourfold bondage. This exposition demonstrated the entanglement of questions of marriage and family with the other strands—religion, politics, society.

It is noteworthy that the ethical principles Stanton used in other aspects of her analysis were also present in the context of marriage and family. While love was the "talisman" of true marriages, it was not sufficient. Justice was never far from the tip of Stanton's tongue. She cited women's clear perceptions of justice, or the training of citizens to honor justice in the family as much as in society at large, as principles by which to guide ethical reflection on these subjects usually seen to be private. She pushed her view of justice, equality, and freedom to the theological statement of the grounds of her case. "Our enlightened ideas of justice" and "the holiest feelings of our nature" were held firmly together in this analysis.

C. The Tyrant Custom

Under the aegis of "social life," the nineteenth century organized a variety of disparate themes. As I show with Anthony, the "social evil" was a subject that referred to sexual practices. Fear regarding race relations in the period centered around the problem of "social equality," the specter of intermarriage between black and white. It was also, however, the period in which "social science" was being born in the works of Comte and Spencer and the Social Science Association. In Stanton's fourfold bondage, the reference to "social" was frequently a catchall term, perhaps best understood as the phenomena that did not obviously fit into politics, family, and religion. We may best be guided by concentrating on Stanton's analysis of education, dress, character, and work, with occasional references to sexual morality. All of these areas of Stanton's commentary were imbued with a strongly moral component. "How can she tolerate our social customs by which womankind is stripped of all true virtue, dignity, and nobility?"[179] was her rhetorical question. As in the other three strands of her full case, Stanton frequently asserted that some aspect of this social arena was the most crucial item in women's situation. Women "will never claim their civil rights until they know their social wrongs."[180] She learned from the Puritan Milton that, "Custom is the most cruel and unrelenting of all tyrants."[181]

One of Stanton's Lyceum Bureau lectures, and a frequent topic of her writing, was "Our Girls," a plea for the adequate and correct education of young womanhood. Like many another liberal before and after her, Stanton's belief in the efficacy of education was a strong one. "Begin with the girls of to-day, and in twenty years we shall revolutionize this nation."[182] The education Stanton proposed was in sharp contrast to the period's notions of education for women, which she characterized as a "system of cramping, restraining, torturing, perverting, and mystifying,"[183] wholly different from true education. "The lesson you learn is nothing unless by it you have discovered your power to think—to think is the whole of education."[184] Thinking and science went hand in hand for Stanton. If the nation was to apply the "science of life" to its moral and political problems (with "the same degree of exactitude that we have already applied to the vegetable and animal creation"), then "woman must be taught to think, to reason—your mothers must be philosophers and scholars."[185] Stanton's notion of thinking was always a wholistic one, reaching beyond the sheerly cognitive or scholarly skills. Book learning without life wisdom was worthless.

> It is not by the intellect that we are peaceful and happy in ourselves. It is not by the intellect that we are kind and sympathizing friends. It is not by the intellect that we take hold of heaven and become like God himself—but as we are kind, noble, truthful, generous, patient, self-sacrificing.[186]

She sought a curricular change that would embody the "superiority of practice over theory," as she explored the changes in education necessary to a true republic. "The merely ornamental in education" went along with the aristocratic idea. She ridiculed those who knew six languages, and the chronology of the English monarchs but nothing of "babies, bread, beef, and biology." This was not, however, a plea for a technical or vocational education such as we know it in the twentieth century. Her point was related to the duties of citizenship in all walks of life. She opposed a double standard in education for scholars and laborers. "When scholars make more use of their hands, and laborers of their brains, when we harness thought and action together, the car of progress will move with new speed in the future."[187]

The case for women's thorough education in mind and body implied coeducation in all levels of schooling.

> Do not sound philosophy and long-experience teach us that men and women should be educated together? The isolation of the sexes in all departments, is an evil greatly to be deplored. . . . Inasmuch, therefore, as we have the same objects in life, namely, the full development of all our powers, and should to some extent, have the same employments, we need precisely the same education; and we therefore claim that the best colleges of the country be open to us. . . . My ground is, that the boy and the girl, the man and the woman, should be always together in the business and pleasures of life, sharing alike its joys and sorrows, its distinction and fame; nor will they ever be harmoniously developed until they are educated together, physically, intellectually and morally.[188]

Stanton, whose own wish to attend school with men was thwarted, believed that mingling the sexes everywhere would obliterate many of the traits of Victorian women.

> Nature intended that boys and girls should be together in the home, in the school, in the world of work. The difference in sex being a difference in mind as well as body, is a healthy stimulus to every faculty. It is the isolation of the sexes that breeds all this sickly sentimentality, these romantic reveries, these morbid appetites, the listlessness and lassitude of our girls. They need the companionship of boys to stimulate them to more active exercise and more vigorous thought.[189]

Education could be summed up as the development of all women's powers of body and soul. The physical education of girls was necessarily related to larger freedoms of body. "One of the essential elements of health is freedom of thought and action. A right to individual life, opinion, ambition. The feebleness of body and mind so universal in women may be attributed mainly to their being forever in a condition of tutelage, a minority."[190] The physical weakness and disability of women in the mythology of the nineteenth century was the result of mistaken notions and false education.

> The childhood of women must be free and untrammeled. The girl must be allowed to romp and play, climb, skate, and swim; her clothing must be more like that of the boy—strong, loose-fitting garments, thick boots, etc., that she may be out at all times, and enter freely into all kinds of sports.[191]

To develop all one's physical powers in a free and active life was but one portion of the needs of development. Self-reliance and independence in many aspects of life was crucial.

> Teach her to go alone, by night and day, if need be, on the lonely highway, or through the busy streets of the crowded metropolis. The manner in which all courage and self-reliance is educated *out* of the girl, her path portrayed with dangers and difficulties that never exist, is melancholy indeed. Better, far, suffer occasional insults, or die outright, than live the life of a *coward* or never move without a protector. The best protector any woman can have, one that will serve her at all times and in all places, is *courage*; this she must get by her own experience, and experience comes by exposure.[192]

Rather than loading women "down with the traditions, proprieties, and sentimentalities of generations of silly mothers and grandmothers," Stanton counseled women to

> Take down your fences everywhere for sex, throw your time-worn theories to the wind, and let your daughters feel that they too have a right to the universe; that their home is the world and their duties wherever they find food for thought or work to do.[193]

Women were to learn that "suffering is not in harmony with God's will; that every pain, sorrow, and wrong is in violation of His law." This shift in understanding is "the first step in this work."[194] It must include the notion that maternity is not a curse, a sorrow, or a humiliation.

Frequently such educational arguments ended with a call for "an entire change in *dress*." The women's costumes of the day were responsible for making them ill, languorous, and uninterested in outdoor exercise. Stanton's commonsense realism pointed out that any man dressed in hoopskirts, tightly laced corsets, and many petticoats to drag in the quite literal mud of the era's city streets would similarly have become languorous and weak. Like many suffragist arguments of the period, God and nature came together in a notion of revelation that indicated the true divine purposes for the development of women's bodies:

> If God had intended that women should dress and move round like churns on castors, he would have made them without legs. If he had intended that in walking they should make no use of arms, but have them pinioned to their sides with their hands in muffs, like chickens skewered to roast, he would have made them without arms like heathen idols.
> If he had intended that they should bring their waists to a circumference of 12", he would kindly have dispensed with a double set of vital organs. In providing them with brains, vital organs, legs, and arms like man, it is evident that Nature intended to fit her for similar emergencies in the journey of life.[195]

Just as she recommended boots and loose-fitting clothes for girls, so for adult women. The feminine clothing was "a continual impediment and vexation" to one who sought the free and untrammeled use of all her faculties. In the 1850s, Stanton, along with a handful of other reforming women, wore the bloomer costume, modified trousers with a knee-length dress or tunic over them. They encountered "constant observation, criticism, ridicule, persecution, mobs."[196] After two years of this treatment, Stanton "gladly went back to the old slavery and sacrificed freedom to repose." Ever afterward, however, her comments on women's dress were especially acerbic. (She noted, for example, that the women who charged the immodesty of seeking public roles were the very women who bared bosoms and arms in ballroom gowns.)

After the debacle over the bloomer costume, Stanton was no longer willing to rest with any halfhearted measures to reform women's dress. "The true idea is for the sexes to dress as nearly alike as possible."[197] Only male clothing was really convenient for free movement; it would protect women from outrages on city streets.

Education and dress were both to be reformed so as to leave women "free and untrammelled"—"free to be, to grow, to feel, to think, to act."[198] The full development of the souls of women had stringent implications for women's *character*, in contrast to the period's notions of proper feminine personality. Stanton was particularly disturbed about the manipulation of others by "women's wiles." She was quick to point out the pernicious implication of this indirect means of attaining women's ends on the family, the church, and politics.

> Wherever there is an oppressed class, they will by trick, art, and management get what they can. If man refused to reason with woman, grant her fair debate, to treat her as a rational being, why, she will talk with the devil, as in Paradise, and then, the home, the state, and the church are all put in jeopardy. The morsels of our social life are repeated in our legislation, and just so long as women have no individual aims, desires, opinions and purposes in life, but secure their ends by echoing, wheedling and managing men, your men will be of the same plastic character, good by policy rather than by principle, led by the nose, by wily politicians, ready to sell their opinions, their votes, their birthrights for a mess of pottage.[199]

Esther and Vashti were good examples of the contrasts in women's characters. Vashti, "bold and uncompromising," was a "strong-minded woman"; she took her stand on high moral principle in refusing to capitulate to her husband's commands.[200] Esther, on the other hand, pretended to subjection but indirectly ruled the king through her feminine wiles. This state of affairs was partly caused by men themselves. "By seeming obedience, and flattery, woman may lead man where she will, but self-assertion in her he cannot brook, whether right or wrong, because he is educated to believe that woman is his subject in nature."[201] She insisted that women should think for themselves, even if they outraged public sentiment.

> Teach the girl it is no part of her life to cater to the prejudices of those around her. Make her independent of public sentiment, by showing her how worthless and rotten a thing it is. It is a settled axiom with me, after much examination and reflection, that public sentiment is false on every subject. Yet what a tyrant it is over us all, women especially, whose very life is to please, whose highest ambition is to be approved. But once outrage this tyrant, place yourself beyond his jurisdiction, taste the joy of free thought and action, and how powerless is his rule over you![202]

Stanton was explicit in linking this claim for women's personal self-assertion with her claims for enfranchisement: "The right to vote is the right of self-assertion."[203] Equally, a certain brand of political rhetoric went with these claims to self-assertion.

> My friends, what is man's idea of womanliness? It is to have a manner which pleases him—quiet, deferential, submissive, approaching him like as a subject

does a master. He wants no self-assertion on our part, no defiance, no vehement arraignment of him as a robber and criminal.[204]

She summed up her claims for women's characters as a "proper self-respect." A self-respecting woman did not allow herself to be treated as less than she was worth. A woman with proper self-respect, with a sense of her own human dignity and pride, did not hesitate to name the condition in which she found herself, however vehement her language concerning bondage, servitude, slavery, oppression under tyranny. She ceased to use euphemistic language, and spoke in clear, direct manner:

> To me, "unlock the doors" sounds better than any words of circumlocution, however sweet and persuasive. . . . Patience and persuasiveness are beautiful virtues in dealing with children and feeble-minded adults, but those who have the gift of reason and understand the principles of justice, it is our duty to compel to act up to the highest light that is in them, and as promptly as possible.[205]

Women needed self-respect in order to achieve the ballot. Equally, to have the ballot would create a greater sense of personal dignity in women:

> If we would rouse new respect for womanhood in the hearts of the masses, we must place woman in a position to respect herself, which she can never do as long as her political status is beneath that of the most degraded, ignorant classes of men. To make women the political equals of their sons, or even of their gardeners and coachmen, would add new dignity to their position. . . . Can you not understand the dignity, the pride, the new-born self-respect which would thrill the hearts of the women of this nation in their enfranchisement?[206]

Self-development was not complete, however, with woman's dress and character in this social strand of Stanton's argument. She looked also to *economic* dimensions of women's condition.[207] The young girl, like her brother, "must be taught to look toward a life of self-dependence and early prepare herself for some trade or profession."[208] Her most comprehensive speeches, such as "The Degradation of Disfranchisement," spoke of women's work. "Society at large . . . has in a measure excluded woman from the profitable industries of the world, and where she has gained a foothold her labor is at a discount."[209]

She was most closely connected to economic questions during the short life of *The Revolution*. That Anthony was attempting to organize working women's associations was no doubt part of Stanton's stimulus. Generally speaking, she saw the economy in terms congenial to her larger theory, in terms of progress, science, and individualism. The movement of civilization ever upward was to create a kind of enlightened economy. "The amount of intelligence we are year by year infusing into wrought iron promises, at no distant day, to relieve the great mass of mankind from long centuries of toil and degradation."[210] Free trade was one way to achieve such progress.[211] The self-development of every individual functioned economically as much as politically or maritally. "The duty of every man to develop his own powers, do what he can with the greatest skill and ease" was the starting point. "Mutual dependence" entered only secondarily, since other self-developing individuals were to supply the needs one could not supply oneself. National questions were strictly analogous to individual ones. England's genius for manufacturing complemented the U.S.'s broad acreage. "Every barrier in the way of imports and exports blocks the wheels of progress, and retards the moral and intellectual development of all the races of man."[212]

Even here, where Stanton was at her worst,[213] she was no apologist for the status quo. An awareness of the actual toll of industrial plants upon the lives of laboring people was the muted background to her enlightened liberalism, her Adam Smithian vision of the economy. "Above the busy hum of industry that gladdens all New England towns, the sighs and wails of the weary and wronged go up daily to heaven, calling for justice and mercy."[214] She visited factories making hoopskirts and pins in Connecticut, just as she visited prisons, and came away aghast:

> beyond the beautiful, polished machinery, and its perfect productions, I see the haggard, hopeless men and women, who never reap the fruits of their own industry, whose lives are one long, constant, struggle for bare necessities, while their employers, living in luxury and ease, realize all the profits of their labor, hoarding the money that should be in circulation and holding the broad acres that should be free to all the children of man. In some factories in Birmingham I was told that little children who should be at school or playing in the sunshine, are shut up to labor ten hours a day for twenty-five cents!! not enough to buy them good bread and milk!! Do not flatter yourselves, good Christian men and women, that the late war ended slavery on this continent.[215]

She ended her piece with something like a call for a social gospel: "let the pulpits of the East preach a few sermons on 'factory life as it is.' "

Stanton devoted an entire (unpublished) manuscript to developing these views of "the true relations of Capital and Labor." They are noteworthy for the prominent place given to ethics and religion in the consideration of their topic. She began with the typical framework of her thought after reading Comte and other scientists. The laws governing human affairs in thought and action was "change, progress, development . . . Hence it is as futile to oppose the new thoughts, demands, reforms, that mark the different stages of human development as it would be to protest against the varied products wrought on the surface of the earth by the ever revolving seasons, days, and nights,"[216]

The healthy discontent she affirmed among women was manifest among laborers. She affirmed not only "combining" but even "testing the strength of their numbers and purposes in strikes, mobs, and riots." She summoned the upper classes of society to "look around," to pay attention to the actual conditions of American life, and to reflect ethically and religiously on what these conditions meant.

> I ask those in the full enjoyment of all the blessings that wealth can give to look around you in the filthy lanes and bystreets of all our cities, the surging multitudes ragged, starving, packed in dingy cellars and garrets where no ray of sunshine or hope ever penetrate, no trick of light or love to cheer their lives. Look in the factories and workshops where young and old work side by side with tireless machines from morn till night through all the days, the weeks, the months, the years, that make up the long sum of life, impelled by that inexorable necessity that knows no law. . . . Look in our furnaces and mines where mid the perils of lurid fires and blasting rocks, deep down in the bowels of the earth begrimed despairing men toil ceaselessly for bread. Look what these unfortunates suffer in our jails, prisons, asylums, look at the injustice in our courts.[217]

Over and beyond these visible conditions, "apparent to most careless observers," she drew attention to "the ceaseless anxiety" and fear for the future that added "an unseen element of torture that can never be measured or understood."

The moral question was uppermost in Stanton's mind. "Is it right," she asked, that the majority should live in poverty so that a minority enjoyed life's blessings? "Is it right" that millions hungered while the few feasted? Or that multitudes were ignorant and dressed in rags while the few developed superior gifts? The Constitution proclaimed as "an abstract question" that every individual had equal natural rights to life, liberty, and the pursuit of happiness.

Those abstract political rights needed to be completed in the concrete opportunities to use them.

> For instance, the natural right to go across the continent is of little value to a man so long as he is compelled by his necessities to remain forever in one place. True, the ideal freedom may bring a passing pleasure, but practically the right is of no possible consequence.[218]

The important ethical differences between groups on the question of labor had to do with whether "poverty is a part of the divine plan that always has and always must exist" or whether it was "the result of human ignorance and selfishness and can be remedied." "To this last class I belong," she announced.

What was to be done therefore to remedy and improve the situation of the masses? The first step was to cultivate "the religious conscience of the people as to the essential sinfulness of these broad inequalities among mankind." I have noted Stanton's arguments for a religious concentration on the duties of this life and the outward conditions of existence rather than on the hereafter and the internal status of souls. Improving the material conditions of life was more important than any doctrinal stand.

> When the Christianity of our metropolis, for example, shall insist on the building of a higher order of tenement houses, on the cleaning of the streets where the poor dwell, on a greatly increased number of public baths, on the enforcement of all those sanitary conditions prescribed by law today . . . they will have accomplished a great work in the salvation of souls.[219]

These changes were more fundamental than, say, education. They were more appropriate to the theology of Jesus than the "nice disquisitions" heard in sermons.

Stanton lived long enough to see the birth of the social gospel and its multitudes of organizations; she affirmed these cooperative ventures. "We hail the work of the Salvation Army, the King's Daughters, the Kindergarten and industrial schools for the children of the poor, the University Settlement, etc. All these, added to our innumerable charities, show that the trend of thought is setting in the right direction."[220] To a certain extent she even shifted the basic terms of her thought, as she began to appreciate cooperation and communion in economic matters. On the fiftieth anniversary of Seneca Falls she called suffragists to agitate "the broader questions of philosophical socialism."[221] "The cooperative idea" was a unifying principle that could gather together "all the fragmentary reforms." Cooperation was a fundamentally American and democratic idea, a natural extension of the claims of the suffrage movement. "It is impossible to have 'equal rights for all' under our present competitive system."

Stanton was no Marxist, however, and there were important ambivalences in her analysis of economic questions. Rather like the view of Shaw I explore later, she found that the harmony of classes with each other was the desideratum. "The word religion means to bind again, to unite those who have been separated, to harmonise those who have been in antagonism,"[222] in contradistinction to the competition of classes and groups. Her appeal was always to the educated classes.

> This radical work cannot be done by what is called charity, but by teaching sound principles of political and domestic economy to our educated classes, showing them that by law, custom, and false theories of natural rights they are responsible for the poverty, ignorance, and vice of the masses.[223]

She was deeply disturbed by the hostility of laborers to woman suffrage. "The worst enemies of woman's suffrage will ever be the laboring classes of men," as she concluded during Anthony's sorties into union organizing.[224] For Stanton economic questions fed rather more directly back into the familial strand of bondage. She argued that women needed to be self-supporting, that financial independence would prevent or heal women's marital woes. In contrast to Anthony, Stanton's emphases were not on trade unions, professions, money, labor, in direct connection with her suffrage cases. The fourfold bondage was a more complicated and comprehensive affair than Anthony's "votes and money."

D. The Degradation of Disfranchisement

Stanton saw her claims for women's political rights as solidly democratic ones, now argued on legal and constitutional grounds, now on broader philosophical ones. This section of my analysis is in a sense the culmination and the undergirding of all Stanton's analysis of injustice to women. I explore first the straightforward democratic cases she made to the American public. The "rubbish of caste and class" vitiated the nation's democratic promise—whether by the aristocracy of men, or by the less-than-democratic sentiments instilled in women themselves by this false system. In this section I also note specific ways the political strand in Stanton's notion of the issue intertwined itself around the other strands of the fourfold bondage. Second, I look at Stanton's high claims for politics, the most exalted of all sciences, the statement of which virtually became a religion. Here I note the ways her claims were embroiled in racism and elitism. Third, I glance at some of her later, little-known, comprehensive statements on the meaning of disfranchisement.

1. By Every Principle of Our Republic

Stanton spoke of suffragists rehearsing the logic of democracy "for the sheer love of it," and most of her speeches bear this out. She pointed to the once stirring principle, "No taxation without representation"—were not women taxed everywhere? If the Founding Fathers said, "We, the people"—were not women people, she asked rhetorically. Was the nation founded on majority rule? Women and blacks, the great disfranchised classes, *were* the majority of the nation. Did government rest on the consent of the governed? Without the vote, women's consent remained to be garnered. Any and every argument advanced by republican theorists during the Revolutionary period, Stanton advanced for woman's enfranchisement. Like the founders, she believed the principles of democratic representation to be unchanging "eternal laws of justice."

> By every principle of our republic, logically considered, woman's emancipation is a foregone conclusion. The great "declarations" by the fathers, regarding individual rights and the true foundations of government, should not be glittering generalities for demagogues to quote and ridicule, but eternal laws of justice, as fixed in the world of morals as are the laws of attraction and gravitation in the material universe.[225]

She was conscious of purloining principles and arguments from the heritage of the nation. It was an advantage rather than a liability of the suffrage cause that her arguments were

> the same our fathers used when battling old King George and the British Parliament for their right to representation, and a voice in the laws by which they were governed. There are no new arguments to be made on human rights, our work today is to apply to ourselves those so familiar to all; to teach man than woman is not an anomalous being, outside all laws and constitutions, but

71

one whose rights are to be established by the same process of reason as that by which he demands his own.[226]

Her work was merely to apply principles "so familiar to all" to herself and other women. She lamented the "inconsistencies of our theory and practice."[227] The same process of reason, the same principles, operated in the case of women as of men in political argument. Since the logic of democracy was on the side of the suffragists, the opponents were left with little reasoning power on their behalf. When men in the Chicago convention saw

> their own guns turned on their defenseless heads, and such fifty-pounders as "taxation without representation," "all men created equal," "no just government can be formed without the consent of the governed," hurled at them, no wonder they left logic and took up ridicule; and now, when we meet them with their own weapons, they say we can not reason. The drunken man always imagines the lamp-posts dancing. Poor R. L. C., in the Chicago convention, really thought his platitudes logic, and our logic sentiment.[228]

The appropriation of this revolutionary rhetoric led Stanton to conclude that without women's enfranchisement, American institutions forfeited their proud democratic claims. "The daughters of the revolutionary heroes of '76"[229] denounced the rank usurpation of their rights, a tyranny based only on custom and prejudice.

> Can it be that here, where we acknowledge no royal blood, no apostolic descent, that you, who have declared that all men were created equal—that governments derive their just power from the consent of the governed, willingly build up an aristocracy that places the ignorant and vulgar above the educated and refined—the alien and the ditch-digger above the authors and poets of the day—an aristocracy that would raise the sons above the mothers that bore them?[230]

Stanton had a truly democratic passion. As her autobiography put it, "I detest the words 'royalty' and 'nobility,' and all the ideas and institutions based on their recognition."[231] Indeed, "aristocracy" was among the mildest of the words Stanton used to describe the state of affairs between the sexes.

> So long as women are not represented in government they are in a condition of tutelage, perpetual minority, slavery.
> You smile at the idea of women being slaves in this country. Benjamin Franklin said long ago, "that they who have no voice in making the laws, or in

the election of those who administer them, do not enjoy liberty, but are absolutely enslaved to those who have votes and to their representatives." I might occupy hours in quoting grand liberal sentiments from the fathers—Madison, Jefferson, Otis, and Adams—in favor of individual representation. I might quote equally noble words from the statesmen of our day. . . . But what do lofty utterances and logical arguments avail so long as men, blinded by old prejudices and customs, fail to see their application to the women by their side? Alas! gentlemen, women are your subjects. Your own selfish interests are too closely interwoven for you to feel their degradation, and they are too dependent to reveal themselves to you in their nobler aspirations, their native dignity.[232]

The division of citizens into male enfranchised and female disfranchised classes was, after the passage of the Fourteenth Amendment, "the last stronghold of aristocracy in the country."

Stanton was as concerned about the stability of republican institutions as any of the founders. Republican inconsistencies between theory and practice, the aristocratic strains in American life resulting from women's disfranchisement, cast in doubt the stability of cherished American institutions.

A government, based on the principle of caste and class, cannot stand. The aristocratic idea, in any form, is opposed to the genius of our free institutions, to our own declaration of rights, and to the civilization of the age. All artificial distinctions, whether of family, blood, wealth, color, or sex, are equally oppressive to the subject classes, and equally destructive to national life and prosperity. Governments based on every form of aristocracy, on every degree or variety of inequality, have been tried in despotisms, monarchies, and republics, and all alike have perished.[233]

Appealing to the immutable laws that reign over human affairs, moral and physical alike, Stanton's bent for a rational science in politics came to the fore. "Whatever is true in theory is safe in practice."[234] Woman's enfranchisement was an "experiment," a novelty in some inessential respects. But equality in more important ways was as old as human society.

The principle of inequality has been thoroughly tried, and every nation based on that idea that has not already perished, clearly shows the seeds of death in its dissensions and decline. Though it has never been tried, we know an experiment on the basis of equality would be safe; for the laws in the world of morals are as immutable as in the world of matter. . . . When we base nations on justice and equality, we lift government out of the mists of speculation into the dignity of a fixed science. Everything short of this is trick, legerdemain, sleight of hand.[235]

Stanton applied these notions of security and science guaranteed by the ballot to other reforms sought by the movement. Without the vote, none of the gains sought or made by women was assured for posterity:

> But be assured that our cause can never rest on a safe, enduring basis, until we get the right of suffrage. So long as we have no voice in the laws, we have no guarantee that privileges granted us today by one body of men, may not be taken from us tomorrow by another.[236]

In fact, this white male nobility was the *worst* of the historical instances of tyranny because of its particular organization. There were several reasons for this judgment. First, the qualification of sex was insurmountable. Stanton was tireless in pointing out that the law classed women with idiots, lunatics, blacks, and criminals—a fine status for the daughters, wives, and mothers allegedly cherished by lawmakers. In fact "our place is lower," for "the negro can be raised to the dignity of a voter if he possesses himself of $250; the lunatic can vote in his moments of sanity, and the idiot, too, if he be not more than nine-tenths a fool."[237] Next, to compare the state of American women with that of English women came naturally to one whose political vocabulary came from the struggle with King George and Parliament. "Woman's position, under our free institutions, is much lower than under the monarchy of England."[238] She entwined class around the status of sex—English noblewomen were eligible to public offices, etc. After the struggles over the Fourteenth Amendment, Stanton further developed this strand of her argument.

The peculiar facts of sex in family, marriage, and social customs tangled with the political strand of the fourfold bondage to deepen the seriousness of women's status.

> Of all kinds of aristocracy, that of sex is the most odious and unnatural; invading as it does, our homes, desecrating our family altars, dividing those whom God has joined together, exalting the son above the mother who bore him, and subjugating everywhere, moral power to brute force.[239]

Both home and government suffered from this unnatural division of the sexes. "The home is in a condition of half orphanage for the want of fathers, and the State suffers for need of wise mothers."[240]

Sometimes these arguments implied that women were better than their oppressors—because educated and refined, on the one hand, because mothers and representatives of morality, on the other. But it is a mistake to read these comments as Stanton's capitulation to Victorian sentiments about women. The period's insipid notions of women's purity and moral influence were as much a part of the problem as part of its solution. The pedestal to which women were raised was another variant on the antidemocratic theme, a positive danger to the republic.

> When you exalt weakness and imbecility above your heads, give it an imaginary throne of power, illimitable, unmeasured, unrecognized, you have founded a throne for women on pride, selfishness, and complacency, before which you may well stand appalled. . . . The most insidious enemy to our republican institutions, at this hour, is found in the aristocracy of our women. The ballot-box, that great leveler among men, is beneath their dignity.[241]

The power attributed to women by public opinion of her day, the "power" of influence, was "wholly irresponsible and hence dangerous."[242] It required the leveling and accountability of the voting booth to temper it—and presumably to educate women out of their less attractive traits. "Influence" represented a portion of the social category of Stanton's fourfold bondage—"that social throne where they tell us our influence is unbounded."[243] This Stanton was firm in rejecting, even in the days when she believed in "sex in soul." The all-pervading light of influence was to pass simultaneously through a prism (to emphasize the individuality of women) and through a burning glass (to give it effectiveness and focus)—both of these metaphors described the ballot. "A direct power over one's own person, an individual opinion to be counted, is better than indirect influence, be it ever so far-reaching."[244]

The traits of character, the self-respect, courage, and education needed for women's independence were linked to politics. The ballot would instill in women a newfound dignity and pride. Equally, women required dignity and pride to assert their rights. When thoughtless women said, "We have all the rights we want," the nation was in a sorry state indeed. What sort of democratic sentiments were to be instilled in the hearts of youth when their mothers were educators such as this? With the suffragist ingenuity that could turn opposition into an argument for her own case, Stanton claimed that the fact that some women did not want to be free and equal was itself the strongest reason for granting women the vote.

> If there are any who do not wish to vote, that is the strongest reason for their enfranchisement. If all love of liberty has been quenched in their souls by their degraded condition, the duties of citizenship and the responsibility of self-government should be laid upon them at once, for their pitiful indifference is merely the result of their disfranchisement. . . . When I hear American women, descendants of Jefferson, Hancock and Adams, say they do not want to vote, I feel that the blood of the revolutionary heroes must long since have ceased to flow in their veins.[245]

Indeed, "woman falsifies herself and blasphemes her God, when, in view of her present social, legal, and political position, she declares she has all the rights she wants."[246]

The false dignity of women of affluence and the lack of political exposure of all women both undermined the democratic institutions of the country.

> Remember woman is the narrow, conservative element, the staunch supporter everywhere of the aristocratic idea. Look at the long line of equipages and liveried servants in 5th Avenue and Central Park, the pageant composed chiefly of women. Think of stalwart men dressed up like monkeys, perched on the back seat of a carriage for ornament. A coat of arms and livery belong legitimately to countries that boast a monarchy, an order of nobility, established church, law of primogeniture, where families live through centuries; but here, where the tallow chandler of yesterday lives in a palace to-day, they are out of place. What a spectacle for us who proclaimed the glorious doctrine of equality a century ago, to be imitating the sham and tinsel of the effete civilizations of the old world, thus degrading the dignity of the idea on which our government is based.
>
> Men in political life cannot afford to do these things. They always have the ballot-box, that great leveller, before their eyes. They keep their kid gloves in their pockets, shake hands all round, and act as if they believed all men equal, especially about election time. This practice they have in the right direction does in time, mould them anew into more liberal ideas than the women by their sides. It is vain to look for a genuine republic in this country until the women are baptized into the idea, until they understand the genius of our institutions, until they study the science of government, and have a direct voice in our legislation; then there will be enthusiasm thrown round our republican idea such as we have never realized before.
>
> The direct effect of concentrating all women's thoughts and interests on home life intensifies her selfishness and narrows her ideas in every direction, hence she

is arbitrary in her views of government, bigoted in religion and exclusive in society; and is ever insidiously infusing her ideas into the man by her side.[247]

Stanton's notion that the country could not truly be democratic until American women were "baptized" into the ideas of democracy was not based on some notion of the innately democratic character of women, but on some thoroughly realistic views of the conditions of political life.

2. The Polling Booth Shall Be a Beautiful Temple

The resemblance of Stanton's suffragist case to the language of the founding period went farther. She too espoused a "civil religion."[248] And like many of the Founding Fathers' equivocations concerning black or propertyless people, Stanton's democratic sentiments could be severely qualified for certain classes of people and under trying political circumstances.

All her life Stanton identified the Reformation and the American Revolution as stemming from the same essential truth, individual rights. Freedom, equality, self-development, the right of individual judgment were high, holy, sacred, grounded in natural law. To refuse to struggle for equal rights was to falsify oneself and to blaspheme God, since God's laws were written on one's soul. Those same laws were the basis of democratic theory. The "jarring discord and confusion in life" that Stanton saw around her was the result of violating those laws.[249] To follow the natural laws, the laws of "change, progress, development," resulted in the growth of humankind toward the perfection God intended. Woman's emancipation, elevation, and enfranchisement had a central role in that great movement toward perfection in Stanton's view long before she became convinced of the differences of sex in soul.

> It is from no captious love of change or power, no shortsighted discontent of my lot in life, no personal hardships or sufferings that I demand for woman her right of suffrage, her right to property, her right to the use and product of all her god-given powers; but because I see that man never can become a God until his mother becomes a divinity.[250]

Political institutions were not simply one social agency among others in the drive toward perfection. In a republic, politics was the location par excellence for the embodiment and manifestation of these religious truths. To vote was "to climb the first rounds of the ladder that they may reach the divine heights where they shall be as gods."[251] This special value of political life came

77

particularly to the fore as Stanton became disenchanted with the churches. In the same debates in the American Equal Rights Association in the late 1860s that divided erstwhile allies over "the Negro's Hour" and that clarified for Stanton the liabilities of self-sacrifice as woman's moral virtue, she articulated a euphoric view of the purification of American political life that was to result from woman's participation.

> Behold, with the coming of woman into this higher sphere of influence, the dawn of the new day, when politics, so called, are to be lifted into the world of morals and religion; when the polling-booth shall be a beautiful temple, surrounded by fountains and flowers and triumphal arches, through which young men and maidens shall go up in joyful procession to ballot for justice and freedom; and when our election days shall be kept like the holy feasts of the Jews at Jerusalem.[252]

This view strikes a reader of the 1980s as incorrigibly idealistic and perhaps slightly amusing as we look back at precious little change in our political life after women's enfranchisement. How did she arrive at such conclusions? Let us look more carefully at the terms in which Stanton couched her arguments.

She was bent on articulating a higher view of politics than the ones she heard around her. Unlike her contemporaries who feared that women were to be sullied by political participation, Stanton would not brook the thought that women were to come "down" to politics. Politics was a high calling, the "most exalted of all sciences." These higher and holier dimensions of political life were the subject of the 1867 speech before the American Equal Rights Association. Stanton set herself straightforwardly to refute the Victorian claim that females would be degraded by the brouhaha and hugger-mugger of politics.

> What thinking man can talk of *coming down* into the arena of politics? If we need purity, honor, self-sacrifice, and devotion anywhere, we need them in those who have in their keeping the life and prosperity of a nation. In the enfranchisement of woman, in lifting her up into this broader sphere, we see for her new honor and dignity, more liberal, exalted, and enlightened views of life, its objects, ends, and aims, and an entire revolution in the new world of interest and action where she is soon to play her part. And in saying this, I do not claim that woman is better than man, but that the sexes have a civilizing power on each other.[253]

At its best, her argument read as a claim for a reciprocal elevating influence between politics and women. This "broader sphere," the science of government, was to procure for women "new honor and dignity, more liberal, exalted, and enlightened views of life." Politics, in other words, would bring enlightenment to women. It was to check the narrowness and complacency Stanton abhorred in pedestalized women. Her notion of civil religion stood on its own two feet, intrinsic to the political life of a democracy.

> When we remember that a nation's life and growth and immortality depend upon its legislation, can we exalt too highly the dignity and responsibility of the ballot, the science of political economy, and the sphere of government? Statesmanship is, of all sciences, the most exalted and comprehensive, for it includes all others.[254]

To this height, women were to be lifted by education and the vote. "To vote is the most sacred right of citizenship—a religious duty,"[255] to be discharged in the full solemnity of a religious act. One of the period's favorite romantic poets had made a similar point.

> To many minds, this claim for the ballot suggests nothing more than a rough polling-booth where coarse, drunken men, elbowing each other, wade knee-deep in mud to drop a little piece of paper two inches long into a box—simply this and nothing more. The poet Wordsworth showing the blank materialism of those who see only with their outward eyes, says of his Peter Bell:
> "A primrose on the river's brim
> A yellow primrose was to him,
> And it was nothing more."
> So our political Peter Bells see the rough polling-place in this great right of citizenship, and nothing more. In this act, so lightly esteemed by the mere materialist, behold the realization of that great idea struggled for in the ages and proclaimed by the Fathers, the right of self-government.[256]

This reference to mere materialism was also Stanton's entrée into the other, more problematic half of her reciprocal argument. "To women it is given to save the Republic." An "entire revolution" was to result from women's enfranchisement.

> It is vain to look for a genuine republic in this country until the women are baptized into the idea, until they understand the genius of our institutions, until they study the science of government, until they hold the ballot in their hands and have a direct voice in our legislation. . . . All must see that this claim for

male suffrage is but another experiment in class legislation, another violation of the republican idea. With the black man we have no new element in government, but with the education and elevation of women we have a power that is to develop the Saxon race into a higher and nobler life, and thus, by the law of attraction, to lift all races to a more even platform than can ever be reached in the political isolation of the sexes.[257]

Here Stanton hinted that the elevation of woman was to develop the Saxon race especially in the evolutionary ladder, and so ("by the law of attraction") bring other races along. This argument for a purified civil religion was couched in terms of individualism and universal suffrage.

The battles of the ages have been fought for races, classes, parties, over and over again, and force always carried the day, and will until we settle the higher, the holier question of individual rights. This is our American idea, and on a wise settlement of this question rests the problem whether our nation shall live or perish.[258]

Sometimes she argued this claim by way of "burying the negro in the citizen," by which she meant seeking the enfranchisement of all individuals of voting age.

We alone have struck the key-note of reconstruction. While man talks of "equal, impartial, manhood suffrage," we give the certain sound, "universal suffrage." While he talks of the rights of races, we exalt the higher, the holier idea proclaimed by the Fathers, and now twice baptized in blood, "individual rights." To women it is given to save the Republic.[259]

So Stanton painted the triumphal picture of the new reign to be inaugurated with woman suffrage, replete with images from the religious tradition. The polling booth would become a temple, election days would be holy feasts, a virtual New Jerusalem would appear as young men and maidens went "to ballot for justice and freedom."

It is important to note that Stanton never asserted that women's higher spiritual capacities were to ennoble politics. She pronounced herself an agnostic on the question of the truth of the sexes' traits. "In the education and elevation of woman we are yet to learn the true manhood and womanhood, the true masculine and feminine elements."[260] Nor was she yet in full cry against other groups in the social order. She honed and expanded her hints of 1854 that the American aristocracy of men was worse than any European equivalent, for the American ruling class of men included the "washed or unwashed, lettered or unlettered, rich or poor, black or white."[261] And in these AERA discussions she equivocated on the educated suffrage. At times she claimed that she had ever argued for universal suffrage, and most of her arguments were directed to this end. When an opponent in the AERA claimed that it was sufficient to argue for one thing at a time, Stanton took her stand on broad philosophical principles:

> To say that politicians always do one thing at a time is no reason why philosophers should not enunciate the broad principles that underlie that one thing and a dozen others. We do not take the right step for this hour in demanding suffrage for any class; as a matter of principle I demand it for all.[262]

Later in the discussion, however, she was willing to step back from this high principle. It was a hypothetical claim: "If we are to have further class legislation, she thought the wisest order of enfranchisement was to take the educated classes first," said the account of the discussion.[263] But that very small "if" was accompanied by various slurs on the ignorant.

> It is a consolation to the "white male," to the popinjays in all our seminaries of learning, to the ignorant foreigner, the boot-black and barber, the idiot—for a "white male" may vote if he be not more than nine-tenths a fool—to look down on women of wealth and education, who write books, make speeches, and discuss principles with the savans [sic] of their age. It is a consolation for these classes to be able to say, "Well, if woman can do these things, they can't vote after all." . . .
> Poor human nature wants something to look down on.[264]

As the contest heated up within the American Equal Rights Association, Stanton was increasingly explicit on both the masculine and feminine "elements" in the universe, and on racism.[265] The next year (1868) she appeared once again before the AERA, with a lengthily argued case for the Sixteenth Amendment—the suffrage amendment. There were six arguments:

1. A government based on the principle of caste and class cannot stand.
2. Manhood suffrage, or a man's government, is civil, religious, and social disorganization.
3. When manhood suffrage is established from Maine to California, woman has reached the lowest depths of political degradation.

TOWARD A TRADITION OF FEMINIST THEOLOGY

4.   The history of American statesmanship does not inspire me with
     confidence in man's capacity to govern the nation alone, with justice and
     mercy.
5.   The present isolation of the sexes is opposed to the teachings of science,
     philosophy, and common sense.
6.   The safety and dignity of woman demands her immediate enfranchise-
     ment.[266]

The first of these arguments I touched on earlier. The fourth put to good use
the political scandals of the day. Since "honorable Senators" had spoken of the
financial ignorance and corruption of the government, there was no reason to
believe that any regime without women in it was a good one. The other four
arguments are worth detailing to inquire more fully into the masculine and
feminine "elements" as well as the racism that saw insults to American
womanhood in extending suffrage to other male groups. I take up numbers
two and five as one piece before looking at arguments three and six together.
     The second point of this case rested on the historical record of the rule of
the masculine element. She began with no complimentary picture of those she
called elsewhere "the self-styled lords of creation."

I urge a Sixteenth Amendment, because "manhood suffrage" or a man's
government is civil, religious, and social disorganization. The male element is a
destructive force, stern, selfish, aggrandizing, loving war, violence, conquest,
acquisition, breeding in the material and moral world alike discord, disorder,
disease, and death. See what a record of blood and cruelty the pages of history
reveal! Through what slavery, slaughter, and sacrifice, through what inquisitions
and imprisonments, pains and persecutions, black codes and gloomy creeds, the
soul of humanity has struggled for the centuries, while mercy has veiled her face
and all hearts have been dead alike to love and hope! The male element has held
high carnival thus far, it has fairly run riot from the beginning, overpowering the
feminine elements everywhere, crushing out all the diviner qualities in human
nature, until we know but little of true manhood and womanhood, of the latter
comparatively nothing, for it has scarce been recognized as a power until within
the last century. Society is but the reflection of man himself, untempered by
woman's thought, the hard iron rule we feel alike in the church, the state, and
the home. No one need wonder at the disorganization, at the fragmentary
condition of everything, when we remember that man, who represents but half
a complete being, with but half an idea on every subject, has undertaken the
absolute control of all sublunary matters.[267]

Stanton had taken off her gloves. "The hard iron rule" of the past, she was
quick to say, did not characterize all male individuals, since "many of the most

beautiful spirits the world has known have been clothed in manhood."[268] Indeed, such negative characteristics were "often marked in woman." Nevertheless, they served more to distinguish the "stronger sex" than they did women.

If the masculine element was more "hard, selfish, and brutal," what of the feminine? Stanton wavered at this point, for good reasons internal to her argument. Since male rule had been "absolute," there was no true understanding of women's nature. "We have simply so many reflections, varieties, and dilutions of the masculine gender,"[269] instead of a balanced picture. Women's characteristics had been repressed, forced to adapt to male conditions, pushed by dependency into traits that please their rulers. "The strong, natural characteristics of womanhood" had been ignored.

> To keep a foothold in society woman must be as near like man as possible, reflect his ideas, opinions, virtues, motives, prejudices, and vices. She must respect his statutes, though they strip her of every inalienable right, and conflict with that higher law written by the finger of God on her own soul. She must believe his theology, though it pave the highways of hell with the skulls of new-born infants, and made God a monster of vengeance and hypocrisy. She must look at everything from its dollar and cent point of view, or she is a mere romancer. She must accept things as they are and make the best of them. To mourn over the miseries of others, the poverty of the poor, their hardships in jails, prisons, asylums, the horrors of war, cruelty, and brutality in every form, all this would be mere sentimentalizing. To protest against the intrigue, bribery, and corruption of public life, to desire that her sons might follow some business that did not involve lying, cheating, and a hard grinding selfishness, would be arrant nonsense. In this way man has been moulding woman to his ideas by direct and positive influences, while she, if not a negation, has used indirect means to control him, and in most cases developed the very characteristics both in him and herself that needed repression. And now man himself stands appalled at the results of his own excesses, and mourns in bitterness that falsehood, selfishness, and violence are the law of life. The need of this hour is not territory, gold mines, railroads, or specie payments, but a new evangel of womanhood, to exalt purity, virtue, morality, true religion, to lift man up into the higher realms of thought and action.[270]

It is remarkable that after this very strong language establishing the sheer lack of information regarding the feminine element, Stanton concluded, equally strongly, with the notion that a "new evangel of womanhood" was the need of the hour. Only one item of some substance appeared as the content of the feminine element—women's love and motherhood:

That great conservator of woman's love, if permitted to assert itself, as it naturally would in freedom against oppression, violence, and war, would hold all these destructive forces in check, for woman knows the cost of life better than man does, and not with her consent would one drop of blood ever be shed, one life sacrificed in vain. With violence and disturbance in the natural world, we see a constant effort to maintain an equilibrium of forces. Nature, like a loving mother, is ever trying to keep land and sea, mountain and valley, each in its place, to hush the angry winds and waves, balance the extremes of heat and cold, of rain and drought, that peace, harmony and beauty may reign supreme. There is a striking analogy between matter and mind, and the present disorganization of society warns us, that in the dethronement of woman we have let loose the elements of violence and ruin that she only has the power to curb.[271]

Even here, the content and meaning of the feminine element were more suggested than stated. The natural analogies of the equilibrium of forces do not particularly invite an uncritical positive rendering of the feminine element. Though hushing the angry winds implies that the feminine may be more peaceful than the male, hushing the winds is not a balance between two opposing forces. And are we to assume that of the "extremes of heat and cold" the feminine is represented by the "cold"? All we are really told is that women, since they give birth, would be unlikely to shed blood; that "in freedom," women's capacities would "naturally" come forth; and that disorganization has resulted from the subjugation of women.

Stanton's fifth argument returned to the masculine/feminine elements of the universe as part of her case for the integration of the sexes in all of life, hence in the polling booth. "I demand the adoption of the 16th Amendment, because the present isolation of the sexes is opposed to the teachings of science, philosophy, and common sense."[272] There was mutual influence between the sexes, on certain specific terms. In education boys were to become more "gentle, pure-minded, and conscientious," while girls were to become "more vigorous in thought and action, less vain and frivolous," by their association with each other. "Just so in politics," she might have said. "When we ask that women be admitted into the world of politics that it may be purified and elevated, it is not that we consider woman better than man, but that the noblest sentiments of both are called out by such associations."[273] "All writers on the science of government"—she cited especially Comte and Spencer—spoke of women in ways that made them "the great harmonizing element of the era we are now entering." When science, philosophy, and common sense were in such concord, how could anyone disagree? Once again this complementarity was not precisely clear. The woman would "harmonize" something in the social order and hence bring about greater peacefulness in the vail of male violence Stanton described; but was she to harmonize two conflicting forces outside herself? Stanton here spoke of woman's "sentiments and affection"; but these, as always with Stanton, needed "development and enlightened direction" in order to play the role for which Stanton had cast her. That role, of making the "first step toward social reorganization," was to be accomplished by women's education, elevation, and enfranchisement, to be sure. The new era was to be one in which government was to be made stable, capital and labor reconciled, intellect and activity harmonized, indeed, "life to be held sacred, the interests of all guarded, labor dignified, the criminal treated like a moral patient, education made practical and attractive and brought within the reach of all."

Whatever confusions there were to Stanton's notion of the natural equilibrium of the sexes, however, it is somewhat clearer, after this identification of social ruin with male rule, and social harmony with female equality, why she was perturbed at the prospect of further male suffrage. Her third major argument portrayed the increased degradation she foresaw as the result for women when male suffrage was extended.

> I urge a Sixteenth Amendment because, when "manhood suffrage" is established from Maine to California, woman has reached the lowest depths of political degradation. So long as there is a disfranchised class in this country, and that class its women, a man's government is worse than a white man's government with suffrage limited by property and educational qualifications, because in proportion as you multiply the rulers, the condition of the politically ostracized is more hopeless and degraded.[274]

Her fear of the rule of the many by the few was exacerbated as the few grew to be greater in number. It also had to do with the character of those who were to be added to the few in power over the many.

> If American women find it hard to bear the oppressions of their own Saxon fathers, the best orders of manhood, what may they not be called to endure when all the lower orders of foreigners now crowding our shores legislate for them and their daughters. Think of Patrick and Sambo and Hans and Yung Tung, who do not know the difference between a monarchy and a republic, who can not read the Declaration of Independence or Webster's spelling-book, making laws for Lucretia Mott, Ernestine L. Rose, and Anna E. Dickinson. Think of jurors and jailers drawn from these ranks to watch and try young girls

for the crime of infanticide, to decide the moral code by which the mothers of this Republic shall be governed.[275]

There it was, starkly. Saxon fathers were the "best orders of manhood," yet their rule might be light in comparison to that of Patrick, Sambo, Hans, and Yung Tung, those stereotypical and trivializing names by which Victorian society referred to minorities and ethnic groups. This was Stanton at her worst, conjuring, by her references to infanticide and motherhood, the sexual fears of the society as arguments for the desirability of woman's enfranchisement. The lower orders of foreigners were juxtaposed to those good American creations, Jefferson's Declaration and Webster's spelling book—the very tactic Stanton abhorred when it was done to her. (It is tempting to quote Stanton to herself: "Poor human nature wants something to look down on.") It was not only the unlettered and unwashed who roused Stanton's ire, but the peculiar American combination of the "iron-heeled peasantry of the Old World and the slaves of the New"[276] ruling American women.

Partly, of course, she was incensed at the ridicule the woman suffrage amendment was receiving in the national press. Partly she was disappointed and angry at the rifts developing with old allies, who saw no way to complete the accomplishments of the abolitionist movement without leaving aside the politically damaging claims of women. She upped the ante:

> Not since God first called light out of darkness and order out of chaos, was there ever made so base a proposition as "manhood suffrage" in this American Republic, after all the discussions we have had on human rights in the last century.[277]

Stanton returned to such themes in her sixth argument. "I urge the 16th Amendment on your consideration, because the safety and dignity of woman demands her immediate enfranchisement." She gave a complicated account of the political effects of previous enfranchisements. Though the arguments were complex and ambiguous, her conclusion was less so: She was certain that "fearful outrages" on women were to result, and it was no accident that she emphasized the South.

> Just as the democratic cry of a "white man's government" created the antagonism between the Irishman and the Negro, which culminated in the New York riots of '63, so a republican cry of "manhood suffrage" creates an

antagonism between black men and all women, that will result in fearful outrages on womanhood, especially in the Southern states.[278]

Like the quantitative principle above, that to multiply the ruling class in number was to make the position of the oppressed even more hopeless, Stanton's case depended on a kind of special ostracism. At the same time, she believed that every move to enfranchise another group was a measure of progress toward universal suffrage. The result of this combination was confusing, as she asserted *both* increased progress and increased degradation for women, at the same time:

> Had Irishmen been disfranchised in this country they would have made common cause with the negro in fighting for his rights; but when exalted above him, they proved his worst enemy. The negro will be the victim, for a generation to come, of the prejudice engendered by making this a white man's government. While the enfranchisement of each new class of white men was a step toward his ultimate freedom, it increased his degradation in the transition period and he touched the depths of human misery when all men but the negro were crowned with citizenship.
>
> Just so with women, while the enfranchisement of all men hastens the day for justice to her, it makes her degradation more complete in the transition period.[279]

Stanton's position was deeply ambivalent. At times she opposed the Fifteenth Amendment, arguing that she would not see another class of men enfranchised before her.[280] On the other hand, she was equally capable of branding the advocacy of property and educational qualifications for the vote as "monstrous injustice":

> After by narrow selfish legislation concentrating the wealth and privileges of a nation in the hands of the few, what monstrous injustice to disfranchise the many because they are poor and ignorant! The shortest way to give a man property and education is to secure him in all the rights, privileges, and immunities of the citizen.[281]

The equivocations of Stanton's positions regarding democracy are best understood as the result of her struggles with political liberalism. She considered herself a liberal, not only in politics but in other realms of life. That liberal men, who agreed with her in principle, indeed from whom she learned her liberalism, could nonetheless do abhorrent things to their own wives, mothers, daughters, was something she saw directly. That she would have

87

been confused about political "advances" that were simultaneously political "regressions" for women, is not surprising; it was not her personal failure,[282] but the failure of liberalism itself. She almost always saw such disjunctions, however, as a theory-practice split; if the theory was sound, there was no choice but to conclude that the idea simply had not been *applied* adequately or thoroughly. (Feminists today might say that the problem was rather one of a dichotomy between public and private, a perspective that casts some doubt on whether the "theory" itself was sound.) Yet she did zero in on some of the crucial points—for example, to be "raised" to a pedestal was a political degradation regardless of the conventional understanding.

There were also ways her religious convictions exacerbated these confusions. To one for whom individual rights were always higher and holier, it should not be surprising that questions of the relative positions of groups could introduce tensions. Similarly, progress was built into her premises, a progress toward an upward plateau on which human beings were to be as gods.

3. The Meaning of Disfranchisement

During the last three decades of the nineteenth century Stanton continued to refine and extend her analyses of the meaning of women's political status. After twenty years of experience, she clarified her views of the ethical and religious stakes in the suffrage movement. She expanded her conceptual apparatus, made creative suggestions for fulfilling the democratic promise, and developed further grounds for the need of women's enfranchisement. In the early and middle 1870s, she refined her understanding of the reasons women were subjugated. In the 1890s, especially "The Degradation of Disfranchisement" and "The Antagonism of Sex" indicate the new ways she struggled with characterizing the movement adequately. (In the 1880s she was frequently in movement from one residence to another, writing the *History of Woman Suffrage*, and gathering her forces for *The Woman's Bible* project.)

The animating principle of much of Stanton's political and social analysis was the problem of the few and the many.

> It has not required much research . . . to discover that all governments to this hour have been administered in the interests of the few rather than the many: that theologians and political economists have laid more stress on divine decrees and the natural law of selfishness than on the purer, higher principles of morals and equity.[283]

The colon in that statement indicated the opposition between the rule of the few over the many and good ethics or true religion. ("The natural law of selfishness," she later added, came from a mistaken notion of the natural law.) "The True Republic" was in certain respects an exposition of the injustice and moral chaos resulting in politics, religion, society, and the home from the tyranny of the few (in the case of the home, the rule of "one despotic will"). Self-government was the only remedy for that chaos. Self-government "involves an understanding of principles, of measures rather than men or policies. Nothing can rescue power from the hands of the few but the education of the many."[284] The remedy was "wisely legislating, all the time, for the interests of the many, rather than the few, diffusing power." She suggested a variation of direct democracy in which all sorts of measures were to be submitted to the people by referendum: taxes, tariffs, public debts, banking, donation of lands to railways, the annexation of territory, or the declaration of war.

Inequality produced "cold hard selfishness on one side and abject hopeless slavery on the other." Here was the cause of woman's subjection, which even

in the best conditions is rooted in selfishness and sensuality. So insidious is its tyranny that I can liken it only to the subjection of the higher faculties, sentiments, and affections of the individual to the gross animal propensities. Of all kinds of slavery the most hopeless and pitiful is that of an individual of genius, power, ambition, bound to the earth by an appetite.[285]

To selfishness and sensuality she added "the same cause that subjugated different races and nations to one another, the law of force, that made might right, the weak the slaves of the strong." In this conflict, "the ballot box is but one of the outposts of progress, a victory that all orders of men can see and understand." Beyond this symbolic drama was another.

Only the few can grasp the metaphysics of this question, in all its social, religious, and political bearings and appreciate the moral effect of according all outward honor and dignity to woman. . . . All the best interests of the race are at stake in her ignorance and degradation.[286]

The irony of this reversal of the relationships between the few and the many is the effect of the elitism in Stanton's perspective. The rule of the few in general she abhorred; on the other hand, she found herself among the few who could truly appreciate the real importance of this entire revolution in the social order.

This same essay honed the requirements for justice for women. Ideal notions of womanhood were not sufficient; nor was it sufficient to treat certain individual women properly.

> Men mistake all the time their reverence for an ideal womanhood for a sense of justice toward the actual being that shares with them the toils of life. Man's love and tenderness to one particular woman for a time is no criterion for his general feeling for the whole sex for all time. That same man that would die for one woman, would make an annual holocaust of others, if his appetites or pecuniary interests required it. Kind husbands and fathers that would tax every nerve and muscle to the uttermost to give their wives and daughters every luxury would grind multitudes of women to powder in the world of work for the same purpose.[287]

Here was a portion of what Stanton meant by making one's judgments on the basis of principles rather than of individual men or policies. No exceptionalism for one's wife or loved ones was to be granted; nor were the period's high-flown phrases on the subject of ideal women. Self-government was a perpetual necessity in all phases of life.

> To say that man may protect woman and represent her interests is to say that man is all-wise and omnipresent, that every woman is blessed with a male saint continually at her side. It is to say that man is cognizant of all her opinions, on every subject of political economy and social ethics, of all her sentiments, affections, ambitions, that he understands all her needs and wants, her mental and moral idiosyncracies and tergiversations, and is ever ready to execute her will. It is to say that man is always just and generous, that he would uniformly consider woman's welfare and sufferings, before his own, or equally with his own, while all history, all systems of jurisprudence, and religion, show him incapable of such chivalry, deficient in such knowledge. Wise men assure us that woman is and must ever be an enigma to man and therein lies her chief attraction! How then can they legislate for a being, the law of whose existence they do not understand?[288]

Indeed, women's rebelliousness and underground resistance went to show that women prefer self-government. "It has taken the whole power of the civil and canon law to hold woman in the subordinate position which it is said she willingly accepts."[289] It was woman's duty to resist subordination, to defend herself against the robbery of her rights as much as against attacks by a robber or assassin. The ballot was "the six-loaded revolver, the sharp shooter" in the battle "to protect the civil and political life of the citizen against oppressors."[290]

"The Degradation of Disfranchisement" was among Stanton's best pieces of work. Its social analysis was comprehensive, detailed, plain. It was critical of other suffragists whose aims were less sweeping and less radical. The distillation of a life's work in untangling the causes and corollaries of women's situation, its rhetoric was of high quality. It opens with an assertion of the radical nature of the injustice done to women, beginning at birth, and closes with a parable of the instinctual nature of the desire for freedom.

"The degradation of disfranchisement begins with the birth into the class or caste to which the individual belongs. . . . The bias of sex is apparent at the very hour of birth," in the tone of triumph in which the sex of the boy is announced or the "minor key" if a girl. Those boy babies are at a premium because "they belong to the ruling class." Stanton notes, "Some tenderhearted gentlemen object to our calling ourselves a distinct class. Well, we object to the fact as they do to the name." The legal and moral differences in the state, church, and home point to the conclusion that the language of class is appropriate. To deny that women and men are different classes

> is as absurd as the idea of the lawyer when talking to his client through the iron door of a prison. After hearing his case, he said, "You can not be imprisoned, you have violated no law." "But," replied the client, "I am in prison." "You can not be." "But I am: if I am not, then open the door." So, I say, if we belong to the same class, then open the door and give us the same freedom you enjoy.[291]

Disfranchisement in a republic was precisely "establishing a privileged class, dividing the people into rulers and subjects." Disfranchisement was "the last lingering shadow of the old spirit of caste that has always divided humanity into classes of greater or lesser inferiority." These distinctions among mankind, including those between Jew and Gentile, black and white, were revolting, "depressing and aggravating to the classes ostracized."

> No one doubts that woman feels all this as well as man: the humiliations of poverty, the bitterness of neglect, the pangs of envy and jealousy of those who enjoy pleasures and luxuries she does not possess. And yet, with the everturning wheel of fortune, these distinctions are transient—yours today, mine tomorrow; the same sad experiences, sooner or later, may come to all.
>
> But the hateful spirit of caste makes insurmountable distinctions that no turning wheel of fortune can change.

The degradation of disfranchisement based on sex was "deeper" and "most unreasonable" of all, partly because it was insurmountable, partly because, in Stanton's view of the masculine and feminine elements of the universe, it antagonized "one vital principle in nature with another, when both are equally necessary to the very existence of the other." This was the reason there had never been a struggle of the human race more complicated than this one. "Our reform is not lifting up an inferior class, but recognizing the rights of equals." Further, it was the "only reform in which no appeal to the narrow self-interest of the dominant powers can be made, because it is the selfish interest of all alike to hold woman in subordination."

The selfish interests of "all alike" meant the interests of the rulers in the state, the rulers in the church, society at large, and the family. "Here, then, is a fourfold bondage, so many cords tightly twisted together, strong for one purpose." Stanton was sharply critical of other suffragists who refused to demand "equality everywhere and the reconstruction of all institutions."

> However stoutly the advocates of suffrage have maintained that political equality for woman would not affect religious faith, nor family life, whenever the question comes up in the halls of legislative or ecclesiastical assemblies, the argument invariably drifts to the divinely-ordained head of the state, the church, and the home. . . . Thus, in spite of all the efforts of the most politic adherents to keep the question of suffrage distinct, the opposition would uniformly consider the question of woman's political equality from every standpoint.

Here the conservatives were right, were even more "clear-sighted . . . as to the ultimate effect" than the radicals themselves. "Let us henceforth meet conservatives on their own ground, and admit that suffrage for woman does mean political, religious, industrial, and social freedom—a new and higher civilization." All those institutions need a complete change to meet woman's wants and needs. Constitutions and laws must be amended; church canons and scripture must be revised; there must be a new domestic altar. "And we do not propose to wait another century to secure all this; the time has come."

Nonetheless, these far-reaching consequences "increase the obstacles in the way of success." The opposition has "the prestige of centuries . . . the force to maintain it, and . . . possession of the throne, which is nine-tenths of the law." What had suffragists in their favor?

> The settled dissatisfaction of half the race, the unorganized protests of the few, and the open resistance of still fewer. But we have truth and justice on our side

and the natural love of freedom, and step by step, we shall undermine the present form of civilization and inaugurate the mightiest revolution the world has ever witnessed.

Brave words, but how was that to be accomplished? The strategy was clear. "By making these demands for liberty in all directions, we should quadruple the agitation, as well as the antagonism." Stanton gave short shrift to other sorts of strategies. She was far more interested in indicating the reasons that this mighty revolution was inevitable. Indeed, "there is a deep unsatisfied longing in the soul of woman for freedom . . . that sooner or later will burst all bounds and carry every barrier before her." Freedom was an instinct, a drive virtually embedded in the organic and biological basis of human life. She told an extraordinary parable to make her point.

In the distant northern plains, a hundred miles from the sea, in the midst of a Laplanders' village, a young reindeer raises his broad muzzle to the north wind, sniffing for the first time the ocean breeze. He stands still and stares at the limitless distance while a man may count a hundred. He grows restless from that moment, but he is yet alone. The next day a dozen of the herd look up from the cropping of the moss, sniffing the breeze, then the whole herd of young deer stand and gaze northward, breathing hard through their wide nostrils, jostling each other and stamping on the soft ground. They grow unruly, it is hard to harness them in the light sledge, the camp grows daily more unquiet. Then the Laps nod to one another, they watch the deer more closely, well knowing, sooner or later, what will happen.

At last, in the northern twilight, the herd begins to move. The impulse is simultaneous, irresistible. Their heads are all turned in one direction. They move slowly at first, biting still here and there at the bunches of rich moss. Presently the slow step becomes a trot, they crowd closely together, while the Laps hasten to gather up their cooking utensils, their wooden gods, all their last unpacked possessions. The great herd break together from a trot to a gallop, from a gallop to a breakneck race. The distant thunder of their united tread reaches the camp for a few minutes and they are gone to drink of the polar sea. Ever swifter and more terrible in their motion, the ruthless herd has raced onward, crowding the weaker to death, careless of the slain, careless of food, careless of any drink, but the sharp salt water ahead of them. And when at last the Laplanders reach the shore, their deer are once more quietly grazing, once more tame and docile, once more ready to draw the sledge whithersoever they are guided.

Once in his life the reindeer must taste of the sea, in one long, satisfying draught, and if he is hindered he perishes. Neither man nor beast dare stand between him and the ocean in the hundred miles of his arrow-like path.

What a picture of human life is this; how like the march and battle of the race in its struggles to satisfy the instincts for freedom; for something of this same longing comes to every human soul, to taste for once the sweet waters of liberty from its fathomless, inexhaustible sources.

The reindeer indeed! Though the comparison is somewhat grotesque, there is something awe-inspiring about this vision, the portrayal of the longing of women to be free as so deeply embedded as to be organic. There is something frightening about it as well: "ever swifter and more terrible in their motion . . . ruthless . . . crowding the weaker to death," the herd was careless of anything except the sweet waters that lie ahead.

Nor was the perspective novel in Stanton's work. From the view of the natural laws Stanton concluded that it was futile to oppose the changes that come in the natural sweep of human stages of development. She used other organic metaphors:

> The great argument for popular government, says George William Curtis, is not the essential righteousness of a majority but the celestial law that subordinates the brute force of numbers to intellectual and moral ascendancy as the immeasurable floods of ocean follow the moon.[292]

That statement is somewhat stunning too, for the ways it implies that the many will be ruled by the few (even by the one) who are intellectually and morally superior. But Stanton was no leveler. To remove the obstacles that stood in the way of the opportunities of those who were naturally superior, and not made so by false and artificial trammels, was in fact part of the argument from the earliest days. Comparison with the Founding Fathers is not amiss here. Like them, she always thought that democracy would be an uplifting force, never a degrading one.

Injustice and Justice

Stanton, together with her cohort Anthony, is generally recognized by historians of the woman suffrage movement as having maintained a clear-eyed focus on justice throughout her career. Indeed, it has been suggested that after these two pioneers passed from leadership of the movement, its characteristic focus shifted from justice to expediency. However that may be, in this section I inquire about the content and formulations of the justice that Stanton so indomitably pursued in her long career. If the diagnosis of injustice "fits" the notion of justice like a theological question fits its correlative answer, what is to be said with regard to Stanton's analysis? What were the epistemological and axiological grounds she cited to support her case that women needed justice? These grounds became for Stanton finally a religious and theological case regarding the woman suffrage movement.

As one of the most systematic theorists of the suffrage drive, Stanton had clear answers to these questions. They were clear answers, moreover, that shaped themselves into a specific pattern, a pattern that I can only call *Enlightenment*, fashioned, contoured, into a usable tool for a woman's struggle. That this pattern of analysis, this mode of thought, if you will, creates problems for her descendants, particularly with regard to her scientific rationalism and her elitism, should not be allowed to obscure her achievement.

On the basis of the preceding pages, several things can be said about the social analysis in Stanton's thought. The multidimensional view she forged of the issue was a very powerful tool for understanding the situation of women. The depth and power of Stanton's work fully merit the accolades historians and suffragists have given her. The intellectual achievement of her approach consisted in three principal strengths. (1) Hers was a comprehensive, holistic analysis. There were flaws, to be sure, in the picture Stanton had of the social order, such as the lack of an adequate economic view. But her aim was to encompass all the relevant human experience within her position, and she came as close to realizing that aim as probably any social analyst ever does. (2) This comprehensiveness was not bought at the price of sacrificing specificity. Each strand in the fourfold bondage marked a particular set of wrongs. The distinct strands were interwoven in such a way that each one perpetuated the others. (3) This view marked out priorities for action within the comprehensively specified perspective. Stanton was less than settled about which strand of the fourfold bondage was the "cause" of the oppression of women; I think that this was also a strength, a measure of her unrelenting intellectual drive to reason out the tangled skein of factors contributing to the situation of women.

The first implication for justice that arises from such a view of injustice to women was that no merely piecemeal or fragmentary program of justice would suit the problem. Justice of lesser scope than the fully interlocking nature of the fourfold bondage was not sufficient. What we have here is grounds for a coalition of feminists, each working on a particular aspect of the total suffragist package. As she said in defense of her biblical project, "all reforms are interdependent . . . whatever is done to establish one principle on a solid basis, strengthens all."[293]

Injustice/justice was not the only thematic "pair" that was held together in Stanton's perspective. It is striking that she encompassed several "dualities" that are usually thought to be, if not strictly incompatible, at least not comfortable companions in usual ethical and religious thought. Masculine and feminine elements of life hardly exhausted these. Burning indignation filled her soul; she was at the same time placid and serene. She was the suffragist apostle of rationality; but women's feelings, especially feelings of moral outrage, were central to her analysis. Theory and practice were major strands of her arguments; the republican theory was sound but not applied in practice. She continually emphasized the great philosophical principles that underlay her reform drive; but access to them seemed to come from either science *or* specific crisis experiences of life.

I do not mean to claim here that Stanton held the members of these pairs in perfect, equipoised, balance in her work. The universal was stressed over the particular; whatever was sound in theory was sound in practice, not the other way around; the enlightened intellect was to be substituted for the vagaries of spontaneous volatile enthusiasm; eternal laws were emphasized rather than the unique and fleeting historical instance. These particular stresses marked Stanton as standing outside the turn of mind of the Bostonians who mediated Romanticism, in large measure, to American life. She never lingered lovingly over uniqueness, tradition, diversity, feeling, art, or genius (except insofar as the latter was exemplified in the American general ideas of freedom and equality). Even individuality was read by Stanton as the respect in which all human beings were *alike*, not different from one another.

Stanton was utterly clear about how these pairs fit together in her ethical and religious view because she had a clear perception of the epistemological grounds for suffrage work. Women alone could articulate the oppression of women, for they alone experienced it concretely, they alone really knew it. What they knew, however, corresponded to the deepest nature of the universe and nature. The way Stanton put these themes together in her work gives us a clearer picture of her notion of injustice and justice.

Stanton was firm in maintaining, from Seneca Falls to the end of her career, that only women could articulate women's oppression with any insight and detail. Only those who had experienced this injustice could really *know* enough about it so as to formulate and appreciate "the nice shades and degrees" of women's wrongs. Concrete experience was essential for the complex and detailed understanding of the issue that produced the analysis. We may add two other points.

Women's experience functioned for Stanton as a principle of verification of the analysis once constructed. The women who responded to her divorce speech knew who had struck a blow for them in the right place. At times she indicated that such an experiential approach was a source of persistence in the pursuit of justice over time, an assurance that she would not change her mind. For example, with regard to marriage, she said that

> I never read a thing on this subject until I had arrived at my present opinion. My own life, observation, thought, feeling, reason, brought me to this conclusion. So fear not that I shall falter. I shall not grow conservative with age.[294]

The experiential base of the analysis was simultaneously the experiential base of the struggle. That is, only women could do the work that proved justice to women possible. That women were touted as dependent on men (and occasionally became so) was false, was a mockery. The widow, for example, or the wife of the drunkard or incompetent, who had met her trials without aid—more, with every hindrance of the laws, conventions, economy, and church in her path—was a practical demonstration of the justice woman suffragists demanded.

> It is into hands like these—to these who have calmly met the great emergencies of life—who, without the inspiration of glory, or fame, or applause, though long years have faithfully and bravely performed their work, self-sustained and cheered, that we commit our cause. We need not wait for one more generation to pass away, to find a race of women worthy to assert the humanity of women, and that is all we claim to do.[295]

Only women could assert women's wrongs; only women were competent to establish women's rights. Women thinking, studying science or literature, proved that women could think just as their brothers could; and by proving that they could, they proved their right to do so. All human capacities were given for the purpose of their development—given by the Creator of Nature.

It is especially remarkable to note how frequently this woman who extolled reasoning spoke in emotive terms about justice. The *feelings* of women struggling were among the evidence she advanced in principle to prove her case. "The deep, settled discontent of woman is proof sufficient that she has *not* all the rights she wants."[296] She spoke frequently of the burning indignation that filled the souls of women, and especially her own, reading the laws; of the love for freedom that burned in women's souls. These feelings of women were moral and ethical evidence of injustice. Indeed, they were a source of ethical contagion in society. "You cannot shut up discord, any more than you can smallpox. There can be no morality where there is a settled discontent."[297] Women's perceptions of their own situations could be trusted—especially when they were in line with principle and not mere expediency—as truthful indicators of their moral situation.

Given this experiential base for a large part of Stanton's analysis, it is evident how two further problems might easily arise. If women's perceptions were to be trusted about their oppression, it followed that the lack of support by masses of women could be presented as counterevidence to her claims. Stanton's answer was forged by the antislavery liberals.

> If, in view of laws like these, there be women in this State so lost to self-respect, to all that is virtuous, noble, and true, as to refuse to raise their voices in protest against such degrading tyranny, we can only say of that system which has thus robbed womanhood of all its glory and greatness, what the immortal Channing did of slavery, "If," said he, "it be true that the slaves are contented and happy—if there is a system that can blot out all love of freedom from the soul of man, destroy every trace of his Divinity, make him happy in a condition so low and benighted and hopeless, I ask for no stronger argument against such a slavery as ours." No! never believe it; woman falsifies herself and blasphemes her God, when in view of her present social, legal, and political position, she declares she has all the rights she wants.[298]

Thus the women who sat back in complacency (as she saw it), who refused to join or support the suffragists, were not a continual testimony against Stanton on her own grounds.[299] That such women falsified themselves *and* blasphemed God, in Stanton's view, was a direct result of her natural law position. Indeed, to falsify oneself and to blaspheme God were virtually the same act. The love of freedom, the pursuit of equality, were naturally implanted in the human soul.

What was it, however, that prevented such women from coming to see and feel the urgency and truth of suffrage? The language Stanton used here was typical Enlightenment language. It was prejudice, custom, tradition, mere popular sentiment, the interests of the powerful, priestcraft, that kept people from recognizing the truths of nature and of Nature's God. However, these forces functioned in slightly different ways for the two sexes.

Women needed particularly to step outside the boundaries of public sentiment; they needed only to "taste the joys of free thought and action" in order to escape the fetters of conventionality. Courage was among the prerequisites of such an experiment, a courage that was of course not encouraged by the young girl's education. Stanton underwent a virtual conversion experience in which her "woman's right to think" came to the fore. Thinking to Stanton ever meant science in her synthesis of thinking, religion, and politics.

For men there were slightly different parameters. The fundamental problem with men was that they did not recognize that the same laws of mind operated in women as in them. "They do not feel as I would" was the rejoinder that Stanton put in the mouths of the Southern slaveholder and the Northern male legislator when confronted by the suffering of blacks and women. Here she was tireless in reiterating that men had to learn that women were not anomalous beings; that the same reasons and processes of reasoning *applied* to women as to men. She believed the republican theory was the only true, and scientific, theory; its flaw was that it had not been practiced with regard to women. Here Stanton's theory of the human person entered the case—and perhaps broke down. Individuality was the fundamental cosmological unity; and individuality meant solitary, interchangeable atoms, related to one another in only incidental ways. To Stanton human beings were not fundamentally social. Society was an "additive" phenomenon, composed of collections of individuals; though she was also convinced that Comte and Spencer had proved that the interests of individuals and of society were not disjunctive, she never had a "relational" view of human nature. There was no real room in her analysis for differences in the conclusions of reasoning, nor legitimate differences between people of different social locations.

Nonetheless, Stanton's elitism and scientism were significantly qualified, in creative ways, by her notion of the epistemology of injustice and justice. While science and reason were pre-eminent paths of the discovery of natural laws, access to truth was also available through crisis and suffering. We might say that for Stanton "the great emergencies of life," whether individual or communal, thrust people back into a state of nature. Suffering provided a vantage point for recognizing eternal truths such as equality, individuality, liberty. She described the American discovery of democratic principles in just this way:

> When by some moral revolution men are cut loose from all their old moorings, and get beyond the public sentiment that once bound them, with no immediate selfish interest to subserve—as, for instance, our fathers in leaving England, or

the French Communes in the late war—*in hardship and suffering they dig down to the hard-pan of universal principles*, and in their highest inspirational moments proclaim justice, liberty, equality for all.[300]

Hardship and suffering, in other words, provided a certain access to the knowledge of justice that was not gained in the ordinary course of life. Hardship and suffering were an ethical "crucible,"[301] we might say.

She specified and amplified this point in terms of women's varied situations at the 1888 International Council of Women. She described the language of women's suffering as a language of universal significance, a moral language, communicated subtly, perhaps "around the edges" of male discourse.

> In welcoming representatives from other lands here to-day, we do not feel you are strangers and foreigners, for the women of all nationalities, in the artificial distinctions of sex, have a universal sense of injustice, that forms a common bond of union between them.
>
> Whether our feet are compressed in iron shoes, our faces hidden with veils and masks, whether yoked with cows to draw the plow through its furrows, or classed with idiots, lunatics, and criminals in the laws and constitutions of the state, the principle is the same, for the humiliations of spirit are as real as the visible badges of servitude. A difference in government, religion, laws, and social customs makes but little change in the relative status of woman to the self-constituted governing classes, so long as subordination in all nations is the law of her being. Through suffering we have learned the open sesame to the hearts of each other. There is a language of universal significance, more subtle than that used in the busy markets of trade, that should be called the mother-tongue, by which with a sigh or a tear, a gesture, a glance of the eye, we know the experiences of each other in the varied forms of slavery.[302]

In these remarks women's suffering functioned in two different directions simultaneously. It was the grounds of a common bond of union among women. Note too that it was between hearts, not minds, that union was formed.[303] Most important, it provided the sense of injustice, the place from which women could formulate principles of opposition to the varied forms of slavery they experienced in their own countries around the world. The sense of injustice women felt was universal. This sense is not easily describable as a "cognitive" sense. Even though the mother tongue was a language of universal significance, it spoke not in propositions or moral rules, but with sighs, tears, gestures, and glances.

What was universal in woman's experience, communicated so readily but so subtly to one another, was the "law of her being," the law of artificial subordination whose other face was the law of natural equality. They were the sighs of a free spirit attesting to its love for freedom; the glances of an equal at an equal; they provided a glimpse of the natural soul "underneath," perhaps, the artificial injustices that prevailed. Suffering produced moral insight; suffering, which provided the access to one another's hearts, also provided insight into the universal principles of justice.

There is no particular mystery or inconsistency in Stanton's frequent use of the language of the emotions for the ethics of her case. The moral and the material laws of the universe were not different in kind. Right reasoning and right feeling went hand in hand. The mind and the heart did not tug in opposite directions, if one lived in accordance with the laws of nature.

When an individual, or a society, was not proceeding in obedience to these great immutable laws, disorganization was the inevitable outcome. It is as true to reverse this statement: "Disorganization," wherever it occurred, was the clue by which one discerned that the natural laws were being violated. Disorganization meant a variety of things to Stanton—ill health, unhappiness, "unbalanced" personal development, sickly children, the separation of the sexes, poverty, crime, agony, sorrow, and suffering. These were all signals of *injustice*. "We cannot play fast and loose with the eternal principle of justice without being caught sooner or later in the net of our own weaving."[304] To respond to the world from motives of policy, from the dictates of public sentiment rather than from reason, to follow blindly traditional authority, were all ways the disorganization and perversion of present society were caused and perpetuated. This, in fact, was one of the ways Stanton responded to the charge that woman suffragists were provoking disorder. She turned such charges on their heads; what Victorians took as order was in reality chaos. One needed only to look around one to see that, if one looked with the proper perspective. That proper perspective was always the perspective of high moral principle.

What did that include for Stanton? First let me note that Stanton used justice in two separate ways in her work. On the one hand, "justice" was a summary of all the moral principles applicable to the case women argued. Injustice summarized the facts of women's oppression in the fourfold bondage; playing "fast and loose with the eternal principle of justice" provoked disorganization of many kinds. Here justice was a fundamental ordering principle that demanded fairness between the sexes, a single standard. This use of justice made it a synonym for "nature." In this use of justice, we might locate all Stanton's claims that women were to be treated in practice exactly as men were; that women were not anomalous beings, as she put it; that the Golden Rule was the single standard; that the same process of reasoning functioned to establish women's rights as did men's; that the same laws of mind and moral feelings were to be accounted for in both cases; that all women suffragists asked for were the same things men had had in the progress of their development.

In this first use of justice, as the summary virtue, so to speak, of her case, there is no doubt that justice was preeminently a rational virtue. "The intellectual and moral sense for justice and equality" was what suffragists appealed to in the only appropriate way, by "fair debate" rather than with womanly wiles.[305] Those who have the gift of reason and understand the principles of justice" were to be compelled promptly to live up to "the highest light that is in them."[306] This combination of rationality and ethics was the "higher law written by the finger of God on one's own soul."

There were other occasions on which justice was only one of the principles[307] Stanton asserted to cover the case of women. She wrote, for example, of "justice, liberty, equality," of "justice and mercy," of "justice and equality," of "justice and freedom," of "justice, religion, and logic." God was frequently spoken of as a God of "justice, mercy, and truth." This use of justice as "justice and—" does not so much imply that the dictates of justice and those of, say, equality, would not be the same, for there was ample reason to see that equality was one of the principles of justice. That she also spoke of "justice and mercy" or of "justice and religion," however, gives us some pause, for mercy is frequently thought to be a quality not *of* justice, but transcending justice.

The reason for this alternate use of justice is found in Stanton's view of progress, I believe. When she asserted that women asked for the same rights that men had obtained in all their progress and development, she was clearly asserting an upward movement to the path of human history in the evolution of civilization. She demanded the "elevation" of women in marked contrast to the "downward" direction of her favored metaphor of injustice, "degradation."[308] Here certain other moral counters overrode and supplemented justice as equality, yet were in close relationship to the principle of justice. The next century, she was sure, was to be "as much purer than the past as our immediate past has been better than the dark ages."[309]

In the statement of her civil religion, purity was the hallmark of religion, justice the hallmark of government. Yet these two ultimately came together. Purity was just, and justice was pure. We might say for Stanton that "all that rises must converge." The ladder of citizenship, which combined education and the ballot, was an upward path leading to the place where human beings were to be as gods.[310] Religion and politics were distinct areas of her thought—and yet they overlapped and virtually coincided in their "highest" moments.

It was not only religion and politics that had this distinct yet overlapping character in Stanton's full thought. She sought equally for higher and holier marriages, for true virtue and dignity in social customs, and for a more rational religion. (It is significant that she rarely spoke of a purified church.) The areas traced in the fourfold bondage were contingent dimensions of human life in history. They were, to be sure, the locus in which the justice Stanton demanded was enacted or not enacted. They were not themselves religious, but the context in which the sacred could be glimpsed, revered, and taken as a guide for practice, The substance, for example, of a higher and holier marriage was not marriage itself, but some religious realities. There were four of them: right reason (or free thinking); the sacred individual and his/her rights; the cosmic laws; and a certain deity. These four, like the strands in the fourfold bondage, were interrelated and interwoven. All four of these religious themes intersected with *each* strand of the fourfold bondage. We could, in effect construct a sixteen-square grid in which this intersection would be clearer. We need, therefore, next to look more closely at the other "half" of Stanton's religious social thought.

THREE

Elizabeth Cady Stanton, Continued: A More Rational Religion

The first step in the elevation of woman to her true position, as an equal factor in human progress, is the cultivation of the religious sentiment in regard to her dignity and equality.

The Woman's Bible

I like Matthew Arnold's definition of religion. He says, "Religion is science couched with emotion." I want women to feel that it is their religious duty to take part in government, the most exalted of all sciences.

Stanton, "Closing Address"

If governments are to make us just, and religions are to make us pure, we must now ask: In what does this religion consist? How does it relate to this justice for women? Stanton's constructive religious position cannot be reduced to or exhausted by her social analysis. Yet it bears a forceful and direct relationship to questions of justice that are at the heart of this investigation.

To today's observer, Stanton's position deserves to bear the name of something like a "feminist theology" or a "feminist ethics." Stanton herself might have been uneasy with these terms. This was not only because truth was truth as she saw it; no prefatory labels, such as "feminist," obscured or added thereto. It was particularly because Stanton was critical of the discipline of theology itself. She asserted that "religion" was a natural human phenomenon, with all the weight that the word "nature" bore for her. "Theology," on the other hand, tended to be an artificial distortion of this natural human bent. There is no possibility of baptizing Stanton a Christian theologian, despite her

105

frequent averral that Jesus, and on some occasions the Protestant Reformation, saw the same truths she espoused.

She was self-consciously a liberal, arguing at times that one had to be a liberal in religion in order to be a feminist. This liberalism gave her as much conceptual trouble as it gave clarity and system to her position. But she was a particular sort of liberal. Her characteristic reasons and warrants, the appeals she made in arguing women's struggle, are readily identifiable. She applauded facts based on scientific inquiry as opposed to custom, superstition, dead ideas of past generations. She assigned a fundamental place to critical thought as opposed to accepting the opinion of authorities or the deceits of priestcraft. She was a believer in inexorable progress and development to a higher level of civilization, provided that people might be brought to follow rather than contravene the natural laws governing the universe. These natural laws were opposed to the customs and artificial trammels of civilization in its perverse stages, but in themselves they were harmonious, orderly, beautiful, and stable. Similarly, the fundamental unit of Stanton's thought was the isolated individual, an imaginary Robinson Crusoe. These are themes of the Enlightenment. Themes of Enlightenment were and are prominent in American feminism;[1] Enlightenment thinkers, such as Condorcet and Wollstonecraft, were among the first to articulate a feminist cause.

It is hardly too strong to say that Enlightenment was Stanton's religion, complete with an account of her conversion experience. This was an Enlightenment that was thoroughly worked and reworked through Stanton's experience of the social struggle to which she devoted her lifetime—and willy-nilly, therefore, through the period in which she lived. This synthesis of Enlightenment with Victoria's culture did *not* result, as it did for so many of her contemporaries, in baptizing American reality in the Christian font, or in proclaiming hers an aura of "sweetness and light" à la the Matthew Arnold she quoted. Rather, as Stanton became more enlightened, she grew more critical of the times in which she found herself and especially of the ecclesiastical institutions that held sway. This was not because Stanton was a female "Miniver Cheevy, born too late." It was because she was a female self-consciously struggling for justice toward herself and those like her. It is not too strong either to say, in the language of our day and not hers, that it was her perceptions of sexism and the struggles to overcome sexism that pushed Stanton into theological creativity.[2]

This chapter examines in detail the structural underpinnings of Stanton's constructive religious thought. "A Woman's Right to Think" identifies the central place that thinking itself, and the issue of authority that accompanied her "conversion" to thinking, played in Stanton's view. "An Imaginary Robinson Crusoe" concentrates on Stanton's individualism, with particular attention to "The Solitude of Self." "The Great, Immutable Laws" indicates Stanton's natural law bias, in which the laws of the cosmos and of ethics were synthesized as the fundamental basis of her feminism. "The God of Justice, Mercy, and Truth" explores the notion of deity that accompanied Stanton's religion, the God who demanded not a stern faith, but a noble life in the woman suffrage struggle. Finally, I conclude with some critical remarks as to the strengths and problems encountered in Stanton's position.

A More Rational Religion

I opened the discussion of the fourfold bondage with an exploration of the "perversion of the religious element in woman." I noted in passing that a notion of a distorted religiousness logically presupposed a perspective on an undistorted or, in Stanton's own language, a healthy or "true" religion. Her point was initially stated negatively. True religion did not hold man and woman "supinely down to endure the dwarfing, crippling, withering of all those powers that in their growth and development would make them more like gods than men."[3] Rather it set them free for progress—not merely technological progress, but moral progress toward the divine, or the Divine Ideal, as she sometimes put it. She summarized her view: "Religion is a perception of the moral laws that govern the universe, a conscientious observance of them, and a worshipping love of their divine author."[4]

Religion raised what it touched to dignity and purity, as when women were to be lifted to the dignity of the ballot box, or government to the dignity of a fixed science. What was pure was sacred; what was sacred was enduring and eternal; what was pure produced honor, respect, joy, and satisfaction; what was pure and sacred was virtuous. All these were "higher" things in life, higher than mere gross materialism. The pure and sacred and virtuous things had a lawlike character; their operation ideally was peaceful, harmonious, beautiful, majestic, worthy of awe. Most sacred of all were individuality and the rights of the individual, which were written in the cosmos and in the human soul; among them were justice, right, equality, freedom, growth and self-development, self-respect, joy in the natural expansion of life. The growth of the individual was a movement toward the development of one's faculties toward their greater purity and freedom. It is difficult to begin such an exposition without repetitively completing the circle; each aspect of Stanton's analysis led immediately into the next.

The analogy between the "moral and the material" was, as Stanton saw it, "striking." Yet she decried the materialism that saw in the polling booth a slip of paper and "nothing more." Sometimes this "blank materialism" was read in language that implied mind/body, spirit/matter dichotomies that contemporary feminist theologians believe to be fundamental to women's oppression. The Esthers of this world, in contrast to the suffragist Vashtis, "drag man down to death, by gross appeal to his sensual appetites."[5] Materialism could become a catchphrase for all that Stanton abhorred—authority, violence, ruin, brute force. But it represented not so much the body per se (which Stanton enjoyed) as the lack of moral principle. (Stanton *never* meant merely "sexual" when she said "moral.") Materialism, in other words, represented an ethical blindness that did not see the connection between specific acts and the principles embodied in them, or perhaps "behind" them, "underlying" them.

Nonetheless, there was the spirit-over-matter mindset deplored by contemporary feminist theologians in Stanton's religious thought. It resulted not from the deprecation of the body or this life in this world (for she opposed speculations about another world or another life). It resulted from the directionality of her language. Rational thought and the high moral principles embodied in its proper operation moved "upward." Reason and justice were the "highest light" that was in human beings. To be an "immortal, high-born soul" was to be rational. Her view was that of a hierarchy of human capacities in which reason and justice were at the apex of the pyramid. Emotion, intuition, the affections needed to be firmly guided by the enlightened intellect, lest they become the "wild enthusiasm" she decried. The "appetites" were to be ruled by the higher faculties.[6] Lowest of all was "brute force," the animating cause of so much violence and ruin. Brute force, superstition, obscenity, fear, intellectual confusion and perplexities, barbarism were all associated with the darkness. "Happiness," for Stanton as for many classical thinkers before her, summarized the highest good; unhappiness went along with darkness and death. Stanton abhorred gloominess in religion. Sin was among the hallmarks of gloomy, confusing, and ignoble creeds—the mere creeds, not to be confused with the substance of religion. The diviner elements in human nature went along with peace and serenity, dignity, purity.

In human beings as they should be, however, it was unthinkable that feeling and reason should not mesh. Her period's notions of women were contrary to "our enlightened ideas of justice and the holiest feelings of our nature." It was only in the unregulated or poorly organized individual that feelings and rationality were separate or disjunct. Pure and holy feelings were conjoined with rational justice. From the Divine Ideal came the teleological purposes of moral development, a virtual synonym for progress. (Any "development" that was not progress was *not* a development, but a backward movement, a dwarfing, crippling, restraining, distortion of human possibility.) In this phase of her thought it was obvious to Stanton that the humiliations of spirit were "as real as the visible badges of servitude"; they were based on the same principle of artificial obstacles to natural development.

A. A Woman's Right to Think

Like many others of her day, Stanton frequently contrasted rationality and thinking with religion. The fetishes of savage people, superstition, fear, blind faith were opposed to reason and science. In women's education, for example, she called for the substitution of "reason for blind faith, science for theological superstition."[7] The "mists of speculation"[8] or airy theorizing about the unknown (which she associated with theology) were equally to be replaced with the "dignity of a fixed science." This contrast between thinking and religion was especially sharply drawn when the subject was women, whose sufferings "were not mitigated until rationalism took the place of religion, and reason triumphed over superstition."[9] In discussions concerning the role played by Christianity with regard to women, Stanton claimed that rationalism and science were responsible for any good done to women, even in antiquity. "The vantage ground woman holds today is due to all the forces of civilization, to science, discovery, invention, rationalism, the religion of humanity chanted in the golden rule round the globe centuries before the Christian religion was known."[10] In such moments, the Christian religion was not even counted as one of the "forces of civilization." In this strand of her arguments, Stanton might easily be identified with secularizing tendencies in the modern period, seeking to unseat religion from its throne in order to set up science.

But this was not the whole story. There was another, and more interesting, element in Stanton's discussion of rational thought. There were moments when Stanton did not contrast, but virtually identified reason and religion with each other. Her memorial accounts of several pioneer feminists were virtually mythic in the repetition of "*Sapere Aude*." The most important of these, for my purposes, were contained in her reminiscences of Lucretia Mott, recounting their initial acquaintance at the 1840 meeting of the World Anti-Slavery Convention in England. Stanton and Mott spent long hours together discussing the convention's action and many another topic in "theology and social life." The denouement of this encounter was described dramatically by Stanton:

> I found in this new friend a woman emancipated from all faith in man-made creeds, from all fear of his denunciations. Nothing was too sacred for her to question, as to its rightfulness in principle and in practice. "Truth for authority, not authority for truth" was not only the motto of her life, but it was the fixed mental habit in which she most rigidly held herself. It seemed to me like meeting a being from some larger planet, to find a woman who dared to question the opinions of Popes, Kings, Synods, Parliaments, with the same freedom that she would criticize an editorial in the *London Times*, who recognized no higher authority than the judgment of a pure-minded, educated woman. When I first heard from the lips of Lucretia Mott that I had the same right to think for myself that Luther, Calvin, and John Knox had, and the same right to be guided by my own convictions, and would no doubt have a higher, happier life than if guided by theirs, I felt at once a newborn sense of dignity and freedom; it was like suddenly coming into the rays of the noonday sun, after wandering with a rushlight in the caves of the earth.[11]

This incident was described by Stanton as though it had the character of a conversion experience. Virtually every phrase requires exegesis to render adequately all that Stanton has compressed into these lines.

"When I first heard from the lips of Lucretia Mott": That being from a larger planet, that pure-minded educated woman, was described here as initiating Stanton into a truth that was religious. "Mrs. Mott was to me an entirely new revelation of womanhood," she said elsewhere in these reminiscences. The phrase "pure-minded, educated woman" implies the equal development of ethics with intelligence.

"That I had the same right to think for myself that Luther, Calvin, and John Knox had": This young female nobody was identified, in her conversion experience, with the male religious geniuses of the Reformation, who were themselves identified with the right to think. This was the positive side of the notion that popes, kings, synods, and parliaments were on a par with any newspaper editorial. The right to question, the right to assertion, were similar religious dimensions of the right to think. It was a small step from this to the Woman's Bible project.

"And the same right to be guided by my own convictions, and would no doubt live a higher, happier life than if guided by theirs": To think for oneself, to be guided by one's own moral convictions, once again paralleled intellect and ethics. Similarly, a higher and a happier life went hand in hand; the upward moral progress of evolution was compatible with personal satisfaction, if one was guided not by external (male) authority, but by one's own (female) authority.

"I felt at once a newborn sense of dignity and freedom": The conversion theme of new birth was associated with Stanton's female dignity, in contrast to the spiritual humiliation of women. Dignity and freedom arose from the right to think and live from one's own authority, as opposed to the restrictions and cramping of living according to public sentiment and custom.

"It was like suddenly coming into the rays of the noonday sun, after wandering with a rushlight in the caves of the earth": The darkness associated with the intellectual labyrinths of Finney's revival doctrines was dispelled. Darkness was exchanged for the "clear sunlight of Truth," that favorite of all images of the Siècle des Lumières. "*Sapere Aude*" had been translated into the experience of a female, converted to this truth by another female, and identified with the Reformation.

The experience of hearing Mott "talk what, as a Scotch Presbyterian, I had scarcely dared to think"[12] reoriented Stanton's religion. She was explicit about this, even though her biography claims that the demystification of Finney's revivalism had already led her into the clear sunlight of Truth. In parting from Mott, Stanton "thanked her for the many religious doubts and fears she had banished from my mind."[13] To this Mott responded, according to Stanton, by drawing a distinction between religion and theology.

> She said, "There is a broad distinction between religion and theology. The one is a natural, human experience common to all well-organized minds. The other is a system of speculations about the unseen and the unknowable, which the human mind has no power or grasp to explain, and these speculations vary with every sect, age, and type of civilization. No one knows any more of what lies beyond our sphere of action than thou and I, and we know nothing."[14]

Stanton "accepted her words of wisdom with the same confiding satisfaction that did the faithful Crito those of his beloved Socrates." Hearing Mott preach in a Unitarian church during this visit to England seemed to her the fulfillment of "an oft-repeated happy dream."

Stanton read the structure of her own conversion to Enlightenment into the lives of her co-workers. She quoted Paulina Wright Davis as saying, "I was not a happy child, nor a happy woman, until in mature life, I outgrew my early religious faith, and felt free to think and act from my own convictions."[15] Of Matilda Joslyn Gage, she reported

> that for which she feels most indebted to him [her father], as she often says—the grandest training given her—was to think for herself. She was taught to accept no opinion because of its authority, but to question the truth of all things. Thus was laid the foundation of Mrs. Gage's reform tendencies and of her non-acceptance of masculine authority in matters of religion and politics.[16]

Margaret Fuller's conversations with women "were in reality a vindication of woman's right to think."[17]

On the basis of this central principle, woman's right to think, she demanded that women declare themselves boldly on the vital issues of the day. In 1890, she exhorted the NAWSA members to comment on all sorts of other public issues besides the woman question. Her language is very much akin to that of her "conversion."

> In this way we make ourselves mediums through which the great souls of the past may speak again. The moment we begin to fear the opinions of others and hesitate to tell the truth that is in us, and from motives of policy are silent when we should speak, the divine floods of light and life flow no longer into our souls. Every truth we see is ours to give the world, not to keep for ourselves alone, for in so doing we cheat humanity out of their rights and check our own development.[18]

"Divine floods of light and life" reiterated the thematic emphasis on the light of truth, associated it with deity, and blended it with the courage needed for freethinking. This was an ethical statement. Silence was associated with mere motives of policy, rather than the high principles on which she took her stand. These few sentences represented almost an Enlightened rendering of the spiritualist "medium."[19]

The central theme on which Stanton's strictures against the churches and her own reconstructed rational religion met was that of *authority*. To substitute each woman's own authority for the external male authorities that reigned in the four realms was her basic aim. Hindu women, Turkish women, Mormon women, American Christian women—all had in common their subjugation backed by religious authority. "Man, of himself, could not do this; but when he declares, 'Thus saith the Lord,' of course he can do it."[20]

The discontent of women at their social situation was exacerbated by the pretention to religious authority: "No man can fathom the depths of rebellion in woman's soul when insult is heaped upon her sex, and this is intensified when done under the hypocritical assumption of divine authority."[21] In the American Christian case, the Woman's Bible project was "to destroy in the minds of women, at least, all authority to superhuman origin" of the biblical text.[22] The negative moment of the program was this centrally Enlightenment project, the demystification of authority. Women were to understand that what they had taken for the divine word was only a human word, and a male word at that:

> Banish the idea of divine authority for these machinations of the human mind, and the power of the throne and the church, of a royal family and an apostolic order of succession, of kings and queens, of popes and bishops, and man's headship in the State, the Church, and the Home will be heard of no more.[23]

Stanton's positive aim in all her feminist work was that each individual woman should find the source of authority in herself alone—not in her husband or other beloved male figures in the family sphere, not in public opinion or the received sentiments of society, not in lawmakers' distorted codes, not in any ecclesiastical body or text. Each *individual* woman was to cast off the shackles of external authority in order to be guided solely by her own sense of truth.

This question of women's own authority was one reason for the profoundly democratic cast of Stanton's work. The most obscure woman, as much as any Reformation giant or king, was to test every thought and practice as to its truth. There was no higher authority than her own judgment in such matters.[24] At times, even late in her life, Stanton conceded that the right of individual judgment was a Christian idea as much as an American idea.[25] But any specific religion was bound to be judged by its affirmation or negation of the right to think. "A religion is pure only as it dignifies man, lifts him above fear and superstition, and leaves him free to think," as she put it in her anti-Catholic polemic. Notions of authority external to the self, in some text or ecclesiastical body, were "materialistic"; and on some occasions these themes of materialism and authority were related to *men*, and not women.[26] It was mere materialism that degraded politics, that saw nothing more in the ballot than a piece of paper put into a box.

Woman's right to think also led, in Stanton's view, to particular conclusions in religious matters. Male authority over women depended on the manipulation of women's feelings; it was inseparable from the false forms of religion by which women were deceived. Priestcraft, recall, duped women into "worship of the saints, pictures, holy days, and inspired men and books" by developing only women's sentiments. The enlightened intellect guided one to the worship of "the living God and the everlasting principles of Justice, Mercy, and Truth."[27] As she put it in one of her early comments on the Bible, "to any thinking person," there was no difficulty in realizing that Paul's comments did not apply to the women of the nineteenth century. Particularly as Stanton entered her free thought period, she became more vehement that it was the religious emotions by which women were subjugated. The church had done "more to degrade woman than all other adverse influences put together. And it has done this by playing on the religious emotions (the strongest feelings of her nature) to her own complete subjugation."[28] The church was at fault for "training her sentiments and emotions at the expense of her reason and common sense." Hence in the more rational religion for which Stanton aimed: "We must turn the tide of her enthusiasm from the church to the state, arouse her patriotism; awaken her interest in great public questions, on which depend the stability of the republic and the elevation of the race, instead of wasting so much time and thought on the salvation of her soul."[29]

There were few occasions indeed on which Stanton sang the praises of any other faculty than reason. One of these rare times was spurred by an Illinois clergyman's denunciations of the women's movement for its "lack of logic" and of "women's intuitions in general." Stanton tried to calm the women of his town "by exalting intuition, and with a pitiful and patronizing tone deploring the slowness, the obtuseness, the materialism of most of the sons of Adam."[30] Thinking for Stanton was never merely a matter of form, as though it were reducible to following a syllogism to its conclusion. Though she spoke of woman suffragists rehearsing the logic of democracy "for the sheer love of it," this Illinois clergyman was "rather morbid on the question of logic."[31] Even here, however, her praise of intuition was set in the context of a critique based on reason.[32]

One of Stanton's lifelong efforts was to convince men that the minds of women operated according to the same "laws" as did their own male brains. That men never did understand this was the result of interests, prejudice, and unthinking custom. This notion of the laws of the mind was another strategy to connect thinking itself with democracy. Each one had the same right to think, the most lowly, the female, along with Luther and Calvin; equally each one thought, ideally, in the same fashion. It was not altogether clear what Stanton saw as the content of the laws of the mind. It was rather more clear that she used this sort of phrase interchangeably with philosophy and science. Joan of Arc's success, recall, was "philosophical, in accordance with the laws of the mind."[33] Similarly, this rationality was neither merely a technical process nor, at the other end of the spectrum, a speculative one. It was highly charged with morality. Her Seneca Falls address was clearest in its enunciation of the connection between the laws of the mind and ethics:

> Moral beings can only judge of others by themselves. The moment they assume a different nature for any of their own kind, they utterly fail. The drunkard was hopelessly lost until it was discovered that he was governed by the same laws of mind as the sober man. . . .
> Let a man once settle the question that a woman does not think and feel like himself, and he may as well undertake to judge of the amount of intellect and sensation of any of the animal creation as of woman's nature. He can know but little with certainty, and that but by observation.[34]

There were only two possibilities Stanton could envisage: to reason correctly, which meant, in accordance with philosophy, science, the laws of the mind, or to reason incorrectly.

> Highly organized minds, governed by principle, invariably give true interpretations; while others, whose law is expediency, coarse and material in all their conceptions, will interpret laws, Bible, constitution, everything, in harmony with the public sentiment of their class and condition.[35]

Since the laws of the human mind were the same in each person, the judgments of all women would be similar to those of "pure-minded, educated" women such as Lucretia Mott. Each individual woman, thinking for herself, would arrive at the same conclusions Stanton reached.[36]

A philosophical approach for Stanton meant articulating the broad principles that were presupposed by particular cases, or particular reforms. These broad principles were generally understood to be universals. Hence Stanton's reiterated emphasis was on womanhood rather than wifehood or motherhood, for womanhood was the "more universal fact" about women. This philosophical bias was also in principle opposed to self-interest; to argue

115

"in harmony with the public sentiment of [one's] class and condition" was to follow the law of expediency and materialism.

These points about the process and substance of thinking held even when Stanton asserted "sex in soul" as well as in body. It was extremely difficult to discern what was meant by the feminine element in the balance of the feminine and masculine elements. It certainly never meant exalting the heart over the mind, as it did to many other Victorians and to her successor, Shaw. A society ruled by the male element was one "untempered by woman's thought"; the new evangel of womanhood was "to lift man up into the higher realms of thought and action."[37] Equal education, coeducation, were the immediate consequences she drew from this motif of the balancing forces.

> In the fuller development of the feminine element in humanity we shall have the impress of woman's thought and sentiment in government and religion, exalting justice and equality in the one, love and tenderness in the other, anger and vindictive punishment having no place in either.[38]

Though to reason correctly was to reason in accordance with science for Stanton, this bias should not obscure the conjunction of "thought and sentiment." Science *and* the crises of life were both occasions on which one could learn the basic truths of equality and justice. Stanton's use of "science" was not the "value-free" use that ears accustomed to twentieth-century positivism have come to associate with science. She saw the nineteenth century preparing the "marriage feast of science and religion."[39] With this view, it is clear how she might say, "I like Matthew Arnold's definition of religion: 'Religion is science touched with emotion.' "[40] This meant not science in a laboratory, for she immediately added that politics was the most exalted of all sciences. It followed, logically, that women were to understand that it was their religious duty to vote, indeed, their most exalted religious duty.

Her interpretation of science, thinking, and philosophy led Stanton astray more than once. Reading about the matriarchate, for example, she was convinced that the *facts* presented by Bachofen, Morgan, and others "cannot be questioned. They seem so natural in the chain of reasoning and the progress of human development."[41] The rationalism in such a statement is obvious; if the theory was right, the "facts" must be there, just as her political principle read, "Whatever is sound in theory is safe in practice." On other occasions, she spoke of thinking as a kind of "brain force." Reading Galton on heredity, she asserted that equality between the sexes was sure to stimulate "a flow and interflow of brain forces that will kindle all their powers, vitalize their best thoughts, and give strength and dignity to their combined action in every department of life."[42] This emphasis on science also accounted for the astonishing arrogance of several of Stanton's statements. Looking to the time when scientists like Comte, Mill, and Spencer asserted that (woman's) moral power would govern (man's) brute force, she found it "wearisome to parley with carping minds today, answer their absurd objections, listen to their stale platitudes and puny insults to womanhood."[43]

Science in its positivist dress did not exhaust her position on such points. An anecdote recounted from one of Stanton's European visits illustrates her in practice, enticing a nonsuffragist woman to think. It sheds some light on the breadth and depth to which such thinking was meant to attain in Stanton's use. She invited a woman not to discard or ignore her feelings as though to become *more* rational by doing so, but to *remember* her feelings in life, and particularly her moral responses:

> After dinner, while the gentleman still lingered at the table, the ladies being alone, an unusual amount of heresy as to the rights of "the divinely appointed head of the house" found expression. A young English-woman, who had been brought up in great retirement, turned to me and said, "I never heard such declarations before; do you ladies all really believe that God intended men and women to be equal, and do you really feel that girls have a right to enjoy as many privileges as boys?" In chorus we all promptly said, "We do," and I added, "If you will recall all the events of your life thus far, and your own feelings at times, you will find that again and again your own heart has protested against the injustice to which you have been subjected. Now," said I, "think a little, and see if you can recall no sense of dissatisfaction at the broad difference made between your sisters and brothers." "Well," said she, "I did often wonder why my father gave the boys half a crown a week for spending money, and us girls a few pence; why so much thought and money were expended on their education, and so little on ours; but as I saw that that was the custom everywhere, I came to the conclusion that they were a superior order of beings, and so thought no more about it, and I never heard that theory contradicted until this evening."[44]

There is no better example of the ways Stanton's method of operation left the aridities of enlightened rationalism and science when she got down to cases. "Think a little," said she—"the ladies being alone." To recall feelings of dissatisfaction, the heart's protest at injustice, was to begin the process of thought. We might say today that Stanton invited this woman to reinterpret her own experience on the basis of this new hermeneutical principle, repressed

117

memories of protest against injustice. We might also say, in light of Stanton's own account of her experience with Lucretia Mott, that she was inviting this woman to discover a different religion—a more rational religion, as Stanton would have it, one that affirmed that "God intended men and women to be equal."

B. An Imaginary Robinson Crusoe

The primacy of the individual was a constant theme in Stanton's exposition of the fourfold bondage in state, church, society, and family, those secondary relations of human existence. In discussing marriage, she brought all such arguments before the bar of individual happiness and development. She admitted no barrier to a woman's sacred right to her own person. It was the natural rights of the individual to which she referred all political discussion. In the churches, as I have shown, ecclesiastical bodies transgressed on women's individual souls and consciences.

"Solitude of Self" was in some ways Stanton's most magnificent statement of the philosophical underpinnings of her position. An address to Congress in 1892, it was immediately printed by NAWSA as a tract. It remains justly famous for its concise, elegant language. Its power came from its sheer grandeur of rhetoric as well as the two traditions Stanton identified as one, the Protestant Reformation and the American Revolution. This piece is remarkable for more than stylistic reasons. Its portrayal of the "immeasurable solitude of self" was adumbrated over the human life cycle, through birth, childhood, young adulthood, age, death. It was equally modulated into the solitude of triumphs and defeats alike, of presidential candidates and prisoners in their cells, of nature and of human companionship. From Jesus to the most ignorant, humble, or vicious, all human beings were alone; this existential solitude of the human condition was a human link to God. Stanton's individualism had been pushed to its final, radical conclusion, and there it overcame much of the unsavory class bias of her earlier statements. Her portrayal of the situation of women, unprepared by society for either ordinary ills or the great emergencies of life, sharpened her case for justice for women.

She began at the beginning, with her metaphysical first principle:

> The point I wish plainly to bring before you on this occasion is the individuality of each human soul—our Protestant idea, the right of individual

conscience and judgment—our republican idea, individual citizenship. In discussing the rights of woman, we are to consider, first, what belongs to her as an individual, in a world of her own, the arbiter of her own destiny, an imaginary Robinson Crusoe with her woman Friday on a solitary island. Her rights under such circumstances are to use all her faculties for her own safety and happiness.

Secondly, if we consider her as a citizen, as a member of a great nation, she must have the same rights as all other members, according to the fundamental principles of our Government.

Thirdly, viewed as a woman, an equal factor in civilization, her rights and duties are still the same—individual happiness and development.

Fourthly, it is only the incidental relations of life, such as mother, wife, sister, daughter, which may involve some special duties and training.[45]

This was the fundamental case, the basic point, the philosophical order of things—cosmos, nation, civilization, relationships.[46] No one reasoned about the rights of men as human beings, citizens, or males from the standpoint of their "incidental relations" such as father, husband, brother, son, but from their individual rights. "Just so with woman." Each human being was an "imaginary Robinson Crusoe." From that status, everything else followed. "The isolation of every human soul and the necessity of self-dependence must give each individual the right to choose his own surroundings." By this Stanton presumably meant that each individual must be equipped to choose freely and to follow freely a course in life, without the "artificial obstacles" she decried in the path of women. Hence, she continued,

The strongest reason for giving woman all the opportunities for higher education, for the full development of her faculties, her forces of mind and body; for giving her the most enlarged freedom of thought and action; a complete emancipation from all forms of bondage, of custom, dependence, superstition; from all the crippling influences of fear—is the solitude and personal responsibility of her own individual life.[47]

This solitude and isolation of each individual had little in common with "inwardness." Woman was "an individual, in a world of her own," firmly connected to social dramas and circumstances of human existence. First, solitude of self was applied to a variation on the fourfold bondage.

The strongest reason why we ask for woman a voice in the government under which she lives; in the religion she is asked to believe; equality in social life, where she is the chief factor; a place in the trades and professions, where she may earn her bread, is because of her birthright to self-sovereignty; because, as an individual, she must rely on herself.[48]

Stanton viewed with contempt any effort to palliate women's dissatisfaction with chivalry. "No matter how much women prefer to lean . . . nor how much men desire to have them do so, they must make the voyage of life alone." The "little courtesies of life" lay only "on the surface"; they faded "into utter insignificance in view of the deeper tragedies in which she must play her part alone."

She proceeded to the life cycle. "We come into the world alone, unlike all who have gone before us." Each human soul was unique (since "Nature never repeats herself"), and this "infinite diversity in human character" implied that each soul was to be uniquely and completely fitted for its own fate. "Friendless children are left to bear their own burdens before they can analyze their feelings; before they can even tell their joys and sorrows, they are thrown on their own resources." In youth each one's bright hopes and bitter disappointments were known only to the self. The girl of sixteen struggled alone against the temptations surrounding her; if she gave up her integrity to follow the crowd she found "plenty of company but not one to share her misery in the hour of her deepest humiliation." This one discovered the "bitter solitude of self." The young wife and mother required individual resources to manage even if she was secure against the ordinary ills of life. Her uneducated counterpart was in far worse position to cope; the solitude of the weak and the ignorant was pitiful as they were "ground to powder" in the struggle for survival. In old age, similarly they must "fall back on their own resources"; with education, informed interest in society, self-development such an old woman's solitude can be "at least respectable." Just as we come into the world alone, so "we leave it alone under circumstances peculiar to ourselves." No woman was spared such a fate. "The Angel of Death even makes no royal pathway for her."

Solitude of self was true for the hero and the outcast, the saint and the sinner. "Alike amid the greatest triumphs and darkest tragedies of life we walk alone." Both the winner and the loser of a presidential campaign had a "solitude peculiarly his own." Some of Stanton's best rhetoric was marshaled to depict the solitude of tragedy:

> In ignorance, poverty, and vice, as a pauper or criminal, alone we starve or steal; alone we suffer the sneers and rebuffs of our fellows; alone we are hunted and hounded through dark courts and alleys, in by-ways and highways; alone we

stand in the judgment seat; alone in the prison cell we lament our crimes and misfortunes; alone we expiate them on the gallows.[49]

This speech contains her strongest language for describing women's situation. We know that she and Anthony censored themselves, tempering their private discussions into less indignant and less bold terms before submitting them to public scrutiny. Here Stanton gave a sense of what might have been said:

> To throw obstacles in the way of a complete education is like putting out the eyes; to deny the rights of property is like cutting off the hands. . . . Shakespeare's play of Titus and Andronicus contains a terrible satire on woman's position in the nineteenth century—"Rude men seized the king's daughter, cut out her tongue, cut off her hands, and then bade her to call for water and wash her hands!" What a picture of woman's position! Robbed of her natural rights, handicapped by law and custom at every turn, yet compelled to fight her own battles, and in the emergencies of life to fall back on herself for protection.[50]

The "fierce storms of life" beat equally on both sexes, but women were yet at a fatal disadvantage since they were not trained to self-protection and resistance as men were. "Whatever the theories of woman's dependence on man, in the supreme moments of life he cannot bear her burdens." The supreme moment was childbirth. "Alone she goes to the gates of death to give life to every man that is born into the world." It was no accident that the next paragraph told of the solitude of Jesus.[51]

> In the highways of Palestine; in prayer and fasting on the solitary mountain top; in the Garden of Gethsemane; before the judgment seat of Pilate; betrayed by one of His trusted disciples at His last supper; in His agonies on the cross, even Jesus of Nazareth in these last sad days on earth, felt the awful solitude of self. Deserted by man, in agony he cries, "My God! My God! Why hast Thou forsaken me?" And so it must ever be in the conflicting scenes of life, in the long weary march, each one walks alone.[52]

Stanton abhorred gloominess in theology and ever sought happiness and serenity; thus this speech was notable for its dark motifs. There was small concession here to human camaraderie and companionship. "Woman's love and sympathy enter only into the sunshine of our lives."[53] In "life's greatest emergencies," where heroism and courage in the face of danger were required, humans were alone. In the terrible disasters of life, in losses of broken friendships and shattered loves, in prison, in darkness, "in the hour of danger and death" people were alone. And linked to God: "In that solemn solitude of self, that links us with the immeasurable and the eternal, each soul lives alone forever."[54] Women have risen to such sublime occasions more than once, untutored though they may have been. But justice to women was to create the possibility of complete individual development. Hence, women "will, in a measure, be fitted for these hours of solitude that come alike to all, whether prepared or otherwise."

This exercise was designed to move the legislators. There was sufficient reason "in the outer conditions of human beings" for advocating liberty and development. "But when we consider the self-dependence of every human soul," the case was strengthened. "Such is individual life. Who, I ask you, can take, dare take, on himself the rights, the duties, the responsibilities of another human soul?"

Though this speech was very late in Stanton's career, the view of the crises of life was one that she had held from her first public years. She commended the cause of woman suffrage and the humanity of women to the female hands that all around one "calmly met the great emergencies of life" as early as 1853.[55] Human life was not a scene of sweetness and light. Rather, "sorrow and suffering . . . envelope the human family like a dark cloud."[56] Victorian notions of chivalry were trivial in the face of human pain and tragedy. "Life is not a tournament . . . where men prance on glossy steeds, and women throw them crowns and flowers, but a scene of suffering and conflict, where the strong and the fortunate ones are in duty bound to bear the burthens of the weak."[57] Hagar, among the strong-minded women of the Bible, was an object lesson for women in the self-reliant and independent qualities essential to the cosmic solitude of self. Exiled by her "natural protector," she wasted no tears, but

> with the calm dignity of despair, she took up the burden of life and went forth, and in the solitude of the wilderness, with great Nature in all her majesty and beauty, she learned the power of the human soul, taught of God, to make for itself a world that no mortal hand can mar, nor foot invade.[58]

Among these crises of life were those of social injustice. Here too it was from one's own soul that one took one's bearings. It was possible to do so because the law of God was "written" on or in the soul. "When the human soul is roused with holy indignation against injustice and oppression, it stops not to translate human parchments, but follows out the law of its inner being, written by the finger of God in the first hour of its creation."[59] This law of one's inner being was, however, no solipsistic law. It corresponded to the law of the universe. "What could sustain mortal men in this awful 'solitude of self,' but the fact, that the great moral forces of the universe are bound up in his organization."[60] When Stanton deplored external authorities of the past or of "creeds, codes, and customs," and looked to her own inner authority, she appealed "to the teachings of my own soul, to the inner and the great outer world that lies beyond human legislation."[61]

What was it that was written on the human soul? The answer is easy, in one sense: justice. "The eternal principles of justice graven on her heart" were "more sacred than canons, creeds, and codes written on parchment by Jesuits, bishops, cardinals, and popes."[62] Woman had the "same keen sense of justice and equality that man has."[63] "Nobler aspirations and native dignity" were written there also—worth, esteem, excellence, human nobility, the very opposites of the false dignity that refused the equality of the ballot box. Each soul had a "high and holy destiny." Written on the human soul was its creation in the divine image, the infinite possibilities of development that reduced all positive laws to naught.

> Inasmuch as God made man in His own image, with capacities and powers as boundless as the universe, whose exigencies no mere human law can meet, it is evident that the man must ever stand first; the law but the creature of his wants; the law giver but the mouthpiece of humanity . . . [the natural rights of the individual] are a component part of himself, the laws which insure his growth and development.[64]

Thus it was the "highest duty of all to seek those conditions in life, those surroundings, which may develop what is noblest and best, remembering that the lessons of these passing hours are not for time alone, but for the ages of eternity."[65] This partially meant "our duty to render earth as near heaven as we may," the possibility of which was granted by the laws of the cosmos.

This correspondence between self and cosmos skipped over human institutions and human society. Stanton moved directly from the individual to the universe without passing through any intermediary stages. No old parchment, but also "no human institutions can bound the immortal wants of the royal sons and daughters of the great I Am—rightful heirs of the joys of time, and joint heirs of the glories of eternity."[66] Stanton occasionally made slim concessions to human interdependence. They were usually slipped into the context of her individualistic point of view.

While, as members of society, all individuals are, in a measure, dependent on each other, yet each human soul is a distinctive creative will-power subject to nothing in God's universe but the law of her being which is better known to herself than it can possibly be to any other creature.[67]

On other occasions she simply proclaimed that "it is a mistaken idea, that the same law that oppressed the individual can promote the highest good of society."[68] Reading Spencer taught her to say that the "interests of the individual and of society lie in the same direction."[69]

It followed that to consider any social, familial, political, or ecclesiastical question from the standpoint of individuality and individual rights was to consider it from the viewpoint of what was most sacred. Individual rights were always a "higher, holier" question for Stanton. Individual rights were the linchpin, the fundamental tenet of the American civil religion, baptized in blood, the only question on which the enduring stability of the nation could be guaranteed.[70]

Those higher, holier, individual rights were pure. This was the reason Stanton spoke so forcefully of the "rubbish of caste and class." The rubbish of disorder and moral chaos was in contrast to the purity of justice.[71] These revolting and disgusting group distinctions cast a shadow over the lives of millions, the shadow of "false ideas of favoritism ascribed to Deity," rather than the clear sunlight of democratic truth.[72] To pursue individual rights and to be guided by one's individual soul was to be on an upward path toward that pure light, the light of the future. "We cannot take our gauge of womanhood from the past, but from the solemn convictions of our own souls, in the higher development of the race."[73] Those solemn convictions led to a time that was "to be as much purer than the past as our immediate past has been better than the dark ages."[74]

Real democracy, based on universal suffrage, was the highest form of government because it developed the individuals within it. Sometimes Stanton spoke of this dimension of individuality as "character," as did so many of her contemporaries. "The value of real character above all artificial distinctions [is] the great lesson of democracy."[75] This "real" character was self-reliant, independent, courageous, free thinking, self-respecting, developing in accordance with its own internal laws. It was a democratic character with freedom and equality. The "love of domination" was the animal inheritance of evolution, a lower dimension of human existence to be turned to its true end, self-government.

"The love of domination" [is] the strong hereditary feature of our animal descent, which prevents the harmonious development of the oppressor as well as the oppressed.

The true use of this love of domination is in governing ourselves. As the chief business of life is character-building, we must begin by self-discipline, as thus only can we secure individual freedom.[76]

Thus the "beauty and power of individual sovereignty"[77] lay not only in the fact that it alone could acknowledge the "nobler aspirations and native dignity of woman"[78] but also in continual progression toward higher realization of self.

It goes almost without saying that Stanton had no use for a view of sin in this solitary, isolated, self-dependent individual. Individual happiness and self-dependence, not individual sinfulness or dependence on God, were the cardinal points. The first law of the soul was self-development, not repentance. Stanton forcefully repudiated "man's degradation and total depravity." The denial of original sin was the premise on which she could build the picture of upward evolutionary progress of civilization and the moral growth of the individual. The pessimism of Ecclesiastes and various liturgical practices were particular adversaries of this evolutionary stance.

The Episcopal service is more demoralizing on this view. Whole congregations of educated men and women, day after day, year after year, confessing themselves "miserable sinners," with no evident improvement from generation to generation. And this confession is made in a perfunctory manner, as if no disgrace attended that mental condition, and without hope or promise of a change from that unworthy attitude.[79]

The inherently moral quality of human existence was a necessary aspect of her notion of reason, which did not need to be corrected or completed by revelation. No fall, no revelation; no fall, no savior.

Original sin was not merely repudiated, it was condemned. Original sin was the cause of "the chains, the indelible scars, the festering wounds, the deep degradation of all the powers of the godlike mind."[80] From this bondage one needed to be "born again into the kingdom of reason and free thought," as Stanton herself had been. Sin and the related prospect of hell were "inflictions on the human family . . . which man has conjured up for himself," inflictions far worse than any nature had in store. "What is a shipwreck to conversion to the gloomy doctrines of Calvin?" Only those who had experienced the

125

"mourning, groaning, fasting, and praying in the slough of despond," those who had "lived all their lives under the dark clouds of vague undefined fears," were able to appreciate the joy of the new birth into free thought. She wrote from her own experience.

> [A]ll the cares and anxieties, the trials and disappointments, of my whole life, are light in the balance with my sufferings in childhood and youth from the horrible dogmas I sincerely believed and the gloomy environments connected with everything associated with the name of religion. . . . I early believed myself a veritable child of the devil, and suffered endless fears lest he should come some night and claim me as his own. To me, he was a personal, ever-present reality, crouching in a dark corner of the nursery. Ah! how many times I have stolen out of bed, and sat shivering on the stairs for hours, where the hall lamp and the sound of voices from the parlor would in a measure mitigate my fears![81]

Original sin was especially terrible for women and children. As Stanton believed in sex in soul, the differences between men and women made a belief in sin more oppressive for women. "Men, with their steady nerves, strong muscles, equable temperaments, trained to reason and self-reliance, in contact with the stern facts of life, cannot comprehend the multiplied and ever-present fears and apprehensions of coming danger that poison the lives of most women and children growing out of their more nervous organization, more fertile imaginations, and that natural timidity that accompanies a sense of helplessness in danger."[82] And original sin was the chief rationale for woman's subjection. *The Woman's Bible* maintained that it was the picture of fallen humanity, and the necessity of salvation, that was the central sticking point of this Christian text. The chief biblical story enjoining subordination of woman linked that point inextricably to the notion of sin. No fall, no revelation; but equally, no fall, no degradation of women. These propositions were indissolubly wedded in Stanton's view.

Further, all theologies of "an angry God, a judgment seat, an all-powerful devil, and everlasting torments in hell" were masculine products, "ideas that emanated from the diseased brains of dyspeptic celibates."[83] All such gloomy notions, all speculations of afterlife, had nothing to do with "the new gospel of the Motherhood of God and of humanity."[84]

> These masculine theologies, all so foreign to the mother-soul, should have no place in our thoughts. They should no longer be permitted to shadow our lives.
> In the fuller development of the feminine element in humanity we shall have the impress of woman's thought and sentiment in government and religion,

exalting justice and equality in the one, love and tenderness in the other, anger and vindictive punishment having no place in either.[85]

Stanton abhorred self-sacrifice in general, but she had plenty of reason in particular to reject it strenuously when applied to women. The sheer reality of the case, the "really real," amounted to the fact that individuals were, willy-nilly, self-dependent. The basic goodness of infinite capacities of individuals made it metaphysically possible for them, and especially individual women, to rely on their own faculties for progress and development.

It also followed from the solitude of self that the rights of all were the same. Just as all minds functioned alike, so their selves in their isolated and self-dependent state were virtually identical, interchangeable. Hence the "rights of every human being are the same and identical."[86] Or as she put it with regard to the political strand of her argument, the suffragist work was "to teach men that woman is not an anomalous being."[87] Any process of reason to determine the rights of men was the only appropriate process to determine the rights of women, whose core of individuality was identical. The individual virtues—self-respect, personal dignity, courage, self-reliance, personal freedom, independence—were the same for all human souls, which operated on the same moral laws. Women had to be educated into this self-reliant mode, taught to go "alone" on the streets, to please themselves first. "Woman . . . has a right to be happy in and of herself; . . . she has a right to the free use, improvement and development of her faculties, for her own benefit and pleasure . . . she should never sacrifice one iota of her individuality."[88] The "most sacred" right of all was the right to one's own (female) person, to all one's God-given powers of body and soul.

It was no doubt for this reason Stanton's notion of the solitude of every individual self, that she often exclaimed over the difficulty of making "men see that women feel the humiliation of their petty distinctions of sex precisely as the black man sees those of color." On her premise, this precisely should not have been difficult, and yet it was. A similar quandary arises in the next section. The great immutable laws of morals were as fixed as those of physics, and yet were transgressed regularly.

C. The Great, Immutable Laws

The analysis of the fourfold bondage was replete with references to the laws undergirding human existence. Marriages foundered when they were not organized in keeping with the laws of their nature. Sometimes these laws were the "laws of attraction" of two equal beings; sometimes they were "physiological truths" that brought imbecility, vice, corruption, and poverty in the wake of their transgression. The area of social customs similarly required the application of reason and science to discover the rational laws of education, dress, character, economy. Politics was based on the "eternal laws of justice," as enduring as the scientific laws of gravitation. Christianity trespassed on the moral law especially in its denigration of the feminine element. The laws of the mind were the same for both sexes. Stanton did not always specify the content of those immutable laws. But enough of their substance was provided to lay the groundwork, the structural principles, of her feminist view.

The great immutable laws were the natural laws of democracy and progress. They represented the eternal archimedean point where the republic and religion met and fulfilled each other. They were primarily ethical; it was "moral laws that governed the universe." Because of the analogy between the moral and the material, however, those ethical laws were described with a strong organic component. That freedom was close to an instinct for Stanton; the organicist bent of her description of those natural laws created problems for the ways she conceptualized freedom. The source of true order, harmonious and beautiful, those laws were finally static. They also provided Stanton with her favored entrée into discussions of God and the true rational religion.

Democracy alone corresponded to the natural laws. All distinctions of family, blood, wealth, color, sex, class, or caste were artificial. Individual rights alone were natural. Even if there was sex in soul, the rights and duties of men and women were the same—individual happiness and development. What was artificial could only perish. Inequality bore the "seeds of death" as it provoked dissension and decline.[89] Equality and freedom alone were life-giving. It was because the nation's "life and growth and immortality" depended on its legislation that statesmanship was the "most exalted of all sciences."[90]

It was in the reform movement that the progress aspect of the natural laws coincided with the democracy aspect of the natural laws. To relieve suffering and promote progress by reference to the great laws was the purpose and meaning of reform movements. The equivalence of life, ethics, democracy, and progress led Stanton to a "medical metaphor." Reform movements were opposed to the inefficient humanitarianism that merely dealt in "symptoms."

> The wise physician who shall trace out the true causes of suffering; who shall teach us the great, immutable laws of life and health; who shall show us how and where in our every-day life, we are violating these laws, and the true point to begin the reform, is doing a much higher, broader, and deeper work than he who shall bend all his energies to the temporary relief of suffering.[91]

Many of the "moral deformities of the race," and the physical deformities too, had their true causes in the violations of cosmic law in the false relations of the sexes. These true causes were "lurking under the shadow of the altar, the sacredness of the marriage institution, or the assumed superiority of man" in the case of marriage.

Reformers were doing a higher work than mere charity. There were several distinct aspects to this elevated view of reform movements. While in theory every soul had its own "native dignity," an inherently elevated status, yet the masses of people were sunk below this standard, whether through poverty, ignorance, vice, or by laws that excluded them from voting. Stanton's views of comparative degradation of various classes of people were complex. Though some women were better educated than some black men, if these black men could vote, women were thereby so much more comparatively degraded; this degradation was all the more humiliating if one was a pure-minded, educated woman, as woman suffragists were. It is very difficult to sort out the reasons Stanton had for her relative judgments here. But one thing is certain. To recognize and protest against oppression was to rise on the scale of elevation. The masses of people who were apathetic were thereby more deeply degraded than those who protested, though nothing else in one's objective situation changed. At least to protest showed some self-respect.

Stanton's democratic position was akin to those of the Founding Fathers. She never saw democracy as a leveling, but always as an uplifting, force. Itself the highest form of government, democracy was to raise its degraded and benighted groups to the highest levels of human possibility, where they become godlike. The natural laws were the laws of progress. To follow, rather than to violate, the laws of existence led one upward in the course of human evolutionary development. Indeed, evolutionary change was itself one of the laws: "Progress is the law of life."[92] "Change is the natural result of growth and development."[93]

That both statesmanship and medicine could be cited by Stanton as pursuing the higher course may be indicative of her nearly biological view of the natural laws. On some occasions it seems that she meant it nearly literally when she said that the nation's "life and growth and immortality" (a conjunction that in itself was fascinating) depended on living in accordance with the natural laws. Natural progress was opposed to unnatural suffering, life to death, as she reflected on society's relationship to the laws of our being. A leg broken by defying the law of gravitation was equivalent to a heart broken in a mismatched marriage when the positive laws of the state refused divorce.

> Our sorrows in life are not caused by the direct fiat of a malevolent Being, but by our own ignorance and indifference to the laws of our being. . . .
>
> I see inexorable law everywhere, cause and effect. Our sufferings and prayers do not mitigate one iota the effect of violated law either in the moral or material world. If we defy the law of gravitation, a broken neck or leg will be the penalty. If we do not exercise the tender emotions of love, friendship, sympathy, and charity, we blunt the moral sense and isolate ourselves from all that is best in human companionship.[94]

This organicist tinge, if I may so put it, of Stanton's view of the moral laws of the universe resulted in several problems in her thought. "Belief is not voluntary and change is the natural result of growth and development." Though Stanton's arguments for free love and individual rights depended on a sense of freedom, the lawlike structure of the world seemed to vitiate free will, choices made by persons, real disagreements as to the substance of policy, and human agency itself. It was "futile" to oppose the changes coming in the next stage of development of the race. By emphasizing the analogies between the moral and the material, Stanton seemed almost to say that the laws of the universe were also the laws of logic. The facts presented by Bachofen had to be true, recall, because they were so logical and in accordance with the truth of theory. The vitiation of free will coupled with her denial of sin also left quandaries as to *how* these immutable laws could be so regularly broken. The law of gravitation, after all, is not abrogated if I step out my window; what occurs is precisely an instance of its functioning. This does not seem to be the same as "setting aside" the moral laws or "playing fast and loose with the eternal principles of justice." Violation of the laws was the result of either ignorance or the selfish interests of the ruling classes. Without a notion of sin somewhere, that selfish oppression of others seems difficult to account for.

These organic aspects of Stanton's uses of the natural law did serve her well when she appealed to the laws of life and health with regard to women's bodies. The strength and vigor of women's bodies, the free use of limbs in exercise unhampered by the trailing draperies of women's costumes, were logical components of such a natural view. Theories of the natural weakness and disability of women were absurd, for nature (or God) did not make women to suffer in weakness. "The first step in this work is to make all women understand that suffering is not in harmony with God's will; that every pain, sorrow, and wrong is in violation of his law."[95] They seem particularly troubling with regard to her emphases on motherhood, however. Motherhood, as the supremely natural function of women, sometimes qualified, or skewed, her atomistic reading of natural individuality and tinged her reflections with female chauvinism.

> Our trouble is not our womanhood, but the artificial trammels of custom under false conditions. We are, as a sex, infinitely superior to men, and if we were free and developed, healthy in body and mind, as we should be under natural conditions, our motherhood would be our glory. That function gives women such wisdom and power as no male ever can possess. When women can support themselves, have their entry to all the trades and professions, with a house of their own over their heads and a bank account, they will own their bodies and be dictators in the social realm.[96]

Her vision of women as "dictators in the social realm," however, should not be read as merely reversing patriarchy to make women the sole rulers of the state. She meant that women were to decide the appropriate fathers of their children, rather than being forced into marriages of vice and violence. The natural bent of her thought left her open to various nineteenth-century scientific notions, such as the hereditary passage of vice to one's offspring. Mentally deficient children, drunkenness, and criminality were the natural result of women's captivity in marriage. Nonetheless, she usually spoke of the complete change that she saw occurring with the transformation of woman's status as a "probable" one:

> It is quite probable that when woman is independent and self-supporting she will choose the father of her children. . . . In exalting moral power above brute force, in the education, elevation, and enfranchisement of woman, one thing is sure, that vice, disease, and crime, drunkenness, deformity and degradation, will find no means of perpetuating themselves. In the restoration of woman we look

for the re-creation of the race, for that great onward step that will accomplish all the partial reforms that now occupy public thought.[97]

Only one thing was certain: "We cannot do our duties until we secure our rights." When she saw the family as the state in miniature, she similarly concluded not that women were to rule solely, but that women were the natural superintendents of prisons, makers of criminal codes, and teachers.

Motherhood also was the reason that the feminine element of civilization was understood to be less violent than the masculine element. Since women knew the cost of giving life, they were less likely to decree the shedding of blood. Masculine/feminine elements had either mutually degrading or mutually elevating influences on each other, depending on whether they were isolated or integrated in all walks of life. Sometimes this was read by way of the "law of attraction" of the sexes, which not only brought them together in marriage but stimulated each to higher, purer effort. Sometimes it was read by way of Victorian piety; men are what their mothers make them, so who is to be surprised that women degraded politically have sons who do not appreciate democracy?

Part of the purpose of the great laws was to assure progress, change, and innovation, as opposed to the weight of tradition's inertia. Each time was to be governed by its own internal dynamic, just as each soul was governed by the laws of its own being. "If we are to be governed in all things by the men of the eighteenth century, and the twentieth by the nineteenth, and so on, the world will be always governed by dead men."[98] Since life and growth, not death, were natural, this was obviously undesirable and a cause of instability. Stanton's analysis therefore aimed to hold together both the continuity of permanence—the great laws, after all, were immutable—with the continuing change and development of history toward its final goal. To depend on the laws of nature ensured the safety of any reform measure proposed. "As to this being an innovation on the laws of nature, we may safely trust nature at all times to vindicate herself."[99]

The hereafter, if there was to be one, was also governed by the same laws of growth and development as this life, or so "we may logically infer."[100] Sometimes Stanton guardedly suggested merely that "the best possible preparation for the next form of existence is to fulfill our duties here."[101] Mostly she sought to turn women's attention firmly to this life. "If the women of this nation will henceforth give all the thought, the time, the force, the enthusiasm, to the practical work of this life, that they have heretofore expended in speculations and preparations for the future, we might bring sunshine into every home, open the prison doors."[102] Such agnosticism about the future world was sometimes coupled with a democratic critique. Notions of predestination especially smelled to her of "a royal heaven, an aristocracy of saints" (not to mention "an arch fiend to torment and a God who laughs at [human] calamities").[103] She deplored telling laborers and women and children that "their miseries here are but the foreshadowing of infinitely worse suffering hereafter." Her liberalism was at its very worst, however, when she suggested that perhaps we might make up some pleasant fiction about the hereafter for the comfort of the present.

> If we think it is not safe to tell them the simple truth, that we know nothing of what lies beyond our mortal horizon, we might at least picture for them some beautiful visions of peace and joy in comfortable homes eternal in the heavens. . . . It is too bad to defraud them of the comforts and necessaries in this life and of all bright hopes in the celestial world hereafter. If some dreams and speculations must be sent forth as a kind of police chart of instruction, pray let them tell of a golden age to come, when the blessings of life shall be shared equally by all the children of earth.[104]

She looked for progress toward the incarnation of the divine laws, but it is hard not to conclude that her position was finally static. This especially was true in the later period when she emphasized the equilibrium of natural forces as metaphors for the masculine/feminine elements of humanity. The counters of her language swing into a rhythm of stability. Exegeting Genesis 1: 27-28, for example, she hymned the praises of progress, to be sure, but the "exact balance" of eternity was the real point.

> Thus Scripture, as well as science and philosophy, declares the eternity and equality of sex—the philosophical fact, without which there could have been no perpetuation of creation, no growth or development in the animal, vegetable, or mineral kingdoms, no awakening nor progressing in the world of thought. The masculine and feminine elements, exactly equal and balancing each other, are as essential to the maintenance of the equilibrium of the universe as positive and negative electricity, the centripetal and centrifugal forces, the laws of attraction which bind together all we know of this planet whereon we dwell and of the system in which we resolve.[105]

133

"These great natural forces must be perfectly balanced or the whole material world would relapse into chaos."[106] "Just so," as she frequently said, with the sexes.

While true religion never held people down, but nerved them to protest and struggle against their degradation, that religion was described not in terms of conflict, but of harmony. "The word religion means to bind again, to unite those who have been separated, to harmonize those who have been in antagonism."[107] I said above that I might characterize Stanton's view as "all that rises must converge." Now it is equally appropriate to say that her view amounted to "all that rises must converge—and rest."[108]

Finally, the immutable laws were Stanton's particular and favored entrée into a doctrine of God. God was the divine lawmaker, legislator, sometimes the "divine author" of the moral laws governing the universe, sometimes these laws themselves. When asked in her later life whether she believed in God, she characteristically and classically responded:

> Yes, as I look about I see law everywhere: the sun, moon and stars, the constellations, the days and nights, the seasons at regular intervals all come and go. The centrifugal and centripetal forces, positive and negative, magnetism, the laws of gravitation, cohesion, attraction are all immutable and unchangeable, one and all moving in harmony together. Hence behind all this, I argue, intelligence, a supreme law, Nature, God, or whatever one may choose to call the eternal forces that set all in motion. As we learn these laws that govern the universe of mind and matter alike in the moral and material world and walk in line with them, we secure health, comfort, happiness, harmony, and that peace that passeth all understanding.[109]

D. The God of Justice, Mercy, and Truth

The "more rational religion" was the groundwork of Stanton's feminist case. It entailed denying the inspiration of the Bible (expurgating it, in fact), denying the fall and redemption. These denials were by no means merely iconoclastic or antireligious acts. They proceeded from a constructive religious impulse. In response to the critics of The Woman's Bible who charged its authors with blasphemy, Stanton claimed, on the contrary, that "in denying divine inspiration for such demoralizing ideas, [the committee of authors] shows a more worshipful reverence for the great Spirit of all Good, than does the Church."[110] To be sure, there was an element of flippancy in this claim.

But on systematic grounds she was supremely in earnest. The great spirit of all good, the great spirit of the universe, the divine ideal, the great oversoul, our ideal first cause, the creator, the infinite intelligence, supreme law, nature, God—"or whatever one may choose to call the eternal forces that set all in motion"—was the final groundwork of her suffragist case. Stanton's characteristic names for God did not include Judge, King, Redeemer, Savior. Her use of deistic names for God was completely appropriate to this student of the Revolutionary Fathers, this woman who saw the polling place as a "holy of holies."

The "God of Justice, Mercy and Truth" was a locution she used from her earliest statements. To be sure, under the influence of her connections with the Boston liberals, Stanton spoke of living in harmony with "the great divine soul of all," or the divine ideal. To the women gathered in the International Council in 1888 she echoed Emerson's language in the claim that "the same great over-soul has been our hope and inspiration."[111] There were also several occasions in which she paralleled the deity with the principles of justice, mercy, and truth. During the time that she still maintained the two types of Christianity, for example, she pointed out that priestcraft deterred women from the worship of "the living God *and* the everlasting principles of Justice, Mercy, and Truth."[112] This juxtaposition was narrowed in the following year, though, when the "living God," that biblical character, was dropped. Instead she asserted that "our God"—i.e., the reformers' God—was "a God of justice, mercy, and truth."[113]

Mostly Stanton buried her positive statements in the hearts of critical claims and polemics, especially those against the churches and clergy. She said little that was explicitly concentrated on divinity. But we can discern the positive outlines of her claims in such comments, which were consistent over the years and cohered with the systematic account that she gave of the suffrage cause. As a liberal, Stanton had little use for a divine reality that was discontinuous with human life, and especially with the highest and best in human life. In concluding this section I concentrate on assembling the explicit comments Stanton made related to the nature of God, the omnipotence of humanity as it struggled toward that deity, and the true worship of this god.

The God of justice, mercy, and truth was above all else the creator of nature and of the great immutable laws of nature. The doctrine of creation was as prominent in Stanton's thought as it is in most natural law theologies. Individual rights were a component part of humanity because God created it so. Self-sovereignty was a link to this God. When she hymned the centrifugal and centripetal forces that undergirded the universe, she saw God "behind all this"—the watchmaker's God, who set the universal laws of movement into motion ("one and all moving in harmony together"), but was not itself moved or in motion.

Though the creator was "behind" the universe, she/he was nonetheless immanent in it. Stanton's God was not particularly concerned with historical events, movements, peoples, but was exemplified in the diviner elements in individual human nature or in Nature. "Mother Earth" passed as deity in some contexts, for Stanton found the "soul of love in matter as well as in mind."[114] This was not, it goes without saying, nature "red in tooth and claw," but benevolent, serene nature in harmony with itself. Stanton thought little of the deity represented in the Old Testament precisely because Jahweh's attributes and activities were so harsh. "Surely the writers had a very low idea of the nature of their God. They make Him not only anthropomorphic, but of the very lowest type, jealous and revengeful, loving violence rather than mercy."[115] On the occasions when she described the "female element" as mercy and love, it made sense that she saw in the women around her something more divine than in the men who ruled:

> It is this underlying faith of women in human nature, this love for the weak and forsaken who most need it, that we would fain see represented in our criminal legislation. The day is dawning in which our creeds and codes are to be essentially modified by this diviner element destined to work to radical reconstruction in society.[116]

In keeping with her notion of the integration of these two elements in the world in order to maintain its balance, such views led her to assert "plurality in the Godhead, a heavenly Mother as well as a heavenly Father, the feminine as well as the masculine element."[117] This view, represented in Genesis 1: 27-28, was one of the few "crumbs of comfort" in the Bible.

Faith in human nature extended not solely to the rejection of sin. I have noted in Stanton's statement of her civil religion that the doctrine of individual rights, pure and sacred, was bridging the gulf between the Creator and the creature. Eve with her maligned apple had declared "humanity omnipotent."[118] With the parallelism that sin-redemption doctrines frequently carry even when rejected, Jesus too had "declared humanity God" on the cross.[119]

Indeed in her latest period Stanton was explicit in calling for the "Worship of God in Man," a religion of humanity, in which "men and women will worship what they see of the divine in each other; the virtues, the beatitudes, the possibilities ascribed to Deity reflected in mortal beings."[120] The grandeur of Nature was matched by the grandeur of human works—the seven wonders of the ancient world, St. Peter's Cathedral in Rome, "tireless machines," the railroads, electricity, even "the new mysteries revealed by physical researches." This late statement was completely in keeping with Stanton's tireless themes. "The new religion will teach the dignity of human nature and its infinite possibilities for development." It was to lead its adherents into the paths of self-respect and high aspiration rather than into the "valley of humiliation"; it would teach practical duties to other human beings in this life rather than "sentimental duties to God" in the next.

These were also the days in which Stanton had discovered the virtues of "cooperation." Though the "solitude of self" appears in this essay, she had changed her mind enough to see that "a loving human fellowship is the real divine communion. The spiritual life is not a mystical contemplation of divine attributes, but the associative development of all that is good in human character."[121] This religion, the "practical righteousness" she had learned at Mott's feet, conceded that Jesus and the prophets had also "taught a religion of deeds rather than forms and ceremonies."

Whether in an explicit religion of humanity or in reform movements, the noble aspirations of human beings, built into their being in creation, were a means of access to deity. Self-development was no merely peripheral or incidental obligation of the human condition; it was a direct link to God. She put her point negatively against clergy who said nothing to rouse women "from the apathy of ages, to inspire them to do and dare great things, to intellectual and spiritual achievements, in real communion with the Great Spirit of the Universe."[122] Women's aspirations to the higher life, upward progress toward self-reliance, cultivation of individual potential, were "real communion" with the deity, rather than the unreal relationship with God fostered by the veneration of saints and parchments. Human beings had "capacities and powers as boundless as the universe."[123] This meant the investigations of science, surely, but it especially meant reform movements.

It is surprising how supinely people endure evils that could be so easily remedied by resistance and determination. The trouble is, most people believe that human affairs revolve like the solar system, and cannot be changed, whereas the will of man is mightier than the elements. It can mould circumstances, all material things, annihilate time and space, bind continents together, and weld the nations of the earth in one.[124]

Democracy was a prime locus for the use of this infinite human capacity:

> May the true women of England and America alike devote their tongues and pens and lives to chase despots, monarchs, emperors, kings and queens, aristocrats and tyrants, to their hiding-places and thus usher in the new age of "Equal Rights for All." Then can we pray in sincerity and faith, "Thy kingdom come on earth as it is in heaven."[125]

The more rational religion that rejected the allegories of the Garden of Eden for Darwin saw the upward movement of the ages from a lower to a higher form of life as a movement toward God. To clear away the rubbish of caste and class was also to clear away the distinctions "between the creature and the Creator."[126]

Stanton's God, incompatible with any false notions, was instead compatible with all truths, and only with truth. God "our Father and Mother" was not given to proposing revelations outside the great book of nature and the reach of human reason. Not a mythological creature, but one whose laws and nature were accessible to ethical and rational scrutiny, the God of justice, mercy, and truth, was served best by the full development of all one's faculties, a process that was "natural" and hence in harmony with science. The God of justice, mercy, and truth was thus served by the impending "marriage" between science and religion. One *argued* for the existence of this God, one inferred it logically from the known facts, by the same processes of reason one put to use on the "science of life." One did not behold this God in a mystical vision or hear deity's murmur in one's heartfelt emotions; religious emotion not guided by enlightened intellect was contrary to the true, rational religion. Confusion, perplexity, speculation, allegories, intellectual labyrinths were foreign to the deity.

The God of justice, mercy, and truth was served best by a "noble life." The "irreligious mode" of politics undermined its dignity, stability, and safety. It was not to churches that one looked for "patterns of purity, goodness, and truth," but to the reformers, antagonists of the churches. True religion made one moral and free, fully developed: "a noble life [was] of more importance than a stern faith." To live thus, guided by the everlasting principles of justice, equality, happiness, truth, was to live in harmony with the underlying arrangements of God's cosmic order, that perfect, immutable, and complete spectacle. Such harmonious lives, organized around individual rights and the natural equilibrium of the sexes, would procure greater power to individuals and the civilization, since "either sex, in isolation, is robbed of one-half its power for the accomplishment of any given work."[127] In any case, to do other than to "walk in line" with the immutable laws was to precipitate moral chaos.

The true worship of such a deity was inextricably intertwined with the moral life, with being guided by one's own moral convictions just as Luther, Calvin, and Knox were. Certainly no Christian worship service that was focused on redemption from sin was adequate to the veneration of the God of justice, mercy, and truth. Since Stanton was never allowed to enter into the "holy of holies" of the republic, the polling booth, great Nature's temple was one of the few places available to her for the ritual re-enactment of her brand of religion. She took up her pen, in her later years, in defense of women's bicycle riding; it was no accident that this prosaic topic could be wedded to the preferred mode of worship:

> I believe that if women prefer a run in the open air on Sunday to a prosy sermon in a close church they should ride by all means. With the soft changing clouds before their eyes, and the balmy air in their lungs, moving along hills, rivers, trees, and flowers, singing with the birds and the praises of the Lord in that temple not builded with human hands, but standing eternal under the blue heavens—this worship is far preferable to playing the role of "miserable sinners" in the church service, and listening to that sanctimonious wail, "Good Lord deliver us."[128]

Between the love of nature and the kingdom of heaven itself were few places in which Stanton would have been likely to worship. It was utterly typical of her that she claimed she would be proud to introduce herself in the next life, that sphere of continued progress, as an American. "I have always said that I did not want to go into the kingdom of heaven disfranchised, and have looked forward with pleasure to introducing myself to St. Peter at the gate as an American citizen."[129]

Living a noble and free life, and the most appropriate means of worshipping deity, were never conjoined in principle for Stanton with relationships and organizations, as they were for Anthony. Stanton's individualism was far too central to her thought. In her very latest years, she became explicit that being alone for thought, in meditation, was also a possible means of access to one's real self.

> There is such a thing as being too active, living too outward a life. Most reformers fail at this point. I cannot find an article on meditation which I intended to send you. But the gist of it was that, in order to develop our real

selves, we need time to be alone for thought. To be always giving out and never pumping in, the well runs dry too soon.[130]

This comment from Stanton's old age may of course reflect an understandable fatigue after fifty years of struggle. It also was perfectly in keeping with her thought. The solitude of self, after all, was a central principle to her—and what could be more solitary than meditation? Indeed, there was a great deal of resistance in Stanton to the active life of reformers; it was Anthony who continually spurred her friend on to action for woman suffrage. It was not untypical of Stanton in her later years to announce that she would not attend the year's suffrage convention. It was not untypical of Anthony that she would nonetheless schedule for Stanton a keynote address, arrive at Stanton's home several days before the convention opened, start her writing the speech, pack her bags, and entrain with her, protesting all the while, to the convention. Some of this reluctance stemmed perhaps from Stanton's alleged "laziness"—or from her genuine sensuality. A good Victorian in some ways, Stanton was un-Victorian in her high regard for all the pleasures of the flesh—sexual passion, good food, rest, and recreation. This too was consistent with her thought. Self-sacrifice for women she abhorred. It was self-cultivation, directing one's own "benevolent instincts" toward oneself, one's own rights, one's own happiness, that pleased the God of justice, mercy, and truth.

Comments and Conclusions

Stanton was a brilliant and systematic theorist and theologian of woman suffrage. Her feminist program involved her in a project of redescribing the human situation, and that in a particularly sweeping and comprehensive fashion. The way Stanton's more rational religion related to each strand of the fourfold bondage was a good indicator of her "operative" concept of positive and essential religion. This more rational religion could not be reduced to conventional or traditional religious topics, but was brought to bear on what are commonly thought to be "secular" phenomena—marriage, society, politics. Her own religious position was the ground on which she could be critical of the religions of man and of the structures of the other three strands of bondage. We might say that religion provided the warrants—that is, the reasons behind the reasons[131]—for Stanton's judgments regarding justice. Geertz suggests that the "heart" of the religious perspective is "the conviction that the values one holds are grounded in the inherent structure of reality, that between the way one ought to live and the way things really are, there is an unbreakable inner connection."[132] The worldview of religion, the model of "how reality is at base put together" and the ethos side, the model of "the way [people] do things and like to see things done," mutually confirm each other and are invoked in support of each other. This was precisely what Stanton's more rational religion provided in her suffrage case—a picture of the fundamental components of the universe that rendered certain actions appropriate and believable, and a set of moral obligations for action that rendered this picture of the universe satisfying and apparent.

Geertz also suggests that it may be well for students of religion to distinguish between the "force" and the "scope" of any particular religious perspective. By force, he means the intensity, the thoroughness with which one holds that perspective, its "centrality or marginality" in the lives of its adherents; by scope, the range of phenomena to which it is regarded as relevant.[133] This seems helpful in understanding the peculiar cast of Stanton's enlightened religion. Stanton read true religion as a happy religion, conducing to cheerfulness and enjoyment of life, even in the fierce struggles of reformers. It is difficult to imagine anyone becoming terribly passionate, burning intensely for the "great immutable laws." The force, in other words, of Stanton's religion was slight. Argument, inference, calm and detached contemplation of the workings of the cosmos and the human mind were all in order, not mountaintop experiences or frenzied emotion.

The scope of Stanton's religion, on the other hand, was of the widest sort. Any and every topic she discussed with regard to the fourfold bondage was eventually referred to individual happiness, the immutable laws of the universe, and to deity however named in a specific context. That Stanton invoked in tandem the Protestant Reformation and the American Revolution was a strong indicator of her brand of civil religion. Both were reinterpreted by their conjunction. The revolution was read as sacred, a religious reformation establishing the new "holy of holies," the ballot box; the Reformation was read as though it had unleashed the rights of individual citizenship into the world. Both were to be purified and fulfilled by the enfranchisement of women, who were to initiate a new departure in the religion of the republic, a step higher on the upward path of progress and development. Women, exercising their rights to think and to equality, would re-enact the works of Luther, Calvin, etc., and by re-enacting this mythic drama of religious reform would redeem society from the chaos in which it inevitably was trapped. The health, happiness, and power of these original sacred acts would be released into the society, in a new beginning that incarnated novelty and true continuity at once.

This reference to novelty should remind us that Stanton was actively seeking transformations in her contemporaries. This gives us slight pause with regard to the way Geertz's conceptual schema regards religious change. When he says that the "defining concern" of religion is acceptance of the wider dimensions of reality, and not action on them, that is only a partial truth with regard to Stanton's religious perspective. If the religions of the day stood in the way of woman's emancipation, they were due for transformation as surely as the secular legal structures. But it was true that for her the laws of the universe were immutable, almost by definition. Stanton's implicit concept of positive and essential religion, of false and true religion, was her way of reconciling the changes sought in her whole life work with eternity. It was a way of calling for religious changes while preserving religion's universal validity. The "redescription" of the eternal verities was her strategy for attaining this end. What was thought to be true was false; what was formerly attributed to deity was attributed to mere males; the authority of tradition was replaced by the authority of each woman thinking for herself; the acme of civilization was declared to be remnants of barbarism and degradation; what was acclaimed as order was seen in no uncertain terms as chaos.

While I called the previous section "a more rational religion," in line with Stanton's own vocabulary, I might well have called it a "more religious religion." For that, in the final analysis, is what Stanton meant by describing as a "false faith" anything in the other religions of the world that opposed women's emancipation.

To describe the fourfold bondage and to redescribe it in religious terms were internally and reciprocally related in Stanton's analysis of the situation of women in her day. She pointed to actual structures, such as the loss of a woman's maiden name in marriage, or violence in the home: facts. That these were not healthy situations for women, that they spelled the degradation of women for Stanton, was obviously a piece of her value structure. But mere disapproval was not all that was at stake. There were more fundamental, more really real, components of this strand of the fourfold bondage that were required for an adequate discussion of them. The marriages, politics, customs, churches she saw about her were not simply "bad," though they were that. They were *false*. To live in harmony with God's laws of equality and individual happiness was the *true* and *pure* relationship. This true state of affairs could

142

not be reached until major social changes occurred pertaining to social customs, individual character, the legal structure, interpretations of Scripture, etc.

It would be equally true to outline Stanton's process of reasoning in the other direction. She *started* (logically, not chronologically) from first principles of individual happiness, women's right to think, the immutable laws set by the just, merciful, and true creator. These were the points to which virtually all discussions of women's fourfold bondage were referred. It "follows" from individual happiness that both individuals party to a marriage must be considered primary in considering the relationship, that one can dissolve any institution into its "atoms," its components. To attempt to distinguish which was "first" in a chronological ordering, say, is to ask the question of the chicken and the egg. Stanton's religion was internally and reciprocally related to her description of fourfold bondage; to separate them is impossible.

Her religion was also the occasion of some confusions in her mode of analysis. In the great emergencies of life, when rough storms beat upon a woman's soul, she was alone with herself and her own resources. Self-sovereignty was simply a fact, a structured aspect of the cosmos. This fact, however, was somehow not recognized in the case of women. Stanton frequently spoke of the need to apply the eternal principles to the case of women—that is, to extend a truth understood and in operation in one area into further areas. She was never very clear about how it could happen that an eternal truth could be unrecognized, how human beings acquired the power to trespass the great immutable laws. This is the same quandary we saw above with regard to the science of politics, which "should" have been as "fixed" in the realm of morals as the physical sciences were fixed in their laws.

These perplexities, however, send us back to the notions of justice in Stanton's thought. Those immutable laws, however static they were in the cosmos, were the source of transformation of human society. They were the principles of movement toward justice and its divine author. The universe was in equilibrium, but human society was emphatically not. It was in chaos and discord, rather than in the harmonic motion of the stars. A mighty revolution, the mightiest of all revolutions, was needed to bring the United States into the state where it *ought* to be and hence most fully *was*. The suffrage reform was complicated precisely because the injustice of woman's state was contrary to the laws of the universe, antagonizing "one vital principle in nature with another." Women were *not* inferior in the cosmological scheme. From the viewpoint of the really real, women were already equal with men, they were

143

already free. Those complications, we might say, came from the contrast between the really real and the merely actual. The metaphysical status of women was trespassed, violated in all realms of society. No wonder that there was pain, agony, violence, ethical contagion. No wonder either that in the headlong rush for freedom some members were trampled. Only when the longing for freedom, the longing to be at one with the universe, was slaked, when the pure and true state of affairs was realized, would there be quiet and harmony. Until women were free, they would be degraded. The only way to salvage some self-respect, to be at least partially in the pure and true state, was to protest, agitate, struggle for the broadest, highest principles of justice.

The "higher" and "lower" places in Stanton's thought were the way to solve the problems bequeathed by the traditional religious views of women. The woman suffrage movement was in conflict with much of Christianity, the received religion. Stanton resolved these conflicts not by removing the cause of woman suffrage from the arena of religion, but by redefining religion in such a way as to make the movement and its purposes religious in their own right. She then proceeded to assert that the religion inherent in the movement, along with the civil religion with which it was virtually synonymous, was "more rational"—that is, higher and purer than Christianity.

It is to Stanton's credit that it was always the conjunction of justice and purity that she sought. Justice was pure, and purity was just. She never lost sight of this fundamental ethical counter as she sought the progress of evolution, for she could never accept a purity that stood outside the struggle for women's rights or that saw itself unconnected to equal rights. "Equal rights for all" was the criterion by which one assessed the kingdom of heaven to be brought on this earth. The fundamental democratic truths were not superseded by the laws of heaven; they *were* the laws of heaven.

The "great immutable laws of progress and development" are an easy target for a disillusioned twentieth-century critique. Yet we should not forget that Stanton herself lived through the Civil War and that she spent the last decades of her life in the New York urban-industrial dislocations. It was not a simple belief in progress that Stanton held, but a complicated one in which both elevation and degradation were simultaneously discerned in one and the same political act. One may wonder whether such views of progress are not far removed from the consciousness of any reformer who is interested in effective change toward justice and not simply in expressive action, in acting out one's anger, or in the Bohemian urge to *épater les bourgeois*.

These reflections, which border on disagreement with Stanton, raise the question of how we are to be critical of Stanton's views, the question of the sorts of terms that can be adequate both to recognizing her achievement and to correcting what is problematic in her work. Suffragists have had more than their share of unfair critiques, whether from scholars who are outright sexists, from scholars who seek to turn them from feminists into socialists, or from contemporary feminists berating their racist and classist assumptions with little analysis of the ways these assumptions might be built into the larger framework of their intellectual positions. Nothing is harder in these matters than to avoid making the virtues of hindsight into moral virtues as well. Stanton's enlightenment belief in progress is never far from either the historian's or the ethicist's pen, as when we today speak of "going beyond" someone's position.

Stanton's insights and presuppositions must be reformulated if we are even to stand beside her, let alone on her shoulders in a tradition. She would have been the last to suggest that feminists were to be guided by the dead past. It should be clear that to critique Stanton's work is to be critical of values that undergird more of American political life and social thought than their strictly feminist incarnation. Since Stanton saw herself applying the "logic of democracy" to the suffragist case, to be concerned about her suffragist case in many ways is to raise questions about American democratic theory. Briefly, let me signal, as initial counters of critique, the distinction between "internal" problems in Stanton's own thought and those questions that are more "external." The former have to do with questions of systematic coherence and consistency; the latter with differences in modes of thought or in the area of historical anachronism—those questions which are somewhat clearer eighty-five years after Stanton's death. While it may be that finally such distinctions break down, yet such a distinction seems prima facie to recommend itself to begin comments on Stanton's work. I look briefly, then, at three places in Stanton's work that seem fruitful for a critical commentary—her individualism, her notions of thinking, and the religion of democracy.

Stanton's individualism is so obvious as to require no further clarification. Twentieth-century explorations of the formation of personality, of historical and social class factors in epistemology, of social roles, and of the crucial nature of language indicate that human beings are social in essential and not merely peripheral ways. When the women's liberation movement builds its critiques of sexism on the basis of concepts such as socialization or the internalization of social norms, it expresses the distance between Stanton's

145

perspective and that of the present, though frequently without explicit argument to that effect. (Even Stanton saw woman as imaginary Robinson Crusoe "with her woman Friday.") I cannot fully enter into arguments about the adequacy or inadequacy of this very American aspect of this position. Yet there are questions that may be raised in this context to indicate some salient directions for future work.

First and most squarely, there are questions concerning the natural individual rights. Stanton was sanguine that the best interests of the individual and society (or the public good, in other language) always lay in the same direction. This postulate seemed to be an act of faith, in the debased sense of the term. I have nowhere found a statement of that view that went farther than its bare assertion, nowhere a consideration of the hard cases in which individual rights and social good seemed to diverge, so that we might be set more clearly on the trail of the meaning of this principle. It was evident how individual rights fit into the rest of her rational religion. Individual rights were sacred, high, and holy, because the cosmos was made up of individual atoms only incidentally related to one another. Sometimes she was sure that if the nation settled the score of individual rights firmly—that is, enacted legislation, social customs, families, and religion that embodied the individuality of women—all else would follow as automatically as the earth revolved around the sun, would follow "naturally," we might say.

This conjunction of the natural consequences of enshrining the true order with the question of individualism is no accident given Stanton's thought. It should alert us to the fundamental question of the status of a natural law theory with regard to feminism. It was Stanton's achievement that she rigorously and systematically articulated a natural law theory that emancipated women. In the tradition nature had mostly been weighed in to prove women's subordination. This was no small accomplishment. On the other hand, the great immutable laws cause no end of confusions in Stanton's own thought, contradictions that she was unable to resolve. Perhaps I ought to follow another principle of this great theorist and admit that the conservatives are right in this respect. We may be uneasy about the status of natural law on other grounds. Now that Stanton has done this work, nature has been called as evidence to prove *both* woman's subordination and woman's emancipation. This might lead one to suspect that no clear and unequivocal perspective on such questions will be forthcoming from nature. To put this another way, from within the context of twentieth-century social science: We may suspect that justice, should it ever reign, will be as artificial as injustice—since in fact all social arrangements have this character.

Such questions, bordering on historical and cultural relativism, raise sharply questions about the status of moral norms and principles. The natural laws and the individual rights that were a part of them were Stanton's means of establishing the grounds of ethical imperatives beyond the customs and laws of the day. They were, as Paul Ricoeur has pointed out, "a protestation," a means of establishing a moral perspective that did not capitulate to the status quo.[134] "*Sapere aude*" and "solitude of self" were critiques of a social order that took for granted certain roles and activities in the two sexes. There is almost a sense in which the individualism of the American tradition never applied to women, only to men. Since the purpose of this cosmological atomism was always to assert that individual women were of greater ethical importance than the relationships in which they were embedded, it was a powerful counter for the freedom of women as individual persons. Can we have a social view of humanity, as constituted by relationships in society, that does not reinstate women as primarily relational beings, defined and limited by the needs and wants of those around them, in contrast to their brothers? Can "autonomy" or individual rights find an ethical grounding from within a relational view as powerful as that articulated by the individualistic natural rights view on which Stanton drew?

In fact these relational/individual questions are hardest, it seems to me, when we consider the question of motherhood. It is odd to assert that Stanton's individualism was at its best on such questions, but that seems precisely the case. When she laid forth the proper order for considering such questions—individual in the cosmos, individual citizen, element of civilization, incidental relations—she relativized her claims regarding the mothering functions of women. This is, I think, the best and most systematic reading of Stanton's position. It seems, however, that it was also the way Stanton tried to eat her cake and have it too—that, in other words, it was where her systematic synthesis broke down. When Stanton spoke about the transformations to occur in American society with the elevation, education, and enfranchisement of women, it was almost always because of some quality she associated with motherhood. We might say today that even that group of women who are or will be mothers may disagree sharply on what that *means* to them, and that it may be well for the women's movement to have some tools of thought that can allow that diversity to appear in creative ways.

The fundamental claim that the right of each individual soul to self-development was the heart of the suffragist case (like the abolitionist or manhood suffrage cases) is alive and well among feminists today. The right of "self-sovereignty" appears not only in the contemporary demand to control one's body, but in more general claims to control one's destiny. There are realms of life in which personal freedom, self-sovereignty as opposed to rule by others, is intrinsic. It may well be that in order to address, with perceptiveness and precision, the ethical problems raised by the situation of women in American life, one requires more than a single fundamental principle—that one must specify the arenas of life and society in which distinct principles are paramount.

The religious valorization of the processes of thinking in Stanton's perspective is one of the most interesting and creative aspects of her work. For women to think about their experiences and situation was a fundamentally ethical and religious act, the source of enlightenment comparable only to the Reformation. That Stanton had this notion at all is fascinating in the midst of a period that many historians have characterized as anti-intellectual. What was important here was not simply that Stanton defended women's capacity to reason in the face of overwhelming stereotypes to the contrary. It was especially her defense of the notion that women had clear perceptions of justice, especially in their own cases. This may well be the single most important aspect of Stanton's work.

On the other hand, there is more than one problem about the ways she thematized such discussions. I have discussed certain facets of these problems, such as the relationship among thinking, science, and philosophy. Her work occurred before the methodological self-consciousness of science and the attendant discussions among social scientists as to how far the scientist may free himself or herself from self-interest. She was uncritical of the problems of applying science to life, as she put it—and certainly uncritical of the quandaries regarding the presuppositions of the human scientist in formation of theory and hypothesis.

These problems are exacerbated for a contemporary ethicist when we recall Stanton's comments regarding the relationship of science to religion. The marriage feast of these two human activities that she foresaw has been postponed, perhaps indefinitely; in quarters where there has not been a hostile divorce, an amicable separation seems to be widely accepted as the best solution. The relationship of facts to religion, and of empirical generalizations to religion, seems in most quarters nonexistent.

Central to the operative notion of thinking in Stanton's work was analogy. Her logic functioned to enunciate a truth in one area, and then to elaborate the analogy with women. Here was a truth from democratic theory: just so with women. Here was a truth from the abolitionist struggle: just so with women. Here was a truth from electromagnetic fields: just so with the sexes. If a statement was true, it applied to women also. This concern with analogy is familiar to the current women's movement as well. How far can such analogies and comparisons, for example, between sexism and other social causes hold? Stanton claimed that sexism was more odious than other social issues, because of the specific nature of the oppressed group—because they were mothers of the oppressors. The metaphor of slavery was not far from any suffragist's tongue. (Slavery was not far from the labor movement's tongue, either, as in "wage slavery.") On what basis is one to argue or discern how far the analogies are warranted and when they become dysfunctional?

Analogies functioned in other ways as well in Stanton's thought. The family, for example, was but the state in miniature, and women were, she thought, well aware how unfit men were to govern there, particularly in matters of education and punishment. Motherhood became ever larger in Stanton's view of women. The mother-child relationship became the analog of the relationship of the lawmaker or law enforcer to the criminal (or the upright to those in vice, the intelligent to the ignorant). This was problematic in two ways at once in Stanton's work. It vitiated her democratic claims, since the lawmaker and the lawbreaker no longer were two equal adults. Also, however, these notions served more and more to characterize women as though they all were mothers, which Stanton abhorred in principle, since some women were never mothers.

The problems of analogy in the reasoning process, and the subsequent problems of empirical investigation and ethics, are matched by the unresolved problems in Stanton's work regarding the relationship of emotion to reason—and therefore, of emotion to ethics. This latter point particularly is not one in which Stanton stands alone; one may search in vain the discussions of twentieth-century ethicists for guidance as to emotion and ethics. It is a concern with some creative potential in Stanton's thought. Women's feelings of dissatisfaction clearly were ethical counters on which she relied heavily; rebellion, indignation, humiliation were all evidence that something was morally awry. And the love of freedom burning in one's breast and the sighs and glances with which women communicated their status were occasions of ethical discernment. Here is matter for further ethical investigation.

Stanton's particular brand of civil religion was a strikingly prominent part of her thought. The right to think, solitude of self, the great immutable laws, and the God of justice, mercy, and truth were the more general grounds on which Stanton could say that politics was the most exalted of all sciences and that the ballot box was the holy of holies of the republic. They were counters of the cosmological structure that proved that the order of late-nineteenth-century America was nothing more than chaos, doomed rather than immortal.

This redescription of Victorian civilization constituted the grounds on which she said "to woman it is given to save the republic." A portion of this suffragist messianism resulted from her sense of the masculine/feminine elements of civilization, for women represented a "new element" that had never before had its day in the life of the nation. Stanton did not rest her case sheerly with this description of the sexes; she usually qualified these statements by saying that we do not really know what women are like under these conditions. The integration of the two sexes in all walks of life was also important, because they had a mutually vivifying or uplifting influence on each other. This sounds very good, but it depends really on what is meant by it, and under some meanings it seems, today, to be empirically untrue. In education, for example, it seems that integrating the sexes in college life has not had the positive effect on women's achievement that Stanton sought—though there is much controversy surrounding "fear of success." In mixed sex conversation as well, there is a certain amount of evidence that in comparison with same-sex conversation, creativity decreases and conformity rises when men and women are together. This surely is not the uplifting influence that Stanton sought; though we have little notion of what she might have thought of "creativity," she was not fond of conformity. It is not at all clear *why* these results occur, but today the arguments regarding "integration" and "segregation" of the sexes are more complicated than even Stanton thought they were.

Stanton herself created some of the confusions between democracy and suffrage theory with her strong statement that there were no new political principles to be articulated in the feminist struggle, only old ones to be applied to new cases. Even within the pages of *HWS* and Stanton's own memoirs, there is a sense of something amiss with this thought. Stanton said in her later life that she did not want simply to purvey "worn-out opinions." *HWS* similarly introduced its printing of "Solitude of Self" with the statement that it was presented *instead* of the "old arguments so many times repeated."[135]

While this interest in novel arguments may represent a variety of things—the banality that attends many years of careful polishing of the republican principles, a stereotypically feminine inconstancy, faddism in reforming circles—I suggest that it was in part an insight into the condition that "old principles newly applied" was not only what is at stake with women's rights.

This is perhaps clearer with the hindsight that a bicentennial celebration of American achievements brings than it was a century earlier. Today it is frighteningly possible that the Equal Rights Amendment bequeathed to us by the suffragists may require *another* century of struggle before its passage. Today the social sciences have taught us a great deal about the psychological mechanisms of sexual and social relationships. The quest for feminist legitimacy in terms of the American democratic ideology encountered stumbling blocks of "irrational prejudice" and "out-worn customs" whose depth in the American political consensus it was not able to gauge and to which the classic statements were not adequate as an alternative.

Stanton's Enlightenment roots are most evident in her desire for a more *rational* religion. We do not understand that rational religion unless we see that the equality of woman was its central component. No religion could be true, scientific, logical if it denigrated the female sex. Twentieth-century scholarship has seriously damaged the notion that rationality is the supremely desirable quality of any religion. But Stanton's nearly positivist understanding of rationality, and justice for women, may be separated from each other. We might also ask—for these notions were inseparable for her—is justice itself a rational virtue? Such points, however, are not intended to imply that either religion or justice is necessarily antirational, irrational. Rather, they open spaces in which differing modes of rationality, or perhaps reasonableness, may be appreciated. Stanton did not (and perhaps could not on her premises) appreciate enthusiasm and emotion in religious matters; nor the peculiar qualities of myth, symbol, and ritual. It remains to be seen, however, how far affirmations of the diversity of religious sensibility can cohere with justice to women.

The clearest thing about Stanton's civil religion, however, was that it was to substitute for the Christian churches. It was odd, in some respects, that Stanton should have moved away from the churches at precisely the time theological liberalism was looming larger in those bodies. Her rejection of original sin was one that many good church people found congenial in the late nineteenth century. In part, however, Stanton anticipated these comments on her position; that isolated individuals should concur with her was not adequate, she pointed out, to the demands of justice. Alas, eighty-odd years after Stanton's death, the denominations are still slow to come to her position. It has taken well into the twentieth century for major denominations to ordain women to the clergy—Presbyterians, United Methodists, Episcopalians, and Lutherans[136]—and there remain ecclesiastical bodies that will not do so as a matter of principle.

In this matter of the churches versus some other sort of religion, Stanton put her finger on a spot that remains exceedingly sore among feminists. Conflicts and painful disagreements persist as to whether the American churches can ever be just and hospitable places for women, and as to the extent and seriousness of sexism in the theologies of American Christendom. Only the last decade has witnessed appreciable numbers of women entering the theological schools of mainline American Protestantism; "feminist theology" has only just been born. We cannot settle here the deeply knotted questions of women's participation in churches; certainly no one can "settle" such questions outside of personal considerations of integrity, commitment, assessments of likelihood of change, etc. Among contemporary feminists who remain related to churches, I find (and I feel) the importance of keeping such questions alive, of "settling" them in some proximate, rather than some final, fashion. Today, similarly, feminists who reject American Christianity are far less likely than Stanton to find the civil religion an appropriate alternative; menstrual rituals and women's art seem far more viable options to many women.

And yet one can wonder about this. American society has, it seems, a voracious capacity to initiate and co-opt small-scale religious experiments. One can wonder, indeed, about the relationship of such explicitly religious phenomena to social change toward justice. As I show in the next chapters, there were yet other possibilities for religion with regard to the woman suffrage, or feminist, activities if we are not uncritical of the notion of religion itself in such matters.

Susan Brownell Anthony: Toward a Theology for a Feminist Praxis

> I would rather *make* history than write it.
> Susan B. Anthony

> Miss Anthony's love of justice links her with the divine.
> Clara Bewick Colby

Susan B. Anthony too operated from a religious stance regarding her lifelong efforts for woman's emancipation. Though certain aspects of her thought show Stanton's influence, and though Anthony constantly sought to point away from herself toward her esteemed friend, there is sufficient discontinuity between them to require a separate analysis.

Less systematic than her old friend, Anthony was in several respects more interesting and creative. Though she looked to Stanton's pen to weld suffragist insights and policies into polished literary form, Anthony had a gift for political rhetoric that was of a different order from Stanton's. While her arguments are somewhat unwieldy, her short phrases are striking: "Pray with your ballots"—"My work is my worship"—"Men who fail to be just to their mothers cannot be expected to be just to each other"—"There is not the woman born who desires to eat the bread of dependence"—"Failure is impossible." These and other sloganlike phrases, like the perpetual underlining of words for emphasis in her written hand, give us glimpses of her character. Stanton was quite right to say that it was "into Miss Anthony's private correspondence one must look for examples of her most effective writings."[1] She was ever the activist, ever the democrat. Far less elitist than Stanton, she rarely sang the praises of science or upward progress.

Woman's powerlessness, dependence, or subjection was to Anthony the synonym for the "injustice" of our "question-answer" framework of analysis. To this she invariably opposed woman's "emancipation"—and the parallels to slavery were both vivid to and self-consciously addressed by her. An agent for the Garrisonian wing of the abolitionist movement in upstate New York, she was greatly influenced by the policies and wisdom of the editor of the *Liberator*. Like Stanton, Anthony was given to listing the dimensions of the social order in which woman's degradation was to be found and in which corresponding efforts for her emancipation were to be made. Anthony, however, saw them differently from her friend. To Stanton's familial, social, political, and religious strands of bondage must be juxtaposed Anthony's political, industrial, and social analyses. Unlike Stanton, she did not analyze these aspects of society autonomously from one another. Anthony found a particular importance in enunciating the industrial, or as we would say today, the economic, aspects of woman's dependence. "Votes and money" was the archimedean lever by which woman's position was to be reformed—and by which woman's reform activities were to be efficacious.

Anthony believed in the redemption of the human world by the moral power of voting and monied womanhood. Her greatest interest for me, however, is less this eschatological vision than the consistency with which she maintained the view that it was reform work, and especially that for equal rights for women, which was "wholly spiritual," indeed an act of worship on her part. This act of worship was not directed so much to the creator of the immutable laws to which Stanton gave her allegiance as to the deity of her Quaker heritage. While this divine presence was, in keeping with the Friend's position, perceived in inwardness, it was also especially encountered in the association with other women seeking a noble purpose in action.

As with Stanton, I begin with a short biographical summary to set the context for Anthony's thought. The next section, "Women's Powerlessness," is an exposition of the definition of the issue as Anthony saw it. To Anthony, women's powerlessness was a broad matter, demonstrating the intertwinement of several aspects of human life in America, including the personal attitudes and feelings of women. She exhorted women to a life of action, of political involvement. "Tame Submission to the Evils Around Them" explores Anthony's particularly astute and intimate understanding of action for women, as well as her trial for voting, one of her characteristically forthright personal acts. I next consider her clear portrayal of the economic dimension of the issue. "The Bread of Dependence" is explored and Anthony's ambiguous efforts to organize workingwomen's associations. "Social Purity" considers a no less characteristic Anthony appeal against "social evils." In the language of the day, "social" verged on "sexual," and this thread of her analysis addressed, fearlessly for the Victorian age, venereal disease, prostitution, rape, bigamy, spouse murder, and infanticide, all of which were traced to their roots in woman's dependence. These three dimensions of her analysis were entangled with each other.

The third major section of this chapter, "Injustice and Justice," pauses to look at the shape of the "answer" to my "question." Here I look at Anthony's stance as an example of *Fiat Iustitia Pereat Mundus*—"let justice be done though the world may perish."

The fourth section, "The Needs of the Oppressed," spells out Anthony's religious view. The social policy of "agitation" for women's rights became a theological position that may be compared with contemporary liberation theology. "Prayer by Action" looks at her explicitly this-worldly social action view of religion. "Freedom of Religion" considers her left-wing Reformation view that dissent in religion was itself of religious importance. And "With Such Women as These" considers themes in her work that we might today call "sisterhood" as a locus of the religious. The final section, in conclusion, finishes my exploration of Anthony's social thought with some critical comments and conclusions.

Biographical Summary

Susan Brownell Anthony (1820-1906) was brought up by an unconventional Quaker family in upstate New York. Unlike Stanton, whose faithful colleague and friend she was to become, Anthony faced no familial opposition to her suffrage work. Her parents' adherence to suffrage and abolition causes preceded her own; they attended the first women's rights convention and signed its Declaration of Sentiments before Anthony herself was attached to the cause. The Anthonys encouraged, supported, and often financed their daughter's work throughout her life. The family home was frequented by reformers such as Garrison, Pillsbury, Mayo, Douglass, Phillips, and W. H. Channing (pastor of the Unitarian Church in Rochester to which the family transferred their membership).

For fifteen years, Anthony earned her living as a schoolteacher, leaving that career only for full-time devotion to various struggles for justice. Her initial exposure to public work came through the Daughters of Temperance, but she soon deserted that cause for the twin struggles of blacks' and women's rights. Her employment history, however, was not irrelevant to her reform work. Beginning in 1853, when she set the New York State Teacher's Convention on its ear by attempting to speak in discussion, that assembly was an annual forum for her resolutions regarding equality in education for blacks and women throughout the 1850s. One of the last public acts of her life was to insure coeducation at the University of Rochester, an effort her biography credited with breaking her health.

In 1854, she made her debut as an indefatigable and indispensable activist, systematizing a New York organization to respond to the state legislature's rebuff of women's property and custody rights. In this campaign, she was dubbed the "Napoleon of the movement," a title that stuck throughout her career. In the 1850s, she was New York State's "general agent" for the American Anti-Slavery Society, and met her trial by mob along with the many antislavery speakers whose campaigns she scheduled and assisted. A Garrisonian, she was passionately committed to principles such as "no union with slaveholders" and "no compromise." The parallels between the two movements were vivid to Anthony. Opposition to the Fugitive Slave Law was readily transferred to sheltering a fugitive battered woman from the forces of her husband, the law, and pressure from abolitionist allies who did not perceive the parallel. She stood firmly, one of the few white abolitionists to do so, committed to opposing racial discrimination in northern cities as well as to ending slavery.

After the postwar split within suffrage ranks, Anthony edited and financed the NWSA paper *The Revolution*. During its brief stormy life, that organ frankly discussed a wide range of taboo topics, including infanticide, prostitution, and labor unions. It did not hesitate to take sides on controversial cases of the hour; its position on Victorian scandals did nothing for its commercial success. In addition, Anthony attempted to create a workingwomen's association. The paper's failure committed her to six years' work to repay its debts.[2] Her diary summed up the efforts of 1871: "6 months of constant travel, full 8,000 miles, 108 lectures. The year's full work 13,000 miles travel—170 meetings."[3]

Her lecture tours culminated in 1875 in the systematic treatment of two themes that had long been brewing in her mind. "Bread and the Ballot" sounded the characteristic Anthony call to women's financial independence; "Social Purity" fearlessly discussed divorce, rape, adultery, infanticide, venereal disease, and prostitution—topics that outraged the nineteenth-century's notions of maidenly delicacy.

Ever a woman of action, Anthony, along with a handful of women elsewhere in the country, attempted to force the issue of woman suffrage by court action in the early 1870s. After a series of women's rights conventions had argued that women were already enfranchised by the Fourteenth Amendment, Anthony cast a Republican ballot in the election of 1872. This act, in conjunction with the ensuing trial (cleverly manipulated by the judge so as not to allow the constitutional issues to arise), consolidated the suffragist realization that none of the preceding remedies of law would suffice to enfranchise women. To achieve a specific amendment to the Constitution became so characteristic of her every effort thereafter that suffrage followers called it, through its successive numerical designations, the "Anthony Amendment."

More than any other activist of her generation, it was Anthony who provided the continuity of the movement. She sought out bright, articulate, promising young women (such as the Reverend Anna Howard Shaw), nurtured their talent, and assured a generation to carry on after the feminist "pioneers." She made sure that suffrage history was a regular part of annual convention activities to educate the newcomers. Becoming "Aunt Susan" to hundreds of the younger women—and eventually to the country as a whole—she was at times fiercely maternal about her "girls," her "half-fledged chickens." By the time of her death in 1906, she had so richly succeeded that her last public words became part of the suffrage legend. Usually only a part of that last speech is remembered: "Failure is impossible." Characteristically, Anthony's comment was a tribute to the rising generation: "With such women consecrating their lives—failure is impossible."

It is sometimes said that Anthony, among others, was responsible for narrowing the feminist platform to the single-minded capture of the ballot. Indeed, as she wrote to one collaborator of the 1890s in preparation for the next convention:

> I want it to be on the one and *sole point* of *women disfranchised*—separate and alone—and *not* mixed up with—or one of—19 *other points of protest*—each of the 19 good and proper perchance—but the very moment we put temperance, land monopoly, labor and capital, anything, however good and needed—we sink woman's *claim to* equality of rights and civil and political down to the common level of the others—whereas we must keep our claim first and most important overshadowing every other.[4]

157

But her earlier concerns for other dimensions of the issue did not altogether desert her in the final decades of her life. In the 1890s, she opposed the nation's lynching campaigns as she had once fought slavery; her solidarity with working people was celebrated when the Knights of Labor made her an honorary member.

Anthony suffered, perhaps more than any other single individual in the women's movement, from the period's stereotypes of female appearance and behavior. She dressed severely, initially from Quaker policy, later perhaps from habit or taste. Her speech was always straightforward, brief, and direct, in contrast to the euphemisms and florid circumlocutions expected of the women of her day. Ever unmarried, despite a series of reported proposals, she was castigated, mocked, stereotyped, and lied about by the press everywhere, the object of personal contumely that Stanton's maternal status and respectable appearance did not provoke.

She is supremely remembered as the organizer of the suffrage movement—its "hands and feet," where Stanton was seen as its "head" (and Lucretia Mott its "heart"). Anthony herself frequently concurred in such a view. She spoke of her work on one occasion as "subsoil plowing."[5] On another, she said, "I have been as a hewer of wood and a drawer of water to this movement. I know nothing and have known nothing of oratory or rhetoric."[6] Her firsthand political experience remains daunting in its scope and length. She spent fifty-odd years of her life agitating for reform, enticing others to join her, and doing the tedious "common work" of reform movements. She engaged speakers, laid out their itineraries in statewide campaigns, arranged publicity both before and after the fact, spoke and lectured herself times beyond enumeration, frequently to hostile crowds. She was interminably fund-raising to forward the cause of agitation. She went door-to-door with petitions; she arranged and gave testimony to congressional committees both state and national; she buttonholed congressmen and more than one president; she demanded a suffrage plank on the platforms of political parties of all sorts. Hers was, of course, a major voice in the creation of suffrage strategies.

Perhaps it is Anthony's outstanding talent as an activist that makes the temptation constant for anyone working on this woman's contribution to speak of her character—that old reliable theme of the nineteenth century. Nothing is more characteristic of the comments about her in the annals of the suffrage records, and in newspapers of the period, whether for good or ill. For this woman's character was a "grand large one" (in the speech of the day); it is easy to see why it provoked adulatory biographies and tributes, though some of the latter should be discounted as a peculiar "genre" of the period. Reading of her "life and work," even in an uncritical treatment, *does* provoke a certain astonishment and admiration. The endurance and energy she brought to the suffrage movement were unsurpassed in either her times or ours. The mere lists of places where she spoke in any given year, even into her seventies, wear away at the reader's sensibility like so many constant drops of water on stone. Yet however important character may be to ethical matters, there is a sense in which contemporaries, not successors, are its best judge.[7] The assessment of Anthony's character, in any case, is not the object of this study.

Rather, I seek here to assess Susan Anthony's thought and theory about women's rights, an exercise in which her contemporaries rarely engaged.[8] As Harriet Stanton Blatch put it, Anthony was "a Deed, not a thinking."[9] To be sure, this task is not so readily accomplished as with Stanton. The standard of consistency and systemization that the latter set is too high for most other suffragists, and perhaps for most other theorists actively engaged in struggle. Anthony's own theoretical efforts were more occasional than systematic—not sporadic, but stimulated by particular occasions, events, campaigns, audiences, individuals, queries. This occasional nature of her work imposes certain specific disciplines on the work of interpretation. But the occasional theorist is not on that account chaotic or inconsistent. One can discern broad outlines in Anthony's thought, thematic emphases that cohere and persist reasonably throughout the vicissitudes of period, popularity, etc.

The lack of critical studies of Anthony's thought is also partly due to the nature of the intimacy between Stanton and Anthony. Since these two women collaborated so closely, it is difficult at times to ascribe responsibility to one or the other for particular thoughts. In her own estimation a less than adequate public speaker, Anthony embarked on lecture tours only when she could not cajole another into doing it or accompanying her—or when she was in great need of money. Frequently she asked Stanton to "load her cannon" so that she might fire in Stanton's absence. She called Stanton her "sentence-maker" and "pen-artist."[10]

For example, Stanton wrote the essay on education that Anthony delivered at the 1853 New York State Teacher's Convention.[11] Equally, at the other end of their long suffrage careers, Stanton wrote several papers delivered by Anthony at the Columbian Exposition in 1893. It is not at all clear, however, which of these two women authored the other manuscripts that reside in Anthony's papers. Where authorship is in doubt, I have tried to leave those speeches out of consideration here. Stanton wrote of their collaboration that "like husband and wife, each has the feeling that we must have no differences in public."[12] This book attempts to sort out some of the differences these two may have had in private. But specific authorship is not always the primary or the most important question. It is rather that there is a pattern, a shape, if you will, to Anthony's thought, which is frequently in contrast to the pattern or shape of Stanton's thought.[13]

Reconstructing Anthony's thought, therefore, is a delicate but not impossible task. We are aided by an early biographer, Ida Husted Harper, who worked with Anthony's cooperation if not her imprimatur. Harper specifically indicates some material authored solely by Anthony.[14] The suffragist's own prolific letters and journals are another clue to her personal style and characteristic emphases when she was operating spontaneously or singly. Occasionally her unprepared remarks at some political gathering were recorded. They provide sufficient evidence for discerning a number of themes unshared by Stanton, or articulated in a fashion strikingly different—her economic emphases, for example, or her specific remarks on the importance of action.[15] Because of these hermeneutical problems attending this collaboration, I have drawn attention, especially in footnotes, to areas of discernible disagreement and discernible agreement between these two figures.

On the questions of religion that are at the heart of this book, Anthony and Stanton diverged as they did on no other topic. It is well known that Anthony opposed the anticlericalism of Stanton's later years. She tried to persuade her friend that the church had progressed as much as any other institution. It might be said that such a rift represented a tactical difference. That was the interpretation of Ida Husted Harper, who claimed that "Miss Anthony felt that it would arouse criticism and prejudice at the very beginning."[16] As I show below, it was rather a principled disagreement resulting from divergent theological positions. Stanton's theoretical approach insisted on demystifying certain ideas; Anthony's praxis orientation saw that action in the world would free women's thought.

Thus, while there is some danger of overestimating the disagreements between them, it exists particularly in the area of their social analysis, their definition of the issue, rather than in their religious thought. The approach followed here, therefore, offers one of the few, if not the only, means for disentangling these two whose hearts, if not their minds, were "eternally wedded." The thought of Anthony offers more hope for thinking about women's friendships, and their central role in religious thought, than Stanton's notion of an "imaginary Robinson Crusoe" woman.

Women's Powerlessness

The issue Susan B. Anthony confronted with her decades of suffrage activism was one she firmly attached to "all good causes," like many another antebellum reformer pursuing abolition, prison reform, rescue of prostitutes, peace, industrial change, and religious transformation all at once. At the turn of the century, when the fate of the Philippines, Hawaii, and Puerto Rico were being weighed in the national balance, Anthony was furious with the younger generation's refusal to speak up on such questions and to link them with woman suffrage. She wrote Clara Bewick Colby,

> I really believe I shall explode if some of you young women don't wake up and raise your voice in protest. . . . I wonder if when I am under the sod—or cremated and floating in the air—I shall have to stir you and others up. How can you not be all on fire?[17]

Anthony found it both congenial and necessary to be "all on fire" for a variety of public questions because of her particular approach to suffrage. She believed that the issue to which her life's work was addressed as the "cause of causes."[18] "The cause of nine-tenths of all the misfortunes which come to women, and to men also," she said, "lies in the subjection of women, and therefore the important thing is to lay the axe at the root."[19] To put it positively, she claimed that "woman suffrage is the one great principle underlying all reforms."[20]

The terms on which she effected this synthesis varied from time to time. In a letter of solidarity to a black meeting in New York City in 1903, protesting black disfranchisement in the South, she was glad to join with those who were "like sufferers" with women. But the trouble lay "farther back and deeper" than simply the disfranchisement of one race.

> When men deliberately refused to include women in the Fourteenth and Fifteenth Amendments to the National Constitution they left the way open for all forms of injustice to other and weaker men and peoples. Men who fail to be just to their mothers cannot be expected to be just to each other. The whole evil

comes from the failure to apply equal justice to all mankind, men and women alike.[21]

On the issue of international peace, she was equally single-minded; and her principle was the same.

There is no possible hope of justice among the nations of the world while there is such gross injustice inside of the highest and best Government of them all. Peace and arbitration are the outgrowth of justice, and while one-half of the people of the United States are robbed of their inherent right of personal representation in this freest country on the face of the globe, it is idle for us to expect that the men who thus rob women will not rob each other as individuals, corporations, and Governments.[22]

At other times, she argued that humanitarian reforms, that staggering list of activities on which women were working "with might and main" to alleviate the "horrors of our semi-barbaric conditions," was work "without knowledge," mere "man-appointed missions," for they failed to deal directly with women's rights.

That cause, that underlying disease producing a bewildering myriad of differing symptoms, was woman's dependence, woman's powerlessness, woman's subjection. These phrases were synonymous to Anthony. Sometimes, revealing the powerful grip the antislavery struggle held on her image of reform work, she called it "sex-slavery."[23] Just as the "peculiar institution" had come to a halt with the Emancipation Proclamation, so she thought that the "answer" to this injustice was women's emancipation. (She wrote President Roosevelt in 1902 that sponsoring the woman suffrage amendment "would be as noble an act as the Emancipation Proclamation of Abraham Lincoln, and would render [him] immortal."[24]) The abolitionists' struggle provided Anthony with specific terms on which she spoke of woman suffrage.

I find three "strands"—to use Stanton's language—in Anthony's social analysis. Inaction, or "tame submission," was a forthrightly political dimension of Anthony's view of the situation of women. Hence in the first section, I explore her view of the "energetic doing of noble deeds" that women required, and her trial for voting. Second, I look at Anthony's economic analysis. Last, I glance at her view of the "social evil."

A. Tame Submission to the Evils Around Them

As the "Napoleon of the Movement," as William Henry Channing dubbed her, Anthony had extraordinary political experience and acumen. Whether or not she possessed the theoretical capacities to systematize her insights, her comments to women and on the subject of women contain a series of reflections on the life of action. These insights are noteworthy for their discernment in interpreting a political way of life to women in the idiom of the nineteenth century, when women had little or no inside exposure to the practice of politics.

The notion of women's powerlessness was directly expressed in Anthony's view of this first aspect of the servitude endured by women. Inaction, acquiescence as a sort of moral slumber, "tame submission to the evils around them,"[25] was at the heart of the need to struggle for the vote. Sometimes she indicated that women lived a "hot-house existence"[26] away from the struggles of the world and politics. The lure of domesticity was one that even this indefatigable reformer felt. "It is so easy to feel your power for public work slipping away if you allow yourself to remain too long snuggled in the Abrahamic bosom of home. It requires great will-force to resurrect one's soul."[27] The coziness of private intimacy was not the only source of women's bondage, however. The lack of self-respect, the lack of allegiance to themselves as women first, idle wishes—all could intervene to keep women from action. Whatever the contributing facts to women's powerlessness, however, "she who would be free, herself must strike the blow."[28]

One of the finest paragraphs to roll from Anthony's pen made several of these points in conjunction. It was, alas, not part of a public presentation. A letter to an English organization, summing up the American state of affairs on women's rights in 1870, lamented the inactivity of the suffrage movement due to the "management of mere politicians" and the expediency of Republicans before the election. Nothing less than some stinging blow, she thought, would move the organizations out of this false security and complacency:

> So while I do not pray for anybody or any party to commit outrages, still I do pray, and that earnestly and constantly, for some terrific shock to startle the women of this nation into a self-respect which will compel them to see the abject degradation of their present position; which will force them to break their yoke of bondage, and give them faith in themselves; which will make them proclaim their allegiance to woman first; which will enable them to see that man can no more feel, speak, or act for woman than could the old slaveholder for his

slave. The fact is, women are in chains, and their servitude is all the more debasing because they do not realise it. O, to compel them to see and feel, and to give them the courage and conscience to speak and act for their own freedom, though they face the scorn and contempt of all the world for doing it![29]

This comment recalled the galvanizing effect of the Fugitive Slave Law of 1850 on reform activity—and perhaps also Garrison's public burning of that law, several judicial decisions, and the United States Constitution itself. Women needed to be roused, to be stirred up, to be awakened from the moral complacency of the times concerning themselves.

I would exhort all women to be discontented with their present condition, and to assert their individuality of thought, word, and action by the energetic doing of noble deeds. Idle wishes, vain repinings, loud-sounding declamations never can bring freedom to any human soul.[30]

This view of moral slumber was the reason for the policy of agitation. Women needed to be "startled" into self-respect, whether by reformers or some external event. Self-respect, individuality asserted, meant to refuse "tame submission." It meant to act and to rouse others to action. It meant especially action for justice, for removing the chains, visible or invisible, that bound human beings in tyranny.

"Agitation" came from a particular brand of antebellum activism. The abolitionist activity of Anthony's family was among the Garrisonians. Agitation was an ethically and religiously based approach to social change that found compromise unacceptable. Her comments on Garrison were unstintingly positive precisely for this reason.

Had the accident of birth given me place among the aristocracy of sex, I doubt not that I should be an active, zealous advocate of Republicanism; unless perchance, I had received that higher, holier light which would have lifted me up to the sublime height where now stand Garrison, Phillips, and all that small but noble band whose motto is "No Union with Slaveholders."[31]

Followers of Garrison brooked no limitation on their language, arguments, or actions because of their unpopularity in the eyes of public opinion.[32]

Anthony's journal recorded her a spokeswoman for the notion that Christ was an agitator:

A young Quaker preacher from Virginia, who happened to be there, said: "Christ was no agitator, but a peacemaker; George Fox was no agitator; the Friends of the South follow these examples and are never disturbed by fanaticism." This was more than I could bear; I sprung to my feet and quoted: "I came into the world not to bring peace but a sword. . . . Woe unto you, scribes and Pharisees, hypocrites that devour widow's houses!" Read the New Testament and see if Christ was not an agitator. Who is this among us crying "peace, peace, when there is no peace?"—and sat down.[33]

Indeed, her diary spoke of Garrison as the "most Christ-like man" she had ever met, because of his actions, his deeds of "Christian benevolence" as opposed to mere "belief."[34]

It was because of her intimate understanding of action that Anthony sought the ballot for women. Women urgently needed to be involved in reform work as part of the prescription for their dependency. Even the WCTU could be an avenue of healthy activity.

She was sure that with a modicum of reform experience, women would soon discover that "kind words, entreaties, and tears avail nothing. Any and every reform work is sure to lead women to the ballot-box."[35] Women fighting to reform society would soon stumble over their own powerlessness and would see the prime necessity of seeking their own power, of being "armed with weapons equal to those of the enemy—votes and money."[36] Tears and prayers, the means by which women were to exercise their "influence" on the public life of Victorian America, would give way to "prayer by action."

Such qualifications were rare with Anthony. Following conscience, maintaining one's self-respect, choosing principles over expediency were the guidelines she set for women's "noble deeds." Her abolitionist training in the school of "No Compromise" was a lesson to which Anthony cleaved even when her erstwhile allies and teachers did not. During the Civil War, when even hard-line abolitionists of old were caught up in the war fervor, she wrote to Anna Dickinson in one of many attempts to keep that popular public orator on the right track:

It seems to me that *Liberator* and *Standard* are gone "stark mad" in their echo of the politicians' cry—"Save the Union." We read no more of the good old doctrine "Of two evils choose neither"—"Do the right and trust the consequences with God."[37]

While it may be a truism that one of the fundamental points of women's rights was to encourage and support women to act, Anthony's fervent espousal of action for women was of a specific sort. She looked to women for "noble deeds" similar to those done in the abolitionist struggle. There are a series of themes to which she regularly returned in articulating this dimension of her work among women: I have described how the motive force of action was found in *moral discontent* with the world. Now I look at several others. (1) One's *conscience*, the "inner light" of Quakers, guided such actions; (2) from conscience was forged adherence to a high moral *purpose*; (3) *courage* was necessary to follow these convictions despite whatever consequences would come; (4) only *"infinite patience"* would allow a reformer to endure to the end; and (5) women required faith in themselves and other women to follow this route.

In Anthony's view, the power of the orator Anna Dickinson (like that of "all true lives") lay in speaking "the absolute truth, not in echoing the popular cry of the multitude. And so long as you look *within* for guidance in the spirit and letter of your utterances, you are safe. To speak as will please the people is always failure."[38] "Expediency," that course of all mere politicians, was perhaps the dirtiest word in Anthony's vocabulary. She stood firmly through the worst years of the 1850s antislavery struggle, when the "masses" were "devoid of conscience and looking only for some new expedient to accomplish the desired good."[39] In those days, the abolitionists "alone . . . have lived the faith the [Founding] Fathers taught"; they were "the people's conscience" and "the real life of this Nation."[40] Of the Civil War and the many bitter conflicts it created in the North, she was sure that "God is *not* in it—but now as of old in the 'still, small voice.' " That still, small voice was the only access to "truth, that will never err, however hard its promptings may be sometimes."[41] That the war brought former abolitionist fighters into harmony with the world around them was incomprehensible.

> I have tried hard to persuade myself that I alone remained mad, while all the rest had become sane, because I have insisted that it is our duty to bear not only our usual testimony but one even louder and more earnest than ever before. . . . The Abolitionists, for once, seem to have come to an agreement with all the world that they are out of tune and place, hence should hold their peace and spare their rebukes and anathemas. Our position to me seems most humiliating, simply that of the politicians, one of expediency, not the abandonment of all our meetings, and am more and more ashamed and sad that even the little Apostolic number have yielded to the world's motto—"the end justifies the means."[42]

In her later years, Anthony became more "politic" about the woman suffrage movement. She made calculations about the sections of the male voting public that could be repelled by certain suffrage arguments. She opposed Willard's bringing temperance literature into the 1896 suffrage drive in California—and Stanton's Bible arguments as well. Earlier she had diverted Stanton from an "open letter" on Frederick Douglass's marriage to a white woman.[43] But even in such cases it was to conscience she repaired as the final court of appeal:

The strongest argument to win the Prohibition men to vote for W.S.—is the very strongest one to drive from us the high license men—So the strongest testimony showing how all women's voting will lessen the ratio of the foreign vote and of the Catholic vote—is just the worst thing—in fact wholly estops all hope of winning the foreign born men's vote—and the Catholic vote—we are between two distracting dilemmas at every step—so I try to keep my talk on general principles—the bettering of women's chances for work and wages, tyranny of taxation—etc. etc.—but it is hardly possible to say anything—that will not hurt somebody—so each of us must be governed by our own true inwardness as to what and how to present our claims.[44]

To accomplish such noble deeds, "true inwardness" needed to be specified as goal or purpose in woman's life. Anthony regularly counseled women to take to their souls some high purpose and to pursue it in season and out. After a visit by a friend, she wrote,

I trust each will take to her soul a strong purpose and that on her tombstone shall be engraved her own name and her own noble deeds instead of merely the daughter of Judge Ormond, or the relict of some Honorable or D.D. When true womanhood shall be attained it will be spoken of and remembered for itself alone.[45]

Another letter from late in her life echoes this theme with regard to her own endeavors: "If I may be said to have made a success of my life, the one great element in it has been constancy of purpose—not allowing myself to be switched off the main road or tempted into bypaths of other movements."[46] Whatever constitutional or temperamental factors contributed to Anthony's ceaseless activity, she herself also attributed it to her strong adherence to a meaningful goal. Even on her few vacations she could not stop work long. When she did give herself over to relaxation, as on her sightseeing tour of Europe with Rachel Foster Avery, she became depressed and "blue . . . from having lived a purposeless life these three months."[47] Her well-known strictures on marriage to her suffragist colleagues came from this concern for women's pursuit of a meaningful, individually chosen, purpose: "I would not object to marriage if it were not that women throw away every plan and purpose of their own life, to conform to the plans and purposes of the man's life."[48] Uncharacteristically, this comment continued with a note of discouragement, which Anthony allowed herself only in the deepest privacy of her journals or in letters to most intimate confidantes. She added, "I wonder if it is woman's real, true nature always to abnegate self." Her belief in strong purposes was sometimes so fervent as to make her insist that their pursuit would triumph over any and all external forces.

> Institutions, among them marriage, are justly chargeable with many social and individual ills but, after all, the whole man or woman will rise above them. I am sure my "true woman" never will be crushed or dwarfed by them. Woman must take to her soul a purpose and then make circumstances conform to this purpose, instead of forever singing the refrain, "if and if and if!"[49]

Generally she was not so sanguine about individual capacities in the absence of institutional support. Money was a prime factor in her views of what was needed to do noble deeds. Her realism about the actual structural conditions underlying reform work was notable in an age singing the praises of "will-power."

To live from one's conscience meant following a series of ethical principles: the end does not justify the means; of two evils choose neither, etc. Her references to courage and conscience meant especially, "Do right and leave the consequences to God." It did not matter particularly to Anthony whether the consequences were hard for the nation or hard for one's personal fortunes. "Expediency" meant choosing a path that was workable in the short run; on a personal level, it meant choosing a course that was comfortable to the reformer, that risked little.[50] This Anthony rejected wholeheartedly, and with a consistency that her contemporaries could rarely match. Moral courage, moral strength, were necessary to face the opprobrium that came from choosing the path of conscience over the objection of multitudes.

> Every day brings to me new conceptions of life and its duties, and it is my constant desire that I may be strong and fearless, baring my arm to the encounter and pressing cheerfully forward, though the way is rough and thorny.[51]

Her private correspondence often echoed such themes.

> Cautious, careful people, always casting about to preserve their reputation and social standing, never can bring about a reform. Those who are really in earnest must be willing to be anything or nothing in the world's estimation, and publicly and privately, in season and out, avow their sympathy with despised and persecuted ideas and their advocates, and bear the consequences.[52]

The abolitionists' noble deeds in fighting the Fugitive Slave Law were no mere metaphors, empty comparisons, or mental images to Susan Anthony. The parallel was an immediate cause for action on women's rights. In 1860 she sheltered and hid the fugitive wife of a Massachusetts politician, a woman beaten, incarcerated in an insane asylum, and denied custody of her children by her husband. Abolitionists and colleagues in the suffrage movement added to the public outcry. Garrison wrote that her action was "hasty and ill-judged, no matter how well-meant," and urged discretion. Anthony replied that the consequences for the movement were irrelevant to her act.

> I cannot give you a satisfactory statement on paper, but I feel the strongest assurance that all I have done is wholly right. Had I turned my back upon her I should have scorned myself. In all those hours of aid and sympathy for that outraged woman I remembered only that I was a human being. That I should stop to ask if my act would injure the reputation of any movement never crossed my mind, nor will I now allow such a fear to stifle my sympathies or tempt me to expose her to the cruel, inhuman treatment of her own household. Trust me that as I ignore all law to help the slave, so will I ignore it all to protect an enslaved woman.[53]

To ignore all law was not the least of the conclusions that followed. Anthony was as willing to face the destruction of social institutions if that was the logical conclusion of her conscience's dictates. This was the policy especially of *The Revolution*. As Anthony put it to President Johnson when she invited him to subscribe to that short-lived but spunky journal,

> Mrs. Stanton and myself for two years have boldly told the Republican party that they must give ballots to women as well as to Negroes, and by means of *The Revolution* we are bound to drive the party to this logical conclusion or break it into a thousand pieces as was the old Whig party, unless we get our rights.[54]

This logic—like the "simple gospel logic" abolitionists had been drumming into people's heads[55]—could occasionally entrap Anthony and her cause itself in its toils. The case of her trial for voting in 1872 is a good example. In the early 1870s, suffrage proponents became convinced for a time that the Constitution already guaranteed women's right to vote. In her 1872 testimony to the Senate Judiciary Committee, Anthony obliquely announced her new policy: "Although I am a Quaker and take no oath, yet I have made a most solemn 'affirmation' that I would never again beg my rights."[56] Accordingly, on Election Day that year, along with a small group of Rochester friends and relatives, and a handful of women elsewhere in the country, Anthony went to the polls.

The trial was a serious travesty of the law and just missed being a farce. The judge refused to allow the jury to deliberate. (Cases against Anthony's codefendants were dismissed; the men who received their votes were given a presidential pardon from Ulysses S. Grant.)[57] When asked if she had any reason why sentence should not be pronounced, Anthony delivered herself so far as one can see of a wholly spontaneous, detailed argument for her rights as a citizen, over many protests from the judge.

> A: All my prosecutors, from the 8th Ward corner grocery politician, who entered the complaint, to the United States Marshall, Commissioner, District Attorney, District Judge, your honor on the bench, not one is my peer, but each and all are my political sovereigns; and had your honor submitted my case to the jury, as was clearly your duty, even then I should have had just cause of protest, for not one of those men was my peer; but, native or foreign, white or black, rich or poor, educated or ignorant, awake or asleep, sober or drunk, each and every man of them was my political superior; hence, in no sense, my peer. Even, under such circumstances, a commoner of England, tried before a jury of lords, would have far less cause to complain than should I, a woman, tried before a jury of men. Even my counsel, the Hon. Henry R. Selden, who has argued my cause so ably, so earnestly, so unanswerably before your honor, is my political sovereign. Precisely as no disfranchised person is entitled to sit upon a jury, and no woman is entitled to the franchise, so, none but a regularly admitted lawyer is allowed to practice in the courts, and no woman can gain admission to the bar—hence, jury, judge, counsel, must all be of the superior class.
>
> Judge Hunt: The Court must insist—the prisoner has been tried according to the established forms of law.
>
> A: Yes, your honor, but by forms of law all made by men, interpreted by men, administered by men, in favor of men, and against women; and hence, your honor's directed verdict of guilty, against a United States citizen for the

exercise of "that citizen's right to vote," simply because that citizen was a woman and not a man. But, yesterday, the same man-made forms of law declared it a crime punishable with $1,000 fine and six months' imprisonment, for you, or me, or any of us, to give a cup of cold water, a crust of bread, or a night's shelter to a panting fugitive as he was tracking his way to Canada. And every man or woman in whose veins course a drop of human sympathy violated that wicked law, reckless of consequences, and was justified in so doing. As then the slaves who got their freedom must take it over, or under, or through the unjust forms of law, precisely so now must women, to get their right to a voice in this Government, take it; and I have taken mine, and mean to take it at every possible opportunity.

Judge Hunt: The Court orders the prisoner to sit down. It will not allow another word.

A: When I was brought before your honor for trial, I hoped for a broad and liberal interpretation of the Constitution and its recent amendments, that should declare all United States citizens under its protecting aegis—that should declare equality of rights the national guarantee to all persons born or naturalized in the United States. But failing to get this justice—failing, even, to get a trial by jury *not* of my peers—I ask not leniency at your hands—but rather the full rigors of the law.

Judge Hunt: The Court must insist—(Here the prisoner sat down.)

Judge Hunt: The prisoner will stand up. (Here Miss Anthony arose again.) The sentence of the Court is that you pay a fine of one hundred dollars and the costs of the prosecution.

A: May it please your honor, I shall never pay a dollar of your unjust penalty. All the stock in trade I possess is a $10,000 debt, incurred by publishing my paper—*The Revolution*—four years ago, the sole object of which was to educate all women to do precisely as I have done, rebel against your man-made, unjust, unconstitutional forms of law, that tax, fine, imprison, and hang women, while they deny them the right of representation in the Government; and I shall work on with might and main to pay every dollar of that honest debt, but not a penny shall go to this unjust claim. And I shall earnestly and persistently continue to urge all women to the practical recognition of the old revolutionary maxim, that "Resistance to tyranny is obedience to God."

Judge Hunt: Madam, the Court will not order you committed until the fine is paid.[58]

These were ringing words, worthy of many a freedom fighter before or after. Many touches bear the stamp of Anthony's personality. "Awake or asleep, drunk or sober, each and every man of them was my political superior." The law was "made by men, interpreted by men, administered by men, in favor of men, and against women." Any slave who got to freedom did it "over, or under, or through the unjust law." To violate the unjust laws, from the motive of human sympathy, was to be justifiably "reckless of consequences." Equally the tradition of civil disobedience has often insisted upon bearing the "full rigors of the law." Audiences who hear this case re-enacted in feminist theater can hardly repress a thrill at "I shall never pay a dollar of your unjust penalty" or at the oratorical flourish of the ending, "Resistance to tyranny is obedience to God." The rub is there nevertheless. Because Anthony would not pay the fine, the case could not be appealed. While there may be plenty of reason to doubt that the Supreme Court would have upheld Anthony—any more than did the Senate her petition to strike the verdict—yet it renders this set piece of direct action something of a quandary. It is a good example of the well-known dilemmas of the ethics of conscience versus the ethics of responsibility. Should Anthony have stayed her moral outrage at the verdict in order to see the case appealed? It is a temptation for a later observer to begin a process of "second-guessing" the political tactics of the suffragist movement. But however one may differ from Anthony here, the position she took was in complete coherence with her desire to speak the "absolute truth," to be reckless of consequences, in the pursuit of justice.

"I shall earnestly and persistently urge all women to the practical recognition of the old revolutionary maxim, that 'Resistance to tyranny is obedience to God.' " No one was more persistent, more constant, in the struggle than Anthony. This sense of the importance of enduring to the end is a theme that can ring with surprisingly contemporary accents to a generation acquainted with burnout as ours is. Anthony saw the need for continual vigilance for women's rights. She frequently put revolutionary slogans to good use: "Women, remember: 'the price of liberty is eternal vigilance.' "[59] In 1902, when William Rainey Harper and a section of his University of Chicago faculty advocated the segregation of the sexes in differing classrooms, Anthony was interviewed by a reporter.

> Yes, we women have to fight continually for our rights and after we get them we have to watch constantly for fear they will be taken away just as we begin to feel safe and comfortable. . . . [Woman herself] has had to fight for every step gained, for every concession made, and it looks now as if she would have to fight ever more strenuously to maintain her hold on what she had obtained.[60]

She was clear that the struggle would, in its entirety, be a lengthy and protracted one. "Oh, if I could but live another century and see the fruition of all the work for women! There is so much yet to be done—I think of so many things I should like to do and say—but I must leave them for a younger generation."[61] Yet her sense that the success of the movement was assured was a firm one. When asked if women would obtain the vote, she replied,

Assuredly. I firmly believed at one time that I should live to see that day. I have never for one moment lost faith. It will come but I shall not see it—probably you will—it is inevitable. We can no more deny forever the right of self-government to one-half our people than we could keep the negro forever in bondage. It will not be wrought by the same disrupting forces that freed the slave, but come it will, and I believe within a generation.[62]

In order to "speak and act for their own freedom," women needed to have "faith in themselves . . . [and] proclaim their allegiance to woman first."[63] She conjured Anna Dickinson to devote herself to the suffrage cause, when that noted orator was, as Anthony saw it, being led astray into other fields, by invoking her "to speak out in words the deep, rich, earnest love for your own sex that I know lies in the inner courts of your being."[64] Women needed especially to "appreciate themselves and their work more than they do."[65] She exhorted women in fledgling labor organizations "to have every confidence in one another, and after they [had] formed a sure, stable, and reliable association, then take a firm stand."[66] Her sense that enduring in the cause would make failure impossible was one that she tied firmly to the presence of the other women in the NAWSA; in the last analysis, "sisterhood," to Anthony, was a religious theme.

B. The Bread of Dependence

Temperance organizing in the early 1850s taught Anthony the central place of money in the situation of women. In 1854, she retraced her steps over the state of New York to discover that of the many groups she had so painstakingly helped to set up the year before, only one remained in existence. This experience was immediately transmuted into a piece of her analysis of the issue:

Thus as I passed from town to town was I made to feel the great evil of woman's utter dependence on man for the necessary means to aid reform movements. I never before took in so fully the grand idea of pecuniary independence. It matters not how overflowing with benevolence toward suffering humanity may be the heart of woman, it avails nothing so long as she possesses not the power to act in accordance with these promptings. Woman

173

must have a *purse* of her own and how can this be, so long as the wife is denied the right to her *individual* and *joint* earnings. Reflections like these, caused me to see and really feel that there was no *true freedom* for woman without the possession of all her property rights, and that these rights could be obtained through *legislation* only, and if so, the sooner the demand was made by petitions to the legislature, and that too at its very next session—How could the work be started, why, by first holding a Convention and adopting some plan of united action.[67]

This journal entry is utterly revealing about Anthony's own impulses. No sooner had she perceived the need than she passed immediately to the prescription for action and a strategy for attacking it. These earliest references to financial independence clearly appear in the context of the use of women's moral influence in reform work. Like some of her references to the ballot, money here appeared as a means to an end, rather than an end in itself.

Votes and money went together in Anthony's analysis. Immediately after stating that she desired to see women asserting their individuality by "doing noble deeds," she continued with an assessment of the ethical damage done by eating the bread of dependence.

What woman most needs is a true appreciation of her womanhood, a self-respect which shall scorn to eat the bread of dependence. Whoever consents to live by "the sweat of the brow" of another human being inevitably humiliates and degrades herself. . . . No genuine equality, no real freedom, no true manhood or womanhood can exist on any foundation save that of pecuniary independence. As a right over a man's subsistence is a power over his moral being, so a right over a woman's subsistence enslaves her will, degrades her pride and vitiates her whole moral nature.[68]

The debates that led to the AWSA/NWSA rifts in the late 1860s similarly saw Anthony citing women's financially powerless state as among the reasons why women should not take a backseat to black (male) enfranchisement:

When Mr. Douglass mentioned the black man first and the woman last, if he had noticed he would have seen that it was the men that clapped and not the women. There is not the woman born who desires to eat the bread of dependence, no matter whether it be from the hand of father, husband, or brother; for any one who does so eat her bread places herself in the power of the person from whom she takes it. Mr. Douglass talks about the wrongs of the negro; but with all the outrages he to-day suffers, he would not exchange his sex and take the place of Elizabeth Cady Stanton.

Mr. Douglass:—I want to know if granting you the right of suffrage will change the nature of our sexes?

Miss Anthony:—It will change the pecuniary position of woman; it will place her where she can earn her own bread. She will not then be driven to such employments only as man chooses for her.[69]

"There is not the woman born who desires to eat the bread of dependence." This was hardly an empirical statement. It approached rather more closely Anthony's own notion of "true womanhood," redefining, indeed, standing on its head, the prevalent cultural notion of womanhood.

By the fall of 1869, Anthony had further developed her notion of the importance of women's economic independence. Hard on the heels of the Civil War and abolitionism, she drew the analogy, once again, to that issue. "Still another form of slavery remains to be disposed of; the old idea yet prevails that woman is owned and possessed by man, to be clothed and fed and cared for by his generosity."[70] "The soul of woman" demanded therefore the "right to own and possess herself."[71] Like Stanton citing each one of the strands of the fourfold bondage as fundamental, Anthony too could claim that "all the wrongs, arrogances, and antagonisms of modern society grow out of this false condition of the relations between man and woman." Since the cause was such a sweeping one, it followed that the remedy would be equally global: "This woman's movement promises an entire change of the conditions of wages and support"—though it was not clear what this meant. Anthony then proceeded to one of the period's mistaken notions on the economic relations of the sexes.

It is said that as a rule man does sufficiently provide for woman, and that she ought to remain content. The great facts of the world are at war with this assumption.

For example, I see in the New York Herald 1,200 advertisements of people wanting work. Upon examination, 500 of them come from women and 300 more are from boarding-house keepers; and we may therefore say that eight hundred of the twelve hundred advertisements are from women compelled to rely upon their own energies to gain their food and clothing. Every morning from 6 to 7 o'clock you may see on the Bowery and other great north and south avenues of New York, troops of young girls and women, with careworn or crime-stained faces, carrying their poor lunch half-concealed beneath a scanty shawl. If the facts were in accordance with the common theory, we should not see these myriads of women thus thrust out to get their living.[72]

This use of factual and statistical material was typical of Anthony's appeals regarding the economic dimensions of women's subjection. Where Stanton spoke of herself most often simply as a "philosopher," Anthony attended to "philosophy and facts."[73] Even in her earliest days, she cited numbers, amounts, concrete indicators of the empirical situation. Reporting the agitation regarding women's rights to speak at the New York State Teacher's Convention of 1853, she did not stop with describing her own brave precedent, or with the statement of the "broad principles" Stanton was fond of, but pointed to the inequalities in the economic status of teachers.

> A woman principal in that city [Rochester] receives $250, while a man principal, doing exactly the same work, receives $650. In this State there are 11,000 teachers, and of these four-fifths are women. By the reports it will be seen that of the annual State fund of $800,000, two-thirds are paid to men and one-third to women; that is to say, two-thirds are paid to one-fifth of the laborers, and the other four-fifths are paid with the remaining one-third of the fund![74]

This period, the late 1860s, was the time of *The Revolution*. Readers were exhorted to "send in your subscriptions and complaints that we may show the chivalry of New York the slavery that exists in the garrets and the cellars of this city." And, as the piece continued, "even in your schools where young girls are teaching for a miserable pittance. Let the 100,000 school teachers demand the ballot and thus double their salaries."[75] Its policy was to feature regular accounts of the situations of working women, their wages, working conditions, needs, as well as reporting occasional labor conventions. As Anthony put it in an appeal for new subscribers, "our clientele are the oppressed of all classes, all people. For such we labor; all such we wish to bless. The least of all our brethren share our sympathy, are included in our hope and purpose of salvation."[76]

It was perhaps Anthony's own experience with working for wages that led her sympathies to the cause of labor. "I join heart and hand with the working people in their trades unions, and in everything else by which they can protect themselves against the oppression of capitalists and employers."[77] Anthony was even instrumental in creating a Working Women's Association in New York. It was hardly a militant or Marxist group, nor was it directly connected to organizing women into unions. Rather it had as its object "the broad platform of philosophizing on the general questions of labor, and to discuss what can be done to ameliorate the condition of working people generally."[78] Reformers met with laboring women to share information and to analyze conditions.

Anthony also worked to organize Woman's Typographical Union No. 1 and a Sewing Machine Operators' Union.[79]

Anthony's interest in working women led her into unfortunate bypasses with other advocates of labor. In early 1869, she had an unfortunate run-in with the male printers' unions of the city. She had always sought a more practical, economically oriented education for young women.

> The salvation of the race depends, in a great measure, upon rescuing women from their hot-house existence. Whether in kitchen, nursery or parlor, all alike are shut away from God's sunshine. Why did not your Caroline Plummer of Salem, why do not all our wealthy women leave money for industrial and agricultural schools for girls, instead of ever and always providing for boys alone?[80]

During the printers' strike, she approached a meeting of the employers at Astor House to propose training women for the printing trades.

> The Working Women's Association appeals to you to contribute liberally for the purpose of enabling us to establish a training school for girls in the art of type-setting at once. There are hundreds of young women now in this city (more than fifty have made personal application to me), who stand ready to learn the trade—women who are stitching with their needles at starving prices, because that is the only work they know how to do. Now gentlemen, if you will help us to money, we will at once start a school; these women must be helped to board, in part at least, while learning the trade. Give us the means and we will soon give you competent women compositors.[81]

The employers offered Anthony "a vote of thanks" and formed a committee to consider her scheme, though little else resulted from that group. The printers' unions, on the other hand, were not so pleased. At their meeting, her proposal

> was denounced as being calculated to prove detrimental to the interests of the working women, inasmuch as it aimed at injuring the status of the men who had hitherto proved themselves to be the most anxious in assisting the women to achieve the position to which they are entitled.[82]

It is not clear that Anthony actually encouraged women typesetters to strikebreaking, although there is some evidence that *The Revolution* was printed in a nonunion shop.[83] Male labor unionists rebuked her, in any case, and she defended herself in a subsequent issue of her paper.

You fail to see my motive in appealing to the Astor House meeting of employers for aid to establish a "training school for girls." It was to open the way for a thorough drill to the hundreds of poor girls to "fit them to earn equal wages with men everywhere," and not to undermine Typographical Union No. 6. I did not mean to give the impression that "Women, already good compositors, should work a cent less per thousand ems than men," and I rejoice most heartily that Typographical Union No. 6 stands so nobly by the Women's Typographical Union No. 1, and demands admission for women to all the offices under its control; and I rejoice also that the Women's Union No. 1 stands so nobly and generously by Union No. 6, in refusing to accept most advantageous offers to defeat its demands.

My advice to all the woman compositors of the city is now, as it has been, ever since last autumn, to join the Women's Union; for in "union alone" there is strength—in union alone there is protection.

Every woman should scorn to allow herself to be made a mere tool of, to undermine just prices for men workers; and to avoid this, "union" is necessary. Hence I say, girls, stand by each other and by the men who stand by you.[84]

Some consequences of this imbroglio followed later in the summer. When Anthony sought to attend the National Labor Congress, Typographical Union No. 6 actively campaigned against seating her in the convention. Dissent in the Working Women's Association also came to the surface. A Mrs. Norton, evidently one of the cofounders and an active member of the organization, was strongly assertive: "This association is useless and a sham, and has never done anything for working women."[85] Anthony's response was ambiguous, blended of one part institutional realism and one part defense of the cause of woman suffrage. Working people were suspicious of being used by suffragists.

I always supposed and believed that this association was not only a reality but a success. I believed it was a good plan to call women together to talk over their interests. And if the Suffrage was sometimes mixed up with the discussions, it was to show how women's interests could best be secured. It was to show how the suffrage was the key to unlock every door to them. . . . If we have failed to accomplish all that we would like to do, we are very much like other people. There are very few persons who do not set before themselves an ideal and strive to bring their work up to that standard. They always fail to attain their ideal but they nevertheless strive after it.[86]

Curiously, Anthony stopped to read from her accounts as treasurer[87] before continuing to blend her policy of "agitation" with her understanding of the need to affirm women:

The grandest work that some mortals can accomplish is to talk, and thereby stir other people up to do something. I am ashamed to say that women do not appreciate themselves and their work more than they do. . . . I tell you women must learn to appreciate themselves more than they do. You don't think much of this talking; I tell you it makes everything in the world.[88]

Shortly thereafter the newly formed NWSA too was the scene of internal disagreement. "It was urged by several ladies that the Suffrage Association should resolve itself into a charitable society, to look after suffering women."[89] Anthony's response was paraphrased by the reporter. The language of social causality and the lessons of the abolitionist movement came together in the rejection of charity approaches to the situation of women. The Working Women's Association was cited parallel with the woman suffrage movement. They were both directed to the same ends, "root" changes in the condition of women. It was a defense of what we today call structural change.

Miss Anthony clearly pointed out the difference between the work of those who devote themselves to individual suffering and those who labor for the establishment of principles that would better the condition of the masses. She stated in an able manner the true philosophy of reform to be the removal of the *cause* of the wrongs complained of—not merely helping individual victims. In olden times she was charged with preaching and not practicing Anti-slavery, because she did not devote all her efforts to aid fugitive slaves, precisely as she was now charged with preaching and not practicing on behalf of Working Women, because she could not aid everyone of the thousands who appealed to her. To help one or one thousand women to better work, and better pay, good and philanthropic work, but does nothing to uproot and destroy the wrong principle upon which government and society is based. Every woman is now born to the condition of dependence, and dependence, sugar coat it as we will, is but slavery. Her every energy and every dollar should be devoted to the radical work of changing the condition of women—giving them, everywhere, *equal* power in making and controlling their own and others' surroundings— giving them an equal chance in the world's great scramble for the prizes of life. As the true reform work for the slaves was the *abolition of the right of property in man*, so now it is the *abolition of the legal and social right of custody and control of woman*. Ordinary benevolence will ever minister to individual suffering—even the Hard-Shell Democratic Fugitive Slave Law man in the olden time would hide the fleeing bondman from the chase of his master, and give him $10 to pass him on to Canada. So everybody now who has common sympathy will aid unfortunate women. But the Working Women's Association, of which she was President, was formed to bring to public notice the facts of women's wrongs from garret to cellar, and thereby compel the people to see, and hear, and feel, and come to the help of the few who are trying to uproot and forever

> destroy the false notion that *women are the subjects of men.* This Woman
> Suffrage movement goes to the root of the evil—demands the ballot—the right,
> the power, in woman's hands to help herself.[90]

It was not merely "ordinary benevolence," charity, that was needed in the case
of women's economic and political dependence. It was "to uproot and forever
destroy" women's powerlessness and subjection. This work was radical, to
change the very conditions under which women lived, to enhance women's
own ability to change those conditions. It was, in other words, to make them
reformers looking for structural change and equipped to achieve it. Without
votes and money, such efforts would be for nought. At times Anthony seemed
to think that efforts of charity and humanitarianism to isolated victims were
"man-appointed missions," not the work that women themselves were to do
on their own. In this context, Anthony's use of "self-help" was distinct from
the "self-made man" of the period. Women were to become independent as
individuals, to be sure, but women's independence struck directly at the
conditions of powerlessness in which they lived.

> My aim is to change the condition of women to self-help; yours, simply to
> ameliorate the ills that must inevitably grow out of dependence. My work is to
> lessen the numbers of the poor; yours, merely to lessen the sufferings of their
> tenfold increase.[91]

Self-help for women was a portion of the whole program of structural change
of the social order, not a panacea in itself.

The maturest and most complete statement of these economic arguments
was made in Anthony's oft-repeated speech, "Bread and the Ballot."[92] This
strong suffrage case was aimed at firmly establishing the connections between
disfranchisement and women's economic disabilities—indeed, at painting a
more accurate picture of these latter, which were by and large unknown to the
American public:

> Disfranchisement is not only political degradation, but also moral, social,
> educational, and industrial degradation. . . . Wherever, on the face of the globe
> or on the page of history, you show me a disfranchised class, I will show you a
> degraded class of labor. Disfranchisement means inability to make, shape, or
> control one's own circumstances. The disfranchised must always do the work,
> accept the wages, occupy the position the enfranchised assign to them. The
> disfranchised are in the position of the pauper. You remember the old adage,
> "Beggars must not be choosers"; they must take what they can get or nothing!

That is exactly the position of women in the world of today; they can not choose.[93]

Industrial reforms and other moves to better the condition of the workingmen (such as public education) did not make headway before this class of men was enfranchised. She reviewed the case for the removal of the property qualification for male American voters, and the continuing political power necessary for trade unions to prosecute their strikes, before pressing her specific point about women.

A continual attack was required on the old canard that women were financially supported by men, and therefore did not need the vote.

Statistics show that there are 3,000,000 women in this nation supporting themselves. In the crowded cities of the East they are compelled to work in shops, stores, and factories for the merest pittance. In New York alone, there are over 50,000 of these women receiving less than fifty cents a day.[94]

It was hardly "ladies" or the wealthy whom Anthony had in mind when she made such statements. From her earliest days in suffrage work, she had expressed solidarity with working women. She asked a collaborator in upstate New York to make a "particular effort to call out the teachers, seamstresses, and wage-earning women generally. It is for them rather than for the wives and daughters of the rich that I labor."[95] In "Bread and the Ballot," she pointed out the obstacles to successful union organizing and strikes of working women due to their disfranchisement. It was these three million working women who were the real crux of the urgent necessity for women's enfranchisement—"so that they may be able to compel politicians to legislate in their favor and employers to grant them justice."[96] One wonders what her audiences made of such a point in this period of paranoia about strikes; equally one wonders how Anthony thought that this argument might have been effective in days when only a few hardy souls favored strikes and unions.

This prime economic speech employed a series of economic metaphors in the place of the slavery metaphors used elsewhere. She spoke of "the monopoly of sex, of all men over all women" as the most "fraught with injustice, tyranny, and degradation" of all monopolies. She understood this firmly as what we might call today a structural reality. The individual goodness or evil of the men in power, their character or motives, was not the point. "It is not because the members of Congress are tyrants that women receive only half pay and are admitted only to inferior positions in the departments."[97] It was "simply in obedience to a law of political economy," which ordained that a government could not "do as much for disfranchised as for the enfranchised."

The invocation of the science of political economy and its laws raised another objection to be answered.

> Again men say it is not votes, but the law of supply and demand which regulates wages. The law of gravity is that water shall run down hill, but when men build a dam across the stream, the force of gravity is stopped and the water held back. The law of supply and demand regulates free and enfranchised labor, but disfranchisement estops its operation.

Here she invoked once again the parallel of slavery: "Did the laws of supply and demand regulate work and wages in the olden days of slavery? This law can no more reach the disfranchised than it did the enslaved."[98] In the case of teachers and principals, the empirical case Anthony knew so well from her own years in education, supply and demand obviously did not work: "The law of supply and demand is ignored, and that of sex alone settled the question."

Though she did not use the Marxist terminology, it was the notion of a reserve labor army dragging down the general rate of wages that she had in mind in making the following link in her argumentative chain. Women's enfranchisement

> ought to be done not only for the sake of justice to the women, but to the men with whom they compete; for, just so long as there is a degraded class of labor in the market, it always will be used by the capitalists to checkmate and undermine the superior classes.[99]

In her later years, her speeches to (male) union membership made similar arguments, claiming that woman suffrage would be a boon to workingmen's interests rather than a peril to them,

> Your own interest demands that you should seek to make women your political equals, for then, instead of their being, as now, a dead weight to drag down all workingmen, a stumbling block in their path, a hindrance to their efforts to secure better wages and more favorable legislation, the working women would be an added strength, politically, industrially, morally. . . . It is the honest, hardworking men, with homes and families, those who have done most to build up this country and who are the bone and sinew sustaining it today, who have most to gain from women's getting the ballot. But the best argument of all is

justice—the sister should have the same rights as her brother, the wife as her husband, the mother as her son.[100]

For her peroration, Anthony stepped outside the realm of economics and into the realm of moral speculation. As in several other aspects of social life in which women's equal participation would lift efforts up to a higher moral plane, so in this one.

> When women vote, they will make a new balance of power that must be weighed and measured and calculated in its effect upon every social and moral question which goes to the arbitrament of the ballot box. Who can doubt that when the representative women of thought and culture, who are today the moral backbone of our nation, sit in counsel with the best men of the country, higher conditions will be the result?[101]

This speech and its arguments are ambiguous, especially to a generation of women who know all too well that enfranchisement had not automatically brought equal pay. Anthony assumed that the "law of supply and demand" would function freely after the vote was gained. But one should not oversimplify her claims.

Her understanding of the relationship of the ballot to economic conditions was complex. In 1899, for example, she was interviewed on the subject of housing for poor people in London. She was straightforward in rejecting "palliatives" and went to the heart of the matter: "The real aim should be to pay them better, give them the value of their work." Reiterating the notion that "it all comes back to enfranchisement," she was blithely simple-minded about the effect of votes for blacks and other ethnic groups:

> Negroes never got the value of their work until they were enfranchised. When the Irish emigrated to the United States they were paid less than native-born men until they were naturalized, and then their pay became equal. They declared that the ballot was worth fifty cents a day to them.[102]

When asked whether the vote "would be worth this to womankind," she backtracked somewhat, claiming that she could not put a precise figure to its value. "But I do say that when women get the ballot they will be on fighting ground. At present they have not arrived." This is rather more like Anthony at her better moments.

Later in her life, she asserted that not only the bare necessities of life must be assured women, but "positions of honor and emolument" as well.[103] The

183

contemporary slogan, equal pay for equal work, was one that came naturally to her. In 1903, when women were being admitted into "all the different trades and professions," she was quick to point out that the economic struggles of women continued.

> The battle now is the same as fifty years ago—to get equal pay for equal work and equal eligibility to the highest salaried positions. . . . It is woman's necessity to earn a living that causes her to take less wages than a man receives. This is an appeal to the parsimony of the employers, for it is a law of economics to get as much work done as possible and as good as possible for the least amount of pay. Women must take what they are offered or nothing.[104]

Hence, she continued, women needed the vote *and* unions. "I do not see any hope of a change in this matter until women are enfranchised and until they combine and control their work and wages as do men." These comments, from a letter to the president of the National Federation of Teachers, could as usual be turned into an argument for the ballot.

> There is no other power given in this republican form of government, whereby the different classes of citizens shall be equalized. Perfect equality of rights—civil and political—is and must continue to be the demand of all self-respecting women.[105]

Here as earlier, however, Anthony's claim for the economic benefits to be gained from the vote were not simplistic. "Even if the right to vote brought to woman no better work, no better pay, no better conditions in any way, she should have it for her own self-respect and to compel man's respect for her," for "he will never feel that she is his equal" so long as her right to vote is not acknowledged.

While Stanton too included the economy in her panoply of programs, Anthony was far more insistent on these questions of women's labor, more deeply involved in deeds to rectify conditions of economic dependence. In her last letter to Stanton, whose characteristic claim at the time was that women needed to demand equality in religion as well as in politics, Anthony's emphasis was on work. "The older we grow the more keenly we feel the humiliation of disfranchisement and the more vividly we realize its disadvantages in every department of life, and most of all in the labor market."[106]

Depending on another for subsistence did more than make women open to the vicissitudes of employers. It also created grave moral difficulties in the personal sphere, in the area of "social purity."

C. The Social Evils

Anthony's exposure to the topics of "social purity" occurred long before she systematized her thoughts with this title in 1875. The strong antebellum stands made on women's right to divorce sprang from concerns that had been prominent in the temperance movement. Drunken men were liable to perpetrate horrors, most often unnamed, on their wives and children. These matters, so sexual, so repressed in the Victorian era, convinced Stanton and Anthony as nothing else did of the uniqueness of women's degradation.

Arguments stressing the parallels between marriage and slavery no doubt also built a foundation for Anthony's frank discussion of the need for social purity. The stories of black women's degradation under slavery, with its systematized rape and violation by male owners, were a regular part of the abolition movement. While to a contemporary reader, "marriage is slavery" looks merely like inflated and inflammatory feminist platform rhetoric, to Stanton and Anthony it was a parallel built on specific outrages.

A series of particularly celebrated cases bore immediately on Anthony's strong stand. The fugitive wife of 1860, beaten by her husband, I mentioned earlier. At least four postwar incidents of notoriety were also occasions for the proponents of women's rights to expand their perspectives. Unemployed and starving, Hester Vaughn was brought to trial for alleged infanticide in a freezing garret while ill. The McFarland-Richardson case turned on divorce and murder; the supposedly vicious ex-husband murdered his former wife's lover, and the couple was married as he lay dying. Laura Fair, in jail in San Francisco for the murder of A. P. Crittendown, was an example, to Anthony, of the inanities of the rhetoric that women were "protected" by men. The Beecher-Tilton case was well known as a celebrated accusation of adultery in which everyone seemed to escape unscathed except Elizabeth Tilton.

This latter case was particularly trying for Anthony. Since she was a close personal acquaintance of almost everyone involved in it, the opinion was widespread that she had the inside story. A good many charges of "free love" were flying at suffragists in this period in any case. During the convention immediately preceding the Beecher trial, a resolution to put the association on record as opposing free love was advanced by Mary Livermore. It was typical of Anthony that she responded to this argument not in terms of abstract moral principles or by defending the integrity or personal moral reputations of reformers. Rather she spoke of women's economic subjection, linking prostitution and marriage:

> This howl comes from the men who know that when women get their rights they will be able to live honestly and not be compelled to sell themselves for bread, either in or out of marriage. There are very few women in the world who would enter into this relationship with drunkards and libertines provided they could get their subsistence in any other way. We can not be frightened from our purpose, the public mind can not long be prejudiced by this "free love" cry of our enemies.[107]

Lecture tours of the early 1870s, undertaken to repay the debts of the short-lived *Revolution*, took her to Utah. Anthony's remarks were surprisingly free from the cant of the period on polygamy. Though she conventionally pictured the despair of a "noble, loving, beautiful spirit" who was awakened suddenly to the idea of monogamy, she did not let the rest of the nation off the hook. Women in plural and monogamous marriages lived in the same situation.

> Woman's work in monogamy and polygamy is one and the same—that of planting her feet on the ground of self-support. The saddest feature here is that there really is nothing by which these women can earn an independent livelihood for themselves and their children, no manufacturing establishments, no free schools to teach. Women here, as everywhere, must be able to live honestly and honorably without the aid of men, before it can be possible to save the masses of them from entering into polygamy or prostitution, legal or illegal. Whichever way I turn, whatever phase of social life presents itself, the same conclusion comes: "Independent bread alone can redeem woman from her curse of subjection to man."[108]

This variety of themes and incidents finally took a systematic form in the lecture of 1875 entitled "Social Purity." Despite the conventions of the day, she addressed in public not only the topics of drunken and licentious husbands—a standard theme for temperance outcry—but rape, abortion,[109] infanticide, prostitution, calling them by name. The only aspect of this range of topics that she evidently could not force herself to name in so many words was venereal disease. She called it instead that "loathsome and contagious disease."

186

The time had come, she asserted, to investigate new measures and new forces to address these social ills. Men alone had been unsuccessful. Women, too, when they went on "man-appointed missions" of relief, had little more success, for they merely aimed to alleviate effects and symptoms without striking at the causes. The "roots" of such social distortions were "not merely moral and social, they extend deep and wide into the financial and political structure of the government." Any move to deal with them would require "more than tears and prayers."[110]

The case of prostitution was a good example for the many-pronged analysis Anthony wished to develop. The causes of prostitution were "said to be wholly different with the sexes," male participation due to an "abnormal passion" and female participation due to destitution, "absolute want of the necessaries of life."[111] This desperate economic situation of women had largely come about through the changes wrought by industrialization, and that on specific terms unequal for the sexes, since nowhere were women equipped or allowed to function adequately in the "world's outer market of work."

> Clearly, then, the first step toward solving this problem is to lift this vast army of poverty-stricken women who now crowd our cities, above the temptation, the necessity to sell themselves, in marriage or out, for bread and shelter. To do that, girls, like boys, must be educated to some lucrative employment; women, like men, must have equal chances to earn a living.[112]

Equal education, however, was only part of the story. Anthony envisioned an economy wholly integrated with women's labor.

> Whoever controls work and wages, controls morals. Therefore, we must have women employers, superintendents, committees, legislators; wherever girls go to seek the means of subsistence, there must be some woman. Nay, more; we must have women preachers, lawyers, doctors—that wherever women go to seek counsel—spiritual, legal, physical—there, too—they will be sure to find the best and noblest of their own sex to minister to them.[113]

Of course, economic change could not occur spontaneously. Women must have the practical political means of creating such conditions. "And the only possible way to accomplish this great change is to accord to women equal power in the making, shaping, and controlling of the circumstances of life. That equality of rights and privileges is vested in the ballot, the symbol of power in a republic."

The marriage relation itself must change, since the current form was founded on the financial control of one partner. "Marriage, to women as to men, must be a luxury, not a necessity; an incident of life, not all of it." Financial control created moral control, and hence the destructive double standard of morality.

> Alexander Hamilton said one hundred years ago, "Give to a man the right over my subsistence, and he has power over my whole moral being." No one doubts the truth of this assertion as between man and man; while, as between man and woman, not only does almost no one believe it, but the masses of people deny it. And yet it is the fact of man's possession of this right over woman's subsistence which gives to him power to dictate to her a moral code vastly higher and purer than the one he chooses for himself. Not less true is it, that the fact of woman's dependence on man for her subsistence renders her utterly powerless to exact from him the same high moral code she chooses for herself.[114]

The sporadic vigilante efforts of women against brothels were merely attacking other females, victims themselves. Why did women not rather turn out their erring husbands? Anthony answered her own rhetorical question.

> But how could they, without finding themselves, as a result, penniless and homeless? The person, the services, the children, the subsistence, of each and every one of these women belonged by law, not to herself, but to her unfaithful husband.[115]

Making this tactic of reform workable required giving women joint ownership. But men made the property laws—and all the others bearing on such causes of social evil as well.

> Neither in the making nor executing of the laws regulating these relations has woman ever had the slightest voice. The statutes for marriage and divorce, for adultery, breach of promise, seduction, rape, bigamy, abortion, infanticide—all were made by men. They, alone, decide who are guilty of violating these laws, and what shall be their punishment, with judge, jury, and advocate all men, with no woman's voice heard in our courts, save as accused or witness, and in many cases the married women is denied the poor privilege of testifying as to her own guilt or innocence of the crime charged against her.[116]

The fundamental basis, not merely the symptoms, of all these social distortions must be attacked, Anthony argued. Other efforts would simply be hopeless or "unphilosophical," as were the efforts of the American Colonization Society or the "Fugitive Slave Societies" for dealing with slavery. "As I see and admit now what none but the Abolitionists saw then, that the only effectual work was the entire overthrow of the system of slavery." The *cause*, the fundamental basis, of all these miscellaneous evils, was woman's dependence.

> The tap-root of our social upas lies deep down at the very foundation of society. It is woman's dependence. It is woman's subjection. Hence, the first and only efficient work must be to emancipate woman from her enslavement. The wife must no longer echo the poet Milton's ideal Eve, when she adoringly said to Adam, "God, thy law; thou mine!" She must feel herself accountable to God alone for every act, fearing and obeying no man, save where his will is in line with her own highest idea of divine law.[117]

There was another side, a brighter side, that followed from all these claims. The human race could be redeemed by the efforts of women.

> If it is through woman's ignorant subjection to the tyranny of man's appetites and passions that the life-current of the race is corrupted, then must it be through her intelligent emancipation that the race shall be redeemed from the curse, and her children and children's children rise up to call her blessed. When the mother of Christ shall be made the true model of womanhood, when the office of maternity shall be held sacred and the mother shall consecrate herself, as did Mary, to the one idea of bringing forth the Christ Child, then, and not till then, will this earth see a new order of men and women, prone to good rather than evil.
>
> I am a full and firm believer in the revelation that it is through woman that the race is to be redeemed. And it is because of this faith that I ask for her immediate and unconditional emancipation from all political, industrial, social, and religious subjection.[118]

The world would be redeemed by women; the world would not be redeemed until women themselves were redeemed from their subjection. These twin points push on to justice and religion in Anthony's work.

These sexual questions were not an independent strand of the social order in her view. Sexual morality was directly traced to the financial and political conditions that caused or perpetuated them. While Stanton too claimed these intimate disorders as part of the degraded situation of women, and argued strongly for divorce and self-support, her arguments were more complex, more intertangled in a wholistic analysis of American life. To Anthony, votes and

189

money, or in her more euphonious phrase, bread and the ballot, stood virtually alone as the twin engines enforcing women's powerlessness.

Injustice and Justice

Reflecting more fully on the shape of injustice and its concomitant justice is not so readily accomplished with Anthony as it was with her old friend Stanton. Anthony was not so systematic as her longtime collaborator, yet no less interesting.

There is little of that language of progress which vitiates much of Stanton's work in the eyes of a later observer. Anthony's metaphors almost never lent themselves to that automatic upward movement of life processes. Her figures of speech tended to be more sociological and historical than did Stanton's use of "life." There seems little either of the masculine/feminine elements of the universe in Anthony's work, whether public or private, though she did believe and claim that women of a broad and catholic spirit would constitute a force for better government.

Anthony wavered, it seems, between thinking that the vote was a small contribution to justice and a large portion of it, so to speak. A deathbed comment pointed in the first direction:

> She never complained, but once when the consciousness of approaching death seemed strongly to impress itself upon her, she said, holding up her hand and measuring a little space on one finger, "Just think of it, I have been striving for over sixty years for a little bit of justice no bigger than that, and yet I must die without obtaining it. Oh, it seems so cruel!"[119]

A decade earlier, she spoke of the amendment campaign in similar terms. "Such a little simple thing we have been asking for a quarter of a century. For over forty years, longer than the children of Israel wandered through the wilderness, we have been begging and praying and pleading for this act of justice."[120] But this "little simple thing" was, as she put it on another occasion, the cornerstone of so much more. Addressing the Ethical Culture Society of New York, she claimed that "the very foundation of ethics is justice, therefore, the highest ethical culture for women must lie in the direction of securing justice for their own sex."[121] Clearly, this statement was partially dictated by rhetorical and occasional reasons. Were Anthony quizzed as regards the grounds of this claim, that justice is the foundation of ethics, I am not certain that she would have been able to respond with a full-blown systematic or philosophical case. But Anthony's focus was so firmly on justice, so many of her arguments and cases returned to the assertion of justice, that it is hard not to see here an intimation of her wider views. As she put it in the context of a speech to a trade union, "the best argument of all is justice."

To achieve structural change on issues of racism or war, one needed to work on issues related to women, in Anthony's view. On some readings this was because "sex-slavery" was at the "root" of these other questions. On other occasions, however, Anthony's principle was articulated differently. As I have noted, "men who fail to be just to their mothers cannot be expected to be just to each other."[122] Or as she put it another way, "it is idle for us to expect that men who thus rob women will not rob each other as individuals, corporations, and governments."[123] It is not clear *why* Anthony thought this was so. It was as though those who were unjust to others near them, so to speak, in social, geographical, or emotional space, were not able to be just to those farther away. This is a very interesting light on the interrelationships of sexism with other social issues, one of the most provocative of all Anthony's claims for a feminist analysis.[124] One wonders, for example, whether it is true. Though history provides sufficient material for wondering whether people are ever just to one another, it seems that men are frequently more just to each other, whether near or far, than they are to women—who are regularly cast as "exceptions" to moral rules. But Anthony's comments remain provocative for an ethical view of the issue of sexism.

She was clear that justice involved more than formalities, whether it was justice for blacks or for women, who, after all, suffered from "sex-slavery."

> Every discussion with antinegro suffrage men demonstrates that it is but the *legal* form, not the *spirit* of slavery that is abolished.
> The physical struggle may be nearly over, but the moral battle for the recognition of the great—the underlying principle of Freedom—*equality* before the law of society, politics, and religion—is but begun. The regeneration of a nation like that of an individual is not the work of a day, but the slow learning to do justice step by step. Hence the work of the true abolitionist has just begun.[125]

"The slow learning to do justice step by step" was to result in, to constitute even, the regeneration of the nation. The "true" abolitionist, like the "true woman," was engaged in a moral battle to see the spirit of freedom and quality, not merely their form, enacted on a daily basis.

Anthony's locutions are striking for their strict, uncompromised, even pure, character—"perfect equality," "genuine equality," "absolute freedom," "real freedom," "absolute truth" were the goals of the movement. That justice in a pure form was her goal accounts in part for the rejection of all expedient, merely political, solutions or means. Justice was the standard by which she measured both expediency and the privilege of Victorian womanhood. To male tributes on her eighty-fifth birthday, she drew the line. "You may compliment women, pet them, worship them, but if you do not recognize their claim to justice, it is all as nothing."[126] This uncompromising standard was continuous from Anthony's antislavery days to her woman suffrage struggle. She expected the abolitionists, the "conscience of the nation," to uphold higher principles than the arguments of political or military necessity of emancipation. "We must, as ever, plant ourselves on the highest ground, and demand emancipation simply as an act of justice to the black man."[127] She meant higher moral ground, not higher evolutionary ground. To do justice from no other motive than justice itself, to act ethically from pure ethical motives, rather than from some other reasons, was the highest, uncompromised, position. It was to go "through the narrow gate."[128] This meant above all acting from the pure light of one's conscience.

Conscience dictated that one never speak the merely pleasing word or depart from the "absolute truth." Conscience was permeated by the "still, small voice" of God—that same God who demanded resistance to tyranny and struggle for democracy. "Heaven," in any case, was the clearest locus of "perfect equality," as in Anthony's final letter to Stanton:

> And, we, dear old friend, shall move on to the next sphere of existence—higher and larger, we cannot fail to believe, and one where women will not be placed in an inferior position but will be welcomed on a plane of perfect intellectual and spiritual equality.[129]

That she continually spoke of the "perfection" of the equality and freedom for which she struggled indicates that this was no worldly standard, no finite, fragmented, or proximate grasp of justice that was the desideratum. It was of little concern to her whether the suffrage movement would destroy the Republican Party or any other social institution in order to assert women's rights. "*Fiat Iustitia Pereat Mundus.*" Such a slogan "fits" Anthony's moral and religious bent.

The slogans that leaped to her lips were all of this character. "Of two evils choose neither" or "do right and leave the consequences to God" were ethical maxims that refused to countenance the haggling trade-offs of day-to-day politics. "Courage and conscience" had to go hand in hand in such a view, since the unpopularity of the reform or the reformer of this radical view could be strenuous. Nor were the demands of the organization to be limited by what was reasonably possible. When Anthony demanded the vote for women in newly annexed territories, she was not moved by the objection that one should temper one's demands to what one could get.

> We are told it will be of no use for us to ask this measure of justice—that the ballot be given to the women of our new possessions upon the same terms as to the men—because we shall not get it. It is not our business whether we are going to get it; our business is to make the demand. Suppose during these fifty years we have asked only for what we thought we could secure, where should we be now? Ask for the whole loaf and take what you can get.[130]

In the long run, "we know that only good can come to the individual or to the nation through the rendering of exact justice."[131]

It was not belief but action that counted for Anthony in such ethical matters. To perceive in conscience was to pass immediately into action. She sought from women "the energetic doing of noble deeds," not belief in particular theories. Anthony abhorred the substitution of "creed and dogma" for action. "We all know what we want, and that is the recognition of woman's perfect equality."[132] In a sense, the "one article in our creed" was intended as the source of unity, of suffragist coalition, rather than the divisiveness of sectarianism.

> In this great association we know no North, no South, no East, no West. This has been our pride for all these years. We have no political party. We have never inquired what anybody's religion is. As we have ever asked is simply, "Do you believe in perfect equality for women?" This is the one article in our creed.[133]

She fought to keep the platform "as broad as the universe," so broad that "upon it may stand the representatives of all creeds and no creeds—Jew and Christian, Protestant or Catholic, Gentile or Mormon, pagan or atheist."[134]

"We have never inquired what anybody's religion is." The NAWSA platform was to allow the utmost liberty to its adherents—except if they proposed what Anthony saw as sectarian religious notions. When Stanton was deep in her anticlerical phase, Anthony refused straightforwardly to circulate her Bible arguments in the California campaign. "I shall no more thrust into the discussions the question of the Bible than the manufacture of wine. What I want is for the men to vote 'yes' on the suffrage amendment, and I don't ask whether they make wine on the ranches of California or Christ made it at the wedding feast."[135] Stanton was not alone in injecting these traditionally religious statements into women's rights work. When a suffragist wrote that she was "especially inspired by God to make the demand," Anthony rebuked her.

> Those who are good Methodists like yourself ought to believe in suffrage already, and therefore your appeals are to be made to the men who are not Methodists, possibly not even Christians, and would be repelled by your presenting any of the religious motives which are so powerful with you and other church members. To prevail with the rank and file of voters, you must appeal to their sense of justice.[136]

It was justice and not religious motives that were to be the watchword of this campaign. How, then, did Anthony's own sense of justice relate to her religious faith?

"Looking up the Needs of the Oppressed"

> After the Berlin meeting Miss Anthony and I were invited to spend a week-end at the home of Mrs. Jacob Bright, that "Aunt Susan" might renew her acquaintance with Annie Besant. . . . Now she could not conceal her disapproval of the "other-worldliness" of Mrs. Besant, Mrs. Bright, and her daughter. . . .
> "Annie," demanded "Aunt Susan," "why don't you make that aura of yours do its gallivanting in this world, looking up the needs of the oppressed, and investigating the causes of present wrongs? Then you could reveal to us workers just what we should do to put things right, and we could be about it."
> Mrs. Besant sighed and said that life was short and aeons were long, and that while every one would be perfected some time, it was useless to deal with individuals here.
> "But, Annie!" exclaimed Miss Anthony, pathetically. "We *are* here! Our business is here! It's our duty to do what we can here."
> Mrs. Besant seemed not to hear her. She was in a trance, gazing into the aeons. . . . It was plain that she could not bring herself back from the other world, so Miss Anthony, perforce, accompanied her to it.
> "When your aura goes visiting in the other world," she asked, curiously, "does it ever meet your old friend Charles Bradlaugh?" . . .

194

Mrs. Besant heaved a deeper sigh. "I am very much discouraged over Mr. Bradlaugh," she admitted, wanly. "He is hovering too near this world. He cannot seem to get away from his mundane interests. He is as much concerned with parliamentary affairs now as when he was on this plane."

"Humph!" said Miss Anthony; "that's the most sensible thing I've heard yet about the other world. It encourages me. I've always felt sure that if I entered the other life before women were enfranchised nothing in the glories of heaven would interest me so much as the work for women's freedom on earth."[137]

This anecdote comes from the autobiography of one of Anthony's protégées in the woman suffrage movement. It was written from memory several years after the fact, and dressed up in the editorial pathetic style Victorians enjoyed in reminiscences. Its provenance also stemmed from a period in its subject's life when a tendency to retail myth and apocryphal stories about her was present both in the general public and among suffragists. It coincides too conveniently with certain dispositions of Shaw herself—the slightly humorous view of otherworldliness, of example, is typically Shaw's own. Yet even healthy skepticism over the veracity of this anecdote ought not to be overdone. The themes expressed as Anthony's conversation cohere with her steady espousal of religious attitudes from other periods, and fortunately, from other sources—the denial of otherworldliness, the crucial nature of social action in general and action for justice to women in particular.

What Anthony saw, with a directness and clarity unequaled by other figures in this study, was the religious nature of organized work toward justice for women.[138] That she was not always able to rise theoretically to spell out this vision will become evident. "Prayer by Action" investigates the ways Anthony's own religious faith was directly and intimately tied to her reform work. "Freedom of Religion" seeks to shed some light on her policy of keeping religious sectarianism off the suffrage platform. "With Such Women as These" looks at the sense in which what we now call sisterhood, the unity of women in the suffrage organization, could overcome even death.

A. Prayer by Action

Anthony's religious and theological positions are not easily discernible. She resisted Stanton's attempts to inject her anticlerical biases onto suffrage platforms. One set of religious resolutions to the NWSA brought her to her feet in opposition:

I was on the old Garrison platform, and found long ago that the settling of any question of human rights by people's interpretation of the Bible is utterly impossible. I hope we shall not go back to that war. We all know what we want, and that is the recognition of woman's perfect equality.[139]

Sometimes she even explicitly called her fight a secular one.

No—I don't want my name on that Bible Committee—*You* fight that battle—and leave me to fight the secular—the political fellows . . . I simply don't want the enemy to be diverted from my practical ballot fight—to that of scoring me for belief one way or the other about the Bible.[140]

Yet it would be a serious misunderstanding of Anthony to read this as an unequivocal statement of the secular nature of the movement to her. What she opposed was rather that "special theories" of a religious or metaphysical sort should be made either a point of suffragist allegiance or the bone of contention within the movement. Her fight was a "practical" one.

Charges that suffragists were heterodox were no doubt part of the problem in Anthony's mind. A letter to Shaw inviting her to preach in Rochester in 1889 teased her about orthodoxy and "any sort of a *doxy*," but it continued with a plea that sheds some light on Anthony's own position. "I just hope you'll talk so *above* all mere creeds and dogmas that no one who hears you will ask a thing [about] your special theories."[141] Anthony detested what she called "mere creeds and dogmas" and all other sorts of "speculations." An earlier encounter with Annie Besant than the one above indicates pungently Anthony's approach.

The truth is, I can no more see through Theosophy than I can through Christian Science, Spiritualism, Calvinism, or any other of the theories, so I shall have to go on knocking away to remove the obstructions in the road of us mortals while in these bodies and on this planet; and leave Madam Besant and you and all who have entered into the higher spheres, to revel in things unknown to me. . . . I will join you at Mrs. Miller's Saturday, and we'll chat over men, women, and conditions—not theories, theosophies, and theologies, they are all Greek to me.[142]

The conjunction expressed between the negative view of "the theories" and the positive importance of removing "obstructions in the road" in this life was also an early part of Anthony's vision. While on the antislavery trail someone in her home area cast a slur on Garrison; her diary recounted her response:

I thought him [Garrison] to be the most Christ-like man I ever knew—said Mr. Pierce (?), "does he believe in keeping the Christian Sabbath, does he believe in the Bible," and various other like questions—I told Mr. P. he had not asked me for a single *scriptural evidence*. Nor does the church require any other evidence, than to say you *believe* thus and so—It is astonishing to see how wholly bound to creed and Dogmas they are. I exposed a good many of my heresies to great surprise of all present. Eliza T. said she would rather that I should be a Slave Holder or believe in slave holding, than a disbeliever in the Plenary Inspiration of the Bible—Thus is it *belief*, not Christian benevolence, that is made the modern test of Christianity—when will the world wake from its stupor and look *truth* strait [*sic*] in the face.[143]

This early general reference to Christian benevolence was later outstripped by phrases such as "human rights," but the point remained the same. It was action and not belief that was for Anthony the deciding factor in judging of spiritual matters. A letter to Isabella Beecher Hooker (who was among the spiritualists in suffrage ranks) was explicit on this point. Declining an invitation to join the family in their summer home, she wrote how she would have enjoyed the chance

to chat over the world of work for our good cause. Of the before and after I know absolutely nothing, and have very little desire and less time to question or to study. I know this seems very material to you, and yet to me it is wholly spiritual, for it is giving time and study rather to making things better in the *between* which is really all that we can influence; but perhaps when I can no longer enter into active practical work, I may lapse into speculations.[144]

This wholly spiritual view was one whose biblical metaphors were blended with the antislavery struggle from which Anthony learned so much. One of her brothers accompanied John Brown on his raid. A visit to the John Brown memorial provoked this reflection:

John Brown was crucified for doing what he believed God commanded him to do, "to break the yoke and let the oppressed go free," precisely as were the saints of old for following what they believed to be God's commands. The barbarism of our government was by so much the greater as our light and knowledge are greater than those of two thousand years ago.[145]

"Looking up the needs of the oppressed and investigating the causes of present wrongs," as the anecdote from the Anthony-Besant encounter put it, was the pivot point of Anthony's religious faith.

A number of characteristically pithy, sloganlike locutions expressed this understanding that work in the "between" was "wholly spiritual." These statements recall significant aspects of antebellum religious thought of the antislavery struggle, especially in the emphasis on the value of direct action over conventional forms of religion. She quoted Douglass or Emerson particularly with regard to the inefficacy of prayer in seeking social change.[146] The meetings of the WCTU were among her favorite places for making such a point.

> Rev. C. B. Gardner said Miss Anthony had given the company some excellent political advice, but he inclined to the belief that the temperance reform could be brought about without woman suffrage. "The women would bring the men around in time; they could accomplish much by their moral influence; in this they resembled ministers." Miss Anthony wished to know if it would not be a good thing, then, to disfranchise the ministers and let them depend entirely on their moral influence. She explained that in what she had said about prayer, she meant prayer by action. She would not have it understood that she did not believe in prayer; she thought, however, that an emotion never could be equal to an action.[147]

To "prayer by action" may be added "pray with your ballots." The parallel with the slavery struggle was concrete in her mind.

> Now my good women, the best thing this organization will do for you will be to show you how utterly powerless you are to put down the liquor traffic. You never can talk down or sing down or pray down an institution which is voted into existence. You never will be able to lessen this evil until you have votes. Frederick Douglass used to tell how, when he was a Maryland slave and a good Methodist, he would go into the farthest corner of the tobacco field and pray God to bring him liberty; but God never answered his prayers until he prayed with his heels. And so, dear friends, He never will answer yours for the suppression of the liquor traffic until you are able to pray with your ballots.[148]

Talking, singing, praying—those oblique methods of "influence" so dear to her era, so covered with religious overtones in popular piety—were all rejected by Anthony. "All spasmodic, sensational religious efforts are transient and fleeting. . . . Kind words, entreaties and tears avail nothing." Yet Anthony did not go so far as to discourage temperance women; the work was "good in itself because anything is better for women than tame submission to the evils around them."[149] Her hope was that with political experience would come the realization that only direct action and effective political power could create enduring and permanent reform, structural change.[150]

The concepts and pungent phrases Anthony used to forge direct links between social action and religion rarely spoke, as did other social activists, of bringing God's kingdom on earth. Rather they had a liturgical stamp. "Prayer by action" was matched by the identity of work and worship:

> I pray every single second of my life; not on my knees, but with my work. My prayer is to lift woman to equality with man. Work and worship are one with me. I can not imagine a God of the universe made happy by my getting down on my knees and calling him "great."[151]

Though her capacity for sustained work was astonishing (on a "quiet day," for example, she might write twenty-four letters), this equation of work and worship should not be read as an example of the Puritan ethic. It was reform work she had in mind, work for justice, as the context made clear—not just any sort of disciplined ascetic activity or work for one's own gain.

Anthony was conscious of the divergence between her religious views and those of the world and churches around her. Sometimes she expressed this as her "heresy."[152] At other times, she went farther. On her terms, many of the so-called infidels were true Christians by her practical test:

> very many of the truly great and good men and women of our day, who are loudly denounced as Infidels are found doing the work of righteousness—feeding the hungry—clothing the naked—visiting the sick and in prison—undoing the bonds of the Slave and letting the oppressed go free—omitting the weightier matters of the Law, Judgment, Mercy, and Faith—what though they with their *lips* declare the *Bible* a mere human production? Do not their very acts, "the fruits by which we are to know them," show that they *believe* the great and immutable truths contained therein, to have emanated from none other than a Divine Source.[153]

Or she simply referred to it as a "different" religion, as was implied by this quote copied into the back of her diary:

> Many are called impious, not for having a worse, but a *different* religion from their neighbors, and many atheistical, not for denying God, but for thinking somewhat peculiarly of him.
> The first and last thing I would say to man is, *think for yourself.*[154]

She had no high regard for orthodoxy. When she heard the Rev. Kate Gannett Wells preach in her brother's Unitarian church in Rochester "on the irreligious in our charities and reforms," she thought it "a strange, old orthodox way of putting *religion* apart from morals."[155] The orthodox were as likely as not to appear in Anthony's mind as the "dear religious bigots."[156] She asserted that "liberals really believe *more—not* less—than the Orthodox."[157] The liberals of whom she spoke with admiration remained within the folds of Christianity. She pronounced Wendell Phillips "matchless" for his sermon "on Christianity a force, a movement, to lift up humanity, not mere devotional emotion—or church organization."[158] And she could be somewhat cavalier about specialized theological questions because "all those theological questions had been discussed and settled by the Quakers long ago."[159]

Inasmuch as her Quaker heritage contributed to the priority she placed on action for equal rights, as opposed to "sectarian creeds," it is relevant here.

> I was born and reared a Quaker, and am one still . . . but today all sectarian creeds and all political policies sink into utter insignificance compared with the essence of religion and the fundamental principle of government—equal rights. Wherever, religiously, socially, educationally, politically, justice to woman is preached and practiced, I find a bond of sympathy, and I hope and trust that henceforth I shall be brave enough to express my thanks to every individual and every organization, popular or unpopular, that gives aid and comfort to our great work for the emancipation of woman, and through her the redemption of the world.[160]

Differences in mere theories were to be laid aside in favor of "the bond of sympathy" wherever justice for women was "preached and practiced."

The love of freedom itself was intrinsic to the human relationship to God. Once, in a slaveholding area, Anthony regarded the young slave girl in her rooming house. "Oh how I long to probe her soul in search of that Divine spark that scorns to be a slave. But then would it be right for me by so doing to add to the burden of her wretched life."[161] At a Mormon meeting in Utah she was deeply moved. "As they sang their songs of freedom, poured out their rejoicing . . . and told of the beatitudes of soul-to-soul communion with the All-Father, my heart was steeped in deepest sympathy with the women around me." Her response was typical; she immediately rose to ask the men, "who were bubbling over with divine spirit of freedom for themselves, if they had thought whether the women of their households were today rejoicing in like manner?"[162] San Francisco was "Godless in its treading of womanhood under its heel."[163]

Anthony also held an instrumental view of woman suffrage, that through women the world would be redeemed. The "Social Purity" lecture was one of her most straightforward statements of this "woman as savior" dimension of her religious view. It was directly connected to her belief that this issue was the "cause of all causes," that woman's dependence was at the "very foundations of society," and hence responsible for other social ills.

The "direction," if I may so put it, of Anthony's reasoning reversed itself within the space of two paragraphs. On the one hand, she began with a social analysis tracing the "ways things contingently are" to their "tap-root" in woman's dependence and subjection. "Therefore, if it is through woman's ignorant subjection to the tyranny of man's appetites and passions that the life-current of the race is corrupted, then must it be through her intelligent emancipation that the race shall be redeemed."[164] The next paragraph, however, begins at the conclusion, announcing not a reasoned argument but a revelation, an intuition perhaps, from which is deduced woman's emancipation: "I am a full and firm believer in the revelation that it is through woman that the race is to be redeemed. And it is because of this faith that I ask for her immediate and unconditional emancipation."[165] Anthony could reverse herself so thoroughly not because her logic was fuzzy, but because the two courses of reasoning were circular. There was no discontinuity between the empirical functioning of society and Anthony's "faith." Both pointed sharply and urgently to the same conclusion, the emancipation of women.

Unlike Stanton's cosmological vision of the eternal laws moving together in harmony, when Anthony spoke—rarely—of heaven or God, the references were almost always to the reform struggle. I opened this section with the note that "if I entered the other life before women were enfranchised nothing in the glories of heaven would interest me so much as the work for women's freedom on earth." Not for her the eternal rest that is usual in Western views. For Anthony, heaven was to be a place of bustling activity, a reformer's paradise. "Oh the world is so full of work for those who work at all—I see no old fashioned *heaven* for me—to sit and sing and glorify."[166]

If it is correct that it was Anthony's work for women's equal rights that was the fundamental locus of her religious faith, that opens the way to understanding some of her other themes as religious in nature. From the standpoint of this hermeneutic, we must understand some allegedly secular emphases in an alternative way. The redefinition of the suffrage struggle itself as her prayer and her worship, for example, provided Anthony with a foundation for the critical appraisal of traditional religion, and particularly that hobgoblin of woman's rights, the Bible. First Amendment principles, especially freedom of speech and religious freedom, attained the status of religious tenets with her; they were not merely instrumental, but intrinsic, to her religious position. Her sense of security in the victory of women's rights, expressed in her famous last public comment before her death, expressed a belief in the fundamental inevitability of her cause. With heaven and the best of earth working together toward justice for women, how could the opposition prevail? It was the conviction of her lifelong friend that progress toward the higher planes was inexorable. It remained to Anthony, uniquely, to cite the association of women as the reason that "failure is impossible."

B. Freedom of Religion

Anthony frowned upon, and used her parliamentary positions to head off, explicitly theological arguments in suffrage conventions. Nothing in all the years of collaboration so separated her from Stanton as the latter's attempts to introduce religion into convention platforms, resolutions, and speeches. In this she followed what she understood to be Garrison's policy, a somewhat ambiguous guideline. She wanted to keep the organization's platform at once "broad" (letting both Christians and atheists free upon it to speak their minds) and antisectarian (committed to no particular policy, save free speech alone).

The struggle for equality was the point of unanimity among suffragists; therefore, they should not be led astray into sectarian comments. Behind the scenes she labored to head off such religious statements. Of Stanton's eightieth birthday speech, her journal recorded that the

> only criticism was that she did not rest her case after describing the wonderful advance made in state, church, society, and home, instead of going on to single out the church and declare it to be especially slow in accepting the doctrine of equality to women. I tried to make her see that it had advanced as rapidly as the other departments but I did not succeed, and it is right that she should express her own ideas, not mine.[167]

Anthony was aware of changes in the religious world. "The cultivated men and women of today are above the need of your book. Even the liberalized orthodox ministers are coming to our aid, and their conventions are passing resolutions in favor of woman's equality, and I feel that these men and women who are just born into the kingdom of liberty can better reach the minds of their followers than can any of us out-and-out radicals."[168] The most well-known occasion on which she stated her position was the *Woman's Bible* controversy of 1896, in which members of NAWSA disowned that text. Anthony was deeply perturbed by this "illiberal" move, and she left the podium to express herself vehemently, and for once at some length, on it. It is a succinct statement of a variety of themes to which Anthony returned frequently.

The one distinct feature of our association has been the right of individual opinion for every member. We have been beset at each step with the cry that somebody was injuring the cause by the expression of sentiments which differed from those held by the majority. The religious persecution of the ages has been carried on under what was claimed to be the command of God. I distrust those people who know so well what God wants them to do, because I notice it always coincides with their own desires. All the way along the history of our movement there has been this same contest on account of religious theories. Forty years ago one of our noblest men said to me, "You would better never hold another convention than allow Ernestine L. Rose on your platform"; because that eloquent woman, who ever stood for justice and freedom, did not believe in the plenary inspiration of the Bible. Did we banish Mrs. Rose? No, indeed!

Every new generation of converts threshes over the same old straw. The point is whether you will sit in judgment on one who questions the divine inspiration of certain passages in the Bible derogatory to women. If Mrs. Stanton had written approvingly of these passages you would not have brought in this resolution for fear the cause might be injured among the *liberals* in religion. In other words, if she had written *your* views, you would not have considered a resolution necessary. To pass this one is to set back the hands on the dial of reform.

What you should say to outsiders is that a Christian has neither more nor less rights in our association than an atheist. When our platform becomes too narrow for people of all creeds and of no creeds, I myself can not stand upon it. Many things have been said and done by our *orthodox* friends which I have felt to be extremely harmful to our cause; but I should no more consent to a resolution denouncing them than I shall consent to this. Who is to draw the line? Who can tell now whether these commentaries may not prove a great help to woman's emancipation from old superstitions which have barred its way? Lucretia Mott at first thought Mrs. Stanton had injured the cause of all woman's other rights by insisting upon the demand for suffrage, but she had sense enough not to bring in a resolution against it. In 1860 when Mrs. Stanton made a speech before the New York Legislature in favor of a bill making drunkenness a ground for divorce, there was a general cry among the friends that she had killed the woman's cause. I shall be pained beyond expression if the delegates here are so narrow and illiberal as to adopt this resolution. You would better not begin resolving against individual action or you will find no limit. This year it is Mrs. Stanton; next year it may be I or one of yourselves, who will be the victim.

If we do not inspire in women a broad and catholic spirit, they will fail, when enfranchised, to constitute that power for better government which we have always claimed for them. Ten women educated into the practice of liberal principles would be a stronger force than 10,000 organized on a platform of intolerance and bigotry. I pray you vote for religious liberty, without censorship or inquisition. This resolution adopted will be a vote of censure upon a woman who is without a peer in intellectual and statesmanlike ability; one who has stood for half a century the acknowledged leader of progressive thought and demand in regard to all matters pertaining to the absolute freedom of women.[169]

The controversy over "religious theories" was abhorrent both in its own right and because it might stifle a contribution integral to women's future emancipation. Anthony linked such controversy directly to religious persecution. Fresh themes were brought into view in this impassioned call for religious freedom: the implication that Anthony was a liberal in religion, the aim at women of a "broad and catholic" spirit (liberals, in fact), the place of the Bible, the necessary sense of fallibility in interpreting God's will while defending each woman's right to express dissent.

Anthony's faith in the redemption of the human race by womanhood was one she tied (privately, to be sure) to liberalism. Women without that "broad and catholic" spirit would not constitute a new balance of moral power in the political arena, that new balance of power which she believed would be triumphant in the battle for social purity and reforming industrial evils. She was self-consciously liberal, though she expressed herself mostly negatively against the "illiberal"—that is, the orthodox—folk. When, for example, the WCTU requested suffrage speakers with the proviso that they should not attack Christianity, Anthony wrote to Shaw:

> Won't that prevent your going, Rev. Anna? I wonder if they'll be as particular to warn all other speakers not to say anything which shall sound like an attack on liberal religion. They never seem to think we have any feelings to be hurt when we have to sit under their reiteration of orthodox cant and dogma. The boot is all on one foot with the dear religious bigots.[170]

(Here the orthodox and the liberals appear as "they" and "we.") That the idealism of liberals[171] was in part a legacy of the abolitionist movement was suggested by her Garrisonian echo that ten women practicing liberal principles would be more effective than masses without them.

It was especially practice and action in the "great world" that would create this liberal spirit in women. Privately to Stanton she kept up her argument over her friend's religious crusading.

> You say, "women must be emancipated from their superstitions before enfranchisement will be of any benefit," and I say just the reverse, that women must be enfranchised before they can be emancipated from their superstitions. Women would be no more superstitious today than men, if they had been men's political and business equals and gone outside the four walls of home and the other four of the church into the great world, and come in contact with and discussed men and measures on the plane of this mundane sphere, instead of living in the air with Jesus and the angels. So you will have to keep pegging away, saying, "Get rid of religious bigotry and then get political rights"; while I shall keep pegging away, saying, "Get political rights first and religious bigotry will melt like dew before the morning sun"; and each will continue still to believe in and defend the other.[172]

Action was related to the persistent pursuit of one's own high ethical purposes formulated in the privacy of one's own conscience. Action on the plane of this mundane sphere was the force that was to emancipate women from bigotry and airy speculations—the special theories Anthony so abhorred. It was not, therefore, that Stanton's biblical project was just politically inexpedient to the suffrage movement. Rather, from Anthony's perspective, Stanton's critiques were ill-conceived in principle. Practical religious action, not theoretical religious notions, was the fundamental counter and criterion.

I need to pause for two subsidiary points. First, Anthony's own conscience, formed in a Quaker matrix, produced certain criteria by which she viewed all discussions of the Bible. Second, she believed that the reliance of women on their own consciences would produce something like a "woman's gospel." For Anthony herself, this led back to action for social justice.

Asked publicly about *The Woman's Bible*, she had recourse to the Friends' position on that text. "My own relations to or ideas of the Bible always have been peculiar owing to my Quaker training. The Friends consider the book as historical, made up of traditions, but not as a plenary inspiration."[173] There is no reason to believe that she was simply taking refuge in the nearest bolt-hole. Her comments in the privacy of her diary indicate that she was "thankful for having been born a Friend—a Quaker. To be born into a free religious world is a blessing indeed."[174]

That the Bible was not "sacred," at least not in any simple sense, was obvious to Anthony. It was equally obvious that it was of human origin, that beliefs to the contrary were a superstition.

> I don't know what better one could expect when our ranks are now so filled with young women not yet out of bondage to the idea of the infallibility of that book. To every person who really believes in religious freedom, it is no worse to criticise those pages in the Bible which degrade woman than it is to criticise the laws on our statute books which degrade her. Everything spoken or written by Jew or Greek, Gentile or Christian, or by any human being whomsoever, is not too sacred to be criticised by any other human being.[175]

This reference to "bondage" to the idea of biblical infallibility should alert us to the "liberation theology" themes of Anthony's religious views. Breaking the chains of bondage and tyranny, whether the literal chains of prisoners and slaves, or the metaphorical chains of mistaken divine authorship, was ever Anthony's work and worship. She cited not simply a belief, but a *real* belief, in religious freedom. The "really real" was less a cosmological counter, as it was for Stanton, than an indicator of the fully consistent *practice* of toleration. Further, this real belief in religious freedom undercut the sacred character of the Bible as it spoke of women. The central principle to which she returned in speaking of the Woman's Bible was the rights of women, in practice and conscience.

> I think women have just as good a right to interpret and twist the Bible to their own advantage as men always have twisted and turned it to theirs . . . It was written by men, and therefore its references to women reflect the light in which they were regarded in those days. In the same way the history of our Revolutionary War was written, in which very little is said of the noble deeds of women, though we know how they stood by and helped the great work; and it is the same with history all through.[176]

The plenary inspiration of the Bible was one of the superstitions whose "lingering skeletons" she rejoiced to see "crumbling on every side."[177] What was not a superstition was "perfect equality of rights" and deeds of Christian benevolence that lifted humanity to that perfection. Anthony never, it seems, described this antithesis to superstition as the rational, scientific truth that her friend Stanton extolled. This was not to say that she thought her position unscientific or antithetical to science. But her silence on such a point, given her allegiance to Stanton, was rather remarkable.

Suffrage conventions featured their speakers in the churches and pulpits of their host cities on the Sundays before and after the convention proper. Anthony's institutional policy, in other words, was that the religious angles of the movement were better off framing, flanking, the conventions than as official parts of their business. But on at least one occasion she was drawn into organizing a session directly on religion. The 1888 International Council of Women, which initiated the series of international meetings, contained a symposium on religion. That event is noteworthy for several reasons.

During its planning, Rev. Antoinette Brown Blackwell urged that ordained women be included in the meeting. In response, Anthony firmly asserted the rights of laywomen. She thought of this meeting as an occasion for speaking "woman's gospel." Keeping with the liturgical bent of her language, it was not surprising that it represented a purer and better worship:

> I have felt all along that we ought to give a chance for the expression of the highest and deepest religious thought of those not ordained of men. Your wish to give the result of your research opens the way for us to make the last day—Easter Sunday—voice the new, the purer, the better worship of the living God. We'll have a real symposium of woman's gospel. It is not fair to give only the church-ordained women an opportunity to present their religious thoughts, and now it shall be fixed so that the laity may have the same. I don't want a controversy or a lot of negations, but shall tell each one to give her strongest affirmation. This forever saying a thing is false and failing to present the truth, is to me a foolish waste of time, when almost everybody feels the old forms, creeds and ritual to be only the mint, anise, and cumin.[178]

The meeting itself, however, was perhaps testimony to the wisdom of Anthony's course of keeping "special theories" off feminist platforms. To today's observer, it was one of the more aberrant meetings held under the wings of the movement. The nineteenth century was a bustling, blooming buzz of religious confusion, with sects and theories springing up hither and thither; probably all of them had some suffragist as an adherent. To this meeting came a good section of the variety possible.

Matilda Joslyn Gage chided the participants for not having once mentioned the divine motherhood, and rehearsed her anti-Christian position. Antoinette Brown Blackwell held forth at length and in great technical detail on her scientifically oriented process theories, establishing the existence of God on the basis of a "rhythmic atom" at the base of existence.[179] Elizabeth Boynton

207

Harbert showed conclusively that "God is love." Isabella Beecher Hooker confessed herself a "Christian Spiritualist" and invoked heroic souls of the past and "spirit molecules" to urge women onward. (She did mention the divine motherhood.) Elizabeth Stuart of Massachusetts described an odd numerological Platonism. Frances Willard admitted that she was a true Methodist. This array, of course, would have been grist for the mills of many a conservative theologian.

To this meeting also came Ednah Cheney of Boston. For her the entire week of activities concerning justice for women had been a religious time. She referred to Theodore Parker's teaching that the two great principles of religion were the brotherhood of man and the fatherhood of God. She reminded the group that "fatherhood" meant motherhood to Parker, that theologian who taught many suffragists to speak of "our heavenly Father and Mother." At the heart of her comments was a denial of the segregation of religion from other political and reforming activities.

> This has seemed to me a most religious meeting all through the week. For though we have said very little about these great religious truths in their abstract expression, the whole drift and tone of the speeches have been in the recognition of these two great truths. I think when we have asked for equal rights and equal opportunities for women, it has been because we have always remembered that woman was the child of God just as much as man, feeling that the poorest and most wronged member of this human race, was our brother and our sister; and so we can carry these great truths always in our hearts and our lives, and they are truths we can all unite on. Perhaps I love the subtleties of metaphysics and theology just as well as anyone. I can enjoy them intellectually, but I think we can all differ in those. We can all come back and unite in these great truths of religion which lie at the base of all morality; and if we could only carry them out into works we should find, if we added to them the wisdom of experience and the wisdom of thought, that today they struck the keynote; that they resolved all our difficulties and all our differences into harmony. . . .
>
> It has been a holy week to those who are not wont to think that religion depends on times and seasons, but on consecration to right purposes and great philanthropic and human enterprises.[180]

Anthony presided over this meeting. She was invariably supportive of every speaker, warm about her right to speak—but noncommittal about the substance of what was said. Cheney's comment that religion was not segregated off onto Sunday mornings but enacted in humanistic activities (together with her call away from the "subleties of metaphysics and theology") drew a rare intervention from Anthony. She could not resist offering a sort of "amen" even while being conscious of her position as chair. She reminded the audience of Mott's motto, "Truth for Authority, not Authority for Truth," and drew the delegates' attention to a poem contained in a pamphlet on sale near the door:

Thou, from on high, perceivest it were better
All men and women should on earth be free;
Laws that enslave and tyrannies that enfetter
Snap and evanish at the touch of thee.[181]

This was a veiled affirmation of Cheney's point. To Anthony it was liberation from the slavery of the laws and all sorts of bondage that was the heart of her religious view. That had been occurring, as Cheney had said, "all through the week."

After the final speaker of the meeting, Anthony returned to her position regarding religious freedom. She "summed up" the session by saying, "Women are not so narrow but that they can come together and talk over their religious beliefs, and see down beneath the whole, the true spirit, the true woman, and be ready to work together despite their differences."[182] Women working together—this note leads to the next section of Anthony's thought.

C. With Such Women as These

"Miss Anthony taught us the sisterhood of woman."[183] One of Anthony's most important legacies to the woman suffrage movement was her search for new leaders of the rising generation to ensure the struggle was to continue after the "pioneers" had gone. Among these strands of affirmation of the presence and power of other women is a thematic emphasis that deserves to be called in today's language "sisterhood." Such emphases are central to understanding her, and to understanding her religious position. Her affirmations of the relationships of women need to be seen in their connection with the history of the movement and her sense of the inevitability of its success.

To this task, however, Anthony's theories and vocabulary were not quite adequate. Perhaps if her old friend Stanton, her pen-artist, had not been so indissolubly welded to individual selfhood, we might have had some greater guidance from the woman suffrage movement on this theme so important to the present women's movement. But Anthony's metaphors and images merit the consideration of this topic here. The "second" generation of suffragists, after about 1900, were somewhat better equipped to appreciate the "relational virtues" in her lifework.[184]

In the opening pages of this section I quoted Anthony's comment to Besant that "if I entered the other life before women were enfranchised, nothing in the glories of heaven would interest me so much as the work for women's freedom on earth." Despite the doubtful provenance of the exact text, the sentiment is one that Anthony expressed frequently in her last years of life. She was almost always agnostic about "the other world," life after death, the immortality of the soul, and the spiritualism that crept in among suffragists after the Civil War. The exceptions are noteworthy in that most of them occur in the context of her affirmation of the relationships of women and her hopes for the struggle for women's rights.

In moods of discouragement, she was consoled by the knowledge that God and other souls joined her in the work of reform:

There is so much, mid all that is so hopeful, to discourage and dishearten—and I feel *alone*—still I know I am *not alone*—but that all the true and good souls, both in and out of the body, keep me company, and that the Good Father more than all is ever a host in every good effort.[185]

Perhaps it was this sense of being in the company of the divine and the faithful that led her to hint, as she approached her own death, that she too would remain with the suffragists.

I have passed as the leader of this association of which I have been a member for so long, but I am not through working, for I shall work to the end of my time, and when I am called home, if there exist an immortal spirit, mine will still be with you, watching and inspiring you.[186]

It is very difficult to know at what point these comments became the legends and sagas of the woman suffrage movement. This is particularly true of her deathbed scenes with Shaw, from which came several similar statements. Shaw quoted Anthony as saying,

I do not know anything about what comes to us after this life ends, but . . . if I have any conscious knowledge of this world and of what you are doing, I shall not be far away from you; and in times of need I will help you all I can. Who knows? Perhaps I may be able to do more for the Cause after I am gone than while I am here.[187]

It was also Shaw's testimony that in her final hours Anthony had a vision of the host of her comrades passing before her, in a suffragist review.

> Their faces pass before me, one by one, I cannot call their names but they are a host of splendid, loyal women and I remember and love them all. How good they have been to me! I wonder if we shall know each other in the hereafter. Perhaps I can do more over yonder than I have done here.[188]

That Anthony promised to be with Shaw in her hour of need, however, was something that Shaw remembered on the more trying occasions of her NAWSA presidency.[189]

We need not decide whether these comments stem from Anthony's own mouth or from suffrage mythology.[190] At least the "perhaps" sounds like Anthony. Nor need we rely solely on such quasi-spiritualist themes for investigating this subject.

The other great suffragist legend stands more chance of being true since it took place in the midst of a large gathering. "Failure is impossible" were the final words of her final public utterance. The phrase became a rallying cry, as perhaps it was meant to become. Once again the context of this stirring line was an affirmation of the other women whose efforts were devoted to the cause. As the *History of Woman Suffrage* has it, she spoke of how

> the great work of the National Association had been placed in her charge; turning to the other national officers on the stage she reached out her hand to them and expressed her appreciation of their loyal support, and then, realizing that her strength was almost gone, she said: "There have been others also just as true and devoted to the cause—I wish I could name every one—but with such women consecrating their lives . . . failure is impossible."[191]

Of course, it is never good reform tactics to admit that you doubt that your cause will ultimately triumph. In this age when everyone hailed progress approaching from the nearest horizon, it was not unusual for reformers to announce blandly that right would surely come topside in the vicissitudes of history. Stanton, for example, relied on her certain knowledge that the great immutable laws of nature were fixed and unwavering; that the direction of civilization was broadly in line with them; that the new age dawning would be higher and better. No doubt Anthony too believed some of this. Yet it was

211

uniquely her contribution to transmute these impersonal cosmological grounds of a reformer's faith into a faith in the officers of her organization. It was "with such women as these consecrating their lives" to the cause that was to see it through to justice done, not merely justice hoped for.

Anthony's faith in the triumph of women's rights had to do with human community. When asked, for example, whether she had grown discouraged in earlier years, she replied, "Never, I knew that my cause was just and I was always in good company."[192] The latter phrase is no less striking than the former. Far from Stanton's individualism, her assumption was that "for weal or for woe we are knit together." Progress would come, she believed, "because I have an abiding faith in all my countrymen and countrywomen."[193]

Far more than anything in Stanton's rational, logical cases, Anthony's appeal was to the emotional bonds tying together women struggling for their rights. She invoked from the younger generation the "deep, rich, earnest love for your own sex."[194] The growing women's friendships were "the most beautiful part" of the annual Washington conventions, drawing together women from all sections of the land.[195] The suffrage association indeed stood "like a Mother Church with her arms wide open to those who want to come in."[196]

Just as the mother church proclaimed its unity of saints throughout all ages, for Anthony, telling the suffrage history, recounting the names and deeds of the "pioneers," was an essential part of this task. The unity of the past generations and of contemporary women with one another in the struggles of the mother church was no mystical unity. It was a very present and proximate, this-worldly task of recounting the names and contributions of former workers. Younger women did not realize that "every single inch of ground" upon which women of the day stood had been the result of the hard work of "some little handful of women of the past."[197] Anthony was constant in bringing forward to the assembled eyes of each convention those older women who were also present. NAWSA conventions featured an evening devoted to woman suffrage history.

> The good of this hour is that it brings to the knowledge of the young the work of the pioneers who have passed away. It seems remarkable to those standing, as I do, one of a generation almost ended, that so many of these young people know nothing of the past; they are apt to think they have sprung up like somebody's gourd, and think nothing ever was done until they came. So I am always gratified to hear these reminiscences, that they may know how others have sown what they are reaping today.[198]

Greeting the 1899 meeting of the International Council of Women, Anthony brought together the thought of the "rising" generation with that of the past generation.

Girls—yes, I call you so, for you are all girls compared to me—you have expressed your joy and thankfulness that you had had an opportunity to be present at this Congress. What do you think I feel, I, who remember the time when woman's cause had no friends outside a little group now called the "pioneers"? What do you think I feel to know that now there is a whole generation of women able to carry on the work when the "pioneers" have passed away.[199]

I noted Anthony's policy of naming all the "sinners" of the history project. She was equally adamant that the names of all supporters should not be slighted.

And then the contest over the *names* which should be mentioned! In vain the writer begged, expostulated and protested that the book would be swamped with them. "It is all the return I can offer for the friendship, the hospitality, the loyalty of those who have made it possible for me to do my work all these years," was the unvarying reply, and not one could be smuggled out from under that watchful eye.[200]

Friendship, hospitality, loyalty—these were themes far from Stanton's individualistic perspective. Anthony was conscious of the contributions of the women who were "life-long privates in the war for equal rights," of the followers as much as the leaders. "It is the like of you who stand firm and true for justice to women, that enable us at the front to stand strong and steady," was her reply.[201] Solidarity among women, "combining," as she put it with regard to trade unions, was of a piece with prayer by action. It was corporate prayer and not Stanton's solitary meditation or communing with great Nature.

Her friendship with Stanton was a special case. To Anthony, its most valued occasions happened when the fires of action were hottest. Asked, upon Stanton's death, what period of their lives she had enjoyed most, she replied,

The days when the struggle was the hardest and the fight the thickest; when the whole world was against us and we had to stand the closer to each other; when I would go to her home and help with the children and the housekeeping through the day and then we would sit up far into the night preparing our ammunition and getting ready to move on the enemy. The years since the rewards began to come have brought no enjoyment like that.[202]

This was typical of Anthony; when the fight was thickest and the two of them had to stand "closer to each other" was when her happiness was deepest. Sisterhood was at its height when action was most fiercely called for. Such a view represents another strand in Anthony's intuitive political genius. "My work is my worship," she said. I might point to the intensification of friendship in the struggle for justice as a miniepiphany of religious social action.

Comments and Conclusions

Anthony's religious views are startlingly different from those expressed by Stanton. Unlike the God of the natural laws who ruled impersonally in Stanton's view, Anthony's deity loved freedom and was served by action for justice. Where Stanton spoke of harnessing thought and action together, Anthony spoke of prayer by action. Nor did she share a civil religion. While her view was straightforwardly democratic in its love of freedom and equality, one may doubt that she could ever have seen her faith incarnated in the ballot box as the holy of holies. The conscience of the nation could never be so readily institutionalized as that—except perhaps in the continual protest against renewed injustice in the "Protestant principle."

To her friend Stanton as much as to church members, she might well have said, "Friends, the time has fully come for us to cease to waste all our precious hours in discussing questions of mystical theology and speculative faith, and adopt the plain practical principles taught by Jesus of Nazareth."[203] In principle, Anthony and Stanton agreed on this point. Both opposed the traditional religiousness which took people away from the world and reform. They had their differences within this broad agreement. To Stanton it was an essential part of the work of reform to demystify outmoded notions; more, the notions of sin and salvation embedded in the orthodox reading of Genesis were at the foundations of women's oppression. To this Anthony never rejoined, so far as I can tell. But practical demystification by work in the world—"outside the four walls of home and the other four of the church," as she put it—was more likely to be effective than theoretical arguments. Women needed to stop "living in the air with Jesus and the angels." There is, I think, a great deal of truth to Anthony's position. Stanton's Voltairean sarcasm and indictments of priestcraft made little headway against the entrenched pieties of Victorian America, that soi-disant Christian civilization. The next chapter describes some

214

of the ways the suffrage cause was reconciled to Christianity—a Christianity that was not the orthodoxy rejected by both Stanton and Anthony, but rather more what Anthony called the "liberalizing orthodoxy."

And yet . . . and yet there remains something unsatisfying about Anthony's view. She did not articulate the theology to flesh out her notion of prayer by action. This view remains a major unwritten work of the woman suffrage movement. There was enough ambiguity in this silence that we may ask, what did a "gospel of womanhood" mean? Anthony was clear enough that such a view must not simply represent the view of the ordained or theologically trained woman; it was to stress its affirmations, not its rebuttals. There is a tantalizing quality about this notion of prayer by action, with its accompanying themes: the work was "radical"—destined not merely to alleviate the symptoms of victimization but thoroughly to change the conditions that created victims; it was not directed to devotional emotion or church organization; the economy and the polity were among its crucial dimensions; it remained in significant ways Christian. Anthony may have been right to reject speculation, creed, and dogma in order to emphasize the practice of moral principles and right action. But Anthony's perspective, insofar as I have been able to reconstruct it, represents the highlights, so to speak, of such a position. It remains to be seen what content would fill out the shadows that remain behind or between these glowing phrases.

Stanton's individualism was of a piece with her rejection of otherworldliness; "one good woman" laboring at a bedside could do more than a regiment of ascetics. To Anthony, whose Quaker background also led her to emphasize true inwardness of the individual, the "beautiful part" of the suffrage struggle was the friendships between the women in NAWSA meetings. The mother church may have made its converts one by one, but once within the fold they were assured of the company of God and other good and true souls, whether living or dead.

One hardly knows what to think about the quasi-spiritualist notion that Anthony promised, tentatively to be sure, to be with her descendants in the struggle for women's rights. Perhaps this point is best left in silence. Yet there is something oddly comforting about this theme in Anthony's work—more comforting than anything in Stanton's position. I would, personally, rather have Susan B. Anthony by my side, for all her quirks, than any amount of centrifugal-centripetal forces of the universe. This is precisely the sort of "devotional emotion" that Anthony abhorred—but it is feminist-devotional rather than traditionally pious.

TOWARD A TRADITION OF FEMINIST THEOLOGY

The comparison of Stanton and Anthony leaves us with something of a theory-practice distinction, in which the former emphasized theory and the latter practice. Yet to contemplate Anthony's work on its own internal grounds leaves us with a slightly different question. Anthony, as she herself said, was accused of not doing anything but talking. This apostle of energetic deeds claimed, on her own behalf, that "this talk makes everything in the world." It is as though from the perspective of the proponent of action, the questions that arise are less those of theory and action than they are of speech and action. This is an immensely provocative thought. In a democratic politics, where the arts of persuasion are so very important, certain kinds of talk are virtually action.

It is a temptation of this final section to align, so to speak, the sections of this work with each other and so to make Anthony out to be a more systematic worker than she was. If we look at the articulated and unarticulated portions of her thought, we may see them thus:

Definition of the Issue:
    Tame Submission   Bread of Dependence   Social Evils

Religion:
    Prayer by Action   ——   With Such Women
    a. Freedom of   as These
       Religion

Underlying Principle of Justice:
    Utmost Liberty   Perfect Equality   ("Sorority")

This works, if I may so put it. It sheds some light on Anthony herself, both in what is present in a quasi-systematic way and in what is not present. That Anthony was ever the apostle of women's action, of freedom in action and thought, is reflected in this chart. It was equally clear to her that women could not be free if they were not equal, as when she said that there will be no true freedom for women to act for temperance until they possess the equal right to property. But I have found no way to articulate this dimension of equality in Anthony's religious views, unless it be in such submerged themes as woman's right equal with man to interpret religious phenomena in her own view. Similarly, to see the speech regarding "social purity" and women's sexuality in the light of something like a principle of "sorority," which was never Anthony's locution, is to see it in its best light. Women talking to other women about their woes, women needed in courts of justice to judge the crimes alleged against other women, women united in struggle with one another to change the legal structure of the nation—these themes were present in Anthony's speech. And similarly, the intertwinement of the principles of justice with one another is clarified somewhat by this schematic presentation. For how could there be justice for women on the themes of social purity unless women had equality with men? And how could there be equality with men unless women too had the freedom to act to change the legal structure of the country?

I have found nowhere recorded Anthony's thoughts about the emphasis on mothering aspects of God that are such a striking part of Stanton's thought. Her references to the "All-Father" do not seem to be matched by the "All-Mother." Viewed from certain twentieth-century feminist theological works, this may make Stanton's position the more "radical" one, particularly among the followers of women's spirituality. Anthony's view of "prayer by action" is equally radical, it seems, in quite a different vein.

FIVE

Anna Howard Shaw: Toward a Theology for a Feminist Christianity

Unlike her two predecessors in the NAWSA presidency, Anna Howard Shaw had formal theological training. An ordained Methodist minister, she was one of the most prominent of a small body of women in ministry who were deeply involved in the woman suffrage movement. Unlike Stanton and Anthony, she did not evoke a multidimensional analysis of the definition of the issue in the woman suffrage movement. She shared with them, however, certain thematic emphases—the importance of republican principles, especially. Like both of them, she saw the suffrage cause as fundamentally religious, but on rather different terms. Like Stanton, she had a strong notion of upward evolution; like Anthony, a more communal understanding of human existence. In this chapter, therefore, I investigate the systematic differences that result even in the articulation of shared notions.

For Shaw, the issue faced by the suffrage movement may be stated with relative simplicity. The injustice facing feminists was the inconsistency between the republic's theories and its practice. Since inconsistency was the "question," the "answer," naturally enough, was consistency. Like Stanton she thought that the right to vote was a natural one inherent in the human person, secured but not bestowed by government; but she did not argue this point. At times, however, she wavered in this belief; whether suffrage was a right or a privilege, women were entitled to it. She skirted the notion that if the country were to give up its democratic pretensions, suffragists would be left without a case. Unlike either of the two pioneers, Shaw was forced to do battle with the small but vocal group of antisuffragists—familiarly called the "antis." Some of her best qualities as an orator were called forth on these occasions; her light touch and humorous jibes at the opposition were characteristic.

Like Anthony, whose protégée she was, Shaw connected woman suffrage to all good causes—temperance, abolishing child labor, and peace chief among them. It is rather more difficult to discern why she did this. At times it seemed that these were the causes in which women were struggling; women, she seemed to think, never advocated anything but improvement. At other times she argued, following Frances Willard of the WCTU, that women needed the ballot to protect the home from drink and vice. Militarism and war were directly antithetical to the spirit of democracy; Shaw supported Wilson wholeheartedly because he promised to make World War I the war to end all wars, to make the world safe for the democratic dream Shaw held. On issues of economic class she waffled; the leisure class was the true working class.

According to Shaw, democracy was a sublime vision emanating from the heart of the Infinite, her preferred name for God. The course of human history was an upward movement toward the practice of these grand visions vouchsafed to reformers by a beneficent deity. She considered the heart primary in this process of visionary reform, unlike Stanton's emphasis on reason. And who but women were especially gifted with heart knowledge? Acknowledging herself a visionary and an idealist, Shaw was unprepared for the sheer technical politics that governed the final years of the suffrage movement.

Shaw shared Stanton's vision of the religion of the republic. Unlike that anticlericalist, however, she believed that the religion of democracy was identical with Christianity. Her eschatological vision of the Kingdom of God throbbed with biblical language. She was only rarely critical of the churches. Shaw was one of that band of NAWSA women who opposed *The Woman's Bible*. Nonetheless, in her private correspondence emerged a picture of American churches in ferment over women's rights and women's roles. Shaw is thus particularly interesting as a case study of the synthesis of feminism (a word she knew and defended), the republican faith, and mainstream American Christianity.

A brief biographical sketch outlines the contours of Shaw's life. The second major section of this chapter, "Consistency in Inconsistency," looks at her view of the definition of the issue. "Democratic Principles" looks at her view of the evolutionary trend of American history to bring it into line with the sublime vision of the Founders. "The Antis" is further marked by her view of consistency. The opposition was so contradictory that "all their arguments come in pairs and answer each other." "The Uplifting of Society" inquires into the many good causes for which women were struggling and the terms on which Shaw integrated them into her suffrage case.

The third major section of this chapter, "Injustice and Justice," looks at the shape of the issue and of the remedies Shaw proposed. Not so much the moralist as the two earlier suffragists, Shaw's sermonic abilities led her into looser claims. The cause was based on "justice and fair play and common sense." Her strong notion of the evolutionary process focused on the possibilities and concomitant responsibilities of human existence.

The fourth section, "Evolving Visions of the Infinite," explores Shaw's religious idealism. The woman suffrage cause was "ethical and religious," as she put it. God operated by sending visions to reformers. Since these were invariably visions of democracy, in Shaw's view, I look at "Democracy the Divine Emanation." "Love, Truth, Beauty" analyzes her quasi-Platonic view of these ideals. "The Churches" explores her muted, and mostly private, sense that the "churches need to be taught a lesson."

Biographical Summary

The family of Anna Howard Shaw (1847-1919) migrated to the United States from England in 1851. They resided first in Massachusetts, where her father was involved in both abolition and impractical business schemes. In 1859, in search of financial success, he sent his family to live in a rudimentary cabin in the wilderness of Michigan. Mrs. Shaw, alone with the four youngest children, had a mental breakdown, leaving the survival of the family to the skills of Anna, twelve, and Henry, eight. Though the father returned for brief periods, he and the oldest sons enlisted at the outbreak of the Civil War. Shaw's early years were thus marked by that pioneering spirit of hard work and "gumption" of which she thought so highly. The children's education was a function of the family books and sporadic encounters with a frontier school.

The young woman early felt a desire to preach—and preach she did, to the frontier trees. Her family seriously opposed this calling.

> It was such a shock to everyone and created such a sensation that my people who had decided upon sending me to Michigan University refused to do so unless I gave them my pledge never to preach. This I could not do, so I again faced what seemed like defeat.[1]

221

The Universalist minister Marianna Thompson and suffragist Mary A. Livermore both supported her aspirations as they passed through rural Michigan. Nonetheless, she had to teach school during the 1860s, frequently the sole meager support of the family. Despite her family's Unitarian background, she was discovered by a Methodist Episcopal presiding elder "of progressive ideas," ambitious to be the first presiding elder to have a woman ordained.[2] Shaw was licensed in 1871 and given many opportunities to preach in the surrounding churches.

In 1876 she cut short her undergraduate study at Albion College to go directly to the Boston University School of Theology (the same year that the faculty added Borden P. Browne, later to be accused, and acquitted, of heresy by the Methodists). While male seminarians roomed and boarded free, she (like her one female predecessor, Anna Oliver, who had graduated by the time Shaw arrived) had to make her own way, living off campus and working to pay for meals. Shaw's autobiography, *The Story of a Pioneer*, understated the trials of those seminary years. She was more than once on the brink of starvation, living on nothing more than milk and crackers. The young student was finally discovered by the Women's Foreign Missionary Society, which contributed financially to her comfort and survival. Her biography did not record active disruption or hampering by her classmates such as was reported by other women in early educational settings. Aside from her starvation—which was, after all, enough—her critiques of those years were mild. Virtually the only comment she made was that "throughout my entire course I rarely entered the classroom without the abysmal conviction that I was really not wanted there."[3] One of the nineteenth century's classic stories of sexist exegesis, however, comes from Shaw's seminary days.

I came across the lesson where, on the mountain top after Pentecost when the people declared the Christians were drunk and Peter defended them saying, "These are not drunken; this is the fulfillment of your own Scriptures of your own prophet, who said, 'In the last days I shall pour out my Spirit upon all flesh and your sons and your daughters shall prophesy.' " And I innocently said to the professor, "What does prophesy mean?" "Well," he said, "it depends on where it is used; in the Old Testament they use it in a double sense, in the sense of foretelling or in the sense of preaching, but in the New Testament it is used wholly in the sense of preaching. When the word prophesy is used in the New Testament it means that they shall preach." "Oh," I said, "then women did preach, did they not, at the time of Pentecost?" He was bitterly opposed to women preaching—didn't want me there. He said, "No, oh no, the women talked to each other." I said "Yes, and what did the men do? Talk to each other?" He said, "Oh no they preached." And I said, "But the two are connected by a conjunction, 'men and women,' and when women talk they talk, and when men talk they preach; is that the way it was?" He said, "We will resume."[4]

One hundred years later we can imagine the impact of such experiences, though Shaw tells little of the human toll upon her.[5] She was especially influenced by the preaching of Phillips Brooks and James Freeman Clarke in Boston, both AWSA members.[6] Like many a woman minister after her, when Shaw was finally given a temporary charge in Bingham, Massachusetts, she quadrupled the membership of this failing church only to be replaced by a man.[7]

Upon her graduation in 1878, she received dual Methodist and Congregationalist calls in East Dennis, Massachusetts. Her request for ordination was refused by the Methodist Episcopal New England Conference of Ministers. She removed to the Methodist Protestant Church, which agreed to her ordination in 1880, after a stormy battle. After several initial conflicts with her Methodist parish, she was well received by the congregation. Her ministry in East Dennis, however, was not sufficiently challenging for her "superabundant vitality." She wanted to work with the bodies as well as the souls of women. By 1883, she had returned to Boston University for medical study. Working among women in the Boston slums for three years, she received her M.D. in 1886. In these same three years she stepped up her involvement with both suffrage and temperance lecturing, which eventually led her away from both medicine and the parish ministry. In 1885 she resigned the parish for a reform and lecture career.

She moved back to Boston, where she came in contact with a wide circle of reformers—the Emersons, Garrisons, Alcotts, Whittier, James Freeman Clarke, Phillips, Minot Savage, Foster Weld, Julia Ward Howe, Frances Willard. By this time her oratorical powers were recognized. She worked as a lecturer for the Massachusetts Woman Suffrage Association before being appointed head of the WCTU Franchise Department.

After hearing Shaw preach on "The Heavenly Vision" at the 1888 International Council of Women, Susan Anthony devoted herself to drawing the silver-tongued Shaw to full-time suffrage work. Though Shaw had been a stalwart member of the rival (and more conventionally religious) AWSA, she was captivated by "Aunt Susan," whose intimate she became for the remainder of Anthony's life. Anthony was her "haven of refuge."[8] Of the little band of "half-fledged chickens,"[9] Shaw was one of the few present at Anthony's deathbed, and preached her funeral sermon. She lived from the early 1890s until her own death with one of Anthony's nieces, Lucy E. Anthony, whom Shaw called her "home-maker."[10] She succeeded her mentor to the position of vice president at large of NAWSA when Anthony became its president in 1892. She accompanied Anthony on scores of successive suffrage campaigns, preaching regularly in churches along the way and winning regular admirers by her skill as a speaker.

Shaw was prized by Anthony not only because of oratorical skills. Anthony was well aware of the damage to the movement from its reputation for religious heterodoxy. Shaw reported that Anthony introduced her not only as a Methodist minister, but as "orthodox of the orthodox."[11] She told her protégée that:

> These people have always claimed that I am irreligious. They will not accept the fact that I am a Quaker—or, rather, they seem to think a Quaker is an infidel. I am glad you are a Methodist, for now they cannot claim that we are not orthodox.[12]

When Carrie Chapman Catt resigned the NAWSA presidency in 1904, Shaw was the natural successor. Suffrage historians point to the association's weaknesses under Shaw. As she said in a symposium debating the merits of "pre-election methods," "I do not know a political method when I see it and I haven't an ounce of political sense, but I do believe heartily in this sort of work,"[13] a statement hardly designed to build confidence in the ranks. On the other hand, her self-deprecation about politics may have been so much bluff. The early years of her term in office were devoted to building the local chapters in an organization she believed too centralized.

> I tell you we have got to hold a series of county conventions and build up the state work or we will have a great headquarters with a small regiment of clerks and not a thing back of it to sustain it. Something must be done. We need not to cut down our Headquarters but we do need to build up our field work, and that is my business and I am going to see to it.[14]

Her sympathy almost always lay with the grass-roots element of the NAWSA organization.[15]

Her gifts lay in oratory, in "speaking and inspiring,"[16] not in administration or in adjudication of differing suffragist interests and conflicts. Perhaps, however, her leadership also suffered from larger social forces that no suffragist organizing genius might have overcome. Between 1897 and 1910, the movement's doldrums, no states were added to the meager four that had enfranchised women. Whatever the reasons, however, by 1910 dissent was rampant within the organization. That year saw several staunch old-time workers, such as Rachel Foster Avery, Harriet Upton Taylor, and Florence Kelley, resign from the NAWSA, inaugurating a period of rapid turnover in the national offices, a series of annual attempts to depose Shaw from her office, and the birth of a rival feminist organization, the Congressional Union, later called the Women's Party. Shaw fiercely opposed the more militant women of the "dreadful" or even "devilish" Congressional Union.[17] Militant methods were "undignified, unworthy—in other words, un-American."[18] In public she was careful to say that, "When men protest so loudly against the militant methods of some women across the sea, they must remember that it is men who withhold from women every other means of protest and defense." She quoted William Pitt's reflections on the American colonists who had "been driven to madness by injustice."[19] When a young NAWSA woman was arrested for "chalking the sidewalks," Shaw's private response was one measure of the distance between her and her beloved Aunt Susan.

> If there is a law against chalking the sidewalks for a meeting and if they have selected you in order to make an example of suffragists and to hurt the suffrage cause, the best way to thwart them would be, according to my view and the view of others, to immediately plead ignorance of the law and pay whatever fine there is upon it. . . . Candidly, I see no more reason why suffragists should violate the law than that anybody else should.[20]

As her letter continued, "there are certain laws of order which should be followed by everybody and that one never loses by doing so." This was a far cry indeed from Anthony's espousal of civil disobedience.

On the one hand, Shaw had the militants to contend with; on the other, there was a growing appreciation of new techniques of organization NAWSA required to bring its campaigns to effective, efficient fruition. Harper, editor of the last volumes of the *History of Woman Suffrage*, says the mood was shifting in the organization as early as 1910. "The dominant note of the convention was the intention henceforth to enter the field of politics"[21]—politics in terms we would recognize today. The next year, the NAWSA board decided to emphasize "political district organization."[22] The association became big business; in 1912 alone, three million pieces of literature under 250 titles

225

were published and distributed.[23] To win the New York State Campaign of 1917, two thousand precinct captains, nearly $700,000, more than eleven thousand meetings, ten million pieces of suffrage literature were used.[24] The NAWSA had a Data Department, an Organization Department, and nineteen "suffrage schools" training women in efficient political methods (with courses in suffrage history and argument, organization, publicity and press, money raising, law).[25] Shaw did not preside over this wing of the movement, with which she was genuinely uncomfortable.[26] She resigned from the presidency in 1915, ostensibly to spend her remaining time in the public speaking at which she excelled. It is no accident that 1915 was also the year that

> it was felt that the general public needed no further education on this subject; the association had become a business organization and the woman suffrage question one of practical politics. Therefore, but one mass meeting was held, that of Sunday afternoon, and the entire week was devoted to State reports, conferences, committee meetings, plans of work, campaigns and discussions of details. These were extremely interesting and valuable for the delegates but not for the newspapers or the public.[27]

Between 1917 and 1919, Shaw chaired the Women's Committee of the Council of National Defense, a federal organization to coordinate women's work in support of the war. Of this she made a stunning success (aided by the fact that she had wisely taken her best NAWSA administrator with her) and received the Distinguished Service Medal in 1919. At the war's close, with ex-President Taft and Lowell of Harvard, she embarked on a tour in passionate support of the League of Nations. During this campaign she contracted what proved to be a fatal case of pneumonia.

Shaw's gifts as a speaker were widely acknowledged in her day. She was frequently called the greatest woman orator who ever lived. But she was no systematic thinker. As she said of herself, "I am quick but I am not so profound."[28] Her gift of repartee and wit does not perhaps weather well in the documents bequeathed to a later generation. For a time the movement created a specific forum, "The Question Box," to display Shaw's extemporaneous skill. One example may provide a glimpse of these flashes.

> Last night someone asked, "What shall we do with a woman who says she has all the rights she wants?" The answer came to me in a flash and I said "Give her another and see how quick she will take it."[29]

One needs, I think, to hear some of her work declaimed to appreciate it. Her verbal genius was the undoing of her recorders. *History of Woman Suffrage* remarked more than once that Shaw never wrote her speeches. In consequence, many are lost forever. Those we do have—carefully reconstructed from stenographic notes of admirers, secretaries, newspaper reporters—have the flavor of the extemporaneous. Even her magazine articles were evidently created by dictating them to her secretary. They are consequently verbose and repetitious. There is, nevertheless, a sufficient amount of material to assess her notion of the issue faced by suffragists and her religious orientation. Indeed, her reconstructed speeches run to over a thousand pages.[30]

Consistency in Inconsistency

For Shaw, as for neither of the two preceding feminists, it is most true to say that she narrowed the issue before the women's movement to the right to vote. This was a direct consequence of her way of formulating the question, the injustice, faced by the woman suffrage movement. The definition of a republic was betrayed by women's disfranchisement. The theories were fine—in fact, sublime and lofty. The practice hardly came up to this level. The inconsistency between the two was so taken for granted as to be unnoticed. As she was fond of repeating, "one remarkable characteristic of men is their consistency in their inconsistency; from the beginning of our life as a people on this continent to the present hour, this consistency in inconsistency has been marked."[31] Hence, consistency between the democratic theory and the practice of American institutions was all Shaw claimed that she sought. She articulated no series of dimensions of human life to which to refer the situation of women. She concentrated on the notion of a republic and its travesty in the absence of women's enfranchisement.

The slow process of evolution through American history was bringing the practice of life into line with its high and noble ideals. Woman suffrage was the last step in the growth to a true republic. Though at times she too spoke of the disfranchisement of women as male aristocracy, she was explicit that it was an "evolutionary, not revolutionary, eraser" that was to remove the last little exclusionary word "male" from the Constitution—a disavowal that puts Shaw at some distance from Stanton. While the latter was also a firm believer in the upward progress of evolution, she was also sure that an entire revolution was at stake in women's education, elevation, and enfranchisement.

Consistency was also Shaw's major argument against the increasingly vocal claims of the antisuffragists. She was a master of the refutation and ridicule of the contradictory arguments by the opponents of woman suffrage, and great portions of her speeches were directed to this end. As she used to say, "The 'antis' never make an argument but they answer it. When I was asked to answer one of their debates, I said, 'What is the use? Divide up their literature and let them destroy themselves.' "[32] Perhaps part of her weakness as a theorist lay just here; she spent more time *reacting* against the errors and insipidities of her opponents than in developing her own train of thought. One point at which the antis *were* consistent, however, was their advocacy of a "statical" condition. Since they were out of touch with the underlying processes of human life as continuous evolutionary change, they could only be losers in the struggle. No matter how bleak the pro-suffrage prospect might have looked, particularly in the years of little forward progress, suffragists were in line with the changing times.

Shaw was interested in a ministry to prostitution, temperance, war, and the cause of working women. The terms in which she took up these causes, however, varied. War and the spirit of militarism were directly opposed to the spirit of democracy—except perhaps for that war President Wilson claimed was to ensure the safety of democracy. Temperance and vice were cases in which women needed to vote to protect the home under changing conditions. Similarly, women had always worked; but when men took women's labor from the home to put it into factories, women needed new weapons to protect themselves. Class-consciousness had no part in Shaw's view; divisiveness in a democracy went against the grain. These and all good causes were connected to her view of the nature of women; they expressed, perhaps, the special spiritual insight women possessed. Shaw approached Stanton's view of the "two natures," but without the latter's emphasis on women's cognitive powers.

Consequently, this section on the definition of the issue proceeds in three parts. The first explores the convolutions of democratic theory opposed to democratic practice. The second assesses Shaw's rebuttals of the opposition—a good location to observe Shaw's humorous approach. The last section inquires into the relations between the suffrage struggle itself and other works of "improvement."

A. Democratic Theory and Practice

Why should women have the vote? The answer to that question was a simple one, familiar to any American with an ear for the tradition of the country.

> God created all men equal and endowed them with certain inalienable rights among which are life, liberty, and the pursuit of happiness. To protect these rights, life, liberty, and the pursuit of happiness—and no man will deny that they are the rights of myself as well as himself—to protect those rights governments are instituted among men, deriving their just powers from the consent of the governed. I have no further argument to offer. It is all there.[33]

She pointed to the definition of a republic in any dictionary. The theoretical claims made on behalf of the American government were vitiated in practice.

> We claim that the great defect in the Government is that it is not what it claims to be, that is, a republic. We believe that "a republic is a form of government in which the laws are enacted by representatives elected by the people," and since one half of the republic are arbitrarily deprived of all powers to elect their representatives, the fundamental principle of a republic is denied and that changes the character of the government itself, and instead of our government being a republic, it is in reality, a form of aristocracy.[34]

"All I ask of men is that they believe what they say."[35] She pushed her point. The question of woman suffrage was easy, it was

> so simple that the wayfarer man, though a fool twice over, may be able to see. It is a question so simple that the strangest thing about it is that there should be any trouble in understanding it. It is simply this—Shall a government declaring itself to be a republic be true to its declaration? Shall a government which claims that it is the right of the people to have a voice in their own government be true to itself? Shall a government be sincere? That is all the question there is before us.[36]

At times Shaw pushed this argument from consistency so far as to skirt the notion that if Americans were to admit that the government was not a republic, suffragists would have no grounds to stand on. She could flatly proclaim, "We must simply consider a republic as either desirable or not. If it is desirable, then let us have it. That is the whole question; there is nothing else involved."[37] She was not unconscious of the anomalous position in which her train of thought placed her.

> I frankly confess that I always feel a degree of embarrassment when I begin to talk upon the subject of woman suffrage, because it is a difficult task to prove to people an absolute truism . . . the difficult task which faces woman suffragists is to try to prove to men who profess to believe in a republican form of government that a republican form of government is desirable.[38]

Paradoxically, this implicit agreement in republican principles, ordinarily a strength of the movement, sometimes appeared to Shaw to be a weakness. Repeating familiar arguments to audiences gave suffragists a slight disadvantage in the conflict with the antis:

> Opponents of woman suffrage are not merely opponents of woman suffrage; they are opponents of democracy. They do not believe in the people; they do not believe in the right of self government; they do not believe in the Declaration of Independence nor in the Bill of Rights, nor in any of the fundamental arguments or articles underlying our national life. They tacitly deny these, and, denying them, they have a ground upon which to argue; but we affirm them, and in affirming them there is no possible ground for argument.[39]

Here were no abstruse cases built on the philosophy of the founders, judicial precedent, or natural law proofs. Everyone agreed about the "broad and high ideals of justice" but they were "afraid to live them."[40] It was not at all clear *why* this failure of nerve should have come over the American people. She simply described the fact. Shaw refused to unbend from this stand to take a position on the knotty intricacies of democratic theory raised in the period.

> I am not here to argue whether the vote is a right or a privilege. If it is a right I want my right. If it is a privilege I want my privilege. I do not care which it is. If it is a privilege demanded for cause, it is a privilege I demand for the same cause for which every man demands it.[41]

She was quite sure, however, that voting was a right, if only because "if it is not a right, our ancestors and our Constitution were all wrong."[42] This Shaw's audiences, one supposes, were rarely willing to concede.

Following Stanton's precedent, she pointed to the logical conclusion of the inconsistency of American life. Without women's enfranchisement, America was not a republic or a democracy, but an aristocracy of sex. Unlike the former's vigorous opposition to any sort of class division that stood in the path of individual sovereignty, Shaw found something to concede in the other kinds of aristocratic rule:

> This is not a Republic, it is an aristocracy. And the most inexcusable aristocracy on earth. There might be some weight in an aristocracy of birth. After generations and generations of birth and training, we might produce a very exceptional man. There might be some excuse in an aristocracy of wealth, for wealth gives opportunity for culture and refinement; the opportunity is not always grasped, but it gives it. There might be such a thing as an aristocracy of military power, for that gives strength and the ability to fight, but when you come to an aristocracy of sex, what under the sun can you say for it?[43]

As the contest across the Atlantic heated up, she drew the parallel. "Soon the divine right of sex will be as obsolete as the divine right of kings in Europe."[44] She turned other phases of the democratic rhetoric to good use.

> And you who talk of a great Government in which the voice of God is heard must remember that if "the voice of the people is the voice of God," you will never know what the voice of God in Government is until you get the voice of the people, and the voice of the people has a soprano as well as a bass. You must join the soprano voice of God to the bass voice of God in order to get the harmony of the Divine voice, and then you will have a law which will enable you to say, We are justly ruled.[45]

After opening one of her speeches regarding the odd ways "from the beginning of our national life American men have been the most consistent in their inconsistency of the men of any nation in the world,"[46] Shaw might build her case in several different directions. It might lead her, for example, to ridicule men's lack of logic:

> They are the sentimental sex. Men have logic; they have reason; they have common sense, until they begin to discuss women, and then they are so sentimental, they begin with stars and moon and nothing gratifies them so much as an anti-suffragist spinster talking of the love of wife and mother.[47]

Such a move would have been aimed at getting men to think about women from the same premises as they used to think about themselves, which Shaw admitted were "tolerably reasonable."[48]

If men could forget our relationship to themselves and think of us as influenced by the same aspirations, the same ambitions, the same hopes as themselves, with the same difficulties and obstacles to overcome in shaping and developing our lives, and then if they would ask "What do we want for ourselves under these circumstances?" and if, when answering that question for themselves, they would answer it for every other human being, there would be no further obstacle to our freedom.[49]

Alternatively, such a case might proceed by reviewing the history of the American republic to mark the object lesson in inconsistency. Typically she would begin from a comment such as "in all times men have entertained loftier theories of living than they have been able to formulate into practical experience."[50] A calm résumé of American political history would note that "men in this country from its beginning have been trying to evolve a republic out of a monarchy, step by step they have proceeded."[51] The Puritans came to these shores for the sake of religious freedom, "the Divine ideal which is the sublimest and supremest ideal in religious freedom which men have ever known"[52]—and immediately made church membership a qualification for voting. The Revolutionary fathers similarly articulated the grand notions of the Declaration of Independence, "the sublimest ideal of democracy which had ever dawned upon the souls of men,"[53] but did not understand its relationship to property. No sooner had the property qualification been removed than "white" became the bone of democratic contention. At last the single word "male" stood alone in the Constitution. Shaw would wind up one of these orthodox, evolutionary views of American progress with the triumphant claim, "God said in the beginning, 'It is not good for man to stand alone.' That is why we women are here with our demand for political enfranchisement."[54]

At times Shaw turned her wit onto these historical scenes. One of her most frequently given speeches, "The Fate of Republics," ended by describing the disappointment of women aware of being so constantly passed over in the usual portrayals of American history. She described a painting with a

ship in the background, between it and the shore is a man carrying what seems to be a woman in his arms, on the beach kneel a company of people, and farther up the beach stand another group with uplifted hands, thanking God for their deliverance. They look like men and women. You wonder what company of people it is, and reach the inscription beneath the picture to learn, that it is not a company of men and women at all, but is a representation of "The Landing of the Forefathers." You instinctively exclaim how kind the forefathers were to carry each other ashore, and how much some of them resemble mothers, but they were not mothers, they were all fathers, every mother of them.[55]

This emphasis on the strictly logical character of Shaw's definition of the issue, however, should not blind us to the revivalist zeal of the work to "bring back an apostate people to the fundamental principles of our national life."[56] The woman suffrage movement was to convert America.

> We are the purest democrats; we are the purest republicans; we are the purest and most liberal minded people politically in the government, because we are the only group of people who stand fundamentally, not only for the rights of women, but for the rights of men, and the rights of children to be born of free mothers, as well as free fathers. We believe that democracy is not a form of government; that democracy is not an institution. Democracy is a spirit, and existed before any government existed, and will exist after governments cease to exist. It is the very essence of human life; it is the essence of the development of the human soul; the right of every human soul to be and become all that it is possible for each human soul to become.[57]

In her later life, when the president of Harvard University and other notables of the time declared democracy a failure, Shaw sprang into the breach. "We are becoming an infidel nation, not infidels in theology, but infidels in fundamental principles of democracy."[58] The reformer, the idealist, had a unique contribution to make in refuting the low view of politics as the affray of interest groups.

> Our condition would be a very serious one if, in looking out on what our politicians call the "arena of politics," we really believed it was the aimless struggles of individuals to secure their own ends. But, think of conditions as we may, realize the extreme evils in the midst of which we are living, the real reformer, who judges not from the day in which he lives but who judges his time through the perspective of time and distance and realizes that underneath the strife and the contention, the dishonesty and the graft, under the sorrow and despair, the joy and the beauty, there is constantly working that which is for ever guiding humanity towards the ultimate end for which humanity and government were made.[59]

Those "ideals" framed by the fathers were pre-existent Platonic essentials that "lured," as Alfred North Whitehead was to put it later, the human race to its ideal end. This democratic faith, however, was one that Shaw firmly articulated in Christian terms.

233

We say the blood of the martyrs is the seed of the church. It is true, but it is no more true of the church than it is of civilization. Development and opportunity have been marked by the bloody feet of men and women who have died that you and I might live and be strong. From the seeds of that great truth shall spring the forces of the future but the seeds must be sown in faith that fails not, watered with the rain of tears and walled about with life that fought and won.[60]

B. The Antis

Rebutting antisuffragists was nothing new, of course, in the history of the suffrage organizations. As Shaw pointed out, in one sense, that was all the movement had ever been doing, since at the time of its inception, everyone was an "anti." "They had the whole earth; all we had was heaven." Toward the turn of the century small groups began to appear specifically organized to combat the woman suffrage movement by making arguments against it. Feminists claimed that such groups were small and unrepresentative of the average woman's opinions. But they were convinced that the real opposition came from the interest of liquor brewers and sellers. As Shaw said in one of her most devastating blows at the antis:

> We do not fear that little band of professional anti-women going around the country advocating home, heaven, and mother. We are not at all disturbed by them. The only purpose they serve is that by holding out their skirts they act as a screen for the liquor traffic, the gamblers, the vicious, and those interested in dance halls and places where young girls are ruined. These people have a good screen behind which they can hide, and carry on their antagonism and their opposition to our movement.
> I am so pained that good women do not know that they are being used for that purpose.[61]

A point that Shaw never wearied of making about the opposition, however, was how inconsistent they were. She let her sense of humor fly freely on such occasions. Especially after 1900 her speeches were full of references to the sheer amusement she derived from listening to the opposition. "The trouble with the anti-suffragists is that they can't see a joke. They can't see how funny their position is."[62] In the middle of a speech to encourage the rank and file of suffrage workers, she painted a religious picture of suffrage work. She pointed out what a privilege it was to be a suffragist, chosen by Him to do His service—and broke off abruptly to say, "And how amusing it is. Talk of

234

fun. There is nothing in the world to be compared with following up an anti-suffragist."[63] She might continue by citing the story of the "beautiful lady from New Jersey who kindly left her husband and her home to come out to North Dakota to tell the North Dakota women their place is at home; they must stay there." This same beautiful lady argued in dry North Dakota that woman suffrage would turn the state wet, and in Montana that women would vote it dry. (Shaw never tired of this story.)

Her most typical approach, however, was to iterate a long line of matching antisuffrage arguments, "as all their arguments come in pairs and answer each other."[64]

> One anti said . . . It is no use to give us the vote, because we wouldn't use it . . . But the other anti said we would vote all the time, and would neglect our homes, our husbands, and our children, and go to the ballot box and vote ten hours a day, day in and day out, year in and year out.
>
> Then they would tell us that it is no use to give women the vote, as they would vote just as their husbands do. . . . And then they said that if women were permitted to vote they would not vote as their husbands do, and would create discord, break up the family, and cause the destruction of the home.
>
> Then the same women would tell you that women have no time to vote; their time is so engaged, they have no time to vote—only men have time to vote. And we pay men twice as much money for their time as we do women. . . . And then the same women will tell you . . . that we are the leisure class, and that men are worked to death supporting us in idleness.[65]

Clergy who quoted Paul that women keep silent in the churches did not notice the incongruity of letting women *sing* in their choirs.

> I know of only one man who is thoroughly consistent in this matter. He is a clergyman in the South. He will not allow a woman to talk in the church or to teach in the Sunday School because she makes a loud noise. He would not even allow her to teach in the infant class if there was a male infant in the class. I have the profoundest respect for that man. He is an idiot, but consistent.[66]

Note that in Shaw's view one could be a consistent fool. We might say that there was a certain "logic of events" or "logic of conditions" inherent in her position as well as the narrower congruity or incongruity of stated propositions. (This may have been what she meant by common sense.) Even if the assertions of the antis were not incoherent internally, they clashed with the reality of American life.

Again they tell us that if we women should vote, we should have to mingle at the polls with horrid men—the same horrid men with whom we live the rest of the year. . . . Even if men are, as our opponents claim, dangerously unworthy, the securest possible place for a woman would be at the polls, since the law forbids any interference with an elector within fifty, or in some states, one hundred feet of the voting booth. The polls, compared to a New York subway, for example, is the safest place imaginable.[67]

One cannot help seeing, in Shaw's anecdotes, the ways certain fears of Victorian civilization were the reasons opponents advanced absurd objections to woman suffrage.

In the Missouri legislature, as I was passing out of the house, where I spoke before the body, one gentleman said, "I do not want my wife to go down to the lower end of my city to vote with 50,000 of the lowest people in town." I could not help saying to him, "Does your wife live in the lowest end of the city?" He replied that she did not. I said "Do you vote there?" He replied, "Why, of course I do not." "Then," I said, "just why should your wife, who has respect enough and intelligence enough to select you as her husband, immediately that she is free rush from her home to vote at the lowest end of the city with the people to whom you refer?"[68]

Her reiterated remarking of the inconsistency and ill-logic of antisuffragists was masterly.

I can not understand a daughter of the American Revolution who is opposed to the enfranchisement of women, who glories in the death of an ancestor who died for the principle of no taxation without representation. I can not understand the inconsistency. I was met by one of these daughters once who asked me why I spent all my time in the furtherance of the woman suffrage movement and why I did not join their society. She said, "Were not your ancestors in the Revolution?" I replied they were, and added, "And they fought hard, but they fought on the wrong side." She said, "I am so sorry for you." I replied, "You need not be; I am not a bit sorry for myself." "Why," she exclaimed, "are you not sorry that your ancestors were on the wrong side?" I have had such a hard time getting on the right side and keeping there I have not had time to worry over my great-grandfather. [Applause and laughter]
    I added, "It does not matter half so much to me where my grandfather stood as where I stand [applause], and the difference between you and me, my dear friend, is that you stand where my great-grandfather stood, and I stand where your's stood." [Laughter and applause]
    The lady did not like it. She did not like my reference to my grandfather. She said, "I descended from a long line of revolutionary ancestors." I answered "Yes,

that is exactly what you have done; you have descended from a long line of Revolutionary ancestors, and I have ascended from a line of Revolutionary ancestors and I would rather ascend from my ancestors than descend from them any time."[69]

This was effective rhetoric. There remains something unsatisfying about the mock naiveté with which she recounted such stories. I suspect that Shaw was speaking the literal truth when she said, "I cannot understand the inconsistency." Just as one wishes that she had reflected rather more deeply about why American men were afraid to live their proud ideals, one wishes that she had mulled over the factors intervening in the logic of the legislator or the Daughters of the American Revolution. Perhaps this is asking too much of someone living before the prophets of the precocious social and psychological forces had come into their own. But the result in Shaw's work is that a certain disparagement of other women crept into her tone.

I was very much amused at the calm way in which the antisuffrage women took the statements of the gentleman who debated for our opponents about the intellectual incapacity of the female sex to grasp problems, and at the calm way in which they took the reflections which he cast upon their sex as a whole, and not only at their calm, but at the ecstatic looks they gave him, when he declared, over and over again, that women are unfitted to vote. I simply could not understand the state of mind of woman who, listening to a man going on like that about her and her own sex, was absolutely, heavenly, blissfully happy over it!

And what interested me still more was to hear the women themselves rise and tell how foolish women are. Why, men know how foolish we are without our standing for two hours to explain it to them—they live with us! And we don't have to explain for hours that we are not wise; if we were, we should not have married some of them![70]

Shaw's light touch was at its best when she turned her skill to depicting the social nonsense, the contradictory factors, in American politics.

By some objectors women are supposed to be unfit to vote because they are hysterical and emotional and of course men would not like to have emotion enter into a political campaign. They want to cut out all emotion so they would like to cut us out. I had heard so much about our emotionalism that I went to the last Democratic national convention, held at Baltimore, to observe the calm repose of the male politicians. I saw some men take a picture of one gentleman whom they wanted elected and it was so big they had to walk sideways as they carried it forward; they were followed by hundreds of other men screaming and

237

yelling, shouting and singing the "Houn' Dawg"; then, when there was a lull, another set of men would start forward under another man's picture, not to be outdone by the "Houn' Dawg" melody, whooping and howling still louder. I saw men jump upon the seats and throw their hats in the air and shout: "What's the matter with Champ Clark?" Then, when those hats came down, other men would kick them back into the air, shouting at the top of their voices: "He's all right!" Then I heard others howling for "Underwood, Underwood, first, last and all the time!" No hysteria about it—just patriotic loyalty, splendid manly devotion to principle. And so they went on and on until 5 o'clock in the morning—the whole night long. I saw men jump on the seats and jump down again and run around the ring. I saw two men run towards another man to hug him both at once and they split his coat up the middle of his back and sent him spinning around like a wheel. All this with the perfect poise of the legal male mind in politics!

I have been to many women's conventions in my day but never saw a woman leap up on a chair and take off her bonnet and toss it up in the air and shout: "What's the matter with" somebody. I never saw a woman knock another woman's bonnet off her head as she screamed, "She's all right!" I never heard a body of women whooping and yelling for five minutes when somebody's name was mentioned in the convention. But we are willing to admit that we are emotional. I have actually seen women stand up and wave their handkerchiefs. I have even seen them take hold of hands and sing, "Blest be the tie that binds." Nobody denies that women are excitable. Still, when I hear how emotional and how excitable we are, I cannot help seeing in my mind's eye the fine repose and dignity of this Baltimore and other political conventions I have attended![71]

When Shaw turned away from the ridicule of her opponents, it was to return single-mindedly to the republic. If one grasped firmly the notion that it was the consistency of the republic's principles and practice that was at stake, all the objections to enfranchisement would immediately be seen to be not only amusing, but fundamentally irrelevant to the question.

This is the sort of thing we have to meet and none of it, you see, has anything to do with the woman-suffrage question. In fact, there is not a single argument advanced by the antisuffragists that has anything to do with the subject. Whether women will vote or not, for example, has nothing to do with the question; whether a woman will vote as her husband does or won't love her husband, has nothing to do with the question. Whether a woman believes in feminism or in socialism or in absolute democracy does not make a particle of difference so far as the question itself is concerned. . . . The only question which concerns us is, "Shall any citizens of a nation calling itself a republic be deprived of their right to representation?"[72]

One area, however, in which Shaw conceded that the antis were consistent was that they opposed change. They had a "statical" view of the role of women. In this of course they ran counter to the evolutionary spirit of the age, and to Shaw's own deepest convictions:

> The antisuffragists' cries are all the cries of little children who are afraid of the unborn and are forever crying, "The goblins will catch you if you don't watch out." So anything that has not been, should not be and all that is is right, when as a matter of fact if the world believed that we would be in a statical condition and never move, except back like a crab.[73]

C. The Uplifting of Society

Stanton and Anthony attempted to ally the cause of women's rights with other social issues, principally temperance, antislavery, and, in Anthony's case, trade unions. By the Progressive Era, American life was awash in good causes of reform. Anna Howard Shaw was no stranger to these reforming efforts; she affirmed the work of social improvement on a variety of fronts. She did so in a slightly different spirit than her two predecessors. I look briefly at the home, the cause of working women, prostitution, and war[74] before I turn to her sermon, "The Heavenly Vision," to investigate the ways Shaw related these issues to each other and to the woman suffrage cause.

Shaw was employed by the Franchise Department of the WCTU before turning to the suffrage associations. Her view shows the influence of Frances Willard, rather than that of Stanton or Anthony. Women needed the ballot to protect the home in the wider community: she rarely spoke of the home and family in critical ways, as did, for instance, Stanton.

> We are told that our place is in the home and most of us would like to be in our place if we had it. We are told that our duty is to our family—most of us would like a chance to do it . . . and yet every woman with a grain of common sense and with simply one convolution spread over with brain matter in her head knows it is absolutely impossible for a woman to keep her home safe unless that community in which that home is is safe.[75]

To discuss the home meant supremely to discuss motherhood and childhood to Shaw, both topics directly related to the ballot. Child development was "the first duty of the State," and the home "the most sacred, the most vitally important factor in Government."[76] In part such descriptions were designed to generalize motherhood so that its obligations were not confined to each woman's own children. It was "not only the right but the duty of every woman to protect *all* children."[77] She called for the creation of "a cabinet minister for the department of the home."[78]

There were two specific directions in which informed and responsible mothers needed to move, toward public safety and against vice. The attacks of the Progressives upon child labor, unhealthy water, and tenement housing, were also Shaw's attacks.

Is there any reason why women should not have a vote in regard to water-works? A woman knows as much about water as a man. Generally, she drinks more of it. See how the street cleaners sweep dirt into heaps on Monday and leave it to blow about until Saturday, before it is taken up. Any housekeeper would know better. Sewers and man-traps spread disease literally and metaphorically.[79]

The public conditions that endangered the home made it imperative to have "better housekeeping in the nation, better housekeeping in the state, and better housekeeping in the city."[80] Shaw's speeches on such topics might serve well as a compendium of the reforms of the Progressive Era. She saw no fine dividing line between municipal improvement and temperance:

Let them examine the accounts of food adulteration, and learn that from the effect of impure milk alone, in one city 5,600 babies died in a single year. Let them examine the water supply, so impregnated with disease that in some cities there is continual epidemic of typhoid fever. Let them gaze upon the filthy streets, from which perpetually rises contagion of scarlet fever and diphtheria. Let them examine the plots of our great cities, and find city after city with no play places for children, except the streets, alleys and lanes. Let them examine the school buildings, many of them badly lighted, unsanitary and without yards. . . . Let them follow the children who survive all these ills of early childhood, until they enter the sweatshops and factories, and behold there the maimed, dwarfed, and blighted little ones, 500,000 of whom under 14 years of age are employed in these pestilential places. Let them behold the legalized saloons and the dens of iniquity where so many of the voting population spend the money that should be used in feeding, housing, and caring for their children. It is infinitely more important that a child shall be well born and well reared than that more children shall be born. It is better that one well born child shall live than that two shall be born and one die in infancy. . . . When the human will is developed, it should fill the place of blind irrational forces in working out the problems of life. Progress should be less and less attained by the blind destruction of the unfit, and more and more by the development of greater adaptation through conscious education.[81]

The country had been fathered to death. "The great need of our country today is a little mothering to undo the evils of too much fathering."[82]

Works of public improvement were those to which the male character was not well suited. The republic had prospered along these lines of life Shaw thought peculiarly masculine—"business enterprise, and inventive genius, the aggressive spirit and warlike nature."[83] The times had changed. The masculine qualities were no longer the ones especially needed by society.

> The problems of Government today are no longer aggressive assaults upon neighboring nations. The problems of our government are constructive—How shall we house, feed, and rear our people? How are we to erect our tenements with light and with air, how equip them with proper fire protection; how shall we make our streets clean; how shall we banish contagious and preventable diseases; how shall we stop the smoke nuisance; how shall we stop sweated business in the homes of the poor; how shall little children's lives be spared from avaricious business which contaminates food and drink? How stop child labor and traffic in girlhood? These are the problems of the Government today which come home to the lives of women and which women understand and feel more keenly than men.[84]

To this challenge the women of the nation had already risen.

> Wherever there is any movement for the uplifting of society to higher planes you will find the women in the forefront. . . . On the lines of philanthropy and religion, and on the lines of social movements for the bettering of the condition of our time, women everywhere are in the forefront. We do today nine-tenths of the philanthropic work, nine-tenths of the church work, and form three-fourths of the church membership.[85]

Indeed, with the possible exception of the antisuffrage women, women were never organized into societies to do harm but always to do good. "So far as is known there has never been an organization of women in our country for any other purpose than some form of good, some form of helpfulness, some form of improvement, or public improvement, either physically, intellectually, or morally."[86] All these works Shaw blessed, in her own terms. Like Stanton, she preferred these works to the distant works of Christian charity. "It is much better for us to be interested in good sewerage, good water supply, good air, and good moral surroundings than to be interested in foreign missions."[87] The

241

great Lyman Abbott took up his cudgels against woman suffrage on the grounds that women with votes would have less time for the works of charity and philanthropy for public improvement. Shaw was firm in putting such efforts into perspective.

> I would like to say "Thank God, there will not be so much need of charity and philanthropy." The end and aim of the suffrage is not to furnish an opportunity for excellent old ladies to be charitable. There are two words that we ought to be able to get along without, and they are charity and philanthropy. They are not needed in a Republic. If we put in the word opportunity instead, that is what Republics stand for.[88]

Women needed the vote to protect the home; they also needed it to protect themselves against exploitation at *work*.

> [Women] have always worked, and the world has never objected to women working. They have toiled from early morn until late at night and through the night, but the world has permitted this to go on and has never entered a complaint against it until the time when the work of women became profitable work, then the world protested against women working in lucrative employments.
>
> In olden times women could control the conditions affecting their labor; they could regulate the hours of their labor; they could regulate the conditions under which they labored, hygienic conditions and the conditions affecting their health and the health of their families. They could regulate the price of the produce which they themselves produced in the home; they could regulate all the conditions affecting their labor; but with the inventive genius of man, who is not satisfied with exploiting man's employment, but determines to exploit woman's employment, since men have come and taken from us the industry, then the necessity for women to protect themselves in the new place in which they find themselves—in the workshop, in the sweat shop, in the factory—has come about. Wherever man has taken woman's work the woman must follow it.[89]

This argument regarding woman's work was partially one that feminists might recognize today. Women worked at home as surely as in businesses.

> I heard a man speaking of the awful results coming to the homes of this country because women were working and what a sad thing it was to think that we had five million women working in this United States, and another gentleman said, "you must have your figures wrong, we have eighteen million of working women in the United States but only five million of them get any pay for their work."[90]

Women worked "whether we are toilers in the factory or toilers in the kitchen, or toilers in educational institutions"—or, indeed, whether they were rich. "There are no harder worked women in this country than some of the women who count their money by the tens and hundreds of thousands." It is somewhat difficult to grasp what Shaw meant here. Partly, the rich "working women" she affirmed were women "who not only give their money but give themselves to the best service of humanity of which they are capable"—not the idle rich. Partly Shaw's reading of womanhood intervened, for she refused to draw class lines between women.

> Now we cannot draw lines in this country; we cannot make distinctions between woman and woman, the heart of each one of us beats the same, the desire of each one of us is toward the same aims in life . . . wherever we may be toiling, we are women, and God made women alike in one thing at least, and that is that the larger majority of them want the best things for the human family wherever it may be.[91]

It is also her understanding of American democracy as opportunity and human "brotherhood," as she almost always called it, that was the reason for such judgments. "There is no such thing in this country as class." Democracy required trust in one another, a trust that was undermined by class divisions. When Shaw was calling the nation back from its infidelity to democracy, class lines were among her favored examples.

> I had a most interesting experience in this matter in New York during the winter when addressing a company of people who belong to what we call the leisure class, but which to my mind is the true working class. They claimed that they were fitted for suffrage; they were ready to exercise it; they were all prepared for everything that was before them; but someone said,—"But if we are permitted to do it, how about that great seething section of our people down on the east side?" Not many days after, I addressed a company of people on the east side. They asked most intelligent questions; they seemed to have a larger grasp of affairs than almost any other company of people I addressed in New York City. After the meeting was over, one of those young girls, working in a sweat shop, said—"No, it is all right as far as we are concerned; we people have been educated in the school of toil and our experiences have taught us. But how could we trust the upper classes of women who live up by the park on Madison and Fifth Avenues?" Neither group of people dared trust the other group of people—so great has our infidelity become, and our lack of confidence in each other.[92]

Sometimes she ended this story by saying, "I wondered at the time if it would not be a good thing for you and a good thing for them if, one day in the year, a shirt waist maker down in the East End counted for as much as a woman up on Fifth Avenue."[93]

At other times she was explicit that the middle class was the favored group—somewhat astonishingly, favored by Jesus. "Leaders of reform movements must always appeal to the saving industrious middle-class of society, of whom Jesus said, 'Ye are the salt of the world.' "[94] It was not clear that she meant "middle class" in any precise way. It was surely not a Marxist class, the owners of the means of production, she had in mind. Neither was it necessarily the blander sociological sense of the white-collar or middle-echelon people who were neither rich nor poor. She had her own sense of the extremes between which the "middle" fell. When categorizing women, the poles were represented rather by those with "every ease and comfort of life," on the one hand, and those women responsible for "sex corruption" in politics by using their wiles to influence rulers behind the scenes. Between *these* two groups fell "the great intermediate group of women," whose silent influence needed to become vocal with the ballot. Here she saw the middle as "the great mass of humanity."[95]

When Charles Eliot attacked the minimum wage along with the suffragist claim that women's wages were among the causes of prostitution, Shaw's passion against the "present commercialized inhumanities of crushing and debasing toil" came to the fore.[96] It was "rose water morality" for Eliot or anyone else to "talk virtue to a starving girl." Not all prostitution, but much of it, was traceable to working conditions.

> When we consider the conditions under which so many of these toiling girls are born and reared, the environment of their early years, the lack of home comforts and training, the brutalizing influences with which abject poverty surrounds them, we must realize that, from the very beginning, they are handicapped in the race of life. This is true of a large part of the factory and shop workers, but not all of them. Many enter the factories from the lower grades of public schools, driven into the labor market by the excessive cost of living, which makes it impossible for the day laborer to provide even the necessities of life for his family. These young girls enter the factories full of hope and courage, dreaming that some day they will work up to something better and get out of the factory into a larger field of service. But the days pass into years and the unnatural life for the young, the miserable conditions under which they toil and the long tedious hours, which seems as if they would never end, sap their courage and blight their hopes and, after striving for years at a machine, trying to live

decently on less than a living wage, they go down, unable to continue the struggle.[97]

Suffragists sought "not a Utopia," but wages and working conditions such that young women and mothers

> may not be robbed of health and youth, that the hours shall not be so many that all their vital energies are sapped and there no longer flows through the veins the quick glow of love and joy and courage. They demand that the young toilers shall be able to feel the thrill of the good and of the beautiful that they may love life and know that the trees and flowers and the songs of birds and the sunshine and the stars and the peace and joy of home and family love, are for them, to fill their lives, and to make them sweet and pure and beautiful. Suffragists declare that these are God's gifts to all his children, to be used and enjoyed by all, and that it is the duty of society and of the government, to see to it that the avenues to the higher physical and moral life are open to women.[98]

The physical and moral health of the community alike were to benefit. Since she stressed that such changes were for the good of "all the young women and mothers of the community," the next generation surely would also be better. "Will that very fact not create a new environment into which children may be born and reared, and lay the foundation for the development of sound character in the life of the whole community?"[99]

War was the cause that took up much of Shaw's last years with her government work and League of Nations. She was clear that the spirit of militarism was utterly opposed to democracy.

> The enthronement of might, of arrogance, of physical force, creates within the human spirit a disregard for justice, of human sympathy and of personal obligations on the one hand and, on the other, it breeds a spirit of cowardice, of servile submissions, and of sullen degrading acquiescence in the injustice and wrong. It is unnecessary to repeat the shocking details of the atrocities inflicted upon women and children of Belgium, Flanders, Poland, Armenia, to realize the debasing effect of militarism on men in times of hatred and war. But we must admit that such violation of right, such cruel barbarism could be possible only as the result of moral delinquencies in times of peace.
> The whole trend of militarism as exemplified in the Prussianism of today is to silence all moral and spiritual aspirations in national life.[100]

She did not confine herself to the Prussian example. There were reasons for thinking that democracy was more greatly threatened than other forms of government by the spirit of war and war preparation.

> To no people is the love of war so perilous as to a democratic one. It makes the principles of civil glory look pale. It accustoms populations to subordination and to the idolatry of individual leaders. More than any other principle, as history has shown, it paves the way for empire.[101]

War and violence were particular enemies of womanhood, from Shaw's perspective. As she personalized the immense toll of casualties from World War I, she forged reasons for women to oppose battle.

> Take up your paper and you will find that 300,000 of the flower of Europe's manhood have been killed in the past nine weeks of the war. I can't understand the significance of that many dead men, but I can look into the face of one dead soldier and tell that he had a mother. If this woman escaped death at childbirth she bore a son, and day by day he grew until she had to look up into the eyes of her boy. And then one day that boy was called by his country and an hour later he was dead—he in the happy peace of glory and she facing the empty years of agony. Then they ask what a woman knows about war?
> But that isn't all. The very flower of a country goes to death in a war, leaving the maimed and the broken and diseased to father the children of future generations. We ought to have the ballot both during war and during peace, for you know that if the women could have settled this war it wouldn't have occurred.[102]

Though she disavowed pacifism, she thought, like Stanton, that "brute force" was among the traits of the masculine character.[103]

In her earlier years, Shaw was strongest in maintaining that opposition to war was inherently female. Men were "inferior to women" in the areas of "morality and purity, temperance and obedience to law, of loyalty to the teachings of religion and a love of peace."[104] In her later years, she modified the content she saw in the "fine and vital contrast" between the two sexes. "While the male is more impersonal and is guided in his conduct by a cause or purpose regardless of individual personal relation, women are more largely influenced by personal relations and immediate needs."[105] Hence she expected that it was "in local and moral issues that the effect of women's influence in politics will be more generally felt." Women, she thought, were less partisan than men.[106] She was sure, whatever the content of these sex differences, that women had a "peculiar spiritual insight,"[107] which was most obvious in reform movements.

Several of Shaw's sermons to reforming women expressed her views of the relationships between these and other good causes. The women gathered at the 1888 International Council were not all possessed of the same programs.

All down through the centuries God has been revealing in visions the great truths which have lifted the race step by step, until today womanhood, in this sunset hour of the Nineteenth century is gathered here from the East and the West, and the North and South, women of every land, of every race, of all religious beliefs, yet we come together here and now with one harmonious purpose—that of lifting humanity, both men and women, into a higher, purer, truer life.[108]

Here was a woman with a vision of the human race free at last from the rum fiend. Here another had a vision of women voting. Yet a third had caught a glimpse of knowledge and learning. Another's vision was of "social freedom," which more hinted than described a single standard of sexual morality. All these visions had their germs of truth. As she told the World's Congress of Representative Women a few years later, "there can be no great movement to which has gathered any number of people but that underlying it, and running all through it is some deep and profound truth."[109] These many reformers gathered with their diverse visions needed to learn several lessons. They needed tolerance of one another's dreams; but simultaneously each needed to be true to her own grasp of the truth.

Whether that which we believe is true or not, if we stand by what we believe to be truth, God will illuminate the path, and we shall by and by know the truth, if we are true to the bit of truth we all possess now; for they who are loyal to truth will find that truth is always loyal to them; and they who hearken to its divine voice shall hear it all about them, and know the voice of truth, and follow it, and the voice of a stranger will they not follow.[110]

Like this last phrase with its echoes of the New Testament, these sermons were redolent of the Christian tradition. The many good visions were all given expressly by God. But there was one higher and better than all these others, the vision of Christian discipleship.

This, then, shall be the heavenly vision. Not that which we behold today, but when every man and woman into whose soul the light of truth has burned goes forth in the name and in the spirit of his Master to give this truth to the world that the world by it may be lifted out of its bigotry and sin, out of its false life into the fullness of a truer and broader living. When every man and woman shall have caught the vision which Paul caught, the vision of Jesus Christ as his Master, and whose own life is transformed and fulfilled in its purpose as the spirit of that Master works upon him, and there is wrought upon his life the miracle of divine truth and of a divine resurrection.[111]

Paul's vision on the road to Damascus was the paradigm of reform, whether one shared the Pauline vision of Jesus as master or not. "Every truth which has been taught to humanity has passed through a like channel. No one of God's human children has ever gone forth to the world who has not had first revealed to him his mission in a vision."[112] From Paul's experience she gleaned several points for reformers.

First, these visions were not given to the reasoning faculties, but to the heart.

> There are other avenues to truth than that which lies through the uncertain by ways of reason. To assume that it were not so is to know why heads and not hearts were made.
>
> Some of the deepest, profoundest truths that have ever come to the knowledge of the race, were felt, not reasoned out. . . . The deepest insights of truth are given not by the intellect, but by love.
>
> Who then, but the mother-heart of the race shall be able to read to its deepest depths the mystery? She shall be able to unearth its profoundest secrets.[113]

Despite her emphasis on the logic—or ill-logic—of the American public, ideals themselves were not given through logic.

Second, Paul was not allowed to rest in the quiet contemplation of that vision. "First the vision, then the purpose of the vision," which was to "carry it to a waiting world." To transmit the vision was to increase its power and enrich its scope.

> There is a giving forth of that which one possesses which enriches the giver, and more, he learns that the more he gives out of his vision to men the richer and larger and fuller it becomes, and the clearer and brighter it grows, until it enriches his whole life and illuminates all his pathway. This was the experience of Paul.[114]

Third, the martyrdom of the first apostle was also part of the "lesson" to be gained from scrutinizing his paradigmatic experience described in Acts.

[Paul] learned the lesson all reformers must sooner or later learn; that the world never welcomes its deliverers save with the dungeon, or the fagot or the cross. No man or woman has ever sought to lead his fellows to a higher and better mode of life without learning the strength and power of the world's ingratitude.[115]

Not content with the Pauline parallel, Shaw identified the persecution and martyrdom of reformers, not once but twice, with the crucifixion of Jesus.

This is the penalty paid by strong and good people who sacrifice themselves for others. They must live without sympathy; their feelings will be misunderstood; their efforts will be uncomprehended. Like Paul, they will be betrayed by friends. Like the Lord Christ in agony of Gethsemane, they must bear their struggle alone; they must be content to live and die like the Divine Master, betrayed and forsaken.[116]

And the greatest test of the reformer's courage comes when, with a warm earnest longing for humanity, she breaks for it the bread of truth which God has put into her hand and the world turns from this life-giving power and asks instead of bread a stone. It crucifies its Savior while it demands to have delivered it a robber.[117]

Once the vision was in place, the logic of consistency followed once more. Just as she invoked American men in general to believe what they said, so did reformers need to believe their reforms, to live from them. "It is impossible for any woman to be a real reformer who is not herself reformed."[118] Perhaps today we would call this the "internalization" of the vision. Shaw spoke of it as "earnestness," or as becoming "possessed" of the truth of the vision.[119] From this line of argument she could develop different paths of exhortations to reformers. For instance, since the vision intuitively gained would lift the world, it followed that Shaw was going to speak of the perfectibility of human nature. This Methodist preacher shared the century's high estimate of humanity.

The true reformer must be possessed of two things—infinite hope and infinite love; but out of the gloom and discouragement, out from error and bigotry that opposes the work, he must look up in hope, hoping even against hope and with his eye following the eye of the Divine Master, he must see man, fallen it is true, but magnificent in his ruin. He must catch the thought which burned in the soul of Christ; that, beneath the vilest outside, there is within a human soul capable of endless growth. Christ saw this, hence he treated all with respect.[120]

She might point instead to the necessary "broad, vigorous, healthful character" that the reformer must have. That strong character required moral courage, faith in God, and obedience to God's laws. The reformer needed faith in God, or at least "some faith in some power, somewhere, upon whom all others were dependent,"[121] so that she might know that "ultimately she shall see somewhere, at some time, the triumph of the truth."[122]

These calls to the higher development of the reformer circled around themes of sacrifice and service. Visions came from the infinite into the finite, and the finite received them not—or slowly. Unlike Stanton's call for women to be just to themselves before being generous to others, Shaw's stance was not controversial in the terms of the day.

> It has been said that it is the greatest sacrifice one can make for a friend to give up one's life for one's love; to sacrifice one's life; to lay down your own to find it in the good of another. But how much richer, how much holier, is the praise of her who lays down her own good, who sacrifices it for the good of another unknown, or for the good of a nation yet unborn. This is the highest test of loyalty to truth.[123]

Like her refusal to discriminate between the bits of truth found in the many reform groups, she was also capable of simply hedging her bets on this point. "All human beings are under obligations first to themselves. If self-sacrifice seems best, then we should practice that; while if self-assertion seems best, then we should assert ourselves."[124] Basically she reversed Stanton's view. Women's visions of reform were fundamentally acts of self-denying love; within the context of service, women were given permission to assert themselves. This was the purpose of the Christian call within these sermons. If one was doing not one's own will but God's, what fearlessness and strength might one not have in submission to the Divine?

> But there is still another and higher vision which reaches above earth, beyond time; a vision which has dawned upon so many of God's children that they are here not to do their own work but the will of Him who sent them. Before their gaze there has dawned the great eternity of truth. Before them lies the great eternity when the earth and the fashion of it shall have passed away. And the woman who recognizes the still higher truth recognizes the great power to which she belongs and what her life and the lives of all of God's children may become, when in submission to that Master she takes upon herself the nature of Him whom she serves; and while she hears the groaning agony about her, and while she bears the blows of oppression and scorn, yet around and about

and through her life is a peace so deep, so full that the hand which rests in the hand of a Divine Master moves with no quiver of fear. The child of God puts her hand in the hand of the Father and knows that where He leads her He gives her His own support of peace, and she gives out her vision to the world in the spirit of the life of Him whom she serves and loves.[125]

The visions of reformers' causes were related to one another on nearly a latitudinarian basis. Whatever seemed right to each reformer was right for that reformer, in Shaw's view. This baptism of subjectivism was in rather stark contrast to the work of both Stanton and Anthony, who argued that all these other works were inefficient or "man-appointed missions," as in Anthony's phrase; or they argued that women seeking them were lacking in self-respect as long as they themselves were politically ostracized.

Shaw was able to present this benign acceptance of all good things because of her view that they represented "infinite possibilities" open to God's children.[126] These possibilities were transforming, transfiguring even, humankind into the glory of the Infinite from which they sprang.

Paul standing in the light of that vision beheld the glory of what a true man might become. He saw all the possibilities that were before him when he took upon himself the service of Him to whom he belonged, and what Paul saw every child of God has seen who has stood in the light of truth, and has seen the possibilities that are his if he will only open his heart and let the truth come in there and illuminate his whole life until he is filled with all the fullness of God. So the child of God, beholding in him the Glory of the Father, shall be changed into the same image from glory to glory as by the spirit of the Lord.[127]

And where was a possibility, there was a responsibility.

Injustice and Justice

I have argued that the question, the injustice, of the question-and-answer structure of the definition of the issue for Shaw was the inconsistency between the high democratic ideals and the American practice that did not come up to that standard. The answer, accordingly, was to bring American theory and practice into harmony with each other, to lift the practice to the level of the ideals. This was a relatively straightforward, uncomplicated view of the wrong to be righted, as Shaw herself noted. Yet there was something ambiguous about this position of Shaw's. She saw life as a dynamic process of change; the ideals toward which life moved were also in growth.

Shaw's use of justice was far less thematized, far looser, than Stanton's. Her comment with regard to the peace settlement after World War I might well stand for much of her thought. This was especially so as she viewed that war as one fundamental to democracy. The terms of the peace, she thought,

> must include the spirit of human brotherhood which is growing in the minds and souls of men as a real and mighty power; that justice, fair play, and a sense of responsibility are vital, energetic forces and must be reckoned in the relations of men and nations.[128]

Justice, fair play, and a sense of responsibility. These were down-to-earth, simple concepts, not deeply structured into a systematic view of ethical rules. The question was "so simple, so clear, so plain. It is a matter of justice and common sense; it is in accord with the fundamental principles of our government."[129] I have remarked on Shaw's use of the infinite regarding democracy. She made a special point of speaking in the same terms regarding that peace. It was "only when by our practice, as well as by our theories, we prove to the world that we believe in the infinite power of justice to right wrongs" that the U.S. could be "in the harbinger of hope to despotic and despairing monarchies."[130] She echoed Anthony's dislike for the merely expedient solution in political matters.

> There is nothing in liberty which can harm either man or woman. There is nothing in justice which can work against the best good of humanity; and when on the ground of expediency this measure is opposed, in the words of Wendell Phillips, "whatever is just, God will see that it is expedient." There is no greater inexpediency than injustice.[131]

This use of justice and liberty hard by each other was not untypical of Shaw. Fundamentally, her view of justice emphasized the principle of freedom, rather than, say, equality or community. This was less the liberating freedom or the freedom of conscience dear to Anthony than it was the freedom of opportunity. "Opportunity is the word which means Americanism," she said.[132] Noble leaders with high ideals "bring us nearer to the fulfillment of the dream of justice and freedom, which has been the inspiration of men and women through all the long, weary march of the world's progress to its present place of civilization."[133] What the country needed to make it a democracy was women who said "that they will be free. We need women with souls at a white heat in their love of liberty and we are getting them."[134] She even spoke of "liberty, justice, freedom," without being conscious, it seems, of the repetition.[135]

Shaw's understanding of freedom and opportunity required responsibility as the necessary corollary of liberty. American democracy was founded on the legacy of freedom. The grateful heirs of that tradition were to live up to it. There was a price to be paid for the "passion for freedom."

> This heritage of what the world has worked out as true and just is not ours simply to enjoy or to add to the widening and deepening of our own personal character and power. The world demands from us an adequate return for our equipment for life, and for the vast opportunities which the toil, the patience, the suffering, the holy service of the pioneers of civilization gave to secure to us our high privilege. But with these opportunities come greater responsibilities. We must never forget that *opportunity* is *responsibility*. It is useless to say, "I have privileges; why place upon me responsibilities from which I shrink and which I do not desire." Responsibilities are not the result of desire or willingness to accept them. Opportunity is responsibility and an heroic soul cheerfully accepts the one with the other.[136]

This note was one of the sore points regarding antisuffrage women. "The cry of the woman who seeks freedom from responsibility while claiming privileges and opportunities is the cry of selfishness and cowardice, and has no place in the ideas of a higher humanity." The women at the turn of the century were vastly blessed—and vastly obligated—by the legacy of the past.

> Today we stand upon the vantage ground of the ages; all the accumulated experience and wisdom of the past are ours for use and guidance. The opportunities which open before us are so numerous that the possibilities which lie within them confuse us, and we scarcely know which one to grasp and patiently follow to its goal. . . . Vastly more is demanded of us than in the past; we cannot escape our obligation.[137]

Possibilities and responsibilities went hand in hand. She was dazzled by the "wondrous powers and wondrous possibilities" available in her time and she called women to catch glimpses of a similar vision. Indeed, at times she saw the meaning of "feminism" as the "development of women from sex degeneracy to human aspirations."[138] This was part of the problem, the injustice, part of what she *meant* by the inconsistency between American theory and practice.

> It is almost impossible to get the average person to treat women as human beings with aspirations and ambitions and hopes and sorrows and joys, with problems to face and decisions to make which have practically no relation to sex but everything to do with life and its responsibilities.[139]

Equally, responsibility led to greater moral development in a more noble direction—perhaps created more possibilities.

> Now there is placed upon women the obligation of service without the responsibility of their actions. The man who leads feels the responsibility of his acts, and this urges him to make them noble. Women should have this same responsibility and be made to feel it.[140]

To aspire to wondrous heights, to the infinite that gave visions of infinite possibility, *and* to be responsible—these were the primary moral counters of Shaw's view. Opportunity and responsibility, "freedom and law, self-assertion and obedience, are essential to the higher, spiritual, moral, as well as the social order. They are as inseparable as are the soul and the body. In their perfect balance the fullest human development may be attained."[141]

Since the visions of human possibility sprang from the infinite, lured humanity upward toward them, and grew themselves in the process of improving the human prospect, there was a certain, shall we say, flexibility in Shaw's view. What I characterized as her subjectivism might well be seen as the dynamism inherent in her position. "The life of the spirit is a continual process of becoming. It is life only when there is growth."[142] This was an organic social process, as Shaw saw it, one in which moral codes were inherited "through social heredity to which all the people composing the group, consciously or unconsciously, contribute."[143] A little bit of right mixed with a little bit of wrong was found in each epoch, as in the Jewish religion that preceded Christianity. "It is because of the fact that that which the world has worked out in a given period as right is the basis on which our ideals of life are built, that our ideals with each new epoch are constantly changing and can never if they are alive remain statical."[144] The real reformer needed a long-term view, a view of the human past and the human future together, to be sustained.

It is no wonder that so many are filled with distrust of humanity and ask in the spirit of the fatalist, "Is it worth while?" Why strive with puny, empty hands and high ideals against such vast forces entrenched within the mighty citadels of power? We might well despair if we viewed life for a day. It is only when viewed as a whole that the real reformer is able with unfaltering faith to follow her vision to its goal. The reformer who believes that there is a power reaching through all the ages and that this power is a constant presence working with unfailing purpose toward a single goal, must believe that we shall ultimately know the meaning and purpose of life.[145]

Divinity was present in the reform movements, which were all democratic movements upward. Indeed, this was the meaning of the advent of Jesus: "henceforth, aspiration and struggle, infinite hunger for unattained aims, were to be present in human life, and women were to share in its struggle and its achievements."[146]

Evolving Visions of the Infinite

Shaw was theologically trained, ordained, and had seven years of parish experience. She preached all over the country on her suffrage campaigns, sure to be occupying a pulpit on the Sunday following or preceding the meeting. Suffragists claimed her as the first woman ever to preach in many European nations. It is perhaps to be expected that Shaw blended together her views of woman suffrage and her religious positions. In addition, her years of great suffragist activity are the years when liberal religion, in one form or another, was sweeping through American churches.

The synthesis of Christianity with the woman suffrage cause was proceeding apace before Anna Howard Shaw came into her prime as a suffrage leader. The AWSA, Shaw's route to suffrage, departed from the position of the NWSA on many counts, but the religious divergence between the two organizations concerns me particularly. The AWSA was noted for its roster of respectable Christian clergy, including bishops and "princes of the pulpit"; most of the early ordained women active in the movement were found in the AWSA.[147] This difference in membership was concomitant with disagreements regarding the relationship of religion to the movement. AWSA speakers were quick to point out that Christianity had elevated womanhood far more than any other world religion or social force. As Gilbert Haven put it in 1875 from the AWSA presidential chair:

> The history of Christianity has been a history of the gradual enlarging of the sphere of woman; and this meeting tonight is one of the effects of Christianity. . . . Christianity has lifted woman to a level with man. It has given her liberty of movement, of faith, of life. It also demands her political deliberation.[148]

This was argued from a variety of grounds, but one thing was clear: these suffragists believed Stanton's anti-Christian polemics to be dead wrong.

Further, where Stanton had eschewed self-sacrifice, indeed had likened it to suttee, the AWSA speakers sung the praises of women's service to others. Julia Ward Howe's speech to the first AWSA convention set the tone of much that was to follow:

> She cautioned women not to do injustice to others, while seeking justice for themselves; advised them that they must prepare for the new responsibilities they coveted; and that they would better learn to command, by learning well how to serve. She closed her grand and inspiring address with this sentence: "Oh! of all the names given to us to ward off the demon and invoke the angel, let us hold fast to this word—service!"[149]

AWSA thinkers pursued a variety of strategies to synthesize the Christian tradition and the reform they sought. Sometimes they distinguished between the Bible and Christianity.[150] Henry Ward Beecher pointed out that "I have looked through the Ten Commandments, and although I find a great many things that you shall not do, I don't find anywhere it says that you shall not vote."[151] What the Bible did enjoin was love—an example of a Christianity so generalized that it did not conflict with anything. Francis Dana Gage identified both Christianity and woman suffrage with the Golden Rule: "Christ was hung upon the cross for daring to say, 'Whatsoever ye would do that men should do unto you do ye the same to them.' What else does woman suffrage mean?"[152] Christianity was allied with progress, barbarism with antisuffrage and the use of physical force.[153] Julia Ward Howe was sure that to enfranchise women was to aid in making America "a Christian nation"; the field was "white with the harvest" as this brand of evangelical feminism looked to a national conversion bringing in the new state and new church side by side.[154]

These and other lines of thought were followed by Shaw in both her younger and later years. She was rarely critical of churches. In Shaw's work can be seen a case study in the terms by which the woman suffrage movement became respectable, in attaching itself to mainline Christianity. But it is important to emphasize that Shaw's work is equally a case study in the terms on which the movement became *effective* in middle America, in which the terms of respectability *and* of Christianity had shifted considerably from the 1840s.

Aside from her own anecdotal reminiscences, there is little documentation of Shaw's seminary career or of her maturation in the parish. The earliest extant work is from 1879, the year she graduated from Boston School of Theology. Like so many women in the ministry then and now, she prepared a survey of "Women in the Ministry." It drew attention to the strong female figures of biblical and early church times, attributed to Tertullian and to the church's increasing prestige and wealth the decline in women's status in the church. Like many similar works, it leaped chronologically from that church father to the earliest women of Methodist history. Only a few pages long, the sketch's importance lies primarily in its closing paragraph, Shaw's summary and exhortations to women.

> The need of women in the service of humanity was never so great as it is today, and they will not hesitate to enter it, by the established and officially recognized channels of the church if they may, but by new ones if they must. These and scores of organized bodies of women doing the real work of the church who, because they were restrained from doing it within, have been compelled to organize outside the church. The ministry of women in the future development of religion is an established fact.[155]

The "real work of the church," in Shaw's mind, was in "the service of humanity." This was the AWSA line of argument integrating the themes of service, the work of women for reform, and the Christian tradition into one seamless whole. Stanton agreed that women were debarred from doing this work within the churches, but she would never have spoken of it as "ministry." Stanton's belief in progress was as firm as that of Shaw, but it was the latter who spoke of ushering in the biblical age of the kingdom of heaven. Shaw's closing exhortation to women might be summarized as, "Let women teach and live the social gospel."

> Let her teach no ecclesiastical system which must be rigid and thus from its very nature retrograde; let her go forth in the services of humanity and not to perpetuate a ponderous institution; let her teach that the Kingdom of Heaven is set up here and now; let her show by example that service is the sum of human excellence; let her declare that love is the fulfillment of the perfect law, that it alone is the dynamic force in human lives which is to redeem the world from its greed, its injustice and its barbarism; let love be the keynote of all her

thinking and acting, for out of it alone can come the great social, moral and religious harmony which shall usher in "the new Heaven and the new Earth wherein dwelleth righteousness."[156]

In this statement a portion of her later themes were prefigured. She always sought women to "go forth in the services of humanity and not to perpetuate a ponderous institution." ("God's Women," an often-repeated reply to a conservative churchman, made just such a point.) The immanent eschatological vision, to be achieved by women's works of love, was never far from her lips, particularly in her sermons to suffragists and other reforming women. In later years she tempered such notions, admitting that the millennium would not automatically come when women were given the vote, but adding that it would not come without that measure. The dynamism above was further explicated in the evolutionary terms of the age. Love never disappeared but it was allied with truth and beauty. The ethical idealism persisted and expanded as Shaw developed her notion of the reformer's vision put into practice.

Shaw's speeches always were redolent with religious references. She echoed many an earlier feminist's critical points. The declaration that "When God wants to put a limit on women, He will do it without the help of the New York Legislature"[157] summarized a good deal of feminist rhetoric back to the Declaration of Sentiments. She spoke movingly of the "soul," which she foresaw as the problem of the twentieth century. Like many another liberal of the period, she spoke frequently of Jesus as "the Divine Master," whose message was too noble and high for his age to comprehend fully. Like feminists before and after her, she had an inchoate notion of Jesus as androgynous; she preached one Sunday on "Jesus Christ, the ideal man" and the following Sunday on "Jesus Christ, the ideal woman."[158] But these themes, and many others like them, were not the heart of her religious reflections on her suffragist activity.

A. Democracy the Divine Emanation

I have quoted Shaw's assertion that "we simply must consider a republic as desirable or not. If it is desirable, then let us have it. That is the whole question; there is nothing else involved."[159] Compare that single-minded political utterance with this equally single-minded comment: "Now all that is meant by the woman suffrage movement lies in that first divine utterance to man: 'It is not good for man to stand alone'—either in the home, or in the state, or even in the Garden of Eden."[160] The reason Shaw could make these apodictic statements, one regarding the democratic republic and the other a Christian revealed truth, was not that she varied her comments with the audience. It was that they were virtually the same point for her. Democracy and Christianity came together in an ideal unity, evolving ever farther and ever upward. Her most succinct statement of the "democracy of Christianity"[161] went, with variations, like this:

> No man is fitted to become a citizen of the Kingdom of Heaven who is not a good citizen on this earth. No man who thinks this earth and its problems unworthy of consideration understands the moving of the Divine Spirit; and anyone who thinks that woman suffrage is not a proper subject for discussion on Sunday afternoon does not comprehend the profound, sublime and divine principles of democracy.
>
> Democracy is not merely a form of government; it is a great spiritual force emanating from the heart of the Infinite, permeating the universe and transforming the lives of men until the day comes when it shall take possession of them, and shall govern their lives. Then will men be fitted to lift their faces to the Source from whence the spirit of democracy flows, and answer back in the spirit, in their recognition of that fundamental principle of democracy: "One is our father, even God, and we are members one of another." And as soon as the spirit of democracy takes possession of us, we shall not quibble as to whether it is male or female, bond or free, Jew or Greek; we shall recognize only that every child has an equal right with every other human child of God, in the things that belong to God. Liberty, justice, freedom, belong alike to God's human children.[162]

Democracy, constantly referred to as "sublime," emanated progressively from the "heart of the Infinite." It transformed, sometimes even transfigured, human life. Democracy was an eternal ideal,

> a spiritual thought which existed before governments dawned upon the world, and because of the ideal it will exist long after this world has been rolled as a scroll and passed away into nothingness. Democracy is a spiritual essence. Democracy is the living spirit of the Most High.[163]

It followed that the movements that were seeking further progress in democracy incarnated the spirit of the Most High. "No human being with the eye of faith can fail to see traversing the whole progress of our movement a divinity shaping our ends, rough-hew them as we may, and that divinity is the divinity of the gospel of democracy."[164]

She was not always precise about the relationships of the democratic faith to the Christian faith. Sometimes the "gospel of democracy" seemed almost to stand on its own two feet. At other times it was rather "the democracy of the gospel" that needed to "permeate the democracy of our land."[165] There is, however, no need to separate these two locutions from each other, for Shaw made no pretensions to precision. Both taught the same lesson. Christianity itself was very general in Shaw's mind. "We are learning from the teaching and example of Jesus that life itself is a religion, that nothing is more sacred than a human being, that the end of all right institutions, whether the home or the church or an educational establishment, is the development of the human soul."[166] The struggle to attain high ideals was as fundamental to Christianity as it was to the reformers' visions.

> The democracy of Christianity teaches us that religion must become more personal and more human, and the more one studies the life of Jesus the more he is impressed with the fact that the one permanent basis of the spiritual life is that community of soul in which each earnestly strives to the attainment of the highest life, yet each in loving fellowship with the whole.[167]

Religion was to be more personal, more human, each striving after high possibilities, "yet each in loving fellowship with the whole." Shaw's use of Genesis to show that it was not good for men to stand alone was complemented by her Pauline view that human beings were members of one body. People were "knit together" (in Anthony's, not Shaw's, phrase) such that any injury to one was an injury to all.

> The democracy of the gospel must permeate the democracy of our land and we must learn that as the hand cannot say to the foot, or the ear to the eye—"I have no need of thee." Neither can the educated say to the uneducated—"I have no need of thee"; nor the rich to the poor—"I have no need of thee." Each has need of the other; each must live and live and grow together, or else the survivors must be chained to the diseased and corrupt body of the outcasts. We cannot separate ourselves from them. We cannot fly from the disease; waking or sleeping it is ever present and pollutes the very air we breathe. If any part of the body is diseased, the whole body is diseased; if any part of the people are wronged, the whole people suffer disbasement from that wrong.[168]

Shaw understood herself to be in continuity with Anthony, for the later realized "that this freedom could not come to any one class or race or sex alone, but must include all to be enjoyed by any."[169] Similarly, Galatians 3:28 was one of the pillars of Shaw's arguments. When the spiritual essence that was democracy was to be complete with women's voting, the unity of humankind would be complete with the apostle's insight.

> It is not that women may vote, but that the human in mankind may triumph. That civilization may conquer barbarism, may triumph over autocracy. That every child of God may have a fair chance to be and to become all that it is possible for it to attain. That democracy, which is not merely a form of government, but the divine law of life emanating from the heart of the Infinite entering into the souls of men and transforming human character until some day it will respond in like spirit to the source from whence it springs. And when it does, we shall know that in Him there is neither male nor female, but all are alike one.[170]

This note that "the human in mankind may triumph" reminds us of the explicitly humanistic note in Shaw's vision. Unlike Stanton's ballot box and the Church of Humanity that were to replace the Church of Christ, Shaw's claim was that "true humanism . . . in its completeness is attributed by all religions to their saviours and founders."[171] This true humanism was also the "ultimate goal" of feminism, which "really had its birth in the Garden of Eden, and Eve, the first feminist, took the first step toward humanism."[172] Note that "true masculinism" was the same aspiration.[173]

Shaw never abandoned this religious view of democracy or of the woman suffrage movement, even in the days when those "political methods" of which she claimed ignorance won over her beloved suffrage association. Her final presidential speech to the NAWSA tried (I think, unsuccessfully) to redefine the democratic faith so as to make it compatible with the changes. She acknowledged that the new methods came "as a revelation and a distinct shock" to the woman who was, like herself, an idealist.[174] Nonetheless, she was firm in reiterating that the woman suffrage movement faced no merely technical problem:

> Back of and running through this political problem of ours is one far deeper and more fundamental without which political emancipation would be futile. Our real problem is ethical and religious. Freedom, true freedom, must come from within, and I believe all will agree with me that our great need today is that our

movement be vitalized by a mighty spiritual force working from within ourselves.[175]

Those who balked at the changes were prey to misunderstanding, to "false theories of politics and political leadership." She tried to clear away Tammany Hall and the political machines from the minds of her audience to prepare the way for a civil religion that could coexist with modern methods.

> If we can but eliminate from our minds the knowledge which most of us have of the abuse and misuse of politics, our contempt for political bossism, and remember that our mission is to secure a better government than we now possess, that politics is the science by which governments are controlled, that the government is as holy as the science of religion, that political leadership in itself is as honorable as religious leadership, and that there is no more sacred nor noble vocation than to be one with the Infinite in the government of the world, then we shall cease to regret the change which has been wrought.[176]

It is interesting to compare Shaw's civil religion with that of Stanton. Both saw politics and government as holy and the reformer's work of bringing society closer to the incarnation of democratic principles as a sacred task. But the theological terms by which they fleshed out the meaning of these general statements had very little in common. Their pro- and anti-Christian stances obviously separated them. Shaw, like her AWSA colleagues, firmly held to the notion that Jesus and Christianity were the real origins of women's steadily increasing gains in the Western world. Both of them looked out over the religious pluralism of this earth to conclude with a statement of their fundamental unity. Stanton discovered how they all alike degraded women; Shaw, on the other hand, claimed that the New Testament, Zoroaster, Buddhist scriptures, Islam, Confucius, Augustine, and Hinduism all taught "one truth—divine love."[177]

Indeed, even the points they shared most closely were articulated on grounds basically different. They agreed, for instance, that each woman was to interpret the divine will for herself alone. To Shaw this was a process of visions received by hearts, whereas to Stanton it was via the enlightened intellect and science. Stanton's belief in sober logic and reasoning would never have allowed her to confess herself a dreamer and an idealist, as Shaw's visionary position affirmed. Though they both had a "two natures" theory of the sexes, Shaw's notions of sacrificing love and the more personally oriented approach of women were never the cosmological vision of Stanton's electromagnetic forces demanding woman's self-assertion.

For both, democracy was divinely ordained. To Shaw, on the one hand, democracy was, we might say, "one in being with the Father," of a part with the divine substance from which it came. To Stanton, on the other hand, democracy was insured by the laws of "whatever one chooses to call the Supreme Force which sets all in motion." Stanton's deity was the Creator, whose action was past. Shaw's references to the Infinite were future-oriented; God was the ground of aspiration and hope. To be sure, the Creator Stanton revered sent one forward with evolution according to the immutable laws; and the Infinite sent one back into time with responsibilities to others. But the contrast was nonetheless present and important.

One point that separated Stanton and Shaw as did no other was Shaw's notion that the "spiritual force" flowing toward humanity from on high was "transforming the lives of men,"[178] working on human lives "the miracle of divine truth and of a divine resurrection."[179] When the eternal truth dawned on Paul, it entered into his soul until he was "filled with all the fullness of God"; likewise the lesser followers "beholding in him the Glory of the Father shall be changed into the same image from glory to glory as by the spirit of the Lord."[180] Human beings needed, in other words, to be converted. Shaw was enough of a Methodist, I suspect, to have the traditional understanding that it was the Holy Spirit that worked the work of perfection on the soul once saved.

> Open the windows of your souls, let the sunshine of God's love rush down into them, and as the world becomes a new world when the sun has risen, so let your poor human lives become new and transformed lives as the sun of God's spirit enters into them. Out of the vision of truth which is within you He is able, by the influence of His spirit upon your life, to work a miracle and bring the truth therein to other lives.[181]

References to sin, original or otherwise, were meager and perfunctory in Shaw's speeches and letters. In her liberalism, man was "fallen, it is true, but magnificent in his ruin."[182] It was the other half, as it were, of the concept that really excited her, the need of transformation. Divine intervention, the power of divine love, was needed to bring humanity to its true form. "Infinite love: This must baptize the reformer. She must be bathed in it and walk in its light."[183] Human nature itself could be changed by the divine power.

The changing of human nature is a slow process, but it is changing, and notwithstanding the frauds in politics and the dishonesty in government, higher ideals are evolving, and it is the mission of the woman suffrage association to continue to emphasize them, and to seek to teach the people—all the people, both men and women—that they are responsible for their development.[184]

Such idealism as she evinced must have brought her more than one criticism, for the following year Shaw took the matter up again. Here "dreams" replaced the "visions" of her earlier years on the pulpit and platform. But the thought was the same:

We are told that to assume that women will help purify political life and develop a more ideal government but proves us to be dreamers of dreams. Yes, we are in a goodly company of dreamers, of Confucius, of Buddha, of Jesus, of the English Commons fighting for the Magna Charta, of the Pilgrims, of the Revolutionists, of the Antislavery men and women. The seers and leaders of all times have been dreamers. Every step of progress the world has made is the crystallization of a dream into reality.[185]

This presidential address ended with an "altar call." The Methodist preacher in her could not resist, after all the reports and details of business, luring other women forward by stating the vision again and inviting them to respond in action by joining the organization.

If you think our organization worthwhile, come and help us make it worth while. If you believe the ideal of self-government a good one; if freedom is worth having; if work for the public good is worth doing; if the problems of human development are worth solving; if it is worth while to be one with the infinite in bringing to pass order and peace and justice in human governments, then our ideal should be our life; the very breath of our body. Thus and thus only shall we honor our cause and be honored by it, and, glorying in it, we too may exclaim, "I count these light afflictions, which I endure for a moment, all joy," if I may but enter into the life of those who in all the centuries have striven for this great truth. From henceforth, let us rejoice and joy in it, for great is our reward, that we are permitted now and here to see its approaching fulfillment![186]

Shaw's sense that human beings could be transformed meant less that they were to be saved from sin than that the ideals should be "the very breath of one's body." To bring the republic's practice into line with its ideals was far more than a superficial transaction.

264

B. Love, Truth, Beauty

It should be clear by now that Shaw was an idealist in more than the debased sense that has become virtually synonymous with "unrealistic" (though there was a tinge of unrealism as well). When she exhorted women and other reformers to "open the windows" of their souls to God's truth, her metaphor appears to be a domesticated or small-scale resonance of Platonic themes, such as the cave. Stanton used such images, which contrast wandering in dark caves with the clear sunlight of truth; yet that worthy hardly spoke of the principles for which she battled in the abstract idealist sense Shaw did.

Like Stanton also, Shaw was given to the use of the "soul." When Stanton queried her own soul *and* nature as to the subjection of woman, she stressed the relatively bloodless analogy between the moral and the material. Shaw's conception was slightly different. "To every man and woman of us here God has given a soul, a soul so divinely attuned that we may hear the very harmonies of heaven; a soul so divinely attuned that we may hear the voice of God speaking with us, and be directed by that voice out and into a high and holy plane."[187] While Stanton's vision was of a cosmos in which all the laws—centrifugal and centripetal forces, positive and negative electricity, etc.—moved in harmony together, it was rather more the harmony of a clock whose discrete parts were mechanically interstructured. Shaw's harmony was of a more fluid sort. She never described its "mechanics"; indeed, the spirit "flowed" and "emanated" from its Source in the nether regions. Shaw's harmonies were *heard*, like the harmony of the symphony, or of the voice of the people in which soprano and bass must be intermingled to make it the voice of God.[188]

Shaw's God was active, directing people to do this or that, speaking.

> Then, oh woman! what may we not prophesy of thee, when thou hast come into perfect harmony with the truth, when thou hast heard its voice speaking in thine own being? What may we not prophesy of thee when from off the altar a living coal shall be pressed to thy lips, and thou shalt speak words all aflame with truth?[189]

This deity had a mind. Sometimes the harmonious work of reformers was to "bring God's thought to the mind of God's children."[190] This, it is not surprising, was especially her tack when it was truth that she had in mind. "[A]ll progress is one. That a reform no more than an individual can live to itself. That truth, all truth, is the atmosphere of the Infinite mind, and is in its

265

source and aim one with God."[191] Most often this God was spoken of in terms of the heart. America needed

> a baptism of the spirit, higher religious ideals, deeper tolerance and sympathy. The human heart must be in accord with the Divine heart if America is to mean more than other countries, and, if we are to be what our mothers and fathers aspired to be, we must all be a part of government.[192]

Truth sprang from the heart, and this is where the truth gained its power to transform. Love taught lessons that the head could never learn. Indeed, "the deepest insights of truth are not given by the intellect but by love."[193] Looking back over her long life to inspire college youth, Shaw found two points distilled from experience that expressed this conjunction.

> There are two things in life which make its struggle, its pain, its losses, its joys and victories worth while. They are,
> First, to be so possessed by a fundamental principle of right that it becomes consuming fire. The other is to have a heart filled with a great love for humanity.
> Possessed by these two passions, no struggle can become too severe, no waiting too wearisome, no life useless.[194]

Reformers were inspired and led by "a great love for humanity, a love which nothing can quench. Which can endure all things and still trust with such an abiding faith that it saves, if not others, at least oneself."[195] This was precisely what Anthony meant to Shaw, that Anthony was possessed by an all-absorbing love.

> On the heights alone such souls meet God. In silent communion they learn life's sublimest lessons. They are the world's real heroes. Hers was an heroic life, by it she teaches us that the philosophy of the Ancients is wrong; that it is not true that men are made heroic by indifference to life and death, but by learning to love something more than life.
> Her heroism was the heroism of an all absorbing love; a love which neither indifference, nor persecution, nor misrepresentation, nor betrayal, nor hatred, nor flattery could quench; a heroism which would suffer her to see and know nothing but the power of injustice and hatred to destroy, and the power of justice and love to develop all that is best and noblest in human character.[196]

The ideals, the possibilities inherent in some human life, were the reasons of the sacrifice of love.

Life is of infinite value; every hour of it should be cherished because of the possibilities enfolded within it. To love something more than life; to cherish an ideal so vastly that life for its sake becomes of vital importance; to live and strive when all else save the ideal seems lost, so that life and all its fullness of meaning shall be at its service, is the most heroic sacrifice that one can make for a great reform of his country, and this is the demand our country and our cause makes upon us today.[197]

This love and all its accoutrements were particularly to be found in women. I have already noted Shaw's view that women were more "personal" than men.

The mother-heart of woman, the mother-heart that reaches out to the race and finds a wrong and rights it, finds a broken heart and heals it, finds a bruised life ready to be broke and sustains it—a woman instinct with mother-love, which is the expression of the Divine love; a woman who, finding any wrong, any weakness, any pain, any sorrow, anywhere in the world, reaches out her hand to right the wrong, to heal the pain, to comfort the suffering—such a woman is God's woman.[198]

Mother love was an expression of the divine love. Shaw's private papers too echo this sense of God as having to do with "life, being, knowledge, sympathy, love, and whatever may be attributed to the Infinite Power."[199] Interestingly, she was not sure about calling God "He" or "She," "even they are not the best as they mean limitation, but at least they have an advantage on 'It.' "[200] But "one of the missions of the woman preacher," as Shaw saw it, was precisely

to people heaven with the feminine thought as well as on earth, and the race must be taught that they can no more be half-orphans in heaven than they are on earth, and that in the spirit of divine life, in the spirit of infinite love, in divinity itself, we have the feminine and the masculine, and God is the eternal parent of us all, the father and mother of the human soul.[201]

Over the years, Shaw's views on the nature of womanhood changed slightly. In her earliest days, the qualifications of her position were such that they seemed to reinforce the period's view of women:

if woman enters upon her tasks wielding her own effective armor, if her inspirations are pure and holy, the Spirit Omnipotent whose influence has held sway in all movements and reforms, whose voice has called into its service the great workmen of every age, shall in these last days fall especially upon women, and if she venture to obey, what is man that he should attempt to abrogate her sacred and divine mission?[202]

In her later years, she pointed to the need of women to develop some traits she thought more masculine.

> By feminism I understand the development of those qualities in human nature which we have generally attributed to the female, as love, sacrifice, gentleness—but which we also find in large degree in the highest type of male[.] [B]ut the qualities which modern feminism demands in addition to these are honesty, honor, loyalty—those qualities which heretofore have been largely dormant in women, but which, under new and changing conditions, she is evolving and bringing into practical service in the business of life.[203]

Just as heaven was to be balanced with the inclusion of both masculine and feminine characteristics, so she argued for a balance in both men and women of the traits of each sex. "The best and noblest men and women are those in whom the different characteristics of each sex are most harmoniously blended." This was illustrated, she thought, by the "modern democratic ideal."[204]

For all the broad agreement between Stanton and Shaw that is readily discerned in these themes, it is noteworthy that Stanton's use of love was rare indeed. When she spoke of love it was almost always within the context of marriage, which was sanctified only by the presence of love between the two partners. There was almost no hint in Stanton's work that the reformer was animated by love, whether infinite or proximate. This was not only because Stanton concentrated on science and the enlightened intellect. It was the broad philosophical principles of justice and equality, the indignation against injustice, moral discontent with the world, or self-respect, which she named as the springs of reform. Even when Stanton concentrated on motherhood, it was in different terms. She believed women to be less harsh in punishment and education; the mothering element in deity was thematized not in terms of God's love but in terms of eliminating the fear of eternal punishment for sin. Paeans of praise to love were absent. This contrast between the two is heightened when we notice that Shaw rarely spoke of judicious self-love except in the terms I have characterized as subjectivist or latitudinarian. Anthony, who loved her own family deeply, used the counters of love almost solely in the context of enticing women to the "deep, rich, earnest love for their own sex" rather than the sacrifice of self. The stress on love for others, duty, and responsibility to others were Shaw's quintessentially Victorian themes luring women to the practice of high ideals. The true reformer, bathed and baptized in infinite love, was drawn to other reforms because "as the magnet draws to itself the needle, so love draws to itself love."[205]

Shaw's reiterated use of "sublime" to characterize democracy is something of a puzzle. There is no hint in her work that she meant this in the classic sense of the distinction between the sublime and the beautiful. It seemed rather to be the superlative of beautiful. The "universally noble spirit of Jesus" was manifest in "His interest in the common life and His love of the beautiful in the world"—which were not, of course, rightly understood by his followers.[206] Young factory workers were also to "feel the thrill of the good and of the beautiful."[207] Citing the sublime led Shaw back either to democracy or to love. One of "life's sublimest lessons" was "learning to love something more than life," as she said of Anthony.[208]

The visions of God were glorious, and it may be the resplendent brilliance of the throne of the most high that was most in Shaw's mind when she spoke of beauty. Stanton's "clear sunlight of truth" was close kin to Shaw's point. But one has rather the sense with Shaw that the eternal truth grasped by the reformer was one that dazzled with its ineffable radiance, rather than permeated by the chill clarity of ideas marshalled in order. (Certainly Stanton never spoke of any "thrill" that ran through her in the illumination of the right to think.) And though Shaw made occasional bows to nature, whose precepts were vindicated in the strides made by women, these hardly occupy the place in her work that they do in Stanton's; they were but a perfunctory nod to a tutelary deity of an earlier generation.

Indeed, it is difficult to know what to think about any of Shaw's "ideals." They were immensely abstract, possessed of little or no content, strangely bloodless. They were holy—so much was clear—and implied qualitative change in those who gave them sway over their lives. I suspect that the empty character of the most fundamental terms in Shaw's thought had its reasons in her use of the infinite. For though the infinite was clothed in some of the richly anthropomorphic images of the biblical God, it is always hard, virtually by definition, to characterize the infinite—except to eschew limitation on it. In harmony with this final term of Shaw's work, there was also infinite love, infinite hope, the infinite power of justice, infinite possibility open to the human species; but there is little more than this to be said. Shaw spoke very little of the empirical changes going on about her that served, in her contemporaries influenced by social science, to categorize and analyze the changing world in which they lived. Unlike Gilman, Addams, Scudder, Spencer, who were busily getting down to the concrete specifics of the possibilities of the new age, Shaw seemed content to describe them as wonderful and unlimited. To refrain from calling Shaw sentimental on this account would require more of the Christian virtue of patience than I possess.

And she was nowhere more sentimental than in her utterly traditional and utterly ordinary use of love. Of all the points on which I would fault Shaw, her uncritical rendering of love stands at the center. Here I can only think it was in large part her analysis of the injustice faced by women that was the clue to the banal Victorian platitudes she voiced on this subject. For Shaw's view on the situation of women lacked precisely the description of the "nice degrees" of women's wrongs that Stanton so assiduously sought. Without any sense of the problems faced by her contemporaries aside from the "simple" thought of whether this was a republic or not, Shaw had no intellectual or emotional leverage by which to think about love—to redefine it, to recast it in terms that would not simply bless the age in which she lived, to qualify in fundamental ways her reading of this shibboleth of her time.

C. The Churches

On only a few occasions was Shaw openly and publicly critical of the American churches. In those rare moments, her criticisms tended to be couched in a language familiar to Christians: "The churches of this day have not begun to conceive of what Christianity means."[209] This was the call of a Christian to other Christians to conform themselves more adequately to the common faith, to return from its erring ways to the Gospel.

Shaw's early public comments on the churches tend to be fairly safe ones. They reinterpret the tradition so as to mediate between the average believer and the "liberals" in woman suffrage. Religious objections to the cause, she thought, tended to come in the "second stage" of a reform. The people raising such obstacles were

afraid that religion born of God, emanating from God, the soul and life of the world, will be overthrown by a few of God's simple human children; and these people fearing that God—I speak reverently—shall not be able to hold His own against a few, think they must stand up in defence of God and the great principle and soul-life of his being, and of our being.[210]

Unlike the sarcasm lavished on the Bible by Stanton, Shaw spoke "reverently." She calmly explained the viewpoint of the new advances in Bible scholarship.

Under the head of religion there are two schools of exegesis, in this country and in the world. There are also two classes of theologians. One gives us what is termed the higher criticism, and one which is called the lower criticism of the Bible, especially of the New Testament. One assures us that the New Testament must be taken literally, and that when it makes certain statements in regard to women, those statements are to be accepted today exactly as they were uttered by Paul hundreds of years ago. The other set of exegetes say that these things are not to be taken literally, but that they are to be interpreted as we interpret all books published at that time, taking into account the circumstances under which they were uttered, the condition of society, and the needs of the people. These are the two schools, and when we come to woman's relation to the government and the relation of men to women, we find the same difference here. The party that declares that the Bible should be taken literally is especially emphatic that it should be taken literally when it speaks anything about the subjection of women. And there are men today who do not believe a single word of that Bible was inspired, except that thought which was in the Bible—that Paul said—wives obey your husbands.[211]

She was clear that she was a liberal; in expressing this stance she pointed to the apostasy of the churches when they weighed in against woman suffrage. Shaw was not, like either Anthony or Stanton, willing to accept the label of "infidel."

Shall I be blamed for standing with those who put the more liberal construction on the word, and which I believe to be in accord with the teachings of Christ, the whole of which may be covered with the Golden Rule? That is the highest law given by the highest authority to human beings. The difficulty with our Christian church today is that it preaches Christ but it practices Moses.[212]

Indeed, "if the trouble is that women are more attached to the liberal churches than to the orthodox, there is one way to change it. Let the orthodox church open its doors and let us come in."[213]

Evolution was clearly compatible with revelation. On the one hand, her point was strictly a historical one; on the other, God too adapted to the ways of the world. "The expanding power of the democratic ideal, in religion as in government, proves beyond question that no type is adapted to all ages, hence, 'The Lord giveth the word' as the need of the world calls and the human mind is able to assimilate it."[214] The new translation of the Bible in the late nineteenth century was precisely in line with this evolutionary improvement.

The King James versions make the Revelation of the word as completed. While the Revised version, with its broader vision, recognizes the unfulfilled revelation

271

and the gradual unfolding of the Word as mankind are able to receive and understand it.[215]

Interestingly, however much Shaw believed that even the high ideals themselves evolved over the ages, the Gospel was ever the same. "The crying need of the world today is for a great spiritual teacher. One who can lead us back to the simple realities of life. Not that we need a new religion, but the old Gospel anew, taught in the language of our age."[216]

Since the world had "at last" learned that women had special spiritual powers (such as "intuitions of the human mind . . . the art of persuasive eloquence . . . heroic conduct based on duty,"[217]) those special capacities needed to be exercised in the service of the spirit. "When God wants a certain thing done that he knows needs a woman to do it, he generally raises a woman and not a man for the position."[218] Like Ruth, Rachel, Deborah, or Miriam, the three Marys of the New Testament were examples of God pressing women into His service. Indeed, "one was a woman who was a theological student learning at the feet of the Master. The other was the first divinely commissioned preacher of the Resurrection. One was the mother of the Lord, doing the greatest public work for the race that has ever been done in the world."[219]

Women had the right to formulate their own religious insights. This we have seen in Stanton and Anthony; in Shaw's perspective, however, such a point was made less because of woman's right to think than because of human responsibility, the accountability before the judgment seat of God.

> Men have no right to define for us our limitations. Who shall interpret to a woman the divine element in her being? It is for me to say that I shall be free. No human soul shall determine my life for me unless that soul will stand before the bar of God and take my sentence. Men who denounce us do so because they are ignorant of what they do. Woman has broken the silence of the century. Her question to God is "Who shall interpret Thee to me?" The churches of this day have not begun to conceive of what Christianity means.[220]

Not only had "the world . . . suffered because [woman] had not kept her divinely appointed place,"[221] but also the churches.

> Too long women failed to recognize their mission, and, instead of inquiring of the Word for themselves and following the direction of the spirit, have accepted established dogmas and interpretations of the Scriptures which have been so large a factor in retarding the development of the more complete and perfectly

rounded character which should measure the growth of free human souls. And the church has been robbed of one of the greatest spiritual forces for human betterment.[222]

Her infrequently given speech, "The White Man's Burden," contained some of these rather orthodox strictures on the churches. Her comments were directed against church leaders, allegedly followers of the Prince of Peace, who espoused military means of conquest. But those were buried in a more general critique.

> Is there a man or woman who feels perfectly satisfied with the attitude of the church in this country on great moral and spiritual much less economic problems? He needs to be but a superficial observer to realize that it has in great measure lost and is more and more losing its hold upon the popular mind and that its influence is not felt as it once was as that of the greatest power for spiritual and moral progress in the earth.[223]

(There was an out built into this language; who could say he or she felt "perfectly" satisfied?) Churches were losing membership hand over fist; even "earnest and loyal ministers" were dissatisfied, because "the church as an institution is failing in its purpose."[224] This was not because people were indifferent to religion, as was shown by "the crowded churches which reach their needs and give them the bread they demand instead of a stone."[225] Churches needed to lay aside their insistence on "an intellectual acceptance of antiquated formulas"; they needed to feel rather "that tolerance in religion which recognizes the diversity of human thought, and the activity of the human mind which produces it." But especially they needed to return to the Gospel.

> If we go behind all forms of belief and grasp the essential principles of that religion which Christ taught, we shall find that the hearts of most men beat with a common purpose and are linked in the union of a common love. The church which is to mold the future will reach its highest powers when it learns that the mightiest influence in all the world is not war but love.[226]

This statement was worthy of a Ben Franklin or an Ednah Cheney within woman suffrage circles. "Behind" the sectarian clamor was the simple religion of Jesus—distilled not into Franklin's eleven principles or Cheney's two, but into that one four-letter word to which Shaw returned again and again. This, as we have already seen, was part of the essence of democracy; it was what

273

Shaw saw "underlying all the tumult and disorder of our time," the "one grand, golden thought, that of the human brotherhood of the world."[227] It is hard to see that any church member of the late nineteenth century would have taken exception to these comments.

Nonetheless, Shaw was well aware that the churches were not all that they should be with regard to women, and the antisuffrage stance of certain folk within the churches could tinge her statements with anticlericalism. Her comments on such points, however, were strictly private. The correspondence that she sent home to Lucy Anthony was redolent of Shaw's encounters with the clergy around the country. From these personal notes, mostly anecdotal in character, comes a glimpse of the American churches in some ferment—of antisuffragist ministers, of clergy supporting the cause, of the changing behavior of laywomen at the grass roots of American religion. There is no way to know, of course, how representative these stories were. But Shaw's view has an intrinsic value here, as well as comparative interest, for these tales indicate a rather different slant on the material of this study than Stanton's or Anthony's religious view.

Shaw found many ministerial stereotypes and behaviors disagreeable.

> I am very nicely entertained here. The lady is jolly, and the house a great big comfortable one, old-fashioned and cheerful. The only drawback is a man, an Episcopal clergyman, no, priest, who stays here over Sunday, and is very pious but just as disagreeable. I have observed that a good deal of austerity passes for piety, and ugliness and conceit for deep religious emotion. I hope when I get to heaven—if I ever do—that I will not have to live near a deeply pious man; if I do I will move and try the society of jolly little devils for a while, and an agreeable change it will be. Heaven deliver me from this awful piety in broadcloth which makes you want to swear or laugh all the time. This I know is a wicked letter, but such a man as this makes me want to be wicked. I think if there is a hell and anything could drive me there it would be this kind of minister.[228]

Any "wickedness" in these comments, which seem strictly harmless, probably came from Shaw's own sense of "reverence," the same sense, perhaps, that kept her blaming herself for her moods of despair.

Naturally enough, good portions of this disagreeable quality, this ugliness, came from the antisuffragist prejudices of the clergy she met. A Methodist minister declared to Shaw that he was ashamed of the M.E. church voting on admitting women at all. I told him that I was, too, and that I believed that the time would come when the church would be as ashamed of it as it was that it ever favored slavery, for it was in the same line. Oh, he said, I am ashamed of women that they want to go to the conference at all. I said, I am ashamed of ministers that question their right to go. The old fellow looked as if he could annihilate me . . . yet last night he asked me to preach for him this a.m. . . . . I am not sorry I preached, for I had a chance at him and them. He introduced me as *Miss* and said I would *speak*, instead of saying *preach*.[229]

(The latter point, the refusal to recognize Shaw's ordination, must have been particularly galling to her.) Like both Stanton and Anthony, Shaw was particularly disturbed about the alliance that churches had with intemperance and vice. "Well, the priest and the saloon and the brothel will walk side by side to the polls tomorrow and the priest and the saloon and the white slave cadet will vote the same."[230] On the other hand, ministerial opposition could backfire to the good of the cause.

The Ministerial Union [of Lima, Ohio] decided not to pray for us and so they wanted me to pray last night and, much as I hated to, I did and I think the ministers wished they had not refused. It has advertised the meeting more than anything that has happened.[231]

Like the antisuffragists in general, clergy opposed to the cause were "unconscious allies."[232] Occasionally she poked fun at these clergymen for being out of touch with their congregations. The Presbyterian church in Danville, Kentucky, for example, was so strict that the minister would not allow the women's missionary society to open its own meetings with prayer. Yet Shaw tells us that "everyone of the teachers [of the girls' school] is a suffragist. They even take the Woman's Journal and the poor men don't know it! It is fun."[233]

Like Stanton, Shaw could be incensed over the disparity between the support of women for the churches and the lack of respect and responsiveness the institution returned to them. She enjoyed getting a dig in here and there when she could.

I am helping in another fight here. The women have worked like slaves to furnish and help build the Methodist Episcopal Church, and when I was coming they asked for it to hold my meetings in as it is the largest church in town. To their amazement they were refused and when a reason was asked for the only reply was that the line had to be drawn somewhere and they proposed to do it there. So last night when a lady in the most cordial manner said to me: "I am commissioned by the trustees of the Methodist Episcopal Church to ask you to preach this Sunday morning," I replied, "Thank you very much for the honor but I must decline as I intend to preach in the Baptist Church." She was taken aback and so were the trustees as they had not been used to women standing by their principles, and when I was asked why I would not preach in the M.E. Church I replied, "I have too much self-respect and too much interest in women and too much contempt for such actions on the part of any church to be made a fool of it." Churches need to be taught a lesson and the best thing would be for women to let the men pay the bills and run the church for a time while they sit back and fold their hands. I expect a committee from the church to wait on me today and I think that they won't want to wait on me again. I shall be as dignified and cold as I know how but very polite. Oh, it's fun.[234]

"The churches need to be taught a lesson"—but not the lesson Stanton wanted them to learn. There is no hint in any of these comments that Shaw connected this behavior to any larger realities, to theological positions. She seemed to have no analytic framework in which to understand such incidents.

All was not always bleak. Shaw noted the support of clergy as well. In Pierre, South Dakota, the churches closed so that people could attend a suffrage meeting; the clergy joined her on the platform, including the Roman Catholic priest of the town.

It is very hard, however, to speak under such circumstances because of the fear that some preacher may be offended, but I think I got along alright. Hope so. The Episcopal minister said to me, "If there is a man who can go out of this house tonight and vote against the amendment there is no hope for him."[235]

She was aware of progress, however slight, occurring in the churches.

I preached in the sleepiest old Congregational Church yesterday. I ought to be flattered over it, but I was especially invited to go there by the pastor and less than forty years ago a woman was led out of the same church by a woman for speaking in prayer meeting. So you see things do move.[236]

To my mind, however, the best of these anecdotes was not one of clergy support for the suffrage movement. In Illinois, in 1897, Shaw encountered a minister whose acquaintance she had made years before. "At the supper table I saw an Episcopalian clergyman, who met me some time ago in Newton, Kansas. One of his members, he said, presided and introduced me and my lecture so affected her that he could not manage her anymore."[237] This brief glimpse of the changing behavior of laywomen in the churches might almost stand as a vindication of Shaw's work with American religion. A laywoman met a clergywoman, and sparks were struck by the encounter. Shaw frequently led worship with other ordained women of her day at the national-level suffrage gatherings. But the responses she recounted from one of these occasions in a Michigan (?) local church seem extravagant. One woman said, "I thought when I saw all you three women in the pulpit I would like to have you baptize my baby this afternoon." And this from a man present: "Why, when the three Disciples were on the Mount of Transfiguration they built an altar; I think you three women ought to do that today, for I thought you were all transfigured; I don't think I was ever so happy in my life."[238] I say these responses *seem* extravagant, but they also seem to ring true. Even today, one hundred years later, laywomen and men both express thrills and shed tears at their first encounters with women leading worship.

Though Shaw could and did take on various bishops and religious notables (such as Lyman Abbott) who cast disparagement on the woman suffrage cause, it was in her later years that she altered her tone to a slightly more critical note. In 1918, she thought that one of the consequences of a developing feminism was to be that, "The laws both secular and sacred which in the past and in many cases still rob women of moral responsibility as well as of their natural rights as human beings, and the mother of the race, will be modified or eliminated as they ought to be."[239] This parallel of the sacred and secular laws was almost Stantonesque. But there was no indication that this new acerbity was a product of Shaw's thinking through her position anew. The emphasis on women's moral responsibility was a theme of her entire career, as is this reference to sublime visions.

> Women are proving that the thumb-screws of social criticism, the fires of persecution, the barbarism of unjust laws, the inspirational restraints of religious dogma combined, are unable ultimately to prevent nature from asserting itself. In dogma she has broken down one barrier after another which withheld from her her spiritual birthright of religious liberty and she is following the sublimest vision which ever dawned upon the soul—the right of every human being to stand in the presence of its creator without human mediation.[240]

Yet these were slim public windows into the dissatisfaction Shaw felt with the institutional church. Though from her earliest days she spoke of the ministry of women as opposed to the building up of a "ponderous institution," and had always thought that any institution that sought to remain "statical" had already "within itself the seeds of decay and death," still it is surprising how little of a negative nature she said of the ecclesia. I think this is a case of Shaw's "loyalty," that same loyalty she thought lacking in the NAWSA during her term of office, and in the female character of her time. To be true to an ideal, to have an "abiding faith" that right would come topside, that "somehow, someplace" the truth would be cherished thoroughly in practice, to trust other people—these were themes of her reformers' sermons. It is not implausible to see them in her relationship to the church as well.

There is a certain poignancy in some of Shaw's remarks on ministry. She refused an invitation to return to preach at her former parish in East Dennis, Massachusetts, on the grounds that "it would hurt me if I stood before them at all not to tell them of a higher, grander faith than any of them know; and yet if they asked me where to find it and how I could only say that I am searching for it."[241] Ministers will, I think, recognize this strand of protectiveness to congregations. On its best side, it is the desire to "translate," shall we say, theological insights into language that can connect with the experience and faith of one's parish. On its worst side, it is theological condescension. (This was Anthony's charge at Stanton for her Bible project, that she was talking down to people.)

While there is more than a little ambivalence about this refusal to criticize the churches, there are as well more systematic reasons for it than the virtue of loyalty. Shaw relied on the aspects of the Christian tradition that were most fully in keeping with woman's freedom: Galatians 3:28, for example, a text that Stanton conveniently forgot. If there was no *theological* ambiguity in the tradition's failure to practice what it preached, just as there was no *political* ambiguity in the democratic situation that also failed to practice what it preached, there was no need to wax indignant à la Stanton.

Many Christian theologians in the Progressive Era were not far from Shaw. I can indicate the shifting understanding of these matters from a social gospel theologian. William Newton Clarke's *Sixty Years with the Bible* was a popular version of his thought under the impact of the higher criticism. He ascribes there to the 1880s the transformation of his opinion regarding women. Interestingly, he suggested that it was the women of his third parish who, by their own freedom in action, won him to an understanding of the limits of Paul's parenetic texts.

> The women were taking part in the meetings of the church, as many of them as wished to do so, with perfect freedom. They knew all about the arguments for

reading Paul's prohibition as local and temporary, at least the Corinthian one, and so had no fear that they were sinning against the Scriptures. But the real reason for their freedom was that in this matter they were not governed by Paul anymore. Some of them had fine gifts for speaking and something to say, and would have found some way to speak their minds if Paul himself had been there with all the weapons that he was supposed to carry. They were acting out their real life from the heart, and the ancient hand was off from them. A few years of such freedom lifted it from me. I came to the conviction that the Christian life of women, as of men, must have free course in the activities that are normal to the age in which they live, and that Paul would be the first to have it so. In fact, I think he would have cancelled the prohibition, if he had foreseen what would come of it through long centuries. Better a little disorder in Corinth, he would have said, than such a handicap on the sex of Phoebe and Priscilla. In later years I have had no trouble with these Corinthian counsels; and since I ceased to believe myself required to accept all arguments in the Bible because they were there, I have not been troubled by the inconclusive reasons for enforcing silence on women that are found in the pastoral epistles. Thus by a long and slow evolution I have come to recognize the normal freedom of the Christian life.[242]

It was a pity, Clarke added, that he "had to unlearn so much upon the way." Well, it was a long way to the day that "the normal freedom of the Christian life" was available to women as well as to him—if, indeed, that day has come yet. There is no way to tell, of course, how or why the women of local parishes came to acquire this expanding sense of freedom. That a woman like Shaw could be ordained, that she had the widest possible exposure in the pulpit, was of a piece with a changing theological climate.

Comments and Conclusions

Shaw's work lacks the substantial weight of Stanton's, and in certain respects it lacks the creative potential of Anthony's. Yet it is an interesting position in its own right. It is important to keep in mind some sense of the singular achievements of Shaw's work lest comparisons among these three figures become more "invidious," in Stanton's language, than illuminating. This is true in all three of the major terms of analysis. In this section I come to terms with the definition of the issue, the view of justice, and the religion in Shaw's suffragist religious social thought. In addition, I reflect on Shaw's sense of humor, an element that is unique in this study.

I have stressed Shaw's angle of vision on the definition of the issue, which at first sight appears to be a strictly logical and rather narrow view of the injustice she fought. The inconsistency between the republic's ideals and its practice was so obvious as to be self-evident to her, and, she thought, obvious to her fellow Americans as well. There was also a certain uneasiness in her awareness of these shared values, since convincing someone of something he or she already believed left one with little to argue. Shaw did not stop to ponder why it was that this question, so simple, so easy that even a fool could understand, was so long in coming home to those who believed it. If she had done so, she might have turned a corner in American democratic theory. But she did not do so—and in a certain measure she was aware of deficiencies in her work. Her correspondence with Lucy Anthony indicated not only her depressions and fears, but a sense, poignant to readers of Virginia Woolf, that she lacked "a room shut off from others and all sorts of intrusions—a room entirely my own."[243] Shaw also lacked Woolf's "five hundred pounds a year," for the NAWSA presidency was not a salaried position.

Was Shaw right? Was the issue a simple one? Was it nothing more than "I am human and you are human and men are human and women are human"?[244] No. At this point Stanton's insight is the correct one. An adequate view of the situation of women can be attained only by seeking both the nice shades and degrees of women's wrongs and their "central point," the unifying factor. This seems to me the only way that a feminist position can attain Shaw's "simplicity," which may gain widespread legitimacy in a social order, without becoming merely simple-minded. Perhaps, in this same vein, Shaw might have benefited from Alfred North Whitehead's later advice to philosophers that they seek simplicity *and* distrust it. Shaw's interest and importance here lie less in the character of the definition of the issue, the social analysis, than in some other dimensions of her view.

She was unabashedly and explicitly an idealist—in a goodly company of dreamers, as she put it, along with Jesus and the Magna Charta and Buddha. She did not possess the later theological view, dangerously on the verge of being sanguine, that if human beings were a mixture of infinite and finite, a certain amount of failure to live up to one's lofty and sublime theories was only to be expected, if not precisely accepted. Nor was she a contemporary of those political scientists who were to conclude that the democratic ideals were rationalizations of more sordid aims, ready-made swaddling clothes to hide the conflict of interests.

Shaw's idealism was not only philosophical idealism of the tradition. It was also idealistic in the sense of "unrealistic." She never had Anthony's down-to-earth view of the need for money, for example, to put across a reform—nor the complicated political methods of precinct organization that may sometimes substitute, or at least complement, financial resources. What reformers needed was in "infinite supply"—spiritual rebirth, infinite love, infinite patience, faith in God. One can think of this dimension of Shaw's thought from several viewpoints.

On the one hand, the very abstract character of this perspective allowed her to slide over many empirical specifics that enriched the new wave of feminist theory in the hands of women armed with social science and an eye to the concrete data of social observation. One thinks of Geertz's call for "thick description" rather than thin, the ability to capture the flavor, the texture, of the particular.[245] This, after all, was one of the aims of the romantic movement, with which Shaw shared the taste for emotion, the infinite, and the sublime. Shaw's stature suffers from the rather unhinged, unattached picture of the situation of women in her time.

On the other hand, women suffragists were engaged in one of the most protracted social struggles the country has ever witnessed. It is difficult to know what human resources were required for these reforming women to maintain their "abiding faith," as Shaw put it. They literally spent lifetimes in this work, and all three of these figures died before achieving the Promised Land. Stanton was aware of the toll, as I noted; to be always pumping out and never replenishing one's resources was the pitfall of many reformers. Anthony's sense that one needed to endure to the end was also based on faith. Even when Shaw sensed that "the old ideals [were] losing their authority and much of their vital hold upon the life of the people,"[246] when the movement demanded "new shibboleths," her answer to the NAWSA stalwarts was that "the re-statement of old truths must help to clear their vision and inspire their zeal."[247] Her work of "speaking and inspiring" must have touched responsive chords in the women of her time, who turned out in force to expend their energy for so little.

Yet Shaw was preaching to the converted, as she knew. This was of course no new thing in American religion or American revivals. Many an awakening in American life, from the Great Awakening down to the lesser spiritual scale of Billy Graham and his kindred, have more to do with rekindling the first warmth than with starting fires in people who never felt them before. Interestingly, it was particularly Shaw's *humor* that has most this character. For one needs to "share the joke" before it is told to find it funny; one needs to be already convinced of the structure of things that makes a story laughable. Laughter is something of a "hidden persuader," there is something less explicit about it than the appeals of reasoned argument. To remain silent in a room full of people laughing and applauding Shaw's sallies must have been hard; we can never know, of course, whether congressmen surrounded by these displays might have slid quietly closer to more positive stands on the suffrage amendment. Though nothing was more explicit than Shaw's call to Americans to renew their democratic faith, her tactics relied on implicit counters of rhetoric to move people to this end.

Shaw thought that suffrage work was fun. Her amusement at the labor, the debates, the conflicts, the silliness of American politics was not unmixed with pain. But it is something of a contrast with the two previous suffragists. It was, however, more akin to Anthony's comment that she enjoyed her friendship with Stanton most when the fires of action were hottest, than it was to Stanton's placid indifference to insult and stupidity. Shaw was, I think, expressing colloquially what Hannah Arendt has called "public happiness"—the sheer joy in political action.[248]

Shaw's light touch expressed also a certain detachment from what it glossed. Humor seems to depend on the ability to stand back from the human drama to perform that slight shift of vision that makes it rather the human comedy. To step back from the day-by-day activity to achieve the "big picture," was something Shaw exhorted reformers to do—to be consoled with the growth toward the sublime across the weary centuries, to glimpse divinity's hand moving in democratic movements. God was the supreme guarantor of the victory of the cause. "If there is a God, if there is any justice in the universe, if there is any relation between cause and effect, this cry for human equality and recognition of women's rights will be heard."[249] This relationship of the woman suffrage movement to divinity was something Shaw shared with her two predecessors, but on different terms.

Shaw's view of life and the universe as "process," a dynamic movement, was a position the twentieth-century feminist will recognize more easily than Stanton's cosmology. Possibilities opened the future before women's wondering eyes; what each could be and become was not preordained but opened to unlimited aspiration. Life's dynamism, its continual change, were Shaw's constant themes; to live was to grow, to move on. Here was perhaps the reason she continually spoke of the "lessons" learned by reformers. She was trying to thematize the changing sense of a spiritual life through time. Feminists who today speak of life as a "journey" or a "pilgrimage," in older language, will recognize these developmental motifs in Shaw. Yet her idealism trapped her at precisely these points. The lessons were always the "old" ones, the paradigmatic ones, which she struggled to restate in new terms without quite bringing that off. The strongest case of her failure to come to grips with novelty was, I think, the "Farewell" speech in which she tried to make peace between her democratic faith and the new methods. But nothing really had changed in her vocabulary and insights. The new view was referred to as the "science" of politics and the "science" of religion, but their relationship to the infinite was constant.

There are other quandaries in Shaw's vision of God and the sublime ideals that came from God besides the rather empty character of the ideals I noted above. Virtues of self-assertion and self-sacrifice were equally blessed. The infinite, it seemed, provided little or no guidance as to the ethical priority of one sort of work over against another. Similarly, logic and emotion simply coexisted in Shaw's thought; they were not integrated in a view that allowed one to see how they might fit together.

Shaw pointed to the one "meaning of democracy, which is that we are one great family of God."[250] But it is by no means clear that she had a less individualistic view than Stanton. True freedom came "from within," as she said; the interior of the soul was attuned to the harmony of God's voice. Her eulogy of Anthony claimed that it was "on the heights alone . . . in silent communion" that such souls "meet God . . . and learn life's sublimest lessons."[251] Reformers grew by giving out their visions to others, to be sure. But the heroism that could count all the misunderstanding and persecution as but light afflictions (since they were for God) seemed to be no more than peripherally related to others. The believer or the visionary had the infinite for company, but not necessarily any other human beings.

The emphasis on novelty and process was complemented by the age-old call to service to others, to sacrifice even life for the love of humanity. Shaw's stress on the responsibility inherent in each possibility was also a check upon the ethical slide from opportunity to opportunism. Women were not to hoard the great good available to them, but to offer back to God and humanity what God and humanity had granted them.

There are several points in Shaw's emphasis on love at which I should pause. It surely stood at the opposite pole from Stanton's, to me entirely justified, rejection of self-sacrificing love for women. Here one can say only that Shaw's uncritical acceptance of certain strands of Victorian piety was just not enough. It certainly opened the door for her message to be eagerly received by thousands of her countrywomen, devout Christians schooled in I Corinthians 13 or accustomed to hearing of the crucifixion as the ultimate word of God's love. The love of humanity in general has been one of the most frequent, and most important counters in ethical thought—and at times, this was surely what Shaw was pointing toward. But whether *responsibility* may be articulated on grounds that do not fall into the pitfalls of self-sacrificing love—which, I think, is among the reasons women keep putting themselves last, and men affirm that they should do so—is an open question of great urgency.

Shaw and the AWSA from which she came forged the terms that made available a genuinely Christian commitment to woman suffrage. This was no mean feat, given the history of the tradition; nor was it unimportant to the daily lives of ordinary churchwomen of the time. For if, as Shaw said, three-quarters of church membership was female,[252] relating the Christian heritage to female emancipation was crucial. Elizabeth Stanton's thought was far in advance of its time; it was startlingly thorough in rethinking the theological assumptions of the day on terms of women's emancipation. But it stood little chance of appealing to the rank and file of American churchwomen. Shaw's exegesis was piecemeal and patchwork; it was sometimes torturously bad, as when she read Paul's prohibition on women speaking as meaning to make a loud noise. It was of course no worse, and frequently better, than Stanton's tendentious comments in *The Woman's Bible*. But the metaphors, the phrases, were familiar enough that Christian women could feel that there was no perturbing discontinuity here. Shaw's call to the Christian institutions to leave the spirit of Moses to follow the spirit of Jesus and freedom defined women suffrage as demanded by the Christian gospel—the gospel of democracy. That she was ordained no doubt lent authority to her message—a small counterpose to the clerical authority that had historically been on the other side.[253]

The themes of love in Shaw's work were also entrées for her to expand on both noncognitive avenues to truth and to stress human transformation. These were dimensions of her perspective that need to be incorporated by any latter-day feminist—whether or not she sees them in terms of "love." There are deeply nonrational, or prerational, factors involved in the opposition or espousal of what is loosely called "feminism" today. Questions related to the status of language and symbolism, of material or institutional conditions, of the socialization process, of culture, hold sway in the intricacies of current feminist thought—as they do in other regions of the twentieth century's attempts to improve upon the legacy of the nineteenth. These are, however, points to which I return in the concluding chapter of this work.

SIX

Conclusion

> It is indeed a crucial difficulty in studying the last century that it continually embarrasses us, as a father often embarrasses a son, by stating with pertinence and superior knowledge positions which we had assumed, without having really examined them, to be obsolete or untenable. Remoter centuries, like more distant forebears, have not this disturbing quality; we are not implicated in their absurdities, and can regard them with complacency. *The nineteenth century compels us to define our own position,* and as this is difficult and often painful, we have (until recently) avoided its society like prodigal sons, or bypassed it with superficial irony.
>
> Basil Willey, *Nineteenth Century Studies*

Like many other historians, theologians, and other intellectuals, Basil Willey assumed that the relationship between "us" and our nineteenth-century forebears was a male-male relationship. There were fathers and sons but not, it seemed, mothers or daughters to be noted. He is perhaps not to be blamed too much for this; until very recently, with the renewal of the concerns and demands of feminists, it was taken for granted that the important figures of any tradition, past or present, were male. As Anna Howard Shaw said, it is "an awful thing to belong to a class of people who when men have forgotten you they do not know they have forgotten anything."[1]

Leaving aside the sexism in his comment, however, Basil Willey was right in this respect. The woman suffragists, like other nineteenth-century figures, compel us to define our own position. This material demands to be grappled with, to be assessed, to be taken account of—surely by their feminist successors but not only by them. These women were challenging the society they lived in—its political structures, the churches, the family, the economy, other reformers, the religion of democracy. Their absence in historical accounts of the nineteenth century, particularly religious and ethical accounts, challenges the regnant interpretations of the period.

Willey was right in yet another respect. Articulating one's own position is painful and difficult. This is perhaps particularly apt in terms of the issues of injustice and justice for women, which stand, as Stanton put it, so closely tied to the self-interest of those in power. Today we would say this differently. We might say that sexual identity, or gender, is such a primordial dimension of self-understanding that any challenge is painful and difficult. We might say that we have internalized sexism so fully and closely that even feminists regularly find new aspects of it in themselves. We might say that it is so unconscious that only something akin to therapy, to moral revolution, to religious conversion, can hope to transform us. We might say, as Mary Daly has done, that patriarchy is truly the one global religion adhered to by many other religions—and that this is therefore a cosmic struggle.

This material calls out to be grappled with in part because we are today re-enacting its dynamics in surprising ways. It is because there is again a woman's movement that we have been put in mind of this section of our common history. It is because there is something called feminist theology that the religious positions of these suffragists are of pressing interest today. The definitions of the issue, the positions on justice, the views of religion that are in these works, will be of especially lively concern to other feminists—whose tradition this is, after all. In this sense it demands to be assessed—critiqued, rejected, appropriated, argued with, incorporated—in the same ways as, say, the Christian tradition demands its own assessment by those who continue to claim to stand within it.

This is not the place to assess this material in all these ways. Such assessments are after all the work of a wider community than one isolated scholar. Coming to terms with these figures in this wider sense is another enterprise, one that begins where this one ends. The tasks that remain in this concluding chapter are dictated by the internal program of the preceding chapters. Chief among the themes, then, that require explicit attention are the notions of social analysis, of justice, of religion that have structured my investigation. I began in each case study the work of comparing these figures with one another, and assessing in some measure the success of their work. Here, therefore, I summarize some of these comments and point to further relevant comparisons. The emphasis in each of these sections is rather on the central question or questions that this material raises, more than on any "answers" I may want to give to them. I point only to as much of my own position as is necessary to provide some reasons for the judgments made.

Definitions of the Issue

I have discussed the different conceptual matrices evolved by these three suffrage leaders as to the issue they faced in the social order. Stanton articulated a fourfold bondage of invidious distinctions of sex that denied the individuality of women. Anthony spoke rather of women's powerlessness, particularly in politics and the economy. Shaw leaned heavily on the notion of inconsistency between the ideals of the republic and the practical treatment of women. Looking in detail at the strengths and weaknesses of this variety of approaches would be tedious and repetitious. Let me instead notice some general things at work in these three analyses. Though they are general in nature, they are nonetheless important for coming to terms with these figures. First, there were criteria generated within the woman suffrage movement itself for the assessment of definitions of issue. Second, certain questions arise concerning the relationship between what I call thematizing women's experience and the uses of science in this analysis of the issue. As I comment on these two points, I refer to sections of each woman's thought that particularly exemplify strengths or failures, or to relevant comparisons between them.

The well-known disagreements concerning narrow or broad notions of the suffragist platform were already well underway among these three figures. This discussion is usually marked out in terms of whether the aims of suffragists were "narrowed" to the vote alone. This perhaps is to misconceive the problem. Even Shaw and Anthony, whose positions were most open to this charge, meant a great deal more than bare enfranchisement. When Anthony said she knew nothing but woman and her disfranchised, she was zeroing in on a prime indicator of woman's powerlessness that extended far beyond the polling booth; when Shaw said the problem was so simple that even a fool could understand it, her summons to the American people to believe what they said extended far and wide into the infinite possibilities inherent in democratic ideals. "Breadth" of platform seems self-evident to those of us who follow in the wake of the woman suffrage movement. We, after all, are picking up where they left off. It requires a prodigious effort of the imagination to conceive what it meant, humanly speaking, for a woman to live disfranchised; I can barely do so except through the medium of what these three women said about the experience. Stanton described it as "degradation" and sometimes as torture: it was like cutting off the hands and tongue. Anthony said it was like

287

slavery. Shaw found disfranchisement so bizarre that she had to laugh at the ridiculous spectacle of people contradicting themselves at every turn.

Whatever it was like as an experience, during these discussions the suffragists generated criteria by which to judge what was adequate to describing the situation of women. Stanton attained a self-consciousness and clarity in articulating such points that was not matched by Anthony or Shaw. She aimed at a view that could "cover the whole range of human experience"—at a comprehensive description of "every invidious distinction of sex" throughout the entire social order. This wholistic view was worked out in the fourfold bondage, the multidimensional analysis of the social order from the perspective of the injustice of women's situation. Each aspect of the analysis, each strand in the cable, was capable of being spelled out in its own right. In addition, she pointed out the internal connections among the strands, interweaving and interlacing the fabric of invidious distinctions together into one tapestry.

It was also Stanton who spoke of seeing "all the nice shades and degrees of woman's wrongs and the central point of her weakness and degradation." As I have understood this notion, it meant a view of women's situation that was complex and subtle enough to perceive fine distinctions. At the same time, the emphasis on the "central point" meant that the analysis did not get lost in these shadings and nuances, but maintained a pivotal criterion of importance. She appreciated the complications in the suffragist struggle in a way that I think her descendants will recognize as familiar. Feminists today have different ways of singling out the reasons for these complications. Informed by depth psychology and sociology, these recent explanations of the complexity of sexism are richer than Stanton's "self-interest." But this approach is far more satisfying than Shaw's vaunted simplicity. A hundred years later it is far more adequate to the puzzles still present, perhaps even more present, in woman's situation—or rather, women's situations.

That I have now to speak of women's situations in the plural recalls a central problem in Stanton's definition of the issue. From her viewpoint there were "heights" to which to rise, and "depths" to which to fall, but very little in between. She had no eye for the relative whole, the patterns of meaning in which one might maintain some proximate values—survival, say, or the kind of virtue possible in certain social situations that were not just but that were not devoid of meaning either. This was certainly because of her class, race, and educational prejudices. It was also because she had no systematic interest in diversity, in the multiform possibilities of human life, if I may revert to Shaw's usage. In the 1990s an adequate feminist analysis requires some tools by which to characterize the diversity of women's situations without losing sight of the central parameters of injustice and justice.

Third, Stanton aimed at a view of the social order that would get at the "causes" of woman's degradation so that the work of suffragists would be "efficient." This was a point she shared with Anthony; Anthony traced the "social upas," the poisonous source of social ills, to woman's degradation. One needed to get at the root rather than chop away at the branches. For Anthony, of course, the roots were powerlessness, especially in terms of votes and money. Stanton, on the other hand, seemed at times to postulate four different approaches, each one "causing" woman's degradation in the other realms, the whole complex causing widespread social disorganization, suffering, pain, ethical contagion.

This complex of notions is a helpful one regarding social analyses of injustice. Its stress on comprehensiveness, complexity, priorities of relevance, and some sense of causality seems to provide a sense of what is necessary to describe adequately women's situations. It needs a certain corrective built into it in order to encompass varying race and class dynamics, which Stanton herself failed to do. Nonetheless, the criteria she articulated go a long way toward making such corrections possible.

Furthermore, within this view, and to a certain extent within the work of Anthony and Shaw, there is a tension generated by what I can only think of as a double emphasis in the ways these criteria worked themselves out in practice. The path of Stanton's thought revolved in an ellipsis, shall we say, around dual foci: science and what we might call a phenomenological description of women's lived experience.

"Woman alone can understand the height, the depth, the length and breadth of her own degradation." Therefore it was only women who could describe, from the "inside," as it were, their own experience of life as it was given; and women alone could do the work to rectify injustice. (This was not to reject male allies but to provide specific checks on the ways they were "integrated" into the cause.) This experiential focus was one she reiterated in a variety of ways. Women were to think for themselves, to be guided by their own convictions; they were to "tell the truth" that was in them rather than to fear the opinions of others. At times, particularly the times of the stress on "sex in soul," it seemed that the truths women perceived were quite other than those men saw: women's perspectives looked to men to be sentimental nonsense.

The truths that women perceived were always guaranteed by the lawlike structure of existence—either the great cosmic dualities in Stanton's later life or the simpler "law of God written on her own soul" from the earlier decades. In either case Stanton was in pursuit of the "broad principles" that "underlie" a reform or all reforms. It was in this latter sense that she turned to science to articulate some "deep structures" inherent in the cause of woman suffrage. To a later observer the ways Stanton oscillated between physical science, social science, and ethics are clear indicators of the period in which she lived. It is no longer possible with Stanton's equanimity to rely on the analogy between the moral and the material.

If there is a question with which to struggle here, it is precisely this combination of the thematic description of women's experiences, richly filled with detail and insight, and the drier, more abstract explorations, perhaps explanations, of the social sciences. Inasmuch as all three women remarked that this was a systematic problem, only the tools by which we can describe systems can attain the comprehensive parameters of the social order. But statistics, and the theoretical positions that give them their meaning, need to be attached creatively to the thematic accounts of women's lived experience. It is in the latter realm that the wellsprings of action have their source. This is surely what Stanton meant by pointing toward a "healthy discontent" needed among women of her era.

In thematizing women's experience these women invoked certain human capacities in each definition of the issue. I do not think it a caricature of these three to view them serially as representing thought, action, and emotion. Stanton stressed the enlightened intellect, women's capacity to reason, as a fundamental part of the constitutive movement toward justice. Anthony's emphasis was on action, whether in the phase of women's powerlessness or the energetic doing of noble deeds that justice required. Shaw leaned heavily on the heart, love, emotion. This is no caricature if we see the ways each maintained a systematic place within her work for the other two capacities. Stanton spoke frequently in emotive terms; Anthony admired her friend's intellectual grasp of the issues; Shaw's analysis stressed theory and practice.

The great unasked question of all three women was the question of imagination. Though Shaw's emphasis on beauty and the heart came nearer to the country of such concerns, she finally shied away; logic and the truth of visions obscured anything like art or imagination. This is, I think, an aspect of the contemporary movement that is quite different in spirit from these forebears. Women's art, poetry, painting, sculpture, dance, and music are important and self-conscious dimensions of this movement, a part of a concentration on "women's culture."

This note regarding one major difference between the woman suffrage movement and the women's liberation movement may be extended. If I were to make phrases in Stanton's alliterative style, I should say that the dimensions of sexism that especially preoccupy this second wave of feminism are those related to symbolism, subsistence, and sexuality.

Questions regarding symbolism—that is, language, art, culture, images, metaphors—are prominent to us as they never were to the suffragists. Though Stanton pointed to the loss of women's maiden names in marriage as a sign of the monopoly of sex, we have seen again and again her references to "man" without expressing the slightest dissent or discomfort. Shaw occasionally jibed at the bizarre humor of sexist language ("they were all fathers, every mother of them"), but these sporadic comments were never thoroughly integrated into the analysis. Of the three, only Anthony ever made a specific point of exclusive language. And this point was made in an early lecture, and seemingly dropped.

The nature of language and of symbols has been at the center of twentieth-century philosophy and theology, especially in England and America. The "systematic ambiguity," to use Ryle's phrase, of the "generic" male terms has been explored and denounced by later feminists; sociolinguistics and communications theories have been summoned to the aid of feminist critiques. These concerns regarding symbols are especially important in the area of religion.

Such concerns, however, tend to be highly abstract and "intellectual." It is sometimes hard to mediate their urgency to the lives of real, living, breathing individuals. This is a problem feminist theory shares with all its intellectual counterparts, as the gap between highly specialized endeavors and the "woman in the street" grows wider. (And that the feminist in religion shares with the national leadership in the churches, regularly accused of getting "out of touch" with members of local parishes.)

Questions related to subsistence—the distribution of wealth, work, well-being—are on the contrary very concrete. Women are overrepresented among the poor, the unemployed, the welfare rolls. We are underrepresented among the rich, the professionals, and the policy-makers of corporations and governments. To hit people "in the pocketbook" is to hit them where it hurts most, according to American political folk wisdom. But it is harder to make the connections between the felt reality of desperation and the wider parameters of the American economy. The jargon of academic economics or its Marxist-influenced alternatives are far removed from the lives of people, the experiential places where the feminist movement has its wellsprings.

Sexuality was a concern particularly with Stanton and Anthony. The critiques of the family particularly noted contraception and women's rights to regulate their sexual relationships in terms of love; Anthony's critiques of the social evils linked such questions with the "bread of dependence." These were forward-looking dimensions of these definitions of the issue, though they went underground as the social pressures of Victorian repression took their toll. The terms of such discussions are different today. The discovery that "ladylike" behaviors were part of the problem and not part of its solution, together with other twentieth-century trends (e.g., the birth control movement, the Freudian legacy, the obscenity trials of great literature, and the uses of obscenity in 1960s politics), have drastically changed the tone and style of this incarnation of women's struggle. The rediscovery of violence against women, and the research of Masters and Johnson, have made "our bodies/ourselves" a crucial dimension of this movement.

Justice

Three sorts of ethical positions resulted from the analyses of the issue. All of them, however, varied between the use of justice as a summary principle and the use of justice as one principle among many. This stance was most marked with Stanton. Her focus on the rationality of justice was complemented by the bipolar masculine/feminine elements in which the feminine elements of pity and compassion were to compensate, not for justice itself, but for stern paternal versions of justice. Anthony's occasional locutions were striking. The perfectionism of her stance was best expressed in the classic phrase, *Fiat Iustitia Pereat Mundus*. Shaw's uses of justice were far looser. "Justice and fair play and responsibility" were necessary to provide women with equal opportunity in the American "race" of life. But it was responsibility that was at the heart of Shaw's ethics.

The suffragists under review here were not disputing about ethics or morality on the level of the metaethics that has been so prominent in the twentieth century. To understand better the nature of these ethical positions, I turn briefly to some suggestions of Chaim Perelman, who surveyed six conceptions of justice with a double question in mind: how to express the fact that these six notions are variants of the same thing (for they are all notions of justice) without eliminating their divergence. This may be profitably accomplished, he suggested, by distinguishing between formal (or abstract) justice and concrete justice.

Formal justice, according to Perelman, is "a principle of action in accordance with which beings of one and the same essential category must be treated in the same way."[2] This formula illuminates *some* of the arguments of the woman suffrage movement. These women *were* talking about the "reclassification" of women into the essential category "human being" or "citizen." I have noted the several ways Stanton expressed such a view: that women were not "anomalous beings," for example. The one item in Anthony's creed was "perfect equality of rights." Shaw frequently said "men are human and women are human and you are human and I am human and no human being has the right to control any other human being."

But this was not all. If it had been, feminists might well have rested their cases with the assertion that "women are human beings" or "women are citizens." Indeed, Stanton frequently made precisely such cases. From revolutionary theory downward it was conceded, nay, vehemently argued, that without the right to vote, the rights of citizens were abrogated. It is of course difficult to know what ever moved the legislators on any of these questions; but it does not seem that this abstract argument, valid as it was, started any great landslide of support for enfranchising women.

Such assertions were not enough. These women also struggled with a description of the social order and its institutions that is not represented by a focus sheerly on membership in the essential category. They showed, for example, that it was *urgent* that women were to be so included, that abuses were widespread. (Recall Anthony's description of the "care-worn or crime-stained faces" of women on the Bowery.) They argued that the republic could not endure, that order was chaos under such conditions. In a social order crisscrossed with a series of issues such as the U.S. was (and is), feminists demonstrated that there was concrete pressing need for these changes, that suffrage was a priority on which to act and act quickly. As they had learned from English common law and the abolitionists, justice delayed was justice denied.

Perelman's "concrete justice" is much closer to the level of ethical discussion in the suffrage movement than "abstract justice."[3] As he notes, the formal definition of justice does not altogether account for the attraction, the felt importance of notions of justice, any more than for the confusion that surrounds such ideas. To understand the lure of such notions of justice we must realize that concrete justice involves "a particular view of the world."[4] The *content* of the rules of justice are not given in abstract justice, but imply their "integration in a system" whose general principles assert what is valuable.[5] To establish the essential characteristics of those between whom justice adjudicates involves "positing a certain scale of values, a determination of what is important and what is not, of what is essential and what is secondary."[6] Perelman seems to see such general systems as akin to worldviews. And that, surely, was true of these women. In each case, the views of injustice and justice were located within a larger religious perspective.

It was equally true that all of them had a social analysis of what was occurring to women in their day and age, of the empirical conditions under which women's lives transpired, of changing historical circumstances. This is why I have stated as my general thesis that there was an internal and reciprocal relationship between the definition of the issue and each woman's religious views. We cannot adequately understand each woman's view of the issue without understanding her religious view, and vice versa. It was *concrete justice*, in each case, that was the single matrix, as it were, that brought together the religious perception and the social analysis. Great Nature's laws were the grounds of the ethical principles Stanton invoked to cover her case; but she invoked them because they were daily transgressed. The commands of Anthony's God to break every yoke and let the oppressed go free were crucial because of the yokes of bondage that were in fact around her. The loving responsible service to humanity of the visions Shaw invoked in her suffragist followers was here and now; to take the vision to a waiting world was an integral part of the vision, whose purpose was not its contemplation, or even its theoretical description, but action to realize it.

All these women appealed to the most general claims about God and the nature of the universe to make their cases. Far from simply noting their disagreements with others, they argued for the falsity of the opposition and advocated religious transformations in their followers and in society as a whole.[7] Strikingly, however, they came close to opposing the adumbration of such subjects for their own sakes. Stanton thought theology was speculative, based on what cannot be known. Anthony echoed such positions in her rejection of "mere belief."

While these suffragists used such familiar principles of justice as equality and freedom, the most important principle with regard to justice was something else. It was the obligation to act to transform injustice into justice—the "practical righteousness" of which the period spoke. This stance was part of

Stanton's opposition to sin. To bewail one's fallen state interfered with, substituted for, action. Sometimes this was justified by way of the obligation to maximize good, since one good woman even doing her traditional tasks of visiting the sick did more than a regiment of saints lamenting sin. Women falsified themselves and blasphemed their God when they did not protest their own condition. To protest, to act, were fundamental, were *more* important than a stern faith, even though Stanton did not achieve the direct clear vision of women's action that Anthony had. To this latter, tears, prayers, entreaties were all to be left behind for the effective action, the struggle for votes and money, the power to achieve just ends. "Idle wishes, vain repinings, loud-sounding declarations" were part of the problems, which only moving to action could mitigate. The moral slumber around her called for agitation, to be "all on fire" for the right. Even Shaw's less militant position had similar principles integral to her view. Suffragists had above all else to be responsible. The vision was enriched as it was given out in action, not as it was hoarded for its recipient's personal contemplation. The spirit of democracy transformed the ones who beheld the vision as they acted to realize it in the world.

We might say that all these suffragists agreed on one thing. There was a prima facie obligation to rectify injustice, which overrode all other obligations. If one was acting for justice for women, that stance alone was far more important than all the other divergences that marked these women's positions off from one another. They were also of one mind that the issue they faced was, as we would say today, a systemic one. It required more than piecemeal effort. The causes of injustice, for Stanton, were expressed in a medical metaphor. Sometimes she claimed that to eradicate the cause of the ethical disease was more "efficient" than merely to deal with symptoms. But there was more than this. The wise physician was doing an inherently higher, nobler work—because, of course, he or she was working in line with the laws of the cosmos. Anthony was also self-conscious about the moral difference between efforts to alleviate suffering, however humanitarian, and social change. Even the hard-core advocate of the Fugitive Slave Law, she said, could be moved to help a victim individually. To be radical meant to change the conditions that created wrongs, to prevent the evils rather than to bind the wounds once made. Shaw too rejected charity and philanthropy, and labored for the day when they would be no longer needed.

Of these three, Anthony alone came closest to an equal emphasis on the three principles of the French Revolution—liberty, equality, sorority. Aside from the anomalous speech on free love, in which Stanton set forth her ethical priorities (first equality, then freedom, wisdom, virtue, religion), she actually had very little notion of freedom. Though she said that she did not know whether men were free agents but it was certain that women were not (which implied the need for freedom), finally progress, like belief, was not voluntary. Evil and suffering, like prosperity and health, came automatically from the determinisms of the cosmic laws. Shaw, on the other hand, stressed equality far less than freedom; aspiration, the freedom to be and to become one's possibilities, was the burden of her view.

But these differences, like their religious divergences, were not judged by these suffragists to be of very great import. Though they had at times fierce disagreements among themselves, they had far more in common than not—and not simply because they were all suffragists. Practical righteousness was what bound these women together, and a determination to see concrete justice done.

If there is a central question regarding justice from the work of these three figures, it is precisely this one. Given an analysis of the issue, what is the appropriate and adequate, ethically satisfying relationship of action for social change to other ethical principles? It is frequently said in ethics that the discipline concerns itself with "doing." But these particular doings are less often specifically related in principle to movements for social change. What was it about this period, or this social issue, that gave rise to this concentration on practical righteousness? How does action for justice relate to theoretical perceptions of justice?

And how, since all these women did so, is this action for justice related to religion? These women were, we might say, members of one church. Though they disagreed on the points in their creed, they recognized their unity—and struggled, at times, to express adequately what they shared.

Religion

Stanton's allegiance to a "more rational religion" founded on immutable laws established by the God of justice, mercy, and truth, was the foundation for declaring false all religions that opposed women's emancipation. Anthony, with her this-worldly bent, refused such "speculations" for the straightforward assertion that her work for suffrage was her worship, that she prayed by action. Shaw's religious thought was tinged with the accents of romanticism, since God's sublime visions of upward evolution were imparted to the heart of the reformer rather than to her head.

More than any doctrinal stances or any other single feature of these religious positions, the astonishing thing is that each of them identified the suffrage struggle as itself the chief locus of religiousness. Stanton likened the woman's suffrage struggle again and again to the work of Luther, Calvin, Knox; woman's right to think, solitude of self, a noble life of protest against injustice were links to the God of justice, mercy, and truth. It was women's religious duty to vote; when women voted, the ballot box was to become the holy of holies. To Anthony the world of work for the cause was "wholly spiritual," a work that took precedence over all the glories of heaven. In promising that she was to remain with her followers, she asserted that solidarity among women in the struggle for justice prevailed over the ultimate enemy, death. Even to Shaw, that allegedly orthodox member of this trio, the NAWSA was qualified to call the nation back from its infidelity to democracy because suffragists were the purest democrats, most at one with the infinite. In contrast to Stanton's later anti-Christian stance, democracy and Christianity were virtually one so far as she was concerned.

Now, if these works can be said to embody a portion of a tradition of feminist theology, three questions arise from these views that are of some enduring importance for that enterprise: (1) Does religion have an intrinsic relationship to justice on this issue? (2) How does this religion relate to "other" religions—say, Christianity or Buddhism? (3) What terms best express women's religious experience?

Does religion have an intrinsic relationship to justice on this issue? This question arises directly out of the identification of the suffrage struggle with these women's theological convictions. They are all strikingly similar to Mary Daly's statement that the women's movement in itself is an ontological revolution. But they recall that statement in three distinctive ways, none of which resembles Daly's use of the ontology of Tillich or the metaphysics of Thomism in *Beyond God the Father*, nor her more original use of "spinning, spooking and sparking" in *Gyn/Ecology*.[8] If we answer yes to such a question as this one, we must note its logical successor: What terms best express this relationship?

One function of these religious beliefs was to ensure that justice to women would be done. Humanity was evolving, thanks to science and rationality, closer to the good order in which justice and purity were to converge, in Stanton's view. To Anthony failure was impossible because of the consecrated women who followed the voice of conscience. To be "one with the infinite in bringing to pass freedom, justice, peace" were the stakes Shaw saw in the movement. They were none of them crude versions of "God is on our side," but they were nonetheless versions of that sentiment, whether the mechanical immutable laws of Stanton, Anthony's belief that fetters "evanish at the touch of Thee," or Shaw's extremely vague notion that the reformer needed "some faith, in some power, somewhere," so that "somehow, at some time" she was to behold the "triumph of truth."

Far more important, these religious views provided the *reasons* for characterizing the empirical condition of women in American life as unjust. Nature or God ordained that the segregating of the sexes was unhealthy; dwarfing, crushing, restraining individual development was contrary to the rights of individual souls. The divine spark of freedom in humanity commanded the liberation of the oppressed. The spirit of the infinite lured humanity toward its possibility of freedom and responsibility, and intended that all should live up to the sublime promise of the visions it sent.

These religious views fundamentally shaped the character of the justice sought by each. Each woman's thought had different highest terms that made a great deal of difference in her political program. Stanton always dealt in universals. There was nothing more typical of her stance than the notion that one took one's bearings off the "more universal fact" of women's existence—womanhood, rather than wifehood or motherhood. The more universal, the nobler and grander; hence Stanton always emphasized principles of the most general application. Anthony dealt rather in the perfection of absolutes. The absolute, etymologically, is the utterly undependent, "free" from dependency on anything aside from itself. Shaw dealt rather in the infinite, in the limitless and inexhaustible. Small wonder that she was vaguer about justice, since definiteness always presupposes limits of some sort. To be sure, the universal, the absolute, the infinite, are members of one species; many a theologian of the tradition has put them together for the purpose of characterizing the divine. But they are subtly different from one another, and their influence in each one's thought provided different ethical counters and programs for action.

What is the relationship of this "civil religion" or "political religion" of suffragism to other religions? Shaw identified them as one. The gospel of democracy and the democracy of Christianity were indistinguishable from each other and from the substance of the woman suffrage struggle. Other great world religions echoed the same sublime truth of love. Anthony never said in so many words that she was Christian (though she always identified herself as a Quaker), or that she was not. She was clear that others considered her an infidel. At times she seemed to intimate that there was a "gospel of womanhood." She found thematic emphases in the tradition that expressed her views; to break every yoke was commanded to the saints of old as surely as to the abolitionist or the suffragist. Stanton wavered as to whether or not one could find germs of truth in Christianity. The right of individual judgment was the point she continually conceded as a Christian idea; the truth of creation of Genesis 1:27-28 was fundamental. But sin, hell, fear of punishment were all masculine products, not feminine ones; they bore with particular heaviness upon women and children. Whether or not such a critique of sin (or one in this form) is apt is not at issue here. It remains an open question whether there may be constructed "models" for sin that do not entangle themselves with women's subordination or with maintaining de facto injustice by sapping the wellsprings of action.

There was something altogether sound about Stanton's way of arriving at her anticlerical and anti-Christian conclusions. Two of these points stand out. (1) Stanton's insistence on a pragmatic criterion for judging ecclesiastical groups on women's rights is helpful and insightful. "Among the clergy we find our strongest enemies" was her early principle. But the later refinement of this pragmatic criterion is more adequate. Isolated individuals were not the touchstone; what mattered was whether organized religious bodies had both gone on public record *and* rectified their theological views about women. Like Anthony's insistence on practice, we may read this view as asserting that it was the churches' "fruits" by which they were to be known. (2) Stanton's refusal to treat Christianity as a special case among world religions seems important, even if, perhaps especially if, the feminist adheres to Christianity. The Christian "legitimation" (in later language) of male domination was to be treated in exactly the same way as that of the Hindu, the Moslem, the Mormon; no special pleading was to be allowed. In the present we may need slightly different approaches to such a comparative view, dependent on the specialized views of the history of religions that have so burgeoned since the late nineteenth century. And, like Stanton's pragmatic criterion, we must investigate not merely myths and symbols related to women, but the practice of these other religious bodies in order to have a balanced view.

How was it possible or likely that the suffrage movement itself became the preferred locus of religiousness for these women? There are, I think, several reasons. I single out here primarily the position of the churches and the legacy of liberalism.

It was not only the sexism of the tradition's theology that contributed to this alternative location of religion for these suffragists, though it is certainly not to be denied that this was so. More specifically, I hypothesize, it was because women did not (and do not) have churches of their own. Contrast, for a moment, the shape of sexism and racism in American life. That segregation has been a fundamental shaping force in the relations of the races has meant, among other things, that black people had churches under their own leadership. Hence it is possible for observers of black religion to say that the black church is "the spiritual face of the black community," as C. Eric Lincoln does.[9] But it is different for women. Churches were "integrated," as Stanton might have put it, but they were not integrated on the basis of the "wholesome intermingling" she sought. Even if the majority of church members were female, leadership was (and is) male. Theologians were (and are) male. That is to say, that the people thematizing and articulating, arguing about, preaching the specific shapes of the religiousness experienced in the churches were male.

The nineteenth century was the era par excellence of the creation of women's institutions—the women's club movement, the women's missionary societies, the Women's Christian Temperance Union, and the woman suffrage movement. There had been other such institutions before, notably in the European High Middle Ages, in which convents and their informal parallels, beguine houses, flourished. Protestant women, however, had no such organizational base until the period of this study. The woman suffrage movement was one segment of the American social order in which women were in control of *both* the organizational structure *and* the channels and content of thought. Women articulated their own cases, explicitly concentrated on their own experiences, developed criteria for distinguishing better and worse accounts of women's situation, exhorted and sustained one another spiritually, encouraged other women, demanded of other women that they do similarly—and discovered their own power in these exercises. Everything else paled beside this one supremely important struggle. The women's rights movement gave meaning to life, established grounds for action and coherent, emotionally satisfying pictures of the world. Small wonder that it was a locus of religion.

This synthesis was also possible because these women were liberals. Remember that this was a time before the liberals and radicals, whether in religion or elsewhere, had parted company. Anthony found no discomfort in characterizing herself a liberal who was doing a radical work. Liberalism provided several components of these religious views: the centrality of ethics, continuity between the divine and the human, a historical temper that affirmed the changing grasp of even religious truth, the rejection of sin, a distinction between the church and religion, and an anti-institutional bias. To praise or to find fault with such positions is, in large measure, to praise or blame American liberalism.[10]

What terms best express women's religious experience(s)? This question is prior, it seems to me, to the question of whether there are religious experiences that may be said to be specific to women—though indeed this question may arise depending on the substance of the answer to the more general point. It is particularly the question of the relationship of "theology" to the civil religion of these three women. There was a certain tension expressed among these figures as to whether "theology" was to be eschewed, particularly in the light of practical righteousness. On the other hand, there was something in the area of religion that was akin to the question of science and women's experience raised in the first section of this chapter. "Science of religion" was used more than once to express something like this: a dimension of critical reflection on religion so as to determine its general scope and import, to determine its truth.

The most creative of these positions was, as I have remarked, the protoliberation theology of Anthony. To pray by action, to worship in one's work for justice, to set aside "mere belief" or dogma for the deed—these were fascinatingly direct locutions that resonated the New Testament phrase that it is "by their fruits you shall know them." Practice in the world was to free women of their bondage to outmoded or shackling superstitions, to provide a principle of theological change. These notions were creative not only because of the straightforward way action for justice was valued. They were notable because of the liturgical flavor, if I may so put it, of such themes. Like the mother church, the suffrage movement rehearsed the deeds and stories of its saints and founders. One wonders indeed how such a provocative trend of thought might be combined with more recent views of ritual that emphasize the drama enacted in symbolic action.

Finally, however, these themes were not developed by Anthony. The more religious she was, in a sense, the more she turned aside from thematizing such notions; the more she acted instead. It was Stanton who pursued and pressed the thorough theological critique of the tradition regardless of where it led.

And it led her to the heart of the Christian doctrines of sin and salvation, which she concluded were incompatible with women's elevation, education, and enfranchisement. This was nothing if not a radical and fundamental critique of the tradition, one that could not be waved aside as unimportant or peripheral. It was also to say that, from Stanton's perspective, logically one *had* to be a liberal to be a feminist.

The harmonious but rather static cosmic laws on which Stanton based so much of her thought are outmoded, antiquated, if I may use her own evolutionary language against her. *"Sapere Aude,"* solitude of self, the mothering aspect of God, are pieces of Stanton's position that ring in our ears rather more tellingly than positive and negative electricity, attraction and repulsion. Solitude of self particularly foreshadowed the existential emphasis in twentieth-century philosophy and theology, though its use of the life cycle is not, to my knowledge, duplicated there. The analogy between the moral and the material has been swept away by the concentration of the last several decades on issues of language and culture. Like imagination, issues regarding the cultural plasticity of human beings and the formative character of language raise questions (or ought to) in current theology that were simply not asked by any of these women.

The dynamism of Shaw's stress on infinite possibilities grounded in God is a view with which we are more familiar and comfortable today. Further, Shaw's sense of humor, her sense of the suffrage comedy, was so very much a part of her that on some days it is the most striking thing about this woman's position. It was of a piece with her stress on freedom, for laughter seems to presuppose a certain detachment from that which it surveys. In some respects this was slightly at odds with Shaw's own sense of a love supremely attached to its object. But whatever else one may say of Shaw, there was something redeeming about her view of the humor of women's situations, which was not divorced from their pain. To laugh at sexism, to find it so bizarre and odd that it was comic—there was something in this stance that imported a note of "grace" into the struggle for justice. If nothing else, it bespoke a certain security about Shaw's feminism that had everything to do with her sense of the hospitality of God and the universe of women's rights.

Finally, the uses of "mother" to characterize deity were part of the religious programs of Stanton and Shaw, and seem strikingly absent in Anthony. It may be no coincidence that the two former women characterized the sexes with differing attributes. Especially for Stanton, to speak of God in feminine terms was to reject certain qualities in deity—stern judgment and retribution especially—that she associated with the worst of male rule. Shaw was far less explicit as to the meaning of this feminine dimension of God. It was to be "more personal and more human," as she said—perhaps to enable the human heart to beat in accordance with the divine heart. In the light of recent controversies about the use of such "feminine" language for God, it is striking to note how relatively minor were such themes. They were submerged within larger motifs—the religion of democracy, most notably.

I have in a measure dissolved the presumptive unity of the suffragists into a series of what are at times rather delicately balanced divergences and convergences. In this study of three figures, there are three theological options, three definitions of the issue, three ways of delineating justice. These women cannot be brought to one common position, their views cannot be summed up with ease and economy. This I regard as a positive result of this work and the method employed in it—especially the in-depth analysis of each figure's work in turn on three specified questions. More "light" has been cast on the ethical and religious positions of these figures than has previously been shed there. These religious and ethical views cannot be appreciated, perhaps cannot even be discerned, if we concentrate on "conventional" views of religion—churches, Bibles, God-language—though obviously these too have an important place within the wider religious notions of these women.

Many tensions and disagreements of current feminists, especially within the area of religion, were alive and well in the earlier women's movement. It is my hope that by uncovering and exploring such earlier positions, our predecessors in the enterprise of feminist theology, more will result than the increased accuracy with which we may regard such distant forebears. To have a tradition, however slight compared with the expanse of the entire Western tradition, opens the horizons within which we move—gives a measure of added solidity, if you will, to such novelties as "feminist theology." By reacting on our self-understanding as actors in historical time, such a tradition may, as any of these women might have put it, enhance our self-respect.

More than this, it may enhance some of the intellectual frameworks within which we work. It is finally my aim that, by viewing our positions refracted through the lenses and mirrors of some earlier embodiments of our projects, we may—as Clifford Geertz has said in another context—"refine the precision with which we vex one another." And, one hopes, we may refine the precision with which we please one another as well. For while feminists are as prone as any other body of people to be especially pleased by their agreements with one another, "sisterhood" ideally seeks also to be pleased by the excellence with which we have our disagreements—and by the solidarity that may, in conscious knowledge of our divergences, yet stand together in action for justice.

On Having a Tradition

[W]ithout tradition—which selects and names, which hands down and preserves, which indicates where the treasures are and what their worth is—there seems to be no willed continuity in time and hence, humanly speaking, neither past nor future, only sempiternal change of the world and the biological cycle of living creatures in it. Thus the treasure was lost not because of historical circumstances and the adversity of reality but because no tradition had foreseen its appearance or its reality, because no testament had willed it for the future. . . . [F]or remembrance . . . is helpless outside a pre-established framework of references.

Hannah Arendt, *Between Past and Future*

Stanton's central principle in religion was that women had the right to interpret tradition and experience, Christian or otherwise, from their own perspectives. She was virtually converted to women's right to think, the same right that Luther, Calvin, and Knox had, whose reappearance identified the woman suffrage movement with the Reformation. Her principle is finally having its historical innings. Books, journal articles, conferences, seminary courses appear and proliferate as more and more women enter theological schools, critique the Christian heritage or other religious heritages, and advance positions of their own. This meager span of historical time has made us today more aware than Stanton ever was or could be of just how difficult it is to achieve the full expanse of woman's right to think in religion.

Whether anything of importance will come from feminist theologians is sometimes questioned; the distinctiveness of such efforts may also be disputed. But the bare principle that women have the right to think for themselves in religion will be contested nowhere today—outside, that is, the walls of fundamentalism and some wings of neo-evangelicalism, no small exceptions. Exercising the right to think, however, requires more than simply sitting down in one's armchair to explore internal mechanisms, though that may be a beginning.

It requires *training*, disciplined attention to church history, theological schools of thought, biblical-critical methods, languages, sophisticated methodological tools, the exploration of other world religions, and the growing fields of women's studies in the academy.

It requires *institutional backing*. Virginia Woolf spoke of the need for women artists to have "five hundred pounds a year and a room of one's own," or money and privacy. We might add today: child care, opportunity, library facilities, teachers sensitive and competent, church structures ensuring fairness in recruitment and hiring, parishes or other support communities that are open and supportive, journals to purvey results for the critical attention of others in one's field.

It requires *trust*. This is perhaps less obvious to people in the field of religion than it should be. The women's movement has learned a great deal about the need for trust in one another as a precondition for speaking one's own piece honestly about the social order and perhaps the greater universe as well. The matrices of relationships among women that may be found in women's centers (though not exclusively there) provide the opportunities for women to scrutinize our experience from our own points of view. Such spaces protect women against retaliation from authority figures and from orthodox notions of what we *should* believe. They provide space to surface and articulate—and come to be confident in—what we *do* believe.

Such theological reflection also requires a certain *tradition*, a body of material in continuity with which the newcomer explores the terrain of the faith and life she or he shares with the predecessors—whether to extend its known boundaries or simply to dwell comfortably and with a certain assurance even in the midst of doubts.

These supportive dimensions of the context for theological honesty are not always found ready-to-hand in theological circles. Nor are they usually discussed as fundamental to the theological enterprise itself. That people do not do theology in a vacuum is as true as that they do not write plays with the genius of Shakespeare or paint like Michelangelo without stringent social conditions underlying and encouraging such efforts.[1] What conditions are optimal for doing theological reflection, with perceptiveness and precision, is a question bearing too little theological investigation in current discussions. It results in a certain disembodied quality about the work of such brilliant figures as Paul Tillich, Reinhold Niebuhr, Alfred North Whitehead. To pay attention to the hidden supports of white male figures in theological studies would repay well as we search for ways and means of doing greater justice to women, blacks or other minority peoples, and the poor.

None of these preconditions for theological reflection could have in principle been considered by Stanton. To be sure, she was clear about the injustice of the claim that women were not logical when women were forbidden education. But her notions of reason prevented her from assigning more than a negative valence to such material conditions. Pure reason, legislating for itself alone and by its own inherent capacity in all human beings, had no need in principle of a tradition or a backlog of insights to be refined, critiqued, extended. Tradition, authority, male rule were one rejected whole.

There was something true about Stanton's position on this point. Public sentiment, education, institutional backing were not in place for her. In their absence, the notion that suffering and crisis produced new insight, that people in such conditions dig down to the "hardpan," the bedrock, of human existence, functioned as an alternative mode of establishing the grounds of thought and its authority, its capacity to achieve novelty that was grounded in the nature of existence. It remains true that the school of hard knocks is frequently the only school to which victimized classes of society are admitted freely.

Nonetheless, Stanton's position cannot be adequate any longer. For in fact she is part of our tradition. Once the insight is gained, it is embodied in a history, an ongoing institutionalized record of action, thought, feeling, imagination, association. To be consolidated, to be worked into a form that passes along the substance of the insight, requires that the thought be seen in a context, modified, refined into its most effective form for its next embodiment. Otherwise it risks being lost again. Again.

Whole essays might be devoted to exploring the implications of the needs for training, institutional backing, and trust, as the context for women doing their own theological reflection today. Here I single out the question of tradition. Just as with Stanton, many of our current theological discussions occur from the presupposition that the theological tradition is to be rejected, ignored, or actively fought in order to do feminist theology. And indeed, this stance is appropriate with regard to the patriarchal tradition. But whether therefore traditions and traditioning are also to be rejected, ignored, or actively fought is an open question. Such questions seem to me to change radically when it is our own tradition that is at stake. Perhaps I can make this somewhat clearer by describing my experience of work—that is, of graduate study, scholarly research, and teaching. I proceed in an experiential vein, despite the fact that this is unusual in scholarly circles, an understanding of scholarship that many feminists are coming to reject.

"The young woman is 'torn, like her brother, *though more painfully*, between the past and the future.' "[2] Though de Beauvoir's aside occurs in the course of reflections on puberty and menarche, it is as readily applicable, perhaps even more appropriate, to the experience of the woman conscious of the depredations of Western history with regard to women—the exclusion, insults, hatred, fear, active persecution or sly ignoring of women, whether by historical actors or the historians who record and recount. Like many other feminists I experienced the wave of critiques of sexism within Christianity with deep pain. I felt intensely vulnerable in the face of such newly investigated material, and angry. The sense of the tradition's corruption was exacerbated as I did graduate study in religion. I read with a tense vigilance that required effort and energy. If I did not maintain a certain level of alertness, I feared to come unprepared to another obnoxious saying on the subject of women—that is, on the subject of me, of me and mine. This was wearying enough in itself. As years passed it seemed that there was something more involved than the sheer anxiety of muscles regularly poised to ward off attacks.

When fatigued, I especially felt the need for my past behind me as I felt the need of the back of the chair in which I sat. As a feminist, my chair no longer had a back. It was rather a high kitchen stool on which I sat to work. If I were to lean back, I would topple—topple into the abyss that lurked there just behind me, the darkness of centuries disappeared. I longed for a tradition—the tradition I once had, of which I was now bereft. In many respects it is precisely such a support that a tradition provides: a place on which to rest, a force that continues one's movement into the future, almost willy-nilly, even while one rests from consciously willed effort to move forward.

To be sure, I rested. This women's movement has been created and sustained from sisterhood. I leaned, sometimes heavily, on the shoulders of the women around me; they leaned back. I discovered strength and authority in that mutuality where before I had seen weakness; I learned slowly that vulnerability and neediness were not opposed to power, but components of it. Nonetheless, there is something dreadfully unnatural about the posture of resting propped up by pressure from the sides. Contemporaneity is not enough. "Behind" me—which is, after all, "where" we in the West locate the past—was a great gaping emptiness.

It was perhaps a function of the sense of daring and novelty I felt about feminist theology in the early 1970s that made it all the more shocking and stunning to realize that such women as the ones in this study were doing precisely the same thing a century earlier. No one had told me about it. Indeed, it seemed as I went along, that nobody knew it. As this study progressed, it became clearer to me that what I had on my hands was a portion of a tradition of feminist theology. I do not think that I can describe or remember the fear that this discovery provoked in me. The fear and anxiety far outweighed the anger. Could this possibly be right? Was I making it up as I went along? I went back, periodically, to manuscript materials in the Library of Congress to make sure that what I had read the day before was still there just as I had recorded it. The importance of what I was finding in the woman suffrage movement weighed on me; I became obsessed with the notion that I would be hit by a car before I finished this project, that it would die with me, or require another near-decade of someone's work to unearth this same material. As I shared my research with students in the History of Feminist Religious Thought at Union Theological Seminary, it seemed to acquire a greater reality, to become less unthinkable that this material should be present a century prior to our existence and projects today.

Filling in a small portion of a tradition of feminist theology with the three figures in this study has not "solved" the problem of my metaphor. Perhaps, indeed, I experience questions of women's history in religion so poignantly and passionately because I have acquired from my Christian roots the habit of leaning on centuries of a tradition. It has *begun* a work of construction; it is as though there is at present a small railing, just a few inches high, around the back of the chair in which I work. It is not a full high back on which to take one's ease in leaning. But it is something, a small check in the small of the back to keep one from toppling.

All metaphors have their limitations. But the association of a certain support with the presence of a tradition is not one of the limits of this one, however homely and in certain respects misleading it may be. Scholars who stub their toes on certain questions have no need to solve them alone or de novo. They repair to their well-stocked libraries to look up Aquinas or Lonergan, Luther or Ebeling or Tillich, to find guidance on how such questions have been previously addressed by great minds. They may decide variously on the answers or the very formulations of the questions in these figures. Perhaps Luther's response was satisfactory, and that question is put to rest; his point may be reinterpreted to make it clearer to deluded colleagues; or scholars may decide

309

that Luther was decidedly wrongheaded and go about the work needed to cope with the puzzlement they feel. Whichever it is, such reflections are immeasurably enriched even by their rejections. Even novelty is shaped and situated within the continuity of the matrix of the "cumulative tradition," in Wilfred Cantwell Smith's phrase, within which faith is borne.[3]

This ordinary scholarly process, for which I was trained at great length, is one that now appears to me to be laden with pitfalls, hitches, distractions, bubbles of anger. In the course of meditating on the faculty of memory and its functions, I turn to, say, Augustine: even as I read about time and remembrance I cannot help recalling that in this same book he praised his mother Monica because, among other reasons, she advised women beaten by their husbands to be *more* obedient.[4] I cannot help wondering whether his blatant sexism in one area did not spill over into these seemingly pure, clean, reflections on memory, which appear to be so abstract, so far afield from wife battering. I begin to read not to see what he says but to find evidence of some taint. More, I wonder if the fact of their unrelatedness is not the more suspect. I wonder, irrelevantly, why Augustine's description of the internal recesses of memory reminds me of vaginal folds. I can, to be sure, arm myself with scholarly weapons to keep these questions at bay. I remind myself of anachronism, evidence, the vagaries of free association as opposed to the rigors of argument, etc. In the end I so bristle with armory that I wonder why any woman would *bother* with the effort it takes to read Augustine profitably. It might have been me, you see, among those women; it might have been my mother, battered and abused by her husband. The suspicion is intolerable; I prefer the darkness behind my chair.

To be aware that past women struggled, if not with Augustine himself, with problems of the same nature, has strengthened my sense of the appropriateness and urgency of those questions. As I lived with the material of this study for a few years, precious few in historical time though long for a graduate project, certain benefits and virtues of having a tradition began to appear to me in addition to the quality of support implicit in my metaphor. There are some truths that reveal themselves only after living with certain ideas for a while. No doubt others, who did not experience the anxiety of the early years of this project, will find other virtues, and perhaps vices as well, of living with a history of feminist theology. Nor are my reflections individual; long discussions and work with others involved in feminist theology have contributed greatly to my sense of the enterprise itself, and my sense of what a tradition may offer us.

First is the matter of a certain *division of labor*. Without a body of material that may be accepted provisionally as given, while exploring certain other questions in depth, the feminist theologian is in a precarious position. She is in effect trying to juggle a much larger number of items than her nonfeminist colleague; she is asking in some ways all questions at once.[5] There is a certain fruitfulness to this intellectual juggling act, to be sure; a certain zest results from learning to live with almost all one's questions unanswered. There are also deadly results. The strain, the fatigue, of being alert to too much at once means that one cannot be alert enough to finer points, to the areas where discontinuity jabs at one's attention, to the small nagging questions arising where even the former feminist paradigm does not quite account for the data.

Another function of a tradition is *sheer reassurance*. Women in theological schools who are disturbed by the tradition's lack of representation of beings like themselves, except in secondary or subordinate roles, or who are angered by the obvious marks of sexism within it, look about for models for the incorporation of their own experience, concerns and priorities in theological reflection. Such women, asking questions whose legitimation is not given in the tradition, that are irrelevant to it, frequently feel close to madness, to falling off the edge of the known world. Sometimes feminists embrace this state as a protest against the alleged sanity of the sexist order. As one feminist song puts it, "We'll keep our thoughts on the edge of madness, and move, sisters, move."

This experience is, I believe, largely a function of not having a tradition that is *fully and generously one's own*. A full and generous relationship with the past provides thousands of slender filaments that connect one, almost bodily, with the world. "Behind" the whole person from head to toe are invisible strands of relatedness to what has gone before. Each one separately is fragile, diaphanous; but in their full extent—the full extent of culture—are one strong bond. To be reminded that someone, some several ones, like me, have been here before, secures me against the winds that blow at the edge of the world, at the crevasse that yawns in front of the present. Thus at the edge of time, at the edge of the world, one may step off into space and not fall into the abyss. Buoyed up in space, secured by the tradition's embrace from behind, one walks forward—perhaps still in fear and giddiness—while the world busily extends the cliff's edge out under one's feet as it catches up. The reassurance of a tradition is not simply the more secure knowledge that one is not mad, that many others have had similar thoughts. It is embedded in the nature of the world. Such thoughts have long occurred in the tradition. But perhaps the lack of such a full and generous temporal connection, its human meaning, is something that men are not well equipped to understand. *The* tradition, after all, is theirs.

The division of labor and the consoling security of the world do not exhaust the functions of traditions. Women ignorant of their past are sometimes about the business of reinventing the wheel, repeating what has already been accomplished as though it were novel.[6] To be sure, some of this is the salutary experience of growing into one's own perspective. The appropriation of a heritage always requires the agent to come anew to some old things—conversion, grace, ultimate concern, whatever. Some novelty is built into this re-experience and rediscovery of what was already there. But reinventing the wheel can also mean not getting farther along on one's journey. In other words, *progress*, that shibboleth of the nineteenth-century liberal view of the world, may be made possible from within a tradition. I do not mean automatic or upward progress.[7] Any woman in a theological school, who, after several years of work, meets an alumna of that institution only to discover that the same battles were being fought years earlier, knows what I mean. The despair of never getting anywhere saps the springs of action and creative thought. The presence of a tradition serves to consolidate, to draw together, resources so that they may be extended, rather than dissipated. Without that sense of the tradition in which one works, there is only the "sempiternal change of the world and the biological cycles of living creatures in it," in Arendt's phrase.

This point is worth emphasizing. Understanding is never a substitute for action, though it must accompany all efforts for action, lest we simply strike out blindly, as I am tempted to do at Augustine. Without some sense of the forms in which we receive our contemporary situation, and the contention of the past over the forms of historical existence, we are bereft of guides for effective action. Social issues have a history. Sexism is not the same the world over, nor has it always taken the forms it takes today. Equally, social reformers have a history, which attaches us to the world and shapes our concrete options. Present experience is a good guide to many things ("trust your experience," as the women's movement says), but without a history of how that experience came to be the way it is, it is easy to slide into thinking that nature or deity ordained it to be just that way. A history of one's own provides ways of seeing the possibilities of movement for the future, of critique of one's experience. So it provides, paradoxically, grounds of hope for the future in a round of daily events whose change may be slight, all too often nearly imperceptible.[8]

Even more important is the critical appropriation of one's heritage, the transmission of some intellectual tools with which to achieve sophistication, more precise distinctions, greater ease of connectedness, the perceptiveness that speaks to one's condition. It is finally *excellence*, which can be possible only on the firm ground of a tradition. The thrill of reading the perfect phrase, the insight, the close argument, made by one who is akin, awakens the possibility that I may do as much, that I may do as well. My capacities are stretched slightly farther than they might otherwise be. Even if my own efforts fall short of the excellence I aim for, at least I develop the capacity to recognize excellence in this area. My capacities for feminist judgment are enhanced; the pool of critical awareness, the matrix from which further work comes, is enriched. I may be part of that sustaining appreciation without which such works do not come to their best embodiment. For judgment, that oddly ephemeral quality, may say, I disagree with this but it is good—and it might be improved if you did so-and-so. I may thus midwife another's work to its full birth.

To think for ourselves today about the questions of women's rights cannot mean repeating the perspectives of these foremothers, reasserting Stanton's position. It is rather to think in the company of these women of a hundred years ago. "Think for yourself" was the open door to freedom for Stanton's enlightened feminism; to question the opinions of any authority, any past point of view, was to create alternative perspectives. By adding these women to the company of those with whom we think, we increase our freedom rather than curtail it.

To say that it is part of a tradition particularly implies that this material is *for use* among contemporary theologians and ethicists, feminist or otherwise. It is not to be treated with disrespect, to be ransacked as though it were merely a grab bag of tools. It is not to be looked to for answers, nor even for vindication of contemporary feminist thought. We need to be respectful of the distance between us and this trio of nineteenth-century feminists.

It is for use, nonetheless, in the same way that other traditions are for the use of their adherents. Their questions were not precisely our questions—but they are generally and broadly our questions, even though we may not always be able to articulate what we share. They outline a latitude of thought, action, and inquiry within which we can recognize ourselves in them and them in us without denying the differences or the critiques we might put to them. This

313

is the way a tradition functions, as a living evolution of questions, watchful attention to the way those questions were pursued, and with fidelity to the questions we in our turn ask in continuity with the questions posed before us and around us. For careful attention to women's experience as it presented itself to them, for steadfast abiding in pursuit of justice, for probing theological questions creatively and courageously, we could not ask for better predecessors. To equip ourselves to walk in their footsteps, to stand beside them, perhaps even to stand on their shoulders, we need the best this culture has to offer us (which includes these three and others like them)—and more: women's history, women's support networks, women's art and culture, women's theology.

One cannot think of this tradition in feminist theology without being poignantly aware that it had disappeared. There is no moment more existentially painful or pedagogically difficult, in teaching women's history, whether intellectual or social, than the moment in which students ask in agony and perplexity: Where did they go? Why was I never told of these women before? How could this have been so easily and completely erased? I am no seer, and I hold no cyclic views of history. I do not know whether the oblivion to which this material had passed will eventually overtake this movement as well. But I shiver at the prospect. To pass unnoticed, unrecognized, from the memories of one's successors, is a fate that is perhaps worse than the actual death that overtakes all mortals. It is up to us to fight to insure that this will never happen again. Knowing the risks, knowing the specific historical shape of our own past, can provide us with some sense of what we are up against, and why this struggle, these actions, are so fundamental in a contingent sense as well as an ultimate sense. Many women go mad for the lack of this tradition; others have died.

It is the feminist theology of today that establishes the framework of references that makes it possible to retrieve its own past. But this retrieval is only the first step along the way of traditioning ourselves into the future. A tradition in its fullest extent is more than one work; it is more than thought. It is institutions more permanent than the mortals who dwell in them. It is the education of generations to come into the use and enjoyment of the riches handed across to them. It is the cultivation of those riches—the selection and naming, the appreciation of their worth in both senses of that word: the rapt contemplation with which we cherish them and the increase in value that we add by our own work with them—the caress of many hands enhancing the polish, the sheen, as it were, on the silverware used, not merely admired, by a family through decades.

Remembering, that dreadfully and wonderfully ordinary act, is one of the few resources we have to bulwark ourselves against the darkness into which such feminist theologies as these fell. Remembering itself is endangered by the lack of a conceptual apparatus within which to organize itself. It will require more than this study. It remains to be seen what frameworks of understanding will emerge to aid us in this task. Continually to retell, to rework, to reassess such thoughts as these is the way that they are remembered. Perhaps, as recent Roman Catholic thinkers have said, the *tradita*, the content of what is remembered, is less important finally than the *traditans*, the act of reinterpretation so as to pass along to the next generation. To reinterpret this work is to keep it alive. It is not only by the stern acts of our "wills" that we resolve to remember. It is by promising to ourselves and to others with us, and by rethinking such thoughts as these suffragists had from within new intellectual frameworks, that we can accomplish these ends. So may we say with the psalmist:

If I forget thee, O Jerusalem,
Let my right hand wither.
Let my tongue cleave to the roof of my mouth.

Notes

CHAPTER ONE

1. Even within the feminist tradition itself there are many other figures whose positions would bear similar scrutiny and investigation. Mary Wollstonecraft, Lucretia Mott, the Grimké sisters, Margaret Fuller, Antoinette Brown Blackwell, Jane Addams, Charlotte Perkins Gilman have similarly articulated theological positions of interest. Nor should we neglect the less well-known suffragists: Matilda Joslyn Gage, Isabella Beecher Hooker, Clara Bewick Colby, Ursula Geistfeld, Phoebe Hanaford, Lucy Stone, Julia Ward Howe, Mary Livermore, Caroline Bartlett Crane, Anna Garlin Spencer, Vida Scudder. There were perhaps thirty ordained women involved with the woman suffrage movement whose careers and thought have barely begun to be studied.
2. Kenneth Burke, *A Grammar of Motives* (Berkeley: University of California Press, 1969). For a brief version of Burke's overall project, see "The Philosophy of Literary Form," in idem, *The Philosophy of Literary Form* (Berkeley: University of California Press, 1971), pp. 1-137, or the "Five Summarizing Essays" in *Language as Symbolic Action* (Berkeley: University of California Press, 1973), pp. 2-100.
3. I use "quasi-systematic" by analogy with "quasi-logical" arguments elucidated by recent studies in rhetoric. See Ch. Perelman and L. Olbrichts-Tyteca, *The New Rhetoric: A Treatise on Argumentation*, trans. John Wilkenson and Purcell Weaver (Notre Dame: University of Notre Dame Press, 1969), pp. 193-95. To delineate the internal structure of each woman's thought is fundamental to my exploration of religious social thought among these suffragists. My aim has not been primarily to write intellectual biographies of these figures. Accordingly, this treatment slights questions of influence, of which intellectual tributaries flowed into these streams.
4. My use of "issue" here has its precedents in the legal senses of the word. Thus we find in the *Oxford English Dictionary*, rev. ed. (1971), "issue."
   "V. 11. *Law.* The point in question, at the conclusion of the pleadings between contending parties in an action, when one side affirms and the other denies. . . . (b) A point on the decision of which something depends or is made to rest; a point or matter in contention between two parties; the point at which a matter becomes ripe for decision. . . . (c) A matter or point which remains to be decided; . . . the decision of which involves important consequences. . . . (d)

A choice between alternatives; a dilemma. 12. At issue. In law, generally of persons or parties . . . in controversy; taking opposite sides of a case or contrary views of a matter; at variance. . . . 13. To join issue. (a) In law, of the parties; to submit an issue (sense 11) jointly for decision. . . . (b) To accept or adopt a disputed point as the basis of argument in a controversy; to proceed to argument *with* a person *on* a particular point, offered or selected. . . . (c) To take up the opposite of a case, or a contrary view *on* a question."

5. For a distinction between focal awareness and subsidiary awareness, from which I have taken this concept, see Michael Polanyi, *Personal Knowledge: Towards a Post-Critical Philosophy* (Chicago: University of Chicago Press, 1954; New York: Harper & Row, 1964), especially pp. 55-65.

6. I have been helped especially to formulate tools for understanding social analysis by Alan B. Anderson. See "The Issue of the Color Line: Some Methodological Considerations" (Ph.D. dissertation, University of Chicago, 1975).

7. As a recent ethical theorist reminds us, "The ordinary run of life is there to prove that justice is only spoken about in generalities, whereas, whenever specific cases come up, injustice is what we almost always hear about." Ch. Perelman, *The Idea of Justice and the Problem of Other Arguments* (London: Routledge and Kegan Paul, 1963), p. 31.

8. Paul Tillich, *Systematic Theology*, 3 vols. in 1 (Chicago and New York: University of Chicago Press and Harper & Row, 1961), 1:56-66.

9. Elizabeth Cady Stanton, Susan B. Anthony, et al., *History of Woman Suffrage*, 6 vols. (New York: Fowler and Wells, 1881-1922; New York: Arno Press, 1969), 5:95. (Hereafter referred to as *HWS*.)

10. Ibid., 5:42.

11. Ibid., 5:267.

12. Mary Craigie, *Christian Citizenship: Would the Extension of the Suffrage to Women Raise the Standard of Christian Citizenship?* (New York: National American Woman Suffrage Association, 1912), p. 3.

13. *HWS*, 4:285.

14. Ibid., 4:279-80.

15. *Report of the International Council of Women Assembled by the NWSA, March 25-April 1, 1888* (Washington, D.C.: Rufus H. Darby, 1888), p. 421. That such expansive and nontraditional ways of describing religion should have surfaced in the woman suffrage movement is not surprising. This time was, as earlier historians have pointed out, "a critical period in American religion." See Arthur M. Schlesinger, Sr., *A Critical Period in American Religion* (Philadelphia: Fortress Press, 1967). Several crucial trends combined to make this so: the new biblical investigations, the discovery of the world's religions beyond the bounds of Christendom, and the social upheavals of the urban-industrial order. New theological directions were born to meet these challenges, most notably liberalism and the social gospel.

16. Such discussions of the constraints upon notions of religion are no novelty to students of this subject. For example, see Frederick J. Streng, Charles L. Lloyd,

Jr., and Jay T. Allen, eds., *Ways of Being Religious* (Englewood Cliffs, N.J.: Prentice-Hall, 1973), pp. 1-22. Similar problems occur for feminist theologians today. For a rich panoply of differences in women's religious stories, including such themes as "the color purple," see The Mudflower Collective, *God's Fierce Whimsy: Christian Feminism and Theological Education* (New York: Pilgrim Press, 1985). Similarly, a recent anthology notes that "what counts as resources for feminist spirituality is very broad . . . it questions not only the content of much religious thought, but asks who is doing that thinking, what counts as theology, and how theology is being done." Judith Plaskow and Carol Christ, eds., Introduction to *Weaving the Visions: New Patterns in Feminist Spirituality* (San Francisco: HarperCollins, 1989), pp. 5-6.

17. I have appropriated such phrases from the work of Clifford Geertz. See especially "Religion as a Cultural System" and "Ethos, World-View and the Analysis of Sacred Symbols," in idem, *Interpretation of Cultures* (New York: Basic Books, 1973), pp. 87-141.

18. Geertz believes that this "unbreakable inner connection" implies that religion's "defining concern is not action upon those wider realities but acceptance of them" (ibid., p. 112). This will not do in the context of this study because these women were seeking deliberate religious changes. We need, in other words, to leave open the question, at least initially, of the place of "action" and "acceptance" with regard to the "wider realities" of which Geertz writes. In the central chapters of this study Stanton's view comes closest to consonance with Geertz; both Anthony and Shaw, on the other hand, had views at odds with such a point. Nonetheless, Geertz's position is still helpful here with the modifications I propose below.

19. "Redescription" is from Mary Hesse, *Models and Analogies in Science* (Notre Dame IN: University of Notre Dame Press, 1966), pp. 157-77. For the extension of this concept beyond the field of metaphor and into texts as a whole, see Paul Ricoeur, "The Hermeneutical Function of Distanciation" and "Creativity in Language," *Philosophy Today* 17 (Summer 1973): 129-41 and 97-111, respectively.

20. Women of the nineteenth century, like those of preceding ages, were expected to be religious, but not to pursue theological reflection. They were not supposed to argue for Christianity or any other religious view, to study it deeply, to explore it intellectually with sophisticated tools, or to follow rigorously a chain of reasoning from premises to conclusion. This is in keeping with the period's boundaries for women in other areas; they might write novels, poems, or even devotional literature, but "harder" writing in the sciences and social sciences was frowned upon. As one scholar has put it, "Not thought, but feeling was held to be the woman's forte, and the Victorians especially distrusted women's pretensions to abstract thinking. Emotional prejudice, they believed, disqualified women from objective judgments upon such matters as history, philosophy, and government. Again and again in the journals, reviewers attacked women attempting philosophic discussions." Elaine Showalter, "Women Writers and the Double Standard," in *Woman in Sexist Society: Essays*

in Power and Powerlessness, ed. Vivian Gornick and Barbara Moran (New York: Basic Books, 1971), p. 462. To correct this prejudice against woman's theological reflection we need not swing to the other extreme, however. My claims here for the theological character of these women's thought are primarily to emphasize the structured, coherent, and perceptive nature of their reflections regarding religion, not to canonize them. That their work is worthy of being seen in the tradition of feminist theology, the central chapters amply demonstrate.

21. I have been helped to see that there are a variety of different phases and enterprises under the rubric "theology" by Bernard Lonergan's eightfold division of the functional specialities in this field. See idem, *Method in Theology* (New York: Herder and Herder, 1972), pp. 125-45.
22. To affirm that such figures were engaged in feminist theology, I need not assert that every thought or category was uniquely feminist. Indeed, as I show below, one open question emerging from these women's works is the degree to which either democratic theory or Christianity was an adequate theory to cover the suffrage struggle—an adequate theory whose only problem was that it was not sufficiently practiced.
23. For a controversial discussion of the notion that the "feminization" of American religion was responsible for the liberal rejection of sin, see Ann Douglas, *The Feminization of American Culture* (New York: Alfred A. Knopf, 1977).

CHAPTER TWO

1. Susan P. Conrad, *Perish the Thought: Intellectual Women in Romantic America* (Secaucus, N.J.: Citadel Press, 1978), p. 102.
2. Aileen Kraditor, ed., *Up from the Pedestal: Selected Writings in the History of American Feminism* (Chicago: Quadrangle Books, 1968), p. 113.
3. That Stanton's speeches and essays were never collected for publication remains a loss to the feminist tradition and to the American tradition of religious social thought. Anthony prodded her friend in this direction: "The dream of my life . . . is that you should take all of your speeches and articles . . . and put your best utterances on each point into one essay or lecture . . . and then publish in a nice volume, just as Phillips culled out his best. Your Reminiscences give only light and incidental bits of your life—all good but not the greatest of yourself." Katherine Anthony, *Susan B. Anthony: Her Personal History and Her Era* (Garden City, N.Y.: Doubleday, 1954), p. 408. As matters now stand, Stanton's work is available only in heavily edited versions or in manuscripts accessible primarily to the professional historian.
4. This from a tribute to John Stuart Mill, among the few men capable of fully appreciating the situation of women in Stanton's eyes. Elizabeth Cady Stanton, "John Stuart Mill," *The Revolution*, August 26, 1869, p. 120. The other male

individual capable of seeing the "nice points in the degradation of sex" was William Henry Channing. *HWS*, 3:922-23.

5. Theodore Stanton and Harriet Stanton Blatch, eds., *Elizabeth Cady Stanton as Revealed in Her Letters, Diary and Reminiscences*, 2 vols. (New York: Harper, 1922), 2:346.

6. Alice Rossi distinguishes between "Enlightenment feminists" and "Moral Crusader feminists." The former were urban, sophisticated, solitary, expressing radical impulses "through the pen" rather than in a social movement. The latter were responsive to religious revivals and their messages of social reform. Her typology is based on social origins rather than intellectual similarities. (My position maintains that Stanton's intellectual emphases were far closer to the classic philosophical and political Enlightenment.) See "Social Roots of the Woman's Movement," in idem, *The Feminist Papers from Adams to de Beauvoir* (New York: Columbia University Press, 1973), pp. 141-81. My account is more in line with Lois W. Banner, *Elizabeth Cady Stanton: A Radical for Women's Rights* (Boston: Little, Brown and Co., 1980): "In her search she was influenced by the natural law and natural right theories of Enlightenment philosophy which implied the existence of an underlying scheme of human development" (p. 84). Banner provides an extremely clear, though frustratingly unfootnoted, guide to Stanton's thought.

    Similarly, the most recent and most complete biography of Stanton, *In Her Own Right: The Life of Elizabeth Cady Stanton*, by Elisabeth Griffith (New York: Oxford University Press, 1984), notes that "Stanton's political philosophy was rooted in the theory of natural rights. Like the abolitionists, Stanton applied eighteenth-century natural rights doctrine to nineteenth-century sexual inequality" (p. 54).

7. Elizabeth Cady Stanton. "The Catholic World," *The Revolution*, April 29, 1869, pp. 264-65. This piece was also notable for its anti-Catholic bias. Stanton asserted that it was "not possible for a foreigner and a Catholic to take in the grandeur of the American idea of individual rights as more sacred than any civil or ecclesiastical organizations."

8. Elizabeth Cady Stanton, *Eighty Years and More: Reminiscences, 1815-1897*, with a new introduction by Gail Parker (New York: T. Fisher Unwin, 1898; New York: Schocken Books, 1971), p. 43.

9. Alice Rossi overlooks this rejection of the Finney revival in classifying Stanton among the moral crusaders. Even more, she neglects Stanton's later connections with the Free Religious Association. This same error is repeated by Nancy Hardesty, Lucille Sider Dayton, and Donald W. Dayton in "Women in the Holiness Movement: Feminism in the Evangelical Tradition," in *Women of Spirit: Female Leadership in the Jewish and Christian Traditions*, ed. Rosemary Radford Ruether and Eleanor McLaughlin (New York: Simon and Schuster, 1979), p. 230. More accurate is Elisabeth Griffith's comment that demystifying revival techniques "allowed her to treat theology analytically." Griffith also says that "her experience initiated a decade of religious indecision" (*In Her Own Right*, p. 21) though she does not explore what that means. Griffith sees clearly

that "Stanton's interest in this subject (religion) was lifelong" but she does not deal with the substance of Stanton's religion between this brush with Finney and *The Woman's Bible*.

10. She recorded Gall and Spurzheim on phrenology, and Andrew Combe's *Constitution of Man* and *Moral Philosophy* (Stanton, *Eighty Years and More*, p. 43). In her early married life she read more Combe ("On Infancy"), the Hahneman homeopathic system, and unspecified works in theology, law, history, poverty. However, the influence of Scottish moral philosophy seems less important than Positivism, especially after the Civil War.

11. Stanton, *Eighty Years and More*, pp. 47-48. While there is no reason to doubt, at this point, that Stanton's brother-in-law demystified revival techniques for her, still this late autobiography "reads back" themes of her later life into these earliest years. There is independent evidence to lead one to believe that Stanton was troubled by religious questions in 1840 and later. She attributed to both Lucretia Mott and William Lloyd Garrison a "conversion" experience, but away from Christianity. See below, footnote 12 to chapter 3.

12. Theodore Parker's *A Discourse of Matters Pertaining to Religion*, 3rd ed. (Boston: C. C. Little and J. Brown, 1847) was his defense of the controversial speech, "The Transient and the Permanent in Christianity."

13. Despite this exposure to American Romanticism, Stanton's constantly reiterated emphasis on rationality seems to place her outside this transcendental school. She never gave more than a nodding acknowledgment to art and culture. Thus it is difficult to see her as a Romantic, as does Susan Conrad's *Perish the Thought*, Chapter 4.

14. Elizabeth Cady Stanton to Susan B. Anthony, n.d., Container 1, Elizabeth Cady Stanton Papers, Library of Congress.

15. For example, Stanton wrote a short, light-hearted piece calling for role reversals in housework. "We think that men are better fitted than women for all the drudgery of domestic life. They can stand fire better, not only on the battlefield, but round the cookstove; they excel as cooks. They are better fitted to wash and iron, and the sewing machine is their peculiar sphere. If women must give birth to children, the least that men can do is help take care of them." Elizabeth Cady Stanton, "Woman's Education," *The Revolution*, June 10, 1869, pp. 362-63. To this a Roman Catholic journal responded by calling it "harlotry." See "A Freeman's Journal," *The Revolution*, July 1, 1869, p. 409. These attacks no doubt confirmed Stanton's sense that "among the clergy we find our most violent enemies." *HWS*, 1:850.

16. Stanton, *Eighty Years and More*, p. 382.

17. Elizabeth Cady Stanton, "Religion for Women and Children," *The Index*, March 11, 1886, Container 3, Elizabeth Cady Stanton Papers, Library of Congress.

18. Stanton's withdrawal from active participation in the new suffrage organization no doubt aided the coalition; after her inaugural address to the NAWSA she immediately got back on the boat for England. Members of the former AWSA directed most of their animus toward Stanton. Shaw, for example, refused the effort "to crowd Mrs. Stanton down our throats" even if it meant deserting her

beloved Aunt Susan's side. Anna Howard Shaw to Lucy E. Anthony, January 20, 1890, Mary Earhart Dillon Collection Series XI, Folder 420, Schlesinger Library. Tensions between former AWSA and NWSA stalwarts persisted in the new organization.

19. An indefatigable publicist for the cause of women's rights, Stanton left more than ample documentation for this study. She presided over the first three volumes of the six-volume *History of Woman Suffrage*. I have particularly relied on this work, an indispensible resource for historians. Nevertheless, wherever and whenever possible, I have consulted the full manuscripts of her speeches, many of which were published as pamphlets. Footnotes comment particularly on the occasions in which *History of Woman Suffrage* editing is an unreliable guide to the whole text. This chapter uses only material from *HWS*, which is unequivocally attributable to Stanton herself. Thus, narrative portions of *HWS* or unsigned articles in *The Revolution* have been left aside unless the internal evidence of literary style and content places it obviously under Stanton's pen. The five volumes of *The Revolution* itself (January 1968-July 1870) are especially important indicators of the transition period of Stanton's thought. The two volumes of *The Woman's Bible* are well-known indicators of Stanton's mature religious thought. Elizabeth Cady Stanton and the Revising Committee, *The Woman's Bible*, 2 vols. (New York: European Publishing Co., 1896-1898; Seattle: Coalition Task Force on Women and Religion, 1974). The collected letters and her later diary, edited by two of her children, are especially helpful for the period in which her critique of marriage was forced to go underground. Her correspondence and papers are in the Library of Congress.

20. Stanton and Blatch, *Stanton Letters*, 2:346.

21. Ibid.

22. Stanton's analysis was intertwined with racism and class bias. These references to *women* of all types, classes, and races may stand as the best of Stanton's work on this topic. Her racism almost always appears in the context of discussing black *men*. Arguments for the educated suffrage, on the other hand, were general ones.

23. Elizabeth Cady Stanton, "The Degradation of Disfranchisement," *The Woman's Tribune*, February 7, 1891, Container 7, Elizabeth Cady Stanton Papers, Library of Congress. A comparison of the full text of this speech with the heavily edited version in *HWS* reveals how much was deleted in the latter, especially her critiques of other suffragists. See *HWS*, 4:176-78.

24. Stanton and Revising Committee, *The Woman's Bible*, 1:11

25. Stanton, "Degradation of Disfranchisement."

26. Ibid.

27. Stanton and Blatch, *Stanton Letters*, 2:346.

28. Stanton, "Degradation of Disfranchisement."

29. Elizabeth Cady Stanton, "The Antagonism of Sex," *National Bulletin*, June 1893, Container 7, Elizabeth Cady Stanton Papers, Library of Congress.

30. Ibid.

31. *HWS*, 1:841-41.
32. Ibid.
33. *HWS*, 1:811-12. The "fourfold bondage" speech is a late articulation (1891). But it can easily be shown that Stanton pursued this quaternity in her social analysis of the 1850s, as the two quotations above indicate. In 1856, for another example, a letter to Lucy Stone enumerates these four dimensions, without giving priority to any: "How is it that woman can longer silent consent to her present false position? [1.] How can she calmly contemplate the barbarous code of *laws* which govern her civil and political existence? [2.] How can she devoutly subscribe to a *theology* which makes her the conscientious victim of another's will . . . ? [3.] How can she tolerate our *social customs* by which womankind is stripped of all true virtue, dignity, and nobility? [4.] How can she endure our *marriage* relations . . . ? I answer, she patiently bears all this because in her blindness she sees no way of escape." *HWS*, 1:860; my emphasis. Similarly, in the 1870s a speech entitled "The True Republic" had four major subdivisions: politics, religion, schooling (or society, in my terms), and the family. See Elizabeth Cady Stanton, "The True Republic," Container 5, Elizabeth Cady Stanton Papers, Library of Congress. This reading of the fourfold bondage, however, should not be taken as a more fixed aspect of Stanton's work than it was. Sometimes she listed more, and sometimes fewer, elements in woman's degradation. But these four dimensions of her analysis represent her most systematic treatment of the issue.
34. Stanton, *Eighty Years and More*, p. 376.
35. These notions of a perverted religiousness of course depended on a view of what constituted a healthy and undistorted religiousness. Her indictment of the churches took its urgency from the belief that "true religion sets man and woman free, it does not hold them supinely down to endure the dwarfing, crippling, withering of all those powers that in their growth and development would make them more like gods than men. Religion is a perception of the moral laws that govern the universe, a conscientious observance of them, and a worshipping love of their divine author." Elizabeth Cady Stanton, "Woman's Pet Virtue," *The Revolution*, September 16, 1869, p. 169.
36. *HWS*, 1:850.
37. Stanton and Revising Committee, *The Woman's Bible*, 1:8.
38. Stanton was evidently unprepared for the storm of controversy that broke over this modest gathering: "I shall never forget my astonishment at having the dream of my young life so severely ridiculed. The demand we made was so rational, the justice so apparent, that I thought the simple statement would convince everyone." Elizabeth Cady Stanton, "Closing Address," *Report of the International Council of Women Assembled by the NWSA* (Washington, D.C.: Rufus Darby, 1888), p. 432.
39. Elizabeth Cady Stanton, *Address of Mrs. Elizabeth Cady Stanton Delivered at Seneca Falls and Rochester, New York, July 19 and August 2d, 1848* (New York: Robert J. Johnston, 1870), p. 3.

40. Early in her suffrage career, Stanton's vision was comprehensive. She projected a book on the subject, and was evidently critical of her predecessors, especially the Grimké sisters and Mary Wollstonecraft, because their perspective was not general enough. So I deduce from a letter of Lucretia Mott to Elizabeth Stanton, October 3, 1848, Container 1, Elizabeth Cady Stanton Papers, Library of Congress. I have not yet found the original letter from Stanton to Mott to which the latter replied. Mott chided Stanton for being hypercritical: "As to the generality of the works extant on the subject, it is more surprising that they saw and wrote as far as they did, than that they did not embrace the whole."

41. Stanton, *Address at Seneca Falls*, p. 4.
42. Ibid., p. 5.
43. Ibid.
44. Ibid., p. 13.
45. Ibid., p. 14.
46. Ibid., p. 6.
47. Ibid., p. 13.
48. Ibid.
49. Ibid.
50. Ibid., p. 11.
51. Ibid., pp. 7-8.
52. Ibid., p. 13.
53. Ibid., p. 18.
54. Ibid., p. 19.
55. Ibid., p. 18.
56. Ibid., p. 19.
57. *HWS*, 1:482-83.
58. Ibid., 1:850. In passing I note Stanton's comment that "there is no better test of the spirituality of a man, than is found in his idea of the true woman."
59. Ibid.
60. Ibid., 1:851.
61. Ibid., 1:496-97.
62. Ibid.
63. Elizabeth Cady Stanton, "The Man Marriage," *The Revolution*, April 8, 1869, pp. 217-18. An early speech on education also emphasized that we "become like God himself . . . as we are kind, noble, truthful, generous, patient, and self-sacrificing." See "Education," Address delivered before the Lyceum of San Francisco, 1850s, Container 4, Elizabeth Cady Stanton Papers, Library of Congress. What Stanton saw amiss in business was "a hard, grinding selfishness." See *HWS*, 2:352. Even when she omitted the language of self-sacrifice, her claims against the fourfold bondage continued to count selfishness among the moral inequities of the current system. "Concentrating all woman's thought and interests on home life intensifies her selfishness and narrows her ideas in every direction, hence she is arbitrary in her views of

government, bigoted in religion and exclusive in society." See Elizabeth Cady Stanton, "Stand by Your Guns, Mr. Julian," *The Revolution*, January 14, 1869.

64. *HWS*, 1:860.

65. For example, "in view of the sorrow and suffering that envelope the human family like a dark cloud, that woman must be selfish, ignorant and unthinking, who can wrap the mantle of complacency about her and say, 'I have all the rights I want.' " Elizabeth Cady Stanton, "I Have All the Rights I Want," *The Revolution*, April 1, 1869, p. 200.

66. *HWS*, 1:859.

67. Ibid.

68. The first issue of *The Revolution* notes that Stanton was to speak in Washington, D.C., on "The Bible Position of Women." *The Revolution*, January 8, 1868, p. 10? (page number deteriorated in New York Public Library copy). She wrote from Wisconsin the next year that at the convention "by special request" she gave her "Bible argument"—evidently it was rather well known. "Editorial Correspondence," *The Revolution*, March 18, 1869. Neither *The Revolution* nor *History of Woman Suffrage* prints this "Bible argument"; one wonders whether Stanton repressed it intentionally in the history. Nor have I found manuscript versions.

69. Elizabeth Cady Stanton, "The Strong-Minded Women of the Bible," *The Revolution*, February 26, 1868. See also idem, "Deborah and Jael," *The Revolution*, May 20, 1869; "Vashti," *The Revolution*, July 22, 1869; "Huldah and Haggar," *The Revolution*, September 16, 1869; "Esther," *The Revolution*, September 30, 1869.

70. Stanton, "Deborah and Jael."

71. She could and did argue from whichever she pleased according to the needs of the moment. "As two quite distinct lines of argument can be woven out of those pages on any subject, on this occasion I selected all the most favorable texts for justice to women, and closed by stating the limits of its authority." So she preached on Genesis 1:27-28. *HWS*, 3:948.

72. Elizabeth Cady Stanton, "The Origin of Woman," *The Revolution*, April 1, 1868, p. 265.

73. Elizabeth Cady Stanton, "Peter and Paul at the Toledo Convention," *The Revolution*, March 25, 1869, pp. 184-85.

74. One wonders, however, what she made of the thought that moral perfectionism was "characterized by the subordination of the individual to the social life." Comte's notion that woman represented the "social" may have made this congenial also, since in effect it meant that men were to be subordinate to women for a change. Stanton quoted only certain parts of Comte. She seemingly left no record of what she thought, for example, of his notion that "practical, temporary, political equality . . . would tend to corrupt the source of feminine purity." "Positive Philosophy, (Part II)," *The Revolution*, April 30, 1868, pp. 262-63. In the late 1880s she read the full text in translation and

"found the parts on woman most unsatisfactory." Stanton, *Eighty Years and More*, p. 395.

75. "Positive Philosophy, (Part I)," *The Revolution*, April 16, 1868, pp. 228-29.

76. Stanton's admissions of the change in her mind appear in a review of a British suffrage essay by Lydia Becker. Becker's argument, according to Stanton, "confounds difference with inferiority. . . . We stood on Miss Becker's ground twenty years ago, because we thought, from that standpoint, we could draw the strongest arguments for woman's enfranchisement. And there we stood firmly entrenched, until we saw that stronger arguments could be drawn from a difference in sex, in mind as well as in body." The review then continued by contending that the difference in sex "gives man no superiority, no rights over woman that she has not over him. We see a perfect analogy everywhere, in mind and matter; and finding sex in the whole animal and vegetable kingdoms, it is fair to infer that it is in the world of thought also. To us it is a beautiful idea. . . . It is a low idea of sex to suppose it merely physical." Indeed, "if a difference in sex involves superiority, then we claim it for woman; for as she is more complicated in her physical organism, fills more offices than man, she must be more exalted and varied in her mental capacities and endowments." See Elizabeth Cady Stanton, "Miss Becker on the Difference in Sex," *The Revolution*, September 24, 1868, p. 185.

77. Elizabeth Cady Stanton, "Reverend Henry Edgar, (Part II)," *The Revolution*, June 17, 1869, p. 276. Edgar was evidently a Comtean antisuffragist. Stanton's two-part response to his sermon defended the ballot against his claim that only the Church of Humanity could achieve any serious results on these issues. In addition he bemoaned the fact that positivism had not arrived early enough to spare women the "metaphysical" stage between theology and positivism. Stanton's use of Genesis came to her aid here: "It is not good for man to be alone, neither in the theological, the metaphysical, nor the positive stage." She did not scorn to occupy a stage in history with Mill, Spencer, and Emerson. See also her "Reverend Henry Edgar, (Part I)," *The Revolution*, June 10, 1869, pp. 360-61.

78. Elizabeth Cady Stanton, "Rev. Joseph Thompson on Woman Suffrage," *The Revolution*, April 22, 1869, p. 248.

79. Ibid. Two weeks earlier Stanton commented on a death in prison: "What Christian mother, in view of facts like these, can say she does not demand a voice in our criminal legislation?" Stanton, "I Have All the Rights I Want." With regard to marriage, society, and politics Stanton will make the same shift toward motherhood

80. Stanton, "Rev. Henry Edgar, (Part I)," p. 360. Indeed, the "law that governs this transition period" was one that accounted for the resistance and ridicule that suffragists incurred. A rational woman might thus sit back, serene in the midst of insults and ignorance, confident that science was to vindicate her position. "The nervousness and opposition of man, his weeping and wailing and gnashing of teeth at the prospective equality of woman are in harmony with the same law, hence sensible women accept sneers and ridicules, sermons, essays,

lectures and letters, and all the twaddle that emanates from the male tongue and pen on this question with a placid smile."

81. Stanton, "Catholic World," pp. 264-65.
82. Ibid.
83. Ibid.
84. Ibid.
85. Ibid., p. 265.
86. Phillips was not surprised that the women's rights advocates opposed the Fifteenth Amendment, because "the Women's Rights movement is essentially a selfish one; not disinterested as the Anti-Slavery cause was. It is women contending for their own rights; the Abolitionists toiled for the rights of others. When women emphasize this selfishness, by turning aside to oppose the rights of others, it is, in truth, no generous spectacle." Stanton responded that the woman's rights movement was not different in kind from the antislavery cause: "We should like to know why a movement among women for the outraged and oppressed of their sex is more 'selfish' than that of man for his sex. Is not the philanthropy of Paulina Wright Davis pleading for the enfranchisement of the black women of the South as pure as that of Wendell Phillips pleading for the black man, or of Frederick Douglass for his own race? Mr. Phillips was first interested in the anti-slavery movement by the murder of Lovejoy, by cruelty and injustice to his own *sex and color*, and he learned to hate the spirit of slavery not from personal observations of its workings on Southern plantations, but through the persecutions, the political, religious and social ostracism which he suffered in his own person in common with all abolitionists. Mobbed, denied the right of free speech, denounced by the press, priest and politicians, his warfare became not so much of pure philanthropy as personal definition and self-assertion. In fact it is persecution that strengthens reformers in their positions and makes their philanthropy, however disinterested in starting, more or less a personal matter." The essay concluded with several specific parallels between the two movements that justified the stand of the women's rights movement against the Fifteenth Amendment. Elizabeth Cady Stanton, "A Pronunciamento," *The Revolution*, July 5, 1869, p. 24.
87. Stanton, "Woman's Pet Virtue," pp. 168-69.
88. Ibid.
89. Ibid.
90. Ibid.
91. Matilda Joslyn Gage, Paulina Wright Davis and Edward M. Davis, Phoebe Cousins, and others of the NWSA held such views. On the other hand, these notions were not uncontroversial even in that organization. In 1878 resolutions on the subject of self-sacrifice came to the NWSA convention.

> *Resolved*, That as the first duty of every individual is self-development, the lessons of self-sacrifice and obedience taught women by the Christian church have been fatal, not only to her own vital interests, but through her, to those of the race.

> *Resolved*, That the great principle of the Protestant Reformation, the right of individual conscience and judgment heretofore exercised by man alone, should now be claimed by woman that, in the interpretation of Scripture, she should be guided by her own reason, and not by the authority of the church.
>
> *Resolved*, That it is through the perversion of the religious element in woman—playing upon her hopes and fears of the future, holding this life with all its high duties in abeyance to that which is to come—that she and the children she has trained have been so completely subjugated by priestcraft and superstition. (*HWS*, 3:124)

These came from the pen of Matilda Joslyn Gage, though Stanton associated herself with them in her autobiography; see Stanton, *Eighty Years and More*, p. 382.

92. Elizabeth Cady Stanton, "Labor," Speech of 1868, Container 4, Elizabeth Cady Stanton Papers, Library of Congress.
93. Ibid.
94. Stanton, "True Republic."
95. Ibid. We may profitably understand these arguments to be a call for a social gospel. What has been noted as the "abolitionist legacy" to that movement thus has its parallel in a portion of the "suffragist legacy." See James M. McPherson, *The Abolitionist Legacy: From Reconstruction to the N.A.A.C.P.* (Princeton: Princeton University Press, 1975). Such themes recur, even more forcefully, in Anthony. But unlike Anthony, whose this-worldliness took the form of "prayer by action" and "liberation," Stanton's individualism always shaped her vision of these religious duties in the world. Her examples never concerned social movements but individuals working one by one. "One good woman laboring at her profession of healing the sick, bearing messages of good cheer to many a bedside, always active on the watch-tower of faith and hope, with a bright face and busy hands, is of more value to her day and generation than a regiment of saints who spent their time weeping and praying over the sins of the people." Elizabeth Cady Stanton, "The Pleasures of Age: An Address Delivered by Elizabeth Cady Stanton on her Seventieth Birthday," n.p., n.d., p. 15, New York Public Library.
96. *HWS*, 4:58-59. These resolutions were evidently written by Clara Bewick Colby but substantially argued for by Stanton.
97. Ibid., 4:57-58.
98. Stanton, *Eighty Years and More*, pp. 381-82.
99. *HWS*, 4: 60-61.
100. Stanton, *Eighty Years and More*, pp. 356-57.
101. Stanton, "Religion for Women and Children."
102. "The vantage ground woman holds today is due to all the forces of civilization, to science, discovery, invention, rationalism, the religion of humanity chanted in the golden rule round the globe centuries before the Christian religion was known." Elizabeth Cady Stanton, *The Bible and Church Degrade Woman*

(Chicago: H. L. Green, 1894?), p. 7. H. L. Green was the office of *Free Thought Magazine*.
103. Ibid., p. 14. Sometimes Stanton read witch persecutions as the outcome of the meeting of Christianity with the old religion of the "matriarchate." As she said, "Woman, as mother and priestess, became woman as witch." See Elizabeth Cady Stanton, "The Matriarchate, or Mother-Age," in Kraditor, *Up from the Pedestal*, p. 146. This essay indicates that she had been reading Morgan, Bachofen, and others through the work of Karl Pearson (*The Ethics of Free Thought*). She also claimed that "Luther eliminated the feminine element wholly from the Protestant religion" (p. 147); and, somewhat heedless of the contradiction, that the elimination of the feminine element (not to say its "wholesale, violent suppression") was what "more than any other one cause, produced the Dark Ages."
104. Stanton, *Bible and Church Degrade Woman*, p. 13.
105. Ibid., p. 18.
106. Ibid., p. 20.
107. Ibid., p. 5.
108. Ibid., p. 12.
109. Stanton and Revising Committee, *The Woman's Bible*, 2:12.
110. *HWS*, 4:60.
111. Stanton, *Eighty Years and More*, pp. 467-68.
112. Stanton and Revising Committee, *The Woman's Bible*, 1:66.
113. Ibid., 1:60.
114. Ibid., 1:20.
115. Ibid., 1:117.
116. Ibid., 1:126.
117. Ibid., 2:116.
118. Ibid., 1:12.
119. Ibid., 2:214.
120. Letter to the Editor, *The Critic*, March 28, 1896; reprinted in Kraditor, *Up from the Pedestal*, pp. 118-19.
121. Stanton and Revising Committee, *The Woman's Bible*, 2:214.
122. *The Woman's Bible* has, however, been taken more seriously by the women's movement today. It has been the subject of discussions, for instance, at the American Academy of Religion starting in the 1970s (see Anne McGrew Bennett, "The Woman's Bible—A Nineteenth-Century Approach" in *From Woman-Pain to Woman-Vision: Writings in Feminist Theology*, ed. Mary Hunt, Minneapolis: Fortress, 1989), 71-78. In 1988, a massive discussion occurred about whether to update *The Woman's Bible*; an editor at HarperCollins tells me it is to appear later in the 1990s as *A Woman's Encyclopedia of the Bible*. The most serious of these considerations was that of Elizabeth Schussler Fiorenza, *In Memory of Her: A Feminist Theological Reconstruction of Christian Origins* (New York: Crossroads, 1987). But see also Ruth Page, "Elizabeth

Cady Stanton's *The Woman's Bible*" in *Feminist Theology: A Reader*, ed. Ann Loades (Louisville: Westminister/John Knox Press, 1990), pp. 16-22.

123. *HWS*, 4:263.
124. Ibid., 5:4.
125. Ibid.
126. Ibid., 5:5.
127. Stanton and Revising Committee, *The Woman's Bible*, 1:9.
128. Ibid., 1:13.
129. Stanton, *Eighty Years and More*, pp. 147-48.
130. Stanton and Blatch, *Stanton Letters*, 2:49.
131. Ibid., 2:48.
132. *HWS*, 1:496.
133. At least one observer of perfectionist social thought in the pre-Civil War era suggests that "unlike the spiritual dissenters, secular radicals would not tamper with the institution of the family." Edward Pessen, "Perfectionist Social Thought in the Jacksonian Era," in *American Social Thought: Sources and Interpretations*, ed. Michael McGiffert and Robert Allen Skotheim, 2 vols. (Reading, Mass.: Addison-Wesley, 1972), 1:283.
134. As Stanton was fond of saying, "The woman is greater than the wife and mother"—by which she meant that individuality was both logically and cosmologically prior to relationships. Later Stanton proceeds from "woman as woman" (i.e., imaginary Robinson Crusoe) to "woman as citizen" to "woman as equal factor in civilization" before coming last to woman in the "incidental relations of life."
135. *HWS*, 1:598.
136. Ibid., 1:599.
137. Ibid., 1:600.
138. Ibid., 1:602.
139. Ibid., 1:603.
140. Ibid., 1:603-4.
141. Ibid., 1:604.
142. Ibid., 1:839-40.
143. Ibid., 1:840.
144. Ibid.
145. Ibid.
146. Ibid.
147. Ibid., 1:842.
148. Ibid.
149. Ibid.
150. Stanton and Blatch, *Stanton Letters*, 2:81. Ten years later she made a similar point: "Women respond to this divorce speech as they never did to suffrage. . . . Oh, how women flock to me with their sorrows. Such experiences as I listen to, plantation never equalled" (2:127).
151. *HWS*, 1:860.
152. Ibid.

153. Ibid.
154. Stanton and Blatch, *Stanton Letters*, 2:70.
155. *HWS*, 1:716-17, note.
156. Ibid., 1:717.
157. Ibid., 1:718.
158. Ibid., 1:719.
159. Ibid., 1:718.
160. Ibid., 1:722.
161. Ibid., 1:720.
162. Elizabeth Cady Stanton, "Speech before a Club of Men and Women in New York City around 1869," Container 5, Elizabeth Cady Stanton Papers, Library of Congress. (Hereafter referred to as "Speech of 1869.")
163. Stanton had little patience with suffragists who tried to make the demands of the movement safe. In the 1890s, for example, she roundly critiqued "the most politic suffragists" who tried to keep the cause separate from religion and family questions.
164. Stanton, "Speech of 1869."
165. Ibid.
166. Ibid.
167. Elizabeth Cady Stanton to Henry B. Blackwell, September 15, 1872, copy, Elizabeth Cady Stanton Folder, Container 29, NAWSA Papers, Library of Congress. On the other hand, Bostonians and AWSA members knew quite well that Stanton had argued for free love. As one of them wrote regarding Stanton, "She would like to have equal license accorded to both, instead of an equal constraint imposed on both." Alice Stone Blackwell to Kitty Barry Blackwell, March 10, 1883, Elizabeth Cady Stanton Folder, Container 29, NAWSA Papers, Library of Congress.
168. Stanton, "True Republic."
169. Ibid.
170. Elizabeth Cady Stanton, "Self-Government," c. 1875, Container 5, Elizabeth Cady Stanton Papers, Library of Congress.
171. Elizabeth Cady Stanton, "Self-Government the Best Form for Self-Development," June 29, 1901, Container 3, Elizabeth Cady Stanton Papers, Library of Congress.
172. Elizabeth Cady Stanton, "Is a National Divorce Law Desirable?" Container 3, Elizabeth Cady Stanton Papers, Library of Congress.
173. Ibid.
174. Elizabeth Cady Stanton, "Are Homogeneous Divorce Laws in All the States Desirable?" *North American Review*, March 1900, p. 406, Container 3, Elizabeth Cady Stanton Papers, Library of Congress.
175. Ibid., p. 407.
176. Ibid., p. 409.
177. Stanton, *Eighty Years and More*, p. 228.
178. Ibid., p. 231.
179. *HWS*, 1:860.

180. Ibid.
181. Elizabeth Cady Stanton, "Washington Gossip," *The Revolution*, March 5, 1868, p. 138.
182. *HWS*, 1:816.
183. Ibid.
184. Stanton, "Education."
186. Elizabeth Cady Stanton, "Woman, a Speech of 1856?" Container 4, Elizabeth Cady Stanton Papers, Library of Congress.
185. Stanton, "Education." In some of these educational speeches, there were distinctly Romantic themes present. Among the few references to art and aesthetics is a call for the young woman to regard herself "precisely as the artist does his painting or statue, ever stretching forward to some grand ideal." The daily lives of women, "every impulse, passion, feeling of your soul, every good action, high resolve and lofty conception of the good and true," were described by Stanton as "delicate touches" that rounded out and perfected a true womanhood. See idem, "Our Young Girls," Container 5, Elizabeth Cady Stanton Papers, Library of Congress.
187. Stanton, "True Republic."
188. *HWS*, 1:849-50.
189. Elizabeth Cady Stanton, "Our Young Girls," *The Revolution*, January 29, 1868.
190. Stanton, "Our Young Girls," Stanton Papers.
191. *HWS*, 1:816.
192. Ibid.
193. Stanton, "Our Young Girls," *The Revolution*.
194. Ibid.
195. Ibid.
196. *HWS*, 1:470-71.
197. Elizabeth Cady Stanton, "Woman's Dress," *The Revolution*, July 22, 1869, p. 41.
198. *HWS*, 1:816.
199. Stanton, "Origin of Woman."
200. Stanton, "Vashti."
201. Stanton, "Esther." Vashti was explicitly compared to the woman's rights women—"boldly asserting the right of every individual soul to self-government, and in fair debate appealing to man's intellectual and moral sense for justice and equality." The Esthers of the age were in complete contrast, for they were "still holding all womanly dignity and independence in abeyance to some ulterior object, [and so] drag man down to death, by gross appeal to his sensual appetites." Nonetheless, Stanton admitted that Esther was "a great woman" since she averted the ruin of her people.
202. *HWS*, 1:816.
203. Stanton, "Catholic World," p. 264.
204. *HWS*, 4:165.
205. Ibid., 4:166. This reference to compelling men to cede justice to women skirts the use of force. Stanton was more than a little prescient as she pointed out

that "the next generation will not argue with their rulers as patiently as we have done, and to so little purpose for half a century." If the legislators were not to take suffrage seriously, the question "will eventually be settled by violence. The wild enthusiasm of women can be used for evil as well as for good." Stanton, "Closing Address," pp. 435-36.

206. *HWS*, 4:159.
207. Indeed at one point Stanton's enumeration of the fourfold bondage was "Church, State, Capital, and Society." Ibid., 4:139.
208. Ibid., 1:816.
209. Ibid., 4:178.
210. "Editorial Correspondence," *The Revolution*, April 8, 1869, p. 210.
211. Here is another disjunction between Stanton and her old friend Anthony, who argued for protectionism rather than free trade. See "What the Press Says of Us," *The Revolution*, May 28, 1868, p. 322.
212. Elizabeth Cady Stanton, "Free Trade," *The Revolution*, April 15, 1869, p. 333.
213. Her theory brooked no opposition from mere facts. It was with "wearisome statistics" that men were "befogging the daughters of Eve with endless arithmetic." Her case was sure in the long run "even if the figures do show the contrary." Ibid.
214. "Editorial Correspondence," p. 210.
215. Ibid.
216. Elizabeth Cady Stanton, "Labor, Speech of 1868," Container 4, Elizabeth Cady Stanton Papers, Library of Congress.
217. Ibid.
218. Ibid.
219. Ibid.
220. Elizabeth Cady Stanton, "Worship of God in Man," *The Open Court*, n.d., Container 3, Elizabeth Cady Stanton Papers, Library of Congress.
221. Nora Stanton Barney, *Life Sketch of Elizabeth Cady Stanton by her Granddaughter* (Greenwich: n.p., 1949), Stanton Biography file, Schlesinger Library. Stanton's letter to the anniversary of Seneca Falls seems to have been unpublished before this privately printed pamphlet.
222. Stanton, "Worship of God in Man."
223. Ibid.
224. Elizabeth Cady Stanton, "National Labor Congress," *The Revolution*, August 26, 1869, p. 120.
225. *HWS*, 1:376. The ambiguity of this phrasing was akin to that of Jefferson himself saying that "we hold" certain truths to be "self-evident." Stanton too did not see the incongruity of saying that republican principles "should be" eternal laws as fixed as physical laws.
226. Ibid., 2:549.
227. Ibid., 2:51; see also 2:185, 321, 411. This phase of Stanton's argument was emphasized and honed by Shaw. In Stanton's critique of the churches she made a similar appeal in her earliest years. The practical type of Christianity resulted from "applying more fully . . . Christian principles to life," as we saw above. As

she devoted more of her later years' work to investigating theology, however, this reasoning shifted. "If the Bible teaches the equality of Woman, why does the church refuse to ordain women to preach?" Stanton and Revising Committee, *The Woman's Bible*, 1:9. The implication was that the practice impugned the theory; and investigating the biblical texts corroborated the insight that the theory itself was false. This line of reasoning about the churches and their theology *never* became Stanton's stance about the democratic tradition. She never called for an alternative political institution or theory to replace the heritage of the Revolution, as she called for a new religion.

228. *HWS*, 2:371.
229. Ibid., 1:595.
230. Ibid., 1:596.
231. Stanton, *Eighty Years and More*, p. 399.
232. *HWS*, 2:509-10.
233. Ibid., 2:350-51.
234. Ibid., 2:411.
235. Ibid., 2:186.
236. Ibid., 1:858.
237. Ibid., 1:596.
238. Ibid.
239. Ibid., 2:351.
240. Stanton and Revising Committee, *The Woman's Bible*, 1:137.
241. *HWS*, 2:281-82.
242. Ibid., 4:161.
243. Ibid., 3:952.
244. Ibid.
245. Ibid., 4:160.
246. Ibid., 1:859. See also Stanton, "I Have All the Rights I Want," in which prisons were the example of a reform that needed women's efforts.
247. Stanton, "Stand by Your Guns."
248. "Civil Religion" was introduced into discussions of American religious phenomena by Robert Bellah, "Civil Religion in America," *Daedalus* 96 (Winter 1967): 1-21. This essay has been reprinted in, for example, *Religion in America*, ed. William G. McLoughlin and Robert N. Bellah (Boston: Beacon Press, 1968), pp. 3-23, and in *American Civil Religion*, ed. Russell E. Richey and Donald G. Jones (New York: Harper & Row, 1974), pp. 21-44. Bellah's original contention was that "there actually exists alongside of and rather clearly differentiated from the churches an elaborate and well-institutionalized civil religion in America . . . [that] has its own seriousness and integrity and requires the same care in understanding that any other religion does." He scrutinized themes in the addresses of American presidents from the founders to Kennedy, and suggested two major shifts in that civil religion during the Civil War and the 1960s.
    Since Bellah's essay, a whole literature on this topic has appeared, complete with critiques of his method and perspective, proposals for further conceptual

clarity, attacks on the alleged theological substance of that civil religion and defenses of it. For guides to some of this material see Richey and Jones, especially "The Civil Religion Debate" by the editors (pp. 3-20), John F. Wilson's "A Historian's Approach to Civil Religion" (pp. 115-38), and Martin E. Marty's "Two Kinds of Two Kinds of Civil Religion" (pp. 136-60).

Insofar as I call Stanton "theologian for a feminist civil religion," I view her in what John Wilson typifies as a "theological-meaning model" (Richey and Jones, pp. 117-22). While Wilson rejects this model as useful to the historian, he does suggest that from it "we might presume to find other presidents or lay leaders in other periods of turmoil returning to and even deepening" the legacy (p. 122). That is precisely the case with Stanton. Themes of death, sacrifice, and rebirth have been associated with the Lincolnian version of the civil religion; these motifs were far from Stanton's position. She resembles rather Jefferson and other founders. For a view of Jefferson emphasizing the superficial character of his moral and religious beliefs, see David Little, "The Origins of Perplexity: Civil Religion and Moral Belief in the Thought of Thomas Jefferson," in Richey and Jones, pp. 185-210. For a sympathetic account, see G. Adolf Koch, *Religion of the American Enlightenment* (New York: Thomas Crowell, 1933).

Recently it has been argued that "the foundations of the connection between women and civil religion . . . were laid during the revolutionary era" even though "the relationship of women to civil religion in America has been different from that of men." See Rosemary Skinner Keller, "Women, Civil Religion and the American Revolution" in *Women and Religion in America: A Documentary History*, vol. 2, *The Colonial and Revolutionary Periods* (San Francisco: Harper & Row, 1983), p. 370; and her "Calling and Career: The Revolution in the Mind and Heart of Abigail Adams," in *That Gentle Strength: Historical Perspectives on Women in Christianity*, Lynda L. Coon, Katherine J. Haldane, and Elisabeth W. Sommer, eds. (Charlottesville: University Press of Virginia, 1990), 190-206.

249. Stanton, "Woman."
250. Ibid.
251. *HWS*, 5:32.
252. Ibid., 2:187.
253. Ibid., 2:186.
254. Ibid.
255. Ibid., 2:187.
256. Ibid.
257. Ibid., 2:188.
258. Ibid., 2:186.
259. Ibid., 2:190.
260. Ibid.
261. Ibid., 2:186.
262. Ibid., 2:190.
263. Ibid., 2:215.

262. Ibid., 2:188.
264. Barbara Hilkert Andolsen, *"Daughters of Jefferson, Daughters of Bootblacks":
     Racism and American Feminism* (Macon: Mercer University Press, 1986), takes
     up Elizabeth Cady Stanton, Anna Howard Shaw, and Carrie Chapman Catt,
     creatively juxtaposing their positions with those of contemporary black women
     such as Anna Julia Cooper, Fannie Barrier Williams, Francis Ellen Watkins
     Harper, and others.
265. The fifth and sixth arguments are in Elizabeth Cady Stanton, "Anniversary of
     the American Equal Rights Association," *The Revolution*, May 13, 1869, pp.
     192-93, rather than in *HWS*, from which I quote for arguments one through
     four. For a similar version of the sixth point, see Elizabeth Cady Stanton,
     "Women and Black Men," *The Revolution*, February 11, 1869, p. 88. This essay
     suggests that Stanton's argument was sparked by a black man's advocacy of
     male domination in a suffrage convention.
266. *HWS*, 3:251-52.
267. Ibid., 2:352.
269. Ibid.
270. Ibid.
271. Ibid., 2:352-53.
272. *The Revolution*, May 13, 1869, p. 291.
273. Ibid.
274. Ibid.
275. *HWS*, 2:353.
276. Ibid., 2:354.
277. Ibid.
278. Stanton, "Women and Black Men." These claims are identical with those she
     made May 13, 1869, in that magazine.
279. Ibid. Stanton's principle was made slightly clearer later on. Until women had
     their full rights, "all minor privileges and concessions are but so many added
     aggravations, and are insulting mockeries of that justice, liberty, and equality
     which are the birthright of every citizen of a republic." *HWS*, 4:145-46. In
     Anthony's more pungent language is a similar principle: "Ask for the whole loaf
     and take what you can get."
280. See "Sharp Points," *The Revolution*, April 9, 1869, p. 212, for a rebuke to
     Stanton's position and her reply. *The Revolution* printed, without a word of
     repudiation, that [Sen.?] Wilson claimed that Stanton and Anthony "during the
     last two years had done more to block reconstruction than all others in the
     land." "The Reign of Terror," *The Revolution*, January 8, 1869, p. 10? On the
     other hand, Stanton claimed "we alone have struck the keynote of
     reconstruction" in demanding universal suffrage. *HWS*, 2:190.
281. Elizabeth Cady Stanton, "Too Many People Vote Now," *The Revolution*, June
     24, 1869, p. 392. Also see idem, "The Ballot," *The Revolution*, March 26,
     1868, pp. 184-85. In these essays Stanton asserted that "to demand education
     before enfranchisement is putting the cart before the horse," because "rulers
     have no interest in the education of the masses until they are voters."

282. The recent generation of women historians have made similar points. I have been immensely aided in understanding Stanton's argument by reflections of Joan Kelly-Gadol. She suggests that when the relationship of the two sexes is under scrutiny in ages past, there is more than one instance in which a "high point" for men is a low point for women. "Suddenly we see these ages with a new, double, vision, and each eye sees a different picture." Joan Kelly-Gadol, "The Social Relation of the Sexes," *Signs* 1 (Summer 1976): 811.
283. Stanton, "Labor."
284. Stanton, "True Republic."
285. Elizabeth Cady Stanton, "The Subjection of Woman," c. 1876, Container 6, Elizabeth Cady Stanton Papers, Library of Congress.
286. Ibid.
287. Ibid.
288. Letter to Convention in Indianapolis, May 21, 1880, Container 1, Elizabeth Cady Stanton Papers, Library of Congress.
288. Stanton, "Self-Government the Best Form for Self-Development."
290. Letter to Convention, May 21, 1880.
291. Stanton, "Degradation of Disfranchisement."
292. Stanton, "Self-Government the Best Form for Self-Development."
293. Stanton and Revising Committee, *The Woman's Bible*, 1:11.
294. Stanton and Blatch, *Stanton Letters*, 2:82-83.
295. *HWS*, 1:842.
296. Elizabeth Cady Stanton, "What Rev. Theodore Cuyler Says," *The Revolution*, June 3, 1869, p. 344.
297. *HWS*, 1:721. Stanton distinguished between kinds of discontent. She cited Emerson's dictum that "healthy discontent" was the first step to progress. But "settled discontent" stood rather for what we might call "victimization." It meant dissatisfaction without protest, without action to rectify the source of discontent. The minority with healthy discontent spoke for the majority with settled discontent, who were sunk in "apathy and deeper degradation." Stanton, *Eighty Years and More*, p. 317.
298. *HWS*, 1:859.
299. Stanton never admitted that the majority of women were content. When she made concessions of numbers—i.e., when she admitted that suffragists were a minority—they were always qualified as to the appearances. "When the majority of women are seemingly happy" or "the satisfaction of the many, if real" were typical statements. Stanton, *Eighty Years and More*, pp. 357, 318. As she grew older, she stressed the intellectual factor involved: "all women are dissatisfied with their position as inferiors, and their dissatisfaction increases in exact ratio with their intelligence and development" (p. 284).
300. *HWS*, 2:511-12, emphasis mine. These metaphors are also fascinating for "pairing"—digging "down" to moral bedrock produced history's "highest" moments.
301. This metaphor is suggested by one of Stanton's comments on ethics. "Visiting Chicago not long since, I saw great pieces of rock of the most wonderful

mineral combination—gold, silver, glass, iron, layer after layer, all welded beautifully together, and that done in the conflagration of a single night which would have taken ages of growth to accomplish in the ordinary rock formations. Just so revolutions in the moral world suddenly mould ideas, clear, strong, grand, that centuries might have slumbered over in silence; ideas that strike minds ready for them with the quickness and vividness of the lightning's flash. It is in such ways and under such conditions that constitutions and great principles of jurisprudence are written; the letter and spirit are ever on the side of liberty" (*HWS*, 1:512).

302. Elizabeth Cady Stanton, "Opening Address," *Report of the International Council of Women*, p. 33.

303. The same speech is explicit about the need for women to "cultivate some esprit de corps of sex, a generous trust in each other." Ibid., p. 37. This principle of solidarity, of fidelity to a specific group and its needs and struggles in the movement, "sisterhood," as we would say today, was not something to which Stanton's individualism completely reached.

304. *HWS*, 4:159.

305. Stanton, "Esther."

306. *HWS*, 4:166.

307. Stanton almost always spoke of principles and virtues rather than values.

308. Compare Stanton's many locutions with a family resemblance to "degradation"—woman was crushed, oppressed, repressed, suppressed. Her condition was subservience, subordination, submission, subjugation, subjection. The bonds of slavery held women "down" (downtrodden, downfallen), just as false religion held women "supinely down." Similarly, her less savory racism and elitism used such directional language; the multitudes were "sunk" in poverty, ignorance, vice; children of ill-assorted marriages were "from beneath"; the "lower orders of foreigners" could vote.

309. *HWS*, 4:60-61.

310. Many of Stanton's moral locutions have a family resemblance to "elevation." Pure, refined, enlightened, high moments were all one "upward" piece. The feminine principle was "to lift" the human race "up into the higher realms of thought and action." *HWS*, 2:352. What was good was high, even exalted. This upward language easily modulated into language of expansiveness; what was higher was also broader, wider, more enlarged, comprehensive, more universal, sometimes deeper as well. She praised "the grandeur of man's conceptions and the magnitude of his works"; greatness, grandeur, glory were associated with high moral principles.

CHAPTER THREE

1. See, for example, the language of unmasking ideological interests, of usurpation and robbery, or the strictures against authority in Mary Daly's *Beyond God the*

Father: Toward a Philosophy of Women's Liberation (Boston: Beacon Press, 1973). Similarly, the introduction to Aileen Kraditor's *Up from the Pedestal* claims that "autonomy," that offspring of the Enlightenment, is what is at stake in the women's liberation movement. On the other hand, recent theorists point to another strand of the intellectual history of feminism in "nonrationalist, nonmaterialist traditions," including mysticism. See Catherine F. Smith, "Jane Lead: The Feminist Mind and Art of a Seventeenth-Century Protestant Mystic," in Ruether and McLaughlin, *Women of Spirit*, p. 185.

2. It is the constructive case for a more rational religion (sometimes a religion of humanity) that Ellen Carol DuBois fails to see in characterizing Stanton purely as a "secularist," as she does in *Elizabeth Cady Stanton, Susan B. Anthony: Correspondence, Writings, Speeches* (New York: Schocken, 1981, pp. 183-87). DuBois is quite right to call attention to Stanton's acquaintance with the British secularist movement in the 1880s (though she does not mention the Free Religious Association) and to her disagreements with the Christian feminism of the WCTU (or the AWSA). But she does not attend at all to the positive case that was implied by these critiques and worked out in some detail by Stanton. This is unfortunate insofar as DuBois's insightful discussion about the meaning of Stanton's defeat within the NAWSA does take up the religious dimensions of her position. A similar disinterest in religion marks DuBois's earlier *Feminism and Suffrage: The Emergence of an Independent Women's Movement in America, 1848-1869* (Ithaca: Cornell University Press, 1978). This work details the controversies and complexities of the late 1860s, especially the arguments about race and labor. It passes in silence the many articles about religion in *The Revolution* and in particular the growing rejection of self-sacrifice as an appropriate moral or religious stance for women.

3. Stanton, "Woman's Pet Virtue," p. 169.
4. Ibid.
5. Stanton, "Esther," p. 194.
6. "So insidious is its tyranny [i.e., the rule of selfishness and sensuality that caused the subjection of woman] that I can liken it only to the subjection of the higher faculties, sentiments, and affections of the individual to the gross animal propensities." Stanton, "Subjection of Woman."
7. Stanton, *Bible and Church Degrade Woman*, p. 4.
8. *HWS*, 2:186.
9. Stanton and Revising Committee, *The Woman's Bible*, 1:80.
10. Stanton, *Bible and Church Degrade Woman*, p. 7
11. *HWS*, 1:422.
12. Ibid., 1:421.
13. Stanton exercised the privileges of hindsight in this memorial account. Her "conversion" was by no means so secure—though Mott did exercise an important religious influence on Stanton. Mott's letter indicates that Stanton was spiritually troubled.

And my dear, what is the result of all the inquiries of thy open, generous, confiding spirit? Art thou settled on the sure foundation of the revealed will of God to the inner sense? Or is thy mind still perplexed with the schemes of salvation, and plans of redemption which are taught in the schools of theology? It is lamentable, that the simple and benign religion of Jesus should be so encumbered with the creeds and dogmas of sects—its primitive beauty obscured by these gloomy appendages of man—the investigations of the honest inquirer checked by the cry of heresy—infidelity! Thou knows how it was in London—thou knows too, that I have no wish to proselyte to any speculative opinions I may hold; but all may know, for I proclaim it abroad, that I long to see obedience to manifested duty—leading to practical righteousness, as the Christian standard—the test of discipleship—the fruit of faith. Then large liberty—unbounded toleration—yes, "religious right," as to forms of worship and abstract theories.

This most excellent charity will not forbid our calling the attention of those, who are superstititously dwelling in the shadows and figures of the *truth*, to what we may deem a more enlightened and better understanding of the law of Christ."

Lucretia Mott to Elizabeth Cady Stanton, 3rd month 23rd, 1841, Container 1, Elizabeth Cady Stanton Papers, Library of Congress. Though Mott was calling Stanton to the simple religion of Jesus, Stanton omitted this from her account of their conversations; rather Mott's references to shadows and enlightenment, and practical righteousness are transmuted into Stanton's civil religion of women's right to think.

Stanton elsewhere attributed her conversion to true religion to William Lloyd Garrison during the same convention in England. "My experience is no doubt that of many others. In the darkness and gloom of Calvinism I was slowly [illegible] off the chains of my spiritual bondage when for the first time I met Garrison in London; five bold strokes from the hammer of his truth and I was free. Only those who have lived all their lives under the dark clouds of vague undefined fears can appreciate the joy of a doubting soul suddenly born again into the kingdom of reason and free thought. . . . To Garrison we owe more than any other one of our day all that we have of religious freedom, but for him I doubt whether our Cheevers or Beechers might yet have found backbone enough to stand where they now do." Elizabeth Cady Stanton, "Antislavery," speech, 1860, Container 4, Elizabeth Cady Stanton Papers, Library of Congress.

14. *HWS*, 1:422-23.
15. Ibid., 1:284.
16. Ibid., 1:801.
17. Ibid. Immediately after Seneca Falls, Stanton wrote to Mott that the publicity about the convention "will start women thinking, and men, too, and when men and women think about a new question, the first step in progress is taken. The

great fault of mankind is that it will not think." (Quoted in Griffith, *In Her Own Right*, p. 58.)

18. Ibid., 4:166. Stanton's advice to the press was similar; authors were to write "what you think in your best moments, when your soul rises above all worldly considerations, and in communion with Great Nature touches the Invisible, the Infinite. . . . When God gives any one of us a new truth, it is not ours to keep but to utter, and if we are not faithful, our souls are darkened and truth finds other messengers." Elizabeth Cady Stanton, "What the Press Says of Us," *The Revolution*, June 18, 1868, p. 372.

19. Little is recorded of Stanton's brush with spiritualism and theosophy. Evidently her encounter with Victoria Woodhull in the 1870s was part of the stimulus here. In 1880, she conversed at dinner about "Nirvana, karma, reincarnation." Stanton, *Eighty Years and More*, p. 324. After her English visit of 1882-1883, she and other members of the family read several works in "occult studies," including Blavatsky's "Isis Unveiled," Sinnett's "The Occult World," and Anna Kingsford's "The Perfect Way" (p. 377). Barbara Welter records that in 1890 the Society for Psychical Research heard a rumor that Stanton had experienced voices and spirit manifestations in a hotel room. Barbara Welter, "Something Remains to Dare," Introduction to *The Woman's Bible*, p. xxxvi, note.

20. *HWS*, 4:60-61.
21. Ibid., 1:419.
22. Stanton and Revising Committee, *The Woman's Bible*, 1:126.
23. *HWS*, 4:176-77.
24. Anthony made similar points in her own Quaker language. What for Stanton was woman's right to think was for Anthony one's "own true inwardness." Anthony too associated conscience with God, who was heard in the "still, small voice." With Anthony, however, these themes were less prominent than with Stanton, and they were far less "philosophical" and "scientific."
25. "The central idea of barbarism has ever been the family, the tribe, the nation—never the individual. But the great doctrine of Christianity is the right of individual conscience and judgment." Stanton, *Eighty Years and More*, p. 31.
26. Man, "with his metaphysics and materialism, is more like the church in its bloody struggles from authority to individualism," whereas woman was like Christ—rather than St. Paul's analogy the other way around. Stanton, "Man Marriage." Here individualism, woman, and the "moral and spiritual" capacities of humanity are associated and opposed to authority, metaphysics, materialism, the church, men.
27. *HWS*, 1:850.
28. Stanton, *Bible and Church Degrade Woman*, p. 12.
29. Ibid., p. 4.
30. *HWS*, 2:372.
31. Ibid.
32. "It amuses me to hear the nonsense these men talk. They say God never intended woman to reason, they shut their college doors against her so that she cannot study that manly accomplishment, and then they blame her for taking

a short cut to the same conclusion they reach in their roundabout, lumbering processes of ratiocination. Do these gentlemen wish us to set aside God's laws, pick up logic on the sidewalks, and go step by step to a point we can reach with one flash of intuition? . . . It is enough to make angels weep to see how the logicians, skilled in the schools, are left floundering on every field before the simple intuitions of American womanhood." Ibid.

33. Stanton, *Address at Seneca Falls*, p. 18.
34. Ibid., p. 3.
35. *HWS*, 2:512; see also 2:214.
36. Cassirer's comment, that the Enlightenment saw reason as an "essentially homogeneous formative power," thus seems entirely apt for Stanton. Ernst Cassirer, *The Philosophy of the Enlightenment* (Princeton: Princeton University Press, 1951), p. 5.
37. *HWS*, 2:351-52.
38. Stanton, "Pleasures of Age," p. 15.
39. Stanton and Revising Committee, *The Woman's Bible*, 2:126.
40. Stanton, "Closing Address," p. 437. So far as I can tell, Matthew Arnold is known for saying religion is "*morality* touched by emotion." Matthew Arnold, *Literature and Dogma: An Essay towards a Better Appreciation of the Bible* (Boston: James Osgood and Co., 1873). Stanton's misquotation was a good indicator of her ability to slide readily between science and ethics.
41. Stanton, *Eighty Years and More*, p. 431.
42. Stanton, "Closing Address," p. 438.
43. Stanton, "Anniversary of American Equal Rights Association," p. 292.
44. *HWS*, 3:930, note.
45. *HWS* contains a truncated version of this piece; many of its most interesting points were edited out; see 4:189-90. The full text is Elizabeth Cady Stanton, "Solitude of Self: Address Delivered by Mrs. Stanton before the Committee of the Judiciary of the U.S. Congress," (n.p., n.d.), Schlesinger Library, p. 1.
46. It is this order that organizes all Stanton's thought and particularly her discussion of the masculine/feminine elements, which are almost always cited as elements "of civilization." Finally they are subordinate to individuality.
47. Stanton, "Solitude of Self," pp. 1-2.
48. Ibid., p. 2.
49. Ibid., p. 3.
50. Ibid., pp. 3-4.
51. It is no accident because more than once Stanton identified women as Christ figures, and because the mother soul, or mother love, was close to the Divine for Stanton. "Everyone knows that morally and spiritually woman is superior to man, and in purity and principle more perfectly represents Christ in his life of sacrifice, while man, with his metaphysics and materialism, is more like the church in its bloody struggle from authority to individualism." Stanton, "Man Marriage," p. 217.

Jesus was always exempted from Stanton's strictures on religion, even though she did not consider him Redeemer. He was the exemplar of whatever virtue

Stanton extolled. When self-sacrifice was uppermost, Jesus embodied that quality. When she rejected self-sacrifice for self-assertion, Jesus represented self-assertion and heroic virtues. Equality was "uttered on Calvary" before being written into the American Constitution. Jesus was an example of the possibilities of human nature. Stanton and Revising Committee, *The Woman's Bible*, 2:116. Indeed, on the cross he "declared man God." *HWS*, 1:717.

52. Stanton, "Solitude of Self," p. 6.
53. Ibid., p. 8.
54. Ibid.
55. *HWS*, 1:842.
56. Stanton, "I Have All the Rights I Want," p. 200.
57. Elizabeth Cady Stanton, "Mr. Forney," *The Revolution*, August 12, 1869, p. 89.
58. Stanton, "Huldah and Haggar," p. 172.
59. *HWS*, 1:859.
60. Stanton, "Worship of God in Man."
61. Stanton, "Anniversary of the American Equal Rights Association," p. 192. She continued in florid nature-loving, fashion: "From yonder hill top, at the setting sun, with Nature in her sweet, confiding moods, one may learn all they care to know of human destiny. In hours like this, I have asked the majestic rivers, mighty forests, and eternal hills that in their yearnings seem to touch the heavens: I have asked the sun, the moon, the stars that for ages have looked down on human weal and woe;—I have asked my own soul in moments of exaltation and humiliation, if woman, who, in thought, can touch the invisible, explore the planetary world, encompass land and sea, was made by her Creator to be a slave, a subject; a mere reflection of another human will? and in solemn chorus, one and all have answered, no! no!! no!!!"
62. Stanton, *Bible and Church Degrade Woman*, p. 19.
63. *HWS*, 2:510.
64. Ibid., 1:679.
65. Ibid., 1:717-18.
66. Ibid., 1:722.
67. Elizabeth Cady Stanton, "Horace Bushnell," *The Revolution*, July 8, 1869, p. 9.
68. *HWS*, 1:717.
69. Elizabeth Cady Stanton, *Suffrage a Natural Right* (Chicago: Open Court Publishing Co., 1894), p. 8.
70. "Individual rights" and "individual conscience and judgment" were great American ideas, underlying our whole political and religious life. *HWS*, 2:508. "The battle of the ages have been fought for races, classes, parties, over and over again, and force always carried the day, and will until we settle the higher, the holier question of individual rights. This is our American idea, and on a wise settlement of this question rests the problem whether our nation shall live or perish." *HWS*, 2:186.

71. I have learned about purity and uncleanness as entrées into religious view of order from Mary Douglass. "Rubbish" is "matter out of place," disordered—"disorganized," Stanton said. Following this line of thought one might say that injustice was taboo for Stanton. See especially Mary Douglass, *Purity and Danger: An Analysis of Concepts of Pollution and Taboo* (London: Routledge and Kegan Paul, 1966).
72. Stanton, "Degradation of Disfranchisement."
73. *HWS*, 1:722.
74. Ibid., 4:61.
75. Stanton, "Opening Address," p. 35.
76. Stanton, *Suffrage a Natural Right*, p. 7.
77. *HWS*, 4:953.
78. Ibid., 2:510.
79. Stanton and Revising Committee, *The Woman's Bible*, 2:99.
80. Stanton, "Antislavery."
81. Stanton, "Religion for Women and Children."
82. Ibid.
83. Stanton, "Pleasures of Age," p. 14.
84. *HWS*, 3:260-61.
85. Stanton, "Pleasures of Age," pp. 14-15.
86. *HWS*, 1:604.
87. Ibid., 2:549.
88. Ibid., 1:860.
89. Ibid., 2:186.
90. Ibid.
91. Ibid., 1:495.
92. Stanton, "Catholic World," p. 265.
93. *HWS*, 1:497.
94. Cited in Alma Lutz, *Created Equal: Elizabeth Cady Stanton, 1815-1902* (New York: John Day, 1940), p. 313.
95. Stanton, "Our Young Girls."
96. Stanton and Blatch, *Stanton Letters*, 2:270.
97. Elizabeth Cady Stanton, "Advice to the Strong-Minded," *The Revolution*, May 21, 1868, p. 315.
98. *HWS*, 2:510.
99. Ibid.
100. Cited in Lutz, *Created Equal*, p. 313.
101. Stanton, "Closing Address," p. 437.
102. Ibid.
103. Stanton, "Antislavery."
104. Stanton, "Religion for Women and Children."
105. Stanton and Revising Committee, *The Woman's Bible*, 1:15.
106. *HWS*, 4:57-58.
107. Stanton, "Worship of God in Man."

108. I cannot go fully here into harmony and dissent in Stanton's view, but it is worth noting the terms on which she held this pair too in a kind of polar tension. Individual rights in the churches, for example, provoked "discussion, dissension, and divisions into endless sects, and creeds, the canons, *all good*, it shows *life* and *thought* there." In the state, on the other hand, the unity of the whole was the "outgrowth" of the doctrine of individual rights; it was the determination of "the *whole* people to have a voice in national questions involving the interests of *all alike*." Stanton, "Catholic World," pp. 264-65, emphasis mine. Stanton finally resolved this tension in favor of harmony, and it may be precisely because she abandoned the churches in favor of the civil religion.

109. Cited in Lutz, *Created Equal*, p. 313.

110. Stanton and Revising Committee, *The Woman's Bible*, 2:8.

111. Stanton, "Opening Address," p. 33.

112. *HWS*, 1:50, emphasis mine.

113. Ibid., 1:496-97.

114. Stanton, *Eighty Years and More*, p. 273. This, and Stanton's use of "Mother-Father" for God, is the most evidence I can see for Griffith's claim that Stanton "created a theology based on an affectionate, androgynous God" (*In Her Own Right*, p. xviii.) Androgynous may be correct. But Stanton linked this deity so closely to the immutable cosmic laws that it is hard, for me at least, to see this God as affectionate.

115. Ibid., pp. 395-96.

116. Elizabeth Cady Stanton, "Prisons and Punishments," *The Revolution*, January 7, 1869, p. 9.

117. Stanton, *Bible and Church Degrade Woman*, p. 9. Stanton had a theory about the causes of masculine deity. Each sex was attracted to its opposite; religious men were of the feminine type, they therefore evolved a masculine deity. "The feminine side of humanity, being the devotional and affectional, evolves the masculine God." However convoluted this may be, she saw with exceptional clarity for the period that among women, "the love of Jesus grows out of sexual attractiveness." Elizabeth Cady Stanton to Harriet Stanton Blatch, April 17, 1880, Container 1, Elizabeth Cady Stanton Papers, Library of Congress.

118. Stanton, "Peter and Paul," pp. 184-85.

119. *HWS*, 1:717.

120. Stanton, "Worship of God in Man." This clipping of Stanton's essay came perhaps from Anthony's scrapbooks.

121. Ibid.

122. Stanton and Revising Committee, *The Woman's Bible*, 2:19-20.

123. *HWS*, 1:679.

124. Elizabeth Cady Stanton, "What the Press Says of Us," *The Revolution*, July 2, 1868, p. 403.

125. Stanton, "Letter from Frances Power Cobbe," *The Revolution*, March 5, 1868, p. 137.

126. Stanton, "Catholic World," pp. 264-65.
127. *HWS*, 4:57-58.
128. Cited in Lutz, *Created Equal*, p. 309.
129. Stanton, "Closing Address," pp. 431-32.
130. Cited in Lutz, *Created Equal*, p. 297.
131. Steven Toulmin, *The Uses of Argument* (Cambridge: Cambridge University Press, 1969).
132. Clifford Geertz, *Islam Observed* (New Haven: Yale University Press, 1968), p. 97.
133. Ibid., pp. 111-12.
134. Ricoeur adds that natural law protested "against the voluntarism of the state, against its pretention to impose the right, and to draw the moral law from positive right." Paul Ricoeur, "The Problem of the Foundation of Moral Philosophy," trans. David Pellauer, *Philosophy Today* 22 (Fall 1978): 187-89. To found justice and moral obligation beyond the enactments of positive law has indeed been among the functions of natural law, as early as Aristotle and the Stoics. See, for example, Ernest Barker, *Principles of Social and Political Theory* (London: Clarendon Press; 1951; New York: Oxford University Press, 1965), pp. 89-136. On the other hand, with regard to women, natural law did not play the role of protestation until at least the modern period. See Susan Mullin Okin, *Woman in Western Political Thought* (Princeton: Princeton University Press, 1979).
135. *HWS*, 4:189.
136. The Methodist Protestant Church did ordain Shaw in the nineteenth century. Merger, however, meant that it took until 1956 for the United Methodist Church to return to that policy. The United Church of Christ today dates its policy of ordaining women from its Congregationalist heritage, which ordained a woman in 1853. Unitarians and Universalists, and a legion of smaller bodies, did affirm clergywomen in the last century, as did several varieties of Baptists. See Constant H. Jacquet, Jr., *Women Ministers in 1977* (New York: Office of Research, Evaluation and Planning, National Council of Churches, 1978).

CHAPTER FOUR

1. Elizabeth Cady Stanton, "Susan B. Anthony," in *Our Famous Women* (Hartford: A. D. Worthington and Co., 1884), p. 65.
2. That Anthony as the proprietor bore these debts alone was a source of some friction with Stanton. When one of the magazine's creditors threatened to sue Anthony, her diary noted that "Mrs. Stanton writes my Sister Mary that *my family ought* to pay—and they don't see with her—they got none of the good from the Revolution—Mrs. Stanton got a great deal—[.]" Susan B. Anthony, Diary, January 27, 1874, Susan B. Anthony Papers, Library of Congress. Money was evidently a source of tension between the two of them even earlier.

"Got a check for $200 on New York bank to send to R. J. Johnson for printing Seneca Falls [speeches] of 1848 with Stanton's first speech—she gave $100 of this—the *very* first she ever contributed to print any of her own speeches even." Ibid., June 26, 1871. The early 1870s were a time of other differences as well. Victoria Woodhull was not the least of these, though Anthony's diary indicates her wavering as to how to view this would-be suffragist. It appears that certain other questions were of long standing between them. "Mrs. Stanton failed to be present at my lecture . . . *she* has never yet heard me give a lecture." Ibid., May 6, 1873. That Stanton's letters to Anthony were always addressed to "Susan" and Anthony's were headed "Mrs. Stanton," may indicate part of their relationship.

3. Ibid., December 30-31, 1871.
4. Susan B. Anthony to Matilda Joslyn Gage, October 21, 1895, Susan B. Anthony Papers, Library of Congress.
5. Ida Husted Harper, *The Life and Work of Susan B. Anthony*, 3 vols. (Indianapolis: Hollenbeck Press, 1898-1908), 1:343.
6. Ibid., 1:507.
7. This statement needs severe qualification since her contemporaries were those who began the process of mythmaking about Anthony that makes her difficult to understand as a human being. This was equally true of her friends and her enemies, whose comments all struggled with the "size" of the woman. Attacks and encomiums alike would provide good material for a study of "civil religion" in American life. In her later years especially, she was virtually canonized by her followers, as two examples will suffice to show.

Under this [early] load of contumely many as well-meaning but weaker women went to the wall, but not so Miss Anthony. The fires of travail burned out of her soul the little dross that nature implanted there and the pure gold which nothing tarnishes was left. Fifty years just round out the period of her public life. Last night as she stood before a vast audience in the Church of Our Father, the lights gleaming on her silvery hair, her strong, true face so framed by it that it appeared almost like a halo. Ibid., 3:1175.

She stood before the audience like a vision of the spirit of prophecy, so imbued with her unselfish longing that the angel of the covenant who has held up her hands and kept her from fainting revealed her as the inspired representative of her great idea. Ibid., 3:1221.

Such accounts say little or nothing about Anthony herself, though they say a great deal about the state of American religion at the time.

8. Interestingly, the only example among the many "tributes" given to Anthony, either in her life or afterward, that mentioned her as a thinker was from Coralie Franklin Cook, who brought greetings from "colored women" on Anthony's eightieth birthday: "Carlyle has said, 'Beware when the great God lets loose a thinker upon this earth.' When Susan B. Anthony was born, a thinker was 'let

loose.' Her voice and pen have lighted a torch whose sacred fire, like that of some old Roman temples, dies not." Ibid., 3:1183. This speech, in fact, is one of the few I have found that expressed something very close to Anthony's own view, especially in its understanding of the place of her work for black people, sisterhood, and social action. I agree with a recent biography of Anthony that suggests that Stanton's comments on their work together "left us with an image of Stanton as the intellectually superior one. . . . Such implicitly hierarchical dichotomies between theory and action inevitably favor the theorists." Kathleen Barry, *Susan B. Anthony: A Biography* [New York: New York University Press, 1988], p. 65.

9. Ibid., 2:544.
10. Ibid., 1:187.
11. See "Educating the Sexes Together," Susan B. Anthony Papers, Library of Congress.
12. *HWS*, 1:459.
13. A good example of these contrasts may be seen in the antislavery manuscripts extant from these two. Those speeches residing in the Anthony papers, definitely in her handwriting, are detailed in their accounts of the effects of slavery on black people; in addition they are noteworthy for the portrayal of racial discrimination in the North. For the latter point, see "Judge Taney." On the former points, see, for example, "Making the Slaves' Case Our Own," "No Union with Slaveholders," "What is American Slavery?" These four speeches are in the Susan B. Anthony Papers, Library of Congress. Stanton's two extant speeches on antislavery are noticeably different in content. They concentrate not on the effects of slavery or racial discrimination on black people, but on the effects of the antislavery struggle on abolitionists, presumably white. The most important of these is said to be one's own religious emancipation—which extends over nearly half one manuscript. See Stanton, "Antislavery," and idem, "Free Speech," Container 4, Elizabeth Cady Stanton Papers, Library of Congress.

These differences may not be definitive, since they may have collaborated on all these speeches. But they are very suggestive. In the absence of a study of the specifically antislavery activities of these women, it is difficult to account for these distinctions. One may hazard that Stanton experienced tension in her antislavery allegiances. The "Antislavery Speech" is unstinting in its praise of Garrison; Anthony's work was also in this wing of the movement. Henry B. Stanton, Elizabeth's husband, on the other hand, was a pillar in the other wing of the movement, the Grimké-Weld group.
14. Harper's hermeneutic bears watching, however. Like many biographies of the period, hers sacrificed any critical assessment for the "human interest" story, and worked too closely to a day-by-day account. While her interpretation was unstintingly adulatory, it nonetheless undervalued Anthony's thinking. When Harper claimed, for example, that it would be valuable to collect all the personal inscriptions Anthony wrote in the two earliest volumes of her biography because they contained "such delicious touches of humor, quaint bits

of philosophy, strong words of wisdom and admonition, tender ones of love and friendship," this might well stand for Harper's view of Anthony. The rest of her work takes us no farther than this. Harper, *Life of Anthony*, 3:1124.

Editorially, Harper's principles of selection are not always clear or what might be desired to a later worker. She referred, for example, to an interview with Anthony regarding discrimination against women in education and business. This interview was not itself cited, but she did cite the editorial bilge spilled elsewhere in rebuttal of Anthony's comments. See ibid., 3:1124-25. She continually cleaned up Anthony's style to make it conform to the stilted and affected language of the time. Some examples appear below.

This is not the place for an extended treatment of Harper herself. But it might be said that the suspicion with which other suffragists, such as Mott, viewed her was not without grounds. See, for example, Susan B. Anthony to Anna Howard Shaw, August 21, 1898, Folder 19, Anthony Family Papers, Schlesinger Library. Her stipulation that Anthony's papers should be burned after the work was completed is shocking, though it is not clear precisely what was lost. Harper wreaked similar destruction on Anna Howard Shaw's material, but without completing the biography. See Lucy E. Anthony to Mary Earhart Dillon, May 5, 1943, Folder 409, Mary Earhart Dillon Collection Series XI, Schlesinger Library.

15. References in this chapter include *HWS* and Harper. Regardless of its problems, Harper's work remains an indispensable sourcebook for students of Anthony. I have consulted the Anthony papers, letters, and diaries in the Susan B. Anthony Papers, Library of Congress, and in the Anthony Family Collection, Schlesinger Library. Anthony was such an indefatigable correspondent that there is little chance of being exhaustive with regard to her letters, catalogued under fifty separate collections in the National Union Catalog of Manuscripts in the U.S. Many of these, however, represent only a few letters related to organizing. There are also Anthony letters in the Elizabeth Cady Stanton Collection, Library of Congress. Some Anthony diaries seem to be missing. I have not been able to find any journals for the years between 1855 and 1865; the notorious 1869 diary, which is thought to have contained confidences from Elizabeth Tilton, is believed destroyed. In addition, there are many pages that have been ripped from the diaries beginning around 1870; it is not clear whether this was to destroy certain evidence, or by whom it was done.

16. *HWS*, 5:5, note.

17. Alma Lutz, *Susan B. Anthony: Rebel, Crusader, Humanitarian* (Boston: Beacon Press, 1959), p. 283.

18. Daly, *Beyond God the Father*, pp. 189-90.

19. Harper, *Life of Anthony*, 2:920.

20. Ibid., 2:898.

21. Ibid., 3:1386-87.

22. Ibid., 3:1199-1200.

23. Katherine Anthony, *Susan B. Anthony*, p. 410.

24. Harper, *Life of Anthony*, 3:1374.

25. Ibid., 1:147.
26. Lutz, *Susan B. Anthony*, p. 67.
27. Harper, *Life of Anthony*, 1:218.
28. Susan B. Anthony, "Working Man's National Congress," *The Revolution*, September 17, 1868, p. 169.
29. Harper, *Life of Anthony*, 1:366.
30. Ibid., 1:169. See also Anthony's reported speeches to the Working Woman's Associations in the late 1860s. For example, "Have a spirit of independence among you, a wholesome discontent, as Ralph Waldo Emerson has said, and you will get better wages for yourselves. Get together and discuss and meet again and again to discuss this question, and all the time have a wholesome discontent, or you will never achieve your rights. You must not work for these starving prices any longer." Susan B. Anthony, "Working Woman's Association No. 2," *The Revolution*, October 1, 1868, p. 198. We have already encountered Stanton's use of "healthy discontent" and the unhealthy "settled discontent."
31. Harper, *Life of Anthony*, 1:133. This positive regard for Republicans was striking in the woman who forged the nonpartisan strategy of the woman's rights movement. Note, however, that in 1872, Anthony and Stanton campaigned for the Republican Party and Ulysses S. Grant on the basis of a woman suffrage "splinter" in the platform. See Katherine Anthony, *Susan B. Anthony*, pp. 272-77. Note that "higher, holier light" echoed, or paralleled, Stanton's locutions.
32. Garrison's language was always apocalyptic. Even on the subject of women's rights, which was never his primary concern, he was "uncompromising." This meant, for example, branding the opposition "malignant, desperate, and satanic," animated by a "brutal, cowardly, and devilish spirit." *HWS*, 1: 549. His view was a totalizing one: "If you can convict a man of being wanting in principle anywhere, it will be everywhere." Ibid., 1:138. For an excellent discussion of the weaknesses of agitation as the basis of the suffrage movement, see DuBois, *Feminism and Suffrage*, pp. 182-85.
33. Harper, *Life of Anthony*, 1:177.
34. Susan B. Anthony, Diary, 1853-1855, Anthony Family Papers, Folder 8, Schlesinger Library. Anthony did have her disagreements with Garrison. She was no anti-institutionalist, as that wing of the abolition movement is reputed to have been. After the Civil War, she refused to join his withdrawal from agitation, arguing that emancipation was only the beginning, not the end, of abolition. Harper, *Life of Anthony*, 1:245-46. The whole spirit of slavery needed eradication and not merely its formal manifestation in laws. Garrison also went with the AWSA in the split of woman suffragist ranks. See *HWS*, 2:265, 322. He signed the AWSA organizing call and held office in that group until his death in the early 1870s.

Nonetheless, Anthony remembered Garrison all her life with the highest praise and frequently cited some wisdom of his as a guide to policy decisions in the suffrage movement. When collaborators of *HWS* sought to whitewash early opposition to the cause, she cited him: "Garrison used to say, 'Where there is a sin, there must be a sinner.' " Harper, *Life of Anthony*, 2:529. In some respects she followed him also in her rejection of explicit religious material on the suffrage platform. "I was on the old Garrison platform, and found long ago that the settling of any question of human rights by people's interpretation of the Bible is utterly impossible. I hope we shall not go back to that war." Ibid., 2:595.

35. Harper, *Life of Anthony*, 2:1012.
36. Ibid.
37. Katherine Anthony, *Susan B. Anthony*, p. 182.
38. Ibid.
39. Harper, *Life of Anthony*, 1:158.
40. Susan B. Anthony, "Speech on the Fourth of July, 1862, Framingham, Mass.," Folder 27, Anthony Family Papers, Schlesinger Library.
41. Katherine Anthony, *Susan B. Anthony*, p. 183.
42. Harper, *Life of Anthony*, 1:215.
43. See ibid., 2:586. Anthony's position on issues of racial justice after the Civil War would bear critical study. At one point she exhorted Stanton to fight racism rather than the Bible: "And like of you ought to stop hitting poor old St. Paul—and give your heaviest raps on the head of every Nabob—man or woman—who does injustice to a human being—for the crime! of color or sex!" Aileen Kraditor, *The Ideas of the Woman Suffrage Movement, 1890-1920* (New York: Columbia University Press, 1965; Garden City: Doubleday, 1971), p. 67. She frequently spoke in black churches and schools. Of the tributes received on her eightieth birthday, she claimed that "none has touched me so deeply as that from the one of darker hue." Harper, *Life of Anthony*, 3:118. Similarly, she rebuked a speaker addressing "anarchistic manifestations of the present day" for not including "the lynching of negroes, the cruelest and worst manifestation of all . . . the mistake was too great not to call his attention to it." Ibid., 3:1240-41. But it is hard not to conclude that these expressions of Anthony's continuing solidarity with black struggle had become merely a private dimension of her work in these later years.

During the controversies over the "Negro's Hour" of the late 1860s, she once espoused the educated suffrage. "The old anti-slavery school say women must stand back and wait until the negroes shall be recognized. But we say, if you will not give the whole loaf to the entire people, give it to the most intelligent first." Namely, women. *HWS*, 2:383.

44. Kraditor, *Ideas of the Woman Suffrage Movement*, pp. 46-47.
45. Harper, *Life of Anthony*, 1:183.
46. Ibid., 2:897-98.
47. Ibid., 2:562.
48. Ibid., 2:644.
49. Ibid., 1:170.
50. She paid a high emotional price for this stance. When she made an allusion to Laura Fair in one of her San Francisco speeches, the audience hissed and the papers gave her a "raking." Susan B. Anthony, Diary, July 13, 1871, Susan B.

Anthony Papers, Library of Congress. Laura Fair was currently in jail for having shot her lover. The public response made it virtually impossible for Anthony to continue the lecture tour in California; she detoured to the Northwest until the brouhaha died down. She referred to the ensuing depression in her diary, as friends from the East came to visit: "But the clouds are so heavy over me—I could not greet them as I would—I never was so dreadfully cast down by an expression or me or my powers." Ibid., July 20-21, 1871. This reference to the clouds, or sometimes shadows, hanging over Anthony is in direct contrast to her praise of living in "God's sunshine." Thus while both Stanton and Anthony share references to light and dark, they were on different terms; Stanton's "caves" and the light of truth were far more Platonic than Anthony's down-to-earth physical metaphors.

Anthony was evidently frequently depressed, despite her constant round of work. It is not unusual in her diary or letters to find such comments as: "The clouds do not lift from my spirit—am simply overwhelmed with feeling that I cannot see my way through the work before me." Susan B. Anthony, Diary, March 22, 1893, Susan B. Anthony Papers, Library of Congress. To Stanton she might write, "Mrs S., I have *very weak moments*—and long to lay my weary head somewhere and nestle my full soul close to that of another in full sympathy—I sometimes fear that *I too* shall faint by the wayside—and drop out of the ranks of the faithful few—." Susan B. Anthony to Elizabeth Cady Stanton, September 27, 1857, Container 1, Elizabeth Cady Stanton Papers, Library of Congress.

51. Harper, *Life of Anthony*, 1:158.
52. Ibid., 1:197.
53. Ibid., 1:203-4.
54. Lutz, *Susan B. Anthony*, p. 140.
55. Susan B. Anthony, "Speech on the Civil War and Slavery," 1861 or 1862, Folder 26, Anthony Family Papers, Schlesinger Library.
56. *HWS*, 2:514.
57. Ibid., 2:949.
58. *HWS*, 2:687-89.
59. Anthony, "Working Man's National Congress."
60. Harper, *Life of Anthony*, 3:1358-59.
61. Ibid.
62. Ibid., 3:1259.
63. Ibid.
64. Katherine Anthony, *Susan B. Anthony*, p. 199.
65. Susan B. Anthony, "Working Woman's Association," *The Revolution*, September 9, 1869, p. 154.
66. Susan B. Anthony, "Working Woman's Association No. 1," *The Revolution*, October 8, 1868, pp. 214-15.
67. Anthony, Diary, 1853-1855 with scattered later entries. Interestingly, on her return to Rochester she went "directly to Mr. Channing, told him of the work

I had planned, he answered, 'Capital, Capital. . . . ' " This quotation appears, with Harper's editing, in Harper, *Life of Anthony*, 1:104.

68. Harper, *Life of Anthony*, 1:169.
69. *HWS*, 2:383.
70. Ibid., 1:333. Subsequent citations in this paragraph are from this same page.
71. Stanton used a similar phrase in the context of the familial strand of bondage. There, however, it meant the "sacred right to one's own body," a veiled sexual reference, rather than this "subsistance question," as Anthony called it.
72. Ibid.
73. Ibid., 3:1206. Stanton's own accounts of the collaboration between them bears this out. "She supplied the facts and statistics, I the philosophy and rhetoric, and together we have made arguments that have stood unshaken by the storms of thirty long years; arguments that no man has answered" (1:459). She goes on to add, "Our speeches may be considered the united product of our two brains."
74. Harper, *Life of Anthony*, 1:102-3.
75. Susan B. Anthony, "Bread and the Ballot," *The Revolution*, January 22, 1868, page number deteriorated in New York Public Library copy.
76. Susan B. Anthony, "The Work of the Hour," *The Revolution*, August 6, 1868, p. 72. This short piece is remarkable for its religious tones. The call for subscribers was virtually an altar call, for the editors of the paper were to make it "a very gospel of salvation."
77. Anthony, "Working Women's Association." Here again was contrast with Stanton. Though the latter also wrote for *The Revolution* essays comparing labor with slavery, Stanton's solidarity with labor was at best tenuous. Her response to the refusal of the National Labor Congress to seat Anthony was rather to point to the antagonism between labor and woman suffrage. "The result has proved what *The Revolution* has said again and again, that the worst enemies of Woman's Suffrage will ever be the laboring classes of men. Their late action toward Miss Anthony is but the expression of the hostility they feel to the idea she represents." Stanton, "National Labor Congress." Anthony's words cited above were her response to these same events.
78. Anthony, "Working Women's Association."
79. See, for example, Anthony, "Working Womens' Association No. 2." She encouraged the sewing machine operators to form a "cooperative shop, furnishing the stock and making the goods." Idem, "Female Labor Question," *The Revolution*, October 29, 1868, p. 259.
80. Lutz, *Susan B. Anthony*, p. 67.
81. Susan B. Anthony, "Printers' Strike," *The Revolution*, February 4, 1869, p. 73.
82. Ibid.
83. Stanton, at least, reported that when the National Labor Congress of 1869 refused to seat Anthony as a delegate, part of the discussion had to do with the "publication of her paper by a 'rat.' " See Stanton, "National Labor Congress." The best general discussion of the problems of the Working Women's Association is DuBois, *Feminism and Suffrage*, chapters 4 and 5.

84. Susan B. Anthony, "The Printers' Strike," *The Revolution*, February 11, 1869, p. 90.
85. Anthony, "Working Woman's Association."
86. Ibid.
87. This fear of being accused of financial chicanery probably went back to the Kansas campaign of 1867. The attack on Stanton and Anthony for their involvement with George Francis Train included allegations that Anthony had misused money to finance his trip. (Anthony was exonerated but deeply hurt.) Kathleen Barry claims to have uncovered new evidence that shows that Train's involvement was secretly planned by Henry B. Blackwell precisely to discredit Stanton and Anthony. See Barry, *Susan B. Anthony*, chapter 5, "The Male Betrayal."
88. Anthony, "Working Woman's Association."
89. Susan B. Anthony, "Woman's Suffrage Meeting," *The Revolution*, September 30, 1869, p. 202.
90. Ibid.
91. Harper, *Life of Anthony*, 2:1011.
92. Harper erroneously titled this speech "Woman wants Bread, not the Ballot," in contradiction to its substance.
93. Harper, *Life of Anthony*, 2:996.
94. Ibid., 2:999. It is not always clear where Anthony got her figures, nor that she was consistent in reciting them. The Washington Convention of 1875 heard Anthony making a similar case: "Man neither supports woman nor protects her. The census reports show that two million women are entirely independent of men in regard to employments. Thousands of women do work outside the home from necessity. A million women are engaged in domestic service providing for their own necessities, and a million more are supporting their families and drunken husbands." *HWS*, 2:584. Nor is it clear from what year Harper took the full version of "Bread and the Ballot" used in her biography. In any case, the point was always a similar one: the "great facts of the world" falsified the notion that women were supported and protected by men.
95. Harper, *Life of Anthony*, 1:140.
96. Ibid., 2:1000.
97. Ibid., 2:1001.
98. Ibid.
99. Ibid., 2:1002.
100. Ibid., 3:1162.
101. Ibid., 2:1002.
102. Ibid., 2:1139.
103. Ibid., 2:844.
104. Ibid., 3:1291.
105. Ibid., 3:1292.
106. *HWS*, 5:741.
107. Harper, *Life of Anthony*, 1:325-326. Stanton and Anthony diverged on this topic. In contrast to Stanton's support of Woodhull, and her privately made

speech affirming free love, Anthony thought Woodhull's affirmation of free love proved that she was directed by "male spirits." Woodhull "was the *first* woman man had succeeded in fashioning to his own ideal—so that *she theoretically accepted* man's *practical* theory of promiscuity or change." Susan B. Anthony, Diary, February 19, 1873, Susan B. Anthony Papers, Library of Congress. I have not found Anthony's reactions to Stanton's speech; they may be among the reasons that the 1869 diary is missing.

108. Harper, *Life of Anthony*, 1:389.
109. Anthony's stand was not one with which today's women's liberation movement would be pleased. The pages of *The Revolution* frequently spoke of abortion as infanticide, feticide, or child murder.
110. Harper, *Life of Anthony*, 2:1004-5.
111. Ibid., 2:1006.
112. Ibid., 2:1007.
113. Ibid., 2:1008.
114. Ibid., 2:1007-8.
115. Ibid., 2:1009.
116. Ibid., 2:1010.
117. Ibid., 2:1011.
118. Ibid.
119. Ibid., 3:1420.
120. *HWS*, 4:223.
121. Harper, *Life of Anthony*, 3:1198-99.
122. Ibid., 3:1286-87.
123. Ibid., 3:1199-1200.
124. It is, humanly speaking, easy to understand stereotypes and caricatures of people rarely encountered. It is perplexing that in the structure of sexism, women and men live in the greatest intimacy with each other, and that women regularly feel their personalities are unperceived in these situations—perhaps even by other women.
125. Anthony, Diary, 1853-1855. This comment referred to the Civil War, evidently written in the back of an earlier diary. Since the parallels between black slavery and "sex-slavery" were so vivid to Anthony, I look to these notions about justice in her antislavery work.
126. Harper, *Life of Anthony*, 3:1350.
127. Anthony, "Speech on the Fourth of July, 1862."
128. Anthony, "Speech on the Civil War and Slavery."
129. *HWS*, 5:742.
130. Ibid., 4:333-34.
131. Harper, *Life of Anthony*, 3:1137.
132. Ibid., 2:595.
133. *HWS*, 4:224.
134. Harper, *Life of Anthony*, 2:631.
135. Ibid., 2:857.
136. Ibid., 2:923.

137. Anna Howard Shaw with Elizabeth Jordan, *The Story of a Pioneer* (New York: Harper, 1915), pp. 214-16. As an example of Harper's dressing up Susan B. Anthony's language, this piece is incomparable: "Well," said Miss Anthony, "I don't know anything better to engage his attention. I am sure I should be interested in every good cause just as I am now, and I think I could do a great deal more good by staying near at hand and helping those who are trying to carry on the reforms of this life than I could by soaring to the stars and consorting with the angels." Harper, *Life of Anthony*, 3:1333. However difficult it may be to separate Shaw's rendition of Anthony from Shaw's own perspective, it is not difficult to see that Harper's stilted and genteel version is much farther from the mark.

138. Stanton saw this clearly about Anthony, though she expressed this point in her own terms: "Hers is, indeed, a sincerely religious nature. . . . She first found words to express her conviction in listening to Rev. William Henry Channing, whose teaching had a lasting spiritual influence on her. To-day Miss Anthony is an agnostic. As to the nature of the Godhead and of the life beyond her horizon she does not profess to know anything. Every energy of her soul is centered upon the needs of this world. To her, work is worship. . . . Her belief is not orthodox, but it is religious. In ancient Greece, she would have been a Stoic; in the era of the Reformation, a Calvinist; in King Charles' time, a Puritan; but in this nineteenth century, by the very laws of her being, she is a Reformer." Stanton, *Eighty Years and More*, pp. 160-61. This comment on Anthony's faith has often been misused. Thus Kathleen Barry quotes the first part of it but not the latter part avowing Anthony's religiousness: "In her autobiography, Elizabeth Cady Stanton described Susan's spirituality as that of an agnostic. Susan never denied the existence of God, but her beliefs were secularized and lodged in the world around her." (*Susan B. Anthony*, p. 96.) Here Barry apparently equates supernaturalism with religion.

139. Harper, *Life of Anthony*, 2:595.
140. Kraditor, *Ideas of the Woman Suffrage Movement*, p. 66, ellipsis in original.
141. Susan B. Anthony to Anna Howard Shaw, January 5, 1889, Folder 18, Anthony Family Papers, Schlesinger Library.
142. Harper, *Life of Anthony*, 2:918.
143. Anthony, Diary 1853-1855 with scattered later entries. This strong statement that Eliza T. would rather Anthony be a slaveholder than reject the plenary inspiration of the Bible is an index of how deeply true it was among ordinary believers as among theological leaders of the nineteenth century that "the inspiration of the Scriptures tended to become the only scandal of Christianity." Martin E. Marty, *The Infidel* (Cleveland: World Publishing Co., 1961), p. 117.
144. Harper, *Life of Anthony*, 2:899. This paragraph's disclaimers about the "before and after" were a regular feature of Anthony's religious thought. When asked directly by an interviewer whether she believed in immortality, she answered, "I don't know anything about heaven or hell or whether I will meet my friends again or not, but as no particle of matter is ever destroyed, I have a feeling that no particle of mind is ever lost. I am sure that the same wise power which

manages the present may be trusted with the hereafter. . . . I'm just as much in eternity now as after the breath goes out of my body." Ibid., 2:859. The significant exceptions to this agnosticism about an afterlife occur in specific contexts of the relationships between women in the suffrage struggle, or that of her family.

145. Ibid., 2:708. "Breaking the yoke and letting the oppressed go free" is from Isaiah 58:6 or one of its parallels. It is important to emphasize these echoes of the Old Testament prophets in Anthony's faith. Barry's biography of Anthony quotes such texts in her mouth (for instance, p. 146) without appearing to notice that these phrases are from the Bible and therefore might have some important relationship to religion.

Barry thus misreads Anthony's faith as related to nature: "Like the transcendentalists who found God immanent in nature, Susan found the richness of her spiritual life in the glories of the natural world" (p. 242). This misreading is unfortunate because Barry has quite thoroughly grasped Anthony's clarity about *action*. Her own theoretical terms apparently prevent her from seeing the connection to religion. (They also let her assert both Anthony's spirituality and her secularity, as in note 138 above, without concern about whether these contradict each other.)

146. She was fond of Emerson's dictum "God answers only such prayers as men themselves answer." Ibid., 1:457. Or as she put it in a temperance speech of 1853, "If we would have God answer our prayers, they must be accompanied by corresponding action." Susan B. Anthony, "Temperance Speech of 1853," Folder 22, Anthony Family Papers, Schlesinger Library.

147. Harper, *Life of Anthony*, 2:709.

148. Ibid., 4:457.

149. Ibid.

150. It was perhaps Theodore Parker's "The Transient and the Permanent in Religion" that stood behind such distinctions. We have seen Stanton's acquaintance with this classic piece of American theology. Anthony's use of these categories is quite different from her friend's position. It was structural change by way of the franchise, not the great immutable laws of nature, that bore the weight of Anthony's use.

151. Harper, *Life of Anthony*, 2:859.

152. An early temperance speech attacked the use of "the anathema of *Infidel*, which is so universally bestowed upon all who dare enter the sacred portals of that hoary institution, the Church, and openly and fearlessly point out wherein it fails to *live* that blessed injunction, 'Love thy neighbor as thyself'—that command on which hangs all the law and the prophets." Susan B. Anthony, "The Church and the Liquor Traffic," Susan B. Anthony Papers, Library of Congress.

153. Ibid.

154. Anthony, Diary, 1853-1855. The citation was attributed to Francis Wright's *Few Days in Athens, or Epicurus*. Anthony copied extracts and quotable quotes

from Carlyle, George Sand, Horace Mann, Mrs. Gaskell, Mme. de Staël into the back of this copybook.

155. Susan B. Anthony, Diary, December 11, 1872, Susan B. Anthony Papers, Library of Congress.

156. Harper, *Life of Anthony*, 2:678.

157. Susan B. Anthony, Diary, June 23, 1873, Susan B. Anthony Papers, Library of Congress.

158. Susan B. Anthony, Diary, December 18, 1870, Susan B. Anthony Papers, Library of Congress. To a sermon of Henry Ward Beecher's, on the other hand, she was far less generous. "H.B. tried [to] show the harmony between Law and supernatural action—said God was over and above his laws and could set them aside—children may be filled with such pap—but not full fledged brains—." Anthony, Diary, September 11, 1870.

159. Harper, *Life of Anthony*, 2:648. She had, of course, specific doctrinal stands. When she heard a Baptist minister in the Midwest who "disavowed the vicarious atonement—said there was not one particle less suffering because of the blood of Christ," her reaction was clear: "This seemed to me a new phase of orthodoxy." Susan B. Anthony, Diary, September 3, 1865, Susan B. Anthony Papers, Library of Congress. She had as little use for doctrines of sin as Stanton did. As she said of the Rev. Thomas K. Beecher, "his theology, as set forth that evening, is a dark and hopeless one. He sees no hope for the progress of the race, does not believe that education even will improve the species. I find great apathy wherever the clergy are opposed to the advancement of women." Harper, *Life of Anthony*, 1:125. Or, as she put it about another Methodist minister, he was "devoid of the first spark of reverence for humanity, therefore must be equally so for God." Ibid., 1:119. When her beloved William Henry Channing announced that he believed in miracles, in even the mildest way ("I never disbelieved in miracles. Man's levelling and tunnelling the mountains is a miracle"), Anthony was "stunned" and thought "it must be—simply the waning intellect returning to childish teachings." Ibid., 2:563. These *doctrines* were peripheral to her view.

160. Ibid., 2:793. This formal statement that the "essence of religion and the fundamental principle of government" are to be found in equal rights seems rather stilted for Anthony, and may be redolant of Stanton's influence.

Anthony referred to the "great immutable laws" that were such a large portion of her friend's position. In the antislavery struggle, for example, she was discouraged by the apathy of the masses, but "in every town there are some true spirits who walk in God's sunshine and do what is right, trusting results to the great Immutable Law." Ibid., 1:158.

161. Anthony, Diary, 1853-1855.

162. Katherine Anthony, *Susan B. Anthony*, p. 261. On this same Utah visit she was reported to have said, sweepingly, "Away with your man-visions! Women propose to reject them all, and begin to dream dreams for themselves" (p. 262).

163. *Life of Anthony*, Harper, 1:396.

164. Ibid., 2:1011.
165. Ibid.
166. Susan B. Anthony to Elizabeth Cady Stanton, February 20, 1861, Container 1, Elizabeth Cady Stanton Papers, Library of Congress. The exceptions to this action-oriented approach occur in the context of her family in crisis. On the death of her brother Merritt, she wrote his daughter Lucy, "Well—let us all be *still*—and know that *law* and *order* rule the universe and us with it." Susan B. Anthony to Lucy E. Anthony, June 8, 1900, Folder 20, Anthony Family Papers, Schlesinger Library. To another niece on her impending marriage, she counselled (surprisingly): "So my dear—all from without is, and will be, right—the within must be the source of help to each and all of us." Susan B. Anthony to Anna O. Anthony, July (?) 7, 1900, Folder 20, Anthony Family Papers, Schlesinger Library.
167. Harper, *Life of Anthony*, 2:847. This despite the fact that one of Anthony's earliest speeches, "The Church and the Liquor Traffic," was just as sharply honed a critique of the churches for participation in the liquor trades. The piece called for a boycott of all individuals and economic matters connected in any way with the production or sale of alcohol, a secondary boycott, in fact.
168. Harper, *Life of Anthony*, 2:856-57.
169. Ibid., 2:853-54.
170. Ibid., 2:678.
171. Liberals identified her expressly as an ally of their cause, albeit in somewhat illiberal fashion in some cases. Jenkin Lloyd Jones and his Liberal Religious Congress not only invited her to speak but claimed her as a vice president of the organization without her consent and indeed over her protests. She did agree to address at least one gathering of that organization. Ibid., 2:804-5, 928.
172. Ibid., 2:857.
173. Ibid., 2:856.
174. Ibid., 3:1215.
175. Ibid., 2:855.
176. Ibid., 2:856, ellipsis in original.
177. Ibid., 1:857.
178. Ibid., 2:634.
179. Blackwell's theological work has been ably described by Elizabeth Cazden, *Antoinette Brown Blackwell: A Biography* (Old Westbury, N.Y.: The Feminist Press, 1983). Ocean, atoms, pulse, and God combined in a fluid unity of images for her as in a 1902 poem, in which the ocean's tides are "like God's own love . . . the slow, time-beating pulse of cosmic life. . . . Athrob! Athrob! in ceaseless ebb and flow/ Systole, dyastole, of breathing sea/ And thy full beating pulse is kin to man's/ The heart throbs of a common joyous life" (p. 240).
180. *Report of the International Council of Women*, p. 421. This statement deserves to stand among the definitive expositions of the civil religion of the woman suffrage movement, but on quite different grounds than Stanton's. Like Benjamin Franklin a century earlier, Cheney was looking for some great truths

that were at the basis of the variety she heard around her, some truths that could unite suffragists, form a basis of harmony rather than dissension. The central truths that Parker taught were at the "basis of all morality"; like Franklin's "publick religion," faith pared away to its core produced ethics. (In contrast to Franklin, however, Cheney's two points were a streamlined version.) The explicitly religious statements she had heard earlier represented an "abstract expression" of something, presumably, more concrete. One of the problems of this perspective is precisely there: The fatherhood of God and the brotherhood of man seem hardly more concrete than the statements of her predecessors. Equally, this view depends on the notion that religion is a *motive*, a motive for action in "great philanthropic and human enterprises" to be sure, but essentially a matter of the private belief of an individual.

181. Ibid., p. 422.
182. Ibid., p. 424.
183. Harper, *Life of Anthony*, 3:1181.
184. That the late nineteenth and early twentieth centuries in theology and other disciplines were marked by their greater appreciation of the "social" virtues will be no surprise. This was equally true of the woman suffrage movement after its initial generation, fed on the individualism of the Enlightenment, passed somewhat from the scene. The lead quote of this section, from 1900, is indicative. Ida C. Hultin claimed that "the work of every woman has touched that of every other." Ibid., 3:1182. Harriet Stanton Blatch's tribute to the friendship of Anthony and Stanton called it the dimension of the movement that would endure long after the victory had been won. Ibid., 3:1186-87. The latter part of the century's convocations were filled with references to "cooperation."
185. Susan B. Anthony to Elizabeth Cady Stanton, September 27, 1857, Container 1, Elizabeth Cady Stanton Papers, Library of Congress.
186. *HWS*, 4:401.
187. Lutz, *Susan B. Anthony*, p. 308.
188. Harper, *Life of Anthony*, 3:1419.
189. Sometimes Shaw associated these beliefs with the blackly despairing moods into which she was thrown—and with an orthodox Easter faith, as when she wrote in 1910: "I should like to go to Mt. Hope and sit beside Aunt Susan's grave and feel close to her, though she too, if Christ arose from the dead, is risen and is here with me now in the blackness of my despair." Anna Howard Shaw to Lucy E. Anthony, Easter A.M., 1910, Folder 427, Mary Earhart Dillon Collection, Schlesinger Library. She also made such remarks on occasions of great celebration. When Wilson finally announced his support for the suffrage amendment, Shaw wrote to Lucy Anthony: "I wonder if Aunt Susan was there." Anna Howard Shaw to Lucy E. Anthony, September 30, 1918, Folder 427, Mary Earhart Dillon Collection, Schlesinger Library. During Anthony's final days, however, Shaw did not include all this embroidery, if embroidery it be, on the story. "Aunt Susan said today the faces of the friends and workers passed before her; she could not call their names but could see their faces and

thought of them so often. She wanted to send a word. I asked if I should give them her love and all she said was, 'Yes, tell them I love them all.' " Anna Howard Shaw to Lucy E. Anthony, March 8, 1906, Folder 427, Mary Earhart Dillon Collection, Schlesinger Library.

190. Such words in Anthony's mouth resonated Christ's promise, "I will be with you always even unto the end of the age." Suffrage myths did not stop at canonizing her. She was spoken of with analogies to the divine mother on more than one occasion. See Harper, *Life of Anthony*, 3:1380, 1411.

191. *HWS*, 5:191-92.

192. Harper, *Life of Anthony*, 2:952.

193. Ibid., 3:1345.

194. Katherine Anthony, *Susan B. Anthony*, p. 199.

195. *HWS*, 4:224.

196. Ibid., 5:31.

197. Ibid., 4:223.

198. Ibid., 4:204.

199. Harper, *Life of Anthony*, 3:1136. Like her calling the younger generation of workers her "half-fledged chickens," Anthony's references to her "girls" were condescending from our understanding today. This was felt occasionally by her contemporaries: "On behalf of the 'girls,' I although sixty years old, beg to thank Miss Anthony for what she has done toward the upraising of womanhood and humanhood. Many of us here present are already grey-haired, but still we confess ourselves inexperienced 'girls,' who receive with thankfulness the inheritance she has given us." Ibid.

200. Ibid., 3:1116.

201. Ibid., 3:1201. Sometimes she was more acerbic, conscious of the times when a public word from one of these quiet ones would have been helpful. Even then she did not deny their importance: "I told some of our friends the other day that, as it had been a few of us who stood at the front that had had to take all the pelting when it was with moral brickbats and ugly epithets, while the women who stayed quietly in their homes got no such treatment, so now when the pelting for those of us who are left is of roses and good words, the women who stood behind us all through the hard times are getting no mention. It cannot be helped and there is a sort of justice in it, you see; but nevertheless, without the support of those quiet ones our work could not have been done." Ibid.

202. Ibid., 3: 1263.

203. Anthony, "Church and the Liquor Traffic."

NOTES TO PAGES 221-224

CHAPTER FIVE

1. Anna Howard Shaw, "Select Your Principle of Life," in "The Collected Speeches of Anna Howard Shaw," ed. Wilmer Albert Linkugel, 2 vols. (Ph.D. dissertation, University of Wisconsin, 1960), 2:856.
2. Shaw and Jordan, *Story of a Pioneer*, p. 58.
3. Ibid., p. 93.
4. Anna Howard Shaw, "We Demand Equal Voting Qualifications," in Linkugel, "Speeches," 2:803-4.
5. She was given to depression even during her greatest triumphs; her correspondence with Lucy Anthony bears frequent testimony to her black moods of despair. Like a good Christian she blamed herself for complaining. "It is so wicked for us ever to complain and I resolve that I never will again." Anna Howard Shaw to Lucy E. Anthony, July 22, 1900, Folder 422, Mary Earhart Dillon Collection Series XI, Schlesinger Library. "I slave continually and it does not seem to count and yet it is my own fault." Anna Howard Shaw to Lucy E. Anthony, no date but 1915, Folder 426, Mary Earhart Dillon Collection Series XI, Schlesinger Library. Some of this was surely fatigue from her countless suffrage campaigns and hardships. Some of it was simply lack of self-esteem. Her colleagues thought she won more people to suffrage than any other single advocate. See Carrie Chapman Catt and Nettie Rogers Shuler, *Woman Suffrage and Politics* (New York: Charles Scribner's Sons, 1923; Seattle: University of Washington Press, 1969), pp. 268-69. Nonetheless, she feared that she "would kill the cause every time" she spoke. Anna Howard Shaw to Lucy E. Anthony, no date but 1908, Folder 425, Mary Earhart Dillon Collection Series XI, Schlesinger Library.
6. Shaw and Jordan, *Story of a Pioneer*, p. 89.
7. Ibid., p. 106.
8. Anna Howard Shaw to Lucy E. Anthony, September 27, 1906, Folder 425, Mary Earhart Dillon Collection Series XI, Schlesinger Library.
9. During their South Dakota campaign together, Anthony took Shaw on her lap, calling the younger woman her "baby." Anna Howard Shaw to Lucy E. Anthony, no date but 1890s, Folder 420, Mary Earhart Dillon Collection Series XI, Schlesinger Library.
10. She wrote Lucy Anthony in terms of endearment we have come to expect from women before the twentieth century: "I am thankful that out of all the world in my hour of need God brought you to me. The future with what it has for us I trust we may be permitted to share together. The rooms are light and cheerful and we can make them very pretty with the wash stand in the back room. Let us settle down to the thought and I will be content anywhere that my home-maker chooses to make our home nest. I want you in it and it will be home to me." Anna Howard Shaw to Lucy E. Anthony, March 6, 1891, Folder 421, Mary Earhart Dillon Collection Series XI, Schlesinger Library. On women's relationships in this period, see Carroll Smith-Rosenberg, "The Female

World of Love and Ritual: Relations between Women in Nineteenth-Century America," *Signs* 1 (Autumn 1975): 1-30.
11. Shaw and Jordan, *Story of a Pioneer*, p. 192.
12. Ibid.
13. *HWS*, 5:262.
14. Anna Howard Shaw to Lucy E. Anthony, September 1906, Folder 425, Mary Earhart Dillon Collection Series XI, Schlesinger Library.
15. Some of the tension in suffrage ranks may have come from the distance between workers in the front lines and those who did not know the field. There was no ambivalence about where Shaw stood in such disagreements. Writing to her beloved Lucy about the bedbugs and dirt of South Dakota campaign, she spared little sarcasm on the more dilettantish suffragists: "Oh, this is fun. I wish some of the rich Massachusetts suffragists could endure it a little. I think those Wianno (Winanno?) people would prefer to smell the salt sea and fan themselves and talk palmistry and hypnotism and ethics and Emerson and agnosticism and their idea of woman suffrage, while they neither subscribe a dollar nor get anyone else to do so to enable us to stop at decent places while we do the work they dream about. And then when one of them condescends to notice one of us we ought to go into spasms over their loveliness. Oh, but this trip I hope has cured me of the folly of self-sacrifice and sentiment. I am through with the whole business. You count in suffrage and among workers not for what you do and give and suffer but for what you have got and keep and talk." Anna Howard Shaw to Lucy E. Anthony, September 9, 1890, Folder 420, Mary Earhart Dillon Collection Series XI, Schlesinger Library. Despite Shaw's efforts to strengthen the grass-roots of the organization, several state campaigns seemed dreadfully mismanaged at the local level. One example of her reflections indicated that she had more political sense than she gave herself credit for in the quotation in the text. "It seems useless and especially so here. Women are so frightened to do anything but must falter and wait and do so little. Mrs. Steinem does try but she is so afraid and so delighted because she has got a few society ladies in her work that she thinks she has everything. I told her she must get into the factories and shops and she said she was going to later on, that Mrs. Upton said she was going to have Rose Schneiderman in the State and that she could have three or four days. I told her she needed three or four people everyday until election, on the street corners, in the yards everywhere. It is that cocksure feeling that because Mayor Wheelock and a few others are standing by they will surely win that frightens me." Anna Howard Shaw to Lucy E. Anthony, May 11, 1911, Folder 426, Mary Earhart Dillon Collection Series XI, Schlesinger Library. See also Anna Howard Shaw to Lucy E. Anthony, October 25, 1910, Folder 425; August 12, 1912, Folder 426, Mary Earhart Dillon Collection Series XI, Schlesinger Library.

In NAWSA in-fighting Shaw could hold her own. While it was not clear what the tension was between her and Carrie Chapman Catt, she advised Anthony to get in the first blow in some altercation between them. "Remember, do as you expect the other fellow to do to you, but do it first." Anna Howard Shaw to Lucy E. Anthony, February 1, 1901, Folder 424, Mary Earhart Dillon Collection Series XI, Schlesinger Library. On the other hand, she thought, that Catt "realized more than anyone else except Aunt Susan, what my work has been for in the suffrage movement" and that, in keeping with Shaw's grass-roots interest, was "because she is out in the field and sees it." Anna Howard Shaw to Lucy E. Anthony, April 5, 1902, Folder 42 , Mary Earhart Dillon Collection Series XI, Schlesinger Library.

16. Anna Howard Shaw to Lucy E. Anthony, June 1916, Folder 426, Mary Earhart Dillon Collection Series XI, Schlesinger Library.

17. Anna Howard Shaw to Lucy E. Anthony, October 7, 1916 and April 1914, respectively, Folder 426, Mary Earhart Dillon Collection Series XI, Schlesinger Library. Shaw thought Alice Paul was only after publicity and that the stories of mistreatment of militant suffragists in American jails were "lies." Anna Howard Shaw to Lucy E. Anthony, June 20 and 21, 1917, Folder 427, Mary Earhart Dillon Collection Series XI, Schlesinger Library.

18. Shaw and Jordan, *Story of a Pioneer*, p. 316.

19. Anna Howard Shaw, "Woman Suffrage and the National Constitution," in Linkugel, "Speeches," 2:621-22.

20. Anna Howard Shaw to Lucy Burns, November 19, 1913, Anna Howard Shaw folder, Box SO, NAWSA Papers, Library of Congress.

21. *HWS*, 5:290.

22. Ibid., 5:313.

23. Ibid., 5:335.

24. Ibid., 5:519, 531.

25. Ibid., 5:538-39.

26. Were I to speculate on the decline of religion within the movement, here is where I would begin. It was the rise of these modern techniques that displaced the inspirational and educational approach of the earlier years. Any "secularization" there was in the woman suffrage movement needs to be explicitly understood not simply as the cessation of references of God, Bible, faith, but as a phase of bureaucratization. But without a systematic study of one or more of the proponents of these new methods, such as Carrie Chapman Catt, it is impossible to make such judgments about the "decline" of religion in the movement.

27. *HWS*, 5:441.

28. Anna Howard Shaw to Lucy E. Anthony, October 9, 1890, Folder 420, Mary Earhart Dillon Collection Series XI, Schlesinger Library.

29. Anna Howard Shaw to Lucy E. Anthony, 1897, Folder 422, Mary Earhart Dillon Collection Series XI, Schlesinger Library.

30. It is unclear what has become of Shaw's voluminous letters, particularly those to Lucy E. Anthony, who was evidently reluctant to part with the material Shaw left her. The Schlesinger Library contains typewritten excerpts from the Shaw-Anthony correspondence, perhaps compiled by Ida Husted Harper. Harper was to have written a Shaw biography; though she never completed this work, she seems to have been responsible for burning "bushels and

bushels" of newspaper clippings. Lucy E. Anthony to Mary Earhart Dillon, May 5, 1943, Folder 409, Mary Earhart Dillon Collection, Series XI, Schlesinger Library. From my correspondence with Dillon, she does not know what became of the originals.

31. Anna Howard Shaw, "The Other Half of Humanity," in Linkugel, "Speeches," 2:219.
32. Anna Howard Shaw, "The Fundamental Principle of a Republic," in Linkugel, "Speeches," 2:274.
33. Anna Howard Shaw, "Woman's Right to Suffrage," in Linkugel, "Speeches," 2:92.
34. Anna Howard Shaw, "The Great Defect in Our Government," in Linkugel, "Speeches," 2:150.
35. Anna Howard Shaw, "It's Coming," in Linkugel, "Speeches," 2:616.
36. Anna Howard Shaw, "Is Democracy a Failure?," in Linkugel, "Speeches," 2:574.
37. Anna Howard Shaw, "A Republican Form of Government," in Linkugel, "Speeches," 2:303.
38. Ibid.
39. Ibid.
40. Shaw, "We Demand Equal Voting Qualifications," 2:790.
41. Shaw, "Woman's Right to Suffrage," 2:92.
42. Shaw, "We Demand Equal Voting Qualifications," 2:795.
43. Ibid., 2:799-800.
44. Shaw, "It's Coming," 2:616.
45. Anna Howard Shaw, "The True Voice of God," in Linkugel, "Speeches," 2:688.
46. Shaw, "We Demand Equal Voting Qualifications," 2:790.
47. Anna Howard Shaw, "Divine Harmony through Equal Suffrage," in Linkugel, "Speeches," 2:190.
48. Shaw, "Great Defect," 2:157.
49. Ibid., 2:160.
50. Anna Howard Shaw, "Enlightened Kansas," in Linkugel, "Speeches," 2:145.
51. Shaw, "Great Defect," 2:155.
52. Anna Howard Shaw, "The Fundamental Principle of a Republic," in Linkugel, "Speeches," 2:261.
53. Ibid.
54. Shaw, "Great Defect," 2:156.
55. Anna Howard Shaw, "The Fate of Republics," in Linkugel, "Speeches," 2:398.
56. Anna Howard Shaw, "Freedom is Coming," in Linkugel, "Speeches," 2:554.
57. Ibid.
58. Ibid., 2:553.
59. Shaw, "Is Democracy a Failure?," 2:568.
60. Ibid., 2:584.
61. Anna Howard Shaw, "The Nature of Democracy," in Linkugel, "Speeches," 2:773. Linkugel suggests that because of this statement in 1913 the

Anti-Suffrage Association forbid its members ever to debate Shaw again (2:757).

62. Shaw, "Republican Form of Government," 2:314.
63. Shaw, "Divine Harmony," 2:194.
64. Ibid., 2:195.
65. Ibid., 2:195-96.
66. Shaw "Woman's Right to Suffrage," 2:97.
67. Shaw, "Other Half of Humanity," 2:233.
68. Shaw, "Nature of Democracy," 2:770.
69. Ibid., 2:761-62.
70. Shaw, "Republican Form of Government," 2:309.
71. Anna Howard Shaw, "The Emotional Sex," in Linkugel, "Speeches," 2:592-93.
72. Shaw, "Republican Form of Government," 2:319-20.
73. Shaw, "Fundamental Principle," 2:272.
74. Shaw did not become involved in the work of American blacks. Like Stanton, she frequently asserted that the disfranchisement of women was especially degrading because American women were ruled by the men of many races and nations. "The United States has subjected its women to the greatest political humiliation ever imposed upon the women of any nation. German women are governed by German men; French women by Frenchmen, etc., but American women are ruled by the men of every country and race in the world." Anna Howard Shaw, "An Insuperable Barrier to Self-Government," in Linkugel, "Speeches," 2:591.

She spoke out against lynching, though it is not clear how early she did so. The extant speech on this subject is very late (1919) and ambivalent. A certain euphemism came over her colloquial style as she hinted at rape, "I have no sympathy, and would never waste a tear on any amount of suffering endured by any man, white or black, who perpetrates that criminal offense against womanhood." She viewed rape in the lurid colors of the day. "There is no form of legal punishment too severe—there is no crime more horrible in all the universe of God." Still she was adamant that lynching was merely mob rule and lawlessness. The black woman "cannot protect herself against the white man any more than the white woman can against the black man." See Anna Howard Shaw, "The Cowardice of the Mob," in Linkugel, "Speeches," 2:991-96.

Her speech on "The White Man's Burden," the ready-made occasion for rampant racism at the turn of the century, was notable for the lack of such statements. It called rather for internal changes in the U.S., and castigated church leadership for allying itself with military force. See Anna Howard Shaw, "The White Man's Burden," in Linkugel, "Speeches," 2:971-86.

Similarly, reviewing the suffrage campaign of 1891 in South Dakota she showed "how Indians in blankets and moccasins were received in the State convention with the greatest courtesy," while eminent women were barely tolerated. She engaged in the invidious comparison of "backward" native Americans with the flower of American womanhood. But she closed with a call to equal justice: "Let all of us who love liberty solve these problems in justice,

367

and let us mete out to the Indian, to the Negro, to the Foreigner, and to the women, the justice which we demand for ourselves, the liberty which we love for ourselves. Let us recognize in each of them that One above, the Father of us all, and that all are brothers, all are one." *HWS*, 4:182-83.
75. Shaw, "Is Democracy a Failure?," 2:582.
76. Anna Howard Shaw, "Farewell," in Linkugel, "Speeches," 2:646.
77. Anna Howard Shaw, "Influence versus Power," in Linkugel, "Speeches," 2:849.
78. Shaw, "Farewell," 2:649.
79. *HWS*, 4:278.
80. Anna Howard Shaw, "The Injustice of Woman's Subjection," in Linkugel, "Speeches," 2:693.
81. Anna Howard Shaw, "Heroic Service in the Cause of Truth," in Linkugel, "Speeches," 2:449-51.
82. Shaw, "Fate of Republics," 2:398-99.
83. Ibid., 2:389-90.
84. Shaw, "Great Defect," 2:175.
85. Shaw, "True Voice," 2:687.
86. Anna Howard Shaw, "For the Common Good," in Linkugel, "Speeches," 2:537-38.
87. Shaw, "Injustice," 2:691-92.
88. Shaw, "Fundamental Principle," 2:278.
89. Anna Howard Shaw, "The Fulfilment of American Ideals," in Linkugel, "Speeches," 2:726.
90. Shaw, "For the Common Good," 2:536-37.
91. Ibid.
92. Shaw, "Freedom," 2:553-54.
93. Shaw, "We Demand Equal Voting Qualifications," 2:794.
94. Shaw, "Heroic Service," 2:444.
95. Shaw, "Is Democracy a Failure?", 2:585-86.
96. Anna Howard Shaw, "Working Women and a Living Wage," in Linkugel, "Speeches," 2:183.
97. Ibid., 2:181-82.
98. Ibid., 2:182-83.
99. Ibid., 2:185.
100. Anna Howard Shaw, "The Degradation of Children and Womanhood," in Linkugel, "Speeches," 2:908.
101. Shaw, "White Man's Burden," 2:981.
102. Shaw, "It's Coming," 2:616-17.
103. She argued against the militant tactics of some suffragists on these same grounds. "I do not believe in war in any form, and if violence on the part of man is undesirable, it is much more so on the part of woman; for woman never appears to less advantage than in physical combats with men." Shaw and Jordan, *Story of a Pioneer*, p. 315.
104. Shaw, "Fate of Republics," 2:390.
105. Anna Howard Shaw, "Feminism," in Linkugel, "Speeches," 2:677.

106. Shaw, "Injustice," 2:690.
107. Shaw, "Feminism," 2:677.
108. Anna Howard Shaw, "Heavenly Vision," in Linkugel, "Speeches," 2:32.
109. Anna Howard Shaw, "Lift Your Standards High," in Linkugel, "Speeches," 2:55.
110. Ibid., 2:62.
111. Shaw, "Heavenly Vision," 2:45-46.
112. Ibid., 2:31.
113. Ibid., 2:29-30.
114. Ibid., 2:38.
115. Ibid.
116. Ibid., 2:39.
117. Ibid., 2:40.
118. Shaw, "Lift Your Standards," 2:57.
119. Shaw, "Heavenly Vision," 2:40.
120. Ibid., 2:42.
121. Shaw, "Lift Your Standards," 2:60.
122. Ibid., 2:61.
123. Ibid., 2:63-64.
124. Anna Howard Shaw, "Let No Man Take Thy Crown," in Linkugel, "Speeches," 2:69.
125. Shaw, "Heavenly Vision," 2:34-35.
126. Ibid., 2:46.
127. Ibid.
128. Shaw, "Degradation," 2:915.
129. Anna Howard Shaw, "Suffrage for Hawaiian Women," in Linkugel, "Speeches," 2:833.
130. Shaw, "Farewell," 2:645. This argument recalls Anthony's sense that America could not hope to bring peace until it was based internally on justice to women.
131. Anna Howard Shaw, "Justice to Woman," in Linkugel, "Speeches," 2:701.
132. Anna Howard Shaw, "What is Americanism?," in Linkugel, "Speeches," 2:666.
133. Shaw, "Heroic Service," 2:465.
134. Shaw, "Is Democracy a Failure?," 2:587.
135. Shaw, "Other Half of Humanity," 2:209.
136. Shaw, "Farewell," 2:640.
137. Ibid.
138. Shaw, "Feminism," 2:674.
139. Ibid., 2:669.
140. Shaw, "Let No Man," 2:70.
141. Anna Howard Shaw, "The Women Who Publish the Tidings Are a Great Host," in Linkugel, "Speeches," 2:85.
142. Shaw, "Farewell," 2:638.
143. Shaw, "Degradation," 2:907.
144. Shaw, "Farewell," 2:640-41.

145. Ibid., 2:636-37.
146. Shaw, "Women Who Publish," 2:82.
147. Phoebe Hanaford, Amanda Way, Amanda Deyo, Celia Burleigh, Anna Garlin Spencer, Mrs. Gillette, Augusta Chapin, Sarah M. Perkins, Florence Kollock, Ada C. Bowles were all affiliated with the AWSA. Only Olympia Brown and Antoinette Brown Blackwell seemed to attend the NWSA meetings as well as those of the AWSA. Regarding the male clergy, there were simply more male members of the AWSA. Henry Ward Beecher, James Freeman Clarke, Bishop Matthew Simpson, Charles G. Ames, Bishop Gilbert Haven are the more well known of the thirty or more easily identifiable (but lesser known) ordained men in the AWSA. It is interesting that Washington Gladden made a brief appearance at an AWSA meeting in New York City in 1872, where he carefully refrained from going on record for the cause. As *HWS* paraphrased his remarks, "he didn't wish to be classed with the opposers to woman suffrage, and yet he didn't see his way clear to espouse it as others on the platform did." *HWS*, 2:815. This statement was a perfect example of the ambivalence that could come over many social gospel leaders on this issue. See Ronald Huff, "Social Christian Clergymen and Feminism During the Progressive Era, 1890-1920" (Ph.D. dissertation, Union Theological Seminary, 1977).
148. *HWS*, 2:841. See also James Freeman Clarke, ibid., 2:768; Henry Ward Beecher, ibid., 2:774; Mrs. M. M. Cole, ibid., 2:807.
149. Ibid., 2:760.
150. See Mary Livermore, ibid., 2:812.
151. Ibid., 2:777.
152. Ibid., 2:857.
153. Ibid., 2:793.
154. Ibid., 2:836.
155. Anna Howard Shaw, "Women in the Ministry," in Linkugel, "Speeches," 2:419.
156. Ibid.
157. Anna Howard Shaw, "The Law of Justice," in Linkugel, "Speeches," 2:106.
158. Shaw, "Other Half of Humanity," 2:211.
159. Shaw, "Republican Form of Government," 2:303.
160. Shaw, "Other Half of Humanity," 2:221.
161. Shaw, "Women Who Publish," 2:83.
162. Shaw, "Other Half of Humanity," 2:208-9.
163. Shaw, "Is Democracy a Failure?," 2:569-70.
164. Shaw, "Freedom," 2:560.
165. Ibid., 2:561.
166. Shaw, "Women Who Publish," 2:84.
167. Ibid., 2:83.
168. Shaw, "Freedom," 2:561.
169. Anna Howard Shaw, "Greater than the Discoverer of a Continent," in Linkugel, "Speeches," 2:957.
170. Shaw, "Select Your Principle," 2:859.
171. Shaw, "Feminism," 2:675.

172. Ibid., 2:674.
173. Ibid., 2:671-72.
174. Shaw, "Farewell," 2:642.
175. Ibid., 2:637.
176. Ibid., 2:642.
177. Shaw, "Lift Your Standards." 2:65
178. Shaw, "Other Half of Humanity," 2:208.
179. Shaw, "Heavenly Vision," 2:46.
180. Ibid.
181. Ibid., 2:45.
182. Ibid., 2:42.
183. Ibid., 2:43.
184. Anna Howard Shaw, "Humanity's Most Potent Weapon," in Linkugel, "Speeches," 2:428-29.
185. Shaw, "Heroic Service," 2:464-65.
186. Ibid., 2:472-73.
187. Shaw, "Lift Your Standards," 2:62.
188. Shaw's metaphors tended to be those of voices, of radiance or fire (open the windows of the soul to God's vision; souls at white heat for liberty, carrying the torches ahead of the multitude), sometimes of water (baptism, flowing), or of plenitude (hearts filled with fullness of God).
189. Shaw, "Lift Your Standards," 2:63.
190. Shaw, "Heavenly Vision," 2:37.
191. Shaw, "Select Your Principle," 2:858.
192. Shaw, "What is Americanism?," 2:666.
193. Shaw, "Heavenly Vision," 2:29. The reformer "longs to bring the heart of the world and the heart of truth together that the truth may exercise its transforming power over the life of the world" (2:40).
194. Shaw, "Select Your Principle," 2:857.
195. Ibid., 2:858.
196. Anna Howard Shaw, "All Absorbing Love," in Linkugel, "Speeches," 2:955.
197. Shaw, "Farewell," 2:639.
198. Anna Howard Shaw, "God's Women," in Linkugel, "Speeches," 2:381.
199. Anna Howard Shaw to Lucy E. Anthony, March 19, 1891, Folder 421, Mary Earhart Dillon Collection Series XI, Schlesinger Library.
200. Ibid.
201. Shaw, "Lift Your Standards," 2:57.
202. Shaw, "Heavenly Vision," 2:28.
203. Shaw, "Feminism," 2:667-68. Shaw may have learned the need of these more manly qualities from her NAWSA presidency. Her farewell speech diagnosed "the cause of most if not all the difficulties which have arisen in our work" as "the failure to recognise the obligations which loyalty demands of the members of an association to its officers and to its own expressed will." Shaw, "Farewell," 2:662.
204. HWS, 5:81-82.

205. Shaw, "Heavenly Vision," 2:43.
206. Shaw, "Women Who Publish," 2:82.
207. Shaw, "Working Women," 2:182.
208. Shaw, "All Absorbing Love," 2:955.
209. Anna Howard Shaw, "Strength of Character," in Linkugel, "Speeches," 2:73.
210. Shaw, "God's Women," 2:370.
211. Shaw, "Woman's Right to Suffrage," 2:95-96.
212. Ibid., 2:97.
213. Anna Howard Shaw, "Open Your Doors," in Linkugel, "Speeches," 2:336.
214. Shaw, "Women Who Publish," 2:83.
215. Ibid., 2:77.
216. Shaw, "Strength of Character," 2:83.
217. Shaw, "Heavenly Vision," 2:28.
218. Shaw, "God's Women," 2:373.
219. Ibid., 2:379.
220. Shaw, "Strength of Character," 2:73.
221. Shaw, "Heavenly Vision," 2:27.
222. Shaw, "Women Who Publish," 2:77.
223. Shaw, "White Man's Burden," 2:976.
224. Ibid., 2:977.
225. Ibid., 2:978.
226. Ibid., 2:978-79.
227. *HWS*, 5: 89.
228. Anna Howard Shaw to Lucy E. Anthony, October 21, 1889, Folder 421, Mary Earhart Dillon Collection Series XI, Schlesinger Library.
229. Anna Howard Shaw to Lucy E. Anthony, November 29, 1890, Folder 421, Mary Earhart Dillon Collection Series XI, Schlesinger Library.
230. Anna Howard Shaw to Lucy E. Anthony, 1912, Folder 426, Mary Earhart Dillon Collection Series XI, Schlesinger Library.
231. Anna Howard Shaw to Lucy E. Anthony, October 13, 1910, Folder 425, Mary Earhart Dillon Collection Series XI, Schlesinger Library.
232. *HWS*, 4:171.
233. Anna Howard Shaw to Lucy E. Anthony, March 19, 1891, Folder 421, Mary Earhart Dillon Collection Series XI, Schlesinger Library.
234. Anna Howard Shaw to Lucy E. Anthony, n.d. (1890s?), Folder 420, Mary Earhart Dillon Collection Series XI, Schlesinger Library.
235. Anna Howard Shaw to Lucy E. Anthony, October 22, 1906, Folder 425, Mary Earhart Dillon Collection Series XI, Schlesinger Library.
236. Ibid.
237. Anna Howard Shaw to Lucy E. Anthony, January 21, 1897, Folder 422, Mary Earhart Dillon Collection Series XI, Schlesinger Library.
238. Anna Howard Shaw to Lucy E. Anthony, April 20, 1891, Folder 421, Mary Earhart Dillon Collection Series XI, Schlesinger Library.
239. Shaw, "Feminism," 2:670.
240. Ibid., 2:672-73.

241. Anna Howard Shaw to Lucy E. Anthony, July 7, 1889, Folder 421, Mary Earhart Dillon Collection Series XI, Schlesinger Library.
242. William Newton Clarke, *Sixty Years With the Bible* (New York: Charles Scribner's Sons, 1909), pp. 153-55.
243. Anna Howard Shaw to Lucy E. Anthony, July 22, 1900, Folder 422, Mary Earhart Dillon Collection Series XI, Schlesinger Library.
244. Shaw, "For the Common Good," 2:547.
245. Clifford Geertz, "Thick Description: Toward an Interpretive Theory of Culture," in *Interpretation of Cultures*, pp. 3-32.
246. Shaw, "Farewell," 2:637.
247. Shaw, "Woman Suffrage and the National Constitution," 2:620.
248. Hannah Arendt, "The Pursuit of Happiness," in *On Revolution*, rev. ed. (New York: Viking Press, 1967), pp. 111-37. However, Arendt's tangible worldly freedom had little in common with Shaw's thought that "true freedom comes from within." Arendt's examples, the visions of heaven in Jefferson and Socrates, the one likening the afterlife to Congress and the other to continuous philosophic dialogue, recall Anthony rather than Shaw; it was Anthony who was sure that nothing in all the glories of heaven would interest her so much as the work for woman suffrage on earth.
249. Shaw, "Is Democracy a Failure?," 2:588.
250. *HWS*, 5:536.
251. Shaw, "All Absorbing Love," 2:955.
252. It is not clear what the precise proportions were. In 1915 Charles Stelzle suggested that men were but one-third of the church rolls, and those mostly older in age. Charles Stelzle, *The Call of the New Day to the Old Church* (New York: Fleming H. Revell Co., 1915), p. 43. Nor is it clear whether these nineteenth- and early twentieth-century proportions of the sexes were continuing a time-honored pattern or represented a new departure. Ann Douglas points to some of the evidence that women had been in the majority in American churches in their earliest days. Douglas, *Feminization of American Culture*, pp. 98-99. Jonathan Edwards, for example, was pleasantly surprised to note that "about the same number of males as females" had been converted in his day, for "by what I have heard Mr. Stoddard say, this was far from what has been usual in years past; for he observed that in his time, many more women were converted than men." See Jonathan Edwards, "Faithful Narrative of the Surprising Work of God," in *The Great Awakening: The Beginnings of Evangelical Pietism in America*, ed. J. B. Bumsted (Waltham: Blaisdell Publishing Co., 1970), p. 41. Nor is there any way of telling whether this shift in the first Great Awakening, if shift there be, was related to the "new measures," among which were the use of women exhorters.
253. As to whether the burden of that male clerical authority had fundamentally shifted toward woman's suffrage at any point before the enactment of the amendment, we do not know. Certainly many well-known church figures had come around. Male ministers whose public support was important enough to be recorded in *HWS* increased from 90 in the years 1876-1885 (vol. 3) to 140

in the period 1883-1900 (vol. 4). Many of these opened services with prayer, by no means to be taken as open-handed support. Beginning around 1890, it was not unusual for *HWS* to point out that in state-by-state campaigns "many ministers" endorsed suffrage. *HWS*, 4:516, 555, 559, 701-2, 820-21, 910, 962-63, 974. By 1905 the Portland *Journal* remarked that "the welcome accorded the women by the Portland pastors was sharply in contrast with the hostility shown by the clergy when the suffrage conventions began in the middle of the last century." *HWS*, 5:140-41. Some of this may have been the "bandwagon effect." Some of it may have been the clerical capacity to reconcile itself to the status quo. Alice Stone Blackwell reported a survey of four denominations in the suffrage states—that is, where women were already enfranchised. There were overwhelmingly supportive clergy responses (for example, eleven to one among Presbyterians) in what was inevitably a self-selected sample of those who responded to the mailing. Of course, supporting the suffrage amendment did not imply that these men favored the ordination of women or other measures of justice.

CHAPTER SIX

1. Shaw, "Nature of Democracy," 2:759.
2. Perelman, *Idea of Justice*, p. 16.
3. My use is slightly different from Perelman's however. In his text the formulas of concrete justice are six: To each the same thing; to each according to his merits; to each according to his works; to each according to his needs; to each according to his rank; to each according to his legal entitlement. Ibid., pp. 17-26. At another point, however, Perelman suggests that there are "Innumerable conceptions of concrete justice" (p. 26).

   I mean rather that "concrete" pertains to specified social and historical circumstances as described in the social analysis. Though these suffragists used a variety of the six formulations, this is less interesting and informative than the social analysis, broadly speaking. In his text it is "equity," a nonformal tendency, which is the "crutch of justice" under specific circumstances (p. 32).
4. Ibid., pp. 27-28.
5. Ibid., pp. 45-59.
6. Ibid., p. 27.
7. Perelman's view seems to be that such general worldviews are emotive rather than cognitive, and hence cannot be "argued." His later work on rhetoric and discursive argument of a "quasi-logical" sort did investigate the forms in which people indicate the reasonableness (rather than the "proof") of such views, by which they invite and persuade others to adhere to them. See Perelman and Olbrichts-Tyteca, *The New Rhetoric*.
8. Mary Daly, *Gyn/Ecology: The Metaethics of Radical Feminism* (Boston: Beacon, 1978).

9. C. Eric Lincoln, *The Black Church since Frazier* (New York: Schocken Books, 1974), pp. 115-16.

10. These theoretical assumptions of liberalism may indeed be fundamental to any feminist theology or ethics. But the empirical fact is that the practical record of liberalism does not appear to be more open than that of the evangelically minded. If we take our bearings from women's leadership inside the churches, it is the sects that have maintained large numbers of women in positions of authority. However, these judgments are complicated by the fact that evangelical orientations seem prone to exceptionalism (i.e., I may preach, but not women in general) and to maintaining devotion to male headship in the home. Equally devastating, in my view, is the fact that such groups retreat from making public demands for social change on such issues.

EPILOGUE

1. At least one major twentieth-century theologian has given a glimpse of the social structures that made it possible for him to pursue his theological gifts. "I am married to a woman who spent a quarter of a century teaching in a woman's college. . . . My wife and I used to have breakfast together. I'd go to my office and see students or write books. My wife had to get the children ready for school, provide for the lunch, and do the housekeeping, in addition to her work as a professor. That is why I say combining the two vocations is very difficult." "An Interview with Reinhold Niebuhr," conducted by John Cogley, *McCall's*, February 1966, p. 91. Niebuhr put his finger on the different relationship between home and work for the two sexes. For the classic analysis of these structures, see Alva Myrdal and Viola Klein, *Women's Two Roles: Home and Work* (London: Routledge and Kegan Paul, 1956); for a more recent view, see Jean Curtis, *Working Mothers* (Garden City: Doubleday, 1976). For a feminist discussion of the social conditions excluding women from the pursuit of art, see Linda Nochlin, "Why Are There No Great Women Artists?" in Gornick and Moran, *Woman in Sexist Society*, pp. 480-510.

2. Simone de Beauvoir, *The Second Sex* (New York: Bantam, 1952), p. 315.

3. See Wilfred Cantwell Smith, *The Meaning and End of Religion* (New York: New American Library, 1964), pp. 139-53. My thanks to my Union Theological Seminary colleague, Professor Jim Washington, for calling my attention to this reference.

4. Saint Augustine, *Confessions*, 9. My thanks to Anne McGlinchey, whose "The Church's Response to Battered Women" (M.Div. thesis, Union Theological Seminary, 1978) brought this reference to my attention.

5. Other structural factors of sexism contribute to the sense of having to do everything at once. Phyllis Chesler has commented on this phenomenon in a different context: "Paradoxically, while women must not 'succeed,' when they do succeed at anything, they have still failed if they're not successful at

everything. Women must be perfect (goddesses) or they're failures (whores). . . . If a woman accomplishes a valuable task, she, unlike men (who, after all, are mortal), *still* has failed if she has, for example, abandoned the daily care of her children or her looks to do so." Phyllis Chesler, *Women and Madness* (Garden City: Doubleday, 1972), p. 277.

6. As a contemporary poet has written: "One serious cultural obstacle encountered by any feminist writer is that each feminist work has tended to be received as if it emerged from nowhere; as if each of us had lived, thought, and worked without any historical past or contextual present. This is one of the ways in which women's work and thinking has been made to seem sporadic, errant, orphaned of any tradition of its own." Adrienne Rich, *On Lies, Secrets and Silence: Selected Prose, 1966-1978* (New York: W. W. Norton, 1979), p. 11.

7. Progress was the characteristic note of these nineteenth-century women's view of history. The last generation of scholarship, however, has largely noted not progress, but ambiguity. Women historians have questioned, for example, the conventional periodization of the Western past on these grounds. The Renaissance, the American Revolution, the Age of Jackson, high points in the traditional perspective, all seem to be regressions for women. See Kelly-Gadol, "Social Relations of the Sexes."

Similar conclusions might be drawn about the periodization of religious history if we take seriously recent research about the status of women in the classic Christian epochs. On the ambiguities of the "patristic period," see Rosemary Radford Ruether, "Mysogynism and Virginal Feminism in the Fathers of the Church," in *Religion and Sexism: Images of Women in the Jewish and Christian Traditions*, ed. Rosemary Radford Ruether (New York: Simon and Schuster, 1974), pp. 150-83; also Elizabeth Schüssler Fiorenza, "Word, Spirit and Power: Women in Early Christian Communities," in Ruether and McLaughlin, *Women of Spirit*, pp. 29-70. On the Reformation, see Jane Dempsey Douglas, "Women and the Continental Reformation," in Ruether, *Religion and Sexism*, pp. 292-318. Ruether and McLaughlin's introduction to the more recent anthology suggests that "the nineteenth century is an important watershed in the history of these traditional models of women's leadership" precisely because "liberalism helped to create a new theology of the relationship between history and transcendent possibility." Ruether and McLaughlin, *Women of Spirit*, pp. 24-27.

8. These general comments about the relationship of having a history to a sense of historical agency into the future should be qualified. The historian's gaze that measures time and change in centuries rather than the smaller scale of months and years has something slightly unworldly about it. This may be the reason for the dissatisfaction with regard to Shaw's reflections about the reformer's history. Recall that she invited her colleagues to view history "as a whole" to find the antidote to despair. "The real reformers" judged from "the vantage ground of all the ages" and saw movement "all down through the centuries." It followed that "infinite hope" was in order, for the reformer was gazing into "the great

eternity of truth." The culmination of the reformer's vision would come at an equally distant date—"by and by," on the worse of her statements. Her perspective dissolved the immediate future foreground of the suffrage movement just as it did the proximate background. It is as though there were a temporal arch cast out in two directions from the present. The span with which one views the past casts an equivalent span toward the future.

Bibliography

Manuscript Collections

Library of Congress, Manuscript Division, Washington, D.C.
   Susan B. Anthony Papers
   National American Woman Suffrage Association Papers
   Elizabeth Cady Stanton Papers

New York Public Library, New York, N.Y.
   The Revolution, January 1868-June 1870
   Smith Family Papers
   Woman Suffrage Scrapbooks

Schlesinger Library, Radcliffe College, Cambridge, Mass.
   Anthony Family Papers
   Anna Howard Shaw Papers, Mary Earhart Dillon Collection Series XI

Books and Articles

Abell, Aaron Ignatius. *The Urban Impact on American Protestantism, 1865-1900*. Hamden: Archon, 1962.

Ahlstrom, Sidney E. *A Religious History of the American People*. New Haven: Yale University Press, 1972.

Albanese, Catherine. "Research Needs in American Religious History." *Council on the Study of Religion Bulletin* 10 (October 1979): 101-5.

Anchor, Robert. *The Enlightenment Tradition*. Berkeley: University of California Press, 1967.

Anderson, Alan B. "The Issue of the Color Line: Some Methodological Considerations." Ph.D. dissertation, University of Chicago, 1975.

Anthony, Katherine. *Susan B. Anthony: Her Personal History and Her Era.* Garden City: Doubleday, 1954.

Anthony, Susan B. "The Church and the Liquor Traffic." Susan B. Anthony Papers. Library of Congress.

_____. Diary, 1853-1855. Anthony Family Papers. Folder 8. Schlesinger Library.

_____. "Speech on the Civil War and Slavery." 1861 or 1862. Folder 26. Anthony Family Papers. Schlesinger Library.

_____. "Speech on the Fourth of July, 1862, Framingham, Mass." Folder 27. Anthony Family Papers. Schlesinger Library.

_____. "Working Man's National Congress." *The Revolution*, September 17, 1868, p. 169.

_____. "Working Woman's Association." *The Revolution*, September 9 1869, p. 154.

_____. "Working Woman's Association No. 2." *The Revolution*, October 1, 1868, p. 198.

Ardener, Shirley, ed. *Perceiving Women.* New York: John Wiley, 1977.

Arendt, Hannah. *Between Past and Future: Eight Exercises in Political Thought.* rev. ed. New York: Viking Press, 1968.

_____. *The Human Condition.* Chicago: University of Chicago Press, 1958.

_____. *On Revolution.* rev. ed. New York: Viking Press, 1967.

Arnold, Matthew. *Literature and Dogma: An Essay towards a Better Appreciation of the Bible.* Boston: James Osgood and Co., 1873.

Barker, Ernest. *Principles of Social and Political Theory.* London: Clarendon Press, 1951; New York: Oxford University Press, 1965.

Barney, Nora Stanton. *Life Sketch of Elizabeth Cady Stanton by her Granddaughter.* Greenwich: n.p., 1949.

Bass, Dorothy, comp. *American Women in Church and Society, 1607-1920.* Auburn Studies in Education, no. 2. New York: Auburn Theological Seminary, 1973.

Beauvoir, Simone de. *The Second Sex.* New York: Bantam Books, 1952.

Bellah, Robert N. *The Broken Covenant: American Civil Religion in Time of Trial.* New York: Seabury Press, 1975.

_____. "Civil Religion in America." *Daedalus* 96 (Winter 1967): 1-21.

Berg, Barbara J. *The Remembered Gate: The Origins of American Feminism; The Woman and the City, 1800-1860.* New York: Oxford University Press, 1978.

Blatch, Harriet Stanton, and Alma Lutz. *Challenging Years: The Memoirs of Harriet Stanton Blatch*. New York: Putnam, 1940.

Bourke, Vernon. *A History of Ethics*. 2 vols. Garden City: Doubleday, 1968.

Branch, E. Douglas. *The Sentimental Years, 1836-1860*. New York: Appelton-Century-Crofts, 1934; New York: Hill and Wang, 1965.

Brandt, Richard B., ed. *Social Justice*. Englewood Cliffs: Prentice-Hall, 1962.

Bullard, Laura Curtis. "Elizabeth Cady Stanton." In *Our Famous Women*.

Bumsted, J. B., ed. *The Great Awakening: The Beginnings of Evangelical Pietism in America*. Waltham: Blaisdell Publishing Co., 1970.

Burke, Kenneth. *A Grammar of Motives*. Berkeley: University of California Press, 1969.

_____. *Language as Symbolic Action*. Berkeley: University of California Press, 1973.

_____. *The Philosophy of Literary Form*. Berkeley: University of California Press, 1971.

_____. *The Rhetoric of Religion: Studies in Logology*. Berkeley: University of California Press, 1970.

Bury, J. B. *The Idea of Progress: An Inquiry into its Growth and Origins*. New York: Macmillan, 1932; New York: Dover, 1955.

Butterfield, Jeanne. "Workers and Organizers, Struggles and Visions: Religion and Nineteenth-Century Women." *Radical Religion* 3 (1976): 30-35.

Carroll, Bernice, ed. *Liberating Women's History: Theoretical and Critical Essays*. Urbana: University of Illinois Press, 1976.

Cassirer, Ernst. *The Philosophy of the Enlightenment*. Princeton: Princeton University Press, 1951.

Catt, Carrie Chapman, and Nettie Rogers Shuler. *Woman Suffrage and Politics*. New York: Charles Scribner's Sons, 1923; Seattle: University of Washington Press, 1969.

Cauthen, Kenneth. *The Impact of American Religious Liberalism*. New York: Harper & Row, 1962.

Chafe, William H. *The American Woman: Her Changing Economic, Social and Political Roles, 1920-1970*. New York: Oxford University Press, 1972.

Chambers, Clarke. *Seedtime of Reform: American Social Service and Social Action, 1918-1933*. Minneapolis: University of Minnesota Press, 1963.

Chesler, Phyllis. *Women and Madness*. Garden City: Doubleday, 1972.

Chevigny, Bell Gale. *The Woman and the Myth: Margaret Fuller's Life and Writings*. Old Westbury: Feminist Press, 1976.

Christ, Carol, and Judith Plaskow, eds. *Womanspirit Rising: A Feminist Reader in Religion*. New York: Harper & Row, 1977.

Clark, Elizabeth, and Herbert Richardson, eds. *Woman and Religion: A Feminist Sourcebook of Christian Thought*. New York: Harper & Row, 1977.

Clarke, William Newton. *Sixty Years with the Bible*. New York: Charles Scribner's Sons, 1909.

Clebsch, William A. *From Sacred to Profane America: The Role of Religion in American History*. New York: Harper & Row, 1968.

Cogley, John. "An Interview with Reinhold Niebuhr." *McCall's*, February 1966, pp. 90-96.

Colby, Clara Bewick. "Elizabeth Cady Stanton." *The Arena* 29 (January 1903): 152-60.

Collins, Sheila. *A Different Heaven and Earth*. Valley Forge: Judson Press, 1974.

Conrad, Susan P. *Perish the Thought: Intellectual Women in Romantic America*. Secaucus: Citadel Press, 1978.

Cooper, James L., and Sheila M. Cooper, eds. *The Roots of American Feminist Thought*. Boston: Allyn and Bacon, 1973.

Cott, Nancy F. *The Bonds of Womanhood: "Woman's Sphere" in New England, 1780-1835*. New Haven: Yale University Press, 1977.

————. "Young Women in the Second Great Awakening in New England." *Feminist Studies* 3 (Fall 1975): 15-29.

————, ed. *Root of Bitterness: Documentary of the Social History of American Women*. New York: E. P. Dutton, 1972.

Cott, Nancy F., and Elizabeth Pleck, eds. *A Heritage of Her Own: Toward a New Social History of American Women*. New York: Simon and Schuster, 1979.

Craigie, Mary. *Christian Citizenship: Would the Extension of the Suffrage to Women Raise the Standard of Christian Citizenship?* New York: National American Woman Suffrage Association, 1912.

Cross, Whitney R. *The Burned-Over District: The Social and Intellectual History of Enthusiastic Religion in Western New York, 1800-1850*. Ithaca: Cornell University Press, 1950; New York: Harper & Row, 1965.

Daly, Mary. *Beyond God the Father: Toward a Philosophy of Women's Liberation*. Boston: Beacon Press, 1973.

————. *The Church and the Second Sex, with a New Feminist Post-Christian Introduction by the Author*. New York: Harper & Row, 1975.

_____. *Gyn/Ecology: The Metaethics of Radical Feminism.* Boston: Beacon, 1978.

Doely, Sarah Bentley, ed. *Woman's Liberation and the Church: The New Demand for Freedom in the Life of the Christian Church.* New York: Association Press, 1970.

Dolbeare, Kenneth M. *Directions in American Political Thought.* New York: John Wiley, 1969.

Douglas, Ann. *The Feminization of American Culture.* New York: Alfred A. Knopf, 1977.

Douglass, Mary. *Implicit Meanings: Essays in Anthropology.* London: Routledge and Kegan Paul, 1975.

_____. *Purity and Danger: An Analysis of Concepts of Pollution and Taboo.* London: Routledge and Kegan Paul, 1966.

Driver, Anne Barstow. "Review Essay: Religion." *Signs* 2 (Winter 1976): 434-42.

DuBois, Ellen Carol. *Feminism and Suffrage: The Emergence of an Independent Woman's Movement in America, 1848-1869.* Ithaca: Cornell University Press, 1978.

_____. "The Radicalism of the Woman Suffrage Movement: Notes Toward the Reconstruction of Nineteenth Century Feminism." *Feminist Studies* 3 (Fall 1975): 63-71.

Duncan, Hugh Dalziel. *Communication and Social Order.* London: Bedminster Press, 1962; New York: Oxford University Press, 1970.

_____. *Symbols in Society.* New York: Oxford University Press, 1968.

Earhart, Mary. *Frances Willard: From Prayers to Politics.* Chicago: University of Chicago Press, 1944.

Farley, Margaret. "New Patterns of Relationship: Beginnings of a Moral Revolution." *Theological Studies* 36 (December 1975): 627-46.

_____. "Sources of Sexual Inequality in the History of Christian Thought." *Journal of Religion* 56 (April 1976): 162-76.

Fiorenza, Elizabeth Schüssler. "Feminist Theology as a Critical Theology of Liberation." *Theological Studies* 36 (December 1975): 605-26.

Fischer, Clare B., comp. *Breaking Through: A Bibliography of Women and Religion.* rev. ed. Berkeley: Center for Woman and Religion, 1979.

Flexner, Eleanor. *Century of Struggle: The Woman's Rights Movement in the United States.* Cambridge: Harvard University Press, 1958; New York: Atheneum, 1971.

Fraser, Dorothy Bass. "Women with a Past: A New Look at the History of Theological Education." *Theological Education* 8 (Summer 1972): 213-24.

Fuller, Margaret. *Woman in the Nineteenth Century.* Edited by Arthur B. Fuller. New York: Tribune Press, 1845; New York: Greenwood Press, 1968.

Gabriel, Ralph Henry. *The Course of American Democratic Thought.* 2d ed. New York: Ronald Press Co., 1956.

Gay, Peter. *The Enlightenment: An Interpretation.* 2 vols. New York: Alfred A. Knopf, 1966-1969.

Geertz, Clifford. *Interpretation of Cultures.* New York: Basic Books, 1973.

_____. *Islam Observed: Religious Development in Morocco and Indonesia.* New Haven: Yale University Press, 1968.

_____, ed. *Myth, Symbol and Culture.* New York: W. W. Norton and Co., 1971.

Gluck, Sherna, ed. *From Parlor to Prison: Five American Woman Suffragists Talk about Their Lives.* New York: Vintage, 1976.

Goldstein, Valerie Saiving. "The Human Situation: A Feminine View." *Journal of Religion* 40 (April 1960): 100-112.

Gornick, Vivian, and Barbara Moran, eds. *Woman in Sexist Society: Essays in Power and Powerlessness.* New York: Basic Books, 1971.

Grimes, Alan P. *The Puritan Ethic and Woman Suffrage.* New York: Oxford University Press, 1967.

Gross, Rita M., ed. *Beyond Androcentrism: New Essays on Women and Religion.* Missoula, Mont.: Scholars Press, 1977.

Hageman, Alice, ed. *Sexist Religion and Women in the Church: No More Silence!* New York: Association Press, 1974.

Handy, Robert T., ed. *The Social Gospel in America: Gladden, Ely, Rauschenbusch.* New York: Oxford University Press, 1966.

Harkness, Georgia. *Woman in Church and Society: A Historical and Theological Inquiry.* Nashville: Abingdon Press, 1972.

Harper, Ida Husted. *The Life and Work of Susan B. Anthony.* 3 vols. Indianapolis: Hollenbeck Press, 1898-1908.

Harrison, Beverly Wildung. "The Early Feminists and the Clergy: A Case Study in the Dynamics of Secularization." *Review and Expositor* 72 (Winter 1975): 41-53.

Hartman, Mary, and Lois W. Banner, eds. *Clio's Consciousness Raised: New Perspectives on the History of Women.* New York: Harper & Row, 1974.

Hazard, Paul. *The European Mind, 1680-1715.* Cleveland: World Publishing Co., 1968.

_____. *European Thought in the Eighteenth Century: From Montesquieu to Lessing.* New Haven: Yale University Press, 1954.

Hesse, Mary. *Models and Analogies in Science.* Notre Dame: University of Notre Dame Press, 1966.

Hewitt, Emily, and Suzanne R. Hiatt. *Woman Priests: Yes or No.* New York: Seabury, 1973.

Heyward, Carter. *A Priest Forever: The Formation of a Woman and a Priest.* New York: Harper & Row, 1976.

Himmelfarb, Gertrude. *Victorian Minds: A Study of Intellectuals in Crisis and of Ideologies in Transition.* New York: Alfred A. Knopf, 1952; New York: Harper & Row, 1970.

Hofstadter, Richard. *The American Political Tradition and the Men Who Made It.* New York: Alfred A. Knopf, 1948; New York: Vintage, 1960.

Hopkins, C. Howard. *The Rise of the Social Gospel in American Protestantism, 1865-1915.* New Haven: Yale University Press, 1940.

Hudson, Winthrop S. *Religion in America.* New York: Charles Scribner's Sons, 1965.

Huff, Ronald. "Social Christian Clergymen and Feminism during the Progressive Era, 1890-1920." Ph.D. dissertation, Union Theological Seminary, 1977.

Jacquet, Constant H., Jr. *Women Ministers in 1977.* New York: Office of Research, Evaluation and Planning, National Council of Churches, 1978.

Kant, Immanuel. *On History.* Edited by Lewis White Beck. Indianapolis: Bobbs-Merrill, 1963.

Katz, Esther, and Anita Rapone, eds. *Women's Experience in America: An Historical Anthology.* New Brunswick: Transaction Books, 1980.

Kelly-Gadol, Joan. "The Social Relations of the Sexes: Methodological Implications of Women's History." *Signs* 1 (Summer 1976): 809-24.

Koch, G. Adolf. *Religion of the American Enlightenment.* New York: Thomas Crowell, 1933.

Kraditor, Aileen. *The Ideas of the Woman Suffrage Movement, 1890-1920.* New York: Columbia University Press, 1965; Garden City: Doubleday, 1971.

_____. *Means and Ends in American Abolitionism: Garrison and His Critics on Strategy and Tactics, 1834-1850.* New York: Vintage Books, 1967.

_____, ed. *Up from the Pedestal: Selected Writings in the History of American Feminism*. Chicago: Quadrangle Books, 1968.

Krichmar, Albert, comp. *The Woman's Rights Movement in the U.S., 1848-1970: A Bibliography and Sourcebook*. Metuchen, N.J.: Scarecrow Press, 1972.

Lageman, Ellen Condliffe. *A Generation of Women: Education in the Lives of Progressive Reformers*. Cambridge: Harvard University Press, 1979.

Lemons, J. Stanley. *The Woman Citizen: Social Feminism in the 1920s*. Urbana: University of Illinois Press, 1973.

Lerner, Gerda. "The Lady and the Mill Girl: Changes in the Status of Women in the Age of Jackson." *Midcontinent American Studies Journal* 10 (Spring 1969): 5-15.

_____. *The Majority Finds Its Past: Placing Women in History*. New York: Oxford University Press, 1979.

_____, ed. *The Female Experience: An American Documentary*. Indianapolis: Bobbs-Merrill, 1977.

Linkugel, Wilmer Albert. "The Speeches of Anna Howard Shaw, Collected and edited with introduction and Notes." Ph.D. dissertation, University of Wisconsin, 1960.

_____. "The Woman Suffrage Argument of Anna Howard Shaw." *Quarterly Journal of Speech* 49 (April 1963): 165-74.

Linkugel, Wilmer Albert, and Kim Griffin. "The Distinguished War Service of Dr. Anna Howard Shaw." *Pennsylvania History* 28 (October 1961): 372-85.

Livingston, James C. *Modern Christian Thought: From the Enlightenment to Vatican II*. New York: Macmillan, 1971.

Lonergan, Bernard. *Method in Theology*. New York: Herder and Herder, 1972.

Lovejoy, Arthur O. *Essays in the History of Ideas*. Baltimore: Johns Hopkins Press, 1948; New York: G. P. Putnam, 1960.

Lutz, Alma. *Created Equal: Elizabeth Cady Stanton, 1815-1902*. New York: John Day, 1940.

_____. "Susan B. Anthony and John Brown." *Rochester History* 15 (July 1953): 1-16.

_____. *Susan B. Anthony: Rebel, Crusader, Humanitarian*. Boston: Beacon, 1959.

McGiffert, Michael, and Robert Allen Skotheim, eds. *American Social Thought: Sources and Interpretations.* 2 vols. Reading, Mass.: Addison-Wesley, 1972.

McGlinchey, Ann. "The Church's Response to Battered Women." M.Div. thesis, Union Theological Seminary, 1978.

McKelvey, Blake. "Susan B. Anthony." *Rochester History* 7 (April 1954): 1-24.

McLoughlin, William G., ed. *The American Evangelicals, 1800-1900.* New York: Harper & Row, 1968.

McLoughlin, William G., and Robert N. Bellah, eds. *Religion in America.* Boston: Beacon, 1968.

McPherson, James M. *The Abolitionist Legacy: From Reconstruction to the N.A.A.C.P.* Princeton: Princeton University Press, 1975.

MacIntyre, Alasdair. *A Short History of Ethics.* New York: Macmillan, 1966.

Marty, Martin E. *The Infidel.* Cleveland: World Publishing Co., 1961.

_____. *Righteous Empire: The Protestant Experience in America.* New York: Dial Press, 1970.

May, Henry F. *The End of American Innocence: A Study of the First Years of Our Own Time, 1912-1917.* New York: Alfred A. Knopf, 1959; Chicago: Quadrangle Books, 1964.

_____. *The Enlightenment in America.* New York: Oxford University Press, 1976.

_____. *Protestant Churches and Industrial America.* New York: Harper & Row, 1949.

Mead, Sidney E. *The Lively Experiment: The Shaping of Christianity in America.* New York: Harper & Row, 1963.

_____. *The Nation with the Soul of a Church.* New York: Harper & Row, 1975.

Melder, Keith. "Ladies Bountiful: Organized Women's Benevolence in Early Nineteenth Century America." *New York History* 48 (July 1967): 231-54.

Miller, Randolph Crump. *The American Spirit in Theology.* Philadelphia: Pilgrim Press, 1974.

Mulder, John M., and John F. Wilson, eds. *Religion in American History: Interpretive Essays.* Englewood Cliffs: Prentice-Hall, 1978.

Myrdal, Alva, and Viola Klein. *Women's Two Roles: Home and Work.* London: Routledge and Kegan Paul, 1956.

Noble, David W. *The Paradox of Progressive Thought.* Minneapolis: University of Minnesota Press, 1967.

Oakley, Mary Ann B. *Elizabeth Cady Stanton*. Old Westbury: Feminist Press, 1972.

Ochs, Carol. *Behind the Sex of God: Toward a New Consciousness— Transcending Matriarchy and Patriarchy*. Boston: Beacon Press, 1977.

Okin, Susan Muller. *Woman in Western Political Thought*. Princeton: Princeton University Press, 1979.

O'Neill, William L. *Everyone Was Brave: A History of Feminism in America*. Chicago: Quadrangle Books, 1971.

Our Famous Women. Hartford: A. D. Worthington and Co., 1884.

Parker, Theodore. *A Discourse of Matters Pertaining to Religion*. 3rd ed. Boston: C. C. Little & J. Brown, 1847.

Patrick, Anne E. "Women and Religion: A Survey of Significant Literature, 1965-1974." *Theological Studies* 36 (December 1975): 737-65.

Peabody, Francis Greenwood. *Jesus Christ and the Social Question*. New York: Grosset and Dunlap, 1900.

Perelman, Ch. *The Idea of Justice and the Problem of Other Arguments*. London: Routledge and Kegan Paul, 1963.

Perelman, Ch., and L. Olbrichts-Tyteca. *The New Rhetoric: A Treatise on Argumentation*. Translated by John Wilkensen and Purcell Weaver. Notre Dame: University of Notre Dame Press, 1969.

Pivar, David J. *Purity Crusade: Sexual Morality and Social Control, 1868-1900*. Westport: Greenwood Press, 1973.

Plaskow, Judith. *Sex, Sin and Grace: Women's Experience and the Theologies of Reinhold Niebuhr and Paul Tillich*. Washington, D.C.: University Press of America, 1980.

Polanyi, Michael. *Personal Knowledge: Towards a Post-Critical Philosophy*. Chicago: University of Chicago Press, 1954; New York: Harper & Row, 1964.

Rawls, John. *A Theory of Justice*. Cambridge: Harvard University Press, 1971.

Reardon, B. M. G. *Religious Thought in the Nineteenth Century*. Cambridge: Cambridge University Press, 1966.

Report of the International Council of Women Assembled by the NWSA, March 25-April 1, 1888. Washington, D.C.: Rufus H. Darby, 1888.

Rich, Adrienne. *On Lies, Secrets and Silence: Selected Prose, 1966-1978*. New York: W. W. Norton, 1979.

Richey, Russell E., and Donald G. Jones, eds. *American Civil Religion*. New York: Harper & Row, 1974.

Ricoeur, Paul. "Creativity in Language." Translated by David Pellauer. *Philosophy Today* 17 (Summer 1973): 97-111.

_____. "The Hermeneutical Function of Distanciation." Translated by David Pellauer. *Philosophy Today* 17 (Summer 1973): 129-41.

_____. "The Problem of the Foundation of Moral Philosophy." Translated by David Pellauer. *Philosophy Today* 22 (Fall 1978): 175-92.

Rosenberg, Charles E. *No Other Gods: On Science and American Social Thought.* Baltimore: Johns Hopkins Press, 1961.

Rossi, Alice, ed. *The Feminist Papers from Adams to de Beauvoir.* New York: Columbia University Press, 1973.

Rothman, Sheila M. *Woman's Proper Place: A History of Changing Ideals and Practices 1890 to the Present.* New York: Basic Books, 1978.

Rueckert, William H., ed. *Critical Responses to Kenneth Burke, 1925-1966.* Minneapolis: University of Minnesota Press, 1969.

Ruether, Rosemary Radford. "The Cult of True Womanhood." *Commonweal,* November 9, 1973, pp. 127-32.

_____. *Liberation Theology: Human Hope Confronts Christian History and American Power.* New York: Paulist Press, 1972.

_____, ed. *New Woman, New Earth: Sexist Ideologies and Human Liberation.* New York: Seabury, 1975.

_____. *Religion and Sexism: Images of Women in the Jewish and Christian Traditions.* New York: Simon and Schuster, 1974.

Ruether, Rosemary Radford, and Eleanor McLaughlin, eds. *Women of Spirit: Female Leadership in the Jewish and Christian Traditions.* New York: Simon and Schuster, 1979.

Russell, Letty M. *Human Liberation in Feminist Perspective—A Theology.* Philadelphia: Westminster Press, 1974.

Ryan, Mary P. "The Power of Women's Networks: A Case Study in Female Moral Reform in Antebellum America." *Feminist Studies* 5 (Spring 1979): 66-68.

Saiving, Valerie. "Androcentrism in Religious Studies." *Journal of Religion* 56 (April 1976): 177-97.

Scanzoni, Letha, and Nancy Hardesty. *All We're Meant to Be: A Biblical Approach to Women's Liberation.* Waco: Word Books, 1975.

Schlesinger, Arthur M., Sr. *A Critical Period in American Religion.* Philadelphia: Fortress Press, 1967.

Schneir, Miriam, ed. *Feminism: The Essential Historical Writings.* New York: Vintage, 1972.

Sellers, James. *Public Ethics: American Morals and Manners*. New York: Harper & Row, 1970.

Sewall, May Wright, ed. *The World's Congress of Representative Women*. 2 vols. Chicago: Rand McNally, 1894.

Shaw, Anna Howard. "All Absorbing Love." In Linkugel, "The Speeches of Anna Howard Shaw," 2:949-56.

_____. "The Degradation of Children and Womanhood." In Linkugel, "The Speeches of Anna Howard Shaw," 2:907-16.

_____. "Divine Harmony through Equal Suffrage." In Linkugel, "The Speeches of Anna Howard Shaw," 2:189-202.

_____. "Equal Suffrage—A Problem of Political Justice." *Annals of the American Academy of Political and Social Science* 56 (November 1914): 93-98.

_____. "Farewell." In Linkugel, "The Speeches of Anna Howard Shaw," 2:635-64.

_____. "The Fate of Republics." In Linkugel, "The Speeches of Anna Howard Shaw," 2:388-401.

_____. "Feminism." In Linkugel, "The Speeches of Anna Howard Shaw," 2:667-683.

_____. "For the Common Good." In Linkugel, "The Speeches of Anna Howard Shaw," 2:533-48.

_____. "Freedom is Coming." In Linkugel, "The Speeches of Anna Howard Shaw," 2:549-64.

_____. "The Fundamental Principle of a Republic." In Linkugel, "The Speeches of Anna Howard Shaw," 2:258-92.

_____. "God's Women." In Linkugel, "The Speeches of Anna Howard Shaw," 2:368-82.

_____. "The Great Defect in Our Government." In Linkugel, "The Speeches of Anna Howard Shaw," 2:149-78.

_____. "Heavenly Vision." In Linkugel, "The Speeches of Anna Howard Shaw," 2:25-48.

_____. "Heroic Service in the Cause of Truth." In Linkugel, "The Speeches of Anna Howard Shaw," 2:433-74.

_____. "The Injustice of Woman's Subjection." In Linkugel, "The Speeches of Anna Howard Shaw," 2:689-96.

_____. "Is Democracy a Failure?" In Linkugel, "The Speeches of Anna Howard Shaw," 2:567-89.

_____. "It's Coming." In Linkugel, "The Speeches of Anna Howard Shaw," 2:615-17.

_____. "Let No Man Take Thy Crown." In Linkugel, "The Speeches of Anna Howard Shaw," 2:67-71.

_____. "Lift Your Standards High." In Linkugel, "The Speeches of Anna Howard Shaw," 2:49-66.

_____. "Men of America on Trial for Democracy." *The Public*, August 24, 1917, pp. 813-14.

_____. "The Nature of Democracy." In Linkugel, "The Speeches of Anna Howard Shaw," 2:757-74.

_____. "The Other Half of Humanity." In Linkugel, "The Speeches of Anna Howard Shaw," 2:207-46.

_____. "A Republican Form of Government." In Linkugel, "The Speeches of Anna Howard Shaw," 2:302-52.

_____. "Select Your Principle of Life." In Linkugel, "The Speeches of Anna Howard Shaw," 2:850-62.

_____. "Strength of Character." In Linkugel, "The Speeches of Anna Howard Shaw," 2:72-73.

_____. "The True Voice of God." In Linkugel, "The Speeches of Anna Howard Shaw," 2:684-88.

_____. "We Demand Equal Voting Qualifications." In Linkugel, "The Speeches of Anna Howard Shaw," 2:789-816.

_____. "What is Americanism?" In Linkugel, "The Speeches of Anna Howard Shaw," 2:665-66.

_____. "The White Man's Burden." In Linkugel, "The Speeches of Anna Howard Shaw," 2:971-90.

_____. "Woman Suffrage and the National Constitution." In Linkugel, "The Speeches of Anna Howard Shaw," 2:618-43.

_____. "Woman's Right to Suffrage." In Linkugel, "The Speeches of Anna Howard Shaw," 2:88-104.

_____. "The Women Who Publish the Tidings Are a Great Host." In Linkugel, "The Speeches of Anna Howard Shaw," 2:74-87.

_____. "Working Women and a Living Wage." In Linkugel, "The Speeches of Anna Howard Shaw," 2:179-88.

Shaw, Anna Howard, with Elizabeth Jordan. *The Story of a Pioneer*. New York: Harper, 1915.

Sherman, Julia, and Evelyn Norton Beck,, eds. *The Prism of Sex: Essays in the Sociology of Knowledge*. Madison: University of Wisconsin Press, 1979.

Sinclair, Andrew. *The Emancipation of the American Woman*. New York: Harper & Row, 1966.

Sizer, Sandra S. *Gospel Hymns and Social Religion: The Rhetoric of Nineteenth-Century Revivalism*. Philadelphia: Temple University Press, 1978.

Sklar, Katheryn Kish. *Catherine Beecher: A Study in American Domesticity*. New Haven: Yale University Press, 1973.

Smith, Timothy L. *Revivalism and Social Reform: American Protestantism on the Eve of the Civil War*. New York: Harper & Row, 1965.

Smith, Wilfred Cantwell. *The Meaning and End of Religion*. New York: New American Library, 1964.

Smith-Rosenberg, Carroll. "The Female World of Love and Ritual: Relations between Women in Nineteenth-Century America." *Signs* 1 (Autumn 1975): 1-30.

_____. "The New Woman and the New History." *Feminist Studies* 3 (Fall 1975): 185-98.

_____. *Religion and the Rise of the American City: The New York City Mission Movement, 1812-1870*. Ithaca: Cornell University Press, 1971.

Sochen, June. *Movers and Shakers: American Woman Thinkers and Activists, 1900-1970*. New York: Quadrangle, 1973.

Stanton, Elizabeth Cady. *Address of Mrs. Elizabeth Cady Stanton Delivered at Seneca Falls and Rochester, New York, July 19 and August 2d, 1848*. New York: Robert J. Johnston, 1870.

_____. "An Address of Elizabeth Cady Stanton on the Divorce Bill Before the Judiciary Committee of the New York Senate, February 8, 1861." Albany: Weed, Parsons and Co., 1861.

_____. "Address in Favor of Universal Suffrage for the Election of Delegates to the Constitutional Convention before the Judiciary Committee of the Legislature of New York, January 23, 1867, on behalf of the American Equal Rights Association." Albany: Weed, Parsons and Co., 1867.

_____. "Address to the Legislature of New York. Adopted by the State Women's Rights Convention Held at Albany, Tuesday and Wednesday, February 14 and 15, 1854." Albany: Weed, Parsons and Co., 1854.

_____. "Anniversary of the American Equal Rights Association." *The Revolution*, May 13, 1869, pp. 192-93.

_____. "The Antagonism of Sex." *National Bulletin*, June 1893. Container 7. Elizabeth Cady Stanton Papers. Library of Congress.

_____. "Antislavery." Speech, 1860. Container 4. Elizabeth Cady Stanton Papers. Library of Congress.

_____. "Are Homogeneous Divorce Laws in All the States Desirable?" *North American Review*, March 1900, pp. 405-9.

_____. *The Bible and Church Degrade Woman*. Chicago: H.L. Green, 1894?

_____. "The Catholic World." *The Revolution*, April 29, 1869, pp. 264-65.

_____. "The Civil and Social Evolution of Woman." In Sewall, *The World's Congress of Representative Women*, 1:327-29.

_____. "Closing Address." In *Report of the International Council of Women*, pp. 431-38.

_____. "Deborah and Jael." *The Revolution*, May 20, 1869.

_____. "The Degradation of Disfranchisement." *The Woman's Tribune*, February 7, 1891.

_____. "Divorce versus Domestic Warfare." *The Arena* 5 (April 1890): 560-69.

_____. "Education." Address delivered before the Lyceum of San Francisco, 1950s. Container 4. Elizabeth Cady Stanton Papers, Library of Congress.

_____. *Eighty Years and More: Reminiscences, 1815-1897*. New York: T. Fischer Unwin, 1898; New York: Schocken Books, 1971.

_____. "Esther." *The Revolution*, September 30, 1869.

_____. "The Ethics of Suffrage." In Sewall, *The World's Congress of Representative Women*, 2:482-88.

_____. "Huldah and Haggar." *The Revolution*, September 16, 1869.

_____. "I Have All the Rights I Want," *The Revolution*, April 1, 1869, p. 200.

_____. "Labor," Speech of 1868. Container 4. Elizabeth Cady Stanton Papers. Library of Congress.

_____. "The Man Marriage." *The Revolution*, April 8, 1869, pp. 217-18.

_____. "The Matriarchate, or Mother-Age." In Kraditor, *Up from the Pedestal*, pp. 140-47.

_____. "National Labor Congress." *The Revolution*, August 26, 1869, p. 120.

_____. "The Need for Liberal Divorce Laws." *North American Review* 139 (March 1884): 234-45.

_____. "On Marriage and Matrimony." *The Index*, September 9, 1870, p. 238.

_____. "Opening Address." In *Report of the International Council of Women*, pp. 32-37.

_____. "The Origin of Woman." *The Revolution*, April 1, 1868, p. 265.

_____. "Our Young Girls." Container 5. Elizabeth Cady Stanton Papers. Library of Congress.

_____. "Our Young Girls." *The Revolution*, January 29, 1868.

_____. "Peter and Paul at the Toledo Convention." *The Revolution*, March 25, 1869, pp. 184-85.

_____. "The Pleasures of Age: An Address Delivered by Elizabeth Cady Stanton on her Seventieth Birthday." N.p., n.d. New York Public Library.

_____. "Reading the Bible in the Public Schools." *The Arena* 17 (June 1897): 1034.

_____. "Religion for Women and Children." *The Index*, March 11, 1886, pp. 435-36.

_____. "Reverend Henry Edgar, (Part I)." *The Revolution*, June 10, 1869, pp. 360-61.

_____. "Self-Government the Best Form for Self-Development." June 29, 1901. Container 3. Elizabeth Cady Stanton Papers. Library of Congress.

_____. "Solitude of Self: Address Delivered by Mrs. Stanton before the Committee of the Judiciary of the U.S. Congress." N.p., n.d. Schlesinger Library.

_____. "Speech before a Club of Men and Women in New York City around 1869." Container 5. Elizabeth Cady Stanton Papers. Library of Congress.

_____. "Stand by Your Guns, Mr. Julian." *The Revolution*, January 14, 1869.

_____. "The Subjection of Woman." C. 1876. Container 6. Elizabeth Cady Stanton Papers. Library of Congress.

_____. "Suffrage." *A True Republic (Perkins Magazine)* 10 (May 1900): 104-5.

_____. *Suffrage a Natural Right.* Chicago: Open Court Publishing Co., 1894.

_____. "The Sunday Opening." *Women's Journal*, March 8, 1893.

_____. "Susan B. Anthony." In *Our Famous Women*, pp. 53-74.

_____. "The True Republic." Container 5. Elizabeth Cady Stanton Papers. Library of Congress.

_____. "Vashti." *The Revolution*, July 22, 1869.

_____. "Where Must Lasting Progress Begin?" *The Arena* 4 (August 1891): 293-98.

_____. "Woman, a Speech of 1856?" Container 4. Elizabeth Cady Stanton Papers. Library of Congress.

_____. "The Woman Question." *The Radical* 3 (September 1867): 18-27.

_____. "Woman's Pet Virtue." *The Revolution*, September 16, 1869, pp. 168-69.

_____. "Women and Black Men." *The Revolution*, February 11, 1869, p. 88.

_____. "Worship of God in Man." *The Open Court*. Container 3. Elizabeth Cady Stanton Papers. Library of Congress.

_____. "The Worst Enemy of Woman is Woman." *The Open Court*, August 4, 1887, pp. 818-28.

Stanton, Elizabeth Cady, Susan B. Anthony, Matilda Joslyn Gage, and Ida Husted Harper, eds. *History of Woman Suffrage*. 6 vols. New York: Fowler and Wells, 1881-1922; New York: Arno Press, 1969.

Stanton, Elizabeth Cady and the Revising Committee. *The Woman's Bible*. 2 vols. New York: European Publishing Co., 1896-1898; Seattle: Coalition Task Force on Women and Religion, 1974.

Stanton, Theodore, and Harriet Stanton Blatch, eds. *Elizabeth Cady Stanton as Revealed in Her Letters, Diaries and Reminiscences*. 2 vols. New York: Harper, 1922.

Stelzle, Charles. *The Call of the New Day to the Old Church*. New York: Fleming H. Revell Co., 1915.

Streng, Frederick J., Charles L. Lloyd, Jr., and Jay T. Allen, eds. *Ways of Being Religious*. Englewood Cliffs: Prentice-Hall, 1973.

Strout, Cushing. *The New Heaven and New Earth: Political Religion in America*. New York: Harper & Row, 1974.

Taylor, Graham. *Religion in Social Action*. New York: Dodd, Mead and Co., 1913.

Tillich, Paul. *Systematic Theology*. 3 vols. in one. Chicago and New York: University of Chicago Press and Harper & Row, 1961.

Toulmin, Steven. *The Uses of Argument*. Cambridge: Cambridge University Press, 1969.

_____. *An Examination of the Place of Reason in Ethics*. Cambridge: Cambridge University Press, 1968.

Trible, Phyllis. *God and the Rhetoric of Sexuality*. Philadelphia: Fortress Press, 1978.

Washbourn, Penelope. *Becoming Woman: The Quest for Wholeness in Female Experience*. New York: Harper & Row, 1977.

Welch, Claude. *Protestant Thought in the Nineteenth Century, 1799-1870*. New Haven: Yale University Press, 1972.

Welter, Barbara. "Anti-Intellectualism and the American Woman: 1800-1860." *Mid-America* 48 (October 1966): 258-70.

_____. "The Cult of True Womanhood: 1820-1860." *American Quarterly* 18 (Summer 1966): 151-74.

_____. "The Feminization of American Religion, 1800-1860." In *Insights and Parallels: Problems and Issues of American Social History*. Edited by William O'Neill. Minneapolis: Burgess Publishing Co., 1973, pp. 305-55.

_____. "Something Remains to Dare." Introduction to Stanton and the Revising Committee, *The Woman's Bible*. New York: Arno Press ed.

_____, ed. *The Woman Question in American History*. Hinsdale, Ill.: Dryden Press, 1973.

White, Morton. *Social Thought in America: The Revolt against Formalism*. Boston: Beacon, 1957.

White, Ronald C. Jr., and C. Howard Hopkins. *The Social Gospel: Religion and Reform in Changing America*. Philadelphia: Temple University Press, 1976.

Whitehead, Alfred North. *Adventures of Ideas*. New York: Macmillan, 1933; New York: Free Press, 1967.

Willey, Basil. *The Eighteenth Century Background: Studies in the Idea of Nature in the Thought of the Period*. London: Chatto and Windus, 1940; Boston: Beacon, 1960.

_____. *More Nineteenth Century Studies: A Group of Honest Doubters*. New York; Columbia University Press, 1956; New York: Harper & Row, 1966.

_____. *Nineteenth Century Studies: Coleridge to Matthew Arnold*. New York: Columbia University Press, 1949; New York: Harper & Row, 1966.

_____. *The Seventeenth Century Background: Studies in the Thought of the Age in Relation to Religion and Poetry*. New York: Columbia University Press, 1935; Garden City: Doubleday, 1953.

Winter, Gibson. *Elements for a Social Ethic: Scientific and Ethical Perspectives on Social Process*. New York: Macmillan, 1966.

Wollstonecraft, Mary. *A Vindication of the Rights of Woman*. London: Joseph Johnson, 1794; New York: W. W. Norton and Co., 1967.

Additional Bibliography, 1991

Albers, James W. "Perspectives on the History of Women in the Lutheran Church—Missouri Synod during the Nineteenth Century," *Lutheran Historical Conference* 9 (1982), pp. 137-83.

Albers, Patricia, and Bea Medecine. *The Hidden Half: Studies of Plains Indian Women*. Washington, D.C.: University Press of America, 1983.

Allen, Paula Gunn. *The Sacred Hoop: Recovering the Feminine in American Indian Tradition*. Boston: Beacon Press, 1986.

_____, ed. *Spider Woman's Granddaughters: Traditional Tales and Contemporary Writing by Native American Women*. Boston: Beacon Press, 1989.

Althur, Thomas, ed. *Procreation or Pleasure: Sexual Attitudes in American History*. Malabar, Fla.: Robert E. Krieger Publishing Co., 1983.

Amott, Teresa L., and Julia A. Matthaei. *Race, Gender and Work: A Multicultural Economic History of Women in the United States*. Boston: South End Press, 1991.

Anderson, Bonnie S., and Judith P. Zinsser, eds. *A History of Their Own: Women in Europe from Prehistory to the Present*. 2 vols. New York: Harper & Row, 1988.

Andolsen, Barbara Hilkert. *"Daughters of Jefferson, Daughters of Bootblacks": Racism and American Feminism*. Macon: Mercer University Press, 1986.

Andolsen, Barbara Hilkert, Christine Gudorf, and Mary D. Pellauer, eds. *Women's Conscience, Women's Consciousness: A Reader in Feminist Ethics*. San Francisco: Harper & Row, 1985.

Andrews, William L., ed. *Sisters of the Spirit: Three Black Women's Autobiographies of the Nineteenth Century*. Bloomington: Indiana University Press, 1986.

Applewhite, Harriet B., and Darline G. Levy, eds. *Women and Politics in the Age of the Democratic Revolution*. Ann Arbor: University of Michigan Press, 1990.

Aries, Philippe and Andre Bejin, eds. *Western Sexuality: Practice and Precept in Past and Present Times*. Anthony Forster, trans. Oxford: Basil Blackwell, 1985.

Bass, Dorothy C. "Sex Roles, Sexual Symbolism and Social Change: A Study in Religious Popular Culture of Nineteenth-Century American Women," *Radical Religion* 4 (1978), pp. 21-27.

Badone, Ellen, ed. *Religious Orthodoxy and Popular Faith in European Society*. Princeton: Princeton University Press, 1990.

Baker, Paula. *The Moral Frameworks of Public Life: Gender, Politics and the State in Rural New York, 1870-1930*. New York: Oxford University Press, 1991.

Banner, Lois W. *Elizabeth Cady Stanton: A Radical for Woman's Rights*. Boston: Little, Brown and Co., 1980.

Barry, Kathleen. *Susan B. Anthony: A Biography*. New York: New York University Press, 1988.

Bataille, Gretchen M., and Kathleen Mullen Sands, eds. *American Indian Women: Telling Their Lives*. Lincoln: University of Nebraska Press, 1984.

Baum, Dale. "Woman Suffrage and the 'Chinese Question': The Limits of Radical Republicanism in Massachusetts, 1865-1876," *New England Quarterly* 56 (1983), pp. 60-77.

Bednarowski, Mary Farrell. "Outside the Mainstream: Women's Religion and Women Religious Leaders in Nineteenth-Century America," *Journal of the American Academy of Religion* 48 (1980), pp. 207-31.

Beecher, Maureen Ursenbach, and Lavina Fielding Anderson, eds. *Sisters in Spirit: Mormon Women in Historical and Cultural Perspective*. Champaign: University of Illinois Press, 1987.

Behnke, Donna A. *Religious Issues in Nineteenth-Century Feminism*. Troy, N.Y.: Whitson Press, 1982.

Belenki, Mary Field, Blythe McVicker Clinchy, Nancy Rule Goldberger, and Jill Mattuck Tarule. *Women's Ways of Knowing: The Development of Self, Voice and Mind*. New York: Basic Books, 1986.

Bennett, Anne McGrew. *From Woman-Pain to Woman-Vision: Writings in Feminist Theology*, ed. Mary Hunt. Minneapolis: Fortress Press, 1989.

Bloch, Ruth. "Untangling the Roots of Modern Sex Roles: A Survey of Four Centuries of Change," *Signs* 4 (1978-79), pp. 237-52.

Blocker, Jack S. "Separate Paths: Suffragists and the Women's Temperance Crusade," *Signs* 10 (Spring 1985), pp. 460-76.

Borden, Ruth. *Women and Temperance: The Quest for Power and Liberty, 1873-1900*. Philadelphia: Temple University Press, 1980.

Boyd, Nancy. *Emissaries: The Overseas Work of the American YWCA, 1895-1970*. N.p.: The Woman's Press, 1986.

Boylan, Anne M. *Sunday School: The Formation of an American Institution, 1790-1880*. New Haven: Yale University Press, 1988.

_____. "Women in Groups: An Analysis of Women's Benevolent Organizations in New York and Boston, 1797-1840," *Journal of American History* 71 (December 1984), pp. 497-523.

Braude, Ann. *Radical Spirits: Spiritualism and Women's Rights in Nineteenth-Century America*. Boston: Beacon Press, 1989.

Brereton, Virginia Lieson. *Training God's Army: The American Bible School, 1880-1940*. Bloomington: Indiana University Press, 1990.

Bridenthal, Renate, Claudia Koonz, and Susan Stuard, eds. *Becoming Visible: Women in European History*. Boston: Houghton Mifflin, 1987.

Brock, Rita Nakashima. "Special Section: Asian Women Theologians Respond to American Feminism," *Journal of Feminist Studies in Religion* 3 (Fall 1987), pp. 103-5.

Brooks, Evelyn. "Feminist Theology of the Black Baptist Church, 1880-1900," in *Class, Race and Sex: The Dynamics of Control*, eds. Amy Swerdlow and Hanna Lesinger. Boston: G. K. Hall, 1983.

Brown, Peter. *The Body and Society: Men, Women and Sexual Renunciation in Early Christianity*. New York: Columbia University Press, 1988.

Brumberg, Joan Jacobs. "Zenanas and Girlless Villages: The Ethnology of American Evangelical Women, 1870-1910," *Journal of American History* 69 (1982), pp. 347-71.

Brundage, James A. *Law, Sex and Christian Society in Medieval Europe*. Chicago: University of Chicago Press, 1987.

Buechler, Steven M. "Elizabeth Boynton Harbert and the Woman Suffrage Movement, 1870-1896," *Signs* 13 (Autumn 1987), pp. 78-97.

Bullough, Vern, and Bonnie Bullough. *Sin, Sickness and Sanity: A History of Sexual Attitudes*. New York: New American Library, 1977.

Bullough, Vern, and James Brundage, eds. *Sexual Practices and the Medieval Church*. Buffalo: Prometheus Books, 1982.

Bushman, Claudia, ed. *Mormon Sisters: Women in Early Utah*. Cambridge: Emmeline Press Ltd., 1987.

Butler, Jon. *Awash in a Sea of Faith: Christianizing the American People*. Cambridge: Harvard University Press, 1990.

Bynum, Caroline Walker, Steven Harrell, and Paula Richman, eds. *Gender and Religion: On the Complexity of Symbols*. Boston: Beacon Press, 1986.

Bynum, Caroline Walker. *Fragmentation and Redemption: Essays on Gender and the Human Body in Medieval Religion*. New York: Zone Books, 1991.

_____. *Jesus as Mother: Studies in the Spirituality of the High Middle Ages*. Berkeley: University of California Press, 1982.

Cannon, Katie Geneva. "Resources for a Constructive Ethic in the Work of Zora Neale Hurston," *Journal of Feminist Studies in Religion* 1 (Spring 1985), pp. 37-51.

_____. *Black Womanist Ethics*. Atlanta: Scholars Press, 1988.

Cazden, Elizabeth: *Antoinette Brown Blackwell: A Biography*. Old Westbury: The Feminist Press, 1983.

Chopp, Rebecca S. *The Power to Speak: Feminism, Language, God*. New York: Crossroads, 1989.

Clark, Anna. *Women's Silence, Men's Violence: Sexual Assault in England, 1770-1845*. London: Pandora Press, 1987.

Clawson, Mary Ann. "Nineteenth-Century Women's Auxiliaries and Fraternal Orders," *Signs* 12 (1986), pp. 40-61.

Cliff, Michelle. " 'Found God in Myself and Loved Her—I Loved Her Fiercely': More Thought on the Work of Black Women Artists," *Journal of Feminist Studies* 1 (1986), pp. 7-39.

Coltelli, Laura, ed. *Winged Words: American Indian Writers Speak*. Lincoln: University of Nebraska Press, 1990.

Coontz, Stephanie. *The Social Origins of Private Life: A History of American Families, 1600-1900*. New York: Verso Press, 1988.

Copeland, Warren R., and Roger D. Hatch, eds. *Issues of Justice: Social Sources and Religious Meanings*. Macon: Mercer University Press, 1988.

Coon, Lynda L., Katherine J. Haldane, and Elizabeth W. Sommer, eds. *That Gentle Strength: Historical Perspectives on Women in Christianity*. Charlottesville: University of Virginia Press, 1990.

Cott, Nancy F. *The Grounding of Modern Feminism*. New Haven: Yale University Press, 1987.

Cott, Nancy F., and Elizabeth H. Pleck, eds. *A Heritage of Her Own: Toward a New Social History of American Women*. New York: Simon and Schuster, 1979.

Countryman, L. William. *Dirt, Greed and Sex: Sexual Ethics in the New Testament and Their Implication for Today*. Minneapolis: Fortress Press, 1988.

Day, Peggy L., ed. *Gender and Difference in Ancient Israel*. Minneapolis: Fortress Press, 1989.

Davis, David Brion. *Slavery and Human Progress*. New York: Oxford University Press, 1984.

Dayton, Donald W., ed. *Holiness Tracts Defending the Ministry of Women*. New York: Garland Publishing, 1984.

Degler, Carl. *At Odds: Women and the Family in America from the Revolution to the Present.* New York: Oxford University Press, 1980.

Dieter, Melvin E. "The Development of Nineteenth-Century Holiness Theology," *Wesley Theological Journal* 20 (1985), pp. 61-77.

Deutsch, Sarah. *No Separate Refuge: Culture, Class and Gender on an Anglo-Hispanic Frontier in the American Southwest, 1880-1940.* New York: Oxford University Press, 1987.

Donovan, Mary Sudman. *A Different Call: Women's Ministries in the Episcopal Church, 1850-1920.* Wilton, Conn.: Morehouse-Barlow, 1986.

Douglass, Jane Dempsey. *Women, Freedom and Calvin.* Philadelphia: Westminster, 1985.

DuBois, Ellen Carol, ed. *Elizabeth Cady Stanton, Susan B. Anthony: Correspondence, Writings, Speeches.* New York: Schocken Books, 1981.

DuBois, Ellen Carol, and Vicki L. Ruiz, eds. *Unequal Sisters: A Multicultural Reader in U.S. Women's History.* New York: Routledge, 1990.

Eisenstein, Zillah. *The Radical Future of Liberal Feminism.* New York: Longman, 1981.

Epstein, Barbara L. *The Power of Domesticity: Women, Evangelism and Temperance in Nineteenth-Century America.* Middletown, Conn.: Wesleyan University Press, 1981.

Erler, Mary, and Maryanne Kowaleski, eds. *Women and Power in the Middle Ages.* Athens: University of Georgia Press, 1988.

Evans, Sara M. *Born for Liberty: A History of Women in America.* New York: The Free Press, 1989.

Fabella, Virginia, and Sergio Torres. *Irruption of the Third World: Challenges to Theology.* Maryknoll, N.Y.: Orbis Books, 1981.

Falls, Helen E. "Baptist Women in Missions Support in the Nineteenth Century," *Baptist Historical Heritage* 12 (1977): 26-36.

Farrer, Claire R. *Women and Folklore: Images and Genres.* Prospect Heights, Ill.: Waveland Press, 1987.

Fisher, Sheila, and Janet E. Halley, eds. *Seeking the Woman in Late Medieval and Renaissance Writings: Essays in Feminist Contextual Criticism.* Nashville: University of Tennessee Press, 1989.

Fiorenza, Elizabeth Schüssler. *Bread not Stone: The Challenge of Feminist Biblical Interpretation.* Boston: Beacon Press, 1984.

_____. *In Memory of Her: A Feminist Theological Reconstruction of Christian Origins.* New York: Crossroads, 1987.

Fliegelman, Jay. *Prodigals and Pilgrims: The American Revolution against Patriarchal Authority, 1750-1800*. New York: Cambridge University Press, 1982.

Forman, Frieda Johles, and Caoran Sowton, eds. *Taking Our Time: Feminist Perspectives on Temporality*. New York: Pergamon Press, 1989.

Fout, John C., ed. *German Women in the Nineteenth Century*. New York: Holmes and Meier, 1984.

Fox-Genovese, Elizabeth. "Two Steps Forward, One Step Back: New Questions and Old Models in the Religious History of American Women," *Journal of the American Academy of Religion* 53 (September 1985), pp. 465-72.

_____. *Within the Plantation Household: Black and White Women of the Old South*. Chapel Hill: University of North Carolina Press, 1988.

Frederickson, George M. *The Arrogance of Race: Historical Perspectives on Slavery, Racism and Social Inequality*. Middletown: Wesleyan University Press, 1988.

_____. *The Black Image in the White Mind: The Debate on Afro-American Character and Destiny, 1817-1914*. Middletown: Wesleyan University Press, 1971.

Freedman, Estelle B. *Their Sisters' Keepers: Women's Prison Reform in America, 1830-1930*. Ann Arbor: University of Michigan Press, 1981.

Friedman, Jean E. *The Enclosed Garden: Women and Community in the Evangelical South, 1830-1900*. Chapel Hill: University of North Carolina Press, 1990.

Gaettens, Marie-Luise. "The Hard Work of Remembering: Two German Women Reexamine National Socialism," in *Taking Our Time: Feminist Perspectives on Temporality*, eds. Frieda Johles Forman and Caoran Sowton, New York: Pergamon Press, 1989, pp. 74-93.

Gifford, Carolyn De Swarte, ed. *Women in American Protestant Religion, 1800-1930*. New York: Garland Publishing, 1985ff. 36 volumes in reprint.

Giddings, Paula. *When and Where I Enter: The Impact of Black Women in Race and Sex in America*. New York: William Morrow and Co., 1984.

Gilkes, Cheryl Townsend. " 'Together and in Harness': Women's Traditions in the Sanctified Church," *Signs* 10 (Summer 1985), pp. 678-99.

Gilligan, Carol. *In a Different Voice: Psychological Theory and Women's Development*. Cambridge: Harvard University Press, 1982.

Glenn, Evelyn Nakano. *Issei, Nisei, War Bride: Three Generations of Japanese American Women in Transition.* Philadelphia: Temple University Press, 1985.

Gold, Penny Schine. *The Lady and the Virgin: Image, Attitude and Experience in 12th-Century France.* Chicago: University of Chicago Press, 1985.

Gordon, Linda. *Heroes of Their Own Lives: The Politics and History of Family Violence, Boston, 1880-1960.* New York: Viking Press, 1988.

Green, Lowell. "Education of Women in the Reformation," *History of Education Quarterly* 19 (1979), pp. 93-116.

Greene, Dana, ed. *Lucretia Mott: Her Complete Speeches and Sermons.* New York: Edwin Mellen Press, 1980.

Griffith, Elizabeth. *In Her Own Right: The Life of Elizabeth Cady Stanton.* New York: Oxford University Press, 1984.

Hampsten, Elizabeth. *Read This Only to Yourself: The Private Writings of Midwestern Women, 1880-1910.* Bloomington: University of Indiana Press, 1982.

Hardesty, Nancy. *Women Called to Witness: Evangelical Feminism in the Nineteenth Century.* Nashville: Abingdon, 1984.

Harley, Sharon, and Rosalyn Terborg-Penn, eds. *The Afro-American Woman: Struggles and Images.* Port Washington, N.Y.: Kennikat Press, 1978.

Harrison, Beverly Wildung. *Making the Connections: Essays in Feminist Social Ethics.* Boston: Beacon Press, 1985.

Hartsock, Nancy. *Money, Sex and Power: Toward a Feminist Historical Materialism.* New York: Longman, 1983.

Hayden, Dolores. *The Grand Domestic Revolution: A History of Feminist Designs for American Homes, Neighborhoods and Cities.* Cambridge: MIT Press, 1982.

Hersh, Blanche Glassman. *The Slavery of Sex: Feminist-Abolitionists in America.* Champaign: University of Illinois Press, 1978.

Heeney, Brian. *The Women's Movement in the Church of England, 1850-1930.* New York: Oxford University Press, 1988.

Hertz, Karl H. "The Role of the Laity in American Christianity," *Mid-Stream* 22 (1983), pp. 326-41.

Heschel, Susannah. *On Being a Jewish Feminist: A Reader.* New York: Schocken, 1983.

Hewitt, Nancy A. *Women's Activism and Social Change: Rochester, New York, 1822-1872.* Ithaca, N.Y.: Cornell University Press, 1984.

Hill, Patricia. *The World Their Household: The American Woman's Foreign Mission Movement and Cultural Transformation, 1870-1920.* Ann Arbor: University of Michigan Press, 1985.

Hine, Darlene Clark. *When the Truth Is Told: A History of Black Women's Culture and Community in Indiana, 1875-1950.* Indianapolis: National Council of Negro Women, 1981.

Hirata, Lucie Cheng. "Chinese Immigrant Women in Nineteenth-Century America," in *Women of America: A History*, Carol Berkin and Mary Beth Norton, eds. Boston: Houghton Mifflin Co., 1979, pp. 224-44.

_____. "Free, Indentured, Enslaved: Chinese Prostitutes in Nineteenth-Century America," *Signs* 5 (Autumn 1979), pp. 3-29.

Howell, Martha C. *Women, Production and Patriarchy in Late Medieval Cities.* Chicago: University of Chicago Press, 1986.

Hull, Gloria T., Patricia Bell Scott and Barbara Smith, eds. *All the Women Are White, All the Blacks Are Men, But Some of Us Are Brave: Black Women's Studies.* Old Westbury, N.Y.: Feminist Press, 1982.

Hunter, Jane. *The Gospel of Gentility: American Women Missionaries in Turn-of-the-Century China.* New Haven: Yale University Press, 1984.

Isasi-Diaz, Ada Maria, and Yolanda Tarango. *Hispanic Women: Prophetic Voice in the Church.* San Francisco: Harper & Row, 1988.

James, Janet, ed. *Women in American Religion.* Philadelphia: University of Pennsylvania Press, 1980.

Janowski, Dolores. *Sisterhood Denied: Race, Gender and Class in a New South Community.* Philadelphia: Temple University Press, 1986.

Jensen, Joan M. *Loosening the Bonds: Mid-Atlantic Farm Women, 1750-1850.* New Haven: Yale University Press, 1986.

Jones, David. *Senapia: Comanche Medicine Woman.* New York: Holt, Rinehart and Winston, 1972.

Jones, Jacqueline. *Labor of Love, Labor of Sorrow: Black Women, Work and the Family, From Slavery to the Present.* New York: Vintage Books, 1985.

Karlsen, Carol. *The Devil in the Shape of a Woman: Witchcraft in Colonial New England.* New York: W. W. Norton, 1987.

Katzenstein, Mary Fainsod. "Feminism and the Meaning of the Vote," *Signs* 10 (Autumn 1984), pp. 4-26.

Kerber, Linda K., and Jane DeHart Mathews, eds. *Women's America: Refocussing the Past.* New York: Oxford University Press, 1982.

Keller, Catherine. *From a Broken Web: Separation, Sexism and Self.* Boston: Beacon Press, 1986.

Kelly, Joan. *Women, History, Theory.* Chicago: University of Chicago Press, 1984.

Kenneally, James J. *The History of American Catholic Women.* New York: Crossroads/Continuum, 1990.

Kennelly, Karen, ed. *American Catholic Women: A Historical Exploration.* New York: Macmillan, 1988.

Kessler-Harris, Alice. *Out of Work: A History of Wage-Earning Women in the United States.* New York: Oxford University Press, 1982.

Kirshner, Julius, and Suzanne F. Wemple, eds. *Women of the Medieval World.* Oxford: Basil Blackwell, 1985.

Kolmer, Elizabeth, comp. *Religious Women in the United States: A Study of the Influential Literature from 1950 to 1983.* Wilmington: Michael Glazier, Inc., 1984.

Kraemer, David, ed. *The Jewish Family: Metaphor and Memory.* New York: Oxford University Press, 1988.

Lang, Amy Shrager. *Prophetic Woman: Anne Hutchinson and the Problem of Dissent in the Literature of New England.* Berkeley: University of California Press, 1987.

Lasser, Carol, and Marlene Deahl Merrill, eds. *Friends and Sisters: Letters between Lucy Stone and Antoinette Brown Blackwell, 1846-93.* Champaign: University of Illinois Press, 1987.

Lawless, Elaine J. *Handmaidens of the Lord: Pentecostal Women Preachers and Traditional Religion.* Philadelphia: University of Pennsylvania, 1988.

Leavitt, Judith Walzer, ed. *Women and Health in America: Historical Readings.* Madison: University of Wisconsin Press, 1984.

Lefkowitz, Mary R. *Women in Greek Myth.* Baltimore: Johns Hopkins University Press, 1986.

Lerner, Gerda. *The Creation of Patriarchy.* New York: Oxford University Press, 1986.

Levy, Barry. *Quakers and the American Family: British Settlement in the Delaware Valley.* New York: Oxford University Press, 1988.

Loades, Ann, ed. *Feminist Theology: A Reader.* Louisville: Westminster/John Knox Press, 1990.

Loveland, Ann C. "Domesticity and Religion in the Antebellum Period: The Career of Phoebe Palmer," *Historian* 40 (1978), pp. 235-51.

MacHaffie, Barbara J. *Her Story: Women in Christian Tradition.* Philadelphia: Fortress Press, 1986.

Mannard, Joseph G. "The 1839 Baltimore Nunnery Riot: An Episode in Jacksonian Nativism and Social Violence," *Maryland Historian* 11 (1980): pp. 13-27.

_____. "Maternity . . . of the Spirit: Nuns and Domesticity in Antebellum America," *U.S. Catholic Historian* 5 (1986), pp. 305-24.

Marshall, Sherrin, ed. *Women in Reformation and Counter-Reformation Europe: Private and Public Worlds*. Bloomington: Indiana University Press, 1989.

McCants, David A. "Evangelicalism and Nineteenth-Century Women's Rights: A Case Study of Angelina E. Grimké," *Perspectives on Religious Studies* 14 (1987), pp. 39-57.

McDaniel, Colleen. *The Christian Home in Victorian America, 1840-1900*. Bloomington: Indiana University Press, 1986.

McKivigan, John R. *The War against Proslavery Religion: Abolitionism and the Northern Churches, 1830-1865*. Ithaca: Cornell University Press, 1984.

McLoughlin, William G. "Billy Sunday and the Working Girl of 1915," *Journal of Presbyterian History* 54 (1976), pp. 376-84.

Meyers, Carol. *Discovering Eve: Ancient Israelite Women in Context*. New York: Oxford University Press, 1988.

Mintz, Steven, and Susan Kellogg. *Domestic Revolutions: A Social History of American Family Life*. New York: The Free Press, 1988.

Misner, Barbara. *"Highly Respectable and Accomplished Ladies": Catholic Women Religius in America, 1790-1850*. New York: Garland Publishing, 1988.

Mollencott, Virginia Ramey. *Women of Faith in Dialogue*. New York: Crossroads, 1987.

Monter, E. William. "Women in Calvinist Geneva (1550-1800)," *Signs* 6 (1980-81), pp. 189-209.

Moraga, Cherrie, and Gloria Anzaldua, eds. *This Bridge Called My Back: Writings by Radical Women of Color*. Watertown, Mass.: Persephone Press, 1981.

Morton, Nelle. *The Journey is Home*. Boston: Beacon Press, 1985.

Mudflower Collective (Kate Cannon, Beverly Harrison, Carter Heyward, Ada Maria Isasi-Dias, Bess Johnson, Nancy Richardson, Mary Pellauer). *God's Fierce Whimsy: Christian Feminism and Theological Education*. New York: Pilgrim Press, 1985.

Neverdon-Morton, Cynthia. *Afro-American Women of the South and the Advancement of the Race, 1895-1925.* Nashville: University of Tennessee Press, 1989.

Noll, William T. "Women as Clergy and Laity in the 19th-Century Methodist Protestant Church," *Methodist History* 15 (January 1977), pp. 107-21.

Oates, Mary J. "The Good Sisters: The Work and Position of Catholic Church Women in Boston, 1870-1940," in Robert Sullivan and James O'Toole, eds., *Catholic Boston: Studies in Religion and Community, 1810-1970.* Boston, Roman Catholic Archdiocese, 1985, pp. 171-200.

_____, ed. *Higher Education for Catholic Women: An Historical Anthology.* New York: Garland Publishing, 1987.

Ochs, Carol. *Women and Spirituality.* Totowa, N.J.: Rowman and Allenfield, 1983.

Ochs, Vanessa L. *Words on Fire: One Woman's Journey into the Sacred.* New York: Harcourt Brace Jovanovich, 1990.

Oden, Thomas C., ed. *Phoebe Palmer: Selected Writings.* New York: Paulist Press, 1988.

Olson, Carl, ed. *The Book of the Goddess, Past and Present: An Introduction to Her Religion.* New York: Crossroads, 1985.

Orsi, Robert A. *The Madonna of 115th Street: Faith and Community in Italian Harlem, 1880-1950.* New Haven: Yale University Press, 1988.

Ostriker, Alicia Suskin. *Stealing the Language: The Emergence of Women's Poetry in America.* Boston: Beacon Press, 1986.

Pateman, Carole. *The Disorder of Women: Democracy, Feminism and Political Theory.* Stanford: Stanford University Press, 1989.

Peiss, Kathy, and Christina Simmons, eds. *Passion and Power: Sexuality in History.* Philadelphia: Temple University Press, 1989.

Pellauer, Mary, Barbara Chester, and Jane Boyajian, eds. *Sexual Assault and Abuse: A Handbook for Clergy and Religious Professionals.* San Francisco: Harper & Row, 1988.

_____. "Understanding Sexism" in *Issues of Justice: Social Sources and Religious Meanings*, Warren R. Copeland and Roger D. Hatch, eds. Macon: Mercer University Press, 1988, pp. 127-52.

Peterson, Susan Carol, and Courtney Ann Vaughn-Roberson. *Women with Vision: The Presentation Sisters of South Dakota, 1880-1985.* Champaign: University of Illinois Press, 1988.

Pickle, Linda Schelbitzki. "Women of the Saxon Immigration and their Church," *Concordia Historical Institute Quarterly* 57 (1984), pp. 146-61.

Plaskow, Judith, and Carol Christ, eds. *Weaving the Visions: New Patterns in Feminist Spirituality*. San Francisco: Harper & Row, 1989.

Plaskow, Judith. *Sex, Sin and Grace: Women's Experience and the Theologies of Reinhold Niebuhr and Paul Tillich*. Lanham, Md.: University Press of America, 1980.

Pleck, Elizabeth. *Domestic Tyranny: The Making of American Social Policy against Family Violence from Colonial Times to the Present*. New York: Oxford University Press, 1987.

_____. "Feminist Responses to 'Crimes Against Women,' 1868-1896," *Signs* 8 (Spring 1983), pp. 451-70.

Pobee, John S., and Barbara von Wartenberg-Potter, eds. *New Eyes for Reading: Biblical and Theological Reflections by Women from the Third World*. Geneva: World Council of Churches, 1986.

Porterfield, Amanda. *Feminine Spirituality in America: From Sarah Edwards to Martha Graham*. Philadelphia: Temple University Press, 1980.

Power, Eileen. *Medieval Women*. New York: Cambridge University Press, 1975.

Powers, Marla N. *Oglala Women: Myth, Ritual, Reality*. Chicago: University of Chicago Press, 1986.

Raser, Harold E. *Phoebe Palmer: Her Life and Thought*. Edwin Mellen Press, 1987.

Reverby, Susan M. *Ordered to Care: The Dilemma of American Nursing, 1850-1945*. New York: Cambridge University Press, 1987.

Riley, Glenda. *The Female Frontier: A Comparative View of Women on the Prairie and the Plains*. Lawrence, KS: University Press of Kansas, 1985.

Rodriguez, Gregorita. *Singing for My Echo: Memories of a Native Healer of Santa Fe*. Santa Fe: Ocean Tree Books, 1988.

Rollins, Judith. *Between Women: Domestics and Their Employers*. Philadelphia: Temple University Press, 1985.

Rowe, Kenneth E. "Methodist Women: A Guide to the Literature," Lake Junalaska, N.C.: The General Commission on Archives and History, the United Methodist Church, 1980.

_____. "The Ordination of Women, Round One: Anna Oliver and the General Conference of 1880," *Methodist History* 12 (April 1974), pp. 60-72.

Ruether, Rosemary Radford, and Rosemary Skinner Keller, eds. *Women and Religion in America: A Documentary History*. 3 vols. San Francisco: Harper

& Row. Vol. I: *The Nineteenth Century*, 1981. Vol. II: *Colonial and Revolutionary Periods*, 1983. Vol. III: 1900-1968, 1986.

Ruether, Rosemary Radford. *Sexism and God-Talk: Toward a Feminist Theology*. Boston: Beacon Press, 1983.

_____. *Women-Church: Theology and Practice*. San Francisco: Harper & Row, 1985.

_____. *WomanGuides: Readings toward a Feminist Theology*. Boston: Beacon Press, 1986.

Ruiz, Vicki L. *Cannery Women, Cannery Lives: Mexican Women, Unionization and the California Food Processing Industry, 1939-1950*. Albuquerque: University of New Mexico Press, 1987.

Russell, Letty, ed. *Feminist Interpretations of the Bible*. Philadelphia: Westminster Press, 1985.

Russell, Letty M., Kwok Pui-lan, Ada Maria Isasi-Diaz, and Katie Geneva Cannon, eds. *Inheriting Our Mothers' Gardens: Feminist Theology in Third World Perspective*. Philadelphia: Westminster Press, 1988.

Ruud, Inger Marie. *Women and Judaism: A Select Annotated Bibliography*. New York: Garland Publishing, 1988.

Ryan, Mary. *Cradle of the Middle Class: The Family in Oneida County, New York, 1780-1865*. New York: Cambridge University Press, 1981.

Salmon, Marylynn. *Women and the Law of Property in Early America*. Chapel Hill: University of North Carolina Press, 1989.

Sanday, Peggy Reeves. *Female Power and Male Dominance: On the Origins of Sexual Inequality*. New York: Cambridge University Press, 1981.

Schlissel, Lillian, et al. *Far from Home: Families of the Westward Journey*. New York: Schocken Books, 1989.

Schlissel, Lillian, Vicki L. Ruiz, and Janice Monk, eds. *Western Women: Their Land, Their Lives*. Albuquerque: University of New Mexico Press, 1988.

Seidenberg, Robert. "The Trauma of Eventlessness," in *Psychoanalysis and Women*, ed. Jean Baker Miller. New York: Penguin Books, 1973, pp. 350-62.

Sklar, Kathryn Kish. "The Last Fifteen Years: Historians' Changing Views of American Women in Religion and Society," in *Women in New Worlds: Historical Perspectives on the Wesleyan Tradition*, eds. Hilah Thomas and Rosemary Keller. Nashville: Abington Press, 1981, pp. 48-68.

Smith, Amanda. *An Autobiography: The Story of the Lord's Dealing with Mrs. Amanda Smith, the Colored Evangelist*. New York: Oxford University Press, 1988.

Smith-Rosenberg, Carol. *Disorderly Conduct: Visions of Gender in Victorian America*. New York: Oxford University Press, 1985.

Spretnak, Charlene, ed. *The Politics of Women's Spirituality: Essays on the Rise of Spiritual Power within the Women's Movement*. Garden City: Doubleday, 1982.

Starhawk. *The Spiral Dance: A Rebirth of the Ancient Religion of the Great Goddess*. San Francisco: Harper & Row, 1979.

Steele, Lois. *Medicine Woman*. Grand Forks, N.D.: University of North Dakota Press, 1985.

Stepsis, Ursula M., and Delores Liptak, eds. *Pioneer Healers: The History of Women Religious in American Health Care*. New York: Crossroads Continuum, 1989.

Stratton, Joanna L. *Pioneer Women: Voices from the Kansas Frontier*. New York: Simon and Schuster, 1982.

Tamez, Elsa. *Against Machismo: Rebem Alves, Leonardo Boff, Gustavo Gutierrez, Jose Miguel Bonino, Juan Luis Segundo and Others Talk about the Struggle of Women*. Oak Park, Ill.: Meyer-Stone Books, 1987.

_____. *The Bible of the Oppressed*. Maryknoll, N.Y.: Orbis Books, 1982.

Taves, Ann. "Mothers and Children and the Legacy of Mid-Nineteenth-Century American Christianity," *Journal of Religion* 67 (1987), pp. 203-19.

_____. *Religion and Domestic Violence in Early New England: The Memoirs of Abigail Abbot Bailey*. Bloomington: Indiana University Press, 1989.

Tax, Meredith. *The Rising of the Women: Feminist Solidarity and Class Conflict, 1880-1917*. New York: Monthly Review Press, 1980.

Thistlethwaite, Susan. *Sex, Race and God: Christian Feminism in Black and White*. New York: Crossroads, 1989.

Thomas, Hilah, and Rosemary Skinner Keller, eds. *Women in New Worlds: Historical Perspectives on the Wesleyan Tradition*. Nashville: Abingdon, 1981.

Thomas, Samuel J. "Catholic Journalists and the Ideal Woman in Late Victorian America," *International Journal of Women's Studies* 4 (1981), pp. 89-100.

Thompson, Margaret S. "Philemon's Dilemma: Nuns and the Black Community in Nineteenth-Century America: Some Findings," *Records of the American Catholic Historical Society* 96 (1986), pp. 3-18.

Thompson, Roger. *Sex in Middlesex: Popular Mores in a Massachusetts County, 1649-1699*. Amherst: University of Massachusetts Press, 1986.

Thurston, Bonnie Bowman. *The Widows: A Women's Ministry in the Early Church*. Minneapolis: Fortress Press, 1988.

Trible, Phyllis. *God and the Rhetoric of Sexuality*. Philadelphia: Fortress Press, 1978.

_____. *Texts of Terror: Literary-Feminist Readings of Biblical Narratives*. Philadelphia: Fortress Press, 1984.

Tucker, Cynthia Grant. *Prophetic Sisterhood: Liberal Women Ministers of the Frontier, 1880-1930*. Boston: Beacon Press, 1990.

Ulrich, Laurel. *Good Wives: Image and Reality in the Lives of Women in Northern New England, 1650-1750*. New York: Knopf, 1982.

Van Kirk, Sylvia. *Many Tender Ties: Women in Fur Trade Society, 1670-1870*. Norman, OK: University of Oklahoma Press, 1983.

Van Voris, Jacqueline. *Carrie Chapman Catt: A Public Life*. New York: The Feminist Press, 1987.

Walters, Ronald G. *The Antislavery Appeal: American Abolitionism after 1830*. New York: W. W. Norton, 1978.

Weatherford, Doris. *Foreign and Female: Immigrant Women in America, 1840-1930*. New York: Schocken Books, 1986.

Weeks, Jeffrey. *Sex, Politics and Society: The Regulation of Sexuality since 1800*. New York: Longman, 1981.

Wegner, Judith Romney. *Chattel or Person? The Status of Women in the Mishnah*. New York: Oxford University Press, 1988.

Welch, Sharon D. *A Feminist Ethic of Risk*. Minneapolis: Fortress Press, 1990.

Wheeler, Leslie, ed. *Loving Warriors: Selected Letters of Lucy Stone and Henry B. Blackwell, 1853 to 1893*. New York: Dial Press, 1981.

Wren, Brian. *What Language Shall I Borrow? God-Talk in Worship: A Male Response to Feminist Theology*. New York: Crossroad, 1989.

Yung, Judy. "A Bowlful of Tears: Chinese Women Immigrants on Angel Island," *Frontiers* 1 (Summer 1977), pp. 52-55.

_____. *Chinese Women of America*. Seattle: University of Washington Press, 1986.

411

Index

Abbott, Lyman, 242, 277
Abolition, 175
  Susan Brownell Anthony and Elizabeth Cady Stanton's different reasons for supporting, 349n
  Susan Brownell Anthony's work for, 156
  as model for suffragists, 293
  differences from woman suffrage movement, 328n
  influence of movement on Susan Brownell Anthony, 164, 165-66, 169-70, 192
  influence of movement on Elizabeth Cady Stanton, 19
  and liberalism, 205
  religious aspects of movement, 198
  split with women's movement, 86
  suffragist support for, 20
  unselfish nature of movement for, 39
  See also William Lloyd Garrison; Racism; Reform; Slavery
Abortion, 356n
Adams, John, 73, 76
Addams, Jane, xiv, 269
AERA
  See American Equal Rights Association
Ahlstrom, Sydney
  A Religious History of the American People, ix
Alcott, Amos Bronson, 19
American Anti-Slavery Society, 156
American Colonization Society, 189
American Equal Rights Association, 20, 78, 81
  See also Suffrage; Suffragists; Woman Suffrage Movement

American Revolution
  as guarantor of individual rights, 38
  fought to secure right of suffrage, 141
American Woman Suffrage Association, 20, 21, 174, 223, 262, 284, 322n-23n, 351n
  feminism of, 40
  membership of, 370n
  and religion, 44, 255-57
  See also National American Woman Suffrage Association; Suffrage; Suffragists; Woman Suffrage Movement
Ames, Charles G., 370n
"The Antagonism of Sex," 88
Anthony, Anna O., 360n
Anthony, Lucy E., 224, 274, 280, 360n, 363n
Anthony, Merritt, 360n
Anthony, Susan Brownell, 20, 21, 22, 50, 55, 60, 70, 94, 225, 278, 281, 288, 291
  on abortion, 356n
  "agitation" activism of, 164-65
  analytical structure used by, 154
  on antislavery, 349n
  biography of, 155-61
  collaboration with Elizabeth Cady Stanton, 159-61
  compared to Anna Howard Shaw, 219, 220, 239, 251, 260-61, 268, 271, 272, 274, 275, 279, 280-81, 282, 285-302, 373n
  compared to Elizabeth Cady Stanton, 153-54, 155, 160-61, 176, 184, 189-90, 193-94, 195-96, 201, 205, 206-7, 212,

214-17, 285-302, 342n, 354n, 355n-56n
contemporaries' view of, 348n, 348n-49n, 362n
depression of, 353n
economic analysis of, 173-85, 187-88
ethics of, 12, 168-69
and Laura Fair, 352n-53n
on friendship with Elizabeth Cady Stanton, 213-14
and George Francis Train, 355n
on God, 358n
on justice, 190-95, 292-96
labor activism of, 176-83
lack of theological training of, 9-10
lecturing of, 156-57, 158, 159
liberation theology of, 301
on life after death, 210-11, 215, 357n-58n
on love, 268
love for humanity of, 266, 269, 283
on marriage, 168, 185-88
on need for women to act politically, 163-73, 193
"occasional" theoretical style of, 3-4, 159-60, 190
on oppression, 8
and organized labor, 354n
and organized religion, xiii
organizes working women's associations, 66-67
on place of religion in reform, 195-202
public image of, 158-59
Quaker influence on, 154, 166, 170, 200, 205-6, 215
racial views of, 156
recent scholarship on, xv
recruiting efforts of, 157
recruits Anna Howard Shaw, 223-24
reform philosophy of, 154, 166, 168-69, 179-80, 192
reform work of, 156, 158
religious views of, xvi, 1-13, 155, 160-61, 193-94, 195-96, 205, 296-304, 357n, 360n
repudiates religious sectarianism in suffrage campaign, 202-9
self-censorship of, 121
on sexism, 5-6
and sexuality, 292

shelters abused wife, 169
"sisterhood" of, 209-14, 215, 217
on "social evils," 155
on "social purity," 185-90
spurs Elizabeth Cady Stanton to continue public appearances, 139-40
suffrage trial of, 157, 170-72
tensions with Elizabeth Cady Stanton, 347n-48n
theology of, 359n, 360n
use of slavery analogy by, 154, 161, 162
on *The Woman's Bible* controversy, 48, 203-4
on woman suffrage and international peace, 162
on woman suffrage as underpinning of social reform, 161-62
women's action as analytical focus of, 290
on women's powerlessness, 154, 161-90, 163, 165, 287-88, 289
on Victoria Woodhull, 355n-56n
on working women, 355n
and work with African-Americans, 352n
See also Suffragists
Antibiblicism, 25
Anticlericalism
See Clergy
Antislavery
See Abolition; Reform; Slavery
Aquinas, Thomas, 309
Arendt, Hannah, 2, 5, 282, 305, 312, 373n
Arnold, Matthew, 17, 45, 105, 106, 116, 343n
Augustine, 310, 312
Authority
importance of women's own, 112-13
Avery, Rachel Foster, 167, 225
AWSA
See American Woman Suffrage Association

Bachofen, J. J., 116, 130
Barry, Kathleen, xv, 355n, 357n, 358n
Barth, Karl, 10
Becker, Lydia, 327n
Beecher, Henry Ward, 58, 185, 256, 359n, 370n
Beecher, Thomas K., 359n

Bell, Peter, 79
Bellah, Robert, 335n-36n
Besant, Annie, 194-95, 196, 197, 210
Between Past and Future, 305
Beyond God the Father, 297
Bible
    antibiblicism, 25
    and infallibility, 206
Bible and Church Degrade Woman, The,
    329n-30n
Bicycling, 139
Blackwell, Alice Stone, 374n
Blackwell, Antoinette Brown, 207, 370n
Blackwell, Henry B., 355n
Blatch, Harriet Stanton, 21, 159, 361n
Bowles, Ada C., 370n
Bradlaugh, Charles, 21, 194-95
Brauer, Jerald C., ix
"Bread and the Ballot," 156, 180-81
Bright, Mrs. Jacob, 194
Brownson, Orestes Augustus, 19
Brooks, Phillips, 223
Brown, John, 197
Brown, Olympia, 370n
Browne, Borden P., 222
Browne, John, 19
Burke, Kenneth, 3
Burleigh, Celia, 370n

Calvin, John, 19, 110, 115, 125, 139, 141,
    297, 305
Carlyle, Thomas, 358n-59n
Cassirer, Ernst, 343n
Catholic Church
    Elizabeth Cady Stanton's bias against,
        321n
    Elizabeth Cady Stanton supports reform
        of, 57-58
    views on woman suffrage, 37-38
    See also Churches; Christianity; Religion
Catt, Carrie Chapman, 224, 337n, 364n-65n,
    365n
Channing, William Henry, 19, 98, 155, 163,
    357n
Chapin, Augusta, 370n
Cheney, Ednah, 8, 208-9, 273, 360n-61n
Chesler, Phyllis, 375n-76n
"Chicago School"

tribute paid to, ix
*Chicago Studies in the History of American
    Religion*
    challenge established ideas, ix-x
    characteristics of, x-xi
    explained, ix
    significance of, x-xi
    subjects covered by, ix-x
Christian Citizenship, 8
Christianity
    in America, 270
    as reform paradigm, 247-51
    attacked as oppressive to women, 21
    calls for reform of, 41
    civilizing influences benefit women, 109
    criticized as segregating women and men,
        43-44
    and democracy, 258-64
    redefined to support woman suffrage, 144
    and sexism, 152, 308, 334n-35n
    two types of distinguished, 20, 30-32
    upheld by the American Woman Suffrage
        Association, 44
    women and, xv-xvi
    and woman suffrage, 214-15, 255-57,
        284, 298-99, 320n
    See also Churches; Clergy; Protestantism;
        Religion; Theology
Churches
    and ordination of women, 347n
    reform work in, 8
    position of women in, 300
    See also Christianity; Clergy; Protestan-
        tism; Religion
Civil disobedience, 170-71
Civil religion, 38, 214, 341n, 348n
    appeal of to feminists, 152
    defined, 335n-36n
    and divine struggle for equal rights, 77,
        79-80
    individual rights as fundamental tenet of,
        124
    and politics, 102-3
    of Anna Howard Shaw, 262-63
    and Elizabeth Cady Stanton, 17, 136,
        141, 150, 151
    and theology, 301
    and woman suffrage, 144, 298-99,
        360n-61n

See also Religion
Civil War
  effect of on abolitionists, 166
  religious causes of, 42
  suffragist work during, 20
Clarke, James Freeman, 223, 370n
Clarke, William Newton, 278-79
Clergy
  failure of to inspire women, 137
  false authority corrupts, 113-16
  ordination of women as, 152, 257, 347n
  and woman suffrage, 49, 202-3, 235, 255,
    274-78, 299, 359n, 370n, 373n-74n
Colby, Clara Bewick, 153, 161, 329n
Collins, Sheila, 1-2
Comte, Auguste, 21, 35-37, 45, 61, 68, 84,
  99, 117, 326n-27n
Condorcet, Marie Jean de, 106
Congressional Union, 225
Connecticut
  factory working conditions in, 67
Conway, Moncure, 21
Cook, Coralie Franklin, 348n-49n
Cooper, Anna Julia, 337n
Council of National Defense, 226
Cousins, Phoebe, 328n
Craigie, Mary, 8
Crittendown, A. P., 185
Curtis, George William, 94

Daly, Mary, 1-2, 286, 297
Dana, Richard Henry, 19
Darwin, Charles, 48, 138
Daughters of Temperance, 156
Daughters of the American Revolution,
  236-37
Davis, Edward M., 328n
Davis, Paulina Wright, 112, 328n
Dayton, Donald W., 321n
Dayton, Lucille Sider, 321n
de Beauvoir, Simone, 308
"Declaration of Sentiments," 6, 19, 22, 50,
  155, 258
"The Degradation of Disfranchisement," 88,
  91-94
Democracy
  as divine ordinance, 138
  and Christianity, 258-64

and civil religion, 263
and feminism, 151
and individuality, 124-25
and militarism, 245-46
and natural laws, 128-29, 144
and predestination, 133
and religion, 8, 271, 273-74
  Anna Howard Shaw on, 229-34, 238,
    242, 243
and suffrage theory, 150-51
and woman suffrage, 71-94, 99-100, 220,
  295, 297, 320n
and women's self-authority, 113-15
Dewey, John, xiv
Deyo, Amanda, 370n
Dickinson, Anna E., 85, 165, 166, 173
Divorce, 55-56, 59-60
  See also Marriage
Douglas, Ann, 373n
Douglass, Frederick, 155, 167, 174-75, 198,
  328n
Douglass, Mary, 345n
Dress
  need for reform of, 63-64
DuBois, Ellen Carol, xv, 340n

Ebeling, Gerhard, 309
Economics
  Susan Brownell Anthony's theory of,
    173-85, 187-88
  Elizabeth Cady Stanton's theory of, 66-70
Edgar, Henry, 327n
Education
  and suffrage, 337n
  theological training for women, 2
  of women, 27, 61-65, 99, 109, 116-17,
    150, 177-78, 187, 333n
Edwards, Jonathan, ix, xi, 373n
Eliot, Charles, 244
Elizabeth Cady Stanton, Susan B. Anthony:
  Correspondence, Writings, Speeches, xv
Emerson, Ralph Waldo, 19, 50, 135, 198,
  223, 338n, 351n, 358n
England
  economic relationship with United States,
    67
  factory working conditions in, 67
  women's status in, 74

Enlightenment
  influence on feminism, 17, 106, 112-14, 117
  influence on Elizabeth Cady Stanton, 95, 98-101, 141, 148, 151, 321n, 343n
Episcopal Church
  confessions of sin in, 125
Equal Rights Amendment, 151
Ethics
  Susan Brownell Anthony on, 168-69
  and emotion, 149
  and justice, 12, 190-93
  and materialism, 108
  and natural laws, 128-29, 147-48
  and religion, 4-5
  Elizabeth Cady Stanton on, 338n-39n
  and woman suffrage, 294, 296
  See also Morality

Factories, 67
Fair, Laura, 185, 352n-53n
"The Fate of Republics," 232-33
Feminism
  analytical construction of, 288-89
  Biblical creation stories and, 34-35
  and civil religion, 152
  construction of, 284
  and democratic ideology, 151
  Enlightenment influences on, 17, 106
  evangelical form of, 256
  ideal of women's self-sacrifice banished from, 40
  and internalized sexism, 286
  and justice, 303-4
  and natural law theory, 146-47
  and religion, 32, 134, 140-41
  and religious liberalism, 10-11, 375n
  and sexism, 288
  of Anna Howard Shaw, 6, 220, 253-54, 258, 261, 268, 277, 280-81, 282-83, 285, 302
  Elizabeth Cady Stanton's contributions to, 15
  and theology, xv-xvi, 1-2, 105-6, 108, 286, 297, 303, 305-15, 319n-20n
  theory versus practice, 88
  types of, 321n
  and women's role in churches, 152

and women's self-authority, 113
  See also Women
Few Days in Athens, or Epicurus, 358n
Fifteenth Amendment, 87, 161, 328n
Finney, Charles Grandison, 18, 19, 21, 111
Foster, Stephen S., 19
Fourier, Charles, 50
Fourteenth Amendment, 20, 73, 74, 157, 161
Fox, George, 165
Franklin, Benjamin, 72-73, 273, 360n-61n
Free love, 295-96, 332n, 355n-56n
  suffragists charged with, 185-86
  and suffragists' critiques of marriage, 55
  and woman suffrage, 56-58
Free Religious Association, 17, 21, 45, 321n
Freud, Sigmund, 292
"Frontier Thesis," x
Fugitive Slave Law of 1850, 164, 169, 171, 179, 295
Fuller, Margaret, 19, 112

Gage, Francis Dana, 256
Gage, Matilda Joslyn, 112, 207, 328n, 329n
Galton, Sir Francis, 116
Gardner, C. B., 198
Garrison, William Lloyd, 19, 154, 155, 156, 164, 165, 169, 196-97, 202, 205, 223, 322n, 341n, 349n, 351n, 351n-52n
  See also Abolition
Gaskell, Mrs., 358n-59n
Geertz, Clifford, 140-41, 142, 281, 303, 319n
Gillette, Mrs., 370n
Gilman, Charlotte Perkins, 269
Gladden, Washington, 370n
God
  Susan Brownell Anthony on, 358n
  feminine construction of, 302-3
  Anna Howard Shaw on, 265-67, 282-83
  Elizabeth Cady Stanton on, 134-40, 346n
Graham, Billy, 281
Grant, Jacquelyn, xvi-xvii
Grant, Ulysses S., 170, 351n
Green, H. L., 330n
Greene, Ann Terry, 19
Griffith, Elisabeth, 321n-22n
Grimké, Angelina, 50, 325n

Grimké, Sarah M., 50, 325n
Gustafson, James M., xiii
Gyn/Ecology, 297

Hamilton, Alexander, 188
Hanaford, Phoebe, 370n
Hancock, John, 76
Handy, Robert T., ix
Harbert, Elizabeth Boynton, 207-8
Hardesty, Nancy, 321n
Harper, Francis Ellen Watkins, 337n
Harper, Ida Husted, 5, 160, 225, 349n-50n, 357n, 365n-66n
Harper, William Rainey, 172
Haven, Gilbert, 255-56, 370n
Hawthorne, Nathaniel, 19
Health, women's, 62-64, 131
"The Heavenly Vision," 223, 239
History of Woman Suffrage, 15, 21, 88, 150, 211, 225, 227, 323n
Holcombe (philosopher), 36
Hooker, Isabella Beecher, 197, 208
Howe, Julia Ward, 20, 223, 256
Hudson, Winthrop, ix
Hultin, Ida C., 8, 361n
Hunt, Ward, 170-71

Index, the, 21
Individualism
    "American idea" of individual rights, 37-38
    and democracy, 124-25
    denied to women, 24
    importance of to Elizabeth Cady Stanton, 16-17, 145-47, 329n, 331n, 344n
    and interdependence, 123-24
    and Protestantism, 118-19
    and republicanism, 119
    and sisterhood, 339n
    and woman suffrage movement, 127
Ingersoll, Robert G., 21
International Council of Women (1888), 8, 100, 135, 207-9, 213, 223, 247
"Issue"
    defined, 317n-18n

James, William, xiv
Jefferson, Thomas, 73, 76, 86, 334n, 373n
Joan of Arc, 28-29, 115
Johnson, Andrew, 169
Johnson, Oliver, 19
Johnson, Virginia E., 292
Jones, Jenkin Lloyd, 360n
Judaism, 43-44, 47, 254
Justice
    Susan Brownell Anthony on, 190-95
    artificiality of, 147
    as apex of rational thought, 108-9
    as argument for woman suffrage, 94-103
    as catalyst for complete development of women, 122-23
    as ethical stake of woman suffrage movement, 6-7
    as focal point for religious and social analysis, 1, 4-5, 11-13
    defined, 292-94
    eternal laws of, 71
    and feminism, 303-4
    purity of, 124, 144
    and religion, 297-98
    and religious diversity, 151
    requirements for, 90
    and sexism, 4
    Anna Howard Shaw on, 251-255
    Elizabeth Cady Stanton on, 60
    struggle for essential to women's equality, 143-44
    suffragists on, 292-96
    for women, 90, 286
    women's individual suffering as access to, 54
    women's perceptions of, 52, 148

Kant, Immanuel, 15
Kelley, Abby, 19
Kelley, Florence, 225
Kelly-Gadol, Joan, 338n
Knights of Labor, 158
Knox, John, 19, 110, 139, 297, 305
Kollock, Florence, 370n

Labor

Susan Brownell Anthony's activism on
    behalf of, 176-83
and working conditions, 67-68
Laws
    biased against women, 50-60
    and civil disobedience, 170-71
    natural, 128-34, 142-43, 146-50, 211,
        347n
    reform of, 188
League of Loyal Women, 20
League of Nations, 226, 245
Lecky, J.J., 21, 45
Lee, Jarena, xvi-xvii
Liberalism
    and abolition, 205
    of Susan Brownell Anthony, 10, 360n
    and feminism, 10-11, 375n
    politics and failure of, 87-88
    and religion, 10-11, 204-5, 255, 263, 271,
        300-302, 375n
    of Anna Howard Shaw, 10, 263, 271
    of Elizabeth Cady Stanton, 10-11, 106,
        133, 135
    and theology, 151, 375n
Liberal Religious Congress, 360n
Liberator, 154, 165
Lincoln, Abraham, 162
Lincoln, C. Eric, 300
Linkugel, Wilmer Albert, 366n-67n
Livermore, Mary A., 185-86, 222
Lonergan, Bernard, 309
Lovejoy, Elijah, 328n
Lowell, A. Lawrence, 226
Lowell, James Russell, 19
Luther, Martin, 19, 31, 38, 110, 115, 139,
    141, 297, 305, 309-10, 330n

McFarland-Richardson case, 185
Madison, James, 73
Mann, Arthur, xi
Mann, Horace, 358n-59n
Marriage
    Susan Brownell Anthony on, 168, 185-88
    campaign for legal change of, 20
    compared with slavery, 185
    natural laws of, 128, 131-32
    as oppressive of women, 50-60
    slavery as analogy for, 54-55, 59

Elizabeth Cady Stanton on, 32
suffrage and revision of laws regarding,
    51-52, 60
See also Divorce
Marty, Martin E., ix
Massachusetts Woman Suffrage Association,
    223
Masters, William H., 292
Materialism
    and ethics, 108
    and morality, 107-8, 113-16
Maternity
    as wider social issue, 239-40
    Elizabeth Cady Stanton on, 21-22, 44,
        51-52, 131-32, 147, 149
May, Samuel J., 19
Mayo, William S., 155
Mead, George Herbert, xiv
Mead, Sidney E., ix
Michelangelo, 306
Mill, John Stuart, 39, 117, 320n
Milton, John, 61
Miscegenation, 60-61
    woman suffrage as antidote for, 86-87
Morality
    and materialism, 107-8, 113-16
    Anna Howard Shaw on, 254
    and women, 125-27
    See also Ethics
Morgan, Lewis Henry, 116
Motherhood
    See Maternity
Mott, Lucretia, 19, 85, 110-11, 115, 118,
    137, 158, 203, 209, 322n, 340n-41n,
    350n

National American Woman Suffrage Associ-
    ation, 8, 20, 112, 118, 173, 193, 211,
    215, 219, 220, 261-62, 278, 280, 297,
    322n-23n, 364n-65n, 371
    bureaucratic expansion of, 226
    conventions of, 212
    under Anna Howard Shaw, 224-26
    and *The Woman's Bible*, 22, 48-49, 203-4
    See also American Woman Suffrage
        Association; National Woman Suffrage
        Association; Suffrage; Suffragists;
        Woman Suffrage Movement

National Labor Congress, 178, 354n
National Woman Suffrage Association, 20, 21, 156, 174, 195
  debates self-sacrifice, 328n-29n
  feminism of, 40
  membership of, 370n
  proposed reorganization of, 179
  refuses to condemn Christianity, 43
  and religion, 255
  See also National American Woman Suffrage Association; Suffrage; Suffragists; Woman Suffrage Movement
Native Americans, 367n
Natural laws, 128-34, 142-43, 146-50, 211, 347n
NAWSA
  See National American Woman Suffrage Association
New York
  economic status of teachers in, 176
  working women in, 175-76, 177-78, 181
New York State Woman's Temperance Convention, 29
Niebuhr, Reinhold, 306, 375n
Nineteenth Century Studies, 285
Norton, Mrs., 178
NWSA
  See National Woman Suffrage Association

Oliver, Anna, 222
Open Court Press, 21
Otis, James, 73

Paine, Tom, 51
Parker, Theodore, 19, 208, 358n, 360n-61n
Parnell, Charles, 58
Patriarchy, xv-xvi, 5, 74-75, 82-84, 89, 91-92, 131-32, 286, 307
Paul, Alice, 365n
Peabody, Elizabeth, 19
Perelman, Chaim, 292-94, 374n
Perfectionism, 331n
Perkins, Sarah M., 370n
Phillips, Wendell, 19, 21, 39, 54, 155, 164, 200, 223, 252, 328n
Pierce, Mr., 197
Pillsbury, Parker, 21, 35, 155

Pitt, William, 225
Plummer, Caroline, 177
Politics
  and civil religion, 102-3
  corruption in, 82
  emotionalism of, 237-38
  and failure of liberalism, 87-88
  need for women's involvement in, 163-73, 193
  and science, 116, 150
  science of, 143
  Elizabeth Cady Stanton on, 70-94
  women as purifiers of, 78-80, 84-85, 136, 141-42
Positivism
  influences Elizabeth Cady Stanton, 35-37
Progressivism, 239-51, 278-79
Prostitution, 187
Protestantism
  and individuality of human souls, 118-19
  See also Christianity; Churches; Clergy; Religion; Theology
"Protestant Synthesis"
  Chicago Studies in the History of American Religion question, ix-x

Quakers
  See Society of Friends

Racism
  of Anna Howard Shaw, 367n-68n
  of Elizabeth Cady Stanton, 80-82, 85-87, 129, 167, 321n, 323n, 339n
  See also Abolition; Slavery Rationalism, 45
Rauschenbush, Walter, xiv
Reform
  as church work, 8
  as required by God, 137-38
  as spiritual act, 154
  blocked by ideal of women as mothers, 53
  Christianity as paradigm for, 247-51
  expediency rejected, 166, 168-69
  Fugitive Slave Law galvanizes, 164
  love for humanity inspires, 266-68
  motivated by injustice, 295
  and natural laws, 128-29, 132

and "practical" Christianity, 41
religious aspects of, 2, 10, 30-32,
195-202, 214, 254-55
and science, 290
Anna Howard Shaw on, 239-51, 376n-
77n
and suffrage, 23
of women's clothing, 63-64
and women's economic dependence, 173-
74
See also Abolition; Temperance; Woman
Suffrage Movement
Reformation, Protestant 141
Religion
and Christian equality, 17
church membership, 373n
defined, xiii, 9, 105, 107, 116
and democracy, 271, 273-74
distinguished from theology, 111
and divine position of women, 64
and economic theory, 68-70
and feminine God, 302-3
and feminism, 134, 140-41, 291
and free-thinkers, 21
infuses suffrage work, 8-9
and justice, 297-98
and liberalism, 10, 204-5, 255, 263, 271,
300-302, 375n
life after death questioned by, 133
male authority as cornerstone of, 112-16
and natural laws, 128-29
original sin repudiated by, 125-26, 136,
151
and patriarchy, 286
perversion of in women, 24-49, 324n
and rational thought, 107-18
and reform, 30-32, 195-202, 214, 254-55
sanctions true marriage, 55-56
and science, 21, 42, 105, 109, 116-17,
138, 148, 301
sexism in, 3
and sexuality, 346n
Anna Howard Shaw on, 270-79
and social ethics, 4-5
Elizabeth Cady Stanton criticizes, 25-30,
32
suffrage as duty of, 39
in the "True Republic," 41-42
womanly influence on, 8

and woman suffrage, 219, 294, 296-304
women's support of criticized, 27, 29-30
See also Catholic Church; Christianity;
Churches; Civil Religion; Clergy;
Judaism; Protestantism; Theology
Religious History of the American People, A,
ix
Republicanism
and individual citizenship, 119
and natural laws, 128-29
and need for democratic home life, 58-60
place of education in, 62
place of religion in, 41-42
and suffrage, 238
and woman suffrage, 71-94, 99, 219, 227,
229-34, 238, 242, 243
women as saviors of, 150, 293
women essential to progress of, 141
and women's self-authority, 114
Republican Party
and woman suffrage, 163, 169, 192, 351n
Revivalism, 111, 322n
Revolution, The, 21, 25, 34, 35, 36, 39, 41,
57, 66, 156, 169, 171, 176, 177-78, 186,
323n, 326n, 337n, 347n, 354n, 356n
Revolution, American
as guarantor of individual rights, 38
fought to secure right of suffrage, 141
Rich, Adrienne, 376n
Richardson-McFarland case, 185
Ricoeur, Paul, 147, 347n
Roosevelt, Theodore, 162
Rose, Ernestine L., 85, 203
Rossi, Alice, 321n
Royce, Josiah, xiv
Ruether, Rosemary Radford, 1-2
Ryle, Gilbert, 291

Sand, George, 358n-59n
Savage, Minot, 223
Schneiderman, Rose, 364n
Science
and politics, 150
and reform, 290
and religion, 21, 42, 105, 109, 116-17,
138, 148, 301
and woman suffrage, 327n-28n
Scudder, Vida, 269

Selden, Henry R., 170
Seneca Falls Convention, 19-20, 24, 26-28, 50, 341n-42n
Sewing Machine Operators' Union, 177
Sexism
　as catalyst for theological creativity, 11
　as push to theological creativity, 106
　challenged by women's liberation movement, 145-46
　in Christianity, 308
　ethics of, 191
　in history, 312
　internalization of, 286
　and justice, 4
　nature of, 356n
　in religion, 3, 334n-35n
　Elizabeth Cady Stanton on, 23-24
　suffragists on, 5-6, 7
　and theology, 152
Sexuality
　as social evil, 60
　and religion, 346n
　Elizabeth Cady Stanton on, 53, 55, 327n
　suffragist critique of, 292
Shakespeare, William, 306
Shaw, Anna Howard, 37, 70, 116, 157, 195, 196, 204, 210-11
　as suffrage leader, 224-26, 261-62, 364n-65n, 371n
　biography of, 221-27
　civil religion of, 262-63
　compared to Susan Brownell Anthony, 219, 220, 239, 251, 252, 260-61, 268, 271, 272, 274, 275, 279, 280-81, 282, 285-302, 373n
　compared to Elizabeth Cady Stanton, 219, 220, 227-28, 230-31, 239, 241, 246, 250, 251, 252, 256, 257, 261, 262-63, 265, 268, 269, 270, 271, 272, 274, 275, 277, 279, 282, 285-302
　critique of, 279-84
　depression of, 361n, 363n
　emotion as analytical focus of, 290
　ethical reasoning of, 12
　feminism of, 6, 220, 253-54, 258, 261, 268, 277, 280-81, 282-83, 285, 302
　friendship with Susan Brownell Anthony, 223-24
　humor of, 234-35, 281-82, 291, 302

　importance of religious beliefs of, 1-13
　metaphors of, 371n
　on class distinctions, 243-44
　on clergy, 274-78
　on democracy, 8, 220, 229-34, 238, 242, 243
　on "democracy of Christianity," 258-64
　on expediency, 252
　on God, 265-67, 282-83
　on home and family, 239-41
　on justice, 251-255, 292-96
　on love, 266-70, 283-84
　on lynching, 367n
　on militant suffrage tactics, 368n
　on morality, 254
　on need for consistency in republics, 227-28
　on reform, 376n-77n
　on religion, 255-58, 270-79, 284
　on sexism, 5-6
　on woman suffrage, 219-20, 255-58, 284, 287-88
　on working women, 242-43, 244-45
　oratory skills of, 226-27
　and organized religion, xiii
　and Progressive reforms, 239-51
　racism of, 367n-68n
　rebuts antisuffragists, 234-39
　relationship with Lucy E. Anthony, 363n
　religious views of, 10, 263, 265-70, 271, 278, 280-81, 282-83, 296-304
　repudiates The Woman's Bible, 49
　static theory of, 4
　theological training of, 9-10
　See also Suffragists
Shaw, Henry, 221
Simpson, Matthew, 370n
Sixteenth Amendment, 81-82, 84, 85, 86
Sixty Years with the Bible, 278-79
Slavery
　Susan Brownell Anthony and Elizabeth Cady Stanton's differing visions of, 349n
　as analogy for marriage, 54-55, 59
　as analogy for treatment of women, 52, 98, 99, 149, 154, 161, 162, 175, 179, 182, 191, 198, 275, 287-88, 328n, 356n
　and opposition to Fugitive Slave Law, 171

religious justifications for, 42
sexual exploitation in, 185
See also Abolition; Racism
Smith, Adam, 67
Smith, Gerrit, 19, 53
Smith, Wilfred Cantwell, 310
Social Gospel, 40-41, 67, 69, 278, 329n
"Social Purity," 156-57, 186-89, 201
Social Science Association, 61
Society of Friends
    as agitators for reform, 165
    influence on Susan Brownell Anthony,
        166, 200, 205-6, 215
Socrates, 373n
"Solitude of Self," 118-27, 137, 139-40, 147,
    150
Spencer, Anna Garlin, 8, 370n
Spencer, Herbert, 45, 61, 84, 99, 117, 124,
    269
Stael, Mme. de, 358n-59n
Standard, 165
Stanton, Elizabeth Cady, 154, 158, 169, 174,
    175, 185, 192, 202, 203-4, 205, 209,
    276, 278, 280, 281, 284, 291
    on "American idea" of individual rights,
        37-38
    anti-Catholic bias of, 321n
    anticlericalism of, 299
    on antislavery, 349n
    attacks religion as oppressive to women,
        21
    on Biblical creation stories, 27, 34-35,
        43-48
    biography of, 18-22
    on broad impact of suffrage for women,
        22-23
    calls for philosophical socialism, 69-70
    calls for reform of Catholic Church, 57-58
    central religious principle of, 305
    changing theory of, 3
    on churches, 324n
    civil religion of, 17, 141, 150, 151,
        262-63, 336n, 341n, 346n
    collaboration with Susan Brownell
        Anthony, 159-61, 354n
    compared to Susan Brownell Anthony,
        153-54, 155, 160-61, 176, 184, 189-90,
        193-94, 195-96, 201, 205, 206-7,
        214-17, 285-302, 342n, 354n,
        355n-56n
    compared to Anna Howard Shaw, 219,
        220, 227-28, 230-31, 239, 241, 246,
        250, 251, 252, 256, 257, 261, 262-63,
        265, 268, 269, 270, 271, 272, 274,
        275, 277, 279, 282, 285-302
    and contemporary feminists, 145-46
    contributions to feminist theory of, 15
    criticizes conservative suffragists, 92-93
    criticizes St. Paul, 27-28, 33
    criticizes theology, 105-6
    critique of, 145-152, 288-89
    on "Declaration of Sentiments," 6
    domestic life of, 50
    early influences on, 19-20
    economic theory of, 66-70
    on education of women, 61-65
    Enlightenment influence on, 106, 111-12,
        117, 141, 148, 151, 321n, 343n
    on feminine wiles, 64-65
    feminism of, 313
    on fourfold bondage of women, 23-24,
        142-43, 288, 324n, 325n-26n
    four sacred aspects of religious social
        thought of, 103
    and free love, 332n, 355n-56n
    friendship with Susan Brownell Anthony,
        213-14
    on God, 134-40, 346n
    on harmony and dissent, 346n
    on housework, 322n
    and individualism, 344n
    on individual rights for women, 16-17
    influence of sexism on theological views,
        106
    on Jesus Christ, 343n-44n
    on justice, 94-103, 286, 292-96
    on lack of opportunity for women, 307
    lack of theological training of, 9-10
    liberalism of, 106, 133, 135
    on love, 268, 283
    on marriage, 32, 50-60
    on materialism and morality, 107-8, 113-
        16
    on maternity, 21-22, 44, 51-52, 131-32,
        147, 149
    natural law views of, 12, 128-34, 142-43,
        146-47, 150, 211, 212

on need for self-government, 88-90
on need to affirm abstract political rights, 68-69
and organized labor, 354n
and organized religion, xiii
on patriarchy, 74-75, 82-84, 89, 91-92
on perversion of religious element in women, 24-49
racism of, 80-82, 85-87, 129, 167, 321n, 323n, 339n
and rationalism, 45
recent scholarship on, xv
rejects Romanticism, 322n
religious liberalism of, 10-11
on religion, xiii, 1-13, 16-18, 20, 30-32, 42-49, 108-18, 140-41, 151, 160-61, 193-94, 195-96, 205, 296-304, 334n-35n, 343n
on religious views of Susan Brownell Anthony, 357n
repudiates original sin, 125-26
self-censorship of, 121
sensualism of, 140
on sexism, 5-6, 149, 334n-35n
on sexuality, 53, 55, 292, 327n, 346n
and sisterhood, 339n
social analysis evaluated, 95-97
and social gospel, 40-41, 67, 69
on "solitude of self," 118-27, 137, 139-40, 147, 150
and spiritualism, 342n
on suffrage, 8, 15-16, 20-21, 22-23, 39, 70-94, 287
on suffragists' use of violence, 333n-34n
support for women's right to divorce, 55-56, 59-60
tensions with Susan Brownell Anthony, 347n-48n
theological critique of, 301-2
and George Francis Train, 355n
and universals, 298
use of analogies by, 149
on viability of existing political theories, 150-51
on woman suffrage, 287
on women antisuffragists, 98-99
on women as individuals, 329n, 331n
on women's bicycling, 139
on women's dress, 63-64

women's experience as analytical focus of, 289-90
on women's health, 62-64, 131
on women's innate longing for freedom, 93-94
on women's lack of freedom, 295-96
on women's oppression by social customs, 60-70
on women's political rights, 70-94
on women's right to claim self-authority, 109-18
on women's self-sacrifice, 39-40
on women's superior religious character, 343n
and writing of *The Woman's Bible*, 46-49
See also Suffragists
Stanton, Henry B., 19, 20, 349n
Stanton, Theodore, 21
Steinem, Mrs., 364n
Stelzle, Charles, 373n
Stoddard, Mr., 373n
Stone, Lucy, 20
Story of a Pioneer, The, 222
Stuart, Elizabeth, 208
Subjection of Women, The, 39
Suffrage
as holy right, 135, 139, 141, 150
as key to women's independence, 165, 174-75
as vehicle for women's self-assertion, 65-66
as weapon for women, 90-91
and education, 337n
essential to women's equality, 143-44
Eve's actions used to argue against, 35
importance of for women, 187
and individualism, 148
justice as justification for, 12
linked with free love, 56-58
linked with improved working conditions, 180-81, 182-84
moral power of, 154
opponents of, 98-99, 219-20, 220-21, 228, 230, 234-39, 241-42, 253, 256, 274-77, 299, 327n, 366n-67n
and religion, 2, 39, 116, 140-41, 297
and revision of marriage laws, 51-52, 60
and science, 327n-28n

Elizabeth Cady Stanton on, 8, 15-16, 20-21, 22-23, 39, 70-94, 287
and temperance, 167
theorists of, 6-7
women's disfranchisement compared with other groups, 74
See also American Equal Rights Association; American Woman Suffrage Association; National American Woman Suffrage Association; National Woman Suffrage Association; Reform; Suffragists; Woman Suffrage Movement
Suffragists
attack restrictions on women, 8
charged with heterodoxy, 196
critiques of, 145
disagreements among, 287
and labor activists, 178
militant tactics of, 368n
and religion, 33, 64, 300-302
respond to sexist theology, 300
social challenges of, 285
social thought of, 5-6
theological creativity of, 11
urge women to political action, 295
See also American Equal Rights Association; American Woman Suffrage Association; National American Woman Suffrage Association; National Woman Suffrage Association; Reform; Suffrage; Woman Suffrage Movement
Susan B. Anthony: A Biography, xv
Suttee, 45-46
Swedenborg, Emanuel, 36
Sweet, William Warren, ix-x

Taft, William Howard, 226
Taylor, Harriet Upton, 225
Teachers
economic status of in New York, 176
Temperance, 37, 185, 186
and antisuffragists, 234
influence of movement on Susan Brownell Anthony, 173
and Elizabeth Cady Stanton, 20
and suffrage, 167, 220, 228
See also Reform; Women's Christian Temperance Union

Theology
and civil religion, 301
criticized by Elizabeth Cady Stanton, 25-26, 105-6
defined, 10
distinguished from religion, 111
and divine characterization, 298
and feminism, xv-xvi, 1-2, 286, 297, 303, 305-7, 309, 319n-20n
liberation forms of, 206
masculine elements repudiated, 126-27
and Progressivism, 278-79
question and answer structure of, 6-7, 11-13
and religious liberalism, 151, 375n
and sexism, 11, 106, 152, 300
suffragist critiques of, 9, 294
traditions of, 305-15
See also Religion
Thompson, Marianna, 222
Tillich, Paul, 2, 6-7, 10, 297, 306, 309
Tilton, Elizabeth, 58, 185, 350n
Train, George Francis, 355n
Transcendentalism, 21
"The Transient and the Permanent in Religion," 358n
Truth, Sojourner, xvi-xvii
Typographical Union No.6, 178

Upton, Mrs., 364n
Upton, Harriet Taylor, 8

Vaughn, Hester, 185

Way, Amanda, 370n
WCTU
See Women's Christian Temperance Union
Webster, Noah, 86
Weld, Foster, 223
Wells, Kate Gannett, 200
Welter, Barbara, 342n
Wheelock, Mayor, 364n
Whitehead, Alfred North, 233, 280, 306
"The White Man's Burden," 273

White Women's Christ and Black Women's Jesus: Feminist Christology and Womanist Response, xvi-xvii
Whittier, John Greenleaf, 19, 223
Willard, Frances, 167, 208, 220, 223, 239
    See also Women's Christian Temperance Union
Willey, Basil, 285
Williams, Fannie Barrier, 337n
Wilson, John, 336n
Wilson, Woodrow, 220, 228, 361n
Wollstonecraft, Mary, 106, 325n
Woman Suffrage Movement, 10, 16, 19-20, 22-23
    charged with free love, 185-86
    and Christian democracy, 258-64
    Civil War work of, 20
    conflicting interpretations of sexism in, 7
    convention format of, 207
    and cooperative socialism, 70
    and "Declaration of Sentiments," 6
    democratic rhetoric of, 71-94, 99-100, 229-34, 238, 242, 243
    and divinity, 282-83
    and Fifteenth Amendment, 328n
    humor in, 234-35, 281-82, 291, 302
    individuality as tenet of, 127
    and justice, 6-7, 94-103
    leadership of, 158-59
    marriages of members of, 57
    militant tactics of, 225
    opens up theological education for women, 2
    opposed by working-class men, 70
    platform of, 193, 287
    and Progressive reforms, 239-51
    reconciled with Christianity, 214-15
    reform scope of narrowed, 227
    and religion, 8-9, 144, 202-9, 219, 294, 318n, 360n-61n
    secularization of, 365n
    and Seneca Falls convention, 341n-42n
    setbacks of, 163
    sisterhood in, 209-14, 215, 217
    social contention in, 6
    split of, 20-21
    strategy of, 157, 167
    and suffrage trial of Susan Brownell Anthony, 170-72

women's control of, 300
and working women, 179-80
    See also American Equal Rights Association; American Woman Suffrage Association; National American Woman Suffrage Association; National Woman Suffrage Association; Reform
Woman's Bible, The, 21-22, 24-25, 45, 46-49, 88, 105, 110, 113, 126, 134, 203-4, 205-6, 220, 284, 323n, 330n
Woman's State Temperance Organization, 30
Woman's Typographical Union No.1, 177
Women
    as morally superior to men, 28-29
    as purifiers of politics, 136, 141-42
    as saviors of republicanism, 150, 189, 201, 204
    and churches, 300, 373n
    creation of institutions by, 300
    disfranchisement of compared with other groups, 74
    economic dependence of, 173-85, 187-88
    education of, 27, 61-65, 99, 109, 116-17, 150, 177-78, 187, 333n
    fourfold bondage of, 23-24, 142-43, 288, 324n, 325n-26n
    health of, 62-64, 131
    importance of personal authority for, 112-13
    importance of suffrage for, 187
    individuality of denied, 7, 24
    and justice, 90, 122-23, 148, 286
    love for humanity of, 267-68, 283-84
    marriage oppressive of, 50-60
    and morality, 125-27
    need for reform of dress for, 63-64
    oppressed by social customs, 60-70
    ordination of, 152, 257, 347n
    perversion of religious element in, 24-49, 324n
    political rights of, 70-94
    powerlessness of, 154, 161-90
    power of indirect influence criticized, 75
    and religion, xv-xvi, 305-15, 319n
    and self-sacrifice, 39-40, 328n-29n
    slavery as analogy for treatment of, 52, 98, 99, 149, 154, 161, 162, 175, 179, 182, 191, 198, 275, 287-88, 328n, 356n

society denies individuality of, 16-17
spiritual powers of, 272
status in England, 74
status under patriarchy, 83-84, 89, 91-92
theological education for, 2
theological reflections of, 2
urged to claim self-authority, 109-18
urged to pursue political action, 163-73,
  193, 295
work of, 66-67, 242-43, 244-45, 355n,
  376n
See also Feminism
"Women in the Holiness Movement: Feminism in the Evangelical Tradition," 321n
"Women in the Ministry," 257
Women's Christian Temperance Union, 165,
  198, 204, 223, 239, 300
See also Temperance; Willard, Frances
Women's Foreign Missionary Society, 222
Women's Liberation Movement
  challenges sexism, 145-46
  critique of sexist language by, 291
  establishing trust within, 306
  imaginative aspect of, 290-91
  and motherhood, 147
  religious aspects of, 2
  sisterhood of, 308
Women's Party, 225
Women's Typographical Union No.1, 178
Woodhull, Victoria, 58, 342n, 355n-56n
Woolf, Virginia, 280, 306
Wordsworth, William, 79
Working conditions, 67
Working Women's Association, 176-77, 178,
  179
World Anti-Slavery Convention, 19, 50, 110
World's Congress of Representative Women,
  247
World War I, 245-46, 252
Wright, Elizur, 19
Wright, Francis, 358n

Zane, Charles, 19

TITLES IN THE SERIES

Chicago Studies in the History of American Religion

Editors

JERALD C. BRAUER & MARTIN E. MARTY

1. Ariel, Yaakov. *On Behalf of Israel: American Fundamentalist Attitudes toward Jews, Judaism, and Zionism, 1865-1945*
2. Bundy, James F. *Fall from Grace: Religion and the Communal Ideal in Two Suburban Villages, 1870-1917*
3. Butler, Jonathan M. *Softly and Tenderly Jesus is Calling: Heaven and Hell in American Revivalism, 1870-1920*
4. Dvorak, Katharine L. *An African-American Exodus: The Segregation of the Southern Churches*
5. Hardesty, Nancy A. *Your Daughters Shall Prophesy: Revivalism and Feminism in the Age of Finney*
6. Harding, Vincent. *A Certain Magnificence: Lyman Beecher and the Transformation of American Protestantism, 1775-1863*
7. Hewitt, Glenn A. *Regeneration and Morality: A Study of Charles Finney, Charles Hodge, John W. Nevin and Horace Bushnell*
8. Hillis, Bryan V. *Can Two Walk Together Unless They Be Agreed?: American Religious Schisms in the 1970s*
9. Jacobsen, Douglas G. *An Unprov'd Experiment: Religious Pluralism in Colonial New Jersey*
10. Kloos, John M., Jr. *A Sense of Deity: The Republican Spirituality of Dr. Benjamin Rush*

(continued, over)

11. Kountz, Peter. *Thomas Merton as Writer and Monk: A Cultural Study, 1915-1951*

12. Lagerquist, L. DeAne. *In America the Men Milk the Cows: Factors of Gender, Ethnicity, and Religion in the Americanization of Norwegian-American Women*

13. Markwell, Bernard Kent. *The Anglican Left: Radical Social Reformers in the Church of England and the Protestant Episcopal Church, 1846-1954*

14. Morris, William Sparkes. *The Young Jonathan Edwards: A Reconstruction*

15. Pellauer, Mary D. *Toward a Tradition of Feminist Theology: The Religious Social Thought of Elizabeth Cady Stanton, Susan B. Anthony, and Anna Howard Shaw*

16. Potash, P. Jeffrey. *Vermont's Burned-Over District: Patterns of Community Development and Religious Activity, 1761-1850*

17. Queen, Edward L., II. *In the South the Baptists are the Center of Gravity: Southern Baptists and Social Change, 1930-1980*

18. Schmidt, Jean Miller. *Souls or the Social Order: The Two-Party System in American Protestantism*

19. Shaw, Stephen J. *The Catholic Parish as a Way-Station of Ethnicity and Americanization: Chicago's Germans and Italians, 1903-1939*

20. Shepard, Robert S. *God's People in the Ivory Tower: Religion in the Early American University*

21. Snyder, Stephen H. *Lyman Beecher and his Children: The Transformation of a Religious Tradition*